Lecture Notes in Computer Science 15649

Founding Editors

Gerhard Goos
Juris Hartmanis

The series Lecture Notes in Computer Science (LNCS), including its subseries Lecture Notes in Artificial Intelligence (LNAI) and Lecture Notes in Bioinformatics (LNBI), has established itself as a medium for the publication of new developments in computer science and information technology research, teaching, and education.

LNCS enjoys close cooperation with the computer science R & D community, the series counts many renowned academics among its volume editors and paper authors, and collaborates with prestigious societies. Its mission is to serve this international community by providing an invaluable service, mainly focused on the publication of conference and workshop proceedings and postproceedings. LNCS commenced publication in 1973.

Osvaldo Gervasi · Beniamino Murgante ·
Chiara Garau · Yeliz Karaca · David Taniar ·
Ana Maria A. C. Rocha · Bernady O. Apduhan
Editors

Computational Science and Its Applications – ICCSA 2025

25th International Conference
Istanbul, Turkey, June 30 – July 3, 2025
Proceedings, Part II

 Springer

Editors
Osvaldo Gervasi (iD)
University of Perugia
Perugia, Italy

Chiara Garau (iD)
University of Cagliari
Cagliari, Italy

David Taniar (iD)
Monash University
Clayton, VIC, Australia

Bernady O. Apduhan
Kyushu Sangyo University
Fukuoka, Japan

Beniamino Murgante (iD)
University of Basilicata
Potenza, Italy

Yeliz Karaca (iD)
University of Massachusetts Chan Medical
Worcester, MA, USA

Ana Maria A. C. Rocha (iD)
University of Minho
Braga, Portugal

ISSN 0302-9743   ISSN 1611-3349 (electronic)
Lecture Notes in Computer Science
ISBN 978-3-031-96996-6   ISBN 978-3-031-96997-3 (eBook)
https://doi.org/10.1007/978-3-031-96997-3

Preface

The compiled 3 volumes (LNCS volumes 15648–15650) consist of the peer-reviewed papers from the 6 Main Conference Tracks of the 2025 International Conference on Computational Science and Its Applications (ICCSA 2025), which was held between June 30 – July 3, 2025 in Istanbul (Türkiye). The peer-reviewed papers of the 68 Workshops are published in a separate set made up of fourteen volumes (LNCS 15886–15899).

The conference was held in a hybrid form, with the large majority of participants in presence, hosted by Galatasaray University, Istanbul, Türkiye. We enabled virtual participation for those who did not attend the event in person due to logistical, political and economic problems, by adopting a technological infrastructure via open-source software (jitsi + riot) and a commercial Cloud infrastructure.

With the 2025 edition, ICCSA celebrated its 25th anniversary, a quarter of a century as a memorable moment that is harmoniously aligned with Istanbul, an extraordinary city located at the crossroads and acting as a bridge connecting Asia and Europe, representing different cultures, beliefs as well as lifestyles, which highlights its intercultural fabric.

ICCSA 2025 marked another fruitful and thought-provoking academic event in the International Conferences on Computational Science and Its Applications (ICCSA) conference series, previously held in Hanoi, Vietnam (2024), Athens, Greece (2023), Málaga, Spain (2022), Cagliari, Italy (hybrid with a few participants in presence in 2021 and completely online in 2020), whilst earlier editions took place in Saint Petersburg, Russia (2019), Melbourne, Australia (2018), Trieste, Italy (2017), Beijing, China (2016), Banff, Canada (2015), Guimaraes, Portugal (2014), Ho Chi Minh City, Vietnam (2013), Salvador, Brazil (2012), Santander, Spain (2011), Fukuoka, Japan (2010), Suwon, South Korea (2009), Perugia, Italy (2008), Kuala Lumpur, Malaysia (2007), Glasgow, UK (2006), Singapore (2005), Assisi, Italy (2004), Montreal, Canada (2003), and (as ICCS) Amsterdam, the Netherlands (2002) and San Francisco, USA (2001).

Computational Science constitutes the main pillar of most present research, industrial and commercial applications, and plays a unique role in exploiting ICT innovative technologies, and the ICCSA conference series has, accordingly, provided ample opportunities to researchers and industry practitioners to discuss new ideas, to share complex problems and their solutions, and to shape new trends in Computational Science. As the conference mirrors society from a scientific point of view, this year's undoubtedly dominant theme was large language models, machine learning and Artificial Intelligence (AI) and their applications in the most diverse technological, economic and industrial fields, amongst the others.

The ICCSA 2025 conference was structured in six general tracks covering the fields of computational science and its applications: Computational Methods, Algorithms and Scientific Applications – High Performance Computing and Networks – Geometric Modeling, Graphics and Visualization – Advanced and Emerging Applications – Information Systems and Technologies – Urban and Regional Planning. In addition, the conference consisted of 68 workshops, focusing on topical issues of utmost importance to science, technology and society: from new computational approaches for earth science, to mathematical methods for image processing, new statistical and optimization methods, several Artificial Intelligence approaches, sustainability issues, smart cities and related technologies, to name some.

In the Main Conference Proceedings, we accepted 71 full papers, 6 short papers and 1 Ph.D. Showcase paper from 269 submissions to the General Tracks of the Conference (with an acceptance rate of 29.9%). In the Workshops proceedings, we accepted 362 full papers, 37 short papers and 2 Ph.D. Showcase papers from a total of 1043 submissions (Acceptance rate 38.4%). We would like to convey our sincere appreciation to the workshops' chairs and co-chairs and program committee members for their diligent work, commitment and dedication.

The success and consistent maintenance of the ICCSA conference series in general, and of ICCSA 2025 in particular, rely upon the support of many people: authors, presenters, participants, keynote speakers, workshop chairs, session chairs, organizing committee members, student volunteers, Program Committee members, Advisory Committee members, International Liaison chairs, reviewers and other individuals in various roles. Thus, we take this opportunity to wholehartedly thank each and everyone.

We additionally wish to thank publisher Springer for their agreement to publish the proceedings, besides sponsoring part of the best papers awards and for their kind assistance and cooperation during the editing process.

We would cordially like to invite you to refer to the ICCSA website https://iccsa.org, where you can find the relevant details regarding this academic endeavor and event of ours.

June 2025

Osvaldo Gervasi
Yeliz Karaca
Beniamino Murgante
Chiara Garau

A Welcome Message from the Organizers

The International Conference on Computational Science and Its Applications (ICCSA) reflects a culmination of meticulous and dedicated efforts and academic endeavors toward the progress of science and technology.

One of the most noteworthy aspects of ICCSA is its fostering of a collective spirit, bringing together a plethora of participants from all over the world. Correspondingly, this merging power manifests itself in the 25th anniversary of ICCSA, which is a quarter of a century, in Istanbul, Türkiye, which connects and acts as a bridge between two continents, namely Asia and Europe. This unique location in the world hosts the 25th year of ICCSA at Galatasaray University, located on Çırağan Avenue by Istanbul's Bosphorus, which is an established international university bestowed with a distinctive past of teaching tradition, research and education exceeding five centuries.

Istanbul, having served as the capital city of four empires, namely the Roman Empire (330–395), the Byzantine Empire (395–1204 and 1261–1453), the Latin Empire (1204–1261) and the Ottoman Empire (1453–1922), is an exceptional city of the Republic of Türkiye founded by Mustafa Kemal Atatürk.

Situated at a strategic location along the historic Silk Road, Istanbul is at the core of extending rail networks which span across Europe and West Asia along with the only sea route between the Black Sea and the Mediterranean.

The cultural, historical and economic pulses of the country are evident in Istanbul whose rooted origins have embraced varying beliefs, lifestyles and populace, which highlights the city's mosaic quality with blended fabric in a constant harmonious flow. This has enabled cultures to grow and be nurtured, which is profoundly rooted in its urban culture.

Computational Science constitutes the main pillar of most present research, industrial and commercial activities besides manifesting a unique role in exploiting and addressing innovative Information and Communication Technologies. Thus, the 25-year-old ICCSA conference series provides remarkable opportunities to get acquainted with leading researchers, scientists, scholars, practitioners and many more while exchanging innovative ideas and initiating new partnerships, associations and bonds.

With the hosting of Galatasaray University, I would personally and on behalf of the Local Organizing Committee, with the members Emre Alptekin, Gülfem Işıklar Alptekin, Cengiz Kahraman, Abdullah Çağrı Tolga and Ayberk Zeytin, like to convey our sincere gratitude and thanks to everyone who exerted their efforts in and contributed to the realization of ICCSA 2025. With these notes and remarks, welcome to Istanbul!

Cordially yours,

On behalf of the Local Organizing Committee.

June 2025   Yeliz Karaca

Organization

Honorary General Chairs

Bernady O. Apduhan   Kyushu Sangyo University, Japan
Kenneth C. J. Tan   Sardina Systems, UK

General Chairs

Yeliz Karaca   University of Massachusetts, USA
Osvaldo Gervasi   University of Perugia, Italy
David Taniar   Monash University, Australia

Program Committee Chairs

Beniamino Murgante   University of Basilicata, Italy
Chiara Garau   University of Cagliari, Italy
Ana Maria A. C. Rocha   University of Minho, Portugal
A. Çağrı Tolga   Galatasaray University, Türkiye

International Advisory Committee

Jemal Abawajy   Deakin University, Australia
Dharma P. Agarwal   University of Cincinnati, USA
Rajkumar Buyya   Melbourne University, Australia
Claudia Bauzer Medeiros   University of Campinas, Brazil
Manfred M. Fisher   Vienna University of Economics and Business,
                              Austria
Pierre Frankhauser   University of Franche-Comté/CNRS, France
Marina L. Gavrilova   University of Calgary, Canada
Sumi Helal   University of Florida, USA & Lancaster
                              University, UK
Bin Jiang   University of Gävle, Sweden
Yee Leung   Chinese University of Hong Kong, China

International Liaison Chairs

Ivan Blečić	University of Cagliari, Italy
Giuseppe Borruso	University of Trieste, Italy
Elise De Donker	Western Michigan University, USA
Maria Noelia Faginas Lago	University of Perugia, Italy
Maria Irene Falcão	University of Minho, Portugal
Robert C. H. Hsu	Chung Hua University, Taiwan
Yeliz Karaca	University of Massachusetts Chan Medical School, USA
Tae-Hoon Kim	Zhejiang University of Science and Technology, China
Vladimir Korkhov	Saint Petersburg University, Russia
Takashi Naka	Kyushu Sangyo University, Japan
Rafael D. C. Santos	National Institute for Space Research, Brazil
Maribel Yasmina Santos	University of Minho, Portugal
Anastasia Stratigea	National Technical University of Athens, Greece

Workshop and Session Organizing Chairs

Beniamino Murgante	University of Basilicata, Italy
Chiara Garau	University of Cagliari, Italy

Award Chair

Wenny Rahayu	La Trobe University, Australia

Publicity Committee Chairs

Elmer Dadios	De La Salle University, Philippines
Nataliia Kulabukhova	Saint Petersburg University, Russia
Daisuke Takahashi	Tsukuba University, Japan
Shangwang Wang	Beijing University of Posts and Telecommunications, China

Local Organizing Committee Chairs

Emre Alptekin	Galatasaray University, Türkiye
Gülfem Işıklar Alptekin	Galatasaray University, Türkiye
Cengiz Kahraman	İstanbul Technical University, Türkiye
A. Çağrı Tolga	Galatasaray University, Türkiye
Ayberk Zeytin	Galatasaray University, Türkiye

Technology Chair

Damiano Perri	University of Perugia, Italy

Program Committee

Vera Afreixo	University of Aveiro, Portugal
Vladimir Alarcon	Northern Gulf Institute, USA
Filipe Alvelos	University of Minho, Portugal
Debora Anelli	Polytechnic University of Bari, Italy
Hartmut Asche	Hasso-Plattner-Institut für Digital Engineering Ggmbh, Germany
Nizamettin Aydın,	İstanbul Technical University, Türkiye
Ginevra Balletto	University of Cagliari, Italy
Nadia Balucani	University of Perugia, Italy
Socrates Basbas	Aristotle University of Thessaloniki, Greece
David Berti	ART SpA, Italy
Michela Bertolotto	University College Dublin, Ireland
Sandro Bimonte	CEMAGREF, TSCF, France
Ana Cristina Braga	University of Minho, Portugal
Tiziana Campisi	Kore University of Enna, Italy
Yves Caniou	Université Claude Bernard Lyon 1, France
Alessandra Capolupo	Polytechnic University of Bari, Italy
José A. Cardoso e Cunha	Universidade Nova de Lisboa, Portugal
Rui Cardoso	University of Beira Interior, Portugal
Leocadio G. Casado	University of Almería, Spain
Mete Celik	Erciyes University, Turkey
Maria Cerreta	University of Naples Federico II, Italy
Ta Quang Chieu	Thuyloi University, Vietnam
Rachel Chien-Sing Lee	Sunway University, Malaysia
Birol Ciloglugil	Ege University, Turkey
Mauro Coni	University of Cagliari, Italy

Suzan Obaiys   University of Malaya, Malaysia
Marcin Paprzycki   Polish Academy of Sciences, Poland
Eric Pardede   La Trobe University, Australia
Ana Isabel Pereira   Polytechnic Institute of Bragança, Portugal
Damiano Perri   University of Perugia, Italy
Massimiliano Petri   University of Pisa, Italy
Telmo Pinto   University of Coimbra, Portugal
Alessandro Plaisant   University of Sassari, Italy
Maurizio Pollino   ENEA, Italy
Alenka Poplin   Iowa State University, USA
Marcos Quiles   Federal University of São Paulo, Brazil
Nguyen Huu Quynh   Thuyloi University, Vietnam
Albert Rimola   Universitat Autònoma de Barcelona, Spain
Humberto Rocha   University of Coimbra, Portugal
Marzio Rosi   University of Perugia, Italy
Lucia Saganeiti   University of L'Aquila, Italy
Francesco Scorza   University of Basilicata, Italy
Marco Paulo Seabra dos Reis   University of Coimbra, Portugal
Jie Shen   University of Michigan, USA
Francesco Tajani   Sapienza University of Rome, Italy
Rodrigo Tapia Mcclung   Centro de Investigación en Ciencias de
                                    Información Geoespacial, Mexico
Eufemia Tarantino   Polytechnic University of Bari, Italy
Sergio Tasso   University of Perugia, Italy
Ana Paula Teixeira   Universidade do Minho, Portugal
Yiota Theodora   National Technical University of Athens, Greece
Giuseppe A. Trunfio   University of Sassari, Italy
Toshihiro Uchibayashi   Kyushu University, Japan
Marco Vizzari   University of Perugia, Italy
Frank Westad   Norwegian University of Science and Technology,
                                    Norway
Fukuko Yuasa   High Energy Accelerator Research Organization,
                                    Japan
Ljiljana Zivkovic   Republic Geodetic Authority, Serbia

General Tracks

1. Computational Methods, Algorithms and Scientific Applications

Computational Biology
Computational Combustion
Computational Chemistry

Computational Fluid Dynamics
Computational Physics
Computational Geometry
Computational Mathematics
Computational Mechanics
Computational Electro-magnetics
Numerical Methods and Algorithms

2. High Performance Computing and Networks

Parallel and Distributed Computing
Cluster Computing
Supercomputing
Cloud Computing
Autonomic Computing
P2P Computing
Mobile Computing
Edge Computing
Workflow Design and Practice
Computer and Network Architecture

3. Geometric Modeling, Graphics and Visualization

Scientific Visualization
Computer Graphics
Geometric Modeling
Pattern Recognition
Image Processing
CAD/CAM
Web3D, Virtual and Augmented Reality

4. Advanced and Emerging Applications

Biochemistry
Bioinformatics
Astrophysics
Biometric Modeling
Environmental, Climate and Weather Modeling
Geology and Geophysics
Nuclear Physics
Financial and Economical Modeling
Computational Journalism

5. Information Systems and Technologies

Information Retrieval
Scientific Databases
Security Engineering
Risk Analysis
Reliability Engineering

Software Engineering
Data Mining
Artificial Intelligence
Machine Learning
Learning Technologies
Web-Based Computing
Web 2.0
Blockchain

6. Urban and Regional Planning

Urban and Regional Growth
Sustainable Urban and Regional Development
Socio-ecological Systems
Open Data/Big Data
Cultural Heritage
Smart and Sustainable Cities
Mobility and Intelligent Transport Systems
Geographical Information Systems
Decision Support Systems
Complexity Assessment and Mapping
Logistics

Sponsoring Organizations

ICCSA 2025 would not have been possible without the tremendous support of many organizations and institutions, for which all organizers and participants of ICCSA 2025 express their sincere gratitude:

Galatasaray University, Istanbul, Türkiye
(https://gsu.edu.tr/en)

African Mathematical Union
(https://www.africanmathunion.org/)

Springer Nature Switzerland AG, Switzerland
(https://www.springer.com)

The University of Massachusetts, USA
(https://www.umass.edu/)

University of Perugia, Italy
(https://www.unipg.it)

University of Basilicata, Italy (http://www.unibas.it)

Monash University, Australia
(https://www.monash.edu/)

Kyushu Sangyo University, Japan
(https://www.kyusan-u.ac.jp/)

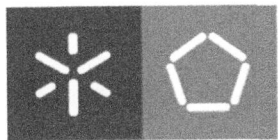

Universidade do Minho
Escola de Engenharia

University of Minho, Portugal
(https://www.uminho.pt/)
Venue
ICCSA 2025 took place in: **Galatasaray University, Istanbul, Türkiye**

Additional Reviewers

Reviewers
The review tasks for each workshop have been carried out by the workshop Organizers and the members of the workshop Program Committee.

Plenary Lectures

Sky Safe with GAI and Post-quantum Computing

Elizabeth Chang

Professor of the Cyber Security and Head of Discipline, University of Sunshine Coast, Australia

Abstract. Professor Chang's talk in this presentation has two distinct parts. To start, she will introduce the landscape of cybersecurity development, attacks, threats, and vulnerabilities, as well as state-of-the-art cyber protection, cyber defence, and cyber incident prevention. This is followed by a discussion of the impact of Generative AI (GAI) and quantum-safe cryptographic computing, highlighting the major issues and challenges in research, education, and training. In conclusion, she will present a vision for Sky Safe solutions, aiming to achieve cyber resilience that supports business and economic stability, enhances human capabilities, and promotes environmental sustainability.

Disaster Preparedness and Risk Profiling in the Digital Era from Earth Observation Lens

Jagannath Aryal

Department of Infrastructure Engineering, University of Melbourne, Australia

Abstract. Natural hazards which turn into disasters result in severe losses of lives, infrastructure, and property. Disasters such as earthquakes and landslides and their impacts on transportation safety, infrastructure resilience, and displacement of people to new places are challenges. To address such challenges, earth observation data and intelligent methods can provide potential solutions in developing decision support systems. This talk will present the state of the in Earth observation for disaster resilience using intelligent methods. In the earth observation space, digitalisation has revolutionised the way we map, monitor, and develop decision support systems. Global case study examples covering earthquake-induced landslides from the Himalayan region will cover the digital capabilities. The digital capabilities will embrace object recognition, interpretation, and their accurate and precise capture to integrate into digital models. The developed digital models from representative case studies can be leveraged in other jurisdictions in profiling risks to protect lives and infrastructure and creating disaster preparedness in the era of digital age and digital economy.

Intelligent Image Enhancement for Real-World Applications in Adverse Atmospheric Conditions

Khan Muhammad

Department of Global Convergence, Sungkyunkwan University, South Korea

Abstract. The adverse impacts of atmospheric conditions such as haze, fog, and low-light environments pose significant challenges for real-world applications reliant on computer vision, including autonomous driving, surveillance, and remote sensing. This keynote explores cutting-edge advancements in intelligent image enhancement, drawing insights from two pivotal studies. The first introduces HazeSpace2M, a comprehensive dataset and novel classification-guided dehazing framework that improves image clarity across diverse atmospheric conditions, addressing the gap between synthetic and real-world dehazing performance. The second focuses on LoLI-Street, a benchmark for low-light image enhancement tailored to urban environments, extending beyond enhancement to enable robust object detection and scene understanding. Taken together, these contributions demonstrate how integrating domain-specific datasets, advanced algorithms, and performance benchmarks can significantly elevate the reliability of computer vision systems under challenging weather and lighting conditions. Attendees will gain valuable insights into the methodologies, datasets, and practical applications driving innovation in this field, with implications for research and industry alike.

In Memory of Carmelo Torre

Unfortunately, Professor Carmelo Torre, one of the cornerstones of the ICCSA Conference, passed away last December, leaving everyone stunned and deeply saddened. His loss has created a profound void within our academic community. Carmelo was not only a respected scholar and dedicated contributor to the success and growth of ICCSA, but also a generous colleague, mentor, and friend to many. His intellectual rigor, warm personality, and unwavering commitment to advancing research will be remembered with great admiration. As we continue the work he helped shape, we honor his legacy and the indelible mark he left on all of us. 'Carmelo Torre graduated in engineering at the Polytechnic of Bari with a thesis on urban planning under Dino Borri's guidance. He began his research career by collaborating with Franco Selicato. During his PhD at the University of Naples Federico II under Luigi Fusco Girard, he specialized in real estate market analysis and multi-criteria evaluation methods. He explored the social impacts of urban transformations with his lifelong friend Maria Cerreta. His first ICCSA participation was in Perugia in 2008, in the session Geographical Analysis, Urban Modeling, Spatial Statistics. Instantly captivated by the conference, his charisma enabled him to involve various Italian scientific communities, including those in real estate and statistics. ICCSA became a yearly commitment for him, where he valued the high editorial quality of the proceedings and the dynamic post-presentation discussions and debates he passionately and expertly enriched. In 2012, alongside Maria Cerreta and Paola Perchinunno, he organized the workshop Econometrics and Multidimensional Evaluation in the Urban Environment (EMEUE), fostering dialogue on critical topics. His influence steadily grew, drawing numerous research groups to ICCSA and establishing real estate and assessment as one of the conference's leading fields. A pillar of ICCSA, he was involved across all facets of the event. Torre's contributions to academic discourse were marked by intellectual rigor and innovative thinking. His conference interventions consistently challenged conventional wisdom, offering insights transcending disciplinary boundaries. Beyond the conference, he passionately advocated for equity and social justice. His left-leaning ideology, though firm, earned respect from those with differing views, thanks to his sincerity and loyalty. He was creative, generous, and always willing to help, even at a personal cost. Despite battling illness, he maintained his characteristic optimism, warmth, cheerfulness, and commitment, supported by his partner, Caterina Rinaldo. His legacy lives on in his ideas, dedication, and unmatched generosity.

Contents – Part II

Information Systems and Technologies

A Deep Learning-Based Computer Vision System for Automated Screw Detection in Vehicle Wheel Boxes: Enhancing Automotive Quality Control with Industry 4.0

Decio Tomio Sakuma⬭, Carlos Marcelo Gurjão de Godoy⬭, and Regina Celia Coelho$^{(\boxtimes)}$⬭

Science and Technology Institute, Federal University of São Paulo, São Jose dos Campos, São Paulo, SP, Brazil
`{decio.sakuma,gurjao.godoy,rccoelho}@unifesp.br`

Abstract. Artificial intelligence (AI) can improve the quality control in the automotive industry. Reliable inspection methods are essential in manufacturing environments, as a single defect can damage a company's reputation. This work presents a practical solution using computer vision and deep learning to detect small screws installed in the wheel boxes of vehicles on a moving assembly line. The system combines a custom image acquisition setup with preprocessing techniques to improve contrast and clarity, followed by object detection using the YOLOv8 algorithm. Synthetic data generated to train the model effectively allowed for more robust performance without relying solely on real-world samples. The system tested outcomes with a screw detection accuracy of 92%, compared to around 71% accuracy from traditional visual inspections. That result suggested that AI-based approaches can significantly enhance quality assurance processes in automotive manufacturing, particularly in fast-paced production settings.

Keywords: Quality inspection · computer vision systems · deep learning

1 Introduction

In the automotive industry, product quality is the driving force behind gaining a competitive edge. Developing technologies to detect defects during manufacturing effectively has become an essential task within this sector [1]. Product quality defects can come from various sources, including machinery failure, operational errors, or failure of existing quality control systems [2]. Such defects can impact product performance and lead to safety concerns. In this context, a single vehicle defect can damage the brand´s reputation and compromise customer loyalty, which has been built over decades.

Visual inspection performed by humans is the traditional method of quality control in the manufacturing industry [3, 4]. This approach may not be feasible for some applications and may have severe consequences in the event of failure, as it is inefficient and prone to errors due to fatigue during repetitive tasks [5, 6]. With the modern trend of Industry 4.0 technologies, computer vision systems and Artificial Intelligence (AI) are increasingly utilized in manufacturing processes for automation, enhancing quality inspection and production efficiency [7–10], as well as reducing the need for manpower by replacing visual inspection [3].

Computer vision, or machine vision technology, is commonly designed to imitate manual inspection. Computer vision is a disruptive innovation that allows computers to perceive the world through cameras and make decisions automatically based on deep learning technology [11]. However, computer vision faces significant challenges, particularly regarding quality defect detection. A purely automated solution is not necessarily the most efficient when applied to quality inspection [5]. In this context, recent vision systems increasingly use deep learning techniques to improve the accuracy and reliability of the quality inspection process [8]. According to [12], deep learning techniques have significantly improved quality control systems for detecting defects in the manufacturing industry. Thus, the major contribution of this work is to demonstrate the role of an AI-based vision systems to manufacturing quality control and deliver product with high- quality products to the end customers.

Efficient computer vision enhances the system's effectiveness by properly training machine learning models with extensive datasets. Consequently, collecting and labeling a significant amount of data presents challenges due to the high diversity of product types and the range of defects that may occur during manufacturing. A balanced dataset of classes is crucial to avoid bias in the algorithm. In this context, utilizing a synthetic dataset can be a feasible method for training AI algorithms, ensuring consistent and reliable detection and classification of defects [12]. Furthermore, synthetic data provides a vast dataset and enables the control and manipulation of various scenarios, producing realistic images.

This study aims to develop a framework for computer vision systems using deep learning to detect quality defects. Our work focuses on the intermediate section of the assembly line, where each vehicle is automatically inspected for the presence of screws in the wheel boxes as it moves along the line. Figure 1 illustrates two types of screws found in the wheel boxes, (a) screw-a and (b) screw-b. We propose a deep learning-based solution to accurately detect small screws, using synthetic data to train the algorithm for outstanding performance. The ultimate goal of this work is for this computer vision system to replace visual inspection completely.

These screws play a pivotal role in properly fixing the plastic cover on the vehicle´s wheel boxes. The plastic cover prevents debris such as rocks, mud, and water thrown by the tires from reaching sensitive components of the suspension, brake, and car body. Thus, the lack of these screws can reduce the strength and durability of that area, potentially increasing safety concerns for the customer or reducing the vehicle´s life cycle.

The remaining sections are structured as follows: Sect. 2 highlights the literature review and related work; Sect. 3 presents the proposed methodology; Sect. 4 describes the obtained results; Sect. 5 offers the discussion; and finally, Sect. 6 includes the conclusions and future research of this work.

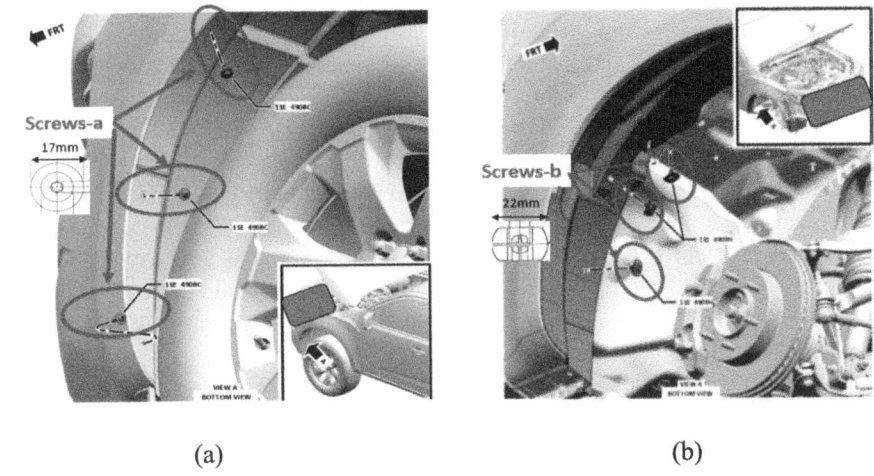

(a)   (b)

Fig. 1. Two types of screws. (a) Screw-a has a 17 mm size and (b) screw-b has a 22 mm size.

2 Literature Review and Related Work

With the concretization of Industry 4.0, the manufacturing process experiences a revolutionary level of automation in the production pipeline that incorporates Artificial Intelligence, Data Analytics, IoT, and more. Such aim is to minimize human intervention for inspection and produce products that meet high-quality standards [8]. In this context, the automation of quality inspection through computer vision and artificial intelligence has generated increasing interest among companies [5, 13, 14].

According to [15], poor product quality can lead to several negative impacts, including financial losses, environmental damage, and resource waste related to materials, personnel, and services. In response, [13] the growing popularity of investments in automated defect detection systems, which reduce labor costs and enhance the consistency and reliability of production processes. They thoroughly investigate two widely used neural network algorithms in industrial object detection systems: YOLO (You Only Look Once) and R-CNN (Region-based Convolutional Neural Network). This work emphasizes the critical role of computer vision in industrial applications, particularly for detecting defects in materials such as fabric, steel, and car rims, demonstrating its potential to improve quality control across diverse manufacturing sectors.

The quality control systems for detecting manufacturing defects have improved by implementing computer vision. However, these systems face challenges, particularly regarding the large datasets needed to train the neural network algorithm, such as YOLO. To address this issue, [12] presents an innovative method to train the AI model YOLO V5 using synthetic data, demonstrating its potential to reduce both the time and costs of data collection. The effectiveness of this method was validated through two industrial use cases: stamped parts and assembly lines. In both cases, the performance of the AI model trained on synthetic data was compared with that of models trained on real datasets. The study highlights the critical role of computational power in generating realistic synthetic images, which are essential for achieving high-quality training outcomes.

Examining related work in image preprocessing techniques, the review presented by [16] shows an interesting article that applies various image preprocessing methods, including Histogram Equalization, CLAHE (Contrast Limited Adaptive Histogram Equalization), image denoising, thresholding, binarization, and morphology transformation. In this work, the authors examined welding defects to verify that the weld spots meet the requirements using machine vision technology.

In summary, computer vision systems coupled with artificial intelligence are increasingly applied in the manufacturing industry to detect quality defects and achieve high accuracy and efficient processes. However, we could not find any papers that predominantly employ a vision system with AI able to detect small screws in the wheel boxes of moving line vehicles, which significantly increases the complexity of achieving high-accuracy performance.

3   Methodology

This section highlights the methodology used to detect and classify the presence of screws in the vehicle's wheel box on the assembly line. To achieve this, a complete computer vision framework was designed, featuring an image acquisition system and an Artificial Intelligence (AI) algorithm for detecting and classifying interesting objects with high confidence and precision, thereby enabling the removal of visual inspections currently performed by humans. Initially, this work consisted in defining the type of hardware and the appropriate setup capable of identifying with optimal quality the presence of all screws fixed in the vehicle. The next step was to develop a dataset to train and test the AI algorithm using synthetic images. Following that, image preprocessing techniques were analyzed to enhance the accuracy of the inspected objects. Finally, the system's results were evaluated using accuracy, precision, and recall. Figure 2 illustrates the proposed development flow for the automatic inspection system with a deep learning architecture.

3.1   Data Acquisition

3.1.1   Hardware

Cameras and lighting are pivotal in developing computer vision systems that detect objects. This proposed system comprises four cameras, eight lighting fixtures, and one central processing unit (CPU). Figure 3 illustrates the leading hardware used in this work.

- Lightning: Infrared light, 850 wave-length, SC75 Model, and 24V.
- Camera: Rolling Shuttle, Monochromatic, aca 3800-10gc, and Basler.
- CPU Matrox Intel core i5, 1Tb
- Cabo Ethernet

3.1.2   Set up and Commissioning of the Hardware

Initially, Process Simulate software was used to evaluate the optimal position for each camera that needed to be installed to achieve the best field of view for object detection.

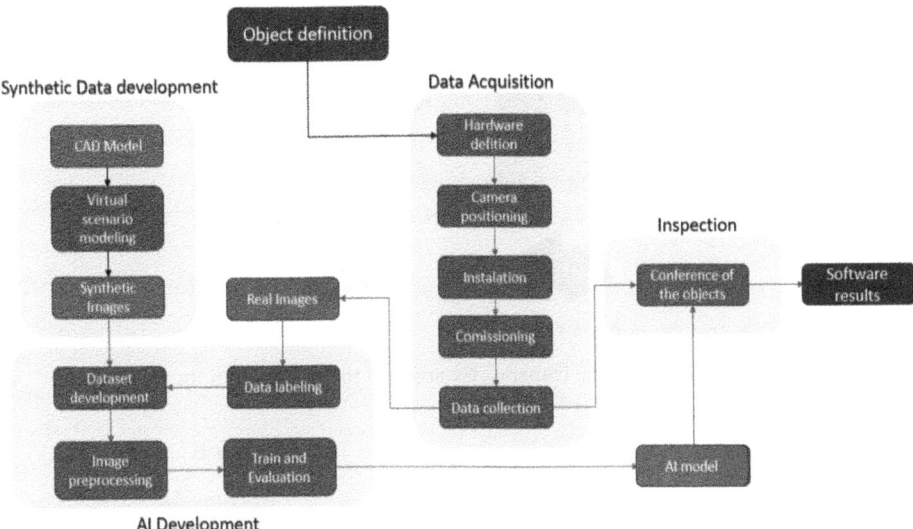

Fig. 2. Automatic Screw Inspection Process Flow

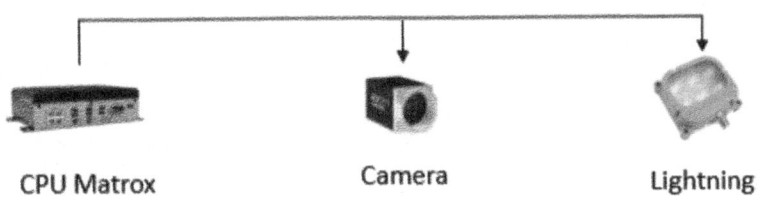

Fig. 3. Main hardware used to detect screws in the vehicle´s wheel boxes

The outcome indicated the necessity of installing two cameras on the right and two on the left sides, as shown in Fig. 4. The optimal position was the camera in "X" view, meaning that camera 1 focuses on the front face, and camera 2 focuses on the rear face. The challenges encountered in this step included adjusting four cameras to detect 27 screws distributed across four wheel boxes in difficult-access areas with varying complexity and size. Figure 5 illustrates an example of the field of view captured in a simulated environment.

3.2 Dataset Development

Real images were collected for dataset development once the data acquisition system was commissioned on the production line. According to [17], many images are required to train machine learning models. This work generated synthetic data to train and validate the proposed artificial neural network in this context.

Firstly, the dataset was developed based on synthetic images generated from CAD (Computer-Aided Design) models. Blender software was utilized for modeling and rendering 3D images. Furthermore, Blender was able to add texture and color and adjust

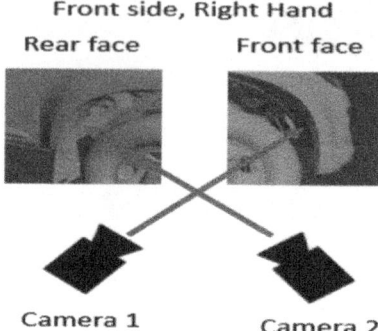

Fig. 4. Position "X" of the cameras. Example of the front part of the Vehicle

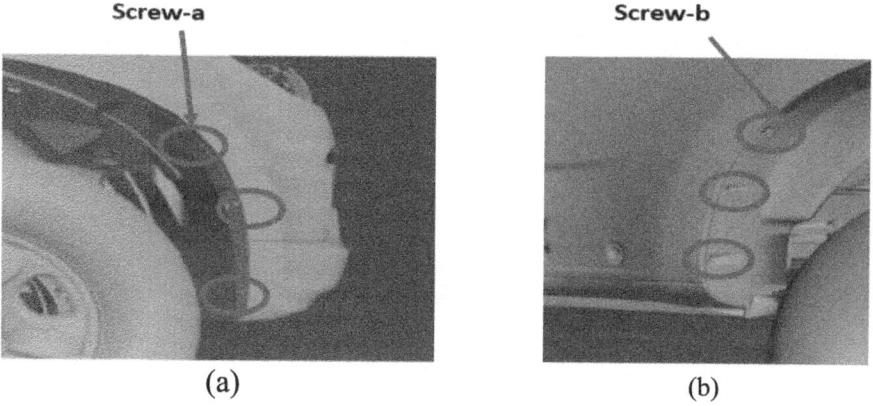

Fig. 5. Two types of screws are fixed in the right/front of the wheel boxes. (a) screw-a positioned in the front face and (b) screw-b positioned in the rear face.

lighting and sharpness, allowing realistic images to be created in a virtual environment. Once the part was modeled, user-friendly integration of Python and PyTorch with Blender automated the development of synthetic data. In addition, real images were captured through the image acquisition system installed in the production line, contributing to the dataset for training and improving the software performance. Figure 6 highlights the comparison of synthetic images (a) and real images (b).

The test dataset was developed using real images collected through the data acquisition system and manually labeled by software developers. Table 1 shows the number of images used to train the algorithm. These images refer to the presence of screw-a and screw-b. Table 2 presents the number of images used to test the AI algorithm. The lower number of screw-b is justified by the number of screws fixed in the vehicle.

3.3 AI Development

One of the characteristics of Deep Learning models is the necessity of representative data for training. In this work, AI development is based on a hybrid dataset for training

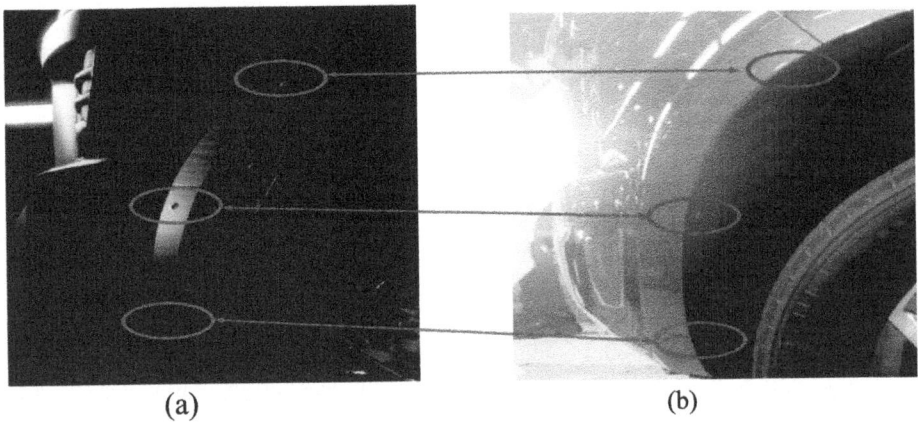

(a)   (b)

Fig. 6. Comparison of synthetic image and real image. The red cycles highlight the screws in the left/front side wheel box. (a) synthetic image and (b) real image.

Table 1. Number of images used to train the AI algorithm.

Dataset	Number of Image by class	
	Screw-a	Screw-b
Synthetic (S)	15389	15767
Real (R)	3262	3105
Hybrid (S + R)	18651	18872

Table 2. Number of images used to test the AI algorithm.

Dataset	Number of Image by class	
	Screw-a	Screw-b
Real (R)	1830	294

and real images for testing, as shown in Table 1. Considering that YOLO is widely recognized for its speed and precision in computer vision tasks [18], we adopted YOLO V8 and tested YOLO V5 and V10 versions. Regarding image preprocessing techniques, CLAHE and Histogram Equalization (HE) were evaluated to enhance the quality of the images and thus obtain better performance.

YOLO (You Only Look Once)

YOLO stands out among single-stage detectors due to its simple architecture, high accuracy, and fast inference speed [19]. Figure 7 illustrates a generic YOLO architecture.

This work prioritized the YOLO V8 due to its improvements in accuracy and processing speed [1, 25], which are essential for our proposed solution's requirement of

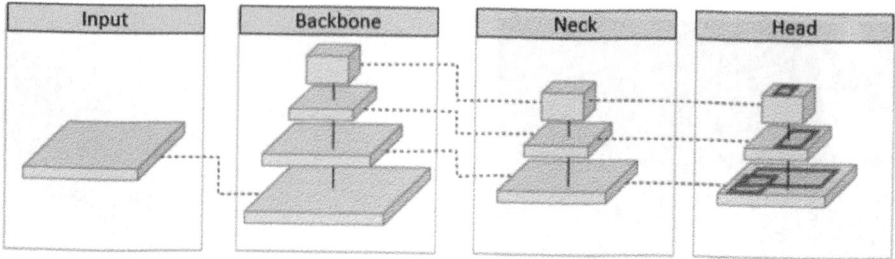

Fig. 7. Generic YOLO architecture.

real-time inspection. This model contains various parameters that can be modified and explored to optimize according to purposes. Table 3 presents some parameters used to develop our AI algorithm, as well as the corresponding parameters for YOLO V5 and YOLO V10. In this test, the dataset consisted of 5000 images, which included only synthetic data.

Table 3. Some parameters used to evaluate the AI algorithm

Parameters	YOLO V5	YOLO 8	YOLO 10
Number of neural layers	22 layers	75 layers	50 layers
Input image size	640 × 640 pixels	960 × 960 pixels	960 × 960 pixels
Initial layer activation function	ReLu	Simoid + SiLu	Simoid + SiLu
End layer activation function	Softmax	Softmax	Softmax

3.4 Image Preprocessing Techniques

Image preprocessing is a pivotal stage in computer vision systems, used to prepare raw images and ensure better results for the next step [20]. This stage aims to solve or minimize inference-related issues, such as noise and lack of image representation [21]. In our work, the CLAHE and HE techniques were evaluated to improve image quality.

According to [22], the HE technique is a method of image preprocessing that enhances the contrast of images. Meanwhile, CLAHE is a variant of HE that aids in preserving an image's local contrast features dynamically. Figure 8 showcases three distinct images: (a) the original image without preprocessing, (b) the image processed with the CLAHE technique, and (c) the image processed with the HE technique. This comparison allows us to evaluate the effectiveness of the preprocessing techniques in enhancing the algorithm's overall performance.

3.5 Performance Metrics

The performance metrics commonly used to evaluate vision systems are accuracy, precision, and recall [2, 8]. A confusion matrix was employed to evaluate our AI algorithm, as

(a)   (b)   (c)

Fig. 8. Comparison of images without preprocessing technique (a), and images using preprocessing techniques (b) and (c).

presented in Table 3. The observed classes identified by the system included the presence of screws, with the ultimate goal set at achieving 95% accuracy. This target is based on level 4 of the FMEA (Failure Mode Effect and Analysis) occurrence table.

Accuracy (Acc):

$$Acc = \frac{TP + TN}{P + N} \tag{1}$$

Precision (PPV):

$$PPV = \frac{TP}{TP + FP} \tag{2}$$

Recall (TPR):

$$TPR = 1 - FN \tag{3}$$

TP = True Positive; TN = True Negative; P = Positive; N = Negative; FP = False Positive; FN = False Negative

The AI classification results were evaluated using the Confusion Matrix based on the model in Table 4. This method was chosen for its simplicity, which aligns with the approach taken by [23].

Furthermore, the results of the proposed framework for computer vision systems were compared with visual inspection. This comparison demonstrates how important automatic vision is to guarantee product quality in the manufacturing process.

4 Results

This section embraces the results that led to the implementation of computer vision systems for detecting small screws in vehicle wheel boxes. Notably, YOLO V8 outperformed both YOLO V5 and YOLO V10 in all metrics, as shown in Table 5. Although YOLO V10 is the latest version, it did not perform better than the previous version in this evaluation.

Table 4. Confusion Matrix to evaluate AI algorithm.

		Predicted class	
		Class 1	Class 2
Annotated class	Class 1	TP	FN
	Class 2	FP	TN

Table 5. Results of the comparison between YOLO V5, V8 and V10.

	YOLO V5	YOLO V8	YOLO V10
Accuracy	73%	87%	42%
Precision	76%	92%	51%
Recall	73%	91%	51%

Table 6 details the results of image preprocessing techniques using CLAHE and HE. Both techniques focus on improving image quality by reducing noise and enhancing sharpness in the original images [14]. However, we have seen the HE's favorable improvements in contrast and sharpness achieved by demonstrating better outcomes than CLAHE.

For AI model evaluation, a dataset of 2,124 real images was used to test the model. The objective was to validate the effectiveness of this model in detecting the presence of 27 screws in the vehicle wheel boxes. Table 7 presents the number of real images from screw-a and screw-b. The lower amount of screw-b is justified by the number of screws fixed in the vehicle.

Table 6. Results of the image preprocessing techniques.

	Original Image	CLAHE	HE
Accuracy	89%	92%	94%
Precision	90%	93%	94%
Recall	94%	97%	98%

Table 7. Number of real images from screw-a and screw-b to AI test.

Classes	Number of Images by class
Screw-a	1830
Screw-b	294

The classification results were evaluated using the confusion matrix, chosen for its practicality and simplicity, according to the approach outlined in [23]. The results of this analysis, including annotated and predicted images, are presented in Table 8 and the Overall performance in Table 9.

Table 8. Results of the AI evaluation using Confusion Matrix.

		Predicted		
		Screw-a	Screw-b	background
Annotated	Screw-a	1798	3	92
	Screw-b	4	283	49
	background	28	8	0

Table 9. Summary of the AI performance

Overall Performance:	
Accuracy	92%
Precision	93%
Recall	99%

The confusion matrix analysis using real images reveals that, from the 1893 images tested, the system correctly predicted 1798 as screw-a, only three as screw-b, and 92 images were considered as background (images identified by the system as screw-a, but there were no screw-a annotations). In another tested class comprising 336 images, the system correctly recognized 283 images as screw-b, only four predicted as screw-a, and 49 as background. In summary, the AI algorithm´s overall performance results in 92% accuracy, 93% precision, and 99% recall.

5 Discussion

This work demonstrated the development and implementation of an AI-powered computer vision system capable of achieving 92% accuracy in identifying the presence of screws in the vehicle's wheel boxes on a moving assembly line. This level of performance enables automated inspection to surpass traditional manual visual inspection methods, significantly enhancing detection rates and preventing customer dissatisfaction caused by product quality issues. Furthermore, the automated inspection system aligns with Level 8 of the FMEA, underscoring its reliability and effectiveness. Such advancements are critical for manufacturers seeking a competitive edge in today's demanding market.

According to Prabhu et al. [14], HE minimizes image distortion and noise. In this study, HE was applied during the image preprocessing stage and compared with CLAHE to evaluate alternative techniques for image enhancement. The results demonstrated that

HE outperformed CLAHE in screw detection tasks, primarily due to its superior ability to process low-contrast images, particularly in complex backgrounds and small areas, as supported by [24].

An extensive and recent search in the electronic databases revealed no prior research addressing the inspection of small screws fixed in vehicle wheel boxes using computer vision systems integrated with AI technology. Consequently, this study fills a critical gap in the field, offering valuable insights for manufacturers seeking to enhance product quality control and optimize production processes.

The proposed AI model's performance demonstrated outstanding results, with all metrics exceeding 90%. Compared to traditional visual inspection methods, which achieve an efficiency of 71%, the system significantly improves quality control accuracy to 92%. This improvement highlights the significant practical implications of AI-driven solutions for the manufacturing industry. It showcases their potential to revolutionize conventional inspection practices, reduce error rates, and ensure process stability and customer satisfaction, consistent with findings reported in [2]. Such innovations are particularly impactful in applications where human vision is limited and high precision is essential, such as detecting missing screws in vehicles.

Furthermore, synthetic data is pivotal in accelerating AI model training, as highlighted in [12]. In this study, the YOLO V8 algorithm was predominantly trained on a synthetic dataset, delivering consistent and precise results. This approach demonstrates that the use of synthetic data is a strategy to reduce data collection time while increasing the volume and diversity of training datasets, as noted in [5].These advances highlight the potential of AI-based systems to provide scalable, efficient, and highly accurate quality inspection solutions in industrial settings.

Our research aligns with and complements the [13], showcasing practical applications of the YOLO V8 algorithm for quality inspection of wheel box´s screws. This addresses the challenge of detecting small components in areas with a limited field of view while also providing real-time results. As mentioned, synthetic data played a pivotal role in this research, enabling efficient training of the proposed algorithm. This is based on the work of [12], who introduced this method to train the YOLO V5 with real and synthetic images.

On the other hand, the present work provides a comprehensive development of the vision system, encompassing all stages—from dataset creation for training to testing the YOLO V8 algorithm. Furthermore, YOLO V5 and YOLO V10 were also evaluated to determine the best version of the algorithm for screw inspection in wheel boxes using synthetic data, further distinguishing from existing research. Finally, the HE technique was crucial to improve the raw image of the screws and enhance the performance of the vision system. This differs from the approach of [16], who used the CLAHE technique to improve the defective weld images in their research.

6 Conclusion and Future Works

This work shows how AI-based vision systems contribute to manufacturing quality control in the automotive industry. Automated solutions replacing manual visual inspection may improve product quality, optimizing efficiency and reliability in manufacturing.

As accuracy and consistency are critical in the automotive industry, these systems can help detect defects in complex assemblies, which improves production lines´ safety and performance.

In the context of Industry 4.0, advanced technologies, such as deep learning integrated with computer vision, have proven reliable for reducing costs, saving time, and increasing operational efficiency. Although the results presented in this paper focus specifically on detecting screws in wheel housings, future research should include the analysis of objects with different shapes, sizes, compositions, and textures. Such expansion would validate the adaptability of these systems for other industrial applications beyond the automotive sector.

Future studies exploring this type of Industry 4.0 perspective could occur to further integrate these tools towards Lean Manufacturing in the context of Quality 4.0. The synergy of these approaches would enable a more comprehensive exploration of emerging concepts and technologies, thereby supporting the development of innovative computational capabilities for the manufacturing industry. These computational capabilities would specifically help the automotive industry, notably in terms of quality optimization and customization of the production chain.

Acknowledgment. The authors are grateful to FAPESP (Fundação de Amparo à Pesquisa do Pesquisa do Estado de São Paulo, Brazil; grant: 2020/09850-0) for the financial support.

Disclosure of Interests. The authors have no competing interests to declare relevant to this article's content.

References

1. Jung, D.Y., Oh, Y.J., Kim, N.H.: A study on GAN-based car body part defect detection process and comparative analysis of YOLO v7 and YOLO v8 object detection performance. Eletronics (2024). https://doi.org/10.3390/electronics13132598
2. Jamal M., Faisal S., Kusumaningrum D.S., Rohana T.: Application of Yolo V8 for product defect detection in manufacturing companies. Journal Sistem Informasi dan Ilmu Komputer Prima. Vol. 8. N. 1 (2024)
3. Ren, Z., Fang, F., Yan, N., Wu, Y.: State of the art in defect detection based on machine vision. International Journal of Precision Engineering and Manufacturing -Green Technology (2022). https://doi.org/10.1007/s40684-021-00343-6
4. Hachem, C.E., Perrot, G., Paivin, L., Couturier, R.: Automation of quality control in the automotive industry using deep learning algorithms. IEEE Xplore (2021). https://doi.org/10.1109/ICCCR49711.2021.9349273
5. Torto, I.R., Campaniço, A.T., Pereira, A., Teixeira, L.F., Filipe, V.: Automatic quality inspection in the automotive industry: a hierarchical approach using simulated data. IEEE 8th International Conference on Industrial Engineering and Application (2021). https://doi.org/10.1109/ICIEA52957.2021.9436742
6. Rahimi, A., Anvaripour, M., Hayat, K.: Object detection using deep learning in a manufacturing plant to improve manual inspection. IEEE International Conference on Prognostics and Health Management (2021). https://doi.org/10.1109/ICPHM51084.2021.9486529

7. Abukhait J.: Dust Detection on Solar Panels: A computer vision approach. Ingénierie des Sistemes d´information. Vol. 29. N. 2 (2024)

8. Asif, S., Akmal, M.U., Koval, L., Knollmeyer, S., Mathias, S.G., Grossmann, D.: Supervised anomaly detection for production line images using data augmentation and convolutional neural network. IEEE 29th International Conference on Engineering Technologies and Factory Automation (2024). https://doi.org/10.1109/ETFA61755.2024.10710718

9. Avola, D., et al.: Real-time deep learning method for automated detection and localization of structural defects in manufactured products. Computer & Industrial Engineering (2022). https://doi.org/10.1016/j.cie.2022.108512

10. Chouchene, A., Carvalho, A., Lima, T.M., Santos, F.C., Osório, G.J.: Artificial intelligence for product quality inspection toward smart industries. IEEE Xplore (2020). https://doi.org/10.1109/ICITM48982.2020.9080396

11. Reyna, M., Delgado, G., Akundi, A., Luna, S., Chumacero, E.: Product digital quality inspection using machine vision systems – a categorical review. 17th Annual System of Systems Engineering Conference (2022)

12. Werda, M.S., Taibi, H., Kouiss, K., Chebak, A.: Generation of synthetic data for deep learning in manufacturing quality control systems. IEEE 22nd Mediterranean Electrotechnical Conference (2024). https://doi.org/10.1109/MELECON56669.2024.10608616

13. Tang, T., Sun, K., Zhao, D., Lu, Y., Jiang, J., Chen, H.: Industrial defect detection through computer vision: a survey. IEEE 7th International Conference on Data Science in Cyberspace (2022). https://doi.org/10.1109/DSC55868.2022.00091

14. Prabhu, A., Sangeeta, K.V., Likhitha, S., Lakshmi, S.: Application of computer vision for defect detection in fruits: a review. IEEE Xplore (2021). https://doi.org/10.1109/CONIT5 1480.2021.9498393

15. Azamfirei, V., Psarommatis, F., Lagrosen, Y.: Application of automation for in-line quality inspection, a zero-defect manufacturing approach. Journal of Manufacturing Systems (2023). https://doi.org/10.1016/j.jmsy.2022.12.010

16. Yun, G., Oh, S., Shin, S.: Image preprocessing method in radiographic inspection for automatic detection of ship welding defects. Applied Science (2022). https://doi.org/10.3390/app120 10123

17. Shahrabadi, S., Castila, Y., Guevara, M., Magalhães, L.G., Gonzalez, D., Adão, T.: Defect detection in the textile industry using image-based machine learning methods: a brief review. Journal of Physics Conference Series (2021). https://doi.org/10.1088/1742-6596/2224/1/012010

18. Usamentiaga, R., Lema, D.G., Pedrayes, O.D., Garcia, D.F.: Automated surface defect detection in metals: a comparative review of object detection and semantic segmentation using deep learning. IEEE Transactions on Industry Applications (2022). https://doi.org/10.1109/TIA.2022.3151560

19. Geetha, A.S., Alif, M.R., Hussain, M., Allen, P.: Comparative analysis of YOLOv8 and YOLOv10 in vehicle detection: performance metrics and model efficacy. Vehicles (2024). https://doi.org/10.3390/vehicles6030065

20. Ebayyeh, A.R.M.A., Mousavi, A.: A review and analysis of automatic optical inspection and quality monitoring methods in electronics industry. IEEE Access (2020). https://doi.org/10.1109/ACCESS.2020.3029127

21. Luo, Q., et al.: Automated visual defect classification for flat steel surface: a survey. IEEE Transactions on Instrumentation and Measurement (2020). https://doi.org/10.1109/TIM.2020.3030167

22. Mustafa, W.A., Kader, M.M.M.A.: A review of histogram equalization techniques in image enhancement application. Journal of Physics (2018). https://doi.org/10.1088/1742-6596/1019/1/012026

23. Malacca, P., Rocha, L.F., Gomes, D., Silva, J., Veiga, G.: Online inspection system based on machine learning techniques: real case study of fabric textures classification for the automotive industry. Journal of Intelligent Manufacturing (2019)
24. Kalyani, J., Chakraborty, M.: Contrast enhancement of MRI images using histogram equalization techniques. International Conference on Computer, Electrical & Communication Engineering (2020). https://doi.org/10.1109/ICCECE48148.2020.9223088
25. Ravichandran, M., Laxmikant, K., Muthu, A.: Efficient vehicle detection and classification using YOLO v8 for real-time applications. Global Conference on Information Technologies and Communication (2023). https://doi.org/10.1109/GCITC60406.2023.10426587

Impact of Distances in an Anomaly Detection Context for Time Series in Software Testing

Kevin Gerardo Polo Ruiz[✉], Alexandre Claudio Botazzo Delbem, and Paulo Sergio Lopes de Souza

University of Sao Paulo (ICMC/USP), Sao Paulo, Brazil
kpruiz11@gmail.com, {acbd,pssouza}@icmc.usp.br

Abstract. Software Testing is a critical stage in Software Development projects, which increases their quality at the cost of an increasing budget. This cost grows as the System Under Test (SUT) has poor testability. Data streaming systems or web servers usually present poor testability because they have constant input rates that often hide faults during testing. For such systems, it is costly to build test cases and verify whether the output is correct for each particular input. Tricorder proposes a methodology for anomaly detection without system requirements, taking into account the unsupervised learning provided by Damicore's methodology. This paper evaluates the behavior of distance measures for time series data within the frameworks of unsupervised machine learning carried out by Damicore, which is applied to software anomaly detection. The study systematically assesses the impact of each distance measure on the resulting accuracy within Damicore by conducting experiments across multiple benchmarks. Our findings reveal that the Levenshtein distance significantly outperforms DTW, NCD, FFT, and Hamming. Conversely, Hamming distance demonstrates the poorest performance. Levenshtein distance, on the other hand, offers an excellent balance between execution time and accuracy, providing an optimal trade-off for efficient and effective fault detection. The findings provide valuable insights into the effectiveness of these measures in enhancing fault detection accuracy, which could be extended to other domains involving anomaly detection of time-series data.

Keywords: Time Series · Anomaly Detection · Agglomerative Clustering · Fault Detection · Software Testing

1 Introduction

In the current age of the Fourth Industrial Revolution, where almost everything is digitally connected [23], new systems tend to be more complex, increasing the presence of integrity and security issues, with possible economic and personal losses. Validation, Verification, and Test (VV&T) activities are required

O. Gervasi et al. (Eds.): ICCSA 2025, LNCS 15649, pp. 18–34, 2025.
https://doi.org/10.1007/978-3-031-96997-3_2

to improve software quality, bringing high costs up to 40% of the whole budget for projects [28]. There is a pressing need for effective testing methodologies applied to software systems with poor testability, which may arise from factors that hinder the generation of test cases, such as legacy system constraints, incomplete or missing documentation, lack of clearly defined requirements, limited access to system internals, or challenges in replicating real-world scenarios [31].

Tricorder [17] is a novel software testing methodology to alert to possible faults, developed due to the need to execute testing in a maintenance scenario. It is a complementary testing methodology used after usual techniques, such as unit and integration testing, have already been applied. Tricorder was conceived thinking in systems with poor testability [24,29,31], like systems that process streaming data or requests on web servers. These systems have a constant rate of inputs that often prevent faults from being detected during preliminary tests. It is highly costly to build test cases and verify that each output is correct for its particular input [17].

Tricorder detects anomalies in the utilization of computing system resources by comparing execution profiles of a modified system version against a well-tested reference version. It leverages Damicore [22], a methodology focused on unsupervised learning. It applies clustering techniques to automatically identify behavioral deviations in the system through anomaly detection principles applied to time-series data. Damicore, as a core module of Tricorder, operates through three sequentially dependent stages: distance matrix generation, tree simplification, and community detection, ensuring a systematic and practical analysis of system behavior.

The construction of the distance matrix by Damicore is a fundamental stage since its representativeness influences the achievements of other steps. This paper evaluates different distance metrics from the literature on time series fault detection in software testing when using Damicore applied to the Tricorder context. Challenging test scenarios are proposed to check their limits in capturing significant differences from software profiles. Most scenarios relate to software maintenance, which requires identifying the presence and absence of faults, i.e., resource consumption anomalies. The number of false positives or negatives is a way to estimate the performance of such a tool. A balance is expected for practical applications, where the cost of false positives (unnecessary bug fixes) and false negatives (missed faults) can be substantial.

This work presents a systematic approach for evaluating the performance of our model. Although this work focuses on exploring and evaluating our methodology within a software testing context, its principles and findings could be extended to other domains involving time-series anomaly detection. For instance, fields such as health monitoring [10] and financial fraud detection [19] could significantly benefit from the insights and results presented in this study.

The remainder of the paper is as follows. Section 2 introduces the distance metrics in the literature that will also be part of this paper. Section 3 presents Tricorder and its relationship with measurements of software profiles used for fault detection based on computer resource usage. Section 4 describes the methodology for evaluating the performance of Tricorder according to each of the metrics, which involves a set of applications and workload scenarios. Section 5 and 6 present results and a detailed analysis. Finally, Sect. 7 highlights fundamental aspects of the proposed study and concludes the paper.

2   Related Work

The related work described in this Section addresses the construction of the distance matrix, which is the focus of our research.

The significance of Dynamic Time Warping (DTW) in time series analysis is well-documented. DTW aligns sequences by stretching or compressing them, which allows for identifying patterns even when there are temporal shifts. This flexibility makes DTW particularly useful for various applications in anomaly detection, being recognized as a robust and stable resource for handling time series data, outperforming Euclidean distance in some contexts using agglomerative clustering [11].

Another essential technique in the literature is the Fast Fourier Transform (FFT), which is frequently used for its efficiency in transforming time series data into the frequency domain. By doing so, FFT simplifies the identification of periodic components and anomalies within the data. This technique's efficacy is extensively discussed in [4], where FFT's role in processing and analyzing time series data is thoroughly explored.

In addition to these traditional methods, our project also investigates utilizing binary information extracted from logs, applying various distance metrics such as the default option in Damicore, Normalized Compression Distance (NCD) [5]. NCD is advantageous because it measures the similarity between sequences based on their compressibility, providing a unique perspective on anomaly detection that is particularly effective for any kind of data, including log data.

Levenshtein distance is another known metric that is applied to convert time series data into string representations. Levenshtein distance for time series data presents promising results for clustering [27], outperforming DTW and Euclidean in different datasets and demonstrating its capability to effectively calculate distances and identify anomalies by assessing the edits required to transform one string into another.

Hamming distance is also found in the literature, especially for time series data represented as fixed-length binary strings. This metric is helpful for its simplicity and effectiveness in counting the differing bits between two sequences. It is particularly well-suited for identifying anomalies in binary data, providing a straightforward method to detect discrepancies and faults in time series.

By leveraging these diverse distance metrics, we aim to enhance Damicore's robustness and accuracy for the detection of anomalies in the utilization of computing resources in the Tricorder context. Each technique brings its strengths to the table, offering unique insights and capabilities that contribute to the comprehensive detection of abnormal behaviors within our datasets.

3   Tricorder and Damicore

Tricorder [17] is a testing methodology designed to detect potential faults during software maintenance by identifying anomalous behavior in computing systems without relying on their internal structure or code. This approach is efficient for systems with low testability, where defining a test oracle is challenging due to the lack of clearly defined expected outputs. Inspired by regression testing, Tricorder compares the behavior of a modified system version against a previously well-tested version, referred to as the "reference," to identify changes in system performance.

As illustrated in Fig. 1a, after a code modification - often made during software maintenance - the behaviors of the reference version and the system version under test are monitored. During multiple executions, resource usage is captured at fixed intervals, generating time-series data used to construct a performance profile that represents the system's functionality. Deviations in these profiles from the expected norms of the reference version indicate a system's unexpected behavior and, consequently, the existence of possible software faults.

Tricorder has been evaluated across various contexts for fault detection, including applications in multiple domains [8] and machine learning systems [3]. Additionally, the methodology accounts for various system resources during execution, depending on the application type. Previous experiments demonstrated that bugs can significantly impact system resources such as CPU, RAM, disk I/O, and GPU [3,8,17].

The anomaly detection phase of Tricorder leverages Damicore [22] to analyze log data, grouping execution traces and identifying anomalous executions that deviate from expected behavior. The Damicore methodology, based on unsupervised learning, is capable of identifying patterns in any data by applying a hierarchical agglomerative clustering that uses modularity optimization to group execution traces from both the reference version and the version under test, enabling effective anomaly detection across diverse datasets. Damicore clusters executions from both versions, and if a cluster consists only of executions from the new version, it indicates the presence of a fault. Illustrated in Fig. 1b, Damicore receives as input a Profile Dataset and has three key steps:

- **Distance Matrix**: A matrix is generated using distance metrics applied between execution logs, with Normalized Compression Distance (NCD) [5] as the default measure. NCD is a compression-based metric derived from Kolmogorov complexity, enabling the measurement of distances between arbitrary data types. This capability ensures Damicore's versatility in handling diverse datasets, making it adaptable to various anomaly detection scenarios. Each element represents the distance between logs from two executions, and the matrix is iteratively updated with new version logs.
- **Phylogenetic Tree**: A hierarchical structure representing relationships between execution traces based on their similarities. In agglomerative clustering, this tree - also known as a dendrogram - illustrates how data points merge, with closer branches indicating higher similarity. In our approach, the

complete graph is reduced to a simplified tree using the Neighbor-Joining algorithm [21]. It provides a visual representation of the clustering process, where closer branches indicate higher similarity, making it helpful in understanding patterns in unsupervised learning tasks.

– **Profile Clusters**: Communities are identified within the tree using the Fast Newman algorithm [18].

Despite its utility, a gap remains in analyzing the impact of time-series distance measures for anomaly detection in the context of fault identification, as discussed in Sect. 2.

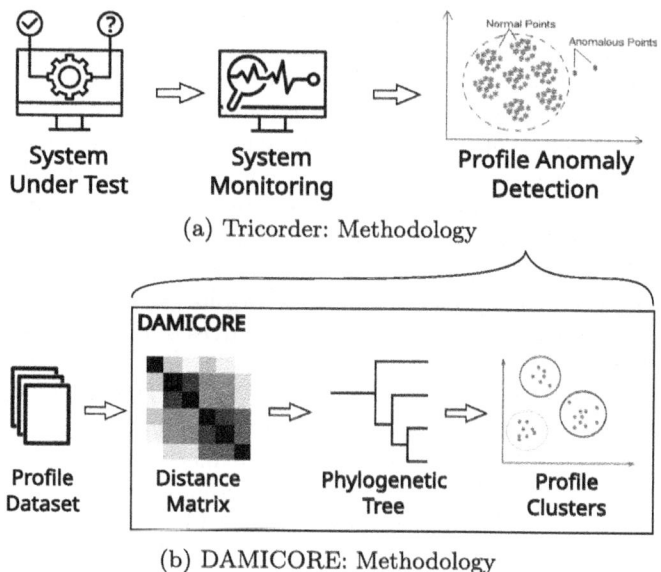

(a) Tricorder: Methodology

(b) DAMICORE: Methodology

Fig. 1. Tricorder and Damicore methodologies.

4   Methodology

In this Section, we outline the methodology applied during the execution of this paper. We begin by defining the scope of applications included in the analysis, most of which have been previously tested using Tricorder [3,17]. These applications were selected, prioritizing highly evaluated and well-documented open-source projects to ensure the reliability and relevance of the analysis. While we recognize the inherent limitation of testing every possible application, the selected set of applications represents a diverse range of characteristics common to many, including streaming services, machine learning projects, and database management systems.

Each application was evaluated using a set of test cases, referred to as workloads in this study, designed to assess key application features comprehensively. To analyze fault detection effectiveness, we tested multiple versions of each system, each containing a different inserted fault. Additionally, to assess potential over-sensitivity, we included a fault-free version, referred to as *CONTROL*, where no anomalies are expected to be detected. The faults were either intentionally introduced by researchers or replicated from real-world issues documented by the community on GitHub [3,32]. This approach ensures that the tests reflect real-world behavior while minimizing selection bias.

4.1 Network Telemetry

Network Telemetry is a streaming application that was initially documented in Tricorder's proposal [16]. In this benchmark, we use data logged already published [15], which contained logs of CPU, RAM, and Disk IO usage during multiple executions of this application. The outline of workloads and faults is as follows:

- Workloads: Defined by the format and size of files the application processes.
  - Format: Binary (BIN), Comma-Separated Values (CSV), and both formats (BINSCV).
  - Size: LOW, MEDIUM, and HIGH sized files.
- Faults
  - BCLEAN: a memory leak.
  - MONO: a parallelism problem.
  - SLEEP: null CPU usage.
  - SWAP: swap memory addresses.
  - INFINITE: high CPU usage.
  - NOBREAK: wrong execution flow.
  - UNLOCK: concurrency desync.

4.2 Voice Cloning

A machine learning application [6,7] that synthesizes audio by cloning the voice from a provided audio with a text. We execute the monitoring stage of Tricorder in this benchmark, according to the workloads and faults defined in previous experiments [3].

- Workloads: Defined by the length of provided audio and text;
  - Audio: Short and Long duration audio.
  - Text: Short, Medium, and Long sized text.
- Faults;
  - API: Missing or wrong API calls.
  - CONC: Problems of concurrence and synchronization.
  - LOGIC: Wrong logic or flow executions.
  - MEMORY: Memory usage problems.
  - MODEL: Misconfigured model.
  - PROCESS: Wrong initialization of variables or methods.
  - TRAIN: Wrong usage of the training set.

4.3   Bert

This benchmark implements the model proposed for solving natural language processing problems [6,7]. We use the data processed by Braga [3], already published [2].

– Workloads: Defined by the Datasets used for training: MRPC, CoLA, MNLI, XNLI, SQuaDv1, and SQuaDv2.
– Faults: Similar to the Voice Cloning benchmark: API, CONC, LOGIC, MEMORY, MODEL, PROCESS, TRAIN.

4.4   Chess Alpha Zero

This benchmark implements a Chess version of the AlphaGo Zero model [20,26], which learns to play by predicting the next move. We use the data processed by Braga [2,3] for our analysis.

– Workloads: Defined by the dataset used for training: OPT, OPT_STEP, EVAL, SELF, and SUP_LEARN.
– Faults: Similar to the Voice Cloning benchmark: API, CONC, LOGIC, MEMORY, MODEL, PROCESS, TRAIN.

4.5   Database

PostgreSQL [9], one of the most used relational database management systems, was executed in the monitoring stage of Tricorder. We defined a new set of faults and workloads.

– Workloads: Defined by the IO operation and the execution load;
    • IO Operation: READ, WRITE, and MIXED.
    • Load: LOW and HIGH size loads.
– Faults
    • DISKSORT: Forces sort operations on disk.
    • HASHJOIN: Forces join using the Hash algorithm.
    • MEMJOIN: Forces join on memory.
    • MONO: Disabling concurrency.
    • INFINITE: High CPU usage.
    • SLEEP: Low CPU usage.

In the context of our research paper, a correct selection of distances is essential to ensure the robustness and generalization of the proposed approach.

In this work, we modify Damicore to evaluate the effectiveness of various distance measures for time series, as introduced in Sect. 2. These modifications aim to address the identified gaps in time-series distance analysis for anomaly detection. Below, we detail the selected distance measures and their relevance to the study:

- Normalized Compression Distance: The default distance metric implemented in Damicore, NCD, measures the similarity between objects based on their compressed sizes. Its versatility lies in being independent of the nature of the data, making it suitable for a wide range of applications.
- Dynamic Time Warping: particularly effective for time-series analysis as it accounts for temporal distortions. We utilize an implementation capable of handling multidimensional time series (See [14,25]).
- Fast Fourier Transform: Employed to analyze the frequency domain characteristics of time-series data. For this study, we use the multidimensional time-series implementation available in SciPy [30].
- Levenshtein: Measures the edit distance between sequences, offering insight into the structural changes in the data [1].
- Hamming: Similar to Levenshtein, Hamming distance evaluates the differences between sequences of equal length, focusing on direct substitutions [1].

By integrating these diverse distance measures, we aim to evaluate their performance comprehensively and identify the most effective approaches for anomaly detection in fault detection contexts.

As presented in Sect. 1, we prioritize accuracy as our primary performance metric for anomaly detection, as it is particularly relevant to our context. Accuracy is defined as the proportion of correctly identified executions where a faulted version triggered an alert and where a non-faulted version did not, relative to the total number of executed workload-version combinations for each application. This metric provides a clear and straightforward measure of detection performance, minimizing unnecessary alerts while maximizing the identification of actual faults. Doing so enhances the robustness and efficiency of the software maintenance process. Other metrics, such as the F1-score, are not considered, as our primary focus is on fault detection rather than balancing precision and recall.

One significant issue identified was the presence of negative branches when employing the neighbor-joining method for Dynamic Time Warping (DTW). This phenomenon was observed particularly with our multidimensional data, where DTW failed to adhere to the triangle inequality. In this context, we applied the Fast Newman method with the inverse of the edge length, which precipitated negative weights. This choice led to the failure of the Fast Newman algorithm. As suggested by [12], a viable solution is to assign a zero value to the negative branches, thereby avoiding negative weights and preserving the network topology. However, this adjustment resulted in zero-length branches, introducing indeterminate weights. To address this, we explored three weight generation strategies: the default inverse option, normalizing lengths for inverse calculation, and applying a constant edge weight of 1, effectively creating an unweighted network (See Table 1).

Finally, we evaluate the influence of these distances on the accuracy of fault detection, where higher accuracy corresponds to superior outcomes. To assess the effectiveness of each distance metric, we will conduct a statistical analysis of their performance. We will generate 100 bootstrapped samples, which will

Table 1. Weight Generation

Name	Weight Value
None	$W = 1$
Inverse	$W = \frac{1}{L}$
Normalize	$W = \frac{1}{1+\Delta+\frac{L-\mu}{\sigma}}$

be calculated in the 25%, 50%, and 75% quartiles, also known as the first, second, and third quartiles. The differences between subsets will be analyzed for each statistical measure, and we will compare the 20% central portion of the sample relative to zero. Based on these comparisons, we will determine whether one strategy offers better, worse, or statistically equivalent accuracy in detecting anomalies. Additionally, we will examine the resource costs associated with this impact, focusing mainly on execution time to identify which distances demonstrate reduced execution duration. Ultimately, we will explore our findings to clarify the underlying explanations for these results.

5   Results

To provide an initial overview of the performance associated with each distance metric, we present the distribution of accuracy values in Fig. 2. This figure depicts the results using boxplots, enabling visualization of key statistical measures such as medians, quartiles, and the spread of the accuracy obtained in all distance metrics evaluated.

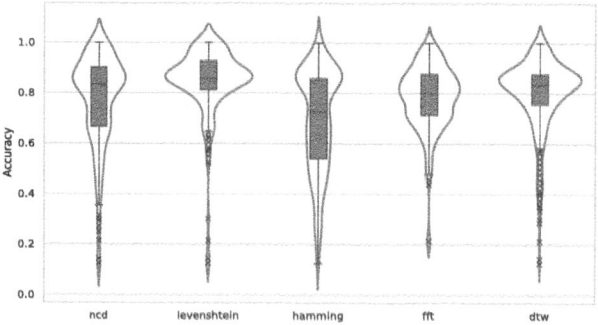

Fig. 2. Accuracy by distance.

Since none of the datasets follow a standard distribution, traditional statistical tests are not applicable. Instead, we applied the bootstrapping analysis detailed in the methodology to examine the quartiles of each distribution. The results of this analysis are summarized in Table 2.

Table 2. Results by distance

	ncd(%)	levenshtein	hamming	fft	dtw
Q_1	66.99 ± 0.76	$\mathbf{81.69 \pm 0.69}$	53.74 ± 1.06	71.26 ± 0.27	75.68 ± 1.1
Q_2	83.17 ± 0.52	$\mathbf{85.75 \pm 0.14}$	71.99 ± 1.32	79.65 ± 0.53	83.87 ± 0.66
Q_3	89.35 ± 0.93	$\mathbf{92.18 \pm 0.77}$	85.89 ± 0.54	86.77 ± 0.86	87.5 ± 0.0

As an example, Fig. 3 displays the bootstrapped distributions of the third quartile computed from 100 resampled datasets for each distance metric. The visualization clearly shows that the Levenshtein distance consistently yields higher third-quartile accuracy scores, while the Hamming distance demonstrates notably lower performance in comparison.

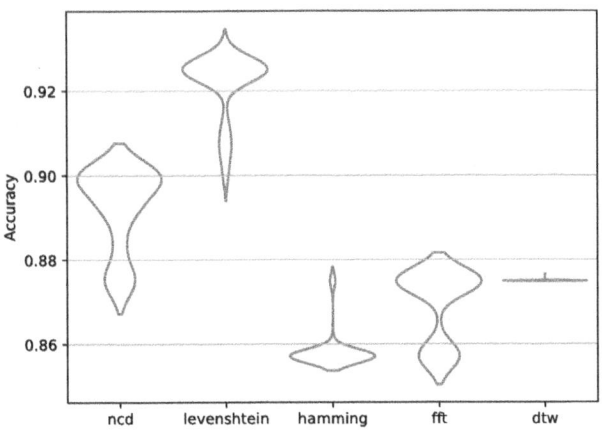

Fig. 3. Q3(75% Quantile) accuracy distribution by distance.

After replicating the analysis across all combinations of distance metrics and identifying negligible differences between bootstrapped datasets, we performed the statistical comparisons outlined in the methodology. Based on these results, we established the following order of accuracy, progressing from lower to higher, within each quartile:

- Q_1: {hamming} < {ncd} < {fft} < {dtw} < {levenshtein}
- Q_2: {hamming} < {fft} < {ncd} < {dtw} < {levenshtein}
- Q_3: {hamming} < {fft} < {dtw} < {ncd} < {levenshtein}

From the evaluation of each quartile, we conclude that the Hamming distance consistently presents the lowest accuracy in every quartile, while the Levenshtein distance shows the highest accuracy. The other distances, namely NCD, FFT, and DTW, fall between these extremes, with their relative performance varying across quartiles.

This consistent pattern suggests that the Levenshtein distance is the most influential metric for our fault detection approach, providing the highest accuracy across all quartiles. Conversely, the Hamming distance is the least effective, yielding the lowest accuracy. The performance of NCD, FFT, and DTW varies, indicating that their effectiveness may depend on the specific characteristics of the data in each quartile. This insight helps guide the selection of distance metrics for optimizing fault detection accuracy in our project.

In previous works, it was expected that Dynamic Time Warping (DTW) would present better results for aligning and comparing time series due to its ability to handle time series with varying lengths and non-linear distortions. However, our results indicate that Levenshtein distance can be more effective for anomaly detection in specific contexts. This effectiveness is likely because anomalies often manifest as local deviations from the norm, and Levenshtein distance excels at identifying such changes.

Table 3. Time Execution in seconds by distance

	hamming	levenshtein	fft	dtw	ncd
1. Matrix	**02.438 $\pm$ 0.030**	40.833 $\pm$ 0.622	44.610 $\pm$ 0.619	49.867 $\pm$ 0.404	94.313 $\pm$ 1.817
2. Others	19.413 $\pm$ 0.080	19.035 $\pm$ 0.091	19.173 $\pm$ 0.342	18.979 $\pm$ 0.078	19.201 $\pm$ 0.077
Total	**21.851 $\pm$ 0.080**	59.868 $\pm$ 0.597	63.784 $\pm$ 0.602	68.846 $\pm$ 0.445	113.514 $\pm$ 1.806

Table 3 presents the response times for community detection using different distance measures, splitting into two stages: "Matrix Distance" and "Others." The total response time is the sum of these two stages. The measures compared include Hamming, Levenshtein, FFT, DTW, and NCD. In the Matrix Distance, we can see:

– Hamming distance is the fastest in computing the matrix distance. This result suggests it is highly efficient for this stage.
– Levenshtein takes a more computationally intensive process for calculating the matrix distance.
– FFT, slightly longer than Levenshtein, highlighting the additional complexity involved in FFT calculations.
– DTW shows a further increase in computation time due to the dynamic programming nature of DTW.
– NCD is the most time-consuming, reflecting its high computational demands for matrix distance calculation.

The "Others" category response times are relatively consistent across all measures. This consistency suggests that the choice of distance measure does not significantly impact the tasks in this stage. All measures' standard deviations are relatively small, indicating stable and consistent response times across different runs. However, NCD shows higher variability in the matrix distance computation, suggesting potential fluctuations in its performance.

6   Discussion

To analyze the trade-off between accuracy and execution time, we present the execution load and accuracy in Fig. 4.

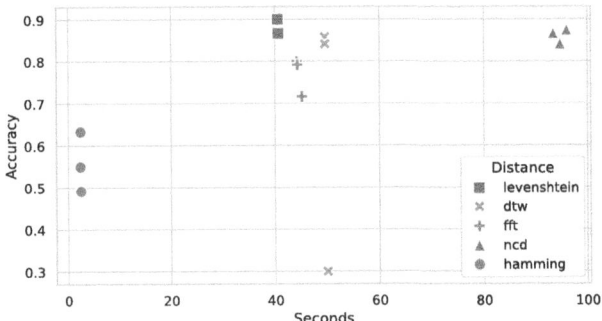

Fig. 4. Time execution vs accuracy.

Our analysis reveals the following insights:

- Efficiency: Hamming distance presented the best results regarding computational efficiency, making it ideal for scenarios where speed is crucial. However, it presents the worst results in accuracy for anomaly detection, which is an essential consideration for applications where accurately detecting anomalies is critical.
- Complexity: Measures like NCD, despite their potentially more prosperous information, come with higher computational costs and variability, which could be a trade-off in time-sensitive applications.
- Balanced Choices: Levenshtein, FFT, and DTW offer moderate trade-offs between computational complexity and richness of information, suitable for applications where moderate computation time is acceptable.

To understand the behavior of each distance, we show the distributions of distances between entities. We separated such entities' data into two groups: a set with reference behavior and a set with anomalous behavior. After this, the distance matrix from combinations of the data is categorized into the following groups:

- *1. Ref vs Ref*: This represents the distance between two reference objects. Since these objects are expected to exhibit normal, non-anomalous behavior, the distance between them should be relatively low. This result indicates that their time series patterns are similar and belong to the same cluster in a typical clustering algorithm used for anomaly detection.
- *2. Def vs Def*: This represents the distance between two anomalous objects. Despite being anomalies, these objects are expected to have similar patterns

of deviation from the norm, leading to a lower distance between them. Identifying this group helps understand common features among different types of anomalies, which can be crucial for refining anomaly detection algorithms.

- *3. Def vs Ref*: This represents the distance between one reference object and one anomalous object. As the behavior of anomalous objects deviates significantly from the reference objects, the distance between them is expected to be higher. This distinction is critical in anomaly detection, as it helps to effectively separate normal time series patterns from those indicative of anomalies.

This categorization helps identify and understand the distinct behavioral patterns between reference and anomalous entities.

In Fig. 5, we show the distributions grouped by the chosen benchmarks. We show slight separability between the group *3. Def vs Ref*, and the other two groups, following the expected behavior. Although the individual datasets yield varying results, the boxplots reveal a consistent trend in the relative ordering among the three data groups.

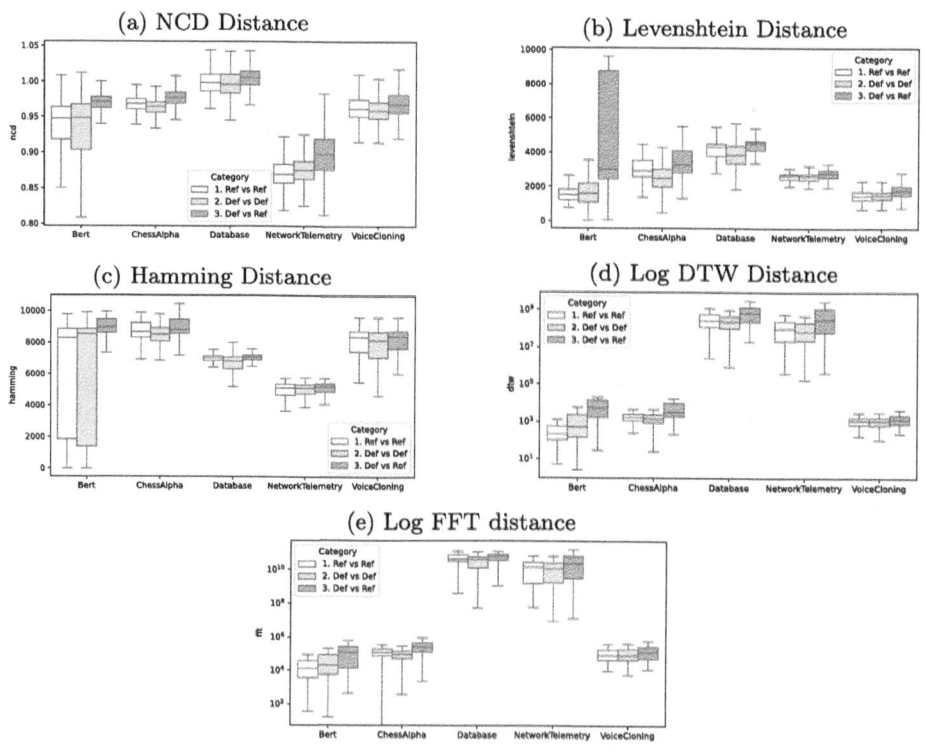

Fig. 5. Distribution for all distances.

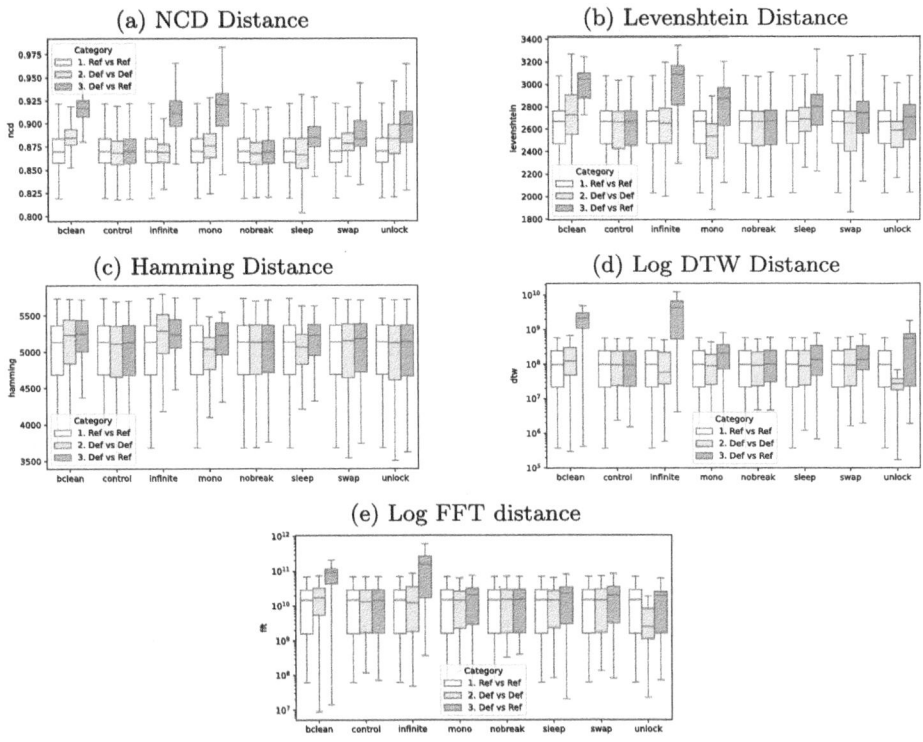

Fig. 6. NetworkTelemetry: Distribution for distances.

To deepen this analysis, we show the distributions of distances in the context of one benchmark, Network Telemetry, the first executed benchmark [17]. As seen in Fig. 6, all distances are visibly capable of detecting differences between objects, with more complications for the Hamming distance. Another notable result is the magnitude of the distributions of distances. Distances with higher accuracy have narrower relative ranges, while those with lower accuracy, such as DTW and FFT, have broader relative ranges. NCD and Levenshtein distances exhibit higher accuracy in distinguishing between reference and anomalous objects. A similar result is presented in the context of voice analysis [13]. Levenshtein out-performs DTW and Euclidean for detecting accents in voice files. This result suggests that these measures are more effective at capturing the underlying differences in behavior, potentially due to their ability to account for more nuanced variations in the data compared to other distance metrics, in contrast to others with higher sensitivity.

7   Conclusion and Future Work

The application of Damicore analysis within the Tricorder context to compare system behavior between well-tested and faulted versions demonstrates that the

Levenshtein distance achieves the highest accuracy for generating a distance matrix while maintaining reasonable execution time. This method outperforms alternatives such as DTW, NCD, FFT, and Hamming distance, paving the way for optimized testing activities within the academic community.

Although this study focuses on fault detection in software systems, the contributions introduced here have the potential to be extended to other fields involving time-series anomaly detection. The principles of this approach, including the application of various distance measures and the systematic evaluation methodology, can benefit domains such as health monitoring and financial fraud detection.

For future work, while our study concentrated on the initial stage of Damicore, subsequent research will explore its later stages, including tree simplification and community detection. By investigating these components and proposing new enhancements, we aim to refine our methodology, leading to more robust, efficient, and effective fault detection processes.

A potential threat to the validity of this study is the reduced diversity of applications and testing coverage. This constraint restricts a broader assessment of Tricorder's flexibility across different functional contexts. To mitigate this threat, we selected five applications from three distinct and widely used domains in the software industry: Streaming, Database, and Machine Learning. Additionally, workloads were designed to maximize feature coverage despite the challenges of generating test cases posed by data variability and volume. While Tricorder and Damicore are application-agnostic, their stability in distinct environments requires further investigation. Future work will expand our experiences across multiple programming languages and frameworks to further validate Tricorder's applicability.

Acknowledgments. The authors would like to thank CAPES (PROEX), CNPq (308445/2021-0) and FAPESP (2013/07375-0, 2019/06937-0, 2019/26702-8) for their financial support which made this research possible.

Disclosure of Interests. The authors declare that they have no conflicts of interest related to this research.

References

1. ax Bachmann: Levenshtein python c extension module. https://github.com/rapidfuzz/Levenshtein (2023)
2. Braga, D.: Tricorder machine learning: Dataset. https://github.com/diegobraga92/TricorderMachineLearning (2021)
3. Braga, D.: Assessing the use of performance data clustering for supporting software testing in the machine learning domain (in Portuguese). Master dissertation in computer science and computational mathematics, University of Sao Paulo, Sao Carlos (2022)
4. Brigham, E.O., Morrow, R.E.: The fast fourier transform. IEEE Spectr. 4(12), 63–70 (1967). https://doi.org/10.1109/MSPEC.1967.5217220

5. Cilibrasi, R., Vitanyi, P.: Clustering by compression. IEEE Trans. Inf. Theory **51**(4), 1523–1545 (2005). https://doi.org/10.1109/TIT.2005.844059
6. Devlin, J.: BERT. https://github.com/google-research/bert (2022)
7. Devlin, J., Chang, M., Lee, K., Toutanova, K.: BERT: pre-training of deep bidirectional transformers for language understanding. CoRR arxiv:abs/1810.04805 (2018). http://arxiv.org/abs/1810.04805
8. Duraes, T.d.J.O.: Evaluating the use of performance profiles applied in software testing in different application domains (in Portuguese). Master dissertation in computer science and computational mathematics, University of Sao Paulo, Sao Carlos (2022)
9. Group, P.G.D.: PostgreSQL database management system. https://github.com/postgres/postgres (2024)
10. Khanizadeh, F., Ettefaghian, A., Wilson, G., Shirazibeheshti, A., Radwan, T., Luca, C.: Smart data-driven medical decisions through collective and individual anomaly detection in healthcare time series. Int. J. Med. Informatics **194**, 105696 (2025)
11. Kotas, M., Leski, J., Moroń, T., Guzmán, J.G.: Hierarchical agglomerative clustering of time-warped series. In: Gruca, A., Czachórski, T., Harezlak, K., Kozielski, S., Piotrowska, A. (eds.) Man-Machine Interactions 5, pp. 207–216. Springer International Publishing, Cham (2018)
12. Kuhner, M.K., Felsenstein, J.: A simulation comparison of phylogeny algorithms under equal and unequal evolutionary rates. Mol. Biol. Evol. **11**(3), 459–468 (1994)
13. Lind-Combs, H.C., Bent, T., Holt, R.F., Clopper, C.G., Brown, E.: Comparing levenshtein distance and dynamic time warping in predicting listeners' judgments of accent distance. Speech Commun. **155**, 102987 (2023)
14. Meert, W., Hendrickx, K., Van Craenendonck, T., Robberechts, P., Blockeel, H., Davis, J.: Dtaidistance (2020)
15. Montes, V.: Tricorder method experimental data (2019). https://doi.org/10.17632/7HC8PK6HTW.1, https://data.mendeley.com/datasets/7hc8pk6htw/1
16. Montes, V.S.: Networktelemetry. https://gitlab.com/vmontes/networktelemetry.git (2020)
17. Montes, V.S.: Software fault detection using clustering of performance profiles (in Portuguese). Master dissertation in computer science and computational mathematics, University of Sao Paulo, Sao Carlos (2020). https://doi.org/10.11606/D.55.2020.tde-04022020-093604, https://www.teses.usp.br/teses/disponiveis/55/55134/tde-04022020-093604/
18. Newman, M.E.J.: Fast algorithm for detecting community structure in networks. Phys. Rev. E **69**(6) (2004). https://doi.org/10.1103/physreve.69.066133
19. Ngai, E., Hu, Y., Wong, Y., Chen, Y., Sun, X.: The application of data mining techniques in financial fraud detection: a classification framework and an academic review of literature. Decis. Support Syst. **50**(3), 559–569 (2011)
20. Pang, M.: Chess alpha zero. https://github.com/Zeta36/chess-alpha-zero (2022)
21. Saitou, N., Nei, M.: The neighbor-joining method: a new method for reconstructing phylogenetic trees. Mol. Biol. Evol. **4**(4), 406–425 (1987). https://doi.org/10.1093/oxfordjournals.molbev.a040454
22. Sanches, A., Cardoso, J.M., Delbem, A.C.: Identifying merge-beneficial software kernels for hardware implementation. In: 2011 International Conference on Reconfigurable Computing and FPGAs, pp. 74–79 (2011). https://doi.org/10.1109/ReConFig.2011.51
23. Sarker, I.H.: Machine learning: algorithms, real-world applications and research directions. SN Comput. Sci. **2**(3), 160 (2021)

24. Sharma, R., Saha, A.: A systematic review of software testability measurement techniques. In: 2018 International Conference on Computing, Power and Communication Technologies (GUCON), pp. 299–303 (2018). https://doi.org/10.1109/GUCON.2018.8675006

25. Shokoohi-Yekta, M., Hu, B., Jin, H., Wang, J., Keogh, E.: Generalizing DTW to the multi-dimensional case requires an adaptive approach. Data Min. Knowl. Disc. **31**(1), 1–31 (2016)

26. Silver, D., et al.: Mastering the game of go without human knowledge. Nature **550**(7676), 354–359 (2017)

27. Tamura, K., Ichimura, T.: Clustering of time series using hybrid symbolic aggregate approximation. In: 2017 IEEE Symposium Series on Computational Intelligence (SSCI), pp. 1–8 (2017). https://doi.org/10.1109/SSCI.2017.8280846

28. Valle-Gomez, K.J., Delgado-Perez, P., Medina-Bulo, I., Magallanes-Fernández, J.: Software testing: cost reduction in industry 4.0. In: 2019 IEEE/ACM 14th International Workshop on Automation of Software Test (AST), pp. 69–70 (2019). https://doi.org/10.1109/AST.2019.00018

29. Vianna, A., Kamei, F.K., Gama, K., Zimmerle, C., Neto, J.A.: A grey literature review on data stream processing applications testing. J. Syst. Softw. **203**, 111744 (2023)

30. Virtanen, P., et al.: SciPy 1.0: fundamental algorithms for scientific computing in python. Nat. Methods **17**, 261–272 (2020). https://doi.org/10.1038/s41592-019-0686-2

31. Voas, J., Miller, K.: Software testability: the new verification. IEEE Softw. **12**(3), 17–28 (1995). https://doi.org/10.1109/52.382180

32. Wanstrath, C., Hyett, P.J., Preston-Werner, T., Chacon, S.: Github, https://github.com/

Analysis of Bitcoin Trends Through the Integration of On-Chain Financial Indicators and Machine Learning

Arthur G. Bubolz[1]([⊠]) [iD], Giancarlo Lucca[2] [iD], Lizandro de S. Oliveira[2] [iD], Thiago Teixeira[1], Rafael A. Berri[1] [iD], Eduardo N. Borges[1] [iD], and Bruno L. Dalmazo[1] [iD]

[1] Federal University of Rio Grande, Rio Grande, Brazil
{arthurgomesbubolz,rafaelberri,eduardoborges,dalmazo}@furg.br
[2] Catholic University of Pelotas (UCPel), Pelotas, Brazil
{giancarlo.lucca,lizandro.oliveira}@ucpel.edu.br

Abstract. With the significant growth of the cryptocurrency market, predicting its short-term movements has become a significant challenge, requiring methodologies that combine both on-chain data and traditional financial indicators to improve prediction accuracy. This work proposes an integrated approach to predicting short-term movements in the cryptocurrency market by combining on-chain data with traditional financial indicators within the framework of the Rainbow Bitcoin Chart. The methodology encompasses data preparation, model development, and performance evaluation, aiming to build a robust and accurate tool for classifying market trends. By integrating blockchain structural analysis with financial signals, this approach seeks to enhance forecast accuracy and support more informed decision-making. The results show that the normalized model with 14-day windows achieved the best performance among the tested configurations, reaching an accuracy of over 75%.

Keywords: Cryptocoin · Bitcoin · On-chain · Machine Learning · Indicators

1 Introduction

In recent decades, the growing adoption of Bitcoin has demonstrated a relevant phenomenon in global financial markets [6]. The analysis of this asset presents challenges and opportunities that drive the development of predictive techniques. Among them, the combination of on-chain data and traditional financial metrics has shown promise [7]. This study proposes a model that integrates this information to improve the forecast of market movements, seeking to overcome the challenges identified in previous research [5].

Although many studies use traditional methods for price prediction [8], there is a limitation in considering the structural aspects of blockchain. Some

O. Gervasi et al. (Eds.): ICCSA 2025, LNCS 15649, pp. 35–50, 2025.
https://doi.org/10.1007/978-3-031-96997-3_3

approaches exploit unsupervised techniques [10] or on-chain data [12], but without integration with financial indicators [28]. Other work focuses on anomaly detection [14] or the use of deep learning [15], but does not directly address the combination of these techniques.

This research focuses on Bitcoin, applying predictive models to identify short-term trends. The challenges include choosing on-chain data, defining model parameters and selecting the ideal time interval [4]. With the increase in interest in cryptocurrencies, methodologies that assist in decision making become essential, especially in markets with high uncertainty [1]. The study seeks to evaluate the effectiveness of machine learning-based models in predicting price movements, contributing to more accurate analysis and informed strategies.

In light of this, the goal of this study is to propose a predictive model that integrates the use of a validated meta-classifier, that is, a model that serves as an additional layer to refine the predictions made by individual classifiers. In this case, the Rainbow Chart is used, a model based on logarithmic curves that segments the Bitcoin price range into different zones, providing a clear view of its historical behavior, allowing the identification of appreciation patterns and possible moments of overbought or oversold, helping to interpret market trends. On-chain data is also used, which are metrics extracted directly from the Bitcoin blockchain, such as transaction volume, active addresses and exchange inflows and outflows for respective predictions. Furthermore, the model will incorporate traditional financial indicators, such as the Relative Strength Index (RSI), an oscillator that measures the speed and magnitude of price variations to identify potential moments of overbought (when the asset may be overvalued) or oversold (when it may be undervalued), helping to make strategic decisions within the market. To accurately predict asset price movements in the short term. This model aims to increase assertiveness in negotiations, taking into account the relevance of Bitcoin as the main cryptoactive on the market and its influence on other cryptocurrencies.

The remainder of this paper is organized as follows. In Sect. 2, we present a brief overview of key aspects to understand this work better. In Sect. 3, we describe the related work, following a methodology used to select the most prominent studies on blockchain forecasting. Section 4 presents an assessment methodology to train the machine learning model. In Sect. 5, we detail the performance evaluation and discuss the obtained results. Finally, in Sect. 6, we conclude the paper with remarks.

2   Theoretical Foundation

In this chapter, fundamental concepts are covered for understanding the rest of the work.

2.1   Fundamentals of Cryptoassets

Digital assets operate in a decentralized manner, using cryptography to ensure the security and authenticity of transactions. These operations are recorded on the blockchain, a distributed ledger that keeps all transactions transparent and immutable, eliminating the need for intermediaries [9].

In the cryptoactive market, technical analysis and financial indicators are essential for predicting trends. Technical analysis evaluates price movements based on historical data, using charts and indicators such as moving averages, RSI and Bollinger bands to identify market patterns and support strategic decisions [10].

Financial indicators organize price history into zones that reflect levels of confidence in the market trend. Through metrics such as volatility bands and logarithmic curves, these indicators simplify the interpretation of financial data, helping to detect bubbles and buying opportunities.

Additionally, on-chain analytics examine data recorded directly on the blockchain, such as transaction volume and active addresses, providing insights into the asset's supply and demand. In the case of Bitcoin, this approach allows you to evaluate market dynamics and anticipate possible price movements [11].

2.2   Machine Learning

Machine learning is an approach that allows an algorithm to learn from a set of labeled data, where the correct answers are already known. The main objective of this technique is to allow the model to map inputs to outputs, enabling predictions or classifications to be made on new, unseen data. Within supervised learning, we find two main categories of problems: regression, which predicts continuous values, and classification, which assigns labels or categories to inputs.

Both techniques are essential in building predictive models, especially in the context of the cryptoactive market, where the ability to predict trends is crucial for making informed decisions (ZEKIYE et al., 2023).

Among supervised algorithms, the choice depends on the characteristics of the data. Linear models such as linear and logistic regression [20] are efficient for simple patterns, while probabilistic algorithms such as Naive Bayes [21] offer probability-based approaches. Tree-based methods, such as decision trees and Random Forest [22], are effective for more complex and multi-variable data.

Furthermore, neural networks are inspired by the functioning of the human brain and are highly effective in detecting complex patterns and non-linear data (KIM et al., 2022). In the financial market, they are widely used to predict prices, detect fraud and perform advanced analysis.

2.3   Blockchain

Blockchain [23] is a technology that works like a distributed ledger, recording transactions in a secure and immutable way, the structure is composed of chained blocks of information where each block stores data from network transactions, along with a unique identifier (hash). This identifier references the block within the chain, ensuring data integrity and allowing historical verification of all recorded transactions.

The network has in its structure the intrinsically linked concept of decentralization, where the need for centralized intermediaries for respective transactions is eliminated. The network is maintained by multiple participants (nodes), where they validate and store transaction information through consensus protocols, in the case of Bitcoin, Proof of Work (PoW). Such mechanisms guarantee reliable and validated recording of transactions.

In addition to its essential role in cryptocurrencies, blockchain has been applied in several areas, such as smart contracts, supply chain tracking and identity authentication. Its ability to provide security, transparency and decentralization makes this technology a promising tool for transforming various industries, enabling more efficient and reliable operations.

2.4 On-Chain Data

Among the main on-chain metrics used to analyze the cryptoactive market [24], Weight Mean stands out, which measures the average weight of transactions processed on the blockchain, considering the adoption of Segregated Witness (SegWit), which reflects the efficiency in the use of block space. Difficulty Mean indicates the average level of difficulty to validate blocks within a given period, being adjusted periodically to maintain network stability; its increase suggests greater competition between miners, while a reduction may indicate a decrease in the participation of these agents.

Reward Mean represents the average of incentives received by miners for each validated block, including both the issuance of new cryptoactives and transaction fees. In the case of Transaction Sum, it corresponds to the total movement on the network in a given period, offering an overview of economic activity on the blockchain. The witness sum (Witness Sum), related to SegWit, measures the total volume of witness data included in transactions, an important factor for evaluating the optimization of block space and network security. Also regarding sums, there is the sum of fees paid (Fee Total Sum) reflects the total transaction fees paid by users within a period, indicating moments of greater congestion on the network, as periods of high demand result in higher fees.

The input sum and output sum metrics quantify, respectively, the total values entered and removed from transactions on the blockchain, which is useful for understanding capital flows and network liquidity. Finally, the total number of blocks mined (Total Blocks) measures the number of blocks validated in a given time interval, reflecting the activity of miners and the regularity in the production of new blocks. These metrics, together, offer a comprehensive view of the network's behavior, helping to identify possible overbought or oversold scenarios and allowing for more informed decisions in the cryptoasset market.

2.5 Rainbow Chart

The Rainbow Chart [25] is a popular indicator that uses logarithmic curves to categorize Bitcoin's price range over time. It is not based on conventional technical analysis, but serves as a visual tool to identify possible market trends, helping investors to contextualize the asset's current price concerning its history.

The structure of the Rainbow Chart is made up of different color bands, which represent pricing zones, the lower layers indicate regions considered undervalued, suggesting opportune moments for buying, while the upper layers signal euphoric zones, which may indicate overbought and a possible risk of correction. These ranges are based on logarithmic models, which adjust Bitcoin's growth curve over the years, taking into account its deflationary nature and appreciation cycles (Figs. 1).

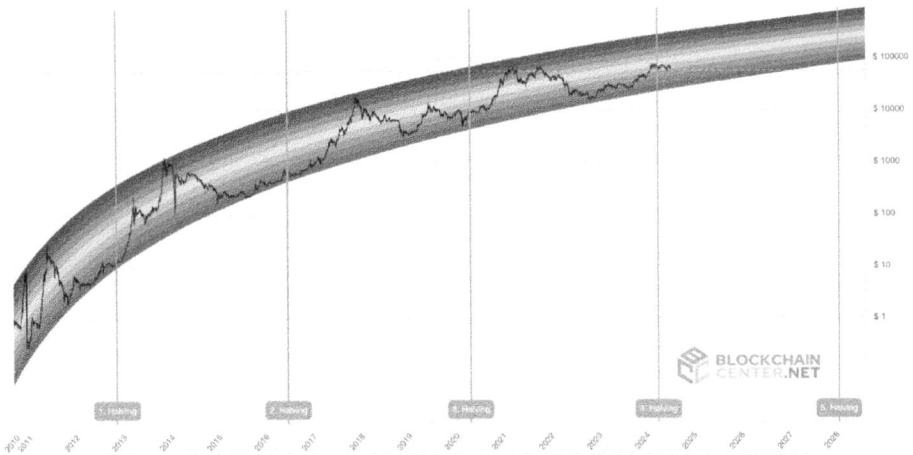

Fig. 1. Rainbow chart indicator. Source: Blockchain Center (2025)

2.6   Trend Forecasting

Trend forecasting [26] is an analytical approach that seeks to identify the future direction of a variable based on historical patterns and contextual factors. In the financial market, this technique does not necessarily focus on predicting exact values, but rather on determining whether the price of an asset is more likely to rise (uptrend), fall (downtrend) or remain relatively stable (sideways movement). The types of forecast may vary beyond these three types, covering different classifications for more significant price changes [13].

In addition to traditional methods based on mathematical and statistical analyses, more advanced approaches, such as machine learning, allow the modeling of complex relationships between multiple variables. Classification models such as decision trees and neural networks can learn non-obvious patterns in data and improve forecast accuracy by providing probabilities of trend continuation or reversal based on a large volume of historical information.

Although trend forecasting is never an exact science, as the market is influenced by unpredictable factors, the combination of different approaches and tools can significantly increase the assertiveness of analyses, allowing for more informed and strategic decisions.

2.7   Evaluation Metrics

The confusion matrix [27] is a fundamental tool in evaluating classification models, allowing you to visualize the model's performance when comparing its predictions with real values, organizing the results into four categories: true positives (TP), when the model hits a positive prediction; false positives (FP), when it incorrectly predicts a positive case; true negatives (TN), when a negative prediction is correct; and false negatives (FN), when it incorrectly classifies a negative case.

Precision is a metric that measures the proportion of correct positive predictions, calculated as Eq. 1. It is especially important when the costs of a false positive are high, such as in anti-fraud systems, as it indicates the reliability of the positive predictions made by the model.

Recall, also called sensitivity, evaluates the model's ability to correctly identify all positive cases defined as Eq. 2. This metric is essential in scenarios where the detection of all positive cases is a priority, such as in the diagnosis of serious diseases, where false negatives can have severe consequences.

The F1-score is a metric that seeks to balance precision and recall, being the harmonic mean between the two values, calculated as Eq. 3. It is useful when there is a trade-off between minimizing false positives and false negatives, ensuring that the model performs well overall without overly favoring one of the metrics.

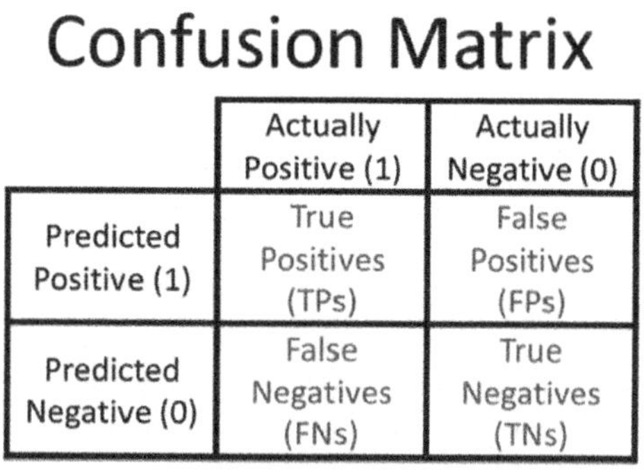

Confusion Matrix

	Actually Positive (1)	Actually Negative (0)
Predicted Positive (1)	True Positives (TPs)	False Positives (FPs)
Predicted Negative (0)	False Negatives (FNs)	True Negatives (TNs)

Fig. 2. Confusion matrix. Fonte: Glassbox Medicine (2025)

$$Precision = \frac{TP}{TP + FP} \tag{1}$$

$$Recall = \frac{TP}{TP + FN} \tag{2}$$

$$\text{F1 Score} = \frac{2 \cdot \text{Precision} \cdot \text{Recall}}{\text{Precision} + \text{Recall}} \qquad (3)$$

3 Related Work

Recent advances in blockchain data analysis and forecasting have been extensively explored in studies such as [9], addressing challenges and proposing innovative solutions. One key area of study involves the extraction, ingestion, and analysis of Ethereum blockchain data, tackling issues related to identifying outliers and suspicious smart contracts. Extracting transaction metadata and mapping smart contract interfaces are considered complex tasks due to the diversity and detail of information within the blockchain. Tools like Pegasus have been employed for data consumption in private blockchains, while machine learning techniques have been applied to clustering and anomaly detection, aiming to identify atypical accounts on the public Ethereum blockchain. However, scalability and data handling issues, along with the inherent complexity of smart contracts, continue to complicate the representation of relevant information.

Another significant field of study involves forecasting Bitcoin volatility through the analysis of on-chain data combined with Tweets posts, particularly from the @whale_alert account, as discussed in [11]. The use of reinforcement learning, specifically Q-learning, enabled the construction of a high-precision predictive model for classifying Bitcoin price variations. Nevertheless, data availability was highlighted as a challenge, especially considering Bitcoin's extensive historical records.

Machine learning has also been applied to analyzing risky cryptocurrencies using techniques like K-means++ for clustering historical data. The research [16] demonstrates that a large percentage of cryptocurrencies vanish from the market within 1,000 days, while only a small fraction have longer lifespans. Variable clustering, followed by normalization and correlation analysis, proved effective in assessing asset quality, though challenges such as algorithmic bias and the subjectivity in selecting change points remain.

Efforts to detect low-latency pump-and-dump schemes led to the proposal in [17], which analyzes 1-minute charts and uses an LSTM autoencoder to forecast cryptocurrency prices and identify anomalies in real time. Although the method showed efficiency, the limited number of samples may restrict its broader applicability.

Ethereum price forecasting has also been investigated through on-chain analysis, leveraging machine learning models that correlate various metrics, such as block size and height, with the cryptocurrency price. Studies like [12] propose evolutionary adjustments to improve prediction accuracy, despite concerns about data inconsistency and correlation.

Self-adaptive deep learning models, such as jSO-LSTM, have been explored in [10] to predict Bitcoin prices, accounting for multiple on-chain metrics. Data normalization and the selection of highly correlated variables have been crucial for model performance, which outperformed conventional methods.

Additionally, frameworks like SAM-LSTM, explored in [8], utilize attention mechanisms combined with LSTM for cryptocurrency price prediction, emphasizing the importance of detecting change points to adapt the model to previously unseen variations. Despite criticisms regarding subjectivity in selecting these points, the model achieved promising results in testing.

Forecasting crypto market phases, particularly to guide investment strategies, has also been addressed in studies like [18] using on-chain data. Predictive models such as SARIMA, LSTM, and CNN were compared, showing the advantage of deep learning methods over traditional approaches, although incorporating actual market movement predictions remains an area to explore.

Innovative approaches for security have been developed in research like [19], where machine learning algorithms are applied to Ethereum smart contracts, featuring unique characteristics like using integers instead of floating points to calculate probabilities. While this methodology proved effective and scalable, its practical applicability still depends on greater integration with the research's end goal.

Anomaly detection in DeFi transactions was explored in [14], using deep learning models like Anomaly VAE-Transformer, which combine variational autoencoders with transformers to assess anomaly probabilities in Olympus DAO data, demonstrating accuracy in correctly detecting anomalies.

Finally, cryptocurrency price forecasting using ensemble deep learning models, which combine CNNs and RNNs, was highlighted in [15] as a promising approach. These models can handle blockchain data's volatility and complex dependencies, surpassing existing methodologies and paving the way for new applications in crypto asset price modeling.

The mentioned studies address the use of on-chain data for various purposes, such as cryptocurrency price forecasting, anomaly detection, and market manipulation scheme identification. While presenting innovative and technically sophisticated approaches, they often focus on direct price predictions or isolated historical trend analysis. Even when normalizing data, they treat context uniformly and disaggregated, limiting the ability to provide a more strategic and contextual view of market movements.

This work aims to fill the gaps left by previous studies by introducing a meta-indicator that considers the market region to guide investment decisions. Instead of merely predicting the future price of Bitcoin or other cryptocurrencies, our model will assess the asset's current position within a predefined market region. Using on-chain data and advanced machine learning techniques, our goal is to determine whether the market is in a bullish or bearish phase and how this may influence buy and sell decisions. This approach will enable more robust and contextual analysis, offering investors a more precise tool for strategic decision-making.

Thus, the study stands out by combining trend forecasts with market region analysis, offering a more holistic and practical approach to cryptocurrency analysis, using Bitcoin as the basis for our experiments. By integrating these elements, we aim to provide a solution that not only indicates potential price movements but also contextualizes these movements within the broader market scenario, allowing investors to make more informed and strategic decisions.

Table 1. Summary of the main characteristics of the related work

Main features	[9]	[11]	[16]	[17]	[12]	[10]	[8]	[18]	[19]	[14]	[15]
Uses technical data	✓		✓	✓	✓		✓	✓			✓
Uses textual data		✓									
Regressive Approach					✓	✓	✓	✓			✓
Classification Approach	✓	✓	✓	✓				✓	✓	✓	
Short Forecast	✓	✓	✓	✓	✓	✓	✓			✓	✓
Long Forecast								✓			
Traditional ML Algorithms	✓		✓						✓		
Deep Learning			✓	✓	✓	✓	✓	✓		✓	✓
Reinforcement Learning		✓									

4 Methodology

The study proposed training a machine learning model using financial and on-chain data, to capture patterns and predict market trends. The data used includes price information, such as opening, maximum, minimum, and closing (Open, High, Low, Close), as well as technical indicators, such as the Relative Strength Index (RSI). The model is guided by the analysis of "Bitcoin's Rainbow Chart", which serves as a reference for identifying the asset's macro trend. We also seek the automated extraction and verification of on-chain data, normalizing it to generate meaningful features, integrating this information into the financial context to enrich the training base and improve the predictive capacity of the algorithm.

The combination of this on-chain data with financial indicators provides a comprehensive and structured analysis, allowing for more assertive and informed information about cryptocurrency market trends. Implementation details are presented in Fig. 3.

In the first step (1 in Fig. 3), the on-chain data is extracted, which provides a detailed view of transactions and activities on the blockchain, in step two (2 in Fig. 3), the historical records of financial indicators are extracted, which offer a traditional perspective on market behavior, step three (3) involves the extraction of the historical records of the base indicator, such as the rainbow chart, which helps in the interpretation of market phases.

With all this data available, in step four 4 in Fig. 3), the data is integrated and normalized, ensuring that it is adequately prepared for the model to understand and process the information coherently. In step five (5), the model is trained, where it learns to identify patterns and trends based on the data provided. Finally, in the sixth stage (6), the model is used to make predictions about the movement of the asset, allowing market movements to be anticipated.

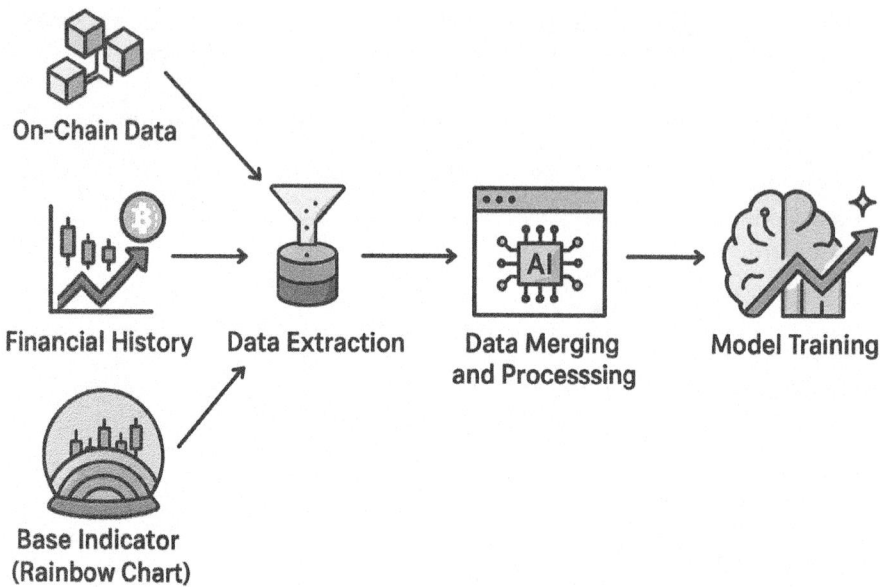

Fig. 3. Conceptual model.

4.1 Normalization

In this part of the work, the process of normalizing the data used will be discussed, detailing the stages of collection, transformation and consolidation of metrics extracted from the Bitcoin network. Normalization is essential to adjust the scale of data, facilitating trend analysis and the application of predictive models.

On-Chain Data: The notebook implements a complete process of collecting, transforming and normalizing on-chain data from the Bitcoin network, with a focus on consolidating daily metrics for trend analysis.

Initially, libraries such as pandas for data manipulation, requests for HTTP requests, BeautifulSoup for HTML analysis, and other auxiliary tools for organizing and processing the files are loaded. The Blockchair platform is used to access the Bitcoin network's block record page, through a GET request, the code captures the HTML content of the page, which is analyzed to extract links to daily block records from 2013 to 2025.

After downloading the files, each record is read and processed to calculate relevant metrics such as average block weight, average difficulty, average USD reward, transaction counts, entries, exits, witnesses, and the total sum of fees paid. The df_to_row function transforms each block DataFrame into a single row with normalized statistics for the respective day, consolidating the information into a format suitable for time series analysis. The normalized records are added to a final DataFrame (`df_result`), with exception handling to deal with empty files or possible reading errors. Finally, the records are ordered by date to maintain temporal coherence.

Financial Data: Initially, Bitcoin's historical data is loaded from CSV files, which were obtained from historical records made available by CoinMarketCap. As the site allows the export of data in CSV format for only one year at a time, it was necessary to perform the removal year by year, each CSV file were representing daily records from a specific year. These files are processed iteratively, treating different delimiters and removing irrelevant columns, such as open, close, high, and low times, as well as the asset name, the date is normalized to daily format, rounding the timestamps, and the resulting DataFrames are concatenated and ordered chronologically.

To model market phases, a logarithmic curve is fitted to closing prices using the curve_fit function from the scipy library. The fitting function follows the form, and the fitted parameters define the base curve. Based on this curve, fixed multipliers determine the price ranges, classifying the asset ranging from the minimum "Fire Sal" level (price much below the predicted value [0.4x]) to the maximum "Super Bubble" level (extremely high price [5x or more]).

Subsequently, RSI is calculated based on a standard 14-day period by analyzing price changes, positive and negative differences are separated to calculate exponential moving averages (EMA) of gains and losses, values presented on the indicator above 70 indicate overbought (possible bearish reversal), while values below 30 indicate oversold (possible bullish reversal).

After adding the Rainbow Chart and RSI, null values are discarded, resulting in a normalized, enriched dataset ready for analysis or to be used as input in machine learning models.

5   Performance Tests and Comparisons

This section aims to present the additional tests carried out to identify the best conditions for forecasting, including the choice of data normalization techniques, the definition of the day intervals used in model selection, and other variables relevant to the forecasting process.

5.1   Description of the Tests

To carry out the tests, a set of data was used in which three additional columns were created based on the closing value of each record. The columns represented the price behavior after 3, 7 and 14 days, with the values classified as 1 when there was an increase in the price and 0 when there was a drop, always concerning the original closing, allowing the problem to be treated as a binary classification task, facilitating the evaluation of the performance of the algorithms.

After creating these columns, the numerical data was normalized by two different methods. The first method consisted of normalization in sliding windows, where values were adjusted to the interval [0, 1] based on blocks of 37 days, a value that represents the median number of days that a rainbow-chart class remains active, which made it possible to capture local patterns and seasonal variations in addition to a more contextualized targeting of the market moment classification that the rainbow-chart indicated. The second method involved global normalization, applied to the entire database, adjusting the values to the same range, but considering all observations. It is important to highlight that normalization was applied exclusively to numerical attributes, since categorical attributes had already been transformed using one-hot encoding, being naturally restricted to the range [0, 1].

To evaluate the effectiveness of each normalization method, k-fold cross validation with 5 divisions was used. The metric used to measure the performance of the algorithms was the average accuracy, calculated from the results obtained in the five folds, enabling a more robust evaluation and reducing the risk of overfitting in the construction of future models, providing a more reliable view of the predictive capacity of the models, with all metrics results for each model presented in the Table 2.

The selection of algorithms used in the cross-validation stage was made with the aim of contemplating different methodological approaches to the binary classification problem, allowing a richer and more comprehensive comparison between linear and non-linear models. Among the linear models, Logistic Regression was chosen, which bases its decision on the sigmoid function to estimate the probability of classes, and Gaussian Naive Bayes, which adopts a probabilistic approach based on Bayes' theorem, assuming independence between variables and normal distribution of data, both included to verify how algorithms with simple structures behave in comparison to more complex and non-linear models.

In the set of non-linear models, three algorithms based on decision trees were selected: Decision Tree Classifier, Random Forest Classifier and Gradient Boosting Classifier, although they share the logic of recursive division of the attribute space, differ in the way they combine the trees, whether individually, in random forests (bagging) or in a sequence of improvements (boosting). In addition to these, the MLPClassifier was also tested, representing artificial neural network methods, the KNeighbors Classifier makes decisions based on the proximity of samples in the attribute space, while the Support Vector Classifier (SVC), seeks an optimal separation between classes through margin maximization in a space possibly transformed by kernels. This diversity of approaches allows us to evaluate not only the accuracy, but also the bias and generalization capacity of each model given the specific nature of the data set.

5.2   Construction of the Model and Final Tests

After carrying out tests with cross-validation, a significant improvement in the performance of the models was suggested in cases where windowed normalization was applied, when compared to normalization considering the complete set of data, providing that windowed normalization allows the models to more

Table 2. Cross-validation results

	acc mean - 3 days		acc mean - 7 days		acc mean - 14 days	
	win	comp	win	comp	win	comp
DecisionTreeClassifier	0.5452	0.5300	0.5616	0.5341	0.6284	0.4789
GaussianNB	0.5979	0.4869	0.6069	0.4876	0.6479	0.4926
GradientBoostingClassifier	0.6057	0.5210	0.6446	0.5360	0.6915	0.5685
KNeighborsClassifier	0.5753	0.5087	0.5950	0.5071	0.6555	0.5391
LogisticRegression	**0.6154**	0.5348	**0.6510**	0.5407	**0.7043**	0.5948
MLPClassifier	0.5971	0.5348	0.6230	0.5267	0.6867	0.5511
RandomForestClassifier	0.6142	0.5265	0.6502	0.5414	0.6948	0.5677
SVC	0.6128	0.5443	0.6308	0.5402	0.6943	0.5711

efficiently capture the underlying temporal relationships in the data, contributing to more robust transfers.

For the construction of the final model and performance evaluation, it was decided to carry out a planned procedure with a horizon of 14 days, since this interval presented the greatest accuracy in the preliminary experiments. Three algorithms representing different approaches were selected: linear regression to capture linear relationships, Random Forest to model nonlinear interactions through decision trees, and an MLP Classifier to explore complex patterns through neural networks.

Each model was optimized using a grid search (Grid Search) with cross-validation, with AUC-ROC as the main metric, to find the best hyperparameter configuration for class discretization. Firstly, the logistic regression model was treated, the best configuration found was with L2 penalty, C equal to 1 and "liblinear" solver, resulting in an approximate AUC-ROC of 0.7789 in the training data and 0.7759 in the test set.

The Random Forest algorithm obtained the best results with 200 estimators, maximum depth of 20, minimum of 2 examples per division and 2 leaves per node, reaching an AUC-ROC of approximately 0.8240 in training and 0.8218 in testing. The MLP Classifier showed better performance with two hidden layers of 50 neurons each, activation function "tanh", solver "adam" and alpha of 0.0001, resulting in an AUC-ROC of 0.8210 in training and 0.8148 in testing.

Finally, the adjusted models with the best hyperparameters were combined in a hard voting Fig. 2, which resulted in a final accuracy of 0.7417, consolidating the contributions of each approach, balancing their strengths to provide a more stable and generalizable solution, being demonstrated through its resulting confusion matrix Fig.5.

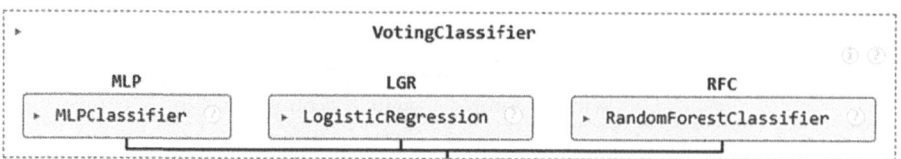

Fig. 4. Ensemble Model Architecture.

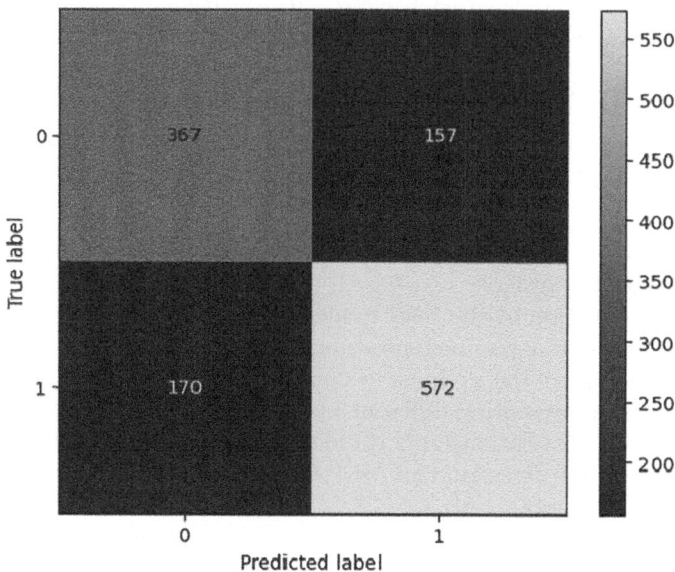

Fig. 5. Confusion Matrix of the model.

6   Conclusions

This work explores cryptocurrency price prediction, proposing an approach that integrates on-chain data, technical indicators, and the Rainbow Bitcoin Chart. Our approach achieved the best performance among all tested configurations, utilizing normalization in moving windows with the dataset and a 14-day forecast horizon. It is believed that over longer intervals, the parameters become more discretized, enhancing the model's ability to make more accurate predictions.

Furthermore, the fact of using windowed normalization strengthens the hypothesis that this method can be more effective than total data normalization. This is because windowed normalization makes the data less sensitive to abrupt variations over time, in addition to aligning more precisely with the meta-indicator used.

Based on the results obtained, it is concluded that the model demonstrates promising performance. This suggests that future research could explore other crypto assets or enhance the current model by integrating additional approaches to refine predictions, leading to significant advancements in the field. For evaluation and transparency of results, we maintain all source codes publicly available in a git repository[1].

Acknowledgements. This work is supported by FAPERGS (24/2551-0001396-2, 23/2551-0000773-8), CNPq (305805/2021-5) and FAPERGS/CNPq (23/2551-0000126-8).

References

1. Kristoufek, L.: BitCoin meets google trends and Wikipedia: quantifying the relationship between phenomena of the Internet era. Sci. Rep. **3**(1), 3415 (2013). Nature Publishing Group UK London
2. Lahmiri, S., Bekiros, S.: Cryptocurrency forecasting with deep learning chaotic neural networks. Chaos Solitons Fractals **118**, 35–40 (2019). Elsevier
3. Dias, M.A., Henriques, M.A.A.: Estudo sobre a relação custo-benefício de mecanismos de consenso Proof-of-Stake para blockchains públicas
4. Greaves, A., Au, B.: Using the bitcoin transaction graph to predict the price of bitcoin. No data **8**, 416–443 (2015)
5. Chevallier, J., Guégan, D., Goutte, S.: Is it possible to forecast the price of bitcoin? Forecasting **3**(2), 377–420 (2021). MDPI
6. Yermack, D.: Is Bitcoin a real currency? An economic appraisal. In: Handbook of Digital Currency, pp. 29–40 (2024). Elsevier
7. Kim, H.-M., Bock, G.-W., Lee, G.: Predicting Ethereum prices with machine learning based on Blockchain information. Expert Syst. Appl. **184**, 115480 (2021). Elsevier
8. Kim, G., Shin, D.-H., Choi, J.G., Lim, S.: A deep learning-based cryptocurrency price prediction model that uses on-chain data. IEEE Access **10**, 56232–56248 (2022)
9. Starikov, V., Kozlyak, R., Opletina, P., Mityagin, S.: Forecasting cascading effects in network models as applied to urban services provision assessment. In: Gervasi, O., Murgante, B., Garau, C., Taniar, D., C. Rocha, A.M.A., Faginas Lago, M.N. (eds.) Computational Science and Its Applications - ICCSA 2024. ICCSA 2024. LNCS, vol. 14813. Springer, Cham (2024). https://doi.org/10.1007/978-3-031-64605-8_30
10. Jagannath, N., et al.: A self-adaptive deep learning-based algorithm for predictive analysis of bitcoin price. IEEE Access **9**, 34054–34066 (2021)
11. Muminov, A., Sattarov, O., Cho, J.: Forecasting Bitcoin Volatility through On-Chain and Whale-Alert Tweet Analysis using the Q-Learning Algorithm. IEEE Access (2023)
12. Jagannath, N., et al.: An on-chain analysis-based approach to predict Ethereum prices. IEEE Access **9**, 167972–167989 (2021)
13. Souza, A.S., Lucca, G., Borges, E.N., Cardoso, F.C., Dalmazo, B.L., Berri, R.: Dataset for Intraday Analysis of B3 stock prices, Harvard Dataverse, Draft Version (2024). https://doi.org/10.7910/DVN/TMB4IG

---

[1] https://github.com/arthur-bubolz/implementation_codes_iccsa.

14. Song, A., Seo, E., Kim, H.: Anomaly VAE-transformer: A deep learning approach for anomaly detection in decentralized finance. IEEE Access (2023)
15. Ali, F., Ravate, S., Nimbore, S.: Ensemble model based on deep learning for forecasting crypto asset futures in markets. In: 2023 3rd International Conference on Smart Generation Computing, Communication and Networking (SMART GEN-CON), pp. 1–8. IEEE (2023)
16. Zekiye, A., Amroush, F., Utku, S., Özkasap, Ö.: AI-assisted investigation of on-chain parameters: risky cryptocurrencies and price factors. In: 2023 Fifth International Conference on Blockchain Computing and Applications (BCCA), pp. 52–59. IEEE (2023)
17. Bello, A. S., Schneider, J., Di Pietro, R.: LLD: a low latency detection solution to thwart cryptocurrency pump & dumps. In: 2023 IEEE International Conference on Blockchain and Cryptocurrency (ICBC), pp. 1–9. IEEE (2023)
18. Casella, B., Paletto, L.: Predicting cryptocurrencies market phases through on-chain data long-term forecasting. In: 2023 IEEE International Conference on Blockchain and Cryptocurrency (ICBC), pp. 1–4. IEEE (2023)
19. Badruddoja, S., Dantu, R., He, Y., Thompson, M., Salau, A., Upadhyay, K.: Making smart contracts predict and scale. In: 2022 Fourth International Conference on Blockchain Computing and Applications (BCCA), pp. 127–134. IEEE (2022)
20. Worster, A., Fan, J., Ismaila, A.: Understanding linear and logistic regression analyses. Can. J. Emerg. Med. 9(2), 111–113 (2007). Cambridge University Press
21. Bayes, T.: Naive Bayes classifier. Article Sources and Contributors, pp. 1–9. BIOMISA, Department of Computer and Software Engineering (1968)
22. Dabiri, H., Farhangi, V., Moradi, M.J., Zadehmohamad, M., Karakouzian, M.: Applications of decision tree and random forest as tree-based machine learning techniques for analyzing the ultimate strain of spliced and non-spliced reinforcement bars. Appl. Sci. 12(10), 4851 (2022). MDPI
23. Di Pierro, M.: What is the blockchain? Comput. Sci. Eng. 19(5), 92–95 (2017). IEEE
24. Stober, A., Sandner, P.: Using on-chain and market metrics to analyze the value of crypto assets. FSBC Working Paper. Frankfurt am Main: Frankfurt School of Finance (2020)
25. Bernardi, D., Bertelli, R.: Bitcoin price forecast using quantitative models. In: Proceedings of the Conference on Quantitative Finance (2021)
26. Dai, Y., Zhang, Y.: Machine learning in stock price trend forecasting. Stanford University, 2, 2023 (2013). Retrieved from http://cs229.stanford.edu/proj2013/DaiZhang-MachineLearningInStockPriceTrendForecasting.pdf
27. Yacouby, R., Axman, D.: Probabilistic extension of precision, recall, and F1 score for more thorough evaluation of classification models. In: Proceedings of the First Workshop on Evaluation and Comparison of NLP Systems, pp. 79–91 (2020)
28. Amorim, M., et al.: Systematic review of aggregation functions applied to image edge detection. Axioms 12(4), 330 (2023). https://www.mdpi.com/2075-1680/12/4/330. https://doi.org/10.3390/axioms12040330

An End-to-End Computer Vision System for Structured Information Extraction from Turkish ID Card Images

Seyf Kazamel[1]([⊠]) [ID], Umut Kocasarı[2] [ID], and Ali Alıcı[1] [ID]

[1] Armut Teknoloji AŞ, Üsküdar 34660, Istanbul, Türkiye
{mohammedk,ali}@armut.com
[2] Technical University of Munich, Arcisstraße 21, 80333 Munich, Germany
umut.kocasar@tum.de

Abstract. This paper introduces an end-to-end computer vision pipeline for automatically extracting key personal information from Turkish ID card images. The system addresses real-world challenges such as invalid images, incorrect card orientation, and older ID card formats by integrating advanced methods for card detection, card format classification, orientation correction, text region segmentation, and optical character recognition (OCR). Specifically, we employ YOLOv5 for ID card detection, CLIP to validate that the image is an official Turkish ID and to distinguish between old and new ID formats, CRAFT and U-Net to segment relevant textual regions, and Tesseract for final OCR. By interfacing with APIs from the Turkish Population Registry, our system performs near real-time ID validation while significantly reducing manual effort. Experimental results indicate over 90% accuracy in identifying and classifying ID cards, with OCR word-level accuracy surpassing 96%, and an end-to-end card-level accuracy of 73% for the pipeline, all with execution times under five seconds. Deployed in production, the system saves manual labor hours and speeds up processing workflows. Our findings underscore the feasibility and business value of automated ID verification, highlighting how deep learning–driven ID processing can streamline operations, mitigate fraud, and enhance the user experience.

Keywords: Computer Vision · Optical Character Recognition (OCR) · Turkish ID Cards · Identity Verification · YOLOv5 · CLIP · CRAFT · U-Net · Tesseract

1 Introduction

Identity verification frequently relies on extracting key details from ID cards, making it essential for applications in banking, online services, and government administration. Manual transcription of ID information is prone to errors, slow, and difficult to scale. Recent advances in deep learning and optical character recognition (OCR) have made it possible to automate ID card data extraction with high accuracy. This is particularly important for Turkish ID cards, which come in both older laminated and newer electronic formats, necessitating robust classification and processing strategies. In real-world use cases, ID images may feature poor lighting, glare, arbitrary rotations, and varied backgrounds, all of which demand efficient, resilient computer vision pipelines capable of fast processing.

Automating the extraction of key personal details (e.g., name, birth date, national identity number) from Turkish ID card images is a challenging task, especially when these images are captured under inconsistent conditions such as uneven lighting, varying angles, or cluttered backgrounds. Accuracy is paramount for ensuring legitimate identities, while efficiency is needed to handle large volumes quickly. Just as important are privacy concerns, which require that sensitive personal data remain secure and, ideally, be processed in-house rather than by third-party services.

Because identity cards contain highly sensitive information, a key motivation for developing an internal system is to avoid sending user data to external information extraction services. Keeping the OCR and extraction process on proprietary servers minimizes exposure of ID images to third parties (aside from the minimal data securely shared with the governmental validation service). This approach substantially reduces the risk of data breaches or misuse by third parties. Moreover, removing the need for routine human review enhances privacy further by limiting additional exposure of personal data.

However, building an entirely in-house, end-to-end ID card extraction system poses several research and engineering challenges. First, robust image classification is required to distinguish valid Turkish ID cards from other documents or photos that might be erroneously uploaded. Second, once an ID card is confirmed, the system must detect, crop, and reorient it—ensuring the text regions line up properly for subsequent extraction. Third, old and new Turkish ID formats exhibit differing text layouts, label languages, and background templates, demanding a mechanism to classify each card's format quickly so the correct downstream model or processing path can be applied. Fourth, localizing and extracting text regions accurately is nontrivial given variations in lighting, orientation, surface glare, and possible obstructions (e.g., fingers holding the card). Finally, maintaining high recognition accuracy on critical fields such as name, surname, date of birth, and ID number is vital to preempt service or authentication errors downstream.

In addressing these challenges, we developed an automated pipeline that integrates modern deep learning components for classification, detection, segmentation, and OCR. Our design leverages: (1) CLIP for zero-shot classification to confirm whether the uploaded image is indeed a Turkish ID card, (2) YOLOv5 for fast and robust card localization, (3) further CLIP-based logic to differentiate old from new ID formats, (4) CRAFT and a U-Net model for pinpointing relevant text fields, and (5) Tesseract for the OCR stage. By unifying these methods in a coherent pipeline, we achieve accurate extraction results under realistic conditions. Lastly, the extracted fields are automatically verified through the Kimlik Paylaşımı Sistemi (KPS) to confirm the correctness of the ID number and personal details, a step that is crucial for reducing fraud and typographical errors.

The remainder of this paper is organized as follows.

- Section 2 reviews relevant works in identity-document processing and the key techniques that underpin modern OCR pipelines.
- Section 3 describes the overall architecture of our system, detailing each processing step, including card detection, orientation correction, and text field segmentation.

- Section 4 outlines the experimental setup and provides quantitative results, illustrating the system's efficacy and performance in practice.
- Finally, Sect. 5 draws conclusions and proposes directions for future work, such as improved OCR strategies, support for additional document types, and enhanced resilience to occlusion or low-quality uploads.

In this work, we show that a dedicated end-to-end computer vision solution can reliably extract ID card information while reducing privacy risks and manual effort in high-volume, real-world environments.

2 Related Works

Optical character recognition (OCR) of identity documents has a long history in the broader field of document processing and pattern recognition. Early approaches often relied on rule-based or classical machine learning strategies for character segmentation, combined with template matching or simple feature extraction techniques (Shaaban et al., 2014). In particular, these older methods were primarily constrained by the need for step-by-step character segmentation (e.g., baseline-based) and suffered from reduced accuracy when confronted with variable-quality images or non-Latin scripts. While effective for their time, these methods depend on handcrafted rules and require substantial domain expertise for each new language or ID format.

More recent methods tend to incorporate deep learning, which improves the robustness of text localization, segmentation, and recognition. For instance, convolutional neural networks (CNNs) and end-to-end pipelines have emerged in various works (Maung & Aye, 2023; Bychkov et al., 2023). These pipelines often integrate region proposal networks or fully convolutional segmentation models for text region detection and then apply attention-based sequence learning or recurrent neural network layers for final text extraction. By leveraging large training datasets, these approaches have shown significant gains in accuracy and generalizability, even under challenging conditions such as poor lighting or skewed orientations (Suddul & Seguin 2024).

Furthermore, some studies focus on specialized mobile-based solutions that require lightweight models and fast inference (Harefa et al., 2022). Such systems often refine or adapt deep learning pipelines to fit real-time constraints in edge devices, illustrating the importance of speed-accuracy trade-offs. Others propose integrated frameworks that apply advanced pre-processing (e.g., generative adversarial networks for image enhancement) or post-processing (e.g., domain-specific correction rules) to further refine OCR outputs (Jobi & Varghese 2023).

Within these more modern systems, identity cards and similarly structured documents receive special emphasis, given the need to handle name fields, national ID numbers, birthdates, addresses, and so forth in a highly reliable manner (Bychkov et al., 2023). Accurate extraction and classification of these text fields opens avenues for streamlined e-KYC (electronic Know Your Customer) and secure onboarding in domains such as finance, governmental services, and telecommunications (Suddul & Seguin 2024).

Existing research demonstrates that combining object detectors, segmentation models, and OCR can significantly improve accuracy and speed in ID recognition. Early methods relied on template matching and manual feature extraction, but they often failed under challenging imaging conditions. Deep learning–based detection models such as YOLO have proven effective for quickly localizing ID cards in cluttered or poorly lit images, while specialized text detectors like CRAFT (Baek et al., 2019) or segmentation models like U-Net (Ronneberger et al., 2015) accurately identify text regions. For OCR, Tesseract (Smith, 2007) remains a strong open-source solution, particularly when text areas are well-segmented. Several studies have validated these approaches: Tavakolian et al. (2020) integrated a deep text detector and face detection for ID card scanning, Cavalcante et al. (2024) combined object detection with OCR for ID badge reading, and Suddul et al. (2024) employed U-Net for text segmentation, all achieving high accuracy in their respective domains.

Building on these insights, our work employs a deep learning pipeline for Turkish ID card images, unifying classification, text region segmentation, and OCR into an efficient end-to-end architecture. We leverage advanced approaches such as object detection, robust segmentation techniques, and open-source pretrained sequence recognition networks while addressing domain-specific challenges like older versus newer card formats. This design focuses on delivering a streamlined, high-performance solution for structured information extraction from Turkish IDs.

3   System Overview

Our end-to-end system is organized as a pipeline of modules, each responsible for a specific task in the ID processing workflow. Figure 1 shows the steps of the pipeline.

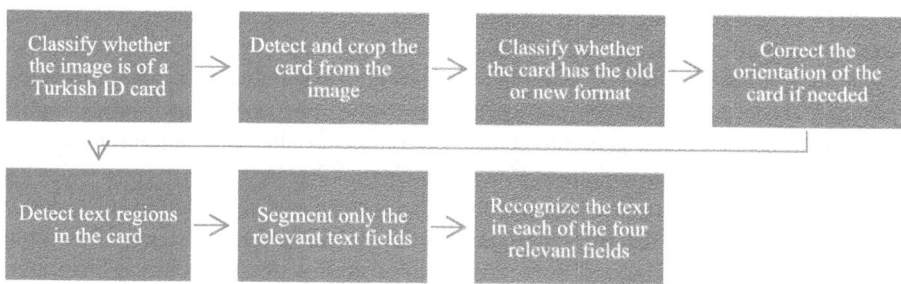

Fig. 1. Information extraction pipeline steps

3.1   Image Classification and Card Preprocessing

The input to our system is an image that is presumed to contain an ID card (often a photo taken by a mobile device). Before we detect and recognize the text on the card, we first check if the photo is of a valid ID card, crop the image to focus on the card, and classify whether the card has the old or new format in order to process it accordingly.

ID Card Identification Using CLIP. We utilize the CLIP model (Radford et al., 2021) in a zero-shot classification manner for ID card identification. We use CLIP's pretrained image encoder and text encoder where we encode the image, and we encode many candidate texts, e.g., "a photo of a Turkish ID card", "a photo of a passport", "a photo of a driving license", "a photo of a person", "a photo of a scene", "a photo of a document", etc. By comparing the cosine similarity of image embeddings to these text embeddings, we can determine if the image is likely an ID card. If the similarity to the correct "ID card" prompt is significantly higher than to generic prompts, we accept the image; otherwise, we flag it as an invalid input. CLIP's ability to understand image content in terms of text is remarkable, and it has been shown to implicitly perform OCR and fine-grained classification during its training. We found CLIP to be robust in filtering out images that were not ID cards (for example, it correctly rejected a few test images of driver's licenses and passports as not being Turkish ID cards, since our prompt was specific).

Card Detection using YOLOv5. Once the image is confirmed to contain an ID card, the next step is to locate the card within the image. Users often upload photos where the ID card is on a table or held in hand against a background. We employ YOLOv5, a one-stage object detector, to detect the bounding box of the ID card. We trained a YOLOv5 model on a custom dataset of ID card images, labeled with bounding boxes over the ID cards. The model treats the ID card as a single object class. YOLOv5 was chosen for its balance of speed and accuracy; it can process images quickly and its smaller models can run on CPU if needed. Compared to two-stage detectors, YOLO's single-shot approach is faster and sufficiently accurate for our needs.

The output at runtime is the bounding box coordinates of the ID card. We crop the image to this bounding box (with a slight margin) to isolate the card. By reducing the image to just the ID card, we eliminate background noise and accelerate the following processing (which can then operate on a smaller image region) (Fig. 2).

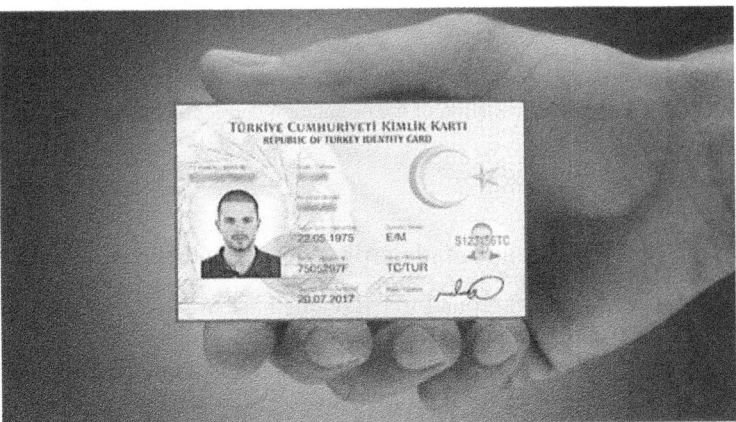

Fig. 2. An illustration of ID card detection in an image (the card in the picture is artificial)

ID Card Format Classification Using CLIP Embeddings. After the image is validated as an ID card, we further classify which type: old vs. new Turkish ID. We do this by again using CLIP. We precalculated the CLIP embeddings of 500 old format and 500 new format ID cards, and at inference time, we compute the embedding of the current card and then calculate its cosine similarity with the reference embeddings. We assign the class of the most similar three embeddings to the current card. This classification is important because the text fields and layout differ. For instance, the old IDs have fields like "Nüfus Cüzdanı" labels, whereas the new IDs have English translations for field labels. Knowing the type allows us to apply appropriate downstream processing.

Orientation Correction and Resizing. The Orientation Correction step is essential for aligning the ID card image before further processing. In this stage, the pipeline utilizes a pre-trained face detection model—specifically, a Single Shot MultiBox Detector with a ResNet-10 backbone—to detect facial features on the card. The process involves rotating the image through four potential orientations (0°, 90°, 180°, and 270°) and evaluating each based on the face detection confidence score. The orientation yielding the highest confidence is selected as the correct alignment, ensuring that any card is properly oriented. After determining the correct orientation, the image is resized to a standard 640×640 dimension, thereby standardizing the input for subsequent text detection and recognition steps (Fig. 3).

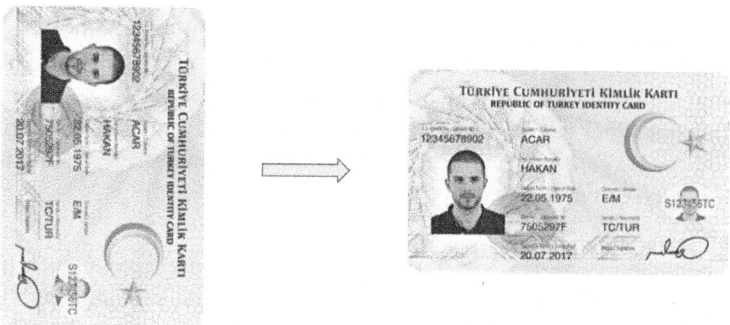

Fig. 3. An illustration of the orientation correction process

3.2   Relevant Text Fields Segmentation with CRAFT and U-Net

After obtaining an upright, background-free ID card image, we first detect all text regions using CRAFT and then segment the four key fields (ID number, surname, name, and date of birth) with a U-Net model. We use different U-Net models depending on whether we are dealing with older or newer ID card layouts.

CRAFT-based Detection: We run CRAFT (Character Region Awareness for Text Detection) to detect potential text regions. CRAFT outputs bounding boxes (and corresponding character density maps) for each region it identifies as text. These bounding boxes can be granular—often detecting individual words or lines.

U-Net Field Segmentation: Next, we apply a U-Net model specifically trained to segment the four relevant fields on the ID card. Rather than highlighting all text pixels, this U-Net produces masks that delineate exactly where the ID number, surname, name, and date of birth should appear. Since the placement of these fields differs between old and new ID layouts, we employ separate U-Net models accordingly.

Combining CRAFT Boxes with U-Net Fields: Once we have the CRAFT bounding boxes and the U-Net's field segmentation masks, we intersect them to isolate only those boxes that fall within the four designated fields. If multiple horizontally aligned bounding boxes belong to the same field, we merge or combine them as needed so that, in the end, each of the four fields is captured by exactly one bounding box. We iteratively merge the closest boxes until only four remain. Finally, we sort these boxes by their vertical or horizontal position to map them consistently to the correct fields (ID number, surname, name, date of birth).

This combined approach leverages CRAFT's strong performance on text detection while using the U-Net segmentation to pinpoint the specific fields of interest. By intersecting the text bounding boxes with the field masks, we ensure we capture the correct regions for each field—even in the presence of background patterns, varying fonts, or different ID card designs (Fig. 4).

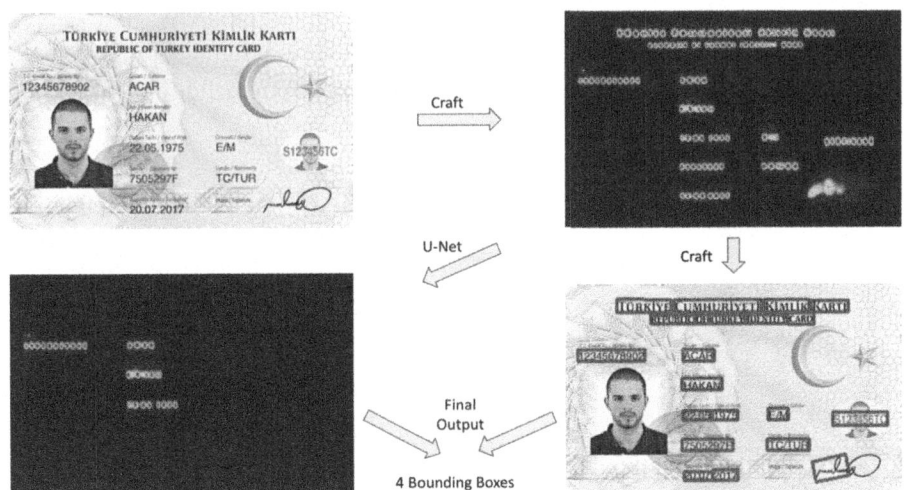

Fig. 4. Using CRAFT to generate the bounding boxes and U-Net segmentation to find the relevant boxes

3.3 Text Extraction Using Tesseract OCR

Once the text regions have been identified, the system extracts the text content from each region using OCR. We utilize Tesseract OCR (version 4.1 with the LSTM engine) configured for both Turkish and English, depending on the field type. Each detected text region (bounding box from the previous step) is cropped from the image and undergoes preprocessing before being fed into Tesseract.

For preprocessing, we apply denoising using `fastNlMeansDenoisingColored` to enhance text clarity. Depending on the field type, we employ different OCR configurations:

- **ID number and birth date:** These fields are processed using the English language model. Additional color thresholding is applied, and multiple Page Segmentation Modes (PSM) are tested, including PSM 3, 6, 7, 8, and 13, to maximize accuracy.
- **Name and surname:** These fields are processed using the Turkish language model. Multiple PSM modes are tested to improve recognition, ensuring accurate extraction of characters such as "Ğ, Ş, İ, Ç, Ö, Ü."

The OCR results undergo post-processing to validate and format the extracted text:

- **ID number:** Must be exactly 11 digits. Any output with non-numeric characters or incorrect length is discarded.
- **Birth date:** Must follow the DD.MM.YYYY format, with valid month and day values.
- **Name and surname:** Punctuation is removed, and outputs are checked for expected uppercase formatting in the Turkish alphabet.

To further enhance accuracy, multiple OCR attempts are made with different pre-processing techniques, including adjusting brightness levels and inverting colors. The results are filtered based on contextual rules to eliminate invalid outputs. The output of this stage is a structured set of textual entries extracted from the ID card, such as Name = "HAKAN", Surname = "ACAR", DOB = "22.05.1975", and ID No = "12345678902". These results are then passed to the validation step to ensure validity before further processing (Fig. 5).

Fig. 5. Using Tesseract OCR to recognize the ID information from the cropped boxes

3.4 Data Verification via API

The final stage of the pipeline is to verify the extracted personal information against an authoritative source. After OCR, we have structured data: e.g., {name: "HAKAN", surname: "ACAR", date_of_birth: "22.05.1975", id_number: "12345678902"}. We utilize the Kimlik Paylaşımı Sistemi (KPS) to validate this data. KPS provides a SOAP-based web service that confirms if a given combination of ID number and personal information is valid. Our verification step takes the OCR results and makes a secure SOAP request to the KPS API with the ID number, first and last name, and year of birth. The API responds with true or false on whether the ID info is valid.

If the information matches exactly (e.g., the name and birth year correspond to that ID number in the government database), we mark the extraction as verified. If not, we flag it: this could mean the OCR made an error (like a misrecognized digit) or that the ID card is not authentic. In case of a mismatch, we leave the process of verifying that card to a human.

This verification step is critical in real deployment scenarios such as automated user onboarding, where just extracting text is not enough and where one also needs to ensure the extracted data is legitimate. By integrating with the KPS API, our system effectively closes the loop from image to validated data. Of course, this step requires access to the government service, which fortunately is available 24/7.

4 Experimental Details and Results

This section summarizes the training setups and performance evaluations of our proposed pipeline for Turkish ID card information extraction. We detail the hyper-parameters and performance metrics for the YOLOv5 detector and the U-Net segmentation models, and we report results for each stage of the pipeline as well as the end-to-end performance.

4.1 YOLOv5 Training and Card Detection

We trained the YOLOv5 model on 1,000 ID card images (500 new, 500 old) using a medium-sized model with an input resolution of 640×640. Data augmentation (mosaic, rotation, horizontal flip, color jitter) was applied to enhance robustness. Key training hyper-parameters are listed in Table 1. During training, we leveraged transfer learning by initializing with YOLOv5 weights pre-trained on COCO and then fine-tuning on our ID card data.

Table 1. YOLOv5 Training Hyper-parameters

Parameter	Value
Optimizer	SGD (momentum $= 0.937$)
Learning Rate	0.01 (cosine decay to 0.0001)
Batch Size	16
Epochs	100
Augmentation	Mosaic, $\pm 5°$ rotation, flip, jitter

On the test set, YOLOv5 achieved a precision of 96.8%, recall of 95.5%, and a mAP@0.5 of 97.2%, with an average inference time of ~15 ms per image on a GPU (Table 2).

4.2 U-Net Training and Segmentation

For segmenting the four key text fields, two U-Net models (one per ID format) were trained using CRAFT's character score maps. The models used a ResNet-34 encoder

Table 2. YOLOv5 Detection Performance

Metric	Value
Precision	96.8%
Recall	95.5%
mAP@0.5	97.2%
mAP@0.5:0.95	92.5%
Inference Time (GPU)	~15 ms per image

Table 3. U-Net Training Hyper-parameters

Parameter	Value
Architecture	U-Net (ResNet-34 encoder)
Optimizer	Adam
Learning Rate	0.001
Batch Size	8
Epochs	50
Loss Function	BCE + Dice
Augmentation	$\pm 10°$ rotation, flip, scaling

optimized with Adam and a combined Binary Cross-Entropy plus Dice loss over 50 epochs. Table 3 lists the hyper-parameters.

The U-Net achieved a pixel accuracy of 98.1%, mean IoU of 90.3%, and Dice coefficient of 94.5%, with an average inference time of ~20 ms per image (Table 4).

Table 4. U-Net Segmentation Performance

Metric	Value
Pixel Accuracy	98.1%
Mean IoU	90.3%
Dice Coefficient	94.5%
Inference Time (GPU)	~20 ms

4.3 Pipeline Steps Evaluation

We evaluated the pipeline steps on 200 Turkish ID card images each. The system integrates CLIP-based card identification, ID photo and format classification, text detection (CRAFT + U-Net), and OCR using Tesseract.

- **ID Card Identification Using CLIP:** The zero-shot classifier achieved 97.5% accuracy. Table 5 shows the confusion matrix for a balanced test set.
- **Overall Pipeline Accuracy:** The end-to-end system achieved a 73% card-level accuracy, defined as the percentage of ID cards for which all four fields were extracted correctly. The main sources of error were occasional OCR misreads and rare missed text field detections under challenging conditions. Card misclassification also contributed to the errors.

Table 5. ID Photo Classification Confusion Matrix

Actual/Predicted	Valid ID Photo	Invalid
Valid ID Photo	98	2
Invalid	3	97

- **ID Format Classification:** The classifier distinguishing new versus old ID formats achieved 95.5% accuracy (Table 6). Minor misclassifications were mostly due to poor lighting conditions.

Table 6. ID Format Classification Confusion Matrix

Actual/Predicted	New ID	Old ID
New ID	95	5
Old ID	4	96

- **ID Card Identification and Classification:** The first three steps of the pipeline, i.e., ID card identification with CLIP, card detection and cropping with YOLOv5, and ID format classification were also jointly evaluated on a dataset of 200 images and yielded an accuracy of 91%.
- **Text Field Detection:** Combining CRAFT and U-Net, the system correctly detected all four expected text fields in 94% of cases. Misdetections were primarily due to low contrast or occlusion in a small subset of images.
- **OCR Performance:** The OCR module yielded a character-level accuracy of 97.5%, a word-level accuracy of 92.0%, and a card-level accuracy of 80% (Table 7). Card-level accuracy is a metric that we introduced because it captures the performance on the ID card information extraction task better than the metrics in the literature. Card level accuracy is the percentage of cards whose information (the four relevant fields) were extracted completely correctly. It is a stringent metric because misrecognizing only one character in any field of the card yields the prediction for the whole card erroneous.

Table 7. OCR Accuracy

Metric	Value
Character-level Accuracy	99.1%
Word-level Accuracy	96.2%
Card-level Accuracy	80.5%

The experimental results demonstrate that our system achieves high accuracy across all processing stages. YOLOv5 robustly detects ID cards, while the U-Net models accurately segment key text regions. The high performance of the classification modules ensures that only valid, correctly oriented images are processed further, thereby enhancing overall system reliability. Although OCR performance is strong, minor errors in low-quality images suggest avenues for future work, such as improved preprocessing and advanced recognition methods. With an overall 73% end-to-end accuracy, the pipeline significantly reduces manual verification effort and underscores the feasibility of automated ID verification in real-world applications.

This result is comparable to findings reported in the literature, such as those by Chandra et al. (2021), who achieved an overall accuracy of 74.2%. It is important to note that their definition of accuracy encompasses the correct prediction of only the full name and the ID card number, whereas our definition also includes the correct prediction of the date of birth.

5 Conclusion and Future Work

We presented an end-to-end computer vision system for extracting and verifying information from Turkish ID card images. The system combines multiple deep learning components in a unified pipeline: YOLOv5 for detecting the ID card in images, CLIP for image validation and classification, CRAFT and U-Net for segmenting relevant text regions, and Tesseract OCR for reading the text. Through a series of preprocessing (cropping, denoising, orientation correction) and postprocessing (OCR result verification and correction), the system achieves a high level of accuracy. It successfully automates what has traditionally been a manual task, handling ID card images in various orientations and conditions and producing structured digital data. Our experimental evaluation showed over 90% accuracy in identifying and classifying ID cards and around 80% card-level accuracy in text extraction, all within an inference time of under 5 s per image. Integrating the Turkish Population Registry API for verification adds an extra layer of reliability, ensuring that the extracted details correspond to a real person.

This study demonstrates the feasibility of a deep learning-driven ID processing system in real-world scenarios. It also illustrates the advantage of combining multiple AI models—each specialized for a sub-problem—into one coherent solution. By leveraging state-of-the-art models (object detectors, image-language models, text detectors, etc.) and existing OCR technology, we were able to build a system relatively quickly that performs competitively.

Future Work: There are several avenues for improvement and extension:

- **Enhanced OCR with Deep Learning:** Replacing or supplementing Tesseract with a modern OCR model (such as CRNN or Transformer-based text recognizer fine-tuned on ID card fonts) could improve the text extraction accuracy. This could be especially beneficial for challenging cases like faint text or uncommon names. It would require assembling a larger training set of annotated ID card text or using synthetic data to train the OCR model.
- **Multi-language and Document Support:** Although we focused on Turkish IDs, the system can be extended to other identity documents (passports, driver's licenses, IDs from other countries). This would involve updating the CLIP prompts, retraining detection on new document types, and using language-specific OCR models. The modular design makes it feasible to maintain one pipeline that handles multiple document types. For instance, the system could first classify the document type (passport vs. ID vs. license) and then route it to the appropriate OCR settings or verification API.
- **Robustness to Occlusion and Damage:** In real usage, an ID card might be partially occluded (e.g., a finger covering a corner) or damaged (faded text, scratches). Future work could incorporate techniques to handle these. For occlusion, one idea is to use multiple frames (if it's a live capture from a video, maybe take the best parts from several frames). For damage, training the text segmentation and OCR on augmented data (with occlusion masks or noise) could help the models become more robust.
- **User Feedback Loop:** In a real application, any time the system fails (for example, cannot verify an ID automatically and requires manual review), that case can be flagged and later added to the training data (active learning). Over time, this can improve the system. Particularly for fields that caused OCR errors, collecting those and retraining a model (or updating a language model for autocorrection) could incrementally push accuracy higher.

In conclusion, our end-to-end system shows that it is practical to automate ID card reading with high accuracy using current computer vision and deep learning techniques. This has significant implications for industries that require identity verification, offering a faster and potentially more secure alternative to manual checking. By continuing to refine the models and expanding the system's capabilities, we move closer to fully automated, reliable ID verification in real-world applications.

Disclosure of Interests. The authors Seyf Kazamel and Ali Alıcı are employed by Armut Teknoloji. Umut Kocasarı was also employed by Armut Teknoloji while implementing this project.

Data Privacy Statement. All processing of private data (ID card images) is performed exclusively on our secure servers which are access-controlled, with no unauthorized external ingress/egress permitted. We ensure that no personally identifiable information is transmitted outside our system and that all data handling complies with applicable privacy regulations and internal security standards.

References

Tavakolian, N., Nazemi, A., Fitzpatrick, D.: Real-time information retrieval from Identity cards. http://arxiv.org/abs/2003.12103 (2020)

Cavalcante, W., Torné, I.G., Camelo, L., Fernandes, R., Printes, A., Bragança, H.: An ID badge information extractor based on object detection and optical character recognition. IEEE Access **12**, 152559–152567 (2024)

Radford, A., et al.: Learning transferable visual models from natural language supervision. In: Proceedings of the 38th International Conference on Machine Learning. pp. 8748–8763. PMLR (2021)

Baek, Y., Lee, B., Han, D., Yun, S., Lee, H.: Character region awareness for text detection. In: 2019 IEEE/CVF Conference on Computer Vision and Pattern Recognition (CVPR), pp. 9357–9366 (2019)

Ronneberger, O., Fischer, P., Brox, T.: U-Net: Convolutional Networks for Biomedical Image Segmentation. In: Navab, N., Hornegger, J., Wells, W.M., Frangi, A.F. (eds.) Medical Image Computing and Computer-Assisted Intervention – MICCAI 2015, pp. 234–241. Springer International Publishing, Cham (2015)

Shaaban, A., Hussein, A., Shokry, E., Alaa-Eldin, O., Rashwan, M., Barhamtoshy, H.: ID card recognition based on ArabicOCR system. Egypt. J. Lang. Eng. **1**(2), 35–49 (2014)

Smith, R.: An overview of the tesseract OCR engine. In: Ninth International Conference on Document Analysis and Recognition (ICDAR 2007), pp. 629–633 (2007)

Bychkov, O., Zubyk, L., Gololobov, D., Isaienkov, Y., Grynkevych, G., Ivanytska, A.: The system for recognizing useful information of the client's ID-card based on machine learning technologies. In: DSMSI (2023)

Jobi, T.R., Varghese, L.: A novel approach for data retrieval from identity cards using deep learning. In: Proceedings of the National Conference on Emerging Computer Applications (NCECA), vol. 5(1), pp. 617–620 (2023)

Suddul, G., Seguin, J.F.L.: A custom-built deep learning approach for text extraction from identity card images. IJ-ICT **13**, 34 (2024)

Maung, S.Z.M., Aye, N.: Text region localization and recognition for ID card identification using deep learning approaches. In: 2023 IEEE Conference on Computer Applications (ICCA), pp. 411–416 (2023)

Harefa, J., Alexander, Chowanda, A., Haikal, E., Fedrick, Antonio Wiranata, S.: ID card storage system using optical character recognition (OCR) on android-based smartphone. In: 2022 International Conference on Electrical and Information Technology (IEIT), pp. 75–79 (2022)

Chandra, A., Stefanus, R.: An end-to-end optical character recognition pipeline for Indonesian identity card. In: 2021 9th International Conference on Information and Communication Technology (ICoICT), pp. 307–312 (2021)

Correlating Socioeconomic Factors and Syphilis Incidence: A Case Study in Brazil

Matheus Tavares[1], Elias Mendes[1], Diego Dias[2(✉)] [iD], Elisa Tuler[1] [iD],
Rodolfo Villaça[2] [iD], Marcelo Guimarães[3] [iD], and Leonardo Rocha[1] [iD]

[1] Universidade Federal de São João del Rei (UFSJ), São João del Rei, Brazil
matheus93t@aluno.ufsj.edu.br, {etuler,lcrocha}@ufsj.edu.br
[2] Universidade Federal do Espírito Santo (UFES), Vitória, Brazil
{diego.dias,rodolfo.villaca}@ufes.br
[3] Universidade Federal de São Paulo (UNIFESP), São Paulo, Brazil
mendeselias2014@aluno.ufsj.edu.br

Abstract. Syphilis is a growing public health concern in Brazil, disproportionately affecting vulnerable populations. Socioeconomic factors, such as education, income, and access to healthcare, significantly influence its incidence. This study compares six statistical methods—Pearson and Spearman correlations, univariate and multivariate linear regression, logarithmic regression, and Poisson regression—to analyze these relationships using data from Minas Gerais, Brazil. The results highlight strong associations between the incidence of syphilis and both educational and health indicators, emphasizing the importance of preventive policies. Methodological comparisons reveal significant discrepancies, with some approaches misestimating the impact of variables due to multicollinearity or data distribution effects. These findings underscore the importance of selecting appropriate statistical models to ensure accurate epidemiological interpretations and support the development of effective public health strategies.

Keywords: Statistical methods · Syphilis · Correlation analysis · Regression models · Data Modeling

1 Introduction

Syphilis is a chronic bacterial infection caused by *Treponema pallidum*, which progresses through distinct clinical stages and can result in severe complications if left untreated [26]. In Brazil, the disease has emerged as a growing public health concern, particularly due to the rising incidence observed in recent years, disproportionately affecting vulnerable populations and diverse social groups. Socioeconomic factors, including educational attainment, income levels, access to healthcare services, and regional disparities, play a critical role in the transmission and persistence of syphilis. A comprehensive understanding of these

O. Gervasi et al. (Eds.): ICCSA 2025, LNCS 15649, pp. 65–80, 2025.
https://doi.org/10.1007/978-3-031-96997-3_5

relationships is essential for developing more effective prevention and control strategies [6].

In this context, computational approaches applied to epidemiology provide valuable tools for analyzing the distribution of syphilis within populations. Statistical methods and machine learning techniques facilitate the identification of patterns, the prediction of trends, and the assessment of the influence of socioeconomic variables on disease incidence. However, the heterogeneity of methodological approaches employed in the literature [6,13,15,19,22] raises concerns about the consistency and comparability of findings. Each statistical method is based on distinct assumptions, offering specific advantages and limitations, and the inappropriate selection of analytical techniques may lead to misinterpretations, ultimately compromising the effectiveness of intervention strategies [23].

To address this issue, the present study aims to compare the application of different statistical methods in analyzing the correlation between syphilis incidence and socioeconomic factors (i.e., education, health, and income). Specifically, we evaluate Pearson correlation [3], Spearman correlation [9], univariate linear regression [1], multivariate linear regression [1], logarithmic regression [2], and Poisson regression [11]. Our analysis focuses on data from selected municipalities in Minas Gerais, one of Brazil's largest and most populous states, characterized by significant regional disparities in socioeconomic development. The study examines the occurrence of gestational syphilis cases [8], using data obtained from the Minas Gerais Transparency Portal[1], the João Pinheiro Foundation[2], and the Minas Gerais Open Data Portal[3]. By assessing the adequacy and robustness of each method, this research seeks to contribute to the standardization of epidemiological analyses and to enhance the understanding of the interrelationships between socioeconomic and epidemiological variables.

While detailed results are presented later in this work, preliminary analyses indicate that educational indicators exhibit the strongest associations with syphilis incidence, underscoring their importance in guiding public policies. Health-related variables, particularly those linked to mortality and healthcare access, also show consistent patterns, while economically disadvantaged populations remain the most vulnerable.

Moreover, methodological divergences observed across models emphasize the importance of selecting appropriate techniques. Certain methods may produce biased coefficients due to data distribution characteristics or multicollinearity, reinforcing the need for a comparative and critical approach.

In sum, our findings highlight the importance of choosing appropriate methodologies to ensure reliable interpretations of the dataset. Moreover, no single strategy consistently captures all relevant correlations, making it essential to consider multiple statistical approaches.

---

[1] https://www.dados.mg.gov.br/vi/dataset/dados_sifilis_ses/resource/c1570999-cbbf-4441-ac53-acd229c36c9f?view_id=e598cfd0-ec9f-48e0-a371-ce1b035d4f91.
[2] https://imrs.fjp.mg.gov.br/Consultas.
[3] https://dados.mg.gov.br/.

2   Related Work

The relationship between disease incidence and socioeconomic factors has been extensively investigated in the literature, particularly in the context of sexually transmitted infections (STIs). Various methodological approaches have been employed to analyze incidence rates and associated risk factors. In general, studies indicate that conditions such as low income, limited education, and restricted access to healthcare services are directly linked to an increase in STI cases [14, 15, 24, 25].

Although multiple studies have identified these conditions as relevant factors, no absolute consensus exists regarding all the determinants that influence STI incidence. Discrepancies arise due to variations in the databases analyzed, selection criteria, and geographic scope of the studies. Additionally, the choice of methodological approaches plays a crucial role in shaping research findings. Various statistical techniques have been used to explore these relationships. For instance, Barbosa et al. [13] investigated risk factors associated with vertical transmission of syphilis in Belo Horizonte, Brazil, employing multivariate logistic regression. Their findings identified low maternal education and inadequate prenatal care as key determinants. In contrast, [19] examined the incidence of congenital syphilis in Recife, Brazil, employing Spearman's correlation to assess the relationship between disease incidence and social inequalities. Their results demonstrated a strong association between higher syphilis incidence and neighborhoods with a lower Human Development Index (HDI). However, neither study explicitly justified the choice of statistical models used for analysis.

Furthermore, spatiotemporal analyses have been applied to understand the distribution of syphilis over time. For example, [22] employed Poisson regression to model syphilis dynamics in São Paulo, Brazil, highlighting seasonal patterns and the impact of public health policies on disease control. Meanwhile, [15] utilized logarithmic regression to assess social inequalities in congenital syphilis incidence in Rio de Janeiro, reinforcing the necessity of targeted interventions for vulnerable populations. These studies, similar to previous ones, applied distinct methodological approaches, often without a clear rationale for their selection. This raises important questions: Which methods are most appropriate for analyzing the relationship between syphilis and socioeconomic factors? Is there a universally optimal approach, or does the choice of method depend on specific epidemiological characteristics? What criteria should guide the selection of an appropriate analytical method?

The diversity of statistical techniques used in the literature reflects the inherent complexity of syphilis epidemiology but also poses challenges to the comparability of results. Different methodological choices can lead to divergent conclusions, complicating the development of consistent public health strategies [23]. In light of this, the present study aims to conduct a comparative analysis of various statistical methodologies used to assess the correlation between syphilis incidence and socioeconomic indicators. The objective is to evaluate the robustness and applicability of each method, contributing to a more standardized and evidence-based approach in epidemiological research.

3   Evaluation Methodology

In this section, we detail the evaluation methodology used to compare statistical and machine learning methods applied in the analysis of the correlation between socioeconomic factors and syphilis incidence.

3.1   Evaluated Methods

Based on the studies presented in the previous section, we consider two correlation methods and four regression methods, as detailed below:

1. **Pearson Correlation:** measures the strength and direction of a linear relationship between two quantitative variables [3]. The coefficient r is:

$$r = \frac{\sum_{i=1}^{n}(x_i - \bar{x})(y_i - \bar{y})}{\sqrt{\sum_{i=1}^{n}(x_i - \bar{x})^2 \sum_{i=1}^{n}(y_i - \bar{y})^2}} \tag{1}$$

2. **Spearman Correlation:** assesses the strength of a monotonic relationship based on ranked values [9]. The coefficient ρ is:

$$\rho = 1 - \frac{6\sum d_i^2}{n(n^2 - 1)} \tag{2}$$

   where d_i is the rank difference and n is the number of observations.

3. **Univariate Linear Regression:** models the relationship between a dependent variable Y and one independent variable X [1]:

$$Y = \beta_0 + \beta_1 X + \epsilon \tag{3}$$

4. **Multivariate Linear Regression:** extends to multiple independent variables:

$$Y = \beta_0 + \beta_1 X_1 + \cdots + \beta_p X_p + \epsilon \tag{4}$$

5. **Logarithmic Regression:** fits data where Y depends on the natural logarithm of X [2]:

$$Y = \beta_0 + \beta_1 \ln(X) + \epsilon \tag{5}$$

6. **Poisson Regression:** models count data where the dependent variable represents the number of events [11]:

$$\log(\lambda) = \beta_0 + \beta_1 X_1 + \cdots + \beta_p X_p \tag{6}$$

   where λ is the expected event rate.

3.2   Analysed Datasets

Our study examines the occurrence of syphilis cases [8] occurring in municipalities of Minas Gerais, one of Brazil's largest and most populous states, characterized by significant regional disparities in socioeconomic development. Specifically, we considered data related to gestational syphilis. This disease, when left untreated, can lead to several complications for the fetus, including: miscarriage, stillbirth, prematurity, low birth weight, and congenital syphilis itself, which can lead to neurological, bone, and skin problems in the baby. It is essential to emphasize the importance of early screening, diagnosis, and treatment of syphilis during pregnancy in order to prevent such consequences and ensure the health of the fetus. These were obtained from Minas Gerais Open Data Portal[4]. In our study, we consider the attributes listed in Table 1.

Table 1. Gestational Syphilis Dataset Attributes

Attribute	Description
_id	Unique Identifier
ID_AGRAVO	Code of the agravo
DT_NOTIFIC	Date of Notification
NU_ANO	Year of Notification
ID_MUNICIP	Municipality
ID_REGIONA	Region
DT_DIAG	Date of Diagnosis
DT_NASC	Date of Birth
NU_IDADE_N	Age in days/months
CS_SEXO	Sex
CS_RACA	Race/Color
ID_MN_RESI	Municipality of Residence
ID_RG_RESI	Region of Residence
ANTSIFIL_N	History of Syphilis at Birth
TRA_ESQUEM	Treatment Regimen
LABC_IGG	IgG Laboratory Test
EVOLUCAO	Case Evolution

The socioeconomic information were obtained from Minas Gerais Transparency Portal[5] and the João Pinheiro Foundation[6]. We selected five cities with

---

[4] https://www.dados.mg.gov.br/vi/dataset/dados_sifilis_ses/resource/c1570999-cbbf-4441-ac53-acd229c36c9f?view_id=e598cfd0-ec9f-48e0-a371-ce1b035d4f91.

[5] https://www.dados.mg.gov.br/vi/dataset/dados_sifilis_ses/resource/c1570999-cbbf-4441-ac53-acd229c36c9f?view_id=e598cfd0-ec9f-48e0-a371-ce1b035d4f91.

[6] https://imrs.fjp.mg.gov.br/Consultas.

the highest incidence of syphilis cases in the state of Minas Gerais, one of the largest and most populous states in Brazil. These cities belong to different regions with varying levels of socioeconomic development (i.e., Belo Horizonte, Juiz de Fora, Ipatinga, Governador Valadares and Montes Claros). We considered the period from 2010 to 2023 and all the available attributes, which correspond to different social indicators: Income, with a sub-indicator of "Management"; Education with sub-indicators "Access" and "Management"; and Health with the sub-indicators "Management", "Hospital medical care" and "Primary care".

Regarding preprocessing strategies, a check for missing data was performed, identifying empty columns and incomplete years. Indicators that presented three or more missing values throughout the period were removed from the study; this amount was chosen because it is equivalent to approximately 20% of the missing data. Although there is no strict consensus in the literature on the exact percentage of missing data that compromises the analysis, some guidelines suggest missing rates greater than 20% can introduce significant biases [4,10,12,21]. At the end of this stage, we were left with a robust set of indicators: 18 Education, 22 Health, and 13 Income indicators, ensuring the comprehensive scope of our study. Finally, we combined the two data collections (syphilis incidence data and socioeconomic data) into a single collection. Finally, we encoded the categorical variables using LabelEncoder [16] and normalized the data using the MinMaxScaler [17] or StandardScaler [18] techniques, ensuring that all indicators were on the same scale and could be compared correctly.

3.3 Experimental Procedures

Our analyses were structured into two lines. First, our goal was to evaluate the quality of the regressions performed by each of the methods. We did this by comparing the function generated with the real data reported in the data collection. The objective was to compare these regression strategies, identifying their limitations in the specific scenario under consideration. To facilitate this comparison, we used the Mean Squared Error (MSE) and the Coefficient of Determination (R^2), two widely used metrics in the evaluation of regression models due to their simplicity and ability to measure the quality of the fits [5].

1. **Mean Squared Error (MSE):** calculates the average of the squares of the differences between predicted and observed values, penalizing more significant errors more severely. MSE helps highlight large discrepancies between predictions and observations due to the quadratic penalization of errors. The smaller the MSE, the better the model fit:

$$\text{MSE} = \frac{1}{n} \sum_{i=1}^{n} (y_i - \hat{y}_i)^2 \tag{7}$$

2. **Coefficient of Determination (R^2):** indicates the proportion of the total variability of the dependent variable that the regression model explains. The R^2 does not provide information about the magnitude of the errors but rather about the proportion of the variability the model explains. It is calculated as:

$$R^2 = 1 - \frac{\sum_{i=1}^{n}(y_i - \hat{y}_i)^2}{\sum_{i=1}^{n}(y_i - \bar{y})^2} \tag{8}$$

where $\bar{y}$ is the mean of the observed values. The value of R^2 ranges from 0 to 1, with values close to 1 indicating that the model explains most of the variability in the data.

In our second analysis, we compared the indicators indicated by each of the strategies analyzed, a crucial step in our research. We applied the correction strategies (Pearson and Spearman) separately and evaluated the five indicators that were associated with the incidence of gestational syphilis, as well as the coefficients related to each of these indicators. We then applied the regression strategies (Univariate and Multivariate Linear Regression, Logarithmic Regression, and Poisson Regression) and evaluated the weights they returned that were associated with the indicators returned by the correlation methods. This comparison was performed separately for each attribute group (educational, health, and income), underscoring the significance of our research in evaluating the complementarity of the strategies considered.

4   Discussion of Results

As mentioned in the previous section, we focused our first analysis on evaluating the predictive performance of the regression models, comparing the predicted values with the actual data. These analyses were performed separately for each city, considering both metrics, R^2 and MSE. In this first evaluation, we considered all the indicators analyzed (health, education, and income), with 80% of the data randomly selected to perform the progression and the evaluation of the result being done on the remaining 20% of the collection. An important observation is that for R^2, a Univariate Linear Regression Linear, the calculation is done for each indicator individually, and, subsequently, the average is calculated. The results can be observed in Tables 2, 3, 4, 5 and 6

Table 2. Results for Belo Horizonte

Metric	Regression Method			
	Logarithmic	Linear Univariate	Linear Multivariate	Poisson
MSE	0.00	0.033	0.00	0.00
R^2	1.00	0.685	1.00	1.00

Our first observation is that some algorithms demonstrate 100% accuracy (R^2) and zero error (MSE). This is properly interpreted as data overfitting, which occurs when a model, in this case a regression model, cannot generalize the data's behavior. It ends up self-adjusting to the data in such a way that it

Table 3. Results for Juiz de Fora

Metric	Regression Method			
	Logarithmic	Linear Univariate	Linear Multivariate	Poisson
MSE	0.00	0.026	0.00	0.00
R^2	1.00	0.722	1.00	1.00

Table 4. Results for Ipatinga

Metric	Regression Method			
	Logarithmic	Linear Univariate	Linear Multivariate	Poisson
MSE	0.00	0.032	0.00	0.00
R^2	1.00	0.70	1.00	1.00

Table 5. Results for Gorvenador Valadares

Metric	Regression Method			
	Logarithmic	Linear Univariate	Linear Multivariate	Poisson
MSE	0.00	0.044	0.00	0.00
R^2	1.00	0.58	1.00	1.00

Table 6. Results for Montes Claros

Metric	Regression Method			
	Logarithmic	Linear Univariate	Linear Multivariate	Poisson
MSE	0.00	0.042	0.00	0.00
R^2	1.00	0.59	1.00	1.00

cannot make effective predictions for new data. This phenomenon occurs when the model memorizes the specific patterns of the training set, including possible noise, instead of capturing the general trend. As a consequence, its performance on unseen data may be significantly lower, making it unsuitable for practical applications. This reinforces the need for adjustments, such as regularization, collection of more data, or the adoption of more robust models to avoid this problem.

Another hypothesis that can explain this issue is Multicollinearity. [7], which occurs when two or more independent variables in a statistical model are highly correlated, making it difficult to determine the individual impact of each one on the dependent variable. This problem mainly affects regression models [20], as it reduces the stability of coefficient estimates and can lead to distorted interpretations of the results. When working with social indicators, multicollinearity can arise naturally, as many of these are interconnected. For example, variables such as per capita income, level of education, and employment rate tend to present

Table 7. Health Indicators

Indicator	Health
Indicator 1	Lung cancer mortality rate
Indicator 2	Breast cancer mortality rate
Indicator 3	Number of doctors per 1000 inhabitants
Indicator 4	Proportional mortality of the elderly population
Indicator 5	Crude mortality rate

Table 8. Education Indicators

Indicator	Education
Indicator 1	School attendance rate for children aged 0 to 3 years old
Indicator 2	School attendance rate for children aged 4 and 5 years old
Indicator 3	Net enrollment rate for elementary school
Indicator 4	Per capita spending on education activities
Indicator 5	Total number of schools offering complete regular elementary school

Table 9. Income Indicators

Indicator	Income
Indicator 1	Disabled people benefiting from BPC
Indicator 2	Total number of BPC beneficiaries
Indicator 3	Elderly people benefiting from BPC
Indicator 4	Per capita income in the formal sector
Indicator 5	Total BPC transfers

strong correlations with each other. Likewise, health indicators, such as infant mortality rate, access to basic sanitation, and life expectancy, often have significant statistical relationships. This problem can generate unstable coefficients, making it challenging to identify which factors really influence the response variable, which highlights the need always to consider different models to perform analyses and thus avoid hasty and perhaps erroneous conclusions.

In our second analysis, which focuses on analyzing the main indicators indicated by each method as the most relevant to explain the incidence of gestational syphilis, for reasons of space, we will consider only the data related to the city of Belo Horizonte, capital of Minas Gerais. As mentioned in Sect. 3.3, we first applied the Pearson and Spearman correlation methods. In this case, we separated our analyses for each group of indicators (education, health and income). In all three scenarios, the five main indicators returned by the two correlations are the same and can be observed in Tables 7, 8 and 9.

Table 10. Correlation Between Indicators from Different Strategies (Health)

Indicator	Regression Method					
	Pearson	Spearman	Logarithmic	Linear Uni.	Linear Multi.	Poisson
Indicador 1	0.856944	0.859341	0.63	0.90	0.44	5.48
Indicador 2	0.829384	0.828571	0.40	0.87	0.32	8.69
Indicador 3	0.828375	0.815385	0.34	0.87	0.23	4.15
Indicador 4	0.827313	0.810989	0.28	0.87	0.19	–
Indicador 5	0.660386	0.677711	-0.62	0.62	0.13	−7.28

Table 11. Correlation Between Indicators from Different Strategies (Education)

Indicator	Regression Method					
	Pearson	Spearman	Logarithmic	Linear Uni.	Linear Multi.	Poisson
Indicador 1	0.907816	0.912088	0.26	0.95	0.18	–
Indicador 2	0.889390	0.894505	0.30	0.93	0.24	–
Indicador 3	0.760739	0.752476	0.55	0.76	0.29	11.60
Indicador 4	0.760739	0.589410	–	0.62	–	−15.83
Indicador 5	-0.792058	-0.792298	–	0.75	–	20.12

In our subsequent analysis, we evaluated the correlation between the main indicators indicated by the Pearson and Spearman correlations and the score assigned to these indicators by the regression methods. Again, we separated our analyses for each group of indicators (health, education and income) and the results can be seen in Tables 10, 11 and 12. In the cells indicated to "–", the regression method was not able to recover the respective indicator.

Table 12. Correlation Between Indicators from Different Strategies (Income)

Indicator	Regression Method					
	Pearson	Spearman	Logarithmic	Linear Uni.	Linear Multi.	Poisson
Indicador 1	0.887070	0.912088	0.38	1.01	0.30	–
Indicador 2	0.868712	0.829670	0.24	0.97	0.19	–
Indicador 3	0.848366	0.818681	–	0.92	–	–
Indicador 4	0.832164	0.811882	–	0.83	–	3.78
Indicador 5	0.828375	0.815385	–	0.87	–	3.93

Analyzing the results, our first observation is that Univariate Linear Regression follows a similar behavior to Pearson and Spearman, with high correction values for the same indicators indicated by these correlation methods, for the three sets of indicators. If only the MSE and R^2 results were considered, Univariate Linear Regression would have been wrongly discarded. Another positive aspect of this regression model is that we can perform an evaluation of how a given variable behaves when describing the incidence of syphilis. To exemplify this analysis, we analyzed two indicators related to education, presented in Fig. 1.

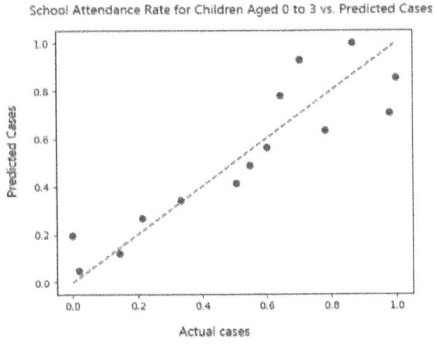 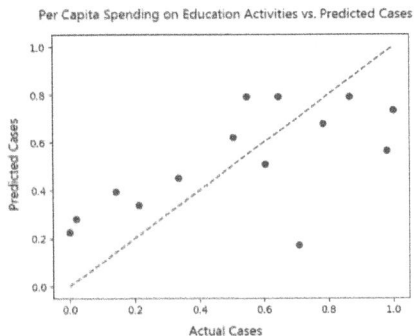

(a) School attendance rate for children aged 0 to 3 years old

(b) Per capita Spending on education activities.

Fig. 1. Individualized Indicator Analysis.

In the images above, we can see how both indicators are behaving in relation to the increase/decrease in cases of gestational syphilis. Contrasting the results of Fig. 1 (a) with the error metrics, we have an R^2 of 0.82 and an MSE of 0.02. In other words, it can reproduce 82% of syphilis cases well, and misses 20%. For Fig. 1 (b), we have an R^2 of 0.42 and an MSE of 0.06. This means that it can abstract only 42% of cases well. This analysis is essential due to reliability. The other algorithms end up analyzing everything together, preventing a more precise analysis, and allowing analysis errors. In addition, we saw that Univariate Linear Regression was the only one that brought coherent values in an analysis.

Another regression model that, despite having suffered from multicollinearity, also showed some positive aspects, was the Poisson. It also has reliability support. In our analyses, when suggesting correlations, it already attributes confidence to these correlations. Showing a robust model for an analysis in our context. Furthermore, it presents itself as a good model for modeling countable variables, which is our case, case count. For the other cases, multicollinearity between the indicators prevented deeper analyses of the indicators from being performed. Again, if one of these models had been chosen for the analyses, without a prior study of how they work and how the data are distributed, it could have led to distorted analyses and erroneous conclusions.

4.1   Qualitative Discussion of Evaluated Methods

Statistical Methods. Pearson's correlation measures the linear relationship between two variables, assuming that the data follows a normal distribution. This method is sensitive to outliers, as it relies on mean and variance. However, it is suitable when the relationship between variables is both proportional and linear. In contrast, Spearman's correlation assesses monotonic relationships, which do not necessarily have to be linear. Since it is based on rank rather than absolute values, it does not require normally distributed data and is less affected by outliers. This makes Spearman's correlation particularly useful for detecting non-linear but monotonic relationships, such as exponential or logarithmic trends.

Our analysis revealed that the data exhibits highly complex, predominantly non-linear relationships. When applying Spearman's correlation, we identified strong associations that Pearson's correlation failed to detect. This suggests that Pearson's method may overlook important patterns. In contrast, Spearman's correlation not only confirmed the relationships detected by Pearson but also expanded the set of identified correlations with greater accuracy. Notably, it was the only method to reveal negative correlations, indicating variables inversely associated with syphilis incidence. Given these findings, we conclude that Spearman's correlation is the most appropriate method for analyzing the dataset used in this study, as it provides a more comprehensive and precise understanding of variable relationships. Considering that this research aims to inform social policies to mitigate syphilis cases, the use of reliable methods such as Spearman's correlation is both fundamental and necessary.

Regression Models. Logarithmic regression employs a logarithmic transformation to model nonlinear relationships. The coefficients are interpreted in terms of percentage changes, making this method particularly useful for variables exhibiting large-scale variation. However, it may introduce distortions when applied to datasets with many values close to zero, and it may not adequately capture non-log-linear relationships.

Univariate linear regression examines the relationship between each independent variable and the dependent variable separately. This approach can reveal strong associations that might otherwise be masked in multivariate regression. However, it does not account for interactions between variables, potentially leading to misleading conclusions by overestimating or underestimating their individual importance.

Multivariate linear regression is particularly suitable when analyzing categorical dependent variables (e.g., presence or absence of an event), allowing for the interpretation of coefficients as changes in the probability of the event occurring. Nevertheless, its application to continuous variables can be less intuitive. Additionally, it assumes independence of observations, which poses a challenge when autocorrelation exists between municipalities or regions, as observed in our dataset. Poisson regression is well-suited for modeling count data, employing a probabilistic approach to estimate uncertainty and highlight statistically significant relationships. Moreover, it allows the incorporation of prior knowledge into the modeling process. However, the interpretation of its coefficients may be less intuitive compared to classical regression methods.

Given the complexity of the relationships within our dataset, relying on a single statistical approach may be insufficient. A combination of methods may be required to fully understand the correlations between syphilis incidence and socioeconomic indicators. Each method presents distinct advantages and limitations, necessitating careful selection based on the specific research objectives. Logarithmic regression is valuable when interpreting marginal effects and percentage-based relationships. Univariate linear regression is useful for identifying initial patterns before developing a more comprehensive model. If the dependent variable is categorical (e.g., presence or absence of syphilis), multivariate linear regression may be more appropriate. Meanwhile, Poisson regression is advantageous when analyzing count data, such as the number of syphilis cases. In our analysis, univariate linear regression emerged as the most suitable method for examining the relationship between syphilis incidence and socioeconomic indicators. Unlike other models, it demonstrated a higher explanatory power, offering deeper insights into individual predictors while avoiding issues related to multicollinearity and model interpretability. Furthermore, its ability to analyze each indicator separately enhances the robustness and clarity of the findings, enabling a more precise evaluation of the factors influencing syphilis incidence. In contrast, other models exhibited limitations such as sensitivity to multicollinearity, reduced explainability, and challenges in handling datasets with a high number of indicators.

4.2   Main Results

Overall, the results demonstrate that the logarithmic, multivariate linear, and Poisson regression models achieved perfect predictive performance across all evaluated cities, with an R^2 of 1.00 and MSE of 0.00. While at first glance this may suggest excellent model performance, such outcomes strongly indicate overfitting, as the models may have memorized the training data rather than generalized underlying patterns. In contrast, the univariate linear regression model showed significantly lower R^2 values, ranging from 0.58 to 0.72 depending on the city, and MSE between 0.026 and 0.044, suggesting a more realistic fit. These findings highlight the importance of carefully evaluating model complexity and addressing potential multicollinearity or data leakage to ensure that predictions are generalizable to unseen data.

5   Conclusion and Future Works

This study aimed to compare different statistical methods for analyzing the relationship between the incidence of gestational syphilis and socioeconomic indicators, specifically health, education, and income. By employing Pearson and Spearman correlation, as well as univariate and multivariate linear regression, logarithmic regression, and Poisson regression models, we obtained a more comprehensive understanding of the interactions among the analyzed variables.

The findings underscore the critical influence of methodological choices on epidemiological analyses. While Pearson correlation exhibited limitations in capturing non-linear relationships, Spearman correlation proved to be a robust approach for detecting monotonic associations. Univariate regression also demonstrated strong explanatory power in modeling socioeconomic indicators. The comparative analysis of municipalities in Minas Gerais with high incidence rates of gestational syphilis revealed distinct patterns across different regional contexts, reinforcing the necessity of segmenting indicators into categories such as health, education, and income. These insights provide a solid statistical foundation for the formulation of targeted and more effective public health policies.

Given these findings, further research is warranted. A logical next step is to extend this analysis to other regions of Brazil, applying diverse statistical approaches and regression models to refine our understanding of the socioeconomic dynamics driving the spread of sexually transmitted infections. This expanded investigation will contribute to the development of more precise and data-driven strategies for the prevention and control of gestational syphilis at a national level.

Acknowledgment. The authors acknowledge partial funding from the Coordination for the Improvement of Higher Education Personnel - Brazil (CAPES) - Funding Code 001, the National Council for Scientific and Technological Development (CNPq), and the Research Support Foundation of the State of Minas Gerais (FAPEMIG). We also thank the Research and Innovation Support Foundation of Espírito Santo (FAPES) for the resources provided through the PROAPEM project (368/2022 - P: 2022-NGKM5) and the PDPG project (129/2021 - P: 2021-GL60J), which were fundamental to the completion of this work.

References

1. de Administração Pública (ENAP), E.N.: Introdução aos modelos de regressão linear. ENAP (2020). https://repositorio.enap.gov.br/bitstream/1/4788/1/Livro_Regress%C3%A3o%20Linear.pdf
2. Bellégo, C., Benatia, D., Pape, L.: Dealing with logs and zeros in regression models. arXiv preprint arXiv:2203.11820 (2022). https://arxiv.org/abs/2203.11820
3. Benesty, J., Chen, J., Huang, Y.: Pearson correlation coefficient. In: Noise Reduction in Speech Processing, pp. 1–4. Springer (2009). https://doi.org/10.1007/978-3-642-00296-0_5
4. Bennett, D.A.: How can i deal with missing data in my study? Aust. N. Z. J. Public Health **25**(5), 464–469 (2001). https://doi.org/10.1111/j.1467-842X.2001.tb00294.x, https://pubmed.ncbi.nlm.nih.gov/11688629/
5. Chicco, D., Warrens, M.J., Jurman, G.: The coefficient of determination r-squared is more informative than SMAPE, MAE, MAPE, MSE and RMSE in regression analysis evaluation. PeerJ Comput. Sci. **7**, e623 (2021). https://doi.org/10.7717/peerj-cs.623

6. Domingues, R., do C. Leal, M.: Incidência de sífilis congênita e fatores associados à transmissão vertical da sífilis: dados do estudo nascer no brasil. Cadernos de Saúde Pública **32**(6), e0008241 (2016). https://doi.org/10.1590/0102-311X00082415
7. Farrar, D.E., Glauber, R.R.: Multicollinearity in regression analysis: the problem revisited. Rev. Econ. Stat. **49**(1), 92–107 (1967). https://doi.org/10.2307/1937887
8. Favero, M.L.D.C., Ribas, K.A.W., Costa, M.C.D., Bonafé, S.M.: Sífilis congênita e gestacional: notificação e assistência pré-natal. Arch. Health Sci. **26**(1), 2–8 (2019). https://doi.org/10.17696/2318-3691.26.1.2019.1137
9. Hauke, J., Kossowski, T.: Comparison of values of Pearson's and spearman's correlation coefficients on the same sets of data. Quaestiones Geographicae **30**(2), 87–93 (2011). https://doi.org/10.2478/v10117-011-0021-1
10. Heymans, M.W., Twisk, J.W.R.: Handling missing data in clinical research. J. Clin. Epidemiol. **151**, 185–188 (2022). https://doi.org/10.1016/j.jclinepi.2022.08.016, https://www.sciencedirect.com/science/article/pii/S0895435622002506, epub 2022 Sep 21
11. Hilbe, J.M.: Negative binomial regression. Cambridge University Press, pp. 40–58 (2011). https://doi.org/10.1017/CBO9780511973420
12. Jakobsen, J.C., Jesper Kjaer, M.G., Gluud, C.: When and how should multiple imputation be used for handling missing data in Randomised clinical trials – a practical guide with flowcharts. BMC Med. Res. Methodol. **17**(1), 162 (2017). https://doi.org/10.1186/s12874-017-0442-1, https://bmcmedresmethodol.biomedcentral.com/articles/10.1186/s12874-017-0442-1
13. Lima, M., Santos, R., Barbosa, G., Ribeiro, G.: Incidência e fatores de risco para sífilis congênita em belo horizonte, minas gerais, 2001–2008. Ciência e Saúde Coletiva **18**(2), 499–506 (2013). https://doi.org/10.1590/S1413-81232013000200023
14. Medeiros, J., Yamamura, M., da Silva, Z., Domingues, C., Waldman, E., Chiaravalloti-Neto, F.: Spatiotemporal dynamics of syphilis in pregnant women and congenital syphilis in the state of são paulo, brazil. Sci. Rep. **12**(1), 585 (2022). https://doi.org/10.1038/s41598-021-04530-y
15. Oliveira, R., Silva, A., Gonçalves, M.: Incidência de sífilis congênita em adolescentes: um estudo epidemiológico na região sudeste do brasil. Revista Paulista de Pediatria **39**(1), 1–8 (2021). https://doi.org/10.1590/1984-0462/2021/39/0101
16. Pedregosa, F., et al.: Scikit-learn: Machine learning in python - label encoding (2011). https://scikit-learn.org/stable/modules/generated/sklearn.preprocessing.LabelEncoder.html
17. Pedregosa, F., et al.: Scikit-learn: Machine learning in python - minmaxscaler (2011). https://scikit-learn.org/stable/modules/generated/sklearn.preprocessing.MinMaxScaler.html
18. Pedregosa, F., et al.: Scikit-learn: Machine learning in python - standardscaler (2011). https://scikit-learn.org/stable/modules/generated/sklearn.preprocessing.StandardScaler.html
19. Ramos, R., Carneiro, G., Oliveira, A., Cunha, T., Ramos, V.: Incidence of congenital syphilis according to inequalities and living conditions in the city of Recife, Pernambuco, Brazil. Revista Brasileira de Saúde Materno Infantil **21**(1), 1–10 (2021). https://doi.org/10.1590/1806-93042021000100002
20. Shrestha, N.: Detecting multicollinearity in regression analysis. Am. J. Appl. Math. Stat. **8**(2), 39–42 (2020)
21. da Silva, M.A., Bustamante-Teixeira, M.T.: Uso da imputação múltipla de dados faltantes: uma simulação utilizando dados epidemiológicos. Cad. Saude Publica **25**(2), 268–276 (2009)

22. da Silva, P., Almeida, J., Santos, M.: A Bayesian approach to understand congenital syphilis distribution: a spatiotemporal analysis in Brazil. Sci. Rep. **11**, 1–10 (2021). https://doi.org/10.1038/s41598-021-04530-0

23. Singh, D.D., Singh, A., Kumar, A., Singh, R.: Selection of appropriate statistical methods for data analysis. Ann. Card, Anaesth. **22**(3), 297–301 (2019). https://doi.org/10.4103/aca.ACA_248_18, https://www.ncbi.nlm.nih.gov/pmc/articles/PMC6639881/

24. Soares, K., Prado, T.N., Zandonade, E., Moreira-Silva, S.F., Miranda, A.E.: Análise espacial da sífilis em gestantes e sífilis congênita no estado do espírito santo, 2011–2018. Epidemiologia e Serviços de Saúde **29**(1), e2018193 (2020). https://doi.org/10.5123/S1679-49742020000100018

25. Souza, V., Mendes, A., Costa, L.: Desigualdades na incidência de sífilis congênita no Brasil: uma abordagem espacial. Revista de Saúde Pública **56**(1), 1–12 (2022). https://doi.org/10.11606/S1518-8787.2022056003800

26. Tsuboi, M., et al.: Prevalence of syphilis among men who have sex with men: a global systematic review and meta-analysis from 2000-20. Lancet Global Health **9**(8), e1110–e1118 (2021). https://doi.org/10.1016/S2214-109X(21)00221-7, epub 2021 Jul 8

RiceAML: An Auto Machine Learning Model to Identify Abiotic Stress-Associated Single Nucleotide Polymorphisms in Rice

Hasnaa Imad Al-Shaikhli[1] , Suhad A. Yousif[1] , Tiba Zaki Abdulhameed[1] ,
and Suzan Jabbar Obaiys[2]([⊠])

[1] Al-Nahrain University, College of Sciences, Computer Science Department,
Baghdad, Iraq
`hasna.imad@nahrainuniv.edu.iq`
[2] Department of Computer System and Technology, Faculty of Computer Science
and Information Technology, Universiti Malaya, 50603 Kuala Lumpur, Malaysia
`suzan@um.edu.my`

Abstract. Identifying core single nucleotide polymorphisms (SNPs) associated with rice abiotic stress traits computationally helps researchers to deepen their understanding of genetic diversity, trait inheritance, yield improvements, and marker-assisted selection in rice breeding. The advancement of recent Artificial Intelligence (AI) can facilitate the identification and prediction of essential SNPs. In this study, a RiceAML model is proposed via utilizing Auto Machine Learning (AML) approach like (TPOT) to classify SNPs of abiotic stress traits in rice. Eight datasets (six individual datasets and two combined datasets) with two DNA sequence lengths 40 and 100 nucleotides, are used. Three encoding approaches are applied to convert DNA sequences into numeric values such as One-Hot, DNA2Vec, and concatenation of both feature vectors. The results showed that the prediction accuracy of the model trained on merged or combined dataset, especially Combined_100, outperformed the prediction accuracy of models trained on individual datasets, particularly when using the One-Hot Encoding, achieving an accuracy of 93.7%. The proposed RiceAML model with related datasets can be accessed through https://github.com/HasnaaImad/RiceAML.

Keywords: Rice · SNP · AI · TPOT AutoML · DNA mining · One-Hot Encoding · DNA2Vec Encoding · Bioinformatics

1 Introduction

Rice (Oryza Sative) is a fundamental staple crop that has played a substantial role in agriculture and human nutrition for over half the world [9,20]. This improves rice genetic research, which is important in global food security.

© The Author(s), under exclusive license to Springer Nature Switzerland AG 2025
O. Gervasi et al. (Eds.): ICCSA 2025, LNCS 15649, pp. 81–96, 2025.
https://doi.org/10.1007/978-3-031-96997-3_6

Researchers and breeders face challenges in optimizing rice quality and quantity through its sophisticated genome architecture and many traits. Specifying core single nucleotide polymorphisms (SNP) related to targeted traits computationally from large genomic data accelerates breeding by reducing irrelevant mutation noise [20].

In the rice genome, Single Nucleotide Polymorphisms (SNPs) are the most popular genetic variation, consisting of altering a single nucleotide base. These variations are important in understanding genetic diversity, trait inheritance, and marker-assisted selection in rice breeding. Identifying SNPs related to popular traits such as yield, disease resistance, and stress tolerance can help breeders develop improved rice varieties more efficiently [6,13,25]. However, the rice genome has an extremely high number of SNP markers, ranging from hundreds of thousands to millions. It is difficult to use all the SNPs for analysis because of the dimensionality and comparably small sample sizes found in breeding data sets. Redundant or irrelevant SNPs add noise, decreasing prediction accuracy. Therefore, effective computational techniques must be employed to predict the most relevant SNPs [20].

Recent developments of machine learning (ML) and deep learning (DL) have remarkably boosted the analysis and employment of SNP data in rice research to address these challenges by enabling deeper analysis of complex and high dimensional SNP data. Farooq et al. [5] comprehensively review how artificial intelligence (AI) is revolutionizing modern plant breeding. The authors highlight the importance of AI in handling large-scale genomic and phenomic data to allow faster genetic gains. Through deep learning, machine learning, and natural language processing algorithms, AI improves trait prediction, variant detection, gene discovery, and genomic selection. Integrating multi-omic data with high-throughput phenotyping allows breeders to reveal complex relationships among traits, leading to increased crop resilience and productivity. The study emphasizes the ability of AI to bridge the genotype-phenotype gap and optimize genome editing tools to create cultivars ready for future challenges.

Another study [10] by Eugene Koh et al. explains the application of AI in the analysis of omics data on plant stress. The authors review more than 4,000 BioProjects and identify widespread drought, heat, and pathogen stress with species such as Arabidopsis thaliana, rice, and maize. It shows how tools such as LLM and AlphaFold can extract methods, build knowledge graphs, and predict gene functions from raw DNA. Despite problems such as inconsistent metadata and explainability, it emphasizes the importance of AI in boosting the study of plant resilience through existing tools and collaboration.

How big data and AI revolutionize plant stress research by interpreting plant reaction to environmental stresses is discussed in [11]. It reports on genomic and transcriptomic data from SRA and GEO on drought, salt, heat, cold, and pathogen stress in Arabidopsis thaliana, Oryza sativa, and Zea mays. AI techniques such as deep learning and large language models identify omics data patterns, make gene function predictions, and support literature mining. Tools such as AlphaFold, Enformer, FloraBERT, and AgroNT optimize stress tolerance predictions. Poor data labeling, interpretability, and unequal access to data are some of the hindrances to its application. The article appeals to interdisciplinary collaboration and more advanced data infrastructure to take AI to greater heights in sustainable agriculture under climate change.

Early crop genomic prediction utilized linear methods such as genomic best linear unbiased prediction (GBLUP), assuming small additive effects for every SNP. ML and DL can capture nonlinear effects (epistasis, dominance) without assuming prior strong requirements. Genomic rice researchers have used various models, from classical ML algorithms (random forests, support vector machines) to more recent DL architectures (convolutional neural networks, recurrent networks, transformers) to predict phenotypes of SNP genotypes or identify SNPs linked to specific traits [26]. What follows is a summary of significant papers from the last years using these methods, categorized by modeling method.

Traditional ML methods have been widely used to handle rice SNP datasets, specifically for feature selection and genomic prediction tasks. Random forests (RF) and gradient boosting (e.g. XGBoost) have worked effectively in the scenario of high-dimension SNP inputs and have feature importance metrics incorporated. For example, a 2024 research study introduced the PlantMine platform [20], which incorporates feature selection into ML algorithms to identify core SNPs (a reduced set of informative markers most predictive of target traits). Three feature selection methods (ANOVA, MIC, F-score) screened approximately 7202 potential SNPs from the 3000 Rice Genomes dataset in PlantMine, and various ML models (XGBoost, SVM, k-NN, Random Forest) were compared to predict flowering time. The best feature selection method, along with the ML model, produced nearly 98% accuracy in discriminating early and late flowering groups using a random forest based on the corresponding SNP subset. Feature selection ML algorithms can effectively manage genome-wide SNP data and also prevent overfitting. The random forest is particularly notable for the detection of SNPs and the increase in predictability. Feature selection improves model interpretability and performance by removing duplicate SNP features. Plant-Mine SNP discovery enables rice breeders to identify key genetic markers for traits such as heading date to prioritize for breeding.

In a crop genomics experiment in 2022 [7], the authors found that classical ML algorithms could outperform deep learning in genotype-to-phenotype predictions when data were sparse. Random forest and XGBoost models performed better than neural networks on 13 of 14 trait prediction tasks, and the top SNPs determined using XGBoost's feature importance were similar to established GWAS trait-associated loci. Properly tuned ML models yield strong performance and improve interpretability. Significant SNP markers can be identified by examining characteristic importance scores such as the XGBoost F score or RF Gini, some of which map to previously identified genes. A model could be reduced to 10% of the SNPs without loss of accuracy, increasing interpretability and speed.

During the study [18], machine learning methodologies are used to discriminate between various stress conditions by analyzing stress-responsive genes in the rice plant. Based on comparative transcriptomic data analysis, the models identify putative genes important for high-level stress tolerance, thus allowing better insight into the genetic underpinnings of stress responses and allowing the generation of stress-tolerant rice cultivars.

Deep learning (DL) has transformed bioinformatics by allowing pattern recognition in large datasets without manual feature engineering. In rice genomics, DL models identify the SNP-associated trait as a classification problem and the quantitative prediction of traits from SNP inputs as a regression problem.

Tan et al. (2022) [4] presented NucleoNet, a novel deep learning framework used to predict rice yields and detect important single nucleotide polymorphisms (SNP) that control yields. NucleoNet outperformed traditional methods such as ordinary least squares (OLS) by leveraging SNP positional data and attention capabilities to identify important genetic markers related to yield. It used 1,536 genotyped SNP markers genotyped in 467 Indonesian rice varieties and tested on 4 environments. In particular, NucleoNet detected several potentially beneficial SNPs in rice breeding programs and highlighted the power of artificial intelligence in the genomic selection of complicated traits.

In 2024, Xu et al. introduced RiceSNP-BST [23], a deep learning framework for predicting SNPs associated with biotic stress traits employing convolutional neural networks. The input to the model consisted of DNA sequences surrounding putative SNP loci in several formats: one-hot representation, DNA2vec embeddings, DNABERT embeddings, and DNAShape features. These features allowed CNN to discover SNPs associated with the trait. RiceSNP-BST was unique in that its 35,749 pairs of SNPs from the GWAS Atlas were used in its training set, with the known pairs being positive and the unrelated SNPs negative. In an independent validation set, the model outperformed baselines such as gradient boosting with improved precision and recall. RiceSNP-BST resulted in an F1-score and AUC of 0.65 and 0.61, respectively, compared to an F1 of around 0.58 by XGBoost. Its generalization performance across species revealed strong learning from unseen data. Genomic task automation eliminates the requirement of tuning CNNs by hand.

A similar approach is followed in early 2025 when the RiceSNP-ABST model or framework [14] was introduced to predict SNPs associated with abiotic stress traits in rice against salinity and drought. It employed CNNs with residual connections to predict SNPs from DNA sequences. Six sets were used to train RiceSNP-ABST because there is poor high-quality data on rice abiotic stress QTLs. Four sequence representation methods (such as RiceSNP-BST: One-Hot, k-mer embeddings), with initial feature selection before CNN modeling, were applied. RiceSNP-ABST's CNN performs better than current machine learning models and past benchmarks. RiceSNP-ABST generalizes well to independent rice data and to other organisms and demonstrates that genomic patterns of stress-responsive variants are captured through learning representations. The model outperforms traditional machine learning methods and multiple state-of-the-art methods in the benchmark data set with a maximum accuracy of 61.38%.

Vourlaki et al. [21] examined the potential improvement in rice trait predictions by combining structural variants (SVs) with single nucleotide polymorphisms (SNPs) using deep learning (DL) methods. Their comparative study of DL models such as multilayer perceptrons (MLP) and convolutional neural networks (CNN) against Bayesian methods showed that DL outperformed conventional modeling approaches in many cases, especially in the case of binary traits like leaf senescence and culm diameter. In particular, adding SVs greatly enhanced predictive power, and SNPs linked to SVs showed high effectiveness. This study emphasizes the great potential that DL and diverse genomic inputs offer to revolutionize rice breeding methods.

Cropformer [22] is an advanced deep learning model with convolutional and attention layers designed in 2024 for predicting crop phenotypes, including rice-specific traits. It is not just applied to rice, but upon testing on five crops (maize, millet, rice, tomato, wheat) on 20+ characteristics, it showcases state-of-the-art deep learning in genomics. Cropformer's architecture integrates CNN layers to capture local haplotype signals and self-attention layers to extract long-range interactions focusing on influential SNPs. Rice genotypes are passed through 1D convolution to identify local linkage disequilibrium signals and then differential weighting by multi-head attention blocks. The architecture greatly improved predictive performance compared to models like rrBLUP and XGBoost. The predictive power was 7.5% better in some characteristics compared to the next-best model. In the case of rice, the cropformer improves predictions of yields and characteristics by capturing epistatic interactions. Crucially, it was designed with interpretability in mind. Once trained on the data, the authors performed haplotype analysis, attention visualizations, SHAP value computation, and clustering to interpret predictions. They selected SNPs with notable weights that could be causal to trait differences. Attention-weighted SNPs in maize identified significant biology associated with height and flowering genes. Likewise, the approach can identify significant SNPs for grain yield or rice disease resistance. The model integrates genomic data with environmental factors to enhance the precision of the predictions. The model's interpretability allows researchers to identify influential genetic markers and environmental factors influencing specific traits, thus facilitating the application of targeted breeding programs.

In this research, a classifier called RiceAML, based on TPOT auto machine learning approach, is proposed to predict the Aboitis Stress-Associated Single Nucleotide Polymorphisms (ABST SNPs) in rice. The first contribution of this work is to check whether auto machine learning will give a machine learning algorithm performance better than the current ones applied individually. To achieve this aim, six benchmark datasets, recently created in [14] with two DNA sequence lengths (40 and 100 bp), are utilized. The second contribution focuses on the study of the effects of combining datasets of the same length on the performance of the proposed model.

This manuscript is organized as follows: Sect. 2 describes the datasets used with the proposed model methodology in detail. Section 3 presents the results of the implementation of ML models with optimized selected features and parame-

Table 1. Summary of datasets with total number of samples for both training and testing stages

Dataset Name (Total Samples)	Training (80%)			Testing (20%)		
	+ve Samples	−ve Samples	Total	+ve Samples	−ve Samples	Total
Random_40 (5118)	2,047	2,047	4,094	512	512	1,024
Common_40 (5118)	2,047	2,047	4,094	512	512	1,024
Rearrange_40 (5604)	2,241	2,241	4,482	561	561	1,122
Random_100 (5140)	2,056	2,056	4,112	514	514	1,028
Common_100 (5140)	2,056	2,056	4,112	514	514	1,028
Rearrange_100 (5604)	2,241	2,241	4,482	561	561	1,122
Combined_40 (15,840)	6,336	6,336	12,672	1,584	1,584	3,168
Combined_100 (15,884)	6,353	6,353	12,706	1,589	1,589	3,178

ters using TPOT. Finally, Sect. 4 summarizes the key contributions of this study and discusses the broader implications of using one-hot and DNA2vec encoding to predict (ABST SNP) in rice.

2   Materials and Methodology

The proposed model consists of four main phases: datasets preparation, sequence encoding and data splitting, constructing the model or classifier, and finally, classifier's performance evaluation as shown in Fig. 1. The description of each phase is explained in detail below.

2.1   Dataset Preparation Phase

The proposed RiceAML model is trained and tested on six recent benchmark datasets, which were created and applied for RiceABST model [14] with two DNA sequence lengths (40 and 100 bp). The RiceAML classifier is further trained and tested on two combined datasets that are created from merging all three datasets with the same DNA sequence length. For instance, a dataset named "Combined_40" is generated from combining datasets "Random_40", "Common_40", and "Rearrange_40" where each sequence has a length of 40 bp as listed in Table 1. It is good to mention that the original datasets' sequence

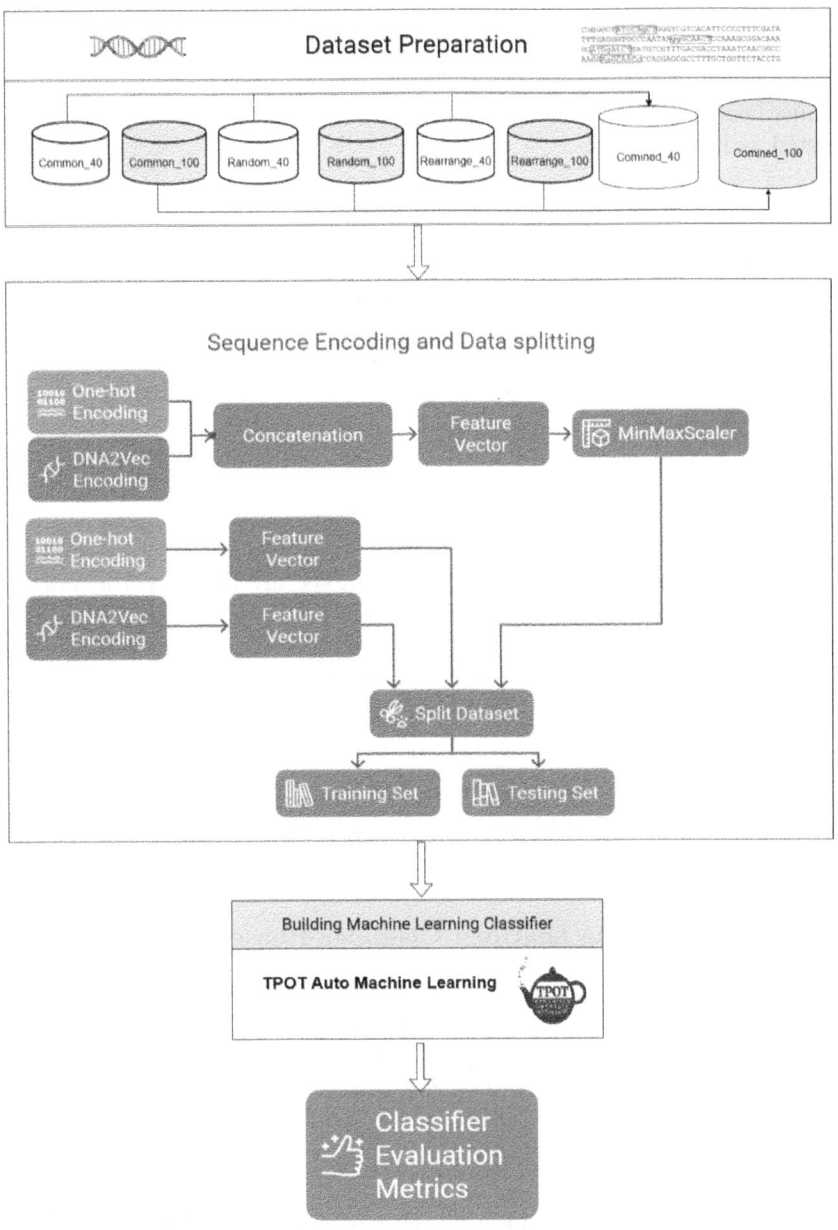

Fig. 1. Proposed model phases.

lengths are 40 or 100 nucleotides, not 41 or 101 nucleotides. For this reason, the names of the datasets in this study are different.

2.2   Sequence Encoding and Data Splitting Phase

To make the dataset instances (sequences) ready for machine learning classifiers, they must be encoded into numeric feature vectors. Thus, three encoding schemes are tested as listed.

- One-Hot-Encoding: The vocabulary set of the DNA sequence consists of the four letters C,G, T, and B. Thus, 4-bit One-Hot Encoding is used [3]. This technique embeds each nucleotide (A, C, G, and T)in a vector. As an example A=(1,0,0,0), G=(0,1,0,0), C=(0,0,1,0), and T=(0,0,0,1). This encoding is easy to generate and simple, but the vectors produced do not carry any contextual information that can help understand the motifs' pattern. The One-Hot-Encoding provides local information, where each DNA sequence nucleotide is considered a feature.
- DNA2Vec Encoding [17] is a DNA sequence embedding technique that uses a shallow neural network (NN) similar to word2vec [8]. The input to the NN are variable k-mers, which are equivalent to the language's vocabulary when word2vec embedding is applied in Natural Language Processing (NLP) applications. The main challenges of DNA2Vec are deciding the value of k, and the range of the surrounding context of the k-mers.
- Concatenation of One-Hot-Encoding and DNA2Vec Encoding into one vector. This is to test whether combining local and contextual relationships can provide more information about the sequence for the classifier. All features were normalized using MinMaxScaler to ensure scale consistency across dimensions.

After generating the feature vectors, the dataset is split into 80% for training and 20% for testing.

2.3   Building Machine Learning Classifier Phase

AutoML automates the process of model development, such as feature selection, hyperparameter tuning, and model evaluation. Some popular AutoML tools are AutoKeras [16], TPOT [15], and H2O.ai [24]. This research uses the Tree-based Pipeline Optimization Tool (TPOT) Auto ML. TPOT applies multiple iterations for feature selection until optimum selected features are passed to the next stage [12,19].

2.4   Classifier Evaluation Metrics Phase

This stage evaluates each classifier generated from the previous stage. Evaluation is based on the Accuracy and Confusion Matrix.

Accuracy is computed by the Eq. 1

$$Accuracy = \frac{TP + TN}{TP + FN + TN + FP} \times 100 \tag{1}$$

Where TP, TN, FN, and FP stands for the total number of True Positive, True Negative, False Negative, and False Positive, respectively. A positive in the Rice trait prediction problem refers to a trait subsequence predicted from the DNA sequence. A TP is the number of Trait subsequences that are correctly classified, and a TN is the number of nontrait subsequences that are also correctly classified. On the other hand, FP is the number of non-trait subsequences incorrectly classified as traits, and FN is the number of trait subsequences incorrectly classified too.

Confusion Matrix is a heat map generated based on the TP, TN, FP, and FN. It illustrates a visualization of the classifier's performance, where higher values of TP and TN indicate better performance.

3 Results and Discussion

In this section, we will present the outcomes of our experiments, starting by loading the dataset and transforming it into an ideal shape to train the model on top of it. Then, we process three different encoding strategies to convert categorical or sequential data to numerical data for machine learning model training. In transforming categorical data to represent digitally, the most prevalent method is the One Hot Encoding method; however, in DNA sequence-based data the DNA2Vec Encoding captures a feature-wise representation of DNA sequences, thus working excellently with biological datasets. Finally, we concatenated the two encoding methods to get more features.

Using TPOT, we automatically optimize and select the best pipeline for every encoding method. The models are assessed based on their key performance metrics: classification accuracy and confusion matrix. Lastly, we show the efficacy of our approach by comparing the results with those of previous studies.

3.1 Results of Different Encoding Methods and Datasets

Based on the horizontal bar chart shown in Fig. 2., higher accuracy results are represented by a dark bar (combined datasets) or a light bar (individual datasets) for each encoding type, so the analysis is broken down into that structure below:

3.2 One-Hot Encoding Results

The combined_100 dataset produced an accuracy result of 0.937, which is higher than all other results by a significant margin, thus demonstrating very high performance. This high accuracy is due to the One-Hot Encoding ability to extract exact positioning information in large aggregated datasets. Individual runs on these datasets achieve an accuracy of 0.583 (rearrange_40), which reflects a significant performance drop from the combined dataset. This large gap shows that single datasets may be underrepresented or non-diverse and that the encoding method can affect accuracy even though a strong encoder is used.

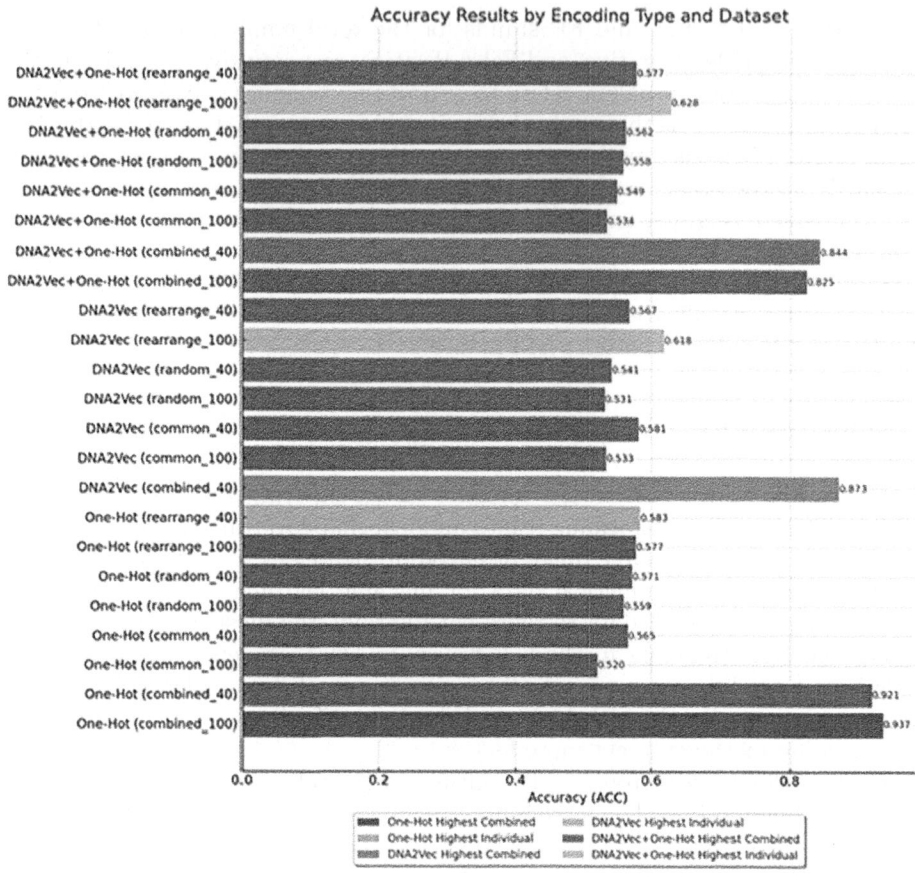

Fig. 2. Accuracy results by applying different encoding type on different datasets.

3.3 DNA2Vec Encoding Results

The best predictor of accuracy was (0.873) in combined_40 dataset with the DNA2Vec Encoding method, which is moderately lower than the One-Hot results, but remains strong. Although the DNA2Vec model can capture semantic similarities between DNA sequences, it may not encode position-specific information as effectively as One-Hot encoding. The best single result for DNA2Vec was in rearrange_100 with an accuracy of 0.618, which was lower than the combined dataset. It illustrates the drop in accuracy that is based on one specific embedding-based approach, which underwrites its trend to increase the data used for better accuracy.

3.4 Concatenated Encoding (One-Hot and DNA2Vec)

While this method did not outperform One-Hot method alone, the combined accuracy of 0.844 was still good. These results suggest that concatenated encoding efficiently combines the advantages of the two approaches, the positional specificity of One-Hot and embedding-based semantic representations of DNA2Vec, to achieve a more balanced and robust prediction performance. The best accuracy seen from individual datasets was produced by rearrange_100 at 0.628, with slight advancements upon DNA2Vec only (0.618) and notably higher than individual One-Hot results (0.583). This result confirms that the advantage of concatenated encoding, as mentioned, is valid for all datasets; as a result, the previous gap between DNA2Vec and other models about positional representation was effectively compensated for.

These results show that the aggregation of datasets always beats the standalone dataset for any encoding strategy, signifying how critical the magnitude of the data is for any predictive storytelling. Of all encoding methods for the combined datasets, one-hole encoding emerges as the single most powerful method. It captures the fine-grained positional features essential for exploring biological sequences. The concatenation approach works effectively for individual datasets, combining the advantages of two encoding methods DNA2Vec scores moderate accuracy, indicating that it may require larger datasets or hybrid approaches for better performance. The score does not appear to improve much with increased training. This visual and analytical comparison method is structured to quickly identify the encoding strategies and their relative strengths. This will ultimately drive decisions about the analysis of biological data and the modeling methods applied in the future.

Finally, we summarize the highest accuracy values among different encoding methods and datasets, showing that the One-Hot Encoding (combined_100) and DNA2Vec concatenated with the One-Hot Encoding (rearrange_100) performed better overall, as shown in Fig. 3. Their confusion matrices are also given to support these results and provide a visualization, as listed in Fig. 4.

Performance analysis of the top results with the TPOT Auto ML classifier based on varying encoding methods, One Hot Encoding, DNA2Vec and One-Hot Concatenated DNA2Vec, for both combined and individual data sets shows that for the combined dataset, the best predictive performance was achieved based on One Hot Encoding (combined_100) with an accuracy (ACC) of 0.937362, an AUC of 0.937365, and an AUPR of 0.906. This impressive result was achieved by the TPOT AutoML pipeline using a well-planned series of preprocessing methods, comprising StandardScaler for feature scaling, and SelectPercentile for keeping about 18% of the most statistically relevant features, and combined parallel Feature Union layers coupling of SkipTransformer (to transfer critical raw feature signals) and Passthrough (to maintain intact numerically encoded raw feature signals). The bagging classifier built on top of this process now only uses 67 trees, no bootstrapping, 61% features, and 66.7% samples to ensure the model diversity and prediction performance are stable.

The highest single result achieved on the individual dataset was using the One-Hot concatenated DNA2Vec Encoding features from the rearrange_100 dataset, which scored an accuracy of 0.628011, an AUC of 0.628002, and an AUPR of 0.580297. The TPOT pipeline executing this individual dataset's best

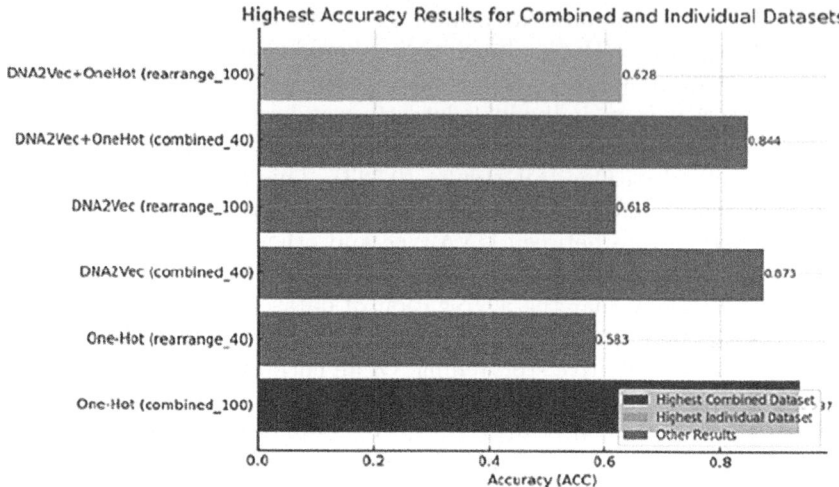

Fig. 3. Highest accuracy results for combined and individual datasets.

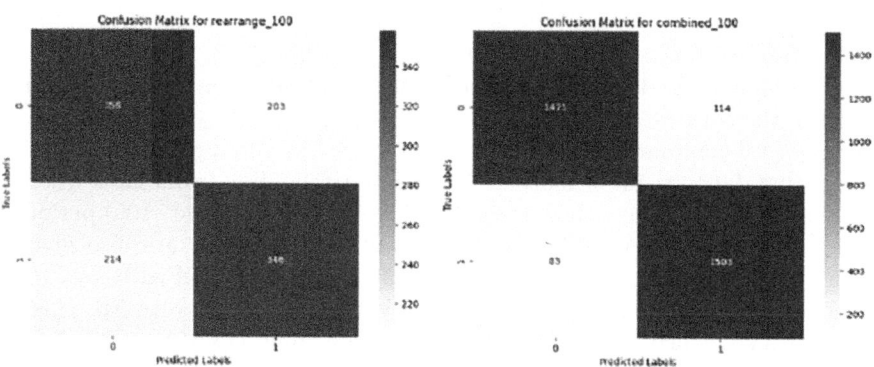

Fig. 4. Confusion matrices of TPOT pipeline models.

result performed extensive preprocessing, with initial scaling of feature values to a global range using MinMaxScaler and multiple nested transformations in twin FeatureUnion layers. A binarizer (threshold = 0.856) and PCA (retaining approximately 51.3% variance) were combined alongside the preserved raw features using a passthrough for optimal representation of the features. At its end, the pipeline arrived at an optimized XGBoost Classifier with regularized hyperparameters (learning_rate = 0.0354, max_depth = 10, subsample = 0.7435, gamma = 0.0154, reg_alpha = 0.00545, reg_lambda = 0.0499, and n_estimators = 100) that mostly finds a compromise between diversity of features, control over complexity, and generalization of prediction.

The findings confirm the great gain of working with combined datasets, especially when using One-Hot Encoding, in obtaining better model performance.

Using TPOT pipelines, selective feature selection and dimensionality reduction in the context of raw signal preservation and ensemble modeling were combined to effectively optimize the final predictive accuracy.

To showcase the state of our new work, we compare our experimental setup and results with the RiceSNP-ABST study [14], one of the latest works for RT-

Table 2. Conceptual and performance comparison between TPOT ML pipeline and CNN-based RiceSNP-ABST models.

Aspect	RiceSNP CNN-Based Model	TPOT ML Pipeline (Proposed Experiment)	Notes
Model Architecture	Automated CNN with residual connections optimized via ENAS	Automated TPOT ML pipelines (XGBoost, Bagging)	CNN vs ML pipeline; CNN captures spatial patterns explicitly.
Datasets	Six training datasets: Random_41, Common_41, Rearrange_41, Random_101, Common_101, Rearrange_101 with two testing datasets (Independent and cross-species).	Eight datasets: Random_40, Common_40, Rearrange_40, Random_100, Common_100, Rearrange_100, Combined_40, Combined_100 (80% for training and 20% for testing).	Multiple datasets used; your method explicitly analyzes encoding strategies.
Preprocessing	Custom preprocessing	Automated within pipeline	Proposed approach enables full automation.
Feature Handling	Learns features from raw data	Selects and transforms features via TPOT	Manual vs automated feature processing.
Best Achieved Accuracy	ACC = 0.6133, AUC = 0.6633 (trained on rearrange_101nt)	ACC = 0.937, AUC = 0.937 (Combined_100, One-Hot encoding)	Proposed model significantly outperforms RiceSNP-ABST.
Individual Dataset Performance	ACC = 0.613 (rearrange_101)	ACC = 0.628 (rearrange_100, One-Hot and DNA2Vec feature vector)	Slightly better individual performance as well.

based trait prediction in rice. In contrast to RiceSNP-ABST, which emphasizes the use of SNP characteristics in attention-based approaches to classification, our experimental design features alternative encoding mechanisms and model architectures designed for improved interpretability and performance. The comparison is made on various factors such as the dataset used, the characteristics represented, the models chosen, the evaluation metrics calculated, and the performance achieved, as shown in Table 2.

4   Conclusions and Future Work

This research presents a comparative evaluation of DNA sequence encoding when used to detect the ABST SNPs in rice. The prediction models were built using TPOT auto machine learning approach, reaching 93.7% with XGBoost model trained on the combined dataset with a sequence length 100 represented with One-Hot encoding.

In general, combined datasets with the two DNA sequence lengths achieved better results. In other words, encoding methods and machine learning algorithms achieve higher accuracy with larger datasets. This is promising situation when analyzing the big genomic data.

Future research should introduce more encoding techniques and larger datasets to uncover the generality of these findings across various crop traits. In particular, integrating these bioinformatics strategies establishes a strong foundation for further genetic work and application for trait prediction, breeding program design, and trait-based data-driven agricultural recommendations in rice and other key crops.

Locating SNPs in DNA rice sequences is similar to the regular motif finding problem in the bioinformatics field. As for future work, motif finding methods or algorithms can be applied not only for predicting SNPs but also for finding their exact locations in the DNA sequences, such as SMF [1] and qSMF [2] algorithms. In our opinion, this can help researchers or breeders to understand which motif(s) (transcription factor binding site(s)) bind to which gene(s) (which affect associated traits).

References

1. Al-Shaikhli, H., de Doncker, E.: SMF: approximate algorithm for the planted (l, d) motif finding problem in DNA sequences. In: Proceedings of the International Conference on Bioinformatics & Computational Biology (BIOCOMP), pp. 123–129. The Steering Committee of The World Congress in Computer Science, Computer ... (2018)
2. Al-Shaikhli, H., de Doncker, E.: qSMF: an approximate algorithm for Quotum planted motif search on ChIP-Seq data. In: 2019 IEEE International Conference on Electro Information Technology (EIT), pp. 434–440. IEEE (2019)
3. Choong, A.C.H., Lee, N.K.: Evaluation of convolutionary neural networks modeling of DNA sequences using ordinal versus one-hot encoding method. In: 2017 International Conference on Computer and Drone Applications (IConDA), pp. 60–65 (2017)

4. Dominic, N., Cenggoro, T.W., Budiarto, A., Pardamean, B.: Deep polygenic neural network for predicting and identifying yield-associated genes in Indonesian rice accessions. Sci. Rep. **12**(1), 13823 (2022)
5. Farooq, M.A., et al.: Artificial intelligence in plant breeding. Trends in Genetics (2024)
6. Feltus, F.A., Wan, J., Schulze, S.R., Estill, J.C., Jiang, N., Paterson, A.H.: An SNP resource for rice genetics and breeding based on subspecies Indica and japonica genome alignments. Genome Res. **14**(9), 1812–1819 (2004)
7. Gill, M., et al.: Machine learning models outperform deep learning models, provide interpretation and facilitate feature selection for soybean trait prediction. BMC Plant Biol. **22**(1), 180 (2022)
8. Goldberg, Y., Levy, O.: word2vec explained: deriving Mikolov et al.'s negative-sampling word-embedding method. arXiv preprint arXiv:1402.3722 (2014)
9. Huang, J., Li, Z., Zhang, J.: Research on plant genomics and breeding (2023)
10. Koh, E., Sunil, R.S., Lam, H.Y.I., Mutwil, M.: Confronting the data deluge: How artificial intelligence can be used in the study of plant stress. Computational and Structural Biotechnology Journal (2024)
11. Koh, E., Sunil, R.S., Lam, H.Y.I., Mutwil, M.: Harnessing big data and artificial intelligence to study plant stress. arXiv preprint arXiv:2404.15776 (2024)
12. Le, T.T., Fu, W., Moore, J.H.: Scaling tree-based automated machine learning to biomedical big data with a feature set selector. Bioinformatics **36**(1), 250–256 (2020)
13. Liu, C.G., Zhang, G.Q.: Single nucleotide polymorphism (SNP) and its application in rice. Yi Chuan= Hereditas **28**(6), 737–744 (2006)
14. Lu, Q., et al.: RiceSNP-ABST: a deep learning approach to identify abiotic stress-associated single nucleotide polymorphisms in rice. Briefings Bioinform. **26**(1), bbae702 (2025)
15. Maher, N., Yousif, S.A.: An automated machine learning model for diagnosing COVID-19 infection. IAES Int. J. Artif. Intell. (IJ-AI) **12**(3), 1360–1369 (2023)
16. Matti, R., Yousif, S.A.: AutoKeras for fake news identification in Arabic: leveraging deep learning with an extensive dataset. Al-Nahrain J. Sci. **26**(3), 60–66 (2023)
17. Ng, P.: dna2vec: Consistent vector representations of variable-length k-mers. arXiv preprint arXiv:1701.06279 (2017)
18. Panahi, B., Hamid, R., Jalaly, H.M.Z.: Deciphering plant transcriptomes: leveraging machine learning for deeper insights. Curr. Plant Biol. 100432 (2024)
19. Ribeiro, P., et al.: Tpot2: A new graph-based implementation of the tree-based pipeline optimization tool for automated machine learning. In: Genetic Programming Theory and Practice XX, pp. 1–17. Springer (2024)
20. Tong, K., et al.: PlantMine: a machine-learning framework to detect core SNPs in rice genomics. Genes **15**(5), 603 (2024)
21. Vourlaki, I.T., Ramos-Onsins, S.E., Pérez-Enciso, M., Castanera, R.: Evaluation of deep learning for predicting rice traits using structural and single-nucleotide genomic variants. Plant Methods **20**(1), 121 (2024)
22. Wang, H., et al.: Cropformer: an interpretable deep learning framework for crop genomic prediction. Plant Communications (2024)
23. Xu, J., et al.: RiceSNP-BST: a deep learning framework for predicting biotic stress–associated SNPs in rice. Briefings Bioinform. **25**(6), bbae599 (2024)
24. Yousif, S.A., Samawi, V.W.: The effectiveness of using AutoML in electricity theft detection: the impact of data preprocessing and balancing techniques. In: International Conference on Computational Science and Its Applications, pp. 68–82. Springer (2024)

25. Zhao, H., et al.: RiceVarMap: a comprehensive database of rice genomic variations. Nucleic Acids Res. **43**(D1), D1018–D1022 (2015)
26. Zhao, L., Walkowiak, S., Fernando, W.: Artificial intelligence: a promising tool in exploring the phytomicrobiome in managing disease and promoting plant health. Plants **12**(9), 1852 (2023)

The Application of Machine Learning Algorithms to Predict Heart Disease

Hadeel Alsolai[(⊠)] [ID]

Department of Information Systems, College of Computer and Information Sciences, Princess Nourah bint Abdulrahman University, P.O. Box 84428, Riyadh 11671, Saudi Arabia
haalsolai@pnu.edu.sa

Abstract. The Early prediction of heart disease at its primary stage, based on symptoms, poses a significant challenge for healthcare organizations worldwide. Machine learning algorithms play a crucial role in predicting and diagnosing heart disease. This paper empirically investigates the application of various types of single machine learning algorithms—Bayes Network, Neural Network, Decision Tree, JRIP—along with one hybrid algorithm (Vote) for heart disease prediction. The study utilizes the heart failure prediction dataset containing 11 features and 918 records. Additionally, two types of feature selection methods— subset and ranking—are employed, each including two techniques: best first, greedy stepwise, Chi-squared, and information gain, respectively. Our empirical findings reveal that the predictive performance of the Vote algorithm surpasses that of other single algorithms. Furthermore, the Vote algorithm outperforms previous studies in most evaluation measures. Concerning feature selection, all methods consistently choose eight attributes, indicating the exclusion of only three attributes— RestingBP, FastingBS, and RestingECG. However, the removal of these attributes does not significantly impact the performance of the prediction algorithms.

Keywords: Heart Disease · Machine Learning · Prediction

1 Introduction

The heart holds a crucial role in the human body by pumping oxygen-rich blood through a network of veins and arteries to various parts of the body. Therefore, it stands as one of the most essential organs, and any form of abnormalities within it is classified as heart disease [1]. Heart diseases continue to be among the primary causes of worldwide fatalities, presenting a significant challenge in the healthcare sector. According to the World Health Organization, heart disease stands as the leading cause of death worldwide, claiming approximately 17 million lives annually, amounting to 30% of global deaths [2]. Additionally, statistics show that between 17% and 45% of patients with heart disease succumb within the first year, while the remaining individuals pass away within five years [3].

Accurately predicting and detecting heart disease in its early stages holds immense significance for successful interventions and improved patient outcomes. Technological advancements, particularly within machine learning algorithms, present promising

O. Gervasi et al. (Eds.): ICCSA 2025, LNCS 15649, pp. 97–115, 2025.
https://doi.org/10.1007/978-3-031-96997-3_7

avenues to enhance predictive models and aid in swiftly identifying individuals suscep-tible to such conditions. Scientists and researchers have invested considerable effort and hard work into conducting several studies utilizing machine learning classifiers to predict heart disease [3–10]. These studies rely on various features, notably gender, heart rate, chest pain type, cholesterol levels, age, and several other attributes. Additionally, several factors play a significant role in elevating the risk of heart disease, including cholesterol levels, diabetes, smoking habits, obesity, family history, and high blood pressure [2]. Nevertheless, manually detecting heart disease based on the aforementioned features poses a challenging task to establish.

This research paper investigates and evaluates the effectiveness of machine learning algorithms in predicting heart disease. Four distinct single algorithms—Bayes Network (BN), Neural Network (NN), Decision Tree (DT), JRIP—alongside the hybrid Vote algorithm, which combines these single algorithms, have been developed. Furthermore, these algorithms are applied to a heart failure prediction dataset comprising 11 features and 918 observations. The study integrates five different datasets related to heart disease, namely Cleveland, Stalog Heart, Long Beach, Switzerland, and Hungarian. Addition-ally, two types of feature selection methods—subset and ranking—are employed, each utilizing two techniques: best first, greedy stepwise, Chi-squared, and information gain, respectively.

The aim of this paper is to clarify the most effective methodologies that facilitate accurate and early identification of individuals at risk of developing heart disease. This is achieved by expanding upon existing knowledge about heart health through the integra-tion of real-world evidence and information derived from comprehensive analysis. The findings are expected to provide valuable insights for developing robust prediction meth-ods, thereby assisting healthcare professionals in early identification and intervention for individuals prone to heart disease.

Essentially, this research strives to bridge complex machine learning techniques with the critical need for precise, early prediction of heart disease. The ultimate objective is to enable more proactive and personalized healthcare approaches.

The goal of this empirical study based on Goal-Question-Metric (GQM) template [11] as follows:

Evaluate: The detecting abilities of heart disease using machine learning classifiers.

Purpose: Detecting heart disease.

Respect: Precision, Recall, F-Measure, Area under carve (AUC) and Accuracy.

Perspective: Machine learning and healthcare researchers.

Context: Heart disease dataset.

In order to achieve the previous goal, we address the following Research Questions (RQ) in our study:

RQ1) Which attributes turn out to be the most important attributes in predicting heart disease?

RQ2) Does the performance of feature selection increase the accuracy of the prediction algorithms of heart disease?

RQ3) Does the performance of hybrid algorithm (Vote) increase the accuracy of the single algorithms of heart disease?

RQ4) Does the performance of hybrid algorithm (Vote) better than the model used by selected previous studies in predicting heart disease?

The remaining sections of this paper are organized as follows: Sect. 2 provides a related work in the heart disease prediction. Section 3 includes a detailed description of the methodology used in this study. Section 4 contains an experiment set up. Section 5 presents results and discussions. Conclusion and future work are conducted in Sect. 6.

2 Related Work

Extensive researches have been published into the problem of predicting heart disease using a variety of machine learning and features. In this section, we present the summary of the selected studies related to prediction heart disease. We consider a total of eight studies published in the well-known journal and conference proceedings. The selected studies have chosen based on the following criteria: (i) papers targeted to predict heart disease. (ii) papers evaluate and compare machine learning algorithms. (iii) papers used different evaluation measures. (iv) papers published recently (after 2019). The main aim of this selection is to determine main gaps in the previous selected studies.

Also, we aim to compare and evaluate our result with these recent studies.

There is a large volume of published studies compared and evaluated several machine learning algorithms and identified the best algorithm that achieved the highest accuracy to predict heart disease. In 2019, Ali et al. [4] developed a novel hybrid algorithm based on X^2 statical model and deep neural network techniques for the diagnosis of heart disease. The proposed algorithm was implemented to remove irrelevant features using X^2 statical model and diagnose heart disease using DNN.

One year later, Pires et al. [5] performed multiple machine learning algorithms, namely Neural Networks (NN), Decision Tree (DT), K-Nearest Neighbors (KNN), Combined nomenclature (CN), Stochastic Gradient Descent (SGD), Support Vector Machine (SVM). The main findings are that SGD achieved the highest prediction accuracy of heart disease by using 5-fold cross-validation. During the same year, Srivastava and Choubey [6] used well-known machine learning models (i.e., DT, KNN, SVM and Random Forests (RF)) to predict heart disease and compared their results with previous nine studies. They stated that KNN attained the highest accuracy (87%) compared with used models as well as the used model by previous nine studies. Aggrawl and Pal [3] created six different algorithms and found the result obtained by RF, along with applying sequential feature selection is the best that gained (86.67%) in term of accuracy performance. Also, Buettner and Schunter [7] built several algorithms and have the same conclusion, where RF outperformed other algorithms and got (84.44%) in term of accuracy.

In 2021, Rani et al. [8] created multiple single algorithms, namely SVM, Naïve Bayes (NB), Logistic Regression (LG), along with two hybrid algorithms RF and Adaptive Boosting (AdaBoost) for detection heart disease. Among these algorithms, again RF produced the optimum performance in term of accuracy (86.6%). During the same period, Kuruvilla and Balaji [9] predicted the heart disease using four types of machine learning classifiers Multilayer Perceptron (MLP), AdaBoost, NB and SVM. The best result is reported by MLP (84.90%).

A recent study by Pan et al. [10] and Li et al. [12] investigated several single and hybrid machine learning algorithms, and the results obtained in these studies reveal that the hybrid algorithms produced the most outstanding performance.

Table 1 presents a summary of the selected studies related to prediction heart disease. This table illustrates datasets and numbers of features and record used in each study, along with pre-processing, evaluation measures and algorithm used. The information proposed in this table helps us to determine main gaps. Also, this table determines algorithm that achieved the best result to enable compare and evaluate our result with these algorithms.

Table 1. Summary of the selected studies related to prediction heart disease.

Study ID	Author	Ref	Year	Dataset/ Numbers of features and record	Pre-processing	Evaluation measures	Algorithm	Algorithm achieved the best result
S1	Ali et al.	[4]	2019	Cleveland heart disease /13 attributes/ 303 records	X^2 statical model to remove irrelevant features	Accuracy, Sensitivity, Specificity, Matthews correlation coefficient (MCC), Area under curve (AUC) and ROC charts	hybrid model X^2-DNN, ANN and DNN	X^2-DNN (93.33%)
S2	Pires et al.	[5]	2020	Statlog (Heart)/13 attributes / 270 records	–	Accuracy, F1measure, Precision, Recall	NN, DT, KNN, CN, SVM and SGD	SGD (87.69%)
S3	Srivastava and Choubey	[6]	2020	Heart Disease /13 attributes / 303 records	Recover the null values	Accuracy, Sensitivity, Specificity, Precision and F-Measure	DT, KNN, SVM, RF	KN (87%)
S4	Aggrawl and Pal	[3]	2020	Heart Failure Clinical Record Data Set 2020 /13 attributes / 299 records	Sequential Feature Selection	Accuracy, Re-call, Precision, AUC and F-Measure	LDA, RF, GBC, DT, SVM, and KNN	RF (86.67%)

(*continued*)

Table 1. (*continued*)

Study ID	Author	Ref	Year	Dataset/ Numbers of features and record	Pre-processing	Evaluation measures	Algorithm	Algorithm achieved the best result
S5	Buettner and Schunter	[7]	2020	Cleveland heart disease /13 attributes / 303 records	NA	Confusion matrix and accuracy	RF	RF (84.44%)
S6	Rani et al.	[8]	2021	Cleveland heart disease /13 attributes / 303 records	Feature selection (genetic algorithm and recursive feature) and sampling (SMOTE)	Accuracy, Sensitivity, Specificity, Precision and FMeasure	SVM, NB, LR, RF, and AdaBoost	RF (86.6%)
S7	Kuruvilla and Balaji	[9]	2021	Framingham heart disease /15 attributes / 4241 records	Feature selection (Correlation Based Feature Selection, Principal Component Analysis)	Accuracy, Precision, Recall, F-Measure and ROC	MLP, AdaBoost, NB and SVM	MLP (84.90%)
S8	Pan et al.	[10]	2022	Cleveland heart disease /13 attributes / 303 records	-	Precision, Recall, F-Measure, Accuracy and AUC	Gradient Boosting, XGBoost, AdaBoost, CatBoost, ANN, RF, SVM, DT and LR	Hybrid (SVM + AdaBoost) 86.88%
S9	Li et al.	[12]	2024	Coronary heart disease/ 7291 records	-	Precision, Recall, F-Measure, Accuracy and AUC	deep neural network, a recurrent neural network model hybrid model	Hybrid model 82.8%

** DNN: Deep Neural Network, NN: Neural Networks, DT: Decision Tree, KNN: K – Nearest Neighbor, CN: Combined nomenclature, SVM: Support Vector Machine, SGD: Stochastic Gradient Descent, RF: Random Forest, LDA: Linear Discriminant Analysis, GBC: Gradient Boosting Classifier, NB: Naïve Bayes, LR: Logistic Regression, AdaBoost: Adaptive Boosting, MLP: Multilayer Perceptron, ANN: Artificial Neural Network, XGBoost: Extreme Gradient Boosting.

The main gaps from aforementioned table are determined as follows:

- Gap 1: Most of the studies have been used datasets that include few numbers of records (e.g., 303 records).
- Gap 2: A limited number of studies have been performed features selection techniques.
- Gap 3: Relatively few studies have been created hybrid algorithms, whereas several studies have been created single algorithms.

Therefore, this study seeks to formulate methodology which will assist to address these research gaps. The methodology used in this paper will be proposed in the next section.

3   Methodology

The methodology is prepared according to the fundings obtained in the selected studies related to prediction heart disease in the previous section. Consequently, three procedures were performed to resolve the identified gaps in section 2 as follows:

- To resolve **Gap 1:** We integrate five different heart disease datasets, namely Cleveland (303 records), Stalog Heart (270 records), Long Beach (200 records), Switzerland (123 records), and Hungarian (294 records).
- To resolve **Gap 2**: We perform two types of features selection methods (subset and ranking) and each types includes two techniques: Subset: Best first and Greedy Stepwise (forwards) and Ranking: Chi-squared and Information Gain. Therefore, the total of features selection techniques is four types, and we take the *intersection* between them (attributes selected by all four types) (see Fig. 1).
- To resolve **Gap 3**: We create Vote algorithm that considered hybrid algorithm and include four single algorithms from different types: BayesNet, Neural Network, decision tree, JRIP.

The paper aims to increase the prediction accuracy of heart disease by comparing between the following:

1. Models created using feature selection and without feature selection.
2. Single algorithms (i.e., BayesNet, Neural Network, decision tree, JRIP) and hybrid algorithm (i.e., Vote).

Figure 2 illustrates methodology of prediction heart disease that used in this study. The methodology includes the following steps:

1. Integrate five heart disease datasets. The total records become 1190 records.
2. Remove duplicated records. 272 records were removed, so the total records become 918 records.
3. Carry out two datasets: without applying feature selection that include 11 attributes and with applying feature selection that include 8 attributes. Four types of features selection techniques were applied and the intersection between them was performed.
4. Create four single algorithms from different types, and create hybrid algorithm from these four single algorithms.

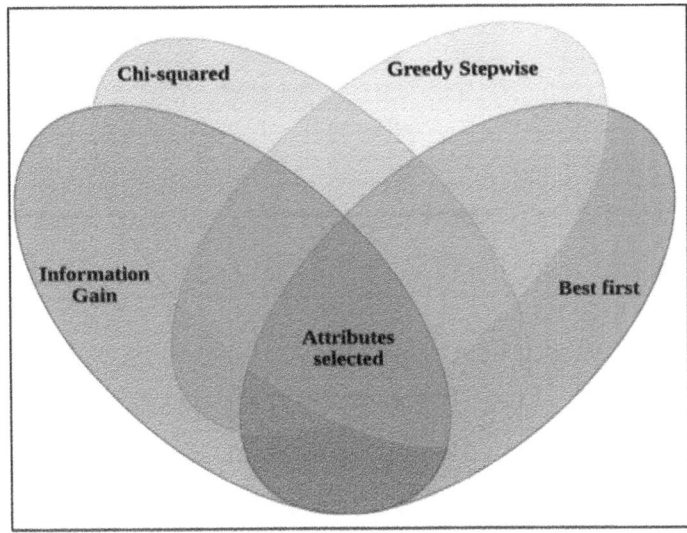

Fig. 1. Method of attributes selected.

4 Experiment Set Up

4.1 Dataset

The heart failure prediction dataset is used in this study and can be obtained from Kaggle from the following link: https://www.kaggle.com/fedesoriano/heart-failure-prediction.

This dataset integrates five different heart disease datasets, namely Cleveland (303 observations), Hungarian (294 observations), Switzerland (123 observations), Long Beach (200 observations), Stalog Heart (270 observations). These datasets Every dataset can be download using the index of heart disease datasets from UCI Machine Learning Repository on the following link: https://archive.ics.uci.edu/ml/machine-learning-databases/heart-disease/.

The total of the heart failure prediction dataset is 1190 observations. However, duplicated observations were removed that include 272 observations, so the final dataset includes 918 observations. The fact that worth mention is that the dataset has no missing values.

4.2 Independent Variables

The heart failure prediction dataset includes 11 independent variables, namely Age, Sex, ChestPainType, RestingBP, Cholesterol, FastingBS, RestingECG, MaxHR, ExerciseAngina, Oldpeak, ST_Slope and one dependent variables Heart Disease. Table 2 provides the description of independent variables of heart disease dataset.

4.3 Dependent Variable

Heart disease is the dependent variable in the heart failure prediction dataset. The machine learning algorithms used in this paper predict heart disease (if a patient has

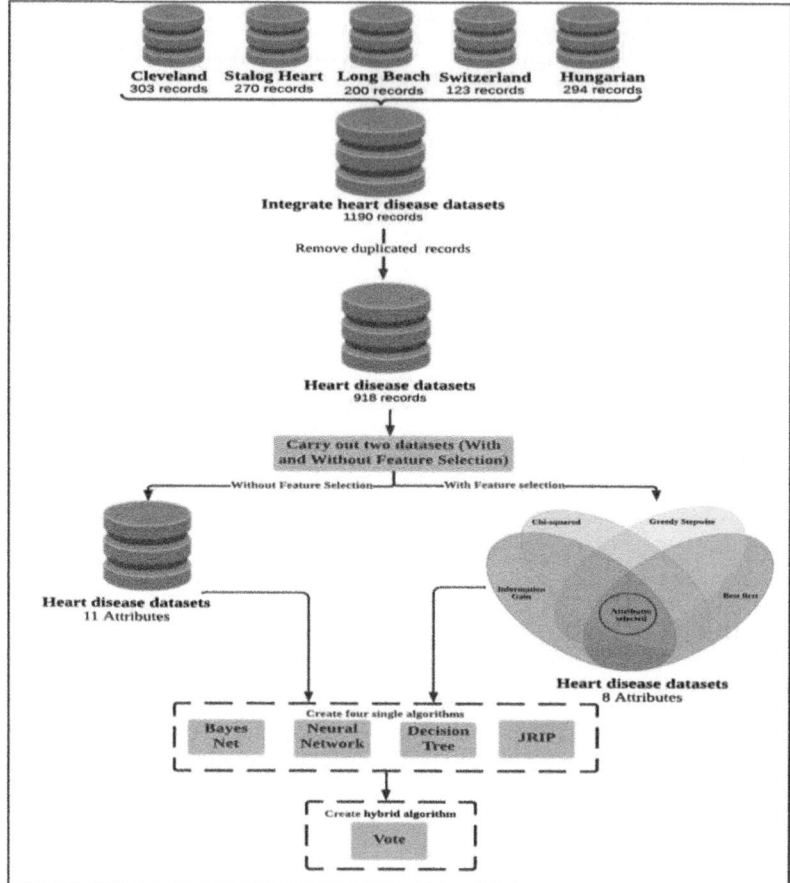

Fig. 2. Methodology of prediction heart disease.

heart disease (True) or not (False). The dataset is considered classification because the dependent variable is Boolean type, and its value class (True) or (False). Figure 3 illustrates the number of values in the dependent variable (heart disease). This figure indicates the dependent variable contain 508 True values and 410 False values. Therefore, the dependent variable is relatively balance and applying sampling techniques to balance datasets is not necessary.

4.4 Feature Selection Methods

Feature selection methods are commonly performed in the dataset to reduce their size and to adjust to the best group for the analysis [13]. Feature selection methods are in general classified into subset and ranking methods. Subset method is identified best suit of feature subset related to the dependent variable [14]. Ranking method is performed in two steps: (i) features are arranged according to a specific statistical measure. (ii) features are selected and sorted according to the highest ranking [15].

- **Best first** can be begun with an empty set of features and identifies the best features for a given dataset by searching forward. In contrast, this method can be begun with a full set of features and identifies the best features for a given dataset by searching backwards. Besides, this method can be begun with any point by searching in both directions to consider all possible features additions and deletions at a given point [16].

Table 2. The description of independent variables of heart disease dataset.

Name	Description	Distinct	Data type	Data values
Age	Age of the patient in terms of years	-	Numeric	Range from 28 to 77
Sex	Sex of the patient that classified into Male (M) and Female (F)	Two	Nominal	M or F
ChestPainType	Chest pain type that classified into Typical Angina (TA), Atypical Angina (ATA), Non-Anginal Pain (NAP) and Asymptomatic (ASY)	Four	Nominal	TA, ATA, NAP or ASY
RestingBP	Resting blood pressure that measures by (mm /Hg)	NA	Numeric	Range from 0 to 200
Cholesterol	Serum cholesterol that measures by mm/dl	NA	Numeric	Range from 0 to 603
FastingBS	Fasting blood sugar that that classified into 1 if FastingBS > 120 mg/dl and 0 otherwise	Two	Numeric	1 or 0
RestingECG	Resting electrocardiogram results that classified into Normal (Normal), having ST-T wave abnormality (T wave inversions and/or ST elevation or depression of >0.05 mV) (ST) and showing probable or definite left ventricular hypertrophy by Estes' criteria (LVH)	Tree	Nominal	Normal, ST or LVH
MaxHR	Maximum heart rate	NA	Numeric	Range from 60 and 202
ExerciseAngina	Exercise-induced angina that classified into Yes (Y) and No (N)	Two	Nominal	Y or N

(continued)

Table 2. (*continued*)

Name	Description	Distinct	Data type	Data values
Oldpeak	ST segment to measure the depression	NA	Numeric	Range from −2.6 to 6.2
ST_Slope	Slope of the peak exercise ST segment that classified into upsloping (Up), flat (Flat) and down sloping (Down)	Tree	Nominal	Up, Flat and Down

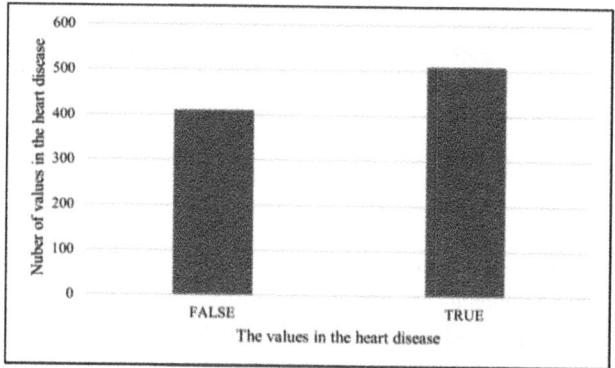

Fig. 3. The number of values in the heart disease.

- **Greedy stepwise** can be started with an empty set of features and identifies the best features for a given dataset by searching forward or backwards. Moreover, this method can be started with a full set of features by doing the same search (i.e. forward or backwards). The search terminates when the addition or deletion of any remaining features effect negatively on the overall performance [17]. The main difference between greedy stepwise and best first is that greedy stepwise can be searched either forward or backward, whereas the best first can be searched in both directions.
- **Chi-squared** aims to select attribute that is highly effect on the dependent variable. It is calculated by testing the independence of two attributes, which are each dependent variable and independent variable. Chi-squared is used only for categorical attributes to determine whether the association between these attributes of the sample would impact their real association in the population [18].
- **Information gain** compares and evaluates the gain of each attribute with the dependent variable. It is calculated how much the amount of information produced by the attributes by measuring the reduction in the surprise. This is performed by dividing dataset according to a specific value of a random variable [19].

4.5 Machine Learning Algorithms

To classify predict if a person has heart disease or not, we create four single well-known algorithms, namely Bayes Net, Neural Network, J48, JRIP, along with one hybrid algorithm (i.e., Vote) that integrate these single algorithms. This section briefly discusses the machine learning algorithms that perform.

- **Bayes Network** performs several quality measures and search algorithms. It provides a collection of random variables and their conditional dependence structure by using a directed acyclic graph. Bayes Network includes information about probability relationships between variables and base class that represents various data structures, including conditional probability, network structure, distributions. Bayesian network is a probabilistic graphical algorithm that based on the Bayes theorem as the following equation [20]:

$$(A|B) = \frac{P(B|A)P(A)}{P(B)} \tag{1}$$

- **Neural Network** has various elements, namely *Input Layers*, which the input variables that provide into the network. *Hidden Layers,* which are the parameters layers that train and *Output Layer*, which are the output of the model. The structure of neural network contains activation function that determine which neurons will be activated and which variables passed to the next layers. Also, the structure of neural network includes cost function that to compute loss of the true and predict results, where neural network aims to reduce this loss [21].
- **Decision tree** provides several decision trees and sets of rules. This performs by dividing the training data into many subsets and each subset has one class. One of the main advantages of the decision is pruned that improve the prediction accuracy and optimize the size of the trees. Pruned replaces a near-leaf node with its child leaves or by adding a smaller sub-tree. Furthermore, the pruned is very beneficial techniques to deal with overfitting dataset or complex rules by decreasing the number of nodes in the tree as well as decreasing the prediction error [22].
- **JRIP** was proposed by William W. Cohen as a new version of IREP, which is abbreviation for Incremental Reduced Error Pruning. is considered rule machine learning algorithm that builds a propositional rule learner. It creates repeated incremental pruning to generate error reduction. JRIP perform better than C4.5 in term of the prediction accuracy due to the running more effectively. Also, another advantage is allowing to increase scalability with large datasets [23].
- **Vote** integrates multiple different single algorithms to produce single result and take advantage from this combination. The combination rule used in Vote is majority voting, which only works with classification problem. Each single algorithm predicts one class in the dependent variable in the test sample. The class which was predicted by the most of algorithms will then be chosen as the result of the vote algorithm [24].

4.6 Performance Measures

In this study, a variety of different performance measures are applied to evaluate and compare the machine learning algorithms in heart disease prediction. We used popular and well-known measures that are suitable for classification problem and calculated from the confusion matrix as shown in Table 3.

Table 3. Confusion matrix

	Predicted Class	
actual class	heart disease (yes)	heart disease (No)
heart disease (Yes)	True Positive (TP)	False Negative (FN)
heart disease (NO)	False Positive(FP)	True Negative (TN)

The following are the performance measures used in this study and computed from the confusion matrix proposed in Table 3:

Precision is the proportion of positive observations that are accurately corrected as shown in Eq. 2:

$$Precision = TP/(TP + FP). \tag{2}$$

Recall is the proportion of the positive observations that are accurately corrected to all the observations in the real class-yes as shown in Eq. 3:

$$Recall = TP/(TP + FN). \tag{3}$$

F-Measure is calculated by using Precision and Recall. Therefore, this measure uses both false positives and false negatives as shown in Eq. 4:

$$F - Measure = 2 * (Precision * Recall)/(Precision + Recall). \tag{4}$$

AUC is a probability curve that plots the TP rate, which is a synonym for recall as shown in Eq. 5:

$$TP\ rate = TP/(TP + FN). \tag{5}$$

against FP rate at different threshold values as shown in Eq. 6:

$$FP\ rate = FP/(FP + TN). \tag{6}$$

It is computed by dividing the area between the two points, and then these areas are integrated to gain the total area.

Accuracy is the percentage of correct classified observations divided by the total number of the observations in the confusion matrix as shown in Eq. 7:

$$Accuracy = (TN + TP)/(TN + FN + FN + FP). \tag{7}$$

The higher of these performance measures (i.e., Precision, Recall, F-Measure, AUC and Accuracy) indicate the better the performance of the machine learning algorithms.

5   Results and Discussion

RQ 1 Which attributes turn out to be the most important attributes in detecting heart disease?

Four types of features selection techniques were performed, which are Best first and Greedy Stepwise (forwards) techniques that belong to subset method, along with Chisquared and Information Gain techniques that belong to ranking method. After that, intersection was applied to determine attributes that selected by all four techniques.

Table 4 illustrates the results of feature selection using subset method that include two techniques: Best first and Greedy Stepwise (forwards). The overall results of two techniques demonstrate that eight attributes were selected and only three attributes were removed from the selection, namely RestingBP, FastingBS and RestingECG.

Table 4. Results of feature selection using subset method.

Attribute	Best first	Greedy Stepwise (forwards)
Age	✓	✓
Sex	✓	✓
ChestPainType	✓	✓
RestingBP	✗	✗
Cholesterol	✓	✓
FastingBS	✗	✗
RestingECG	✗	✗
MaxHR	✓	✓
ExerciseAngina	✓	✓
Oldpeak	✓	✓
ST_Slope	✓	✓

Table 5 shows the results of feature selection using ranking method that include two techniques: Chi-squared and Information Gain. It is apparent from this table that all the attributes were selected except three attributes FastingBS, RestingBP and RestingECG. Data from this table can be compared with the data in Table 3 which shows that the results of feature selection using either subset method or ranking method are the same. To answer **RQ1,** eight attributes turn out to be the most important attributes in detecting heart disease, which are ST_Slope, ChestPainType, ExerciseAngina, Oldpeak, MaxHR, Cholesterol, Age and Sex, whereas three attributes turn out to be the least important attributes in detecting heart disease (i.e., FastingBS, RestingBP and RestingECG). Therefore, these three were removed from of heart disease dataset.

RQ2) Does the performance of feature selection increase the accuracy of the prediction algorithms of heart disease?

Figure 4 presents the results of algorithms with applying feature selection methods (after removing three attributes), along without applying feature selection methods

Table 5. Results of feature selection using ranking method.

Rank Number	Attribute	Chi-squared	Information Gain	Selected Attribute
1	ST_Slope	355.9184	0.29932	✓
2	ChestPainType	268.0672	0.22504	✓
3	ExerciseAngina	224.2809	0.18997	✓
4	Oldpeak	190.1125	0.16143	✓
5	MaxHR	155.8043	0.12748	✓
6	Cholesterol	94.2807	0.08337	✓
7	Age	87.0136	0.0696	✓
8	Sex	85.6463	0.06849	✓
9	FastingBS	65.5861	0.05488	✗
10	RestingBP	19.3133	0.01552	✗

(including whole eleven attributes). The results indicate that applying feature selection methods on the algorithms produced either worsen performance or the similar performance. To answer **RQ2**, applying feature selection does not increase the accuracy of the prediction algorithms of heart disease.

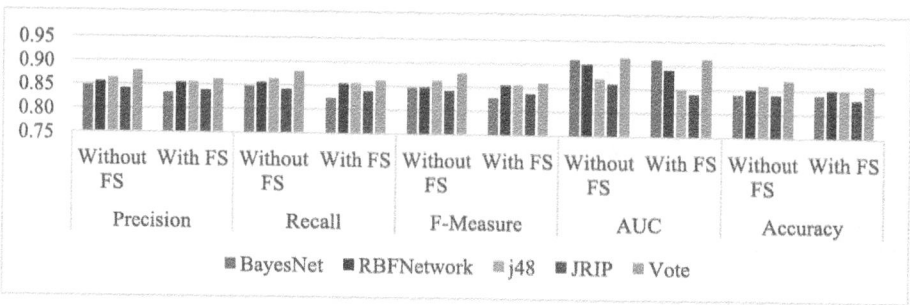

Fig. 4. Results of algorithms with and without feature selection methods.

RQ3) Does the performance of hybrid algorithm (Vote) increase the accuracy of the single algorithms of heart disease?

Figure 5 and Fig. 6 provide the results of hybrid algorithm (Vote) that integrates four single algorithms (i.e., BayesNet, Neural Network, decision tree, JRIP) with applying feature selection and without applying feature selection; respectively. In both figures, the performances of single algorithms (i.e., BayesNet, Neural Network, decision tree, JRIP) were compared against hybrid algorithm (Vote). In order to response RQ3, taken together, these results show that hybrid algorithm (Vote) increase the accuracy of the single algorithms of heart disease across all evaluation measures (i.e., precision, recall, F-measure, AUC and accuracy). Therefore, this study recommends using hybrid algorithm (Vote) to predict heart disease.

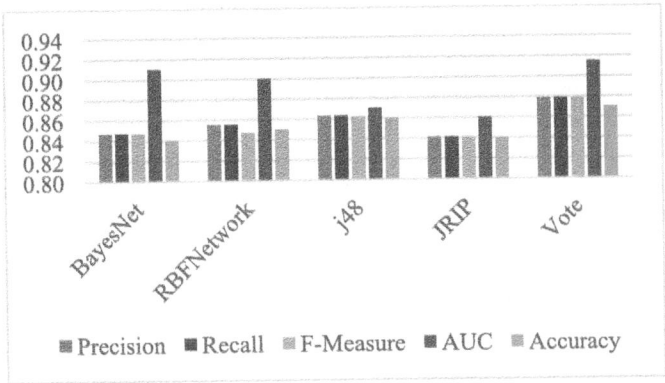

Fig. 5. Results of hybrid algorithm (Vote) with feature selection.

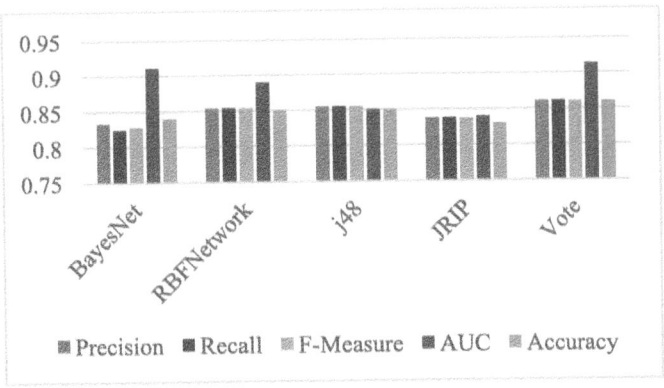

Fig. 6. Results of hybrid algorithm (Vote) without feature selection.

RQ4) Does the performance of hybrid model (Vote) better than the algorithm used by selected previous studies in predicting heart disease?

Five evaluation measures, namely accuracy, AUC, precision, recall and F1-measure were used to evaluate different machine learning algorithms in the current study. We extract these evaluation measures from each selected previous study to compare the performance of hybrid algorithm (Vote) used in the current study with the best algorithm in the selected previous studies. However, some studies did not provide the results of all these measures, such as S1 and S5.

In term of accuracy, the current study reached to 87%, which is considered better than all studies except two studies (S2 and S8) that reported a little bit higher or the same result; respectively. However, there are much higher difference between the accuracy in the current study and S1 that reported 91.57%, which is (4.57%) higher than current study. However, the current study achieved better performance than S1 in term of AUC. Also, the fact that worth mention is that S1 used deep learning algorithm that is much more time-consuming than simple algorithm and it is not recommended for small datasets.

Regarding AUC, the current study and S8 had the best AUC value (92%), where AUC is considered more reliable and informative measure for the prediction problem. In term of the remaining measures, the current study performed better performance than other studies. Furthermore, the current study achieved superior results compared to recent studies S9 published in 2024, across all evaluation measures. To answer **RQ4**, the performance of the current study is better than the previous selected studies in most evaluation measures (See .Table 6).

Table 6. Results of algorithm in the selected previous studies and current study.

Study ID	Ref	Algorithm	Best Algorithm	Accuracy	AUC	Precision	Recall / Sensitivity	F1Measure
S1	[4]	hybrid model X^2-DNN, ANN and DNN	X^2-DNN	**91.57%**	88%	--	87.80%	-
S2	[5]	NN, DT, KNN, CN, SVM and SGD	SGD with 5-fold cross validation	87.69%	-	87.67%	87.69%	86.78%
S3	[6]	DT, KN, SVM, RF	KN	87%	88.5%	83%	73%	77%
S4	[3]	LDA, RF, GBC, DT, SVM, and KN	RF	86.67%	73%	82%	82%	81%
S5	[7]	RF	RF	84.44%	-	-	-	-
S6	[8]	SVM, NB, LR, RF, and adaboost	RF	86.6%	-	85.71%	84.14%	81.50%
S7	[9]	MLP, Ada-Boost, NB and SVM	MLP	84.90%	62%	78%	79%	66%

(continued)

Table 6. (*continued*)

Study ID	Ref	Algorithm	Best Algorithm	Accuracy	AUC	Precision	Recall / Sensitivity	F1 Measure
S8	[10]	Gradient Boosting, XGBoost, AdaBoost, CatBoost, ANN, RF, SVM, DT and LR	Hybrid (SVM + AdaBoost)	86.88%	**92%**	85.18%	85.18%	85.18%
S9	[12]	deep neural network, a recurrent neural network model hybrid model	Hybrid model	82.8%	80%	87.08%	88.57%	87.82%
Current study		BayesNet, Neural Network, decision tree, JRIP and hybrid model (Vote)	Hybrid model (Vote)	87%	**92%**	**88%**	**88%**	**88%**

6 Conclusion

This paper has empirically investigated the application of four single algorithms, along with namely Bayes Network, Neural Network, Decision Tree, JRIP, along with one hybrid algorithm (Vote) in predicting heart disease. These algorithms have performed on the heart failure prediction dataset that include 11 features and 918 records. Furthermore, the application of features selection methods has explored including subset and ranking methods and each types includes two techniques, best first, greedy stepwise, Chi-squared and information gain; respectively.

This study presents interesting finding and empirical evidence for both Machine learning and healthcare researchers. The result of our empirical study shows that the prediction performance of Vote algorithm is better than other single algorithms. Furthermore, it was observed that the performance of Vote algorithm outperforms the previous selected studies in most evaluation measures. Regarding the application of feature selection, eight attributes have selected by all methods, which means only three attributes have removed from the selection, namely RestingBP, FastingBS and RestingECG. The deleting of these attribute does not really affect on the performance of the prediction algorithms.

Several important limitations need to be considered. First, the dataset comprising "11 features and 918 records", may not fully represent predicting heart disease, suggesting that larger datasets could strengthen the algorithms. Second, the algorithms were used without parameter tuning. Applying structured hyperparameter optimization in future studies could improve algorithm performance.

Acknowledgment. The authors gratefully acknowledge the financial support provided by the Graduate Studies and Scientific Research Vice-Rectorate at Princess Nourah bint Abdulrahman University, through the Management of Conferences and Seminars. Thanks are also extended to the Artificial Intelligence in Healthcare Researcher Chair at Princess Nourah bint Abdulrahman University.

References

1. Kumar, R., Rani, P.: Comparative analysis of decision support system for heart disease. Adv. Math. Sci. J. **9**(6), 3349–3356 (2020)
2. Latha, C.B.C., Jeeva, S.C.: Improving the accuracy of prediction of heart disease risk based on ensemble classification techniques. Inform. Med. Unlocked **16**, 100203 (2019). https://doi.org/10.1016/j.imu.2019.100203
3. Aggrawal, R., Pal, S.: Sequential feature selection and machine learning algorithm based patient's death events prediction and diagnosis in heart disease. SN Comput. Sci. **1**(6), 1–16 (2020)
4. Ali, L., Rahman, A., Khan, A., Zhou, M., Javeed, A., Khan, J.A.: An automated diagnostic system for heart disease prediction based on X^2 statistical model and optimally configured deep neural network. IEEE Access **7**, 34938–34945 (2019). https://doi.org/10.1109/ACCESS.2019.2904800
5. Pires, I.M., Marques, G., Garcia, N.M., Ponciano, V.: Machine learning for the evaluation of the presence of heart disease. Procedia Comput. Sci. **177**, 432437 (2020)
6. Keshav Srivastava, D.K.C.: Heart disease prediction using machine learning and data mining. Int. J. Recent Technol. Eng. (IJRTE) **9**(1), 212–219 (2020)
7. Buettner, R., Schunter, M.: Efficient machine learning based detection of heart disease. In: 2019 IEEE International Conference on E-health Networking, Application & Services (HealthCom), 14–16 Oct. 2019, pp. 1–6 (2019). https://doi.org/10.1109/HealthCom46333.2019.9009429
8. Rani, P., Kumar, R., Ahmed, N.M., Jain, A.: A decision support system for heart disease prediction based upon machine learning. J. Reliab. Intell. Environ. **7**(3), 263–275 (2021)
9. Kuruvilla, A.M., Balaji, N.: Heart disease prediction system using correlation based feature selection with multilayer perceptron approach. IOP Conf. Ser. Mater. Sci. Eng. **1085**(1), 012028 (2021)
10. Pan, C., Poddar, A., Mukherjee, R., Ray, A.K.: Impact of categorical and numerical features in ensemble machine learning frameworks for heart disease prediction. Biomed. Signal Process. Control **76**, 103666 (2022)

11. Basili, V.R., Rombach, H.D.: The TAME project: Towards improvement oriented software environments. IEEE Trans. Software Eng. **14**(6), 758–773 (1988)
12. Li, F., Chen, Y., Xu, H.: Coronary heart disease prediction based on hybrid deep learning. Rev. Sci. Instrum. **95**(1) (2024). https://doi.org/10.1063/5.0172368
13. Jović, A., Brkić, K., Bogunović, N.: A review of feature selection methods with applications. In: 2015 38th International Convention on Information and Communication Technology, Electronics and Microelectronics (MIPRO), pp. 1200–1205. IEEE (2015)
14. Shahana, A.H., Preeja, V.: Survey on feature subset selection for high dimensional data. In: 2016 International Conference on Circuit, Power and Computing Technologies (ICCPCT), 18–19 March 2016, pp. 1–4 (2016). https://doi.org/10.1109/ICCPCT.2016.7530147
15. Cilia, N.D., De Stefano, C., Fontanella, F., Scotto di Freca, A.: A ranking-based feature selection approach for handwritten character recognition. In: Pattern Recognition Letters, vol. 121, pp. 77–86 (2019). https://doi.org/10.1016/j.patrec.2018.04.007
16. Lei, X., Pingfan, Y., Tong, C.: Best first strategy for feature selection. In: [1988 Proceedings] 9th International Conference on Pattern Recognition, 14 May–17 Nov. 1988, vol. 2, pp. 706–708 (1988). https://doi.org/10.1109/ICPR.1988.28334
17. Caruana, R., Freitag, D.: Greedy attribute selection. In: Machine Learning Proceedings 1994, pp. 28–36. Elsevier (1994)
18. Haryanto, A.W., Mawardi, E.K., Muljono: Influence of word normalization and chi-squared feature selection on support vector machine (SVM) text classification. In: 2018 International Seminar on Application for Technology of Information and Communication, 21-22 Sept. 2018, pp. 229–233 (2018). https://doi.org/10.1109/ISEMANTIC.2018.8549748
19. Gao, K., Khoshgoftaar, T.M., Wald, R.: Combining feature selection and ensemble learning for software quality estimation. In: International Florida Artificial Intelligence Research Society Conference, pp. 47–52 (2014)
20. Yang, X.-S.: Introduction to Algorithms for Data Mining and Machine Learning. Academic press (2019)
21. Hopfield, J.J.: Neural networks and physical systems with emergent collective computational abilities. Proc. Natl. Acad. Sci. **79**(8), 2554–2558 (1982)
22. Drazin, S., Montag, M.: Decision tree analysis using WEKA. In: Machine Learning Project II, University of Miami, vol. 1, no. 3 (2012)
23. Cohen, W.W.: Fast effective rule induction. In: Machine Learning Proceedings 1995, pp. 115–123. Elsevier (1995)
24. Kuncheva, L.I.: Combining Pattern Classifiers: Methods and Algorithms. Wiley (2014)

Designing and Evaluating Heterogeneous Ensembles for Blood Glucose Level Forecasting

Mamoune Benaida⬤, Ibtissam Abnane⬤, and Ali Idri$^{(\boxtimes)}$⬤

Software Project Management Research Team, ENSIAS, Mohammed V University,
Rabat, Morocco
{mamoune_benaida, ali.idri}@um5.ac.ma, ibtissam.abnane19@gmail.com

Abstract. Accurate forecasting of blood glucose levels (BGL) in individuals with type 1 diabetes mellitus (T1DM) is crucial for effective disease management. This study focuses on advancing BGL prediction by performing a comparative evaluation of single machine learning models and heterogeneous ensembles. The main objective of this study is to determine the optimal model configuration for accurate and reliable blood glucose predictions by examining various optimization strategies. For this purpose, several machine learning techniques were used, including Long Short-Term Memory (LSTM), Convolutional Neural Networks (CNN), Gated Recurrent Units (GRU), Support Vector Regression (SVR) and Deep Belief Networks (DBN). All these models were incorporated into various ensembles and fine tuned using Particle Swarm Optimization (PSO), Random Search (RS) and Bayesian Optimization (BO). We evaluated these models using metrics such as Root Mean Square Error (RMSE), Mean Absolute Error (MAE), Mean Magnitude Relative Error (MMRE) and Predictive Level at 25% (PRED). Our findings demonstrated that PSO fine-tuned models, particularly those using GRU, performed exceptionally well. Most significantly, the PGRU model achieved a RMSE of 7.87 mg/dl. Ensembles optimized using RS and PSO, in particularly ERME and EPAV, outperformed all others, with RMSE values of 12.25 mg/dl and 12.26 mg/dl, respectively. Statistical validation through the Scott-Knott test (SK) and Borda Count (BC) analysis corroborated that PSO significantly enhanced accuracy in both individual and ensemble models. In conclusion, this study underscores the high efficacy of PSO in optimizing BGL forecasting models. Additionally, heterogeneous ensembles offer more consistent and reliable predictions than single models, thereby providing a promising solution for real-time diabetes management.

Keywords: Diabetes Mellitus · Blood Glucose Level · Time Series Forecasting · Ensemble Learning · Heterogeneous Ensembles · Optimization Techniques

© The Author(s), under exclusive license to Springer Nature Switzerland AG 2025
O. Gervasi et al. (Eds.): ICCSA 2025, LNCS 15649, pp. 116–133, 2025.
https://doi.org/10.1007/978-3-031-96997-3_8

1   Introduction

T1DM is a lifelong autoimmune condition that results in the destruction of insulin-producing beta cells in the pancreas, causing complete deficiency of insulin [1]. This disease predominantly affects children and young adults, with an increasing global incidence. According to the International Diabetes (IDF) Federation, the incidence of T1DM increases by approximately 3% annually, particularly among children and adolescents [2]. This upward trend emphasizes the importance of developing effective management strategies to reduce the associated health risks and improve the quality of life of individuals with T1DM.

Complications associated with T1DM can manifest acutely and chronically. Acute complications, such as diabetic ketoacidosis, present a significant life-threatening risk due to severe insulin deficiency [3]. The development of chronic complications has been associated with long-term uncontrolled BGL levels, among them cardiovascular disease, neuropathy, retinopathy, and nephropathy [3]. These complications can lead to significant impairment in patients' quality of life and impose substantial financial burdens on healthcare systems [4]. Effective management of T1DM necessitates continuous glucose monitoring to prevent such complications [5].

By providing real-time blood glucose data, Continuous glucose monitoring (CGM) systems have played a significant role in the management of type 1 diabetes, enabling patients to accurately adjust their insulin therapy and lifestyle. The integration of artificial intelligence and predictive algorithms into these systems enables the prediction of blood glucose trends, aiding patients in avoiding the potentially harmful conditions of both hyperglycemia and hypoglycemia. These predictive capabilities are essential components in the development of artificial pancreas systems. These systems automate insulin delivery, enhance glycemic control, and reduce the risk of long-term complications.

In order to advance the management of T1DM, it is necessary to address the issue of time-series forecasting. This process involves predicting future BGLs based on historical data. The development of accurate predictive models for blood glucose values holds significant potential to empower both patients and healthcare professionals by furnishing them with actionable information regarding insulin dosages, dietary intake, and physical activity [5]. A comprehensive approach to the management of T1DM is imperative to decrease the risk of serious glycemic complications. Traditional statistical models, including the Autoregressive Integrated Moving Average (ARIMA) model, have been used to predict BGL. However, these models are limited by the complexity of the non-linear, dynamic nature of glucose metabolism. Indeed, linear models, which form the basis of ARIMA models, are unsuited to the complexity of high-frequency data generated by CGM systems.

In recent years, machine learning (ML) and deep learning (DL) techniques have offered more robust solutions for BGL forecasting [6,7]. Models such as SVR, DBN, CNN, LSTM, and GRU have demonstrated significant potential for effectively capturing both short- and long-term dependencies in glucose data [8]. Each model demonstrates distinct strengths: SVR is effective in high-dimensional spaces [9], DBNs excel at learning hierarchical data representations [10], CNNs are proficient at modeling local patterns in time-series data [11], and LSTMs and GRUs are well-suited for sequential data, addressing the vanishing gradient problem that affects traditional RNNs [7,10]. These advances have significantly improved the accuracy of BGL forecasting.

Although single models have been successful in predicting BGLs, ensemble methods, which combine multiple models, have proven to be a powerful strategy for improving accuracy. Heterogeneous ensembles are particularly promising because they leverage the strengths of various models [12]. For example, a GRU may excel in capturing long-term trends, whereas a CNN is better at identifying short-term fluctuations. Despite their potential, the use of heterogeneous ensembles in BGL forecasting remains underexplored, and further research is required to determine the optimal combination of models for enhanced performance.

To enhance the performance of both the single models and ensembles, optimization techniques such as RS, BO, and PSO are employed to fine-tune the hyperparameters. RS explores the hyperparameter space by randomly sampling configurations, whereas BO uses a probabilistic model to make more informed choices about which hyperparameters are likely to yield the best results. Inspired by the social behaviors of birds and fish, PSO iteratively refines candidate solutions to find optimal configurations. Integrating these techniques into heterogeneous ensembles for BGL forecasting introduces a novel and powerful approach for improving prediction accuracy.

Numerous studies have already explored the use of traditional models, such as ARIMA and advanced ML/DL models, such as SVR, DBN, CNN, LSTM, and GRU for BGL prediction. These models were also explored in previous studies [6,10]. However, a gap remains in evaluating heterogeneous ensemble models systematically, particularly when optimized with techniques such as PSO, RS, and BO in the context of One-Step Ahead Forecasting (OSF). This study aimed to bridge this gap by developing and assessing a comprehensive framework for building and optimizing heterogeneous ensembles for BGL forecasting.

This study addresses the following research questions:

- RQ1) Is there any single predictive model that outperforms others for BGL forecasting?
- RQ2) Which heterogeneous ensemble provides the most accurate and reliable BGL predictions?
- RQ3) How do heterogeneous ensembles compare to their constituent singles in BGL forecasting?
- RQ4) How do different optimization techniques improve the performance of single and ensemble models for BGL forecasting?

The rest of the paper is structured as follows: Sect. 2 presents the ML/DL and optimization techniques used, Sect. 3 provides a review of related work; Sect. 4 outlines the methodology for developing and evaluating models and ensembles; Sect. 5 presents the results and answers to the research questions. Threats to validity are discussed in Sect. 6, and Sect. 7 concludes the paper with key findings and future research directions.

2   Background

This section provides a comprehensive background on the ML/DL single techniques and the optimization techniques used.

2.1   Single Models

In the context of BGL forecasting, several ML/DL models have been employed to improve the prediction accuracy. Each of these models has unique strengths, leveraging different aspects of the data to enhance forecasting performance. This section provides an overview of the single models utilized in the study: SVR, DBN, CNN, LSTM, and GRU.

Support Vector Regression. SVR is a concept introduced by Vapnik in 1992 [13], is an extension of support vector machines. It was developed for regression tasks that utilize an insensitivity loss function, designated as ϵ-insensitivity, with the objective of mapping input data into a higher-dimensional feature space. The aim of this approach is to identify a function that, although remaining within a specified range of ϵ values relative to the target values, maintains the simplicity of the initial model. This approach is designed to enhance the generalizability of the results obtained.

Deep Belief Networks. Introduced by Geoffrey Hinton in 2006 [14], DBNs are sophisticated neural networks consisting of multiple layers of probabilistic models with hidden stochastic variables. These networks use a generative model, typically a Restricted Boltzmann Machine (RBM), to pre-train each layer individually. In this method, the output of one layer serves as the input to the next, making it easier for DBNs to learn generative representations of data. After pre-training, the network was fine-tuned using supervised techniques such as back-propagation to improve its discrimination capabilities.

Convolutional Neural Networks. The conceptualisation of CNNs can be traced back to the 1980 s [15], with Yann LeCun. The inspiration for CNNs derived from the study of the animal visual cortex. These networks have acquired major importance in the field of image recognition and sequential data analysis. The application of CNNs is based on the use of convolutional filters to identify the proprities of input data. Such networks are typically characterized by their standard architectures, which include convolutional layers, pooling layers, and fully connected layers. When applied to time series data, one-dimensional CNNs effectively capture temporal dependencies, making them particularly useful for predicting BGL by using sequential data to improve prediction accuracy [7].

Long Short-Term Memory. LSTMs as introduced by Hochreiter and Schmidhuber [16], solve the problem of gradient vanishing in traditional recurrent neural networks (RNNs). These networks are designed with the intention to capture long-term dependencies in sequential data, making them particularly well suited to video, speech, and time-series tasks. Their architecture integrates memory cells with a cell state and three key gates: input, forget, and output. The function of these gates is to regulate the flow of information, thereby enabling selective retention and updating [7,16].

Gated Recurrent Units. GRUs, as proposed in 2014, by Kyunghyun Cho et al. [17], represent a variant of recurrent neural networks (RNNs) that aims to reduce their computational complexity by combining the input and forget gates of the LSTM model into a unified update gate. This approach has been shown to reduce computational complexity and accelerate the network training process. The efficacy of GRUs in handling long-term dependencies, particularly in scenarios involving shorter sequences, has been demonstrated. Moreover, GRUs have exhibited noteworthy efficacy in domains such as image and speech recognition, attaining results that are comparable to those of LSTMs despite their more streamlined design.

2.2 Optimization Techniques

Optimization techniques play a significant role in adjustment of model parameters, thereby ensuring optimal performance. Indeed, the accuracy and predictive capability of a model are closely related to its parameter tuning, which varies according to the considered data sets. Consequently, optimization methods are indispensable for identifying the optimal values that will maximize the efficiency of a model. This study will focus on three such approaches: RS, BO, and PSO methods.

Random Search. RS is a robust optimization methodology for tuning the hyperparameters of ML and DL models. As distinct from grid search, RS employs a random sampling method, whereby values are selected from predefined ranges. This process is repeated iteratively, with performance evaluated at each iteration until a predetermined criterion is fulfilled [18]. This approach has the advantage to explore extensive hyperparameter spaces without requiring an exhaustive search, making it well-suited for high-dimensional spaces where optimal values are often not known.

Bayesian Optimization. BO has become a widely used technique in ML/DL research for hyperparameter optimization due to its ability to identify the optimal parameters. This technique employs a probabilistic model, most often a Gaussian process (GP), in order to estimate the performance of different parameter combinations. In addition, to select the next set of hyperparameters to be assessed, BO uses a learning function, generally the Expected Improvement (EI) or Upper Confidence Bound (UCB) [19]. This approach reduces the number of evaluations required, making BO particularly useful for optimizing complex DL models.

Particle Swarm Optimization. Developed by Kennedy and Eberhart in 1995 [20], is a meta-heuristic inspired by bird flocking and fish schooling. It optimizes problems by iteratively adjusting each particle's position based on its own experience and that of its neighbors, aiming to improve solutions relative to a fitness function. PSO is particularly effective for high-dimensional, complex problems, as it often finds optimal solutions in a single run. Key parameters include the number of iterations, swarm size, velocity limits (v_{min}, v_{max}), learning factors (c_1, c_2), and inertial weight (w).

3   Related Work

Recent advances in BGL forecasting increasingly involve the use of ML and DL techniques, in contrast to traditional statistical models such as AR methods. These techniques excel because of their ability to automatically extract and learn data representations, making them well-suited for time-series predictions in T1DM patients.

Early studies introduced neural networks for BGL predictions. Zecchin et al. [21] implemented an artificial neural network with polynomial extrapolation for 30-minute BGL forecasting, laying the foundation for ML applications in healthcare. Mirshekarian et al. [22] later showed that LSTM models outperformed SVR for 30- and 60-minute BGL predictions, demonstrating DL's advantage in managing temporal dependencies. Li et al. [23] further improved the accuracy by combining CNN and RNN in a hybrid model, effectively handling CGM data by leveraging both spatial and temporal feature extractions.

In addition to LSTM and CNN architectures, ensemble learning has emerged as a promising approach for improving BGL prediction accuracy. Alfian et al. [24] demonstrated that XGBoost outperformed models such as SVR and decision trees, yielding lower RMSE values for 30- and 60-minute forecasts. Liu et al. [25] further validated ensemble methods, using a tree-based ensemble with majority voting-based feature selection, which enhanced the accuracy by identifying key glucose indicators. Optimizations such as BO, as applied by Wang et al. [26] to a LightGBM model, showed significant performance gains. RNNs also remain central in glucose forecasting, with El Idrissi et al. [11] and Sun et al. [27] confirming superiority of LSTM over AR models and baseline methods for sequential data prediction in healthcare.

Literature shows that deep learning techniques, particularly LSTM and CNN models, outperform traditional methods in BGL prediction. Integrating ensemble learning and optimization techniques, such as BO further boosts predictive accuracy, indicating a promising future for these models in real-time diabetes management systems.

4   Framework Design

This section outlines our empirical framework for BGL forecasting in T1DM, covering data preparation, performance measures, framework architecture, single-model configurations, and ensemble construction. We also describe the significance tests used to evaluate the model performance. Experimental evaluations were conducted on Google Colaboratory to leverage GPU capabilities, using Keras 2.3.1 [28] with TensorFlow API 2.2.0 [29].

4.1   Data Description

The Diabetes Research in Children Network (DirecNet) dataset [30] includes historical BGL data from 110 T1DM patients aged 3–17, collected from 2000 to 2002. With BGL values recorded every 5 min via CGM sensors, the dataset spans 73,085 records, ranging from 40 to 400 mg/dl with an average of 177.90 mg/dl. To ensure data quality, only patients with at least 200 records were included, resulting in 108 patients with an average of 620 BGL records per patient.

4.2   Performance Measures

To assess BGL predictions, we used MAE and RMSE metrics, which provide insights into model accuracy by measuring the closeness between predicted values $\hat{x}_i$ and actual values x_i [31]. These metrics quantitatively evaluate prediction accuracy, with the formulas for MAE and RMSE given as follows:

– **Mean Absolute Error:**

$$MAE = \frac{1}{n}\sum_{i=1}^{n}|\hat{x}_i - x_i| \tag{1}$$

– **Root Mean Square Error:**

$$RMSE = \sqrt{\frac{1}{n}\sum_{i=1}^{n}(\hat{x}_i - x_i)^2} \tag{2}$$

To improve our BGL prediction accuracy, we employed the MMRE and PRED metrics, which provided insights into the comparison between predicted and actual values [10].

– **Magnitude Relative Error:**

$$MRE = \left|\frac{x - \hat{x}}{x}\right| \times 100 \tag{3}$$

– **Mean Magnitude Relative Error:**

$$MMRE = \frac{\sum_{i=1}^{n}\left|\frac{x_i - \hat{x}_i}{x_i}\right| \times 100}{n} \tag{4}$$

- **Prediction Level:** The PRED metric is determined by the proportion of predictions that fall within a specified threshold p, which is conventionally set to 25%. The formula for PRED is given in Equation (5).

$$Pred(p) = \frac{K}{n} \times 100 \tag{5}$$

In this context, x and $\hat{x}$ denote the actual and predicted values, respectively, and n represents the total number of predictions. In addition, K signifies the number of predictions with an MMRE that falls within the specified error threshold p.

4.3   Significance Tests

To validate the results and facilitate model comparison, we employed statistical tests, beginning with the SK test. This non-parametric method ranks models based on performance by utilizing hierarchical clustering within an ANOVA to identify significant differences [32]. Furthermore, we implemented the BC method to aggregate the SK rankings. The BC method allocates points according to rank, thereby ensuring fairness and minimizing bias [33]. In our study, the BC method was applied across four metrics (RMSE, MAE, MMRE, and PRED), with the technique achieving the highest score considered the most favorable.

4.4   Abbreviations Used

To shorten the names of singles and ensembles, the following abbreviation rule was adopted:

- **For single models,** the format used is:
  Optimization technique-Single model name
  where optimization techniques are abbreviated as follows: R for RS, P for PSO, and B for BO.
  For example, PGRU refers to a GRU model optimized using PSO.
- **For heterogeneous ensembles,** the format is:
  E-Optimization technique-Combination rule
  where combination rules are abbreviated as follows: AV for Mean, ME for Median, IR for Inverse Ranked Weighted Mean.
  For example, EPAV refers to a heterogeneous ensemble composed of five ML/DL single models optimized using PSO, with the mean used as the combination rule.

4.5   Framework Architecture

The framework architecture used in this study is outlined in seven distinct steps, as illustrated in Fig. 1. These steps comprise the entire process from data preparation to model optimization, training, and evaluation. A comprehensive description of each step of the framework is provided below.

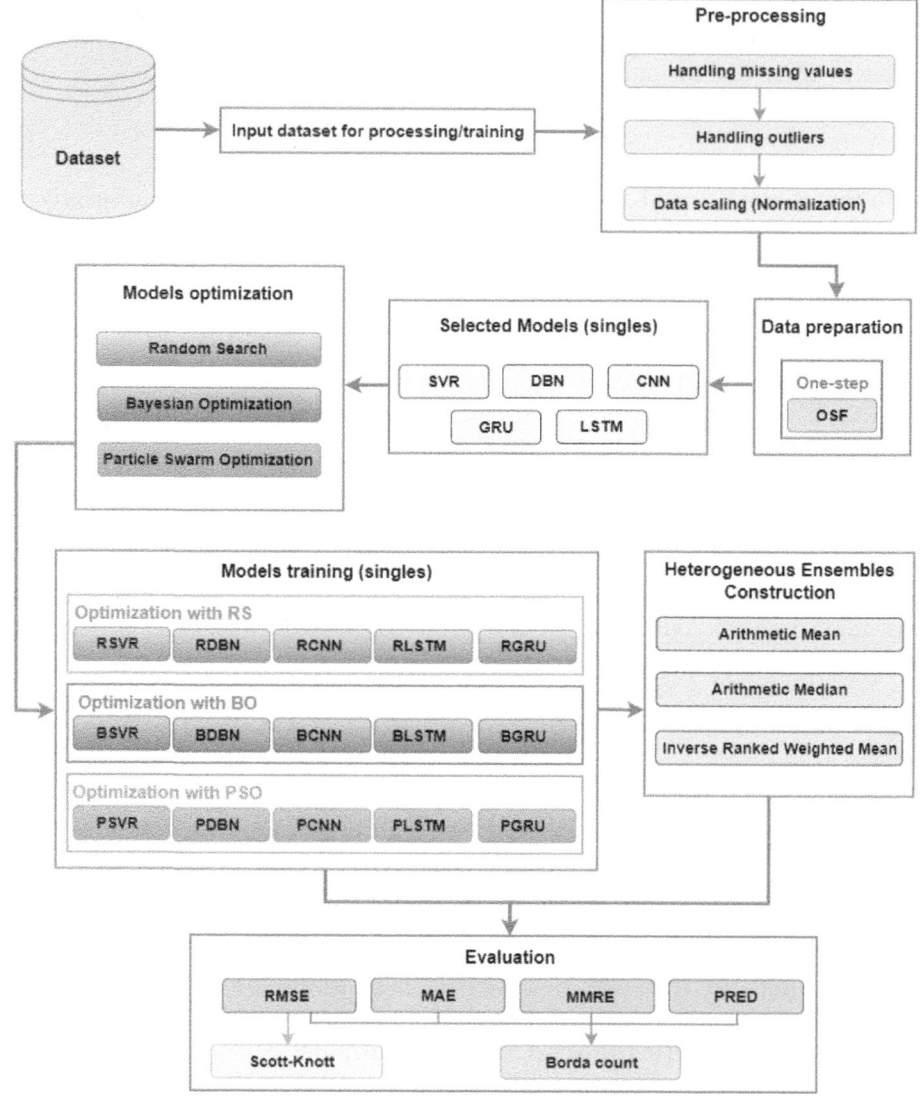

Fig. 1. Overview of the framework architecture.

Step 1) Pre-processing: The initial phase involved importing the dataset for further processing and training. Pre-processing is a crucial part of this step, where missing values are handled, outliers are addressed, and data scaling is performed. This ensures that the data are clean and standardized, which is essential for accurate modeling.

Step 2) Data Preparation for Models: In this step, the prepared data are organized for modeling using OSF forecasting strategies.

Step 3) Model Selection and Optimization: Models were optimized using BO, RS, and PSO to explore the key parameter ranges. For GRU and LSTM, the hidden layer units were tuned, with GRU exploring a wider range (64–128 for the first layer, 32–64 for the second) than LSTM (32–64 for the first, 16–32 for the second). CNN optimization included filter counts in convolution layers and hidden units (32–128), while SVR focused on continuous hyperparameters like regularization C (0.1–2) and kernel parameter γ (0.1–1). DBNs optimized hidden layer units (32-256), learning rates (0.01–1), and training parameters. BO used discrete unit/filter ranges, RS uniformly sampled parameters, and PSO employed lower and upper bounds for a global search.

Step 4) Model Training: This phase involves training each selected and optimized model on the prepared data, ensuring that they are well-fitted and capable of accurate predictions.

Step 5) Heterogeneous Ensembles Construction: After training individual models, we constructed heterogeneous ensembles using methods such as Arithmetic Mean (AV), Arithmetic Median (ME), and Inverse Ranked Weighted Mean (IR). These ensembles combine the model strengths to enhance the overall prediction accuracy through model diversity.

Step 6) Model Evaluation: The models and ensembles are evaluated using the RMSE, MAE, MMRE, and PRED metrics, which quantitatively assess prediction accuracy by measuring the alignment with actual values.

Step 7) Model Comparison: Significance tests, including the SK and BC test, were used to statistically compare the models. The SK test ranks models by performance, whereas the BC method aggregates these rankings to select top-performing models, ensuring a fair and unbiased comparison.

5   Results and Discussion

This section addresses key research questions by analyzing the model performance for BGL forecasting. Performance metrics and SK test results provide detailed model comparisons, whereas BC rankings supplement the analysis with comparative model rankings. Each research question was answered through an in-depth discussion based on these results (Tables 1, 2, 3).

Table 1. Performance comparison of RS ensembles and their singles for OSF.

Techniques	RLSTM	RGRU	RCNN	RSVR	RDBN	ERAV	ERME	ERIR
RMSE(mg/dl)	13.27	**8.03**	24.69	12.17	18.52	13.63	12.25	12.92
MAE(mg/dl)	10.19	**6.13**	19.98	9.66	14.29	10.47	9.31	10.05
MMRE(mg/dl)	6.59	**3.89**	11.71	6.22	8.98	6.3	5.76	6.31
PRED(25%)	98.36	**99.92**	95.44	99.35	95.74	99.05	99.09	98.92

Table 2. Performance comparison of PSO ensembles and their singles for OSF

Techniques	RLSTM	RGRU	RCNN	RSVR	RDBN	ERAV	ERME	ERIR
RMSE(mg/dl)	12.98	**7.87**	22.6	12.17	15.02	12.84	12.26	12.58
MAE(mg/dl)	9.88	**6.09**	17.89	9.62	11.58	9.79	9.33	9.71
MMRE(mg/dl)	6.35	**3.84**	11.57	6.11	7.46	6.12	5.83	6.31
PRED(25%)	98.79	**99.98**	94.42	99.41	97.68	99.22	99.14	99.07

Table 3. Performance comparison of BO ensembles and their singles for OSF

Techniques	RLSTM	RGRU	RCNN	RSVR	RDBN	ERAV	ERME	ERIR
RMSE(mg/dl)	13.25	**7.96**	23.98	15.62	22.64	14.61	13.21	14.01
MAE(mg/dl)	10.18	**6.15**	19.37	12.43	17.62	11.31	9.92	10.67
MMRE(mg/dl)	6.51	**3.8**	12.22	7.89	11.19	6.95	6.14	6.47
PRED(25%)	98.76	**99.97**	93.31	97.1	92.06	98.52	98.64	98.83

5.1   Evaluation of Singles for BGL Forecasting. (RQ1)

The PGRU model was identified as the best-performing single model with an RMSE of 7.87 mg/dl, making it the most accurate model for BGL forecasting.

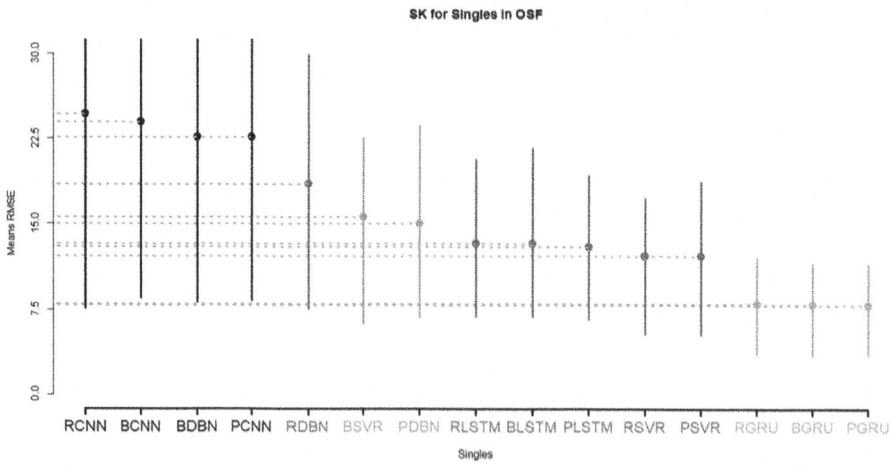

Fig. 2. Plot of SK test for singles in OSF.

Figure 2 presents the SK test results, identifying PGRU as statistically superior, with other GRU-based models like RGRU and BGRU closely following (RMSEs of 8.03 mg/dl and 7.96 mg/dl, respectively) in the top performance group. This grouping underscores the effectiveness of GRU models for BGL forecasting, given their ability to capture long-term dependencies. In contrast, CNN-based models, such as RCNN, with higher RMSEs (e.g., 24.69 mg/dl), were placed in a lower performance group, highlighting GRU architectures as better suited for time-series predictions in this domain.

Table 4. BC ranking for singles, ensembles and their combination for OSF of the top 10 best models based on SK test.

Techniques	Singles		Ensembles		Ensembles and their Singles	
BC Rank	Model	Score	Model	Score	Model	Score
1st	PGRU	59	ERME	34	PGRU	95
2nd	BGRU	56	EPME	32	BGRU	92
3rd	RGRU	53	EPAV	28	RGRU	89
4th	PSVR	48	EPIR	24	PSVR	80
5th	RSVR	44	EBME	17	ERME	78
6th	PLSTM	40	ERAV	16	EPME	76
7th	BLSTM	36	ERIR	16	RSVR	74
8th	RLSTM	32	EBIR	9	EPAV	69
9th	PDBN	28	EBAV	4	EPIR	64
10th	BSVR	24	-	-	ERIR	55

In addition to the SK results, the BC rankings presented in Table 4 reinforce the performance of PGRU, placing it first among single models with a score of 59 and first overall, including ensembles, with a combined score of 95. This highlights the consistency of PGRU across various metrics and optimization techniques.

5.2 Evaluation of Heterogeneous Ensembles for BGL Forecasting. (RQ2)

ERME was the most accurate and reliable heterogeneous ensemble, with an RMSE of 12.25 mg/dl. The SK test presented in Fig. 3, grouped this ensemble into the highest performance cluster. The EPME ensemble also performed well, with an RMSE of 12.26 mg/dl, and was placed in the same performance group, demonstrating that PSO can still provide competitive results in ensemble configurations.

The SK results indicated that the EBAV ensemble, with an RMSE of 14.61 mg/dl, performed lower, suggesting BO is less effective in tuning ensembles than RS and PSO for BGL forecasting. The BC rankings in Table 4 further contextualize ensemble performance: ERME ranked first with a score of 34, followed by EPME with 32, and EPAV ranked third with 28. This underscores the advantages of RS and PSO in enhancing the ensemble accuracy and reliability.

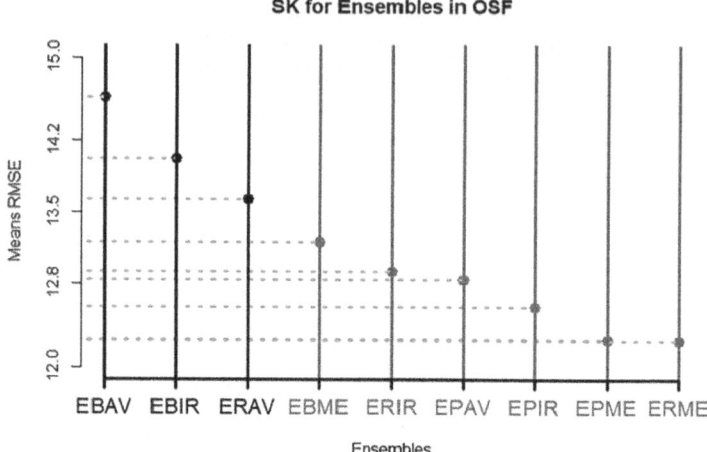

Fig. 3. Plot of SK for heterogeneous ensembles in OSF.

Table 5. Comparison of ensembles and their singles for 5 min forecasting.

	Techniques	Min	Mean	Median	Max
RS	Singles	8.03	15.34	13.27	24.69
	Ensembles	12.25	12.93	12.92	13.63
PSO	Singles	7.87	14.13	12.98	22.6
	Ensembles	12.26	12.56	12.58	12.84
BO	Singles	7.96	16.69	15.62	23.98
	Ensembles	13.21	13.14	14.01	14.61
All	Singles	7.87	15.38	13.27	24.69
	Ensembles	12.25	13.14	12.92	14.61

5.3 Evaluation of Heterogeneous Ensembles Vs Their Constituent Singles in BGL Forecasting. (RQ3)

Figure 4 illustrates the SK test, which identifies single models as belonging to the top performance cluster. However, heterogeneous ensembles consistently outperformed single models across key metrics, such as the mean, median, and maximum RMSE, as shown in Table 5. For instance, while PGRU achieved a low RMSE of 7.87 mg/dl, ensembles showed more stable and consistent performance. Notably, single models reached a maximum RMSE of 24.69 mg/dl, whereas ensembles had a lower maximum RMSE of 14.61 mg/dl, demonstrating their ability to reduce extreme errors and enhance the reliability of BGL forecasting. Across all optimization techniques (PSO, RS, and BO), ensemble models achieved consistently lower mean and median RMSE, proving their effectiveness in improving both accuracy and stability compared to single models.

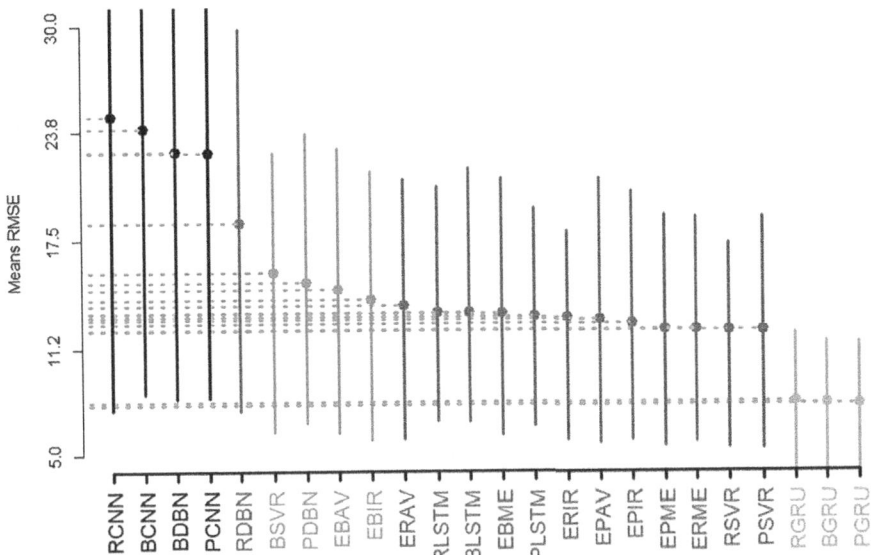

Fig. 4. Plot of SK for singles and ensembles in OSF.

5.4 Evaluation of Optimization Techniques of Singles and Ensembles for BGL Forecasting. (RQ4)

PSO has emerged as the most effective optimization technique for both individual models and ensembles. The SK test revealed that the PSO-optimized models and ensembles consistently ranked in the highest performance groups, with PGRU and EPAV achieving the highest RMSE scores. In contrast, RS also provided competitive results, particularly for ensembles like ERME (RMSE: 12.25 mg/dl), but showed greater variability when applied to individual models, as evidenced by RCNN's poor performance.

BO, while effective in certain cases, was placed in a lower performance group according to the SK test. For instance, BGRU performed well with an RMSE of 7.96 mg/dl, but EBME had higher variability, with an RMSE of 13.21 mg/dl, leading it to be ranked in a lower performance cluster.

Overall, PSO's ability to balance global and local optimization searches makes it the most reliable method, especially for optimizing complex models such as GRU and LSTM, as well as ensemble configurations. The SK test confirmed the superiority of PSO, statistically placing its optimized models ahead of the others across both individual and ensemble configurations.

Table 6 prensents the number of occurences of each optimization technique in the BC analysis reinforcing the effectiveness of PSO. PSO-optimized models appeared 12 times in the top 10 rankings, accumulating a total score of 643, while RS-optimized models appeared 10 times with a score of 491, and BO-

Table 6. Number of occurrences of each optimization technique for top 10 best models based on SK test for singles, ensembles and both.

	Singles		Ensembles		Ensembles and Singles		Total	
	Occurrences	Score	Occurrences	Score	Occurrences	Score	Occurrences	Score
RS	3	129	3	66	4	296	10	491
BO	3	116	3	30	1	92	7	238
PSO	4	175	3	84	5	384	12	643

optimized models appeared 7 times with a score of 238. These results highlight the consistency and effectiveness of PSO in optimizing both single models and heterogeneous ensembles for BGL forecasting.

The findings of this study, supported by the SK test and BC rankings, indicate that PSO-optimized ensembles are the most effective approach for BGL forecasting. The GRU-based models optimized with PSO consistently performed better than the other models, confirming that recurrent architectures are well-suited for handling temporal dependencies in glucose data. Additionally, the superiority of PSO for ensemble configurations suggests that evolutionary optimization techniques should be considered in the future developments of BGL forecasting systems.

6   Threats to Validity

This section considers potential threats to the validity of our study, classified into three categories (internal, external and construct validity). We describe the actions undertaken to counter these threats, reinforcing the robustness and reliability of our findings.

Internal Validity. Internal validity refers to ensuring reliable results and minimizing bias. We used 4-fold cross-validation, which is more robust than a random train-test split and reduces overfitting. In addition, an early stopping mechanism was applied to prevent overfitting during training. To avoid bias from poor hyperparameter choices, optimization techniques, such as RS, BO, and PSO were employed to fine-tune the models effectively.

External Validity. External validity concerns the generalizability of research findings. To ensure broader applicability, we used a dataset of 110 patients with diabetes that offered diverse representation. This contrasts with studies that used smaller datasets and improves the relevance of our findings. We focused on 5-minute prediction horizons, although factors such as physical activity, diet, and stress were not fully considered. Testing these external factors in real-world settings is crucial for validating their practical applicability.

Construct Validity. Construct validity refers to the extent which our performance measures reflect the underlying constructs of model performance. To strengthen the construct validity, we used four metrics: RMSE, MAE, MMRE, and PRED, to ensure a comprehensive evaluation. We applied the SK and BC methods for the balanced model assessment. The SK test clusters models based on RMSE, minimizing variance within clusters and maximizing variance between them, supported by statistical tests such as ANOVA. This method provides a clear ranking of models based on their performance. The BC method aggregates rankings from multiple metrics (MAE, RMSE, MMRE, PRED), assigns points to models and determines the overall rank. This approach ensures fair comparison by simultaneously considering multiple criteria.

7   Conclusion and Future Works

In this study, we evaluated various ML/DL models, including LSTM, CNN, GRU, SVR, and DBN, as well as heterogeneous ensembles, for BGL forecasting in individuals with type 1 diabetes. We aimed to identify the most accurate and reliable models for OSF using optimization techniques such as PSO, RS, and BO.

RQ1: Is there any single predictive model that outperforms others for BGL forecasting?

The results showed that GRU optimized using PSO outperformed the other models. The PGRU model achieved the best performance, with an RMSE of 7.87 mg/dl, indicating its effectiveness in capturing short-term dependencies in BGL data. This highlights the suitability Of GRU for time-series forecasting in diabetes management.

RQ2: Which heterogeneous ensemble provides the most accurate and reliable BGL predictions?

Among the ensemble configurations, the ERME model provided the most reliable forecasts, achieving an RMSE of 12.25 mg/dl, followed by EPME with a quite similar RMSE of 12.26 mg/dl. The combination of different models in the ensemble mitigated the weaknesses of the single models, leading to more stable and accurate predictions.

RQ3: How do heterogeneous ensembles compare to their constituent singles in BGL forecasting?

Heterogeneous ensembles consistently outperformed their constituent single models, showing more robust performance. For example, while the PGRU model had a lower RMSE, the ensemble models provided more balanced and reliable predictions across different metrics, particularly in mitigating single model variability.

RQ4: How do different optimization techniques improve the performance of single and ensemble models for BGL forecasting?

PSO has emerged as the most effective optimization technique, significantly enhancing the performance of both single models and heterogeneous ensembles. The PSO-optimized models consistently ranked among the top performance groups, as validated by the SK test and BC rankings.

Future research should explore long-term multi-step forecasting, incorporate additional physiological data, and develop adaptive models. Additionally, further investigation into other evolutionary optimization techniques, such as genetic algorithms, could improve the model performance. These approaches will enhance real-time diabetes management systems.

References

1. Burrack, A., Martinov, T., Fife, B.: T cell-mediated beta cell destruction: autoimmunity and alloimmunity in the context of type 1 diabetes. Front. Endocrinol. **8** (2017)
2. Chiang, J., et al.: Type 1 diabetes in children and adolescents: a position statement by the american diabetes association. Diabetes Care **41**, 2026–2044 (2018)
3. Mattila, T., Boer, A.: Influence of intensive versus conventional glucose control on microvascular and macrovascular complications in type 1 and 2 diabetes mellitus. Drugs **70**, 2229–2245 (2010)
4. Colberg, S., Kannane, J., Diawara, N.: Physical activity, dietary patterns, and glycemic management in active individuals with type 1 diabetes: an online survey. Int. J. Environ. Res. Public Health. **18** (2021)
5. Kovatchev, B., Gonder-Frederick, L., Cox, D., Clarke, W.: Evaluating the accuracy of continuous glucose-monitoring sensors: Continuous glucose-error grid analysis illustrated by TheraSense Freestyle Navigator data. Diabetes Care. **27** (2004)
6. Benaida, M., Abnane, I., Idri, A., El Idrissi, T.: Machine and deep learning predictive techniques for blood glucose level. Inform. Syst. Technol, pp. 476–485 (2022)
7. El Idrissi, T., Idri, A.: Evaluating a comparing deep learning architectures for blood glucose prediction. In: Biomedical Engineering Systems And Technologies: 13th International Joint Conference, BIOSTEC 2020, Valletta, Malta, February 24–26, 2020, Revised Selected Papers 13, pp. 347–365 (2021)
8. Shahid, S., Hussain, S., Khan, W.: Predicting continuous blood glucose level using deep learning. In: Proceedings of The 14th IEEE/ACM International Conference on Utility and Cloud Computing Companion, pp. 1–5 (2021)
9. Kitchainukoon, N., Sae-Bae, N.: Predicting blood glucose levels with machine learning techniques. In: 2023 IEEE 6th International Conference On Knowledge Innovation And Invention (ICKII), pp. 515–519 (2023)
10. Benaida, M., Abnane, I., Idri, A.: Deep learning based one step and multi-steps ahead forecasting blood glucose level. Expert Systems, pp. e13393 (2023)
11. El Idrissi, T., Idri, A.: Deep learning for blood glucose prediction: CNN vs LSTM. In: Gervasi, O., Murgante, B., Misra, S., Garau, C., Blečić, I., Taniar, D., Apduhan, B.O., Rocha, A., Tarantino, E., Torre, C.M., Karaca, Y. (eds.) ICCSA 2020. LNCS, vol. 12250, pp. 379–393. Springer, Cham (2020). https://doi.org/10.1007/978-3-030-58802-1_28
12. Wadghiri, M., Idri, A., Idrissi, T., Hakkoum, H.: Ensemble blood glucose prediction in diabetes mellitus: a review. Comput. Biol. Med. **147** (2022)
13. Vapnik, V., Golowich, S., Smola, A., et al.: Support vector method for function approximation, regression estimation, and signal processing. Adv. Neural Inform. Process. Syst. 281–287 (1997)
14. Ren, Y., Mao, J., Liu, Y., Li, Y.: A novel DBN model for time series forecasting. IAENG Int. J. Comput. Sci. **44**, 79–86 (2017)

15. LeCun, Y., Bengio, Y.: Convolutional networks for images, speech, and time series. In: The Handbook of Brain Theory And Neural Networks, pp. 255–258 (1998)
16. Hochreiter, S., Schmidhuber, J.: Long short-term memory. Neural Comput. **9**, 1735–1780 (1997)
17. Cho, K., Merriënboer, B., Gulcehre, C., Bahdanau, D., Bougares, F., Schwenk, H., Bengio, Y.: Learning phrase representations using rnn encoder–decoder for statistical machine translation. In: Proceedings of The 2014 Conference on Empirical Methods in Natural Language Processing (EMNLP), pp. 1724–1734 (2014,10). https://aclanthology.org/D14-1179
18. Bergstra, J., Bengio, Y.: Random search for hyper-parameter optimization. J. Mach. Learn. Res. **13** (2012)
19. Frazier, P.: A tutorial on Bayesian optimization. ArXiv Preprint ArXiv:1807.02811 (2018)
20. Wang, D., Tan, D., Liu, L.: Particle swarm optimization algorithm: an overview. Soft. Comput. **22**, 387–408 (2018)
21. Zecchin, C., Facchinetti, A., Sparacino, G., De Nicolao, G., Cobelli, C.: Neural network incorporating meal information improves accuracy of short-time prediction of glucose concentration. IEEE Trans. Biomed. Eng. **59**, 1550–1560 (2012)
22. Mirshekarian, S., Shen, H., Bunescu, R., Marling, C.: LSTMs and neural attention models for blood glucose prediction: comparative experiments on real and synthetic data. In: 2019 41st Annual International Conference Of The IEEE Engineering In Medicine And Biology Society (EMBC), pp. 706–712 (2019)
23. Li, K., Daniels, J., Liu, C., Herrero-Vinas, P., Georgiou, P.: Convolutional recurrent neural networks for glucose prediction. IEEE J. Biomed. Health Inform. **24**, 603-613 (2020) https://nottingham-repository.worktribe.com/output/2302666
24. Alfian, G., Syafrudin, M., Rhee, J., Anshari, M., Mustakim, M., Fahrurrozi, I.: Blood glucose prediction model for type 1 diabetes based on extreme gradient boosting. IOP Conf. Series: Materials Sci. Eng. **803** (2020)
25. Liu, J., Wang, L., Zhang, L., Zhang, Z., Zhang, S.: Predictive analytics for blood glucose concentration: an empirical study using the tree-based ensemble approach. Library Hi Tech. **38**, 835–858 (2020)
26. Wang, Y., Wang, T.: Application of improved LightGBM model in blood glucose prediction. Appl. Sci. (Switzerland). **10** (2020)
27. Sun, Q., Jankovic, M., Bally, L., Mougiakakou, S.: Predicting blood glucose with an LSTM and Bi-LSTM based deep neural network. In: 2018 14th Symposium on Neural Networks and Applications (NEUREL), pp. 1–5 (2018)
28. Chollet, F., et al.: Keras. Seattle, WA, USA (2015)
29. Abadi, M., et al. TensorFlow: a system for Large-Scale machine learning. In: 12th USENIX Symposium on Operating Systems Design And Implementation (OSDI 16), pp. 265–283 (2016)
30. DirecNet Diabetes Research in Children Network (DirecNet). (2020 3). https://public.jaeb.org/direcnet/
31. El Idrissi, T., Idri, A., Kadi, I., Bakkoury, Z.: Strategies of multi-step-ahead forecasting for blood glucose level using LSTM neural networks: A comparative study. In: HEALTHINF 2020 - 13th International Conference on Health Informatics, Proceedings; Part of 13th International Joint Conference on Biomedical Engineering Systems And Technologies, BIOSTEC 2020, pp. 337–344 (2020)
32. Scott, A., Knott, M.A.: Cluster analysis method for grouping means in the analysis of variance. Biometrics. **30**, 507–512 (1974,9)
33. Borda, J.: Memoire sur les elections au scrutin. Mémoires De L'académie Royale, pp. 657–664 (1781)

Measuring Team Productivity in Agile Development: A Scrum-Based Process

Marcela Guerrero-Calvache[1]([⊠]) [iD], Giovanni Hernández[2] [iD],
and María Clara Gómez-Álvarez[3] [iD]

[1] Institución Universitaria Pascual Bravo, Medellín, Colombia
sandra.guerrero@pascualbravo.edu.co
[2] Universidad Mariana, San Juan de Pasto, Nariño, Colombia
gihernandez@umariana.edu.co
[3] Universidad Nacional de Colombia Sede Medellín, Medellín, Colombia
mcgomez@unal.edu.co

Abstract. Team productivity in agile software development (ASD) is perceived as an abstract concept that is still evolving. It works as a fundamental indicator in organizations since it provides information about how a team behaves. Recent studies have revealed that team productivity is composed of determinants, influencers and impact factors. In recent years, the widespread dominance of agile methods in organizations has led to use mainly Scrum in software industry, which is a teamwork management framework used in complex projects. In this sense, it is interesting to establish a system that allows an agile team working with Scrum to incorporate the measurement and improvement of productivity in its activities. In this project, we propose a structured process for measuring team productivity that is aligned with the Scrum framework. The construction of the process was elaborated in two phases. In the first phase, the proposed process is designed, and a representation is elaborated. In the second phase, a validation of the designed process is performed, evaluating the acceptance in a software industry context. As a result, a Scrum-aligned team productivity measurement process was designed. This process is represented by business process models using BPMN notation and supported by a set of artifacts. In addition, the proposed process is validated by 77 software industry professionals organized in 19 Scrum teams. It is possible to establish a process for measuring team productivity in ASD for the following moments: planning, execution, and evaluation. By implementing the proposed measurement process with professionals, a high level of acceptance was obtained.

Keywords: Agile Software Development · Productivity Measurement Process · Team Productivity · Team Productivity Factors

1 Introduction

When talking about productivity, the term used since centuries ago in the economic framework is evoked, relating two relevant dimensions: quantity and quality [1]. Subsequently, software engineering coined the concept in the last three decades of the 20th century, specifically in the late 1970s, reflecting a classical perspective closely aligned with the models of that time [2].

© The Author(s), under exclusive license to Springer Nature Switzerland AG 2025
O. Gervasi et al. (Eds.): ICCSA 2025, LNCS 15649, pp. 134–149, 2025.
https://doi.org/10.1007/978-3-031-96997-3_9

With the advent of the Agile Software Development (ASD) manifesto, the mindset and working methods underwent a significant change [3]. The traditionalist position was left behind to adopt an approach that combines flexibility without compromising the stability of the projects and where people play a leading role in the processes [4].

Nowadays, different organizations, regardless of their context, in which they operate, are using agile methodologies to develop their operations. This is because they provide a strong organizational framework with positive aspects such as alignment with the business, greater customer satisfaction and continuous collaboration [5].

In the literature, it has been observed that the definition of team productivity in ASD is perceived as an abstract concept [6, 7], which is still evolving. This concept not only acts as a crucial indicator in organizations [8, 9] but is also shaped by determining, influential and impacting factors [6–8, 10–13].

These factors are categorized into four groups [8, 14]: *Meaning*, factors that analyze how development team members perceive productivity, either individually or in general terms; *Impact*, factors that affect the team and can negatively, positively or neutrally influence its behavior [8, 14]; *Flexibility*, factors that affect team performance when faced with conditions that require adaptation and change [8, 14]; and *Socio-Human*, factors that focus on the human qualities essential to achieving high levels of team performance and ensuring the success of the software development process [8, 14].

In ASD, productivity is used as an indicator [8, 9] to evaluate the team's performance and efficiency in delivering its tasks [7]. A software development team must incorporate productivity measurement and improvement in its activities [15, 16]. To achieve this goal, it is essential to understand its behavior, which is achieved through the use of metrics. These metrics allow the collection of relevant information to understand performance objectively and guide the continuous improvement of the work process [16].

The widespread use of agile methods in organizations has led them to opt for Scrum [5], a flexible, fast framework used to manage highly complex projects [17].

Scrum was conceived in the 1990s by Ken Schwaber and Jeff Sutherland [18] in response to common problems in project execution: slowness, cost overruns, delivery delays, and lack of customer satisfaction [19]. Its objective is to transform the traditional process into one that prioritizes incremental and iterative deliveries, embracing an adaptive and self-directed approach to generate value quickly [3, 19]. According to the seventeenth agile report exposed by Digital.ai [5], 63% of agile users at team level use Scrum being since 2006 the most popular framework in history.

The motivation for this paper arises, from the above description, which is to propose a productivity measurement process for Scrum teams considering the factors that affect it organized in the categories of: Meaning, Impact, Flexibility and Socio-Human; with their corresponding evaluation metrics.

The paper is organized as follows. Section 2 describes the related work, Sect. 3 presents the methodological process used, Sect. 4 the results, Sect. 5 describes the discussion, and Sect. 6 details the conclusions.

2 Related Works

The study [20] analyzed the metrics used in the evaluation of eleven factors that influence team productivity within ASD, classified into the categories of *Meaning*, *Impact* and *Flexibility*. This analysis was conducted through a systematic mapping of the literature following Petersen's protocol [21]. As a result of this process, 37 primary research available in the bibliographic databases of IEEE Xplore DL and Scopus. The findings highlight the definition of the factors analyzed, the identification of specific productivity metrics associated with each of them, and an attempt at mathematical formalization of some of these metrics.

In the research [14], they conducted a comparative analysis of productivity perceptions among ASD team members based on 63 factors identified in a preliminary Systematic Literature Mapping. Their study was guided by Kitchenham and Pfleeger's [22] protocol for survey development in Software Engineering. The collection of 82 responses from software industry professionals made it possible to establish that productivity is a crucial indicator of improvement within the team's processes and the fulfillment of the client's objectives. Furthermore, productivity can be measured through various factors. The above included a categorization of the factors in terms of Meaning, Flexibility, Impact and Socio-Human highlighting the relevance of 22 of them.

A systematic literature review focused on metrics used to assess team productivity in the context of ASD [23] identified ten main articles following a specific protocol. The results revealed the existence of 21 team productivity metrics, especially highlighting the measurement of early and frequent software delivery and the value added by tasks to the software product.

Machuca and Gasca [24] proposed a gamification-based model that seeks to impact team productivity through intervention in the Socio-Human Factors (SHF). The study presents an innovative proposal that incorporates three thematic areas in Software Engineering: gamification, SHF in software development contexts, with the objective of strengthening skills and abilities; and serving as a strategy to improve productivity.

3 Methodology

In software engineering (SE), a process is defined as a series of activities to be carried out within a specific time frame, using resources to produce work products [25]. Specific roles perform these activities and can be subdivided into tasks, each with an assigned level of responsibility, with the goal of achieving the desired results [25].

That is why, through an SE process, we intend to methodically establish a set of activities that serve as a reference for ASD teams to measure productivity. The process is emphasized in Scrum teams and consists of two phases: design and validation.

Figure 1 details the measurement process in the exposed stages.

3.1 Phase 1: Process Design

This section presents the systematic way in which the proposal of a process for measuring team productivity from the ASD approach is elaborated is presented. The activities carried out in the design of the process are described below.

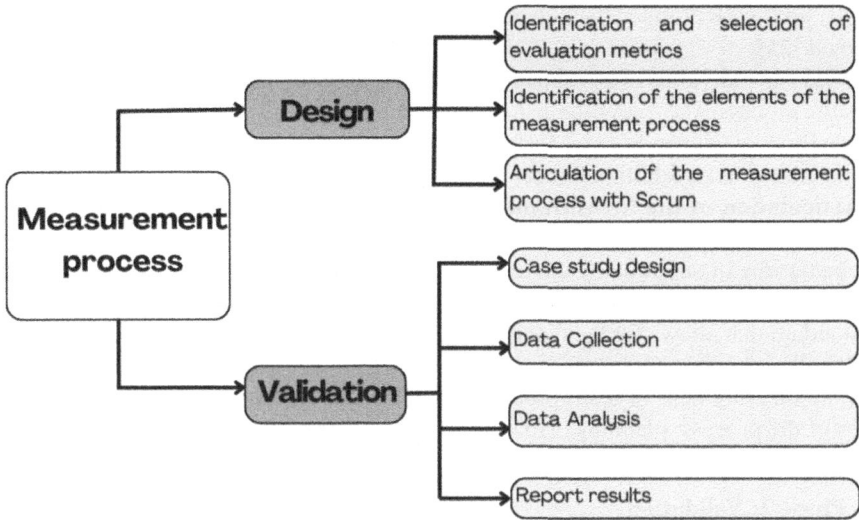

Fig. 1. Stages of the measurement process.

Note: All figures and tables are elaborated by the authors unless otherwise stated.

Identification and Selection of Evaluation Metrics. Metrics are essential in organizations [26] and must be aligned with agile principles such as frequent delivery of value, flexibility and continuous communication with the customer [26, 27]. However, defining metrics is not a trivial task because they can be categorized in different ways depending on the approach adopted [28]. This phase seeks to establish metrics for the evaluation of 22 productivity factors identified in a previous study [14].

Identification of the Elements of the Measurement Process. This part seeks to establish the elements that will be part of the process and, in turn, relate it to Scrum. The elements to be considered are described as follows.

Event. It is an event that allows the team to review its progress and adapt to changes. In Scrum, events enable the work to be visible to those who perform it as well as to those who receive it [18]. The events suggested by Scrum are: Sprint, Sprint Planning, Daily Meeting, Sprint Review and Sprint Retrospective [18].

Metrics. Indicates the way to collect and analyze data in order to produce objective information about a variable that is desired to know and that this contributes to learning, in this case, about a team [23].

Activity. Involves one or more types of work items and how to perform them [29]. An activity consumes certain resources, generates some work product and a role executes it. For the process of measuring team productivity in ASD, activities will be considered and addressed within each of the events proposed by Scrum. It should be noted that the measurement activities should be relevant to the needs of the organization. They should consume little time and effort for the ASD team to implement them [26].

Resources. These are the necessary components for the ASD team to carry out the measurement. There are two types of elements: inputs, which are necessary to start an activity, and work products, which are the results generated once that activity has been executed [25].

Roles. An individual or a group of people who carry out a task or responsibility within a specific process. The roles established for this process follow the Scrum framework and include Product Owner, Scrum Master and Developers [3, 18]. In addition, Stakeholders are considered as an additional role.

Articulation of the Measurement Process with Scrum. This section articulates metrics, activities, resources, and roles defined with the Scrum events, in order to have a systematic way of adoption by the teams in the productivity measurement. To elaborate the representation, the Business Process Management Notation (BPMN) is used, which is a standard that allows for the detailed representation of high-level business processes. BPMN allows the processes to be represented based on central objectives [30], in this case, the measurement of team productivity. The representation is carried out in three stages of the process: planning, execution and evaluation.

3.2 Phase 2: Validation

In this section is presented the systematic approach used to validate the process proposed in Phase 1. The activities performed in the validation follow the protocol proposed by Runeson and Host [31] for the Case Study (CS).

Case Study Design. The objective of this stage is to define what the CS is intended to achieve, what is to be investigated and the context in which the information is to be obtained.

Data Collection. In this stage, the aim is to establish the technique to be used for data collection. According to Lethbridge [31] the techniques to achieve this purpose can be direct methods, indirect methods and independent analysis of work artifacts. For this case study, the survey is taken into consideration as a direct method.

Five important moments were considered when constructing the validation instrument. First, the objective of the instrument was defined. Secondly, the population to which the validation instrument will be applied is established. Next, the duration of the validation is estimated. As a next step, the resources for the application of the instrument are established. Finally, the activities to be developed are selected.

On the other hand, it describes how the implementation of the designed instrument was carried out. Details are included on: execution of planned activities, resource management and interaction with participants.

Data Analysis. Once the data have been collected, the analysis is performed by identifying the most relevant findings. The analysis can be qualitative or quantitative. This case study performs a quantitative analysis considering the participants' perceptions on the productivity measurement process established.

Report Results. To finalize the validation, a results report was prepared based on the participants' perceptions. With the descriptive analysis of the data, positive aspects and aspects to be improved for the process were established.

4 Results

The results obtained are presented in accordance with the methodological design established in Sect. 3.

4.1 Phase 1: Process Design

Establishment of Team Productivity Metrics in ASD. Identifying productivity metrics is a crucial step in the measurement process. To carry out this task, productivity factors were grouped into the following categories: Meaning, Impact, Flexibility and Socio-Human (22 factors in total). The productivity factors are set out in Fig. 2.

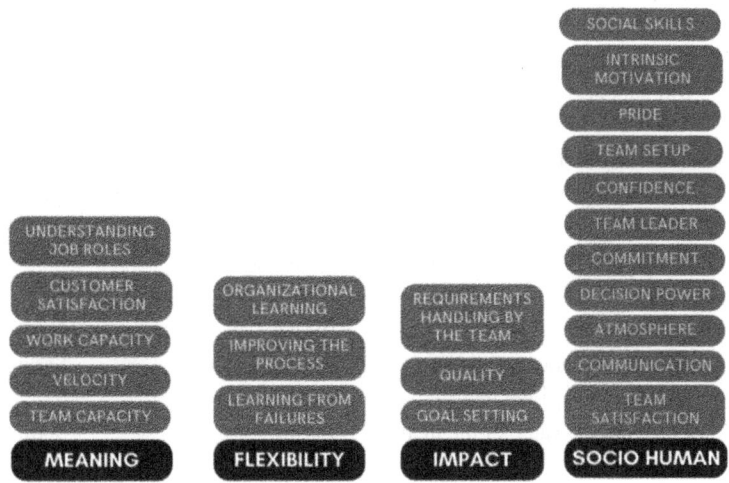

Fig. 2. Productivity factors considered in the study.

For the factors Meaning, Impact, and Flexibility, the metrics identified in [20] were selected, which are determined through a systematic mapping of literature using the IEEE Xplore and Scopus bibliographic databases.

Regarding the factors belonging to the Socio-Human category, the metrics identified in previous works carried out in [32–36] were selected.

Identification of Measurement Process Activities and Alignment with the Scrum Framework.

Currently, the Scrum framework does not provide concrete guidelines for measurement. Therefore, this study proposes a prescriptive process as a contribution to the framework, specifically focused on improving productivity measurement.

Table 1 shows the identified activities and the role that would develop them to plan, execute, and evaluate the measurement of team productivity in ASD considering the Scrum events.

The following presents the different stages of the process, each illustrated with diagrams detailing the activities and resources involved. Each of these figures uses BPMN

Table 1. Measurement process activities linked to Scrum.

Phase	Activity	Scrum Event	Scrum Role
Planning	Introduce factors for measuring productivity	Sprint Planning Meeting	Scrum Master
	Select Productivity Factors	Sprint Planning Meeting	Scrum Master
	Identify the metric(s) or evaluation indicators for each selected factor	Sprint Planning Meeting	Scrum Master
	Establish the form and measure in which a metric can be evaluated	Sprint Planning Meeting	Scrum Master
	Determine the type of rating scale to be used and the set of values that comprise it	Sprint Planning Meeting	Scrum Master
	Identify the resources or tools that will support the process of measuring factors	Sprint Planning Meeting	Scrum Master
	Establish the period the team will be subjected to the measurement process	Sprint Planning Meeting	Scrum Master
Execution	Coordinate data recording for measurement	Sprint	Scrum Master
	Select metric	Sprint	Scrum Team
	Record the data required for measurement of the metric	Sprint	Scrum Team
	Calculate the value of the metric from the collected data	Sprint	Scrum Master
Evaluation	Elaborate a graphical representation of the behavior of the results of the metric	Sprint Retrospective	Scrum Master
	Interpret the results of the graphical representation of the behavior of the metrics	Sprint Retrospective	Scrum Master
	Establish regulation and improvement actions	Sprint Retrospective	Scrum Team
	Synthesize regulatory and improvement actions	Sprint Retrospective	Scrum Master
	Specify action plan	Sprint Retrospective	Scrum Master

(Business Process Model and Notation), employed in the **Bizagi Modeler** tool, to clearly and visually represent the key elements in each phase of the process. Through this representation, the flow and interaction between activities throughout the cycle are made easier to understand.

Figure 3 shows the Planning stage, outlining the key activities and resources required to set the foundation for the process.

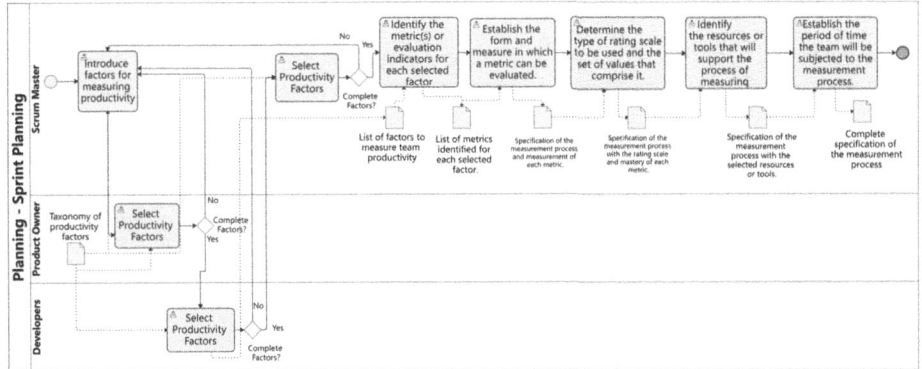

Fig. 3. Planning phase of the productivity measurement process.

To support the Planning stage, artifacts were developed to support the process. Figure 4 details the artifact created for the Planning stage.

Category							
Factor							
Attribute (Metric)	Measurement	Form	Type of Measurement Scale	Measurement Scale	Resource Type	Resource	Period

Fig. 4. Artifact to specify planning.

The *category* corresponds to one of the four classification categories to which a productivity factor could belong (Meaning, Impact, Flexibility, Socio-Human). The *factor* is associated with one of the 22 team productivity factors in ASD. The *attribute* represents the evaluation metrics or indicators according to the productivity factor. The measure is the value or symbol that is assigned to the attribute. The *form* is the formula used so that an attribute can be measured. The *type of measurement scale* is the subjective assessment scheme selected to classify the measure; according to the proposal [23, 28], these can be Likert Scale, Forced Classification, Verbal Frequency Scale, Ordinal Scale, Comparative Scale, Numerical Scale, etc. The *measurement scale* represents the set of values that are part of the subjective assessment scale according to the type selected. On a Likert scale, for example, the values could be Very high, High, Medium, Low, Very Low [23, 28]. The *resource type* is the one used for the measurement process (Physical, Computational Tool, Human, etc.). The *resource* refers to the resource that will support the measurement process. The *period*, which refers to the period of time in which the metric must be calculated.

Figure 5 illustrates the **Execution** process using BPMN. This figure visually represents the activities and flow involved in the Execution stage, providing a clear understanding of how the process unfolds and the interactions between its key elements.

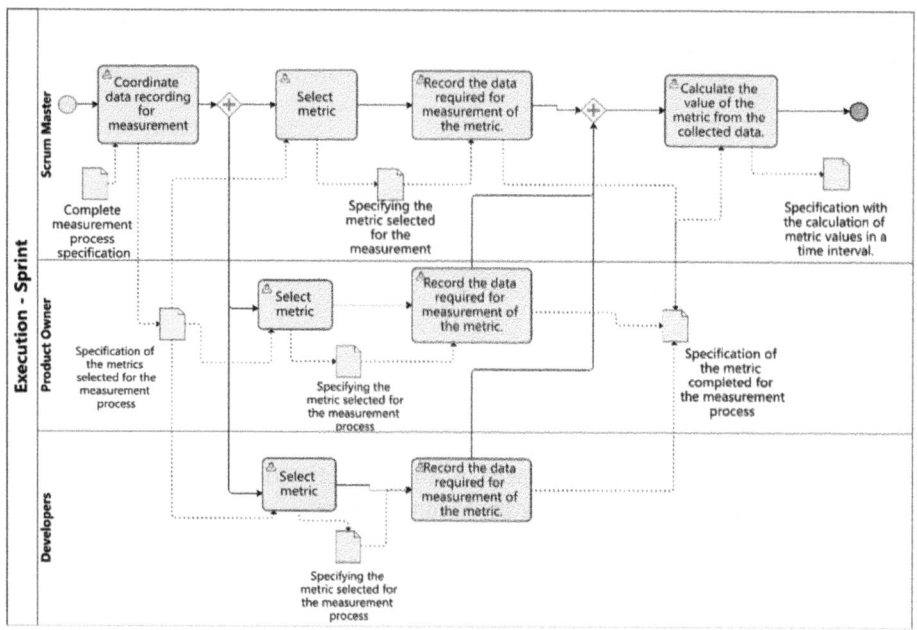

Fig. 5. Execution phase of the productivity measurement process.

As a support resource for the execution stage, the artifact presented in Fig. 6. Was created.

Category				
Factor				
Attribute				
Form				
Period	Variables			
	Variable 1	Variable 2	...	Variable m
Period 1 value				
Period 2 value				
...				
Period value n				

Fig. 6. Artifact to specify execution.

Category, Factor, Attribute, Form, and Period represent the same data displayed in the planning artifact. The *Variables* refer to the values that are captured to obtain the measurement in a specific period.

Finally, to support the **Evaluation** stage, the process is represented (see Fig. 7), and an artifact is created to specify the evaluation (see Fig. 8), along with another to specify the recommendations resulting from the analysis of the metrics (see Fig. 9).

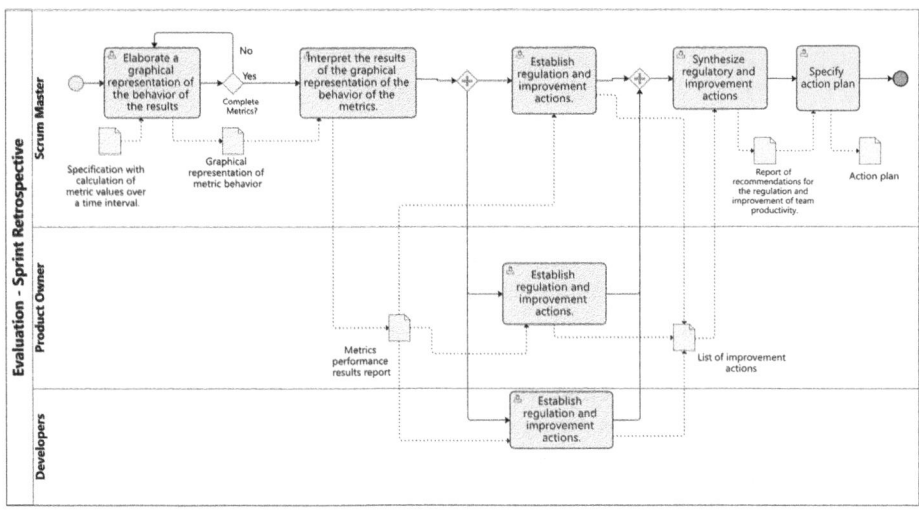

Fig. 7. Evaluation phase of the productivity measurement process.

Category	
Factor	
Attribute	
Form	

Graphical representation of the measurement	Report of results of the behavior of the metric	
	Date	
	Observations	
Sprint 1 Sprint 2 Sprint 3 ... Sprint N		

Fig. 8. Artifact to specify evaluation.

Category, Factor, Attribute, Form represent the same data displayed in the planning artifact. The *Variables* refer to the values that are captured to obtain the measurement in a specific period.

This report details the regulation and improvement actions that the team must implement.

4.2 Phase 2: Validation

Below are the results of the phases of the protocol proposed by Runeson and Host [31] for the Case Study (CS).

Recommendations report	
Date	
ID	Recommendations

Fig. 9. Artifact to specify the recommendations report.

Case Study Design. The purpose of the CS was to validate the process proposed in Phase 1 in order to measure team productivity in the development of a software product of medium complexity using Scrum. This was applied in a real operational scenario with software industry professionals during 6 weeks.

Data Collection. During April and May 2024, CS was held to validate the process of measuring team productivity in ASD with professionals from the software industry. A total of 77 professionals participated, organized in 19 teams.

The teams worked on a project using the Scrum guidelines as a framework for work management, developing two sprints of 3 weeks each. The development of the CS was carried out in three moments.

The first moment corresponded to the planning phase of the process. Prior to the application of the CS, the teams were made aware of the importance of measuring team productivity in ASD. In addition, the productivity measurement process proposal was socialized, including the identification of factors and metrics, together with the activities to be carried out and some artifacts that were created for the collection of information.

In the second moment, the participants were guided in data collection during the development of each Sprint using the artifacts designed to support the process.

In the third moment, at the end of each Sprint, the results were analyzed and interpreted. In this space, participants reflected on the productivity measurements generated in each of the iterations and made a report of results and recommendations.

Data Analysis and Report Results. To collect the participants' perceptions about the proposed process for measuring team productivity in ASD, a survey was developed and administered to the 77 participants. The variables analyzed were: the level of acceptance of the proposal, the difficulties encountered, positive aspects, aspects to include and aspects to improve.

The following section presents the sociodemographic characteristics of the survey participants. These characteristics include gender, age, and professional experience, which provide context for the analysis of the survey results.

The results obtained from the survey revealed that 79.2% of the respondents are male (61), while the remaining 20.8% are female (16).

Regarding the age of the respondents, it was observed that 37.7% of the participants are between 24 and 31 years old, 24.7% are in the 32 to 39 age range, 20.8% are between 40 and 47 years old, and 16.9% are between 48 and 55 years old.

Concerning the amount of time the professionals have been working in software development projects, it is evident that 39% have more than twelve years of experience in the field, 26% have between 1 and 4 years, 20.8% have between 5 and 8 years, and 14.3% have between 9 and 12 years.

Figure 10 shows that the proposal obtained an acceptance level of 97.4% at the High and Very High levels, representing 75 professionals. The above means that the process of measuring team productivity in Scrum has been relevant to evaluating a team performance by proposing a set of activities and artifacts that contribute to the achievement of this objective.

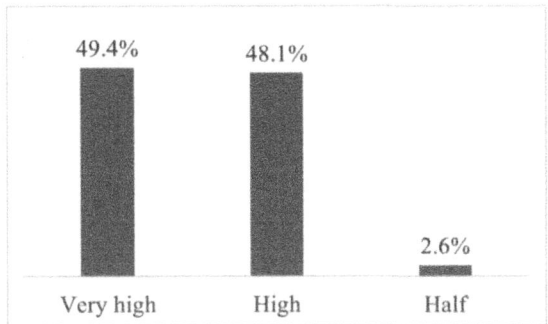

Fig. 10. Level of acceptance of the proposal by professionals.

When investigating the positive aspects, in Fig. 11, it can be seen that the participants fundamentally highlight that the proposal provides artifacts to measure productivity in an organized and systematic way. In addition, there is a systematic process that guides the measurement of productivity from planning to evaluation. Finally, the proposal adapts to the Scrum framework.

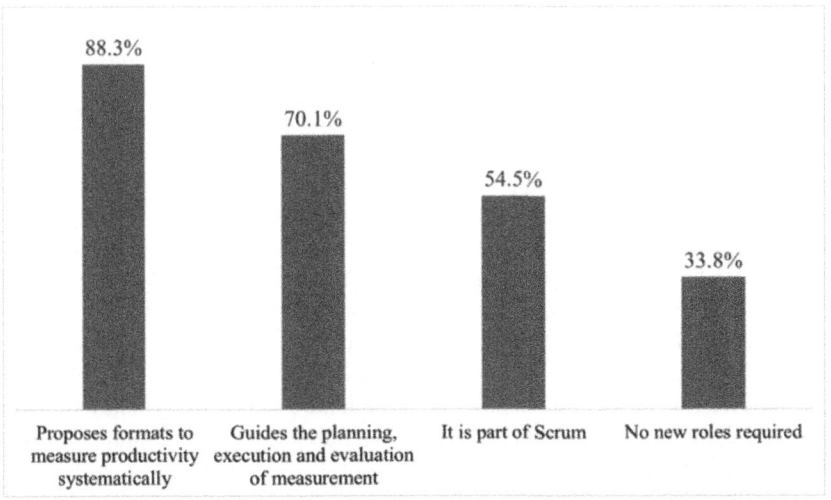

Fig. 11. Positive aspects of the proposal according to the professionals.

Regarding the difficulties expressed by the population object of the validation, when measuring team productivity, it is highlighted that 11.7% (9 professionals) stated that they had had problems when recording the data in the measurement devices, 7.8% (6 professionals) in understanding some factors such as work capacity; and 3.9% (3 professionals) in defining the assessment scales.

According to the data collected, the participants mentioned that one aspect they would like to include in the proposal is the automation of the measurement process through the use of a software tool.

Regarding aspects that could be improved, 74% consider that no additional contribution is required. 16.9% suggest creating a computer tool to automate the measurement process. Finally, 9.1% of participants suggest providing an instruction manual to facilitate the understanding of the factors and the recording of data in the templates that support the process.

After reviewing the measurement process results, one suggestion providing an instruction manual for using the proposal was implemented. A software product that supports the measurement process during all stages is considered a future work line.

5   Discussion

The measurement process consists of several components and is divided into three stages. It began with the definition of specific metrics for the 22 relevant productivity factors, selected through a systematic literature mapping (SMS) and significant studies in the field. The objective of this review was to establish precise definitions for each factor and their measurement indicators using various metrics.

Subsequently, we established the activities, resources and roles to be considered in the evaluation process, dividing them into three key moments: Planning, Execution and Evaluation. For each of these moments, artifacts were designed to specify the results of the tasks. These artifacts provide a clear and defined structure to guide the implementation of the process, ensuring its coherence and effectiveness.

Finally, the defined components were integrated and adapted to the framework and dynamics of the agile Scrum method, taking advantage of its existing structures and ceremonies to facilitate the effective implementation of the process. The process is represented using the business process model proposed by [30] using the BPMN notation.

In this way, the agile Scrum approach and the objective of measuring and improving productivity in a specific software development context synergized [37].

During the validation stage of the measurement process, both the positive aspects of the proposal and those to be improved were identified, as well as the difficulties encountered. It was observed that the proposal obtained a high degree of acceptance, exceeding 90%, which indicates that, in this population, the established measurement process is effective for evaluating productivity in ASD teams. The idea of providing greater support to the measurement process through the creation of an instruction manual to guide the steps to be followed, as well as the automation of the process through a computer tool, is proposed.

6   Conclusions

The research contributed to establishing a team productivity measurement process in ASD for the moments Planning, Execution and Evaluation, which is integrated to the Scrum framework. The measurement process through previous studies, manages to consolidate a set of 22 productivity factors classified into the categories: Meaning, Impact, Flexibility and Socio Human.

Implementing the proposed measurement process with software industry professionals achieved a high level of acceptance. The main difficulty encountered was in capturing the necessary data to carry out the measurement. In addition, the participants suggested the creation of a resource to guide the adoption of the proposal and the development of a computer tool to support the proposed process.

The level of abstraction required to plan the productivity measurement process allowing the identification of a high level of complexity generated in the professionals. In this sense, it is proposed, as future work, to use strategies such as gamification to reduce the level of complexity.

References

1. Romero Navarrete, I.: Evaluación de filosofías y técnicas para el mejoramiento de la productividad y calidad. Tesis de licenciatura, Universidad de Sonora, Hermosillo (1994). http://tesis.uson.mx/digital/tesis/docs/5553/Capitulo2.pdf
2. Hernández-López, A., Colomo-Palacios, R., García-Crespo, Á.: Medidas de productividad en los proyectos de desarrollo de software: una aproximación por puestos de trabajo. Tesis, Universidad Carlos III de Madrid (2014). https://core.ac.uk/download/pdf/29406077.pdf
3. SCRUMstudy.: La Guía para el Cuerpo de Conocimiento de Scrum (Guía SBOK), 4th edn., vol. 4, no. 69. SCRUMstudy (2022)
4. Beck, K., et al.: Manifiesto por el Desarrollo Ágil. Sitio web (2001). https://agilemanifesto.org/iso/es/manifesto.html
5. Digital.AI.: The 17th State of Agile Report (2023). https://digital.ai/es/resource-center/analyst-reports/state-of-agile-report/
6. Scott, E., Charkie, K.N., Pfahl, D.: Productivity, turnover, and team stability of agile teams in open-source software projects. In: 46th Euromicro Conference on Software Engineering and Advanced Applications (SEAA), pp. 124–131 (2020). https://doi.org/10.1109/SEAA51224.2020.00029
7. Mashmool, A., Khosravi, S., Joloudari, J.H., Inayat, I., Gandomani, T.J., Mosavi, A.: A statistical model to assess the team's productivity in agile software teams. In: 2021 IEEE 4th International Conference and Workshop Óbuda on Electrical and Power Engineering (CANDO-EPE), pp. 11–18 (2021). https://doi.org/10.1109/CANDO-EPE54223.2021.9667902
8. Fagerholm, F., Ikonen, M., Kettunen, P., Münch, J., Roto, V., Abrahamsson, P.: How do software developers experience team performance in lean and agile environments? ACM Digital Library (2014). https://doi.org/10.1145/2601248.2601285.
9. Sarpiri, M., Gandomani, T.J: A case study of using the hybrid model of scrum and six sigma in software development. Int. J. Electr. Comput. Eng. 11(6), 5342–5350 (2021). https://doi.org/10.11591/ijece.v11i6.pp5342-5350
10. Jung, M., Chong, J., Leifer, L.: Group hedonic balance and pair programming performance: affective interaction dynamics as indicators of performance. In Proceedings of the SIGCHI Conference on Human Factors in Computing Systems, pp. 829–838 (2012). https://doi.org/10.1145/2207676.2208523

11. Sjoberg, D.I.K.: An empirical study of WIP in kanban teams. ACM Digital Library. doi **10**(1145/3239235), 3239238 (2018). https://doi.org/10.1145/3239235.3239238
12. Dorairaj, S., Noble, J., Malik, P.: Understanding lack of trust in distributed agile teams: a grounded theory study. In: 16th International Conference on Evaluation Assessment in Software Engineering (EASE 2012), pp. 81–90 (2012). https://doi.org/10.1049/ic.2012.0011
13. Melnyk, K., Hlushko, V., Borysova, N.: Decision support technology for sprint planning. Radio Electron. Comput. Sci. Control, 135–145 (2020). https://doi.org/10.15588/1607-3274-2020-1-14
14. Guerrero-Calvache, M., Hernández, G.: Team productivity factors in agile software development: an exploratory survey with practitioners. Appl. Inf., 261–276 (2024).https://doi.org/10.1007/978-3-031-46813-1_18
15. Oliveira, E., Conte, T., Cristo, M., Mendes, E.: Software Project managers' perceptions of productivity factors: findings from a qualitative study. In: Proceedings of the 10th ACM/IEEE International Symposium on Empirical Software Engineering and Measurement (ESEM 2016), pp. 1–6 (2016). https://doi.org/10.1145/2961111.2962626
16. Hernández, G., Navarro, A., Jiménez, R., Jiménez, F.: Cómo los Profesionales Perciben la Relevancia de las Métricas de Productividad para un Equipo Ágil de Desarrollo de Software. Revista Ibérica de Sistemas y Tecnologías de Información **E32**, 596–609 (2020). https://dialnet.unirioja.es/servlet/articulo?codigo=9262435
17. Dingsøyr, M.A., Dybå, T.K., Nilsen, T.P.R.M.: A decade of agile methodologies: towards explaining agile software development. J. Syst. Softw. **85**(6), 1213–1221 (2012). https://doi.org/10.1016/j.jss.2012.02.033
18. Schwaber, K., Sutherland, J.: The Scrum Guide: The Definitive Guide to Scrum: The Rules of the Game (2020). https://scrumguides.org/docs/scrumguide/v2020/2020-Scrum-Guide-US.pdf
19. Sutherland, J.: SCRUM: El arte de hacer el doble de trabajo en la mitad del tiempo (2016)
20. Guerrero-Calvache, M., Hernández, G.: Métricas para la evaluación de factores de productividad de equipo en desarrollo ágil de software: un mapeo sistemático de literatura. TecnoLógicas **27**(59), e2918 (2024). https://doi.org/10.22430/22565337.2918
21. Petersen, K., Vakkalanka, S., Kuzniarz, L.: Guidelines for conducting systematic mapping studies in software engineering: an update. Inf. Softw. Technol. **64**, 1–18 (2015). https://doi.org/10.1016/j.infsof.2015.03.007
22. Kitchenham, B.A., Pfleeger, S.L.: Personal opinion surveys. In: Guide to Advanced Empirical Software Engineering, pp. 157–181. Springer (2008). https://link.springer.com/chapter/10.1007/978-1-84800-044-5_3
23. Hernández, G., Martínez, Á., Jiménez, R., Jiménez, F.: Métricas de productividad para equipo de trabajo de desarrollo ágil de software: una revisión sistemática. TecnoLógicas **22**, 63–81 (2019). https://doi.org/10.22430/22565337.1510
24. Machuca-Villegas, L., Gasca-Hurtado, G.P.: Toward a model based on gamification to influence the productivity of software development teams. In: 2019 14th Iberian Conference on Information Systems and Technologies (CISTI), pp. 1–6 (2019). https://doi.org/10.23919/CISTI.2019.8760813
25. IEEE Computer Society: Software engineering competency model (SWECOM) (2014). https://ieeecs-media.computer.org/media/education/swebok/swecom.pdf
26. Choraś, M., et al.: Measuring and improving agile processes in a small-size software development company. IEEE Access **8**, 78452–78466 (2020). https://doi.org/10.1109/ACCESS.2020.2990117
27. Jain, P., Sharma, A., Ahuja, L.: The impact of agile software development process on the quality of software product. In; 2018 7th International Conference on Reliability, Infocom Technologies and Optimization (Trends and Future Directions) (ICRITO), pp. 812–815 (2018). https://doi.org/10.1109/ICRITO.2018.8748529

28. Fenton, N., Bieman, J.: Software Metrics: A Rigorous and Practical Approach, 3rd edn. CRC Press (2014)
29. OMG: Essence-Kernel and language for software engineering methods (2018). https://www.omg.org/spec/Essence
30. White, S.A., Miers, D.: Guía de Referencia y Modelado BPMN (2009). https://users.dcc.uchile.cl/~nbaloian/DSS-DCC/Software/ModeladoBPMN.pdf
31. Runeson, P., Höst, M.: Guidelines for conducting and reporting case study research in software engineering. Empir. Softw. Eng. **14**(2), 131–164 (2009). https://doi.org/10.1007/s10664-008-9102-8
32. Machuca-Villegas, L., Gasca-Hurtado, G.P., Puente, S.M., Marcela, L., Tamayo, R.: Factores sociales y humanos que influyen en la productividad del desarrollo de software: Medición de la Percepción. RISTI **41**, 488–502 (2021). https://www.risti.xyz/issues/ristie41.pdf
33. Machuca-Villegas, L., Gasca-Hurtado, G.P.: Towards a social and human factor classification related to productivity in software development teams. Adv. Intell. Syst. Comput. **1071**, 36–50 (2020). https://doi.org/10.1007/978-3-030-33547-2_4
34. Machuca-Villegas, L., Gasca-Hurtado, G.P., Restrepo Tamayo, L.M., Puente, S.M.: Social and human factor classification of influence in productivity in software development teams. Commun. Comput. Inf. Sci. **1251**, 717–729 (2020). https://doi.org/10.1007/978-3-030-56441-4_54
35. Machuca-Villegas, L., Gasca-Hurtado, G.P., Morillo Puente, S., Restrepo Tamayo, L.M.: An instrument for measuring perception about social and human factors that influence software development productivity. J. Univ. Comput. Sci.Comput. Sci. **27**(2), 111–134 (2021). https://doi.org/10.3897/jucs.65102
36. Machuca-Villegas, L., Gasca-Hurtado, G.P., Muñoz, M.: Measures related to social and human factors that influence productivity in software development teams. Int. J. Inf. Syst. Project Manage. **9**(3), 43–67 (2021). https://doi.org/10.12821/ijispm090303
37. OMG: Business Process Model and Notation (BPMN), Version 2.0 (2010). https://www.omg.org/spec/BPMN

Generating Local Rules in Fuzzy Rule-Based Classification Systems

Maroua Lejmi[1,2](✉) ⓘ, Bertrand Cuissart[1] ⓘ, Ilef Ben Slima[3,4] ⓘ,
Nida Meddouri[6] ⓘ, Jean-Luc Lamotte[1] ⓘ, and Amel Borgi[5] ⓘ

[1] Université Caen Normandie, ENSICAEN, CNRS, Normandie Univ, GREYC UMR
6072, Caen 14000, France
lejmi.maroua@gmail.com
[2] Université de Tunis El Manar, Faculté des Sciences de Tunis, LIPAH, LR11ES14,
2092 Tunis, Tunisia
[3] ISMAIK, University of Kairouan, Kairouan 3100, Tunisia
[4] SM@RTS: Laboratory of Signals, Systems, Artificial Intelligence and Networks,
Digital Research Center of Sfax, 3021 Sfax, Tunisia
[5] Université de Tunis El Manar, Institut Supérieur d'Informatique, Faculté des
Sciences de Tunis, LIPAH, LR11ES14, 2092 Tunis, Tunisia
[6] Laboratoire de Recherche de L'EPITA, LRE, Le Kremlin-Bicêtre, Paris, France

Abstract. Fuzzy Rule-Based Classification Systems (FRBCS) have
emerged as a powerful model in machine learning and decision-making,
with its capability of handling imprecision and providing understandable
models in diverse applications. The generated rules can sometimes be difficult to interpret in FRBCS, when dealing with a large number of rules.
Additionally, a high number of attributes requires a larger set of rules to
accurately model them which leads to an increased computational complexity. It is also crucial to consider the rules length and generate rules
with short premises in order to improve the system's interpretability.
Researchers use various techniques to reduce the number of attributes
as well as the number of rules. Within this article we are interested in a
technique based on attributes regrouping. We study a particular method
called SIFRA, which we relied on to generate local fuzzy rules in the
simple fuzzy grid with the aim of improving the system performance and
maintaining its interpretability and explainability.

Keywords: Supervised learning · Fuzzy Rule-Based Classification
Systems · Fuzzy rules · Attributes regrouping

1 Introduction

In this paper, we are interested in supervised learning, particularly in Rule-Based
Classification Systems (FRBCS). Their effectiveness consists in their comprehensive models based on linguistic variables where rules can be explicitly formulated and easily interpreted [14]. A FRBCS provides additional flexibility than an

O. Gervasi et al. (Eds.): ICCSA 2025, LNCS 15649, pp. 150–165, 2025.
https://doi.org/10.1007/978-3-031-96997-3_10

ordinary rule-based system by allowing gradual evaluations and handling uncertainty [3]. It should be noted that in Fuzzy Rule-Based classification Systems, all attributes are numerical. In FRBCS design, the number of fuzzy rules grows exponentially with the increase in the number of attributes. This makes the model computationally expensive, especially with high-dimensional data, which in turn results in a degraded interpretation [14]. To overcome this problem, various methods are employed beforehand. These methods involve techniques like attributes selection, rules extraction, rules induction, and attributes regrouping. The last technique can also play a role in reducing complexity by creating simpler models. The attributes regrouping technique in FRBCS, has been effectively applied by various approaches such as SIFCO [20], which uses linear correlation to detect related attributes that will be gathered together and used in fuzzy rules generation. SIFCO uses measures based on statistical concepts. However, there may be other types of linkage between variables that cannot be calculated by statistical measures. Thus, another attributes regrouping method in FRBCS, called SIFRA [4], was proposed to detect associations between both numerical and categorical variables. It consists of determining related groups of attributes based on an association rules concept, precisely the Frequent Itemsets Mining. It is used to calculate a coefficient called the association degree between attributes [11]. In this context, we are interested in the SIFRA approach. SIFRA was compared to the selection attributes method and rules selection approach [10, 13]. The results in terms of classification rate have shown that SIFRA outperforms various state-of-the-art methods [4]. The attributes regrouping approach introduced in SIFRA offers a way to reduce the complexity of FRBCS by regrouping related attributes and generating fuzzy rules for each group of attributes separately. We focused on the determination of associated attributes step of this method because they introduced a captivating technique. It consists of determining frequent itemsets between attributes intervals to outline the linkage between these attributes. In this paper, we propose a new contribution for the generation of candidate fuzzy rules in FRBCS. It consists of finding interesting rules in the fuzzy grid inspired by the SIFRA proposed technique of searching linked attributes. We applied our method to some UCI classification datasets and the results reveal the feasibility of the proposed method.

This paper is organized as follows. In Sect. 2, we recall the basic concepts of FRBCS. In Sect. 3, we present some of state-of-the-art methods. In Sect. 4, the SIFRA method is briefly described. Section 5 is devoted to the introduction of the proposed contribution. Before concluding, we discuss in Sect. 6 the experimental results obtained by computer simulations using different datasets.

2   Fuzzy Rule-Based Classification Systems

FRBCS automatically generate a set of IF-THEN fuzzy rules from numerical data in the learning phase. The classification phase uses a reasoning method to classify new objects. Diverse rule generation methods in FRBCS have been proposed in the literature. Fuzzy decision trees have been used in rule-based learning to construct fuzzy rules from numerical data [21] in order to handle situations where the decision is not binary but rather fuzzy. Neural networks offer another alternative for generating fuzzy rules [15,16]. An innovative contribution has been proposed to simplify real-world complex problems. It involves generating fuzzy rules in FRBCS and is based on a granular reduct. This approach is a type of consistency-preserving attribute reduction method aimed at finding a minimal attributes set while maintaining the predefined consistency level unchanged [17].

Another well-known method from the literature, which is of particular interest to us, is the simple fuzzy grid method [9]. It is one of the earliest methods proposed in this field. It generates the fuzzy rules using a fuzzy grid, which involves partitioning the input space into subspaces and constructing a rule for each subspace. Like all supervised methods, the system described in [9] consists of two main phases: a learning phase and a classification phase. They are detailed in the following sections.

2.1   Learning Phase

In the learning phase, we employ the simple fuzzy grid as in [9]. In fact, the simple fuzzy grid partition has been widely used in pattern recognition and fuzzy reasoning [4]. It is important to note that the notations presented in [9] are used in this section.

We consider a two-dimensional pattern classification problem with two numerical attributes: X_1 and X_2 with C classes and m given training patterns. Each pattern belongs to one of the C class labels $(y_1, y_2, \ldots, y_c)$. The extension of this approach to N attributes is straightforward. The first step is the fuzzy partitioning step where each of the attributes X_1 and X_2 is partitioned into k fuzzy subsets: $A_1^k, A_2^k, ..., A_k^k$ where each A_i^k subset is defined by a membership function. There are several membership functions in the literature such as triangular, trapezoidal and Gaussian functions [19]. In this study, we have employed the triangular membership function which is one of the most encountered in practice. After completing the fuzzy partitioning step, a simple fuzzy grid is obtained, as shown in Fig. 1 (with $k = 3$). The second step is the construction of the fuzzy rules. For each fuzzy subspace $A_i^k \times A_j^k$ of the fuzzy grid, a fuzzy rule labeled R_{ij}^k is generated, accompanied by its certainty factor (CF) as illustrated in equation (1). If a subspace does not contain instances, the algorithm does not allow a rule to be generated in this region. The conclusion and the certainty factor CF are determined as proposed in [9].

$$R_{ij}^k : \text{If } X_1 \text{ is } A_i^k \text{ and } X_2 \text{ is } A_j^k \text{ then } E = (X_1, X_2) \text{ belongs to } y_{ij}^k \text{ with } CF = CF_{ij}^k \tag{1}$$

Where:

- R_{ij}^k: is the label of fuzzy If-then rules,
- k: is the number of fuzzy subsets for the two axes,
- A_i^k and A_j^k: are fuzzy subsets,
- y_{ij}^k: is the consequent (one of the C classes $\{y_1, y_2, ..., y_c\}$),

– CF_{ij}^k: is the certainty factor of the fuzzy if-then rule.

The conclusion and the certainty factor are determined as follows:

1. For each class y_t, the sum of the compatibility degrees of the training examples belonging to this class is calculated, with respect to the premise of the rule:

$$\beta y_t = \sum_{Y(E_p)=y_t} \mu_i^k(X_{1p}) * \mu_j^k(X_{2p}) ; \quad t = 1, 2, ..., C \tag{2}$$

where:
   – y_t: a class among the C classes $y_1, y_2, ..., y_c$
   – $E_p = (X_{1p}, X_{2p})$: a learning example,
   – $Y(E_p)$: the associated class to the example E_p,
   – μ_i^k, μ_j^k: membership functions of A_i^k and A_j^k.
2. Find the class y_a that has the maximum value of βy_t; assign this class as the consequent of R_{ij}^k ($y_{ij}^k = y_a$).

$$\beta y_a = max\{\beta y_1, \beta y_2, ..., \beta y_c\} \tag{3}$$

3. CF_{ij}^k is determined as:

$$CF_{ij}^k = \frac{|\beta y_a - \beta|}{\sum_{t=1}^C \beta y_t} \quad with \quad \beta = \sum_{y_t \neq y_a} \frac{\beta y_t}{C-1} \tag{4}$$

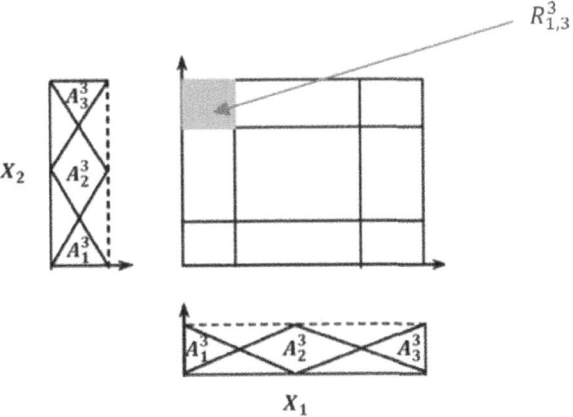

Fig. 1. A fuzzy grid with 2 attributes and 3 fuzzy subsets for each attribute [4]

2.2   Classification Phase

This phase consists of finding the class that will be associated to a new object. Several methods are used in FRBCS such the single winner rule method [9]. Other studies have used another classification method, called the Weighted Vote Method, which takes into account the votes of several rules that match the example to be classified [6,8]. In this work, we applied the single winner rule method. The class y_a that will be associated to a new pattern $E' = (X'_1, X'_2)$ using the previously generated rules set, denoted S_R, is determined as follows :

1. For each class y_t, $t = 1, 2, \ldots, C$, calculate α_{y_t} as:

$$\alpha_{y_t} = max\left\{\mu_i^k(X'_1) * \mu_j^k(X'_2) * CF_{ij}^k \, / \;\; y_{ij}^k = y_t; R_{ij}^k \in S_R\right\} \tag{5}$$

2. Find class y_a which maximizes α_{y_t}:

$$\alpha_{y_a} = max\left\{\alpha_{y_1}, \alpha_{y_2}, ..., \alpha_{y_C}\right\} \tag{6}$$

When two or more classes reach this maximum, the object cannot be classified.

3   Background

In this section, we present some methods from related work that were proposed in the context of fuzzy systems such as attributes selection, rules extraction and attributes regrouping. In [13], a method was proposed for fuzzy feature selection. This method selects the most relevant features capable of distinguishing between classes. It uses the membership degrees of positive and negative patterns in the fuzzy sets in order to compute the relevance of features to the classes. The generation of rules in fuzzy rule-based classifiers was done by using the selected features and their effective fuzzy sets. In [12], another approach was introduced, which proposes an iterative feature selection in fuzzy rule-based binary classifier. The algorithm presents an iterative framework for feature selection and then extracts fuzzy bicluster rules instead of deterministic rules. This helps retaining more useful information in the fuzzy rules and improving the performance. In [5], the authors employed a rules induction technique that combines rough set and fuzzy set theories to obtain a reduced set of interpretable rules with short premises. The technique of rules extraction was proposed in [18], based on an incremental feature selection process. The method begins by extracting an initial minimal set of attributes, referred to as a granular reduct. Then, it generates fuzzy rules based on the selected set of attributes. Additionally, the granular reduct and the fuzzy rules are incrementally updated as new objects are added. Contrarily to feature selection, attributes regrouping retains all attributes. However, the complexity is reduced by handling subsets of the original attributes where, each subset is a projection of the data into a lower dimensional subspace. In this context, a method called SIFCO was proposed in [20]. It is based on a linear correlation search. The SIFCO method gathers attributes that are correlated into groups of attributes and treats each group independently. In [4], an approach called SIFRA was proposed, which simplifies the FRBCS by introducing a method for grouping attributes based on their associations. It detects several types of associations, not only linear correlation. In the following, we describe the SIFRA method, which served as an inspiration for our contribution.

4   SIFRA

SIFRA is a supervised learning method that offers an attributes regrouping technique to create groups of attributes. Then each group is used separately to construct a fuzzy rule base. Later, these bases are aggregated together to form the global rules base, which is used in the classification phase. The attributes regrouping approach was effectively used in FRBCSs by various methods notably SIFCO [20] which uses linear correlation to detect related attributes and SIFRA [4], which consists of determining related groups of attributes based on the Frequent Itemsets Mining concept of Association Rules (AR) [11]. The main objective of SIFRA is to reduce the complexity of FRBCS which are especially complex when treating a dataset with many attributes. The attributes regrouping approach used in SIFRA helps to decompose the searching space into smaller groups of attributes and treat each group separately. This choice is motivated by the effectiveness of ensemble methods [7] in improving predictive performance and enhancing interpretability by dividing complex problems into smaller, more manageable subproblems. SIFRA consists in 3 phases: the attributes regrouping phase, the learning phase, and the classification phase. We focus on the attributes regrouping phase, the following two phases are identical to those used in FRBCS as described in Sect. 2 [9]. The attributes regrouping method in SIFRA includes 3 main steps: mining frequent itemsets, detection of associated attributes, and selection of the final groups of attributes. We provide in the following subsections a description of each step in the attributes regrouping method. The interested reader can refer to the work [4] for more details on this approach.

4.1   Mining Frequent Itemsets

In order to search for frequent itemsets, a specific algorithm such as Apriori is used [1]. An itemset is considered frequent if its support value is greater than a predefined threshold named *minsupp*. The support refers to the frequency of occurrence of an itemset. In our context, attributes are numerical and an itemset is a set of attributes intervals. First, a discretization is used to split into intervals the numerical attributes and map them into boolean ones. Different types of discretization can be used [4]. In SIFRA, the Equal Width Interval (EWI), which divides the numerical range into intervals of equal size and ensures a uniform partitioning of the data space, was used. Apriori is later performed and frequent itemsets are obtained, where each frequent itemset represents a set of related intervals.

4.2 Detection of Associated Attributes

In order to detect the related attributes, the authors in [4] have proposed an association grid which highlights the associations between attributes intervals. When two intervals form a frequent itemset, the cell corresponding to their intersection represents a related region, colored in grey as shown in Fig. 2. Through these regions, we can determine the association between the attributes by computing an association degree β that takes into account the number of the linked regions as well as their density.

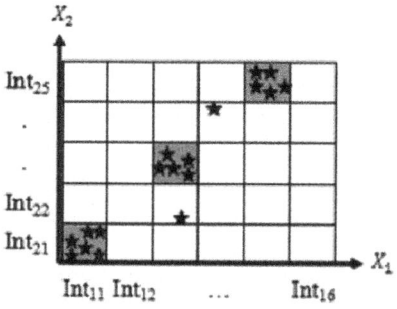

Fig. 2. An association grid example [4]

4.3 Selection of the Final Groups of Attributes

The final step is the selection of the final groups of attributes. A filtering step is used to select the most relevant groups, those with a high association degree β and a high cardinality [4]. After determining the associated groups of attributes, each group is treated independently by a FRBCS [9] as described in Sect. 2. The global rules base is then obtained by the union of the different rule bases and is denoted GR.

5 Proposed Contribution

Our contribution is based on the generation of fuzzy rules in the simple fuzzy grid. In classic FRBCS, when the fuzzy grid is employed, the number of the generated fuzzy rules is very high and increases with the increase of the number of attributes. For N attributes partitioned into k subsets, the number of rules is k^N. For example, if we consider a dataset with 12 attributes, each partitioned into 3 subsets, the number of generated rules is $3^{12} = 531441$. SIFRA reduces this problem by the attributes regrouping method. When the N attributes are divided into groups, the number of rules NB_{rules} is calculated as follows:

$$NB_{rules} = \sum_{i=1}^{n} k^{N_i} \leq \prod_{i=1}^{n} k^{N_i} = k^{\sum_{i=1}^{n} N_i} = k^N \qquad (7)$$

where:

- n is the number of groups of related attributes.
- the groups of attributes constitute a partition of the entire set of attributes ($\sum_{i=1}^{n} N_i = N$).
- N_i is the number of attributes for the group g_i.

For example, with SIFRA, if the 12 attributes are divided into 3 groups, the first with 6 attributes, the second with 4 attributes and the third with 2 attributes, then the number of rules generated is $3^6 + 3^4 + 3^2 = 819$ which is significantly lower than 531441. The SIFRA method overcomes the problem of the explosion in the number of fuzzy rules in FRBCS, but it may miss generating some interesting rules during the attributes regrouping phase. In fact, SIFRA takes into consideration the number of linked regions and their density as two factors in the detection of associated attributes. With this approach, not all the linked attributes are used to generate the fuzzy rules. More precisely, the linkage between two intervals of two attributes does not necessarily imply a linkage between the two attributes in SIFRA. This is because either these attributes can have very few linked regions, or the amount of data in these regions is significantly lower compared to the total amount of data. The case of very few linked regions is illustrated in the association grid AG2 in Fig. 3 where only one region is formed. By ignoring these attributes in the filtering step of SIFRA, some linked regions will be neglected, accordingly some attributes will not be considered together later while generating the fuzzy rules whereas potentially, these attributes might enhance the classification rate. So, there may be interesting rules that remain unexplored in SIFRA due to its attributes regrouping phase.

In our work, we aim to address the problem of a large number of fuzzy rules in classic FRBCS while maintaining good system classification performance. Unlike SIFRA, our contribution does not include an attributes regrouping step. In our contribution, instead of generating all the rules from each cell of the simple fuzzy grid, as described in Sect. 2 [9], we choose to select some cells based on the association between attributes intervals. The process consists of searching frequent intervals of attributes imitating the Mining Frequent itemsets technique that was proposed in the SIFRA method. SIFRA presents this step to determine the associated attributes and regrouping them based on this association. On the other hand, we employ it to search for related intervals between attributes in the fuzzy grid for the purpose of generating fuzzy rules in some specific and interesting regions in the grid which reduces the number of fuzzy rules obtained by the FRBCS. This approach may generate fuzzy rules not generated by SIFRA.

Our method begins by applying a discretization step to split the numerical attributes into intervals and then detects those that are related through the algorithm of frequent itemsets mining, Apriori, as SIFRA (Sect. 4). When a set of intervals is determined to be frequent by Apriori, their corresponding intersection is then considered as related. Our contribution focuses on choosing these related intervals in the simple fuzzy grid in order to generate a local fuzzy rule in each of the related cells. Our method implies two solutions as shown in Fig. 3. In the first solution, we begin by determining the linked regions between attributes using the association grid. Once these regions are detected, we do not apply the regrouping phase as SIFRA, we only take into account the related regions and we generate a fuzzy rule in each of them exclusively as demonstrated in the left side grids of Fig. 3 (a rule is generated in each greyed-out cell). This allows us to take into account the regions that could have been neglected in the SIFRA method and lost during the selection step. The obtained rule base is called : the Local Rules base denoted LR. An excerpt of local rules and those generated by SIFRA is provided in the appendix A to highlight the differences between the two approaches. Since some fuzzy rules obtained by our first solution do not appear in the SIFRA method and vice versa, we proposed a second solution where GR (the Global Rules base generated by SIFRA) and LR are combined to enrich each other. We denoted this rules base CR (Combined Rules base). Figure 3 represents the two solutions, additionally the SIFRA process to effectively illustrate the proposed ideas.

In order to clarify the method, consider two association grids that illustrate the related regions between attributes as shown in the example in Fig. 3. For a simpler explanation, we present two-dimensional grids. However, these grids can be multidimensional depending on the number of attributes. The grid AG1 represents the association between X_1 and X_2, and the second grid AG2 illustrates the association between X_4 and X_5. While generating the Local Rules Base (LR), we consider only the related regions, i.e., regions that surpass the support threshold while applying Apriori. Consequently, a fuzzy grid with the same size as each association grid is generated and fuzzy rules are then constructed. In this example (Fig. 3), three fuzzy rules are derived from the first fuzzy grid and only one fuzzy rule is generated in the second fuzzy grid since the two other regions containing examples (Int4,4 x Int5,4) and (Int4,1 x Int5,1) do not form linked regions. As explained in the previous section, the generation of the Global Rules Base (GR) of SIFRA is preceded by a regrouping attributes step which requires a minimum association between the attributes in order to form groups of attributes. In this example, the attributes X_1 and X_2 are considered associated and form a group of attributes. However, X_4 and X_5 have only one linked region so they are not associated and AG2 is not considered in SIFRA. In this case, one fuzzy grid is generated for X_1 and X_2, and fuzzy rules are derived from all grid cells including related and unrelated regions (see FG1 in Fig. 3).

For attributes partitioning, we employ the Equal Width Interval (EWI) and Equal Frequency Interval (EFI) discretization methods. EWI, which was already used and tested in SIFRA, does not account for data distribution, which may lead to intervals with sparse or unrepresentative data. To address this limitation, we propose the use of EFI in addition, which divides the variation domain of the attribute into a predefined number of intervals so that each interval contains approximately the same number of data points. This ensures that all intervals have a sufficient amount of data, making them more suitable for frequent item-sets mining by avoiding intervals with low support. The applied discretization methods are parametric and require a predefined number of intervals k, set by the user. There are methods that do not use a pre-determined parameter, such as supervised discretization methods [2]. They consider the class information and seek to select the intervals that best discriminate the class, unlike unsupervised discretization methods that divide attributes into a specific number of intervals, regardless of their discriminating capacity. We aim to use supervised techniques as perspective.

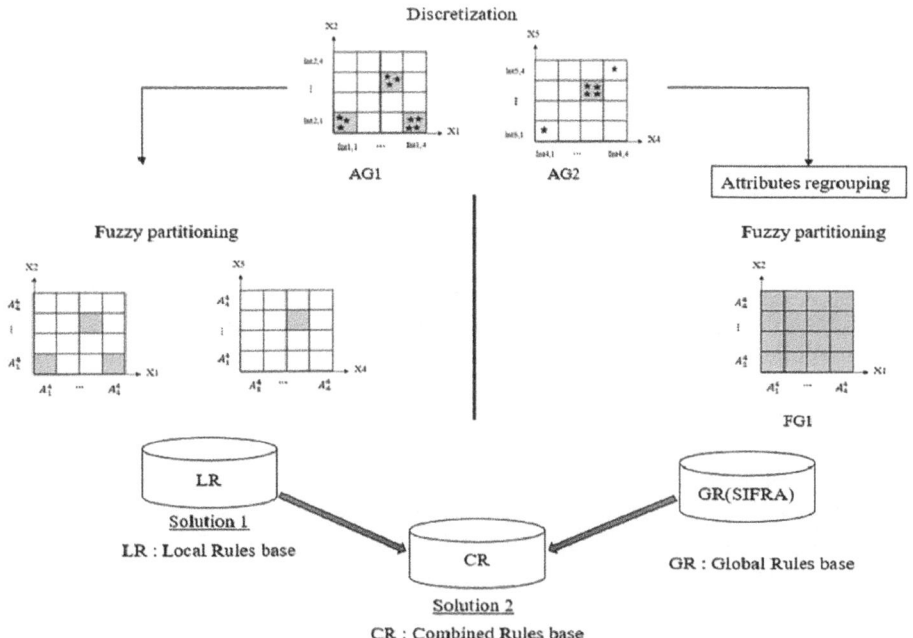

Fig. 3. Schematic representation of the proposed method

6   Experimentation and Test Results

Our contribution was implemented using the library from the WEKA 2 platform[1]. The data structures from WEKA were also adopted. Additionally, we

---
[1] https://ml.cms.waikato.ac.nz/weka/.

relied on the SIFRA system. We used a part of the code (specifically for frequent itemset generation with Apriori and the classification phase). During the learning phase, we integrated our own code to modify the rules generation phase. We conducted experiments with 7 databases from UCI[2] described in Table 1. We chose these databases because they have different sizes and a different number of classes. We recall that in the context of FRBCS, all attributes are numerical.

Table 1. Databases used in the experimentations.

Database	Number of instances	Number of attributes	Number of classes
Iris	150	4	3
Diabetes	768	8	2
Glass	214	9	7
Ecoli	336	7	8
Wine	178	13	3
Heart-statlog	270	13	2
Vehicle	846	18	4

For the experiments, we have three parameters that should be set: the discretization and the minimum support *minsupp* used for the application of Apriori and the discretization used in the fuzzy partitioning in the learning phase of the FRBCS. These parameters were set empirically and a complementary study will be conducted in the future to examine the impact of the parameters on the results. While determining the thresholds of different parameters, we noted from the tests that the choice of appropriate values is highly data-dependent. For this reason, we tested several values of these parameters and choose the best results obtained for each database. As a reminder, in our contribution, the discretization and the number of intervals used for Apriori have to be the same used in the fuzzy partitioning as explained in Sect. 5. We tested two types of discretization: Equal Width Interval (EWI) and Equal Frequency Interval (EFI) with different number of intervals. We used EFI for all tested databases except Iris. In general, EFI gives better results since it divides the attributes according to frequency, which ensures that the regions between the attributes contain data. EWI is not very effective because, when dividing by intervals, some regions contain no data, while some intervals are densely populated, and others have only few instances. However, in Iris, when the attributes are divided into 3 partitions, the intervals are more dense. In Table 2, we present the different thresholds set for each parameter: *minsupp*, the type of discretization, and the number of intervals k. These values were used in all methods, namely LR (Local Rules Base), CR (Combined Rules base), and GR (the Global Rules base generated by SIFRA).

---

[2] https://archive.ics.uci.edu/datasets.

Table 2. Tested parameters.

Database	$minsupp$	Discretization	k
Iris	0.1	EWI	3
Diabetes	0.2	EFI	4
Glass			
Ecoli			
Wine			
Heart-statlog			
Vehicle			

Table 3. Experimental results

Database	LR		CR		GR (SIFRA)	
	Classification rate %	Number of rules	Classification rate %	Number of rules	Classification rate %	Number of rules
Iris	90.6	33	**91.3**	39	84.6	14
Diabetes	**72.5**	25	71.74	32	70.7	34
Glass	**50.4**	35	48.13	45	44.85	33
Ecoli	63.09	54	**66.36**	60	62.5	20
Wine	**86.51**	46	86.51	51	84.8	50
Heart-statlog	**67.4**	138	67.4	158	58.8	41
Vehicle	43.02	168	42.9	179	**45.70**	70

In order to provide a comprehensive evaluation and comparison of our method, we choose the Classification Rate and the Number of Rules as indicators. For the evaluation, we used the tenfold crossvalidation technique.

The outcomes obtained from our proposed solutions and the SIFRA approach are given in Table 3. In general, our two approaches give better results than SIFRA for six datasets among the seven tested. Our proposed Local Rules Base (LR) consistently outperforms the Global Rules Base (GR) for Iris, Diabetes, Ecoli, Glass, Wine and Heart-statlog in terms of classification rate. This amelioration is due to the fact that LR contains rules that do not exist in GR (they were not generated in SIFRA), which proves that these rules can be more effective and contribute well to the classification. Better results are given with the Combined Rules Base (CR) for Iris and Ecoli. In these two databases, LR has higher classification rate than GR, however when their rules are combined the results are improved, which demonstrates that the local fuzzy rules can enhance the classification of the global system. Also the two rule sets have interesting rules that complement each other when performed together. Moreover, this reflects that some of the rules in LR have a better quality than GR since CR chooses rules from both LR and GR for the classification. SIFRA outperforms LR and CR for Vehicle which is a dataset with higher number of attributes. We note that our method performs better on small databases. However, our contribution

LR generates a higher number of rules than SIFRA with five databases. This is due to the fact that we extract more rules in the fuzzy grid without regrouping the attributes. Concerning the rules length, our local rules have shorter premises then the SIFRA rules because they do not cover all attributes intervals. Overall, CR has higher number of rules because it combines rules from LR and GR. SIFRA has been compared with other state-of-the-art methods. It presents better results for classification rates in most cases compared to FRBCS. It also showed good performance when compared to ensemble methods [4].

7   Conclusion

We provide in this work a new method to improve the generation of fuzzy rules in a FRBCS inspired by the SIFRA method, which implies an approach of regrouping attributes based on the associations between their intervals. We proposed a generation of local fuzzy rules in the simple fuzzy grid extracted from the related intervals of attributes. Our contribution demonstrates a significant improvement in classification rates across most of the tested databases with an appropriate number of rules. In future work, we plan to reduce the number of rules and, more generally, to carry out an in-depth analysis to detect the most relevant ones. We also propose to perform tests with more high-dimensional databases and make more comparisons with recent methods and other methods that have been compared with SIFRA [4]. Thus, it could be interesting to combine feature selection methods with our approach in the pre-treatment phase.

Acknowledgments. This work has been achieved thanks to the financial support of PHC UTIQUE 2022 "Paprica", project number 22G1405 (partnership of the French Ministry of Europe and Foreign Affairs and the Tunisian Ministry of Higher Education and Scientific Research)

A   Appendix: Global and Local Rules

To highlight the difference between the global rules generated by SIFRA and the local rules, we present the results of the SIFRA rules in comparison with those generated by our proposed method. This is illustrated through the example of the Iris database. The four attributes of this data set, namely SepalLength, Sepal-Width, PetalLength, and PetalWidth, are displayed with their respective indices: 0, 1, 2, and 3. In this test, each attribute is partitioned into three intervals. Class labels, namely Iris-setosa, Iris-versicolor, and Iris-virginica, are denoted by their indices 0, 1, and 2.

A.1   Global Rules (GR)

Global rules (GR) are the fuzzy rules generated by the SIFRA method, after a regrouping attributes phase. As input, the method receives all the attributes and identifies those that have significant associations. Then, during the selection phase, it retains the related groups that exceed a minimum association threshold, as explained in Sect. 4. In the example below of Fig. 4, we present the related groups followed by the global rules. Two related groups were identified, where each group has two associated attributes. The first group, (0, 2), consists of attribute 0 and attribute 2, which are highlighted in red. The second group, (1,3), contains attribute 1 and attribute 3, which are highlighted in green. During the fuzzy rules generation step, only rules involving attribute pairs (0, 2) and (1, 3) were generated.

A fuzzy rule is represented as follows: [[0, 1], [2, 1], 0, 0.9557560104405949], where each pair in square brackets corresponds to an attribute and its associated interval, for example, [0, 1] denotes attribute 0 with interval 1, and [2, 1] denotes attribute 2 with interval 1. The third element (0) indicates the class label, and the final value (0.9557560104405949) represents the rule's certainty factor (CF).

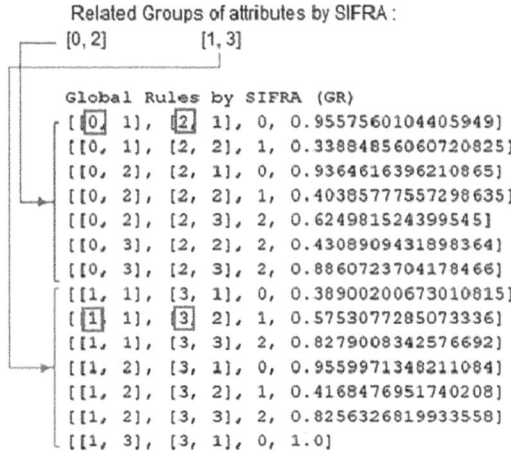

Fig. 4. Global rules generated with Iris dataset

A.2   Local Rules (LR)

Local rules are generated in our method by taking into consideration the frequent intervals between attributes. Once an attribute contains a frequent interval, a rule is generated using that interval. If two intervals belonging to two different attributes are detected as associated and frequent (frequently occurring together), a rule is created for the region combining both attributes with their respective intervals, and so on. For example, in Fig 5, attribute 0 is frequent in two intervals 1 and 2, so a rule is generated with each interval (rules framed in orange). Only one rule can be detected between the attributes 0 and 3 because they only have one intersection considered frequent, which is between the first interval of each of these attributes: [0, 1], [3, 1] (the rule framed in red in Fig 5).

As a result, many combinations between multiple attributes can be formed, though not across all their intervals, as shown by Fig 5. Only the linked regions between attributes identified as frequent are considered. This is the key difference between our rules and those generated by SIFRA.

```
Local Rules (LR)
[0]    [[0, 1], 0, 0.5969465796315772]
       [[0, 2], 1, 0.11608961770909035]
[1]    [[1, 1], 1, 0.3462686340908218]
       [[1, 2], 2, 0.026455024953271736]
[2]    [[2, 1], 0, 0.9478487563799768]
       [[2, 2], 1, 0.35714284532869367]
       [[2, 3], 2, 0.7028780883751137]
[3]    [[3, 1], 0, 0.9186746683396233]
       [[3, 2], 1, 0.4365078993395103]
       [[3, 3], 2, 0.8319671657001529]

[0, 1]    [[0, 1], [1, 2], 0, 0.7082024849919638]
          [[0, 2], [1, 2], 1, 0.09211819312396635]
[0, 2]    [[0, 1], [2, 1], 0, 0.9557560104405949]
          [[0, 2], [2, 3], 2, 0.624981524399545]
[0, 3]    [[0, 1], [3, 1], 0, 0.9448676323584767]
[1, 2]    [[1, 1], [2, 2], 1, 0.566089792391725]
          [[1, 2], [2, 2], 1, 0.30847424516440786]
[1, 3]    [[1, 1], [3, 2], 1, 0.5753077285073336]
          [[1, 2], [3, 2], 1, 0.4168476951740208]
[2, 3]    [[2, 1], [3, 1], 0, 0.9876735047584314]
          [[2, 2], [3, 2], 1, 0.652690471839652]

[0, 1, 2]    [[0, 1], [1, 2], [2, 1], 0, 0.9807008210900543]
             [[0, 2], [1, 2], [2, 2], 1, 0.37349825540177967]
[0, 1, 3]    [[0, 1], [1, 2], [3, 1], 0, 0.9769783473477771]
             [[0, 2], [1, 2], [3, 2], 1, 0.4892444841348519]
[0, 2, 3]    [[0, 1], [2, 1], [3, 1], 0, 0.9892136675834491]
[1, 2, 3]    [[1, 1], [2, 2], [3, 2], 1, 0.7044421193519913]
             [[1, 2], [2, 2], [3, 2], 1, 0.6391673226696912]
[0, 1, 2, 3]    [[0, 1], [1, 2], [2, 1], [3, 1], 0, 0.9959358957085745]
                [[0, 2], [1, 2], [2, 2], [3, 2], 1, 0.6555817027360848]
```

Fig. 5. Local rules generated with Iris dataset

References

1. Agrawal, R., Srikant, R.: Fast algorithms for mining association rules. In: Proceedings of the 20th International Conference Very Large Data Bases, VLDB, vol. 1215, pp. 487–499. Santiago, Chile (1994)
2. Aristodimou, A., Diavastos, A., Pattichis, C.S.: A fast supervised density-based discretization algorithm for classification tasks in the medical domain. Health Inform. J. **28**(1), 14604582211065396 (2022)
3. Bardossy, A., Duckstein, L.: Fuzzy Rule-Based Modeling with Applications to Geophysical. CRC Press, Biological and Engineering Systems (2022)
4. Ben Slima, I., Borgi, A.: Supervised methods for regrouping attributes in fuzzy rule-based classification systems. Appl. Intell. **48**(12), 4577–4593 (2018). https://doi.org/10.1007/s10489-018-1224-0

5. Bollaert, H., Palangetić, M., Cornelis, C., Greco, S., Słowiński, R.: FRRI: a novel algorithm for fuzzy-rough rule induction. Inf. Sci. **686**, 121362 (2025)
6. Cordón, O., Del Jesus, M.J., Herrera, F.: A proposal on reasoning methods in fuzzy rule-based classification systems. Int. J. Approx. Reason. **20**(1), 21–45 (1999)
7. Dietterich, T.G.: Ensemble methods in machine learning. In: Multiple Classifier Systems, pp. 1–15. Lecture Notes in Computer Science, Springer, Berlin, Heidelberg (2000)
8. Ishibuchi, H., Nakashima, T., Morisawa, T.: Voting in fuzzy rule-based systems for pattern classification problems. Fuzzy Sets Syst. **103**(2), 223–238 (1999)
9. Ishibuchi, H., Nozaki, K., Tanaka, H.: Distributed representation of fuzzy rules and its application to pattern classification. Fuzzy Sets Syst. **52**(1), 21–32 (1992)
10. Ishibuchi, H., Yamamoto, T.: Rule weight specification in fuzzy rule-based classification systems. IEEE Trans. Fuzzy Syst. **13**(4), 428–435 (2005)
11. Lejmi, M., Ben Slima, I., Borgi, A.: Attributes regrouping by genetic algorithm in fuzzy inference systems. Proc. Comput. Sci. **207**, 1037–1046 (2022)
12. Li, H., Wang, C., Huang, Q.: Employing iterative feature selection in fuzzy rule-based binary classification. IEEE Transactions on Fuzzy Systems (2024)
13. Mansoori, E.G., Shafiee, K.S.: On fuzzy feature selection in designing fuzzy classifiers for high-dimensional data. Evol. Syst. **7**, 255–265 (2016)
14. Marbun, M., Sitompul, O.S., Nababan, E.B., Sihombing, P.: Framework for Optimizing The Performance of Fuzzy Grid Partition for Rules Generation. In: 2022 IEEE International Conference of Computer Science and Information Technology (ICOSNIKOM), pp. 1–7. IEEE, Laguboti, North Sumatra, Indonesia (Oct 2022)
15. Mazieres, A.: Cartographie de l'apprentissage artificiel et de ses algorithmes. Université Paris Diderot, Manuscrit de thèse (2016)
16. Mitra, S., Hayashi, Y.: Neuro-fuzzy rule generation: survey in soft computing framework. IEEE Trans. Neural Netw. **11**(3), 748–768 (May 2000). https://doi.org/10.1109/72.846746, conference Name: IEEE Transactions on Neural Networks
17. Niu, J., Chen, D., Li, J., Wang, H.: Fuzzy rule-based classification method for incremental rule learning. IEEE Trans. Fuzzy Syst. **30**(9), 3748–3761 (2021)
18. Niu, J., Chen, D., Li, J., Wang, H.: Fuzzy rule-based classification method for incremental rule learning. IEEE Trans. Fuzzy Syst. **30**(9), 3748–3761 (2022). https://doi.org/10.1109/TFUZZ.2021.3128061
19. Sadollah, A.: Introductory chapter: which membership function is appropriate in fuzzy system? In: Fuzzy Logic Based in Optimization Methods and Control Systems and Its Applications. IntechOpen (Oct 2018)
20. Soua, B., Borgi, A., Tagina, M.: An ensemble method for fuzzy rule-based classification systems. Knowl. Inf. Syst. **36**(2), 385–410 (2013)
21. Wang, X., Liu, X., Pedrycz, W., Zhang, L.: Fuzzy rule based decision trees. Pattern Recogn. **48**(1), 50–59 (2015)

Leveraging Large Language Models for Natural Language Processing Based Tasks in the Legal Domain: A Short Survey

Yavuz Balı[1,2(✉)] and Birol Çiloğlugil[3]

[1] Institute of Natural Sciences, Department of Computer Engineering,
Ege University, 35100 Bornova, Izmir, Turkey
9122001744@ogrenci.ege.edu.tr
[2] Intelligent Application Department, Huawei R&D Center, Istanbul, Turkey
[3] Faculty of Engineering, Department of Computer Engineering, Ege University,
35100 Bornova, Izmir, Turkey
birol.ciloglugil@ege.edu.tr

Abstract. The integration of natural language processing techniques (NLP) into the legal domain has opened up new possibilities for automating, analyzing, and improving access to legal information. However, the complex and specialized terminology of legal texts has always been a significant challenge for the NLP area. To overcome this challenge, research studies in the law domain conducted with NLP techniques can be categorized into the following tasks: classification, information extraction, summarization, information retrieval, legal judgment prediction. Recent advancements in large language models (LLMs) have significantly contributed to NLP tasks across various domains, including the aforementioned tasks in the legal domain. The ability of large language models to reason and understand the deep context of texts has shown promising capabilities for understanding legal language and overcoming legal challenges. Therefore, this paper explores the existing tasks addressed by NLP in the legal domain and delves into LLM-based approaches which address these NLP tasks. Moreover, the datasets and evaluation criteria for LLMs have been examined, and the challenges and key limitations of LLMs in the legal domain have been identified. Hallucination, lack of domain-specific knowledge, and lack of interpretability have been determined as the challenges for the reliable application of large language models in the legal field. Finally, opportunities for future research have been discussed.

Keywords: Law · Legal Domain · Large Language Models · Natural Language Processing

1 Introduction

It was asserted by [16] in 1987 that technology will standardize and automate a significant portion of legal services, and these advancements were defined as

O. Gervasi et al. (Eds.): ICCSA 2025, LNCS 15649, pp. 166–178, 2025.
https://doi.org/10.1007/978-3-031-96997-3_11

Legal Tech. The processes within the legal domain are predominantly textual. Hence the domain is inherently a significant research area for Natural Language Processing (NLP). In this regard, there are many studies and approaches to facilitate legal processes. In particular with the development of artificial intelligence technologies, the volume of studies in Legal Tech is increasing considerably.

Rapidly enhancing artificial intelligence technologies affect many domain and change information processing approaches. These enhancements affect the legal domain as it affects other fields [19]. Hence, novel methods are being developed to address legal challenges. The volume of electronic legal documents and legal texts increases exponentially with digitization in the legal domain [1]. The types of documents encompass a broad range, including legal norms, contracts, court rulings, and patents. They are typically detailed and lengthy, with an inherently complex structure that makes exploration challenging [4]. As it depends on high volume of written text, law is an essential application field of NLP [23]. As a result, reasoning and comprehension can be difficult for legal documents [28]. In particular, the unique terminology of legal texts makes its significantly difficult to understand and analyze. The complexity and high amount of legal texts constitute crucial challenges even for the legal professionals [35].

One of the state-of-the-art techniques in the area of natural language processing, Large Language Models (LLMs), have significantly proven their superior performance in understanding natural language. In particular, the GPT-3 model developed by OpenAI attracts attention with its ability to produce human-like texts in diverse language tasks [6]. The models have made significant advancements in natural language processing by effectively learning the contextual and semantic features of language, thereby facilitating near-human performance in a wide range of language tasks [6]. One of the promising enhancements in the field of LLMs and their potential applications is the execution of legal tasks [33]. LLMs have demonstrated notable performance in various legal tasks [36]. Furthermore, the ability of Large Language Models to learn the contextual and semantic depths of the language carries great potential in understanding the difficult terminology of legal texts.

This paper deals with the examination of tasks addressing the difficulties in the area of law and the analysis of how recent studies leverage Large Language Models to address these tasks. We aim to overview the approaches to the challenges in the field of law with the emergence of Large Language Models. Thus, the contributions of this paper can be identified as listed below:

- An overview of the key Natural Language Processing (NLP) tasks that constitute the focus of research in the legal domain.
- An analysis of the suggested approaches leveraging Large Language Models for these tasks.
- An analysis of the data sources utilized by the approaches leveraging Large Language Models.
- An examination of the evaluation metrics employed by these approaches and the performance measures of Large Language Models.

The paper is organized follows: Sect. 2 reviews the tasks in the legal domain using natural language processing techniques, Sect. 3 delves into the novel approaches applied to these handle tasks by utilizing large language models, Sect. 4 presents the data resource used in the papers dealing with large language models, and Sect. 5 demonstrate an explanation of the evaluation strategies and evaluation metrics employed by LLMs, Sect. 6 provides a discussion about the limitations of large language models on natural language processing tasks in the legal domain, and Sects. 7 concludes the paper with final remarks.

2   Challenges and Tasks of the Legal Domain

The exponentially increasing volume of legal information, such as cases and legal documents, has encouraged many challenges in the legal domain. There are many studies on the challenges to help stakeholders in the legal domain. Particularly novel enhancements in the area of artificial intelligence have accelerated the efforts to tackle the challenges. One of these approaches is text classification. For lawyers and legal researchers, examining and researching big volume of legal texts, with new documents getting published constantly, is a time-consuming and challenging process. Vatsal et al. [34] states that classifying and searching US Supreme Court decisions published on the website requires a lot of manual effort by legal researchers. To address this challenge, they proposed automatic classification of court decisions by using artificial intelligent methods. They used the BERT [9], which is a transformer model. Moreover, in [23], the performance of machine learning and deep learning methods is evaluated for binary classification of case texts as "violation" and "no violation". They demonstrated that deep learning methods offer better performance than traditional statistical approaches. Shaheen et al. [27] also performed classification of legal documents according to their relevant areas by utilizing transformer models. In contrast to traditional classifications, they specifically addressed the challenge of large multi-label text classification.

On the other hand, several research studies have been conducted by [7,17, 20], to extract meaningful entities in the legal texts in order to automate the document analysis process of legal stakeholders. These studies leveraged the BiLSTM model, which is one of the deep learning techniques, for information extraction in legal documents and texts.

Working with legal texts emerge as another challenge due to their long-drawn and difficult to grasp structure. Therefore, text summarization is considered as another task to deal with these long-drawn and difficult to grasp texts. Considering the fact that the volume of electronic documents is increasing constantly, Banedetto et al. [4] recommended language-specific summarization and headline generation techniques to enhance accessibility of documents and make them easy to use. They also benefit from transformer models to tackle this challenge.

Lawyers and many legal researchers spend a significant amount of time searching for the most relevant legal document to support or refute a particular point of assertion. Also, this task is particularly challenging given the need for high recall where high volume of legal documents is involved [31]. Accordingly, numerous research studies address the information retrieval as one of the main tasks in the legal domain. Thomas et al. [31] presented a legal research recommender system developed to suggest relevant precedents by extracting arguments from legal documents. The system aims to provide contextually meaningful decisions to the user by combining stages such as argument segmentation and case ranking. Tagarelli et al. [30] proposed a legal text mining approach that overlaps with retrieval-based tasks by automatically extracting and classifying legislative articles on the Italian civil code using the LamBERTa framework they developed.

As another task encountered in legal domain, Legal Judgment Prediction (LJP) focuses on predicting judgment results (including crimes, relevant articles, and length of sentence) from the fact description of a specific case [42]. Civil individuals may have difficulty finding answers to legal problems because they are not familiar with legal texts or provisions. Through LJP, legal support can be provided to civil individuals. Furthermore, in order to be able to provide references for research, numerous legal stakeholders could benefit from legal judgment prediction. For instance, in order to increase the interpretability of judgment prediction models, the proposed QAjudge model establishes the decision-making process in a human-like manner through question-answer structures [42]. The model selects relevant questions by taking into account legal principles, produces answers to them according to the case text, and makes a decision prediction based on these answers. A key strength of the approach is its ability to enhance the transparency and efficiency of the judicial process by reducing redundant questioning via reinforcement learning.

Considering the examined research studies, five distinct tasks emerge regarding the challenges in the legal area. These studies aim to tackle the tasks with different approaches and to open new directions to overcome the challenges. Table 1 presents the task categories and relevant research studies for each category based on the utilized approach as LLM based and non-LLM based.

3   Addressing Legal Challenges with Large Language Models

Recent studies have demonstrated that large language models possess strong reasoning capabilities and a deep understanding of linguistic and domain-specific semantics [6]. Given these abilities, LLMs hold significant potential in the legal domain, where the terminology is complex and precise language use is critical. Recently, LLMs have shown significant development and have been employed to a wide range of NLP downstream tasks across different domains [13]. For instance, the inherent verbosity and complexity of the legal documents may limit the accessibility of legal workers and practitioners to keep track of the updates [3]. Therefore, LLMs have great promise for the legal domain, since many researchers conduct studies on downstream tasks by using LLMs.

Sargent et al. [26] stated that large volumes of unclassified legal information are difficult to research and analyze. To tackle this challenge, they proposed

Table 1. Comparison of Research Approaches by Task and Model Type

Task	Model Type	Representative Studies
Classification	Non-LLM	[8, 9, 23]
	LLM	[15, 26]
Information Extraction	Non-LLM	[7, 17, 20]
	LLM	[5, 10]
Summarization	Non-LLM	[4]
	LLM	[3]
Information Retrieval	Non-LLM	[30, 31]
	LLM	[14, 35]
Legal Judgment Prediction	Non-LLM	[42]
	LLM	[25, 36]

to establish a new legal taxonomy that accurately classifies summary judgment decisions of United Kingdom according to specific legal issues. They benefit from the potential of large language models for topic classification on the summary judgment decisions. Since the traditional models and methods are inadequate for capturing the complex and nuanced nature of legal language, the power of large language models to capture deep meanings is emphasized [15]. Izzidien et al. [15] highlighted the potential of large language models in classification by achieving 87.13% accuracy with formulation of appropriate prompts. Closed-set prompting strategies [38] are adopted with a predetermined topic list. Thereby, accuracy was increased by limiting the inference to a specific focal point. They also introduced advanced prompt approaches with few-shot learning strategies [2] by guiding the model with examples and constraints. They demonstrated the applicability of LLMs in legal domains through solely prompt formulation, without any fine-tuning [12].

After getting trained on high volume of text from various resources, LLM models can be useful to generate coherent and contextually relevant text based on given prompts [10]. Owing to the formulate prompts, LLMs can be used for different tasks without an additional training process. Ribeiro et al. [10] aimed to extract eight different legal elements (conclusion, subject matter, reasoning, etc.) from UK Employment Court decisions. Breton et al. [5] also compared large language models with classical BERT-based and rule-based methods for the information extraction tasks. They are demonstrated that more context-sensitive and flexible inferences can be made compared to traditional methods, especially since prompt strategies such as one-shot and zero-shot [2] are used. Both studies show that the context-capturing and flexible understanding capabilities of LLMs outperform traditional methods on the information extraction task. They proposed methods for the challenges in the legal domain by formulating prompt strategies to information extraction task without the need for a training process. In contrast, Baneddetto et al. [3] stated that while the LLMs are multilingual, most of the training samples are in English. For instance, merely 0.11% of the training samples used for Llama 2 [32] are in Italian. They deals the challenge of summarizing in Italian languages while preserving the legal context although as most existing summarization systems are English-based. To overcome this challenge, they carried out a study with fine-tuning [12] to LLM architectures. In this studies, the fine-tuned models clearly outperform the results assessed by both ROUGE [22] and human evaluations. The results demonstrated that LLMs are powerful tools for summarizing information-dense texts in legal area.

The reasoning capability of LLMs has paved the way for development of new approaches to address numerous challenges in NLP. Unlike traditional information retrieval methods which rely solely on textual similarity, they have approached case selection as a semantic matching problem by enriching it with causal inferences [35]. In this study, first, the case texts were converted into semantic representations using LLM. Afterwards, the causal approach is discussed with a comparative decision mechanism and the articles of law affecting the outcome of the case with the help of the model. Therefore, by taking advantage of the deep understanding capabilities of the LLMs, they not only retrieved the given legal case descriptions but also produced interpretable descriptions for the retrieved documents. Thus, they closed the gap between retrieval performance and interpretability of retrieval causes. Huang et al. [14] also took a similar approach, by relying on the semantic understanding of LLMs to select related and unrelated information from related documents. In this study, continual training [11] and fine-tuning [12] methods were used to provide legal domain knowledge to general purpose trained models. These studies have revealed novel approaches for the information retrieval tasks by exploiting the reasoning capabilities of LLMs.

With inferential reasoning capabilities, LLMs have the potential to perform well on tasks such as legal decision prediction Legal Judgment Prediction (LJP) [25,36]. Wei et al. [36] used the CoT [37], which is an LLM technique with a step-by-step thought process, to extract critical elements such as important events, personals, and circumstances in an annotated manner. They used the extracted information for training of the Deep Neural Network (DNN) model they proposed. Consequently, the proposed model learns the final judgment decisions while also ensuring logical consistency. These inferences increase the interpretability of the model because it has demonstrated not only the model's decision predictions but also the reasoning behind the decisions. Peng et al. [25] used the retrieval augmentation generation (RAG) [21] method to improve the performance of the LJP and the consistency of the predictions. They have created a database to keep information about the indictments with the Athena framework they proposed, and integrated a semantic search mechanism into the model by using vectorization. Thereby, to tackle the lack of internal knowledge of LLMs, they have brought relevant legal information from the external knowledge base, and have included the information in the estimation process of the model. They demonstrated a significant performance increase in LJP tasks in the evaluations.

4   Data Resources in the Field of Law for Large Language Models

In law domain, large data resources can be accessed directly because legal documents and litigation processes are publicly available. The United Kingdom published the Cambridge Law Corpus (CLC) [44], which is a comprehensive open-sourced dataset, to support legal AI research. The dataset includes 250,000 UK court decisions and incorporates raw text, rich metadata and expert annotations. This dataset is a great resource for studies on NLP in legal texts [10,15,26]. By leveraging LLMs, CLC dataset was used as analysis and test dataset to carry out document analysis [15] and topics classification [26] tasks, respectively. Ribeiro et al. [10] preferred the $UKET_{ori}$ dataset, which is a subset of CLC, for their study. From the original $UKET_{ori}$ dataset which comprises of 52.339 cases, they have chosen a subset of 260 cases to use stratified sampling to achieve statistically robust findings.

LLMs demonstrate generalized inference performance due to training on large-scale datasets. Accordingly, several studies have demonstrated that downstream tasks could be addressed with prompting strategies without model training [2,15,26]. However, Benedetto et al. [3] asserted that models need to be fine-tuned in areas such as the legal field where the language is semantically difficult to understand and have complex language structures. Training LLMs has been known to require vast amounts of data [33]; however, field knowledge can be learned with a relatively smaller dataset by utilizing advanced fine-tuning methods [3]. They collected Italian Legal News to fine-tune the LLM. There are 3296 articles in total and the number of news articles significantly varies across different areas. They aimed to increase the model's knowledge of Italian law through fine-tuning methods. Furthermore, Breton et al. [5] used a small dataset where 1339 expressions were identified and annotated with French expressions from 200 documents selected by experts from the Luxembourg Traffic Code [29]. They used the dataset for testing and fine-tuning operations. The performance of fine-tuned models were evaluated on relatively small data sets by [3,5]. In both studies, an increase in the performance of models has been observed.

As a larger dataset with more than 2.6 million criminal cases, CAIL2018 [39], has been valuable a data resource for many studies [14,25,35]. Additionally, comprehensive evaluations has been performed by using subsets created from the CAIL2018 dataset [25,35]. Thus, it has been considered as a major resource for the Information Retrieval task in law domain. On the other hand, Huang et al. [14] used the Chinese Legal Corpus dataset, which was sampled from many datasets by the authors, to increase the legal knowledge of their model. In addition, they extended the JEC-QA [43] dataset with additional explanations to evaluate model performance.

Wang et al. [35] used the COLIEE [18] dataset as an evaluation resource in their study. The COLIEE is a publicly available dataset established by the COLIEE competition, which was organized at the International Conference on Artificial Intelligence and Law (ICAIL). They preferred using a subset of the COLIEE dataset to retrieve relevant articles from the Japanese Civil Code. The test set included 319 new questions, where participants were given the task of retrieving relevant articles from 768 Civil Code articles. This dataset was used to compare LLMs with traditional models. In [36], a subset of the Chinese private lending cases dataset [24] was utilized for model training and testing. The dataset includes a total of 70.485 records. Reject, Partially Support, and Support have been used as the judgment labels for the claims in this dataset.

As a summary, it can be concluded that seven distinct data resources have been utilized by LLMs in the legal domain. Table 2 presents a list of these data resources and their usage purposes by LLMs. Cambridge Law Corpus and CAIL2018 have been observed as the most widely used data resources, as each of them is utilized by three different research studies. Besides, testing is determined as the most common purpose of usage with eight studies, followed by training with five studies.

Table 2. The Data Resources of LLMs in Legal Domain and Their Usage Purposes

Reference	Data Resources	Purpose of Usage
[10]	Cambridge Law Corpus	Testing
[15]	Cambridge Law Corpus	Document Analysis
[26]	Cambridge Law Corpus	Testing
[3]	Custom Data	Training, Testing
[5]	Custom Data	Training, Testing
[14]	CAIL2018, JEC-QA	Training, Testing
[25]	CAIL2018	Testing
[35]	CAIL2018, COLIEE	Testing
[36]	[24]	Training, Testing

5   Evaluation Strategies for LLMs in Law Domain

As more complex AI methods emerge, evaluating task performance becomes more difficult. Hence, evaluating LLMs is quite a challenge on its own. Several studies especially focused on addressing the evaluation of the tasks in legal domain. Traditional performance evaluation metrics such as Accuracy, Precision, Recall and F1-score are widely used [15, 25, 26, 36]. Classification tasks are evaluated in a direct comparative manner on labeled data. LJP tasks are evaluated in a manner similar to classification tasks, which are assessed directly using labeled data [5, 36]. Wang et al. [36] also addressed the judgment selection as a binary classification problem. They preferred classification accuracy as a criterion to evaluate their comparison algorithms. Breton et al. [5] presented a novel approach to address the inherent limitations of traditional evaluation metrics when applied to LLMs for the information retrieval tasks. To overcome these limitations, an advanced evaluation framework that incorporates a detailed analysis of True Positive examples and the combined use of the Levenshtein distance [40] was presented.

Generator outputs for the summarization task can not be evaluated directly as a match between the ground truth and the prediction. Instead, quantitative metrics such as ROUGE [22] and BERTScore [41] are preferred [3]. ROUGE measure the overlap between automatic summaries and reference summaries to assess their quality. On the other hand, BERTScore evaluates the semantic similarity of texts and measures the degree to which the summaries produced by the model overlap with the reference summaries.

Although there are many evaluation criteria, manual evaluation with experts is still widely used [3, 10, 14, 26]. These studies interpret model performance based on the evaluations of field experts. Furthermore, the hallucination problem of LLMs is a major problem widely stated by researchers. The hallucination problem in LLMs refers to the generation of plausible-sounding but factually incorrect or entirely fabricated content. The assessment hallucinations is a major assessment challenge addressed by current studies, and measuring hallucinations in the predictions is utilized as an assessment criterion [13, 14]. Hu et al. [13] examined hallucination evaluation for LLMs with their benchmark called LegalHalBench. They proposed the Non-Hallucination Status Rate method which defines a comparative rate for hallucination in LLMs.

6   Discussion

Addressing the tasks with natural language processing techniques in the field of law is quite challenging due to the complex and nuanced nature of legal language [15]. The studies using LLMs capture deep meanings to overcome the challenging tasks listed in Table 1. However, relying solely on the generalized training of LLMs proves inadequate to address complex tasks [3, 14]. Moreover, since the majority of training data for LLMs is composed of English texts, their capacity to interpret legal documents in other languages remains limited [3]. Therefore, training models to increase knowledge in the legal domain appears to enhance task performance [3].

Table 3 provides an overview of studies utilizing Large Language Models in legal domain. It is observed that the Cambridge Law Corpus and the CAIL2018 datasets are the most commonly employed with three studies each. Cambridge Law Corpus and the CAIL2018 are utilized in [10, 14, 15, 25, 26, 35] respectively. Furthermore, in terms of evaluation criteria, human evaluation appears to be a frequently adopted approach [3, 10, 14, 26], with researchers often relying on domain experts to assess model outputs. The review of the studies reveals that evaluating Large Language Models in the legal domain remains a particular challenge.

It has been demonstrated by [35, 36] that the reasoning capabilities of LLMs have great potential to overcome challenges in the legal domain. While LLMs are

Table 3. Overview of Studies in Legal Domain Using Large Language Models

Article	Task	Data Resource(s)	Evaluation Criteria
[10]	Information Extraction	Cambridge Law Corpus	Human Evaluation
[5]	Information Extraction	Custom Data	F1 Score, Recall, Precision
[15]	Classification	Cambridge Law Corpus	F1 Score
[26]	Classification	Cambridge Law Corpus	F1 Score, Human Evaluation
[3]	Summarization	Custom Data	ROUGE, BERTScore, Human Evaluation
[14]	Information Retrieval	CAIL2018, JEC-QA	Accuracy, Human Evaluation, Non-Hallucination Status Rate
[35]	Information Retrieval	CAIL2018, COLIEE	Accuracy
[25]	Legal Judgment Prediction	CAIL2018	Accuracy
[36]	Legal Judgment Prediction	[24]	F1 Score, Recall, Precision

rarely adopted as base models in research, they commonly function as auxiliary components or decision-making aids. However, LLMs cause concerns in tasks due to hallucination problems and lack of interpretability. In domains such as law, where the reasoning behind justification is of critical importance, the interpretability of artificial intelligence model outputs is crucial. Novel approaches to improve the interpretability of models have been proposed to address the lack of interpretability [36,37]. Besides, approaches that benefit from external resources such as RAG have been observed to prevent hallucinations and increase the consistency of the models [25].

Especially in decision-making positions that directly affect human life, such as in the field of law, LLMs pose a significant risk to direct people to false information. Addressing concerns of hallucination, bias, and lack of interpretability in LLMs is a major requirement for AI technologies in law. In addition, the basic rules of the law which vary depending on the region, country and situation make it difficult to propose a general evaluation method for LLMs in the field of law.

7   Conclusion

In this paper, we discussed the tasks addressed with natural language processing techniques in the legal domain and examined the novel approaches developed with LLMs for these tasks. The deep contextual understanding capabilities of LLMs have been demonstrated to have great potential in tasks which require high reasoning and capture semantically challenging language structures in the legal domain. Novel approaches for legal domain emerge from particularly the reasoning capabilities of LLMs. Additionally, it has been demonstrated that LLMs are more successful in performance than traditional methods. Although LLMs can be applied to legal challenges without requiring training, fine-tuned models have been established to be more successful in grasping the deep context of legal texts.

Hallucination, bias, and lack of interpretability in the LLMs may raise serious concerns. Reducing hallucination and addressing ethical concerns are of crucial importance to increase the application of LLMs in the field of law. Furthermore, the lack of a standard for evaluation and the difficulty of assessing the hallucinations constitute major challenges for application of LLMs in the legal domain. Mitigating these concerns requires the establishment of robust, high-quality datasets and standardized benchmarks. Therefore, generating enhanced datasets and developing new benchmarks are essential steps toward improving the trustworthiness and applicability of LLMs in legal contexts.

References

1. Abanoz, B.: Hukuki bilgiye dijital erişim. Marmara Üniversitesi Hukuk Fakültesi Hukuk Araştırmaları Dergisi **26**(1), 190–203 (2020)
2. Agrawal, M., Hegselmann, S., Lang, H., Kim, Y., Sontag, D.: Large language models are few-shot clinical information extractors (2022). https://arxiv.org/abs/2205.12689
3. Benedetto, I., Cagliero, L., Ferro, M., Tarasconi, F., Bernini, C., Giacalone, G.: Leveraging large language models for abstractive summarization of italian legal news. Artif. Intell. Law 1–21 (2025)
4. Benedetto, I., La Quatra, M., Cagliero, L.: LegITBART: a summarization model for Italian legal documents. Artif. Intell. Law 1–31 (2025)
5. Breton, J., et al.: Leveraging LLMs for legal terms extraction with limited annotated data. Artif. Intell. Law 1–27 (2025)
6. Brown, T.B., et al.: Language models are few-shot learners (2020). https://arxiv.org/abs/2005.14165
7. Çetindağ, C., Yazıcıoğlu, B., Koç, A.: Named-entity recognition in Turkish legal texts. Nat. Lang. Eng. **29**(3), 615–642 (2023)
8. Chen, H., Wu, L., Chen, J., Lu, W., Ding, J.: A comparative study of automated legal text classification using random forests and deep learning. Inform. Process. Manage. **59**(2), 102798 (2022)
9. Devlin, J., Chang, M., Lee, K., Toutanova, K.: BERT: pre-training of deep bidirectional transformers for language understanding. CoRR **abs/1810.04805** (2018). http://arxiv.org/abs/1810.04805
10. Ribeiro de Faria, J., Xie, H., Steffek, F.: Information extraction from employment tribunal judgments using a large language model. Artif. Intell. Law 1–22 (2025)
11. Gururangan, S., et al.: Don't stop pretraining: adapt language models to domains and tasks (2020). https://arxiv.org/abs/2004.10964
12. Howard, J., Ruder, S.: Universal language model fine-tuning for text classification (2018). https://arxiv.org/abs/1801.06146
13. Hu, Y., Gan, L., Xiao, W., Kuang, K., Wu, F.: Fine-tuning large language models for improving factuality in legal question answering. arXiv preprint arXiv:2501.06521 (2025)
14. Huang, Q., et al.: Lawyer llama technical report. arXiv preprint arXiv:2305.15062 (2023)
15. Izzidien, A., Sargeant, H., Steffek, F.: LLM vs. lawyers: identifying a subset of summary judgments in a large UK case law dataset. arXiv preprint arXiv:2403.04791 (2024)
16. Jacobs, G.L.: Legal technology: present and future trends. Legal Econ. **13**, 29 (1987)

17. Ji, D., Tao, P., Fei, H., Ren, Y.: An end-to-end joint model for evidence information extraction from court record document. Inform. Process. Manage. **57**(6), 102305 (2020)
18. Kim, M.Y., Rabelo, J., Goebel, R., Yoshioka, M., Kano, Y., Satoh, K.: Coliee 2022 summary: Methods for legal document retrieval and entailment. In: JSAI International Symposium on Artificial Intelligence, pp. 51–67. Springer (2022)
19. Küçük, D., Can, F.: Hukuki metinlerin otomatik işlenmesinde yapay zekâ teknolojilerinin kullanimi. Bilişim Hukuku Dergisi **6**(1), 1–23 (2024)
20. Leitner, E., Rehm, G., Moreno-Schneider, J.: Fine-grained named entity recognition in legal documents. In: International Conference on Semantic Systems, pp. 272–287. Springer (2019)
21. Lewis, P., et al.: Retrieval-augmented generation for knowledge-intensive NLP tasks (2021). https://arxiv.org/abs/2005.11401
22. Lin, C.Y.: Rouge: a package for automatic evaluation of summaries. In: Text summarization branches out: Proceedings of the ACL-04 workshop, pp. 74–81 (2004)
23. Mumcuoğlu, E., Öztürk, C.E., Ozaktas, H.M., Koç, A.: Natural language processing in law: prediction of outcomes in the higher courts of turkey. Inform. Process. Manage. **58**(5), 102684 (2021)
24. MLY NLP: LJP-MSJudge: a multi-scale dataset for legal judgment prediction. https://github.com/mly-nlp/LJP-MSJudge (2023). Accessed 26 March 2025
25. Peng, X., Chen, L.: Athena: Retrieval-augmented legal judgment prediction with large language models (2024). https://arxiv.org/abs/2410.11195
26. Sargeant, H., Izzidien, A., Steffek, F.: Topic classification of case law using a large language model and a new taxonomy for UK law: AI insights into summary judgment. Artificial Intelligence and Law, pp. 1–49 (2025)
27. Shaheen, Z., Wohlgenannt, G., Filtz, E.: Large scale legal text classification using transformer models. arXiv preprint arXiv:2010.12871 (2020)
28. Shukla, A., et al.: Legal case document summarization: Extractive and abstractive methods and their evaluation (2022). https://arxiv.org/abs/2210.07544
29. Sleimi, A., Sannier, N., Sabetzadeh, M., Briand, L., Dann, J.: Automated extraction of semantic legal metadata using natural language processing. In: 2018 IEEE 26th International Requirements Engineering Conference (RE), pp. 124–135 (2018). https://doi.org/10.1109/RE.2018.00022
30. Tagarelli, A., Simeri, A.: Unsupervised law article mining based on deep pre-trained language representation models with application to the italian civil code. Artif. Intell. Law **30**(3), 417–473 (2022)
31. Thomas, M., et al.: Quick check: a legal research recommendation system. In: NLLP@ KDD, pp. 57–60 (2020)
32. Touvron, H., et al.: Llama 2: Open foundation and fine-tuned chat models (2023). https://arxiv.org/abs/2307.09288
33. Trozze, A., Davies, T., Kleinberg, B.: Large language models in cryptocurrency securities cases: can a GPT model meaningfully assist lawyers? Artif. Intell. Law 1–47 (2024)
34. Vatsal, S., Meyers, A., Ortega, J.E.: Classification of us supreme court cases using BERT-based techniques. arXiv preprint arXiv:2304.08649 (2023)
35. Wang, Z., Ding, Y., Wu, C., Guo, Y., Zhou, W.: Causality-inspired legal provision selection with large language model-based explanation. Artif. Intell. Law 1–25 (2024)
36. Wei, B., Yu, Y., Gan, L., Wu, F.: An LLMs-based neuro-symbolic legal judgment prediction framework for civil cases. Artif. Intell. Law 1–35 (2025)

37. Wei, J., et al.: Chain of thought prompting elicits reasoning in large language models. arXiv preprint arXiv:2201.11903 (2022)
38. White, J., et al.: A prompt pattern catalog to enhance prompt engineering with Chatgpt (2023). https://arxiv.org/abs/2302.11382
39. Xiao, C., et al.: Cail2018: A large-scale legal dataset for judgment prediction (2018). https://arxiv.org/abs/1807.02478
40. Yujian, L., Bo, L.: A normalized levenshtein distance metric. IEEE Trans. Pattern Anal. Mach. Intell. **29**(6), 1091–1095 (2007)
41. Zhang, T., Kishore, V., Wu, F., Weinberger, K.Q., Artzi, Y.: Bertscore: evaluating text generation with bert. arXiv preprint arXiv:1904.09675 (2019)
42. Zhong, H., Wang, Y., Tu, C., Zhang, T., Liu, Z., Sun, M.: Iteratively questioning and answering for interpretable legal judgment prediction. In: Proceedings of the AAAI Conference on Artificial Intelligence. vol. 34, pp. 1250–1257 (2020)
43. Zhong, H., Xiao, C., Tu, C., Zhang, T., Liu, Z., Sun, M.: JEC-GA: a legal-domain question answering dataset. In: Proceedings of the AAAI Conference on Artificial Intelligence, vol. 34, pp. 9701–9708 (2020)
44. Östling, A., et al.: The Cambridge law corpus: A dataset for legal AI research (2024). https://arxiv.org/abs/2309.12269

Analysis of Weightlifting Success Predictability Using Machine Learning

Joaquin Camaran[1], Yuna Ukawa[1], Thiago Reis[1], Christopher Taber[1],
William G. Hornsby[2], Alex Long[1], Mehul Raval[3], N. Sertac Artan[4], Tolga Kaya[1],
and Samah Senbel[1(✉)]

[1] Sacred Heart University, Fairfield, CT 06855, USA
{Camaranj,Ukaway,reist2}@mail.sacredheart.edu, {taberc,longa9,
kayat,senbels}@sacredheart.edu
[2] West Virginia University, Morgantown, WV 26506, USA
william.hornsby@mail.wvu.edu
[3] Ahmedabad University, Ahmedabad, India
mehul.raval@ahduni.edu.in
[4] New York Institute of Technology, New York 11568, USA
nartan@nyit.edu

Abstract. Machine learning techniques are used extensively in sports to help optimize athletes' performance and maximize their chances of winning. Weightlifting requires quick and calculated decision-making by the coach and athlete to determine optimal load selection when progressing through lifting attempts during competition. When an optimal load-selection strategy is employed, the probability of success in competition is maximized. An XGBOOST machine learning model was developed to predict the success of weightlifting attempts in competition. The model was trained on an extensive dataset, including the performances of more than 14,000 athletes observed throughout 11 years of competition. We also included data from the 2024 Summer Olympic Games as a test dataset. The data contained information about the athletes' sex, age, competition weight class, previous lifting performance, and previous competition placings. The accuracy of our predictions varied among the different weight classes, with a maximum accuracy of 89% for female athletes in the clean and jerk event. The outcome of our work is that, in general, the performance of female lifters is more predictable than males. Furthermore, the performance of the athletes competing in the lightest and heaviest weight classes for each sex category is the most predictable. Interestingly, prediction accuracy differs between lift attempts and lifting events performed during competition, with the initial attempt of the clean and jerk being the most predictable.

Keywords: Machine Learning · Prediction · Sports Analytics · Weightlifting

1 Introduction

Machine learning (ML) techniques have become increasingly ubiquitous in competitive sports in recent years. Among the various applications of these analytical techniques, ML have been used in predictive modeling and relational analysis of athlete injury risk,

O. Gervasi et al. (Eds.): ICCSA 2025, LNCS 15649, pp. 179–199, 2025.
https://doi.org/10.1007/978-3-031-96997-3_12

performance optimization, competitive outcomes, optimal roster selection, and athlete rankings [1]. ML have also become pervasive in sports management and promotion, as various analytical techniques have been used to provide recommendations for ticket pricing, and even in sports betting, where ML has been used to improve predictions of competitive outcomes. The sporting applications of ML have been studied extensively in soccer [2], followed by basketball [3], handball [4], and volleyball [5] due to the immense popularity of these sports. The wealth of publicly available data has enhanced the potential use cases for ML in sports due to the potential to generate and train models that may yield relatively accurate predictions using historical performance data for individual athletes, teams, or a specific competition.

Weightlifting is a sport where athletes compete by performing two events, the barbell snatch and the barbell clean and jerk [6]. Competitors are allowed three attempts in the snatch, followed by three in the clean and jerk, to complete each movement with the greatest load possible while meeting specific standards for each movement. Ultimately, the objective is to lift the greatest load possible in each event, which is then summed to equal the athlete's competition total. The athlete who achieves the greatest two-lift total during a specific contest is considered the victor. Therefore, the challenge of the sport is to maximize the athlete's total by having them lift the greatest load possible in each event, within the athlete's capabilities for that given competition day.

Weightlifting is a weight-class sport with multiple classes for males and females. Athletes endeavor to compete with the highest body weight possible under their weight class upper limit, allowing them to maximize their competition potential [7]. By choosing the appropriate weight class for their height and anthropometric characteristics, athletes optimize the amount of muscle mass they can possess in relation to their total body mass, further enhancing their ability to produce force against the external loads encountered in competition [8]. The number of weight classes in modern weightlifting has varied based on the competition year, ranging from 15 to 20 categories for males and females combined [9].

During the competition, coaches and athletes must work together strategically to determine appropriate load selections for each event, and each attempted lift to maximize the athlete's neuromuscular and technical abilities, enabling the athlete to achieve their greatest total. Load selection for each attempted lift is heavily influenced by an athlete's previous training and competition history, the forecasted performance expectations for each athlete determined immediately before a competition, and the athlete's performance in each preceding attempt completed during an ongoing competition. The art of coaching during a Weightlifting meet, then, lies in the selection of optimal initial loads for each event, which are then followed by sensible increases in load with successive attempts. Appropriate determination of initial or opening loads and relevant increases in load during successive attempts during each event enables the athlete to achieve the highest possible placement in competition by successfully completing lifts at or near the athlete's maximum ability. In Weightlifting, no standard increase in load is recommended when progressing through lifting attempts; however, considering historical performance outcomes, coaches often select a load that results in a 2–5% increase between attempts, depending on the athlete. By optimizing load selections between attempts, coaches contribute to an athlete's potential for completing lifting attempts and achieving the intended outcome of posting the highest total possible.

In this work, A ML model was developed to analyze the efficacy of historical load selection strategies in Weightlifting to gain the critical insight necessary to provide recommendations to coaches and athletes for optimal load selection strategies during competition. The model was trained using a publicly available dataset of weightlifting performance data collected during competitions over eleven years. The model aimed to predict the optimal load lifted by each athlete observed by considering successful lifting attempts, unsuccessful lifting attempts, and load increases between attempts. Furthermore, to improve the performance of the model, athlete sex and competition weight class were also considered.

2 Related Work

Ball et al. [10] presents an excellent analysis of all USA powerlifting competitions between 2012 and 2016. They study the effect of age and weight on the performance of athletes over the years, concluding that women's peak performance declines faster than men's peak performance, and women seem to reach their peak sooner than men and decline sooner than men.

A related model was developed by Chavda et al. [11] to predict the optimal performance zones for different competition levels based on the data of 15 male athletes over multiple competitions. Their objective was to predict the optimal body mass for the athletes, while we are interested in predicting the weight lift to attempt based on thousands of lifts by both male and female athletes. Also, they observe that a lighter person can generally lift a greater percentage of their weight than a heavier person. In addition, men, in general, can lift a heavier ratio of their weight compared to women.

Chau [12] presents a machine learning model based on swarm optimization to predict the competition score based on a dataset of 5500 athletes' optimal squat, bench, and deadlift records over 30 years. They established a score prediction model based on the characteristics of male powerlifters and a machine learning method. The model uses the age, body weight, weight class, best squat, best bench, and best deadlift features of powerlifters, and the WOA algorithm is used to improve the model's predictive ability.

Xiang et al. [13] also uses machine learning to predict weightlifting capacity but with a different target: to prevent injury in workers whose job demands them to lift weights. They used computer vision to determine the stressed parts of the body when lifting boxes and used a large dataset to predict the maximum weight a certain person can lift without a knee, back, or shoulder injury or strain.

Kauhanen et al. [14] showed that the relationship between body weight and lifted weight is nonlinear and developed a LOWESS-based regression model for performance normalization. They concluded that the proposed formulas could serve as an objective method to assess male weightlifters' performance, independent of body weight, age, or skill level. This suggests that body weight's nonlinear effect may partially explain differences in prediction accuracy across weight classes.

Our study takes a different approach from previous ML models by considering not only competition level, sex, age, body weight, and weight class but also the outcomes of prior attempts within each performance. Instead of incorporating physical attributes beyond body weight, the model focuses on attempt-specific load selections and outcomes, as well as the ratio between load increases and body weight. This approach aims to optimize load selection for the next attempt as a strategic means of improving weightlifting performance.

3 Methodology

The data used in this work was collected from the public records of Weightlifting competitions at different levels between 2005 and 2016. We also collected data from the Summer Olympics 2024 to use as a test case for our prediction model. The data was aggregated into one set with 14643 rows and 24 columns for analysis as shown in Table 1.

The data required minimal cleaning. Approximately 10 records were removed due to erroneous data entry. The "Country" and "Name" fields had several instances of missing and misspelled data, but this did not affect our analysis and prediction results, as these columns were not included in the analysis.

This research aimed to help athletes and coaches select optimal load increases between lifting attempts to maximize their potential to complete each lifting attempt. Towards that end, we utilize ML to predict the success/fail of each lift based on the different fields, as well as previous lifts and their success load. Therefore, we had six values to predict, one for each lift. Table 2 shows the fields used for each prediction.

Then, the model was run with 18 different subsets of the data:

1. All athletes (14643 athletes)
2. All male athletes (9089 athletes)
3. Men Weight class 56 kg only (731 athletes)
4. Men Weight class 62 kg only (1041 athletes)
5. Men Weight class 69 kg only (1343 athletes)
6. Men Weight class 77 kg only (1458 athletes)
7. Men Weight class 85 kg only (1303 athletes)
8. Men Weight class 94 kg only (1198 athletes)
9. Men Weight class 105 kg only (1069 athletes)
10. Men Weight class 105 + kg only (946 athletes)
11. All female athletes (5564 athletes)
12. Women Weight class 48 kg only (684 athletes)
13. Women Weight class 53 kg only (816 athletes)
14. Women Weight class 58 kg only (920 athletes)
15. Women Weight class 63 kg only (940 athletes)
16. Women Weight class 69 kg only (836 athletes)
17. Women Weight class 75 kg only (708 athletes)
18. Women Weight class 75 + kg only (696 athletes)

Therefore, the model was run a total of 108 (18x6) times, each time with a different set of rows and columns. The dataset was divided into a stratified training group (80%) and a testing group (20%) for each prediction model. Due to the data imbalance of the win/fail groups in most data subsets, we used the SMOTE method to create artificial data to balance the groups.

Table 1. Attributes of the Weightlifting dataset

Attribute	Description
Name	Athlete's name
Age	Athlete age in years (13–64, Mean 24.12, SD 4.57)
Sex	1 = Male, 2 = Female
Weight	Weight of Athlete in kg (42.79–192.14, Mean: 76.5, SD 22.04)
Competition Level	5 categories: Olympic(468), World (3575), Continental(6194), National (4264), and local (106) levels
Weight class	8 men's weight classes: 56, 62, 69, 77, 85, 94, 105, 105 + kgs, and 7 women's weight classes: 48, 53, 58, 63, 69, 75, 75 + kgs
Snatch1 load	Load attempted in first Snatch lift in kg (22–206, Mean: 108.26, SD: 34.85)
Snatch1Win	Binary value, 0 = fail (24.55%), 1 = succeed (75.45%)
Snatch2 load	Load attempted in second Snatch lift in kg (24 - 211, Mean: 111.62, SD: 35.27)
Snatch2Win	Binary value, 0 = fail (37.77%), 1 = succeed (62.23%)
SnatchJump1	Difference between Snatch2 load and Snatch 1 load
SnatchJump1Percent	SnatchJump1 divided by the players' weight
Snatch3 load	Load attempted in third Snatch lift in kg (24–216, Mean: 113.99, SD: 35.52)
Snatch3Win	Binary value, 0 = fail (54.48%), 1 = succeed (45.52%)
SnatchJump2	Difference between Snatch 3 load and Snatch 2 load
SnatchJump2Percent	SnatchJump2 divided by the players' weight
CJ1 load	Load attempted in first Clean & Jerk lift (25–251, Mean: 134.95, SD: 41.69)
CJ1Win	Binary value, 0 = fail (20.99%), 1 = succeed (79.01%)
CJ2 load	Load attempted in second Clean & Jerk lift (28–263, Mean: 139.09, SD: 42.31)
CJ2 Win	Binary value, 0 = fail (41.47%), 1 = succeed (58.53%)
CJ Jump1	Difference between Clean and Jerk 2 load and Clean and Jerk 1 load
CJ Jump1Percent	Clean and Jerk Jump 1 divided by the players' weight
CJ3 load	Load attempted in third Clean & Jerk lift (30–352, Mean: 141.86, SD: 42.75)
CJ3 Win	Binary value, 0 = fail (63.1%), 1 = succeed (36.9%)
CJ Jump2	Difference between Clean and Jerk 3 load and Clean and Jerk 2 load
CJ Jump2Percent	Clean and Jerk Jump 2 divided by the players' weight

Table 2. Attributes used for predicting the success of each lift

Prediction Target	Attributes
Snatch1Win	Age, Sex, Weight, Competition level, Weight_class, Snatch1load
Snatch2Win	Age, Sex, Weight, Competition level, Weight_class, Snatch1load, Snatch1Win, Snatch2load, SnatchJump1, SnatchJump1Percent
Snatch3Win	Age, Sex, Weight, Competition level, Weight_class, Snatch1load, Snatch1Win, Snatch2load, Snatch2Win, SnatchJump1, SnatchJump1Percent, Snatch3load, SnatchJump2, SnatchJump2Percent
CJ1Win	Age, Sex, Weight, Competition level, Weight_class, Snatch1load, Snatch1Win, Snatch2load, Snatch2Win, SnatchJump1, SnatchJump1Percent, Snatch3load, SnatchJump2, SnatchJump2Percent, CJ1load
CJ2Win	Age, Sex, Weight, Competition level, Weight_class, Snatch1load, Snatch1Win, Snatch2load, Snatch2Win, SnatchJump1, SnatchJump1Percent, Snatch3load, SnatchJump2, SnatchJump2Percent, CJ1load, CJ1Win, CJ2load, CJ Jump1, CJ Jump1Percent
CJ3Win	Age, Sex, Weight, Competition level, Weight_class, Snatch1load, Snatch1Win, Snatch2load, Snatch2Win, SnatchJump1, SnatchJump1Percent, Snatch3load, SnatchJump2, SnatchJump2Percent, CJ1load, CJ1Win, CJ2load, CJ Jump1, CJ Jump1Percent, CJ3 load, CJ Jump2, CJ Jump2Percent

Multiple prediction models were experimented with to find the most suitable model for the prediction data, and the optimal results were obtained by the XGBoost model, followed by the Random Forest model. Therefore, the XGBoost model was selected and run 108 times. For each run of the model, accuracy, precision, and recall were used as measures of quality, and are presented in the appendix, with analysis in the following section.

4   Results

4.1   Preliminary Data Analysis

Before analyzing the running machine learning model's output, we did some preliminary analysis of the dataset.

4.1.1   Feature Importance

It is crucial to study the factors that primarily contribute to the outcome of a lifting attempt. We use correlation-driven feature importance in Python to obtain a ranked list of features that affect the chance of winning for each lift. Table 3 shows the top 5 features for each lift. Note that since the type of competition is a category feature, we used one-hot encoding for our analysis to separate the competition type into five binary features:

isLocal, isNational, isCont, isWorld, and isOlympic. Also, some features are co-related negatively as shown in the table.

Table 3. Feature importance table for the six lifts.

Rank	Snatch1Win	Snatch2Win	Snatch3Win	CJ1Win	CJ2Win	CJ3Win
1	isNational	isCont	isCont	isCont	isCont	cj2Win
2	Age (-ve)	snJmp1Percent (-ve)	snJmp2Percent (-ve)	isNational	isNational	Age (-ve)
3	isCont	isNational	isNational	Age (-ve)	Age (-ve)	cjJmp1Percent (-ve)
4	Sn1 load(-ve)	Snatch1Win	snJmp1Percent (-ve)	Sex	cjJmp1Percent (-ve)	Cj 2 load(-ve)
5	Sex	Age (-ve)	Sex	CJ 1 load (-ve)	Sex	cjJump1 (-ve)

In the first five lifts, the most important feature is the competition level with the continental, and national level meets particularly, where athletes tend to perform their best. Age is also important in all lifts with a negative co-relation. Sex (1 = male, 2 = female) shows that women's chances are generally better. The Jump percentage is also an important feature

4.1.2 Load Choice Analysis

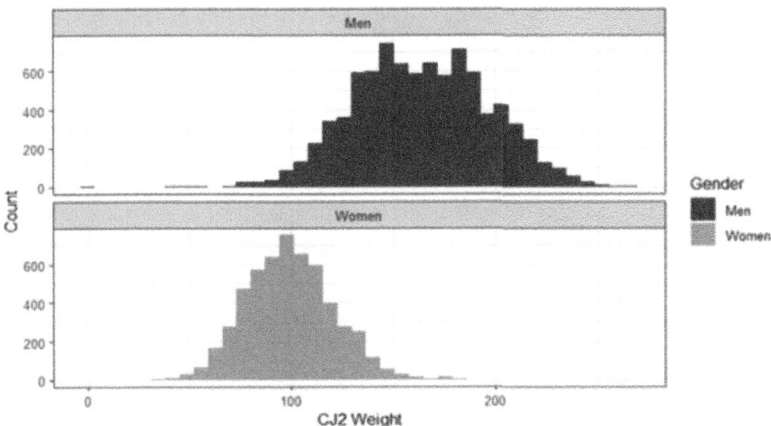

Fig. 1. Range of chosen loads of the Clean and Jerk 2 lifts

We note that there is generally a different pattern in load choices and jumps for all lifts between men and women. Figure 1 shows the range of chosen loads for Clean and Jerk 2 lift as a sample. We note a difference in the range of lifts, with men having a much bigger range of choices and a generally higher average naturally. Similar patterns were obtained for all other lifts.

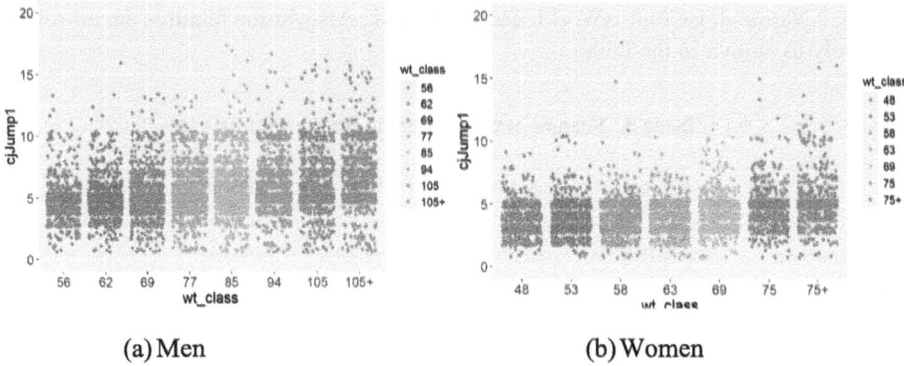

(a) Men   (b) Women

Fig. 2. Clean and jerk jump 1 comparison across different weight classes

Another difference between the sexes is their choice of the jump in loads between lifts, with men mostly going for a jump of 5–10 kgs and women between 3–5 kgs. While the range of attempts from men to women showed a noticeable difference, the trend between higher jumps and having higher loads remained the same for both sexes. Also, the average CJ 1 jump also rises as you increase in weight classes. Figure 2 shows the difference in jump choice for both sexes for the different weight classes between CJ1 and CJ2. Similar results are obtained for the other three jumps.

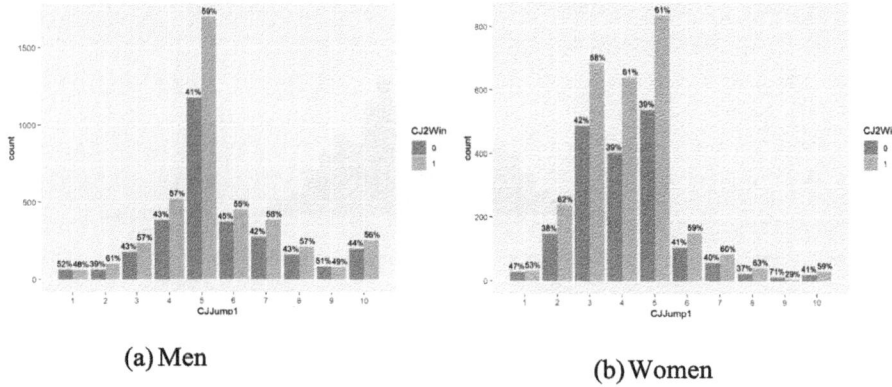

(a) Men   (b) Women

Fig. 3. CJ jump 1 Success and Fail percentage across different jump choices.

In Fig. 3, We analyze the patterns across the different load jumps through all lifts. Each number on the x-axis shows two bar plots. A red one indicates the number of participants who attempted and failed this jump, and a blue one shows the number of participants who tried and succeeded in the jump in that load.

The blue bars with the highest percentage should be considered the safest jumps, though you must also consider the number of people who attempted it. Jumps 3–5 have the most attempts and, therefore, are a more accurate representation of your chances of succeeding or failing a jump of those loads. Figure 3 shows the results for CJ2 lift of the all-men and all-women groups as a sample. Note the strong preference for men of all weight classes for CJ1 jump1 at 5 kilos with a win rate of 59%. Women had more variety in jump choices, with most choosing 3–5 kilos.

4.2 Machine Learning Results

This section reviews the results of running the XGBOOST machine learning model to predict a win in all lifts for all 18 groups specified in Sect. 3. For each model, we measured the accuracy, precision, and recall. In this section, we concentrate on the accuracy of the predictions. The complete results for accuracy, precision and recall can be found in the appendix.

As a sample, here are the results for predicting a CJ1win for women in the $75 + $ kg weight class:

- Confusion matrix:

  Loss [9 9]
  Win [6 109]

- Accuracy: 89%
- Weighted Precision: 88%
- Weighted Recall: 89%

We note the relatively good accuracy (89%) for this weight class, but our goal in this paper is not to reach a high accuracy but rather to compare the predictability of the different lifts, weight classes, and sexes.

4.2.1 Sex Differences in Predictability

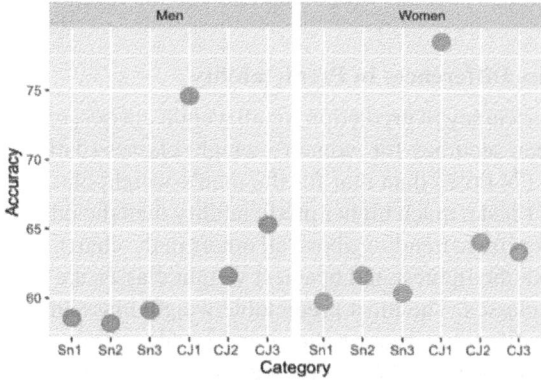

Fig. 4. Comparison of accuracy of prediction for the All-men and all-women groups for all lifts

Figure 4 shows the accuracy for all lifts for our testing set's all-men and all-women groups. The mean accuracy for all-Men was 62.9%, while that of all-women was 64.6%. We note the higher prediction accuracy for women across all lifts except the last lift, CJ3. We also note an increase in prediction accuracy over the different lifts with an almost linear increase, as shown in the Fig. 4. The exception is the CJ1 lift, which shows a much higher prediction accuracy than the other lifts.

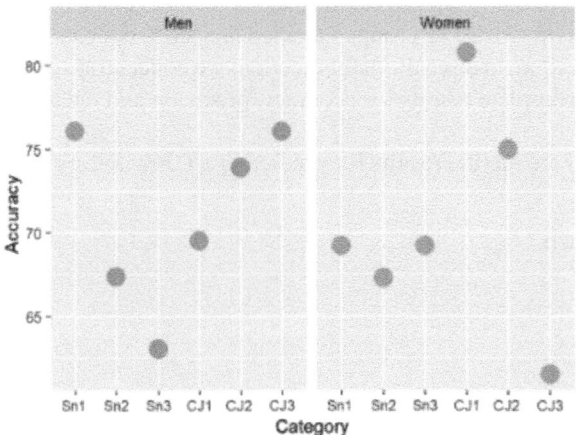

Fig. 5. Comparison of accuracy of prediction for the All-men and all-women groups for all lifts during the 2024 summer Olympics

Slightly different results were obtained when we used the 2024 Olympics data as our test set, as shown in Fig. 5. We observe the same pattern of linear increase over lifts for women but a very different pattern for the men's dataset. Still, the accuracy was generally much higher, with men having a slightly higher predictability: The mean accuracy for all-Men was 71.0%, while the mean accuracy for all-Women was 70.5%. Note that the Olympic dataset is much smaller, with 98 athletes, so the results are limited.

4.2.2   Weight Class Differences in Predictability

Figure 6 shows the accuracy of prediction for all weight classes, ordered by weight class. We observe the mean accuracy for women's weight classes (dark blue trend line) was, on average, higher (74.06%) than that for the men's weight classes (purple trend line) (72.60%). Also, CJ1 had a much higher predictability than the other 5 lifts for both men and women (blue dots trace trending above all others in the chart). Moreover, a U-shaped trend line shows that the lightest and heaviest weight classes are more predictable than the middle-weight classes. The most predictable weight class among all classes for all lifts was the women 75 + kg class, as shown in Fig. 6B.

Figure 7 shows the accuracy results for each weight class separately, ordered by the lifts in turn. The prediction accuracy decreases with each consecutive snatch lift and CJ lift, with the most predictable results being with CJ1. We observe a generally higher level of accuracy when each weight class is predicted separately with a much higher

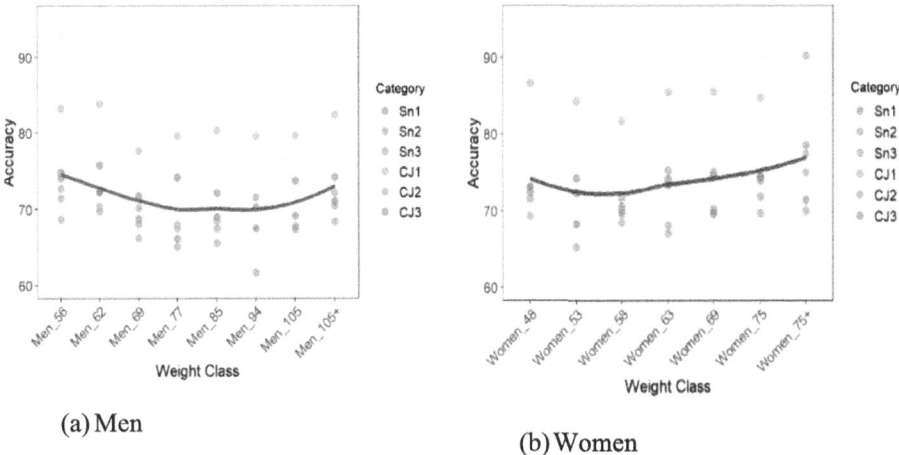

Fig. 6. Accuracy results for all weight classes

prediction rate in general, compared to the results of trying to predict the all-men and all-women groups, as shown in Fig. 4.

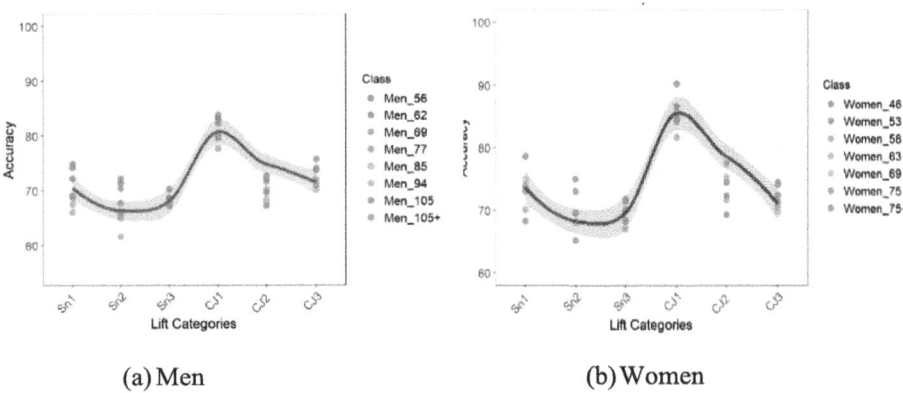

Fig. 7. Accuracy results for all lifts by weight class ordered by lift

Another interesting observation is the more extensive range of accuracy measurements for female athletes across weight classes compared to the men's weight classes as well as the generally higher accuracy of prediction for female athletes.

On running our models with the 2024 summer Olympics data as our test set, we got much better prediction results for all weight classes even though the test size was much smaller (98 athletes in most classes). A key difference was in the men's weight classes in general. Figure 8 shows the average accuracy for the different weight classes for men & women in both the regular test set and the Olympics one. The women followed the same pattern of predictability and were generally more predictable in the Olympics, particularly with the first four lifts. The men's weight classes, in contrast, showed a very unusual pattern with higher-than-average predictability in snatch 1, snatch 2, CJ2 & CJ3, with a significant drop in predictability for snatch 3 and CJ1.

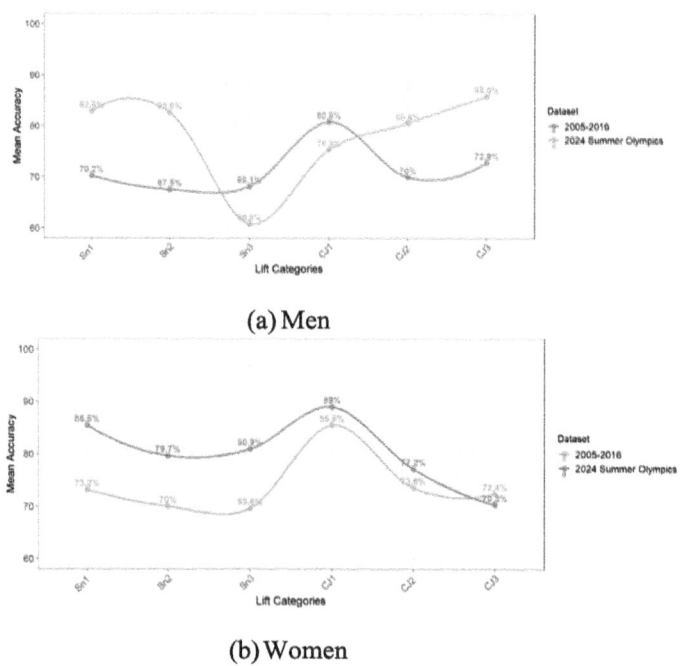

(a) Men

(b) Women

Fig. 8. Accuracy of predicting the 2024 Summer Olympics results

4.2.3 Comparison of Prediction Among the Extreme Weight Classes

In this section, we look at the predictability for the four weight classes with the most difference from the others: the men's lightest weight class (56 kg), the men's heaviest weight class (105 + kg), the women's lightest weight class (48 kg) and the women's heaviest weight class (75 + kg). Those are the most predictable weight classes according to Fig. 6. Figure 9(a) shows the accuracy for the lightest men's weight class (orange) and the heaviest men's weight class (green) against the average for all weight classes (blue line). We observe that both groups have a better accuracy than the average line but are relatively similar in predictability. Figure 9(b) shows the accuracy for the lightest men's weight class (purple) and the lightest women's weight class (yellow) against the average for all weight classes (blue line). We observe that both weight classes are more predictable than average, with the women's weight class slightly more predictable on Snatch 2, Snatch 3, and CJ1 lifts.

Figure 9 (c) shows the accuracy for the lightest women's weight class (yellow) and the heaviest women's weight class (blue) against the average for all weight classes (blue line). Unlike the men's weight class, the women's heaviest weight class is generally more predictable than the lightest weight class. Figure 9(d) shows the accuracy for the heaviest men's weight class (red) and the heaviest women's weight class (yellow) against the average for all weight classes (blue line). Note the big difference in predictability, with the women's heaviest weight class being the most predictable.

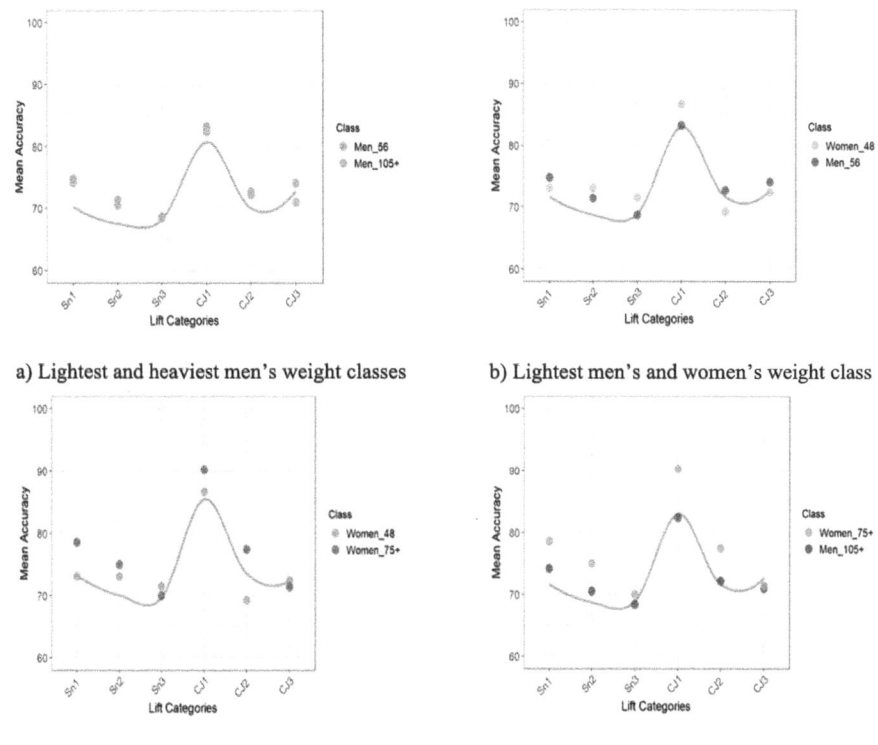

a) Lightest and heaviest men's weight classes   b) Lightest men's and women's weight class

c) Lightest and heaviest women's weight classes   d) Heaviest men's and women's weight class

Fig. 9. Comparison of prediction accuracy for the extreme classes

4.2.4   Win and Fail Precisions

In this section, we compare the win precision (percentage of all wins that were predicted as wins) and the loss precision (percentage of all losses that were predicted as losses) for the "All-men" and "All-women" groups. Figure 10(a) shows that the best win precisions are for the snatch 1 and CJ1 lifts at around 80% and go down with further lifts. On the contrary, Fig. 10(b) shows that the best loss precision is snatch 3 and CJ3 (around 65%), which is generally much lower than the win precision. Figure 10(c) shows the weighted precision for both groups, and we notice that in all three charts, women are consistently more predictable than men in both wins and losses.

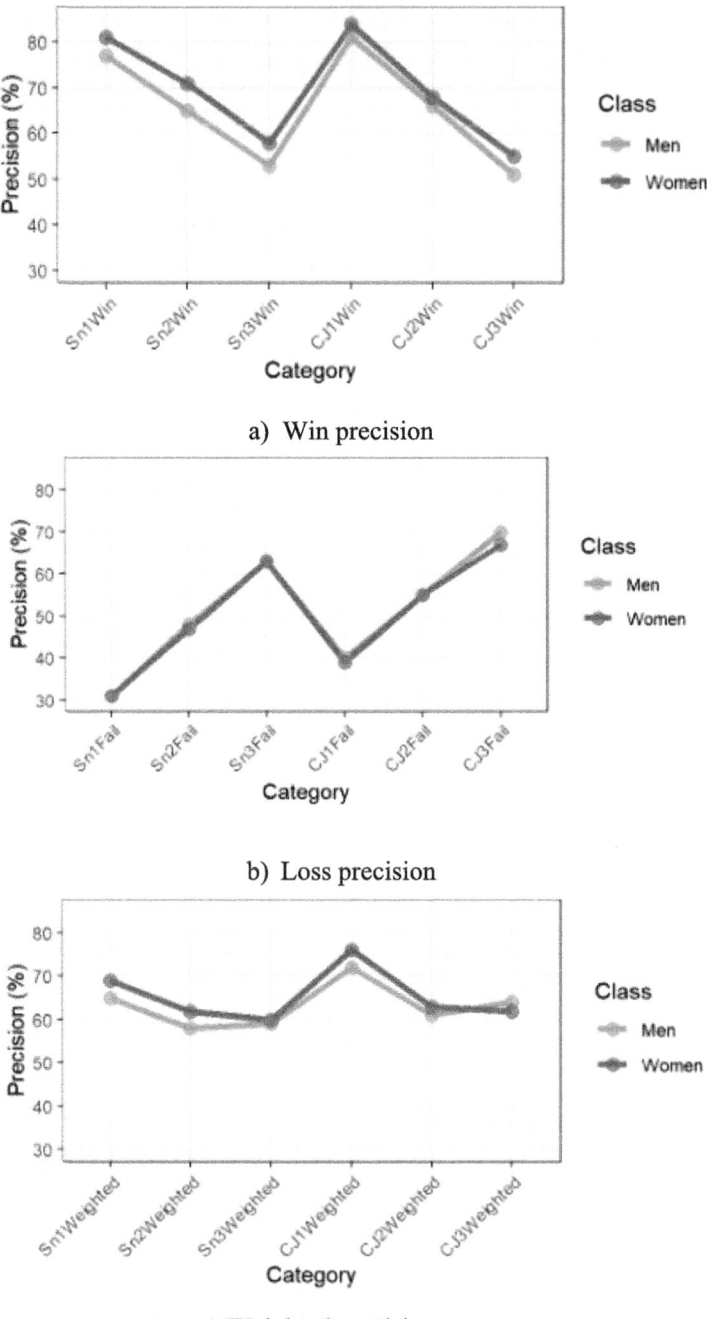

a) Win precision

b) Loss precision

c) Weighted precision

Fig. 10. Win and loss precision for the All-men and All-women groups

5   Discussion

Based on the results shown in Sect. 4, we can ascertain that using a machine learning model to predict the outcome of a lift would be a valuable tool for fast decision-making by coaches and athletes to choose a suitable load to attempt between lifts. Nonetheless, the prediction results differ for both sexes, the different lifts, competition levels, and weight classes. We present four outcomes from this work:

- Women weightlifting athletes are generally more predictable, according to Figs. 4, 6 and 10. This is observable in all weight classes as well as in the all-women group.
- The accuracy and precision of prediction differ a lot by the different lifts, according to Figs. 4, 7 and 10. Generally, the CJ1 lift for all weight classes is the most predictable. The XGBOOST model performs better when predicting success for lifts Snatch 1 and Clean and Jerk 1, as well as when it predicts a fail for lifts Snatch 3 and CJ 3.
- When using the 2024 summer Olympics as a test set, we noted that our model performed much better on this data set than our testing dataset, with a prediction of up to 89% for some weight classes. Also, we note that women athletes' results had a similar pattern but better prediction results across lifts compared to the regular test set. Meanwhile, the men athletes showed a different pattern when competing in the Olympics, with the Clean and Jerk 3 lift being the most predictable.
- Generally, the most predictable classes are the lightest and heaviest weight classes for both male and female athletes. The women's 75 + kg weight class was generally the most predictable in load selection success for all lifts, with highly unpredictable lifts in Snatch 3 and more predictable ones in CJ3.

It would be interesting to train an ML model to predict performance based on the individual's history of lifts in previous competitions as well, but that is out of the scope of this paper and is our future work after collecting historical public data for the different athletes over multiple levels of competition and time, thereby giving a temporal view of their performance as well.

6   Conclusion

In this paper, we develop a machine learning XGBOOST predictor to predict the success of a weight lift based on the athletes' sex, weight class, age, competition level, previous loads, and previous wins. The model was trained with a large dataset of over 14,000 records collected over 11 years. The results of the 2024 Summer Olympics were also used to test our model. We observed that the quality of the prediction varies significantly among the different weight classes, sexes, and lifts. We conclude that it is best to base the prediction on having each weight class separately, even though we would have a smaller dataset. Also, women's performance outcomes are generally more predictable than men's. We observed that, in general, the lightest and heaviest weight classes for each sex have the most predictable performance, with the women's 75 + kg class the most predictable in general. Also, the model predicts success better than failure in the Snatch 1 and Clean and Jerk 1 lifts and does best in the Snatch 3 and Clean and Jerk 3 when predicting failure of a lift. We recommend practitioners should use the model to help when preparing tactics for competition .

Appendix

(See Tables 4 and 5)

Table 4. XGBOOST prediction metrics for the all-men group and the men's weight classes

	Men only (9089 Records)	Men 56 kg (731 Records)	Men 62 kg (1041 Records)	Men 69 kg (1343 Records)	Men 77 kg (1458 Records)	Men 85 kg (1303 Records)	Men 94 kg (1198 Records)	Men 105 kg (1069 Records)	Men 105 + kg (946 Records)
Snatch 1 Accuracy	59%	75%	72%	69%	66%	69%	68%	69%	74%
Snatch 2 Accuracy	58%	71%	72%	66%	65%	66%	62%	68%	71%
Snatch 3 Accuracy	59%	69%	70%	68%	67%	67%	68%	67%	68%
CJ1 Accuracy	75%	83%	84%	78%	80%	80%	80%	80%	82%
CJ2 Accuracy	62%	73%	70%	70%	68%	68%	72%	67%	72%
CJ3 Accuracy	65%	74%	76%	72%	74%	72%	70%	74%	71%
Sn1 Fail precision	31%	51%	41%	43%	43%	43%	45%	44%	48%
Sn1 Win Precision	77%	86%	84%	78%	79%	86%	78%	88%	87%
Sn1 Weighted Precision	65%	77%	74%	69%	68%	75%	69%	77%	77%
Sn2 Fail precision	48%	65%	69%	57%	60%	56%	54%	58%	57%
Sn2 Win Precision	65%	76%	74%	75%	69%	73%	68%	73%	78%
Sn2 Weighted Precision	58%	72%	72%	68%	65%	66%	62%	67%	71%
Sn3 Fail precision	63%	70%	72%	72%	73%	71%	72%	69%	69%
Sn3 Win Precision	53%	67%	68%	62%	61%	61%	61%	65%	68%
Sn3 Weighted Precision	59%	69%	70%	68%	68%	67%	68%	67%	68%
CJ1 Fail precision	40%	75%	66%	57%	61%	60%	56%	56%	55%
CJ1 Win Precision	81%	84%	87%	81%	84%	84%	83%	84%	86%

(*continued*)

Table 4. (*continued*)

	Men only (9089 Records)	Men 56 kg (731 Records)	Men 62 kg (1041 Records)	Men 69 kg (1343 Records)	Men 77 kg (1458 Records)	Men 85 kg (1303 Records)	Men 94 kg (1198 Records)	Men 105 kg (1069 Records)	Men 105 + kg (946 Records)
CJ1 Weighted Precision	72%	82%	83%	75%	78%	78%	77%	78%	80%
CJ2 Fail precision	55%	70%	65%	70%	65%	66%	70%	62%	63%
CJ2 Win Precision	66%	74%	73%	70%	70%	71%	72%	71%	77%
CJ2 Weighted Precision	61%	73%	69%	70%	68%	69%	71%	67%	72%
CJ3 Fail precision	70%	77%	80%	74%	77%	76%	76%	77%	76%
CJ3 Win Precision	51%	67%	66%	63%	66%	62%	56%	66%	64%
CJ3 Weighted Precision	64%	74%	75%	71%	73%	71%	69%	73%	71%
Sn1 Fail recall	46%	63%	50%	42%	53%	65%	50%	75%	63%
Sn1 Win recall	63%	79%	79%	79%	71%	70%	75%	67%	78%
Sn1 Weighted recall	59%	75%	72%	69%	66%	69%	68%	69%	74%
Sn2 Fail recall	49%	67%	57%	69%	57%	60%	58%	53%	57%
Sn2 Win recall	64%	75%	82%	64%	71%	69%	64%	77%	78%
Sn2 Weighted recall	58%	71%	72%	66%	65%	66%	62%	68%	71%
Sn3 Fail recall	68%	77%	82%	75%	71%	76%	70%	77%	70%
Sn3 Win recall	48%	58%	53%	59%	63%	55%	64%	55%	67%
Sn3 Weighted recall	59%	69%	70%	68%	67%	67%	68%	67%	68%
CJ1 Fail recall	28%	30%	50%	32%	45%	38%	36%	40%	36%
CJ1 Win recall	88%	97%	93%	92%	91%	93%	92%	91%	93%

(*continued*)

Table 4. (*continued*)

	Men only (9089 Records)	Men 56 kg (731 Records)	Men 62 kg (1041 Records)	Men 69 kg (1343 Records)	Men 77 kg (1458 Records)	Men 85 kg (1303 Records)	Men 94 kg (1198 Records)	Men 105 kg (1069 Records)	Men 105 + kg (946 Records)
CJ1 Weighted recall	75%	83%	84%	78%	80%	80%	80%	80%	82%
CJ2 Fail recall	53%	62%	60%	58%	61%	68%	56%	56%	58%
CJ2 Win recall	68%	81%	77%	80%	74%	69%	82%	75%	80%
CJ2 Weighted recall	62%	73%	70%	70%	68%	68%	72%	67%	72%
CJ3 Fail recall	81%	83%	85%	87%	87%	82%	82%	83%	75%
CJ3 Win recall	37%	58%	58%	43%	48%	53%	46%	58%	65%
CJ3 Weighted recall	65%	74%	76%	72%	74%	72%	70%	74%	71%

Table 5. XGBOOST prediction metrics for the all-women group and the women's weight classes

	Women only (5564 Records)	Women 53 kg (816 Records)	Women 58 kg (920 Records)	Women 63 kg (940 Records)	Women 69 kg (836 Records)	Women 75 kg (708 Records)	Women 75 + kg (696 Records)
Snatch 1 Accuracy	60%	68%	70%	73%	75%	74%	79%
Snatch 2 Accuracy	62%	65%	70%	68%	70%	70%	75%
Snatch 3 Accuracy	60%	68%	68%	67%	70%	72%	70%
CJ1 Accuracy	79%	84%	82%	85%	85%	85%	90%
CJ2 Accuracy	64%	72%	72%	75%	75%	74%	77%
CJ3 Accuracy	63%	74%	71%	74%	70%	74%	71%
Sn1 Fail precision	31%	43%	42%	49%	48%	42%	40%
Sn1 Win Precision	81%	82%	84%	83%	92%	83%	89%

(*continued*)

Table 5. (*continued*)

	Women only (5564 Records)	Women 53 kg (816 Records)	Women 58 kg (920 Records)	Women 63 kg (940 Records)	Women 69 kg (836 Records)	Women 75 kg (708 Records)	Women 75 + kg (696 Records)
Sn1 Weighted Precision	69%	72%	74%	75%	82%	74%	81%
Sn2 Fail precision	47%	58%	62%	57%	53%	58%	61%
Sn2 Win Precision	71%	70%	76%	76%	76%	76%	79%
Sn2 Weighted Precision	62%	65%	70%	69%	69%	69%	74%
Sn3 Fail precision	63%	73%	70%	69%	73%	70%	67%
Sn3 Win Precision	58%	62%	66%	65%	68%	74%	73%
Sn3 Weighted Precision	60%	68%	68%	67%	71%	72%	70%
CJ1 Fail precision	39%	58%	60%	68%	73%	75%	67%
CJ1 Win Precision	84%	89%	86%	89%	87%	85%	93%
CJ1 Weighted Precision	76%	83%	80%	84%	84%	83%	90%
CJ2 Fail precision	55%	68%	66%	74%	68%	71%	68%
CJ2 Win Precision	68%	75%	76%	76%	77%	77%	81%
CJ2 Weighted Precision	63%	72%	72%	75%	74%	74%	77%
CJ3 Fail precision	67%	79%	74%	77%	76%	78%	73%
CJ3 Win Precision	55%	66%	63%	68%	60%	69%	70%
CJ3 Weighted Precision	62%	74%	70%	74%	70%	74%	71%
Sn1 Fail recall	53%	57%	58%	55%	80%	41%	50%
Sn1 Win recall	62%	72%	74%	80%	73%	84%	84%

(*continued*)

Table 5. (*continued*)

	Women only (5564 Records)	Women 53 kg (816 Records)	Women 58 kg (920 Records)	Women 63 kg (940 Records)	Women 69 kg (836 Records)	Women 75 kg (708 Records)	Women 75 + kg (696 Records)
Sn1 Weighted recall	60%	68%	70%	73%	75%	74%	79%
Sn2 Fail recall	51%	54%	67%	64%	46%	55%	45%
Sn2 Win recall	68%	73%	72%	71%	81%	78%	88%
Sn2 Weighted recall	62%	65%	70%	68%	70%	70%	75%
Sn3 Fail recall	63%	71%	73%	66%	64%	80%	71%
Sn3 Win recall	58%	64%	63%	68%	76%	63%	69%
Sn3 Weighted recall	60%	68%	68%	67%	70%	72%	70%
CJ1 Fail recall	26%	48%	46%	53%	35%	24%	56%
CJ1 Win recall	91%	92%	91%	94%	97%	98%	96%
CJ1 Weighted recall	79%	84%	82%	85%	85%	85%	90%
CJ2 Fail recall	46%	66%	67%	52%	52%	67%	58%
CJ2 Win recall	76%	77%	75%	89%	87%	80%	87%
CJ2 Weighted recall	64%	72%	72%	75%	75%	74%	77%
CJ3 Fail recall	76%	80%	80%	83%	75%	79%	73%
CJ3 Win recall	44%	65%	55%	60%	62%	68%	70%
CJ3 Weighted recall	63%	74%	71%	74%	70%	74%	71%

References

1. Reis, F.J., Alaiti, R.K., Vallio, C.S., Hespanhol, L.: Artificial intelligence and machine-learning approaches in sports: concepts, applications, challenges, and future perspectives. Braz. J. Phys. Ther. **28**, 101083 (2024)
2. Pillitteri, G., et al.: Relationship between external and internal load indicators and injury using machine learning in professional soccer: a systematic review and meta-analysis. Res. Sports Med. **32**(6), 902–938 (2024)
3. Senbel, S., et al.: An Evaluation of the determinants of performance in NCAA division I women's basketball: a dual-season investigation. In: International Sports Analytics Conference and Exhibition, pp. 228–234. Springer Nature Switzerland, Cham (2024). https://doi.org/10.1007/978-3-031-69073-0_20
4. Felice, F., Ley, C.: Predicting handball matches with machine learning and statistically estimated team strengths. J. Sports Anal. **11** (2025)
5. de Leeuw, A.W., van der Zwaard, S., van Baar, R., Knobbe, A.: Personalized machine learning approach to injury monitoring in elite volleyball players. Eur. J. Sport Sci. **22**(4), 511–520 (2022)
6. Chiu, L.Z., Schilling, B.K.: A primer on weightlifting: from sport to sports training. Strength & Condition. J. **27**(1), 42–48 (2005)
7. Zaras, N., Stasinaki, A.N., Spiliopoulou, P., Hadjicharalambous, M., Terzis, G.: Lean body mass, muscle architecture, and performance in well-trained female weightlifters. Sports **8**(5), 67 (2020)
8. Ford, L.E., Detterline, A.J., Ho, K.K., Cao, W.: Gender-and height-related limits of muscle strength in world weightlifting champions. J. Appl. Physiol. **89**(3), 1061–1064 (2000)
9. Garhammer, J., Takano, B.: Training for weightlifting. Strength Power Sport **2** (2003)
10. Ball, R., Weidman, D.: Analysis of USA powerlifting federation data from January 1, 2012–June 11, 2016. J. Strength Condition. Res. **32**(7), 1843–1851 (2018)
11. Chavda, S., Comfort, P., Lake, J.P., Bishop, C., Turner, A.N.: Predicting weight category-specific performance zones for Olympic, world, and European weightlifting competitions. J. Strength Condition. Res. **37**(10), 2038–2045 (2023)
12. Chau, V.H.: Powerlifting score prediction using a machine learning method. Math. Biosci. Eng. **18**(2), 1040–1050 (2021)
13. Xiang, Y., Cruz, J., Zaman, R., Yang, J.: Multi-objective optimization for two-dimensional maximum weight lifting prediction considering dynamic strength. Eng. Optim. **53**(2), 206–220 (2021)
14. Kauhanen, H., Komi, P., Häkkinen, K.: Standardization and validation of the body weight adjustment regression equations in Olympic weightlifting. J. Strength Condition. Res. **16**(1), 58–74 (2002)

CausalBioCF: Causal Counterfactuals for Machine Learning Interpretability

Gabriel Covello Furlanetto[1]([⊠])(ID), Alexandro Baldassin[1](ID), and Aleardo Manacero[2](ID)

[1] Department of Statistics, Applied Mathematics and Computer Science, Universidade Estadual Paulista (UNESP), Avenida 24A, 1515 - Jardim Bela Vista, Rio Claro, SP 13506-900, Brazil
{gabriel.furlanetto,alexandro.baldassin}@unesp.br
[2] Department of Computer Science and Statistics, Universidade Estadual Paulista (UNESP), Rua Cristóvão Colombo, 2265 - Jardim Nazareth, São José do Rio Preto, SP 15054-000, Brazil
aleardo.manacero@unesp.br

Abstract. Machine learning methods have been widely used to support decision-making, but most of the time, decisions cannot be easily explained. Therefore, providing explanations about the results generated by them becomes important. This is particularly relevant in high-risk decision scenarios in order to protect all the participants, as occurs, for example, in financial applications such as credit analysis. This work proposes CausalBioCF, a new method of explainability of machine learning algorithms based on counterfactuals. CausalBioCF combines a low-cost bioinspired optimization technique with domain-knowledge causal relationships to find more viable counterfactuals. The main novelty of CausalBioCF is the integration of counterfactual generation methods and traditional causality analysis. Compared to state-of-the-art systems such as DiCE, our experimental evaluation shows that CausalBioCF performs favorably, particularly when metrics such as sparsity and distance are considered. Furthermore, we show that existing systems such as DiCE can be improved by taking into account causal relationships.

Keywords: Counterfactuals · Causal Inference · Genetic Algorithm

1 Introduction

Machine learning algorithms are gradually being used in many decision-making contexts [16]. Their applications are found in low-risk scenarios, such as in the indication of media content [11,42], and high-risk contexts, such as in medical [9] and financial fields [2]. Therefore, it is important that the choices based on the data generated by these systems are reliable and allow the understanding of how the system is making its predictions, requiring transparency in the algorithms developed.

O. Gervasi et al. (Eds.): ICCSA 2025, LNCS 15649, pp. 200–217, 2025.
https://doi.org/10.1007/978-3-031-96997-3_13

In this context, the concept of counterfactual interpretability becomes relevant. According to Wachter et al. [48], a counterfactual is a slight modification in a set of facts that could lead to a different conclusion in a given analysis. Thus, providing an alternate factual scenario would help users understand why a specific result was reached and how it can be modified to a desired situation. As an example, consider the case of a 20-year-old single bank customer whose income is $1000/month with high school education and whose application was denied (factual); it can be said that a counterfactual for this scenario would indicate that if his income was $1500/month and education level was college, he would have his application approved.

Many counterfactual generation algorithms have been proposed since the work presented by Watcher et al. [48]. Among their main challenges are [50]: the *inefficiency*, given that proposed algorithms are dependent on optimizations and/or deep neural networks, which can be extremely slow; the necessity of *high-quality approximation* for a better explanation, which often ends up generating non-feasible disturbances of the original data; the necessity of taking into account the *relationship between variables*, such as the causal dependence between attributes, since it is essential for ensuring feasible counterfactuals; and the necessity for *insertion of domain knowledge* by experts to generate restrictions that ensure the feasibility of hypothetical situations.

The proposed system described in this paper, CausalBioCF, leverages techniques in the literature so that domain knowledge can be obtained and utilized in the generation of counterfactuals by means of bioinspired optimization algorithms. This approach is specifically designed for tabular data, ensuring that the counterfactuals generated are both meaningful and applicable within structured datasets. The domain knowledge generation algorithm uses statistical analysis to obtain data intervals/distribution and possible causal relationships between them [23]. This work serves as a foundation for using causal relationships to impose constraints that enhance the quality of the counterfactuals generated. The results obtained indicate that bioinspired optimization algorithms can be adapted to produce more feasible and contextually appropriate counterfactuals within the framework of the applied model. CausalBioCF tackles the aforementioned challenges, particularly the difficult task of finding causal relationships without requiring expert input.

CausalBioCF presents two main features. Firstly, it improves the task of obtaining domain knowledge for the application, thus eliminating or reducing human interference as much as possible. Secondly, it relies on bioinspired optimization methods, as they are simple to implement, more adaptable, and require less computational processing than *auto-encoders* that are commonly used to generate counterfactuals [29,52]. The main contributions of this work are:

- The use of causality as a key constraint for the generation of more feasible counterfactuals. Furthermore, we also show how causality can also improve the counterfactuals generated by other systems such as DiCE;
- An innovative approach that combines generation of counterfactuals through bioinspired algorithms and the definition of constraints through domain knowledge obtained with existing statistical techniques to improve the counterfactuals quality.

This work is organized as follows. Section 2 presents the background and related works. Section 3 describes the methodology used to develop this work. The setup for the experimental evaluation is described in Sect. 4, followed by the results and analysis in Sect. 5. Conclusions are presented in Sect. 6.

2   Background and Related Work

The field of counterfactual generation has gained increasing attention in recent years, driven by the growing demand for transparent and interpretable machine learning models [12, 47]. Several approaches have been developed to provide users with actionable feedback on model decisions, particularly in high-risk domains such as healthcare and finance [2, 9].

Among the works in the literature, Guidotti et al. [12] propose a classification of counterfactual generation methods into algorithm families, highlighting different approaches to generation. On the other hand, Verma et al. [47] take a broader perspective, analyzing counterfactual explanations in the context of interpretability and algorithmic recourse [22, 46, 47].

Based on these previous works, we can generally classify counterfactual generation methods in the literature into four main categories: optimization-based, perturbation-based, generative-based, and causal-based methods. This classification provides a structured way to analyze different approaches while highlighting the distinct strategies each category employs to ensure actionable and feasible counterfactuals. Each of these methods defines constraints differently. Optimization-based approaches enforce constraints through minimization limits of a loss function. Perturbation-based methods define constraints through functions that generate controlled modifications to the input data. Generative-based methods leverage deep learning models, such as transformers, Generative Adversarial Networks (GANs), or Autoencoders, to synthesize counterfactuals. Lastly, causal-based methods incorporate cause-effect relationships as intrinsic constraints to maintain causal validity.

This classification aligns with the perspectives of Guidotti et al. [12], who emphasize structural differences among counterfactual generation approaches. While their work categorizes methods into optimization-based, heuristic-based, instance-based, and decision tree-based, our classification extends this perspective by integrating perturbation and generative techniques, as well as explicitly considering causal constraints. Furthermore, Verma et al. [47] highlight the importance of evaluating counterfactuals beyond their generation process, advocating assessment criteria such as validity, sparsity, and minimal action. Rather than proposing a taxonomy, their work focuses on comparative evaluation frameworks. By incorporating these principles, our classification not only organizes counterfactual generation methods but also ensures that quality assessment remains integral to the discussion.

Thus, we structure the presentation of related works based on these four categories while using Verma et al.'s evaluation framework to guide the validation of the proposed approach.

2.1 Optimization-Based

This family is a union of optimization and heuristic-based families proposed by Guidotti et al.. Counterfactual generation is obtained through optimization strategies and uses a loss function to minimize the distance to the factual point as a minimization problem. These methods rely on mathematical equations to find optimal or near-optimal solutions. Another option of optimization is to find counterfactuals through local heuristic optimization, such as a genetic algorithm, that iteratively minimize a cost (loss) function. These methods are usually more efficient than the purely mathematical algorithms, but generally this efficiency comes at the cost of local solutions rather than global solutions. Some of the main works that exemplify this approach are **D**istribution-**A**ware **C**ounterfactual **E**xplanation (DACE) [20], **D**iverse **C**ounterfactual **E**xplanations (DiCE) [28], **C**ounterfactual **E**xplanations for **R**obustness, **T**ransparency, **I**nterpretability, and **F**airness (CERTIFAI) [44], and SkylineCF [49].

For linear programming algorithms [6], challenges include the need for high computational processing costs, especially in high-dimensional space problem and convergence to suboptimal counterfactuals, since algorithms get stuck in local minima. These algorithms also face challenges such as lack of plausibility, the generation of unrealistic counterfactuals, and difficulties in selecting the optimal objective function to satisfy all quality criteria, including proximity, plausibility, sparsity, and others. In contrast, heuristic-based optimization algorithms face fewer issues, are flexible and more time efficient but are still subject to provide less accurate or optimal solutions. Furthermore, it is necessary to define hyperparameters such as mutation rate or population size, which can significantly impact performance [12].

2.2 Perturbation-Based

Perturbation-based methods explore small variations in input attributes in order to identify plausible counterfactuals. The perturbations are generally generated by methods like a gradient or, in some cases, randomly. As an example of this approach, we can cite **N**earest **I**nstance **C**ounte**f**actual **E**xplanations (NICE) [4], **C**ounter**F**actuals **N**ow (CFNOW) [31], **F**easible and **A**ctionable **C**ounterfactual **E**xplanations (FACE) [36], **G**enerating **RA**ndom **C**ontrastive sampl**E**s (GRACE) [26], and Growing Spheres [25]. The main challenge in these algorithms is to define the limitations of the generated perturbations, ensuring that the generated counterfactuals are plausible and feasible.

2.3 Generative

Generative approaches leverage neural networks or probabilistic models to synthesize realistic counterfactuals. Examples of generative methods are Counte**R**-GAN [29], and **C**ounterfactual **C**onditional **H**eterogeneous **A**utoencoder (CCH-VAE) [33]. The main challenges of these methods are ensuring the feasibility of counterfactuals, as generative models (such as GANs or VAEs) often produce examples that do not fully align with real data distributions [47]. Furthermore, the high computational costs of training generative models and their complexity pose significant difficulties.

2.4   Causal

To address causal analysis, the concept of causality is defined in the sense that it must be based on premises rather than only on statistical associations or correlations, which can lead to erroneous conclusions. As suggested by Judea Pearl [35], associative and causal relationships can be distinguished as follows:

- **Associative relationship:** consists of any relationship of distributions observed together among a set of variables. Examples include correlation, dependence, conditional independence, etc.;
- **Causal relationship:** consists of relationships that cannot be defined only through a distribution. Examples include influence, effect, confusion, disturbance, etc.

It can be seen that causality is a complex concept but important for several areas of research, such as statistics, economics, epidemiology, computer science, and philosophy. According to Nogueira et al. [30], causality can be defined as the influence by which an event contributes to the production of other events. Thus, causality seeks to explain relationships between distinct events of which different variables are part. Other authors such as Pearce and Lawlor [34] also seek to define causality in a simplified way. According to them, in a case in which a variable X is a cause of a variable Y, Y depends on X to determine its value, that is, the variable Y uses the information provided by X to obtain the assumed value. This definition suggests that the variable X plays a causal role in determining the variable Y and that a change in X can result in a corresponding change in Y, indicating a cause-and-effect relationship between the variables. It is important to emphasize that this definition is based on a causal and dependent perspective between variables.

In this scenario, causality has been widely used to improve the performance of Machine Learning algorithms [35] as well. By capturing causal relationships between variables, mainly through graph-based methods such as Structural Causal Models (SCM) [35], some authors have proposed causal classifiers [32] that outperform traditional models.

Counterfactuals are also frequently used as a means of assessing causality or estimating outcomes over time. Methods for estimating time-varying outcomes were initially introduced in epidemiology and are heavily based on simple linear models [27]. The goal here is to estimate the average (non-individual) effects of treatment variations in time using counterfactuals.

Examples of research in this family that leverage causality to generate counterfactuals and enhance explainability in Machine Learning algorithms include the work of Shao et al. [43]. In this study, Structural Causal Models are utilized to measure causality between variables, producing counterfactuals with superior quantitative and qualitative evaluation metrics. However, as cited by the authors, the primary limitation of this approach lies in its reliance on expert knowledge to generate SCM graphs.

2.5   CausalBioCF's Approach

Counterfactual generation existing methods often perform well in one area (e.g. proximity, sparsity, or feasibility) while compromising another (e.g., execution time or interpretability). Furthermore, bioinspired optimization techniques remain underexplored, presenting opportunities for more efficient algorithms. Our approach seeks to address these limitations by integrating bioinspired optimization techniques and obtaining domain knowledge from a causal model to generate feasible counterfactuals while maintaining computational efficiency. Unlike other works, CausalBioCF uses causality to replace expert-provided domain knowledge, employing the results of causal analysis to define mutable and immutable features to generate high-quality counterfactuals. The approach is part of the family of causal counterfactual generation algorithms.

3   CausalBioCF

The proposed approach, CausalBioCF, considers statistical and causality analysis techniques to automate the acquisition of domain knowledge. This knowledge is used as constraints, improving the quality of counterfactuals generated without the need for specialist knowledge.

Figure 1 shows the overall structure of the proposed approach. The main information that must be fed to CausalBioCF is as follows:

– **Classifier model and Model input:** classifier model is a black-box machine learning model or statistical function that takes input data (model input), such as a tuple, composed of numeric, categorical, or other data formats, to determine the class or the probability of belonging to a given class. In CausalBioCF, these components determine the class of the factual instance and check if the individuals generated by the genetic algorithm belong to the opposite class, forming a population of valid counterfactuals. For example, a credit analysis classifier takes inputs such as age, education, profession, and income and classifies the credit application as approved or denied based on learned patterns;
– **Data Sample:** A set of real labeled data that exemplifies the input and output scenarios for a machine learning model. This data will serve as the basis for calculating causal inference, ranges of continuous variables, possible categories for attributes, among other domain knowledge information.

From these inputs, CausalBioCF can infer the domain knowledge required by the classifier, through its causal and statistical analysis module, generate counterfactuals (counterfactual generating component) and deliver them, in the desired quantity, to the end user with model result, aiming to provide explanations for the model's decision.

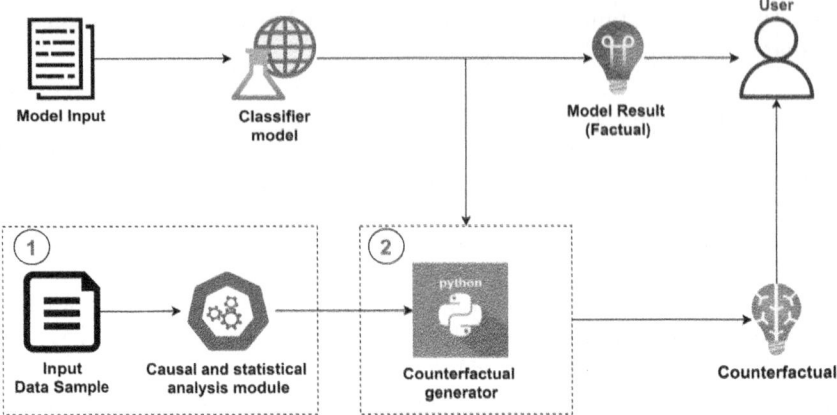

Fig. 1. CausalBioCF architecture.

The two main modules of CausalBioCF are presented using two numbered dashed boxes in Fig. 1. Module 1 includes the actions responsible for analyzing the features (input variables for the classification model) and the relationship between them through data samples. When we refer to relationships, this includes causal inference, variation intervals, possible categories for each feature, and the correlation between them. A more consistent sample will return better results in the form of constraints that will be used in the generation of counterfactuals. Module 2 is responsible for using the domain knowledge obtained from the previous module in order to generate viable, unique, diverse, and valid counterfactuals.

Thus, it can be noted that CausalBioCF addresses the challenge of manual intervention of specialists by using generated domain knowledge and ensuring that viable counterfactuals, closer to the factual, can be generated. Furthermore, this approach performs sufficiently fast with the use of a genetic algorithm.

In the following subsections, we describe in more detail each of the two main modules of CausalBioCF.

3.1 Causal Inference

In order to identify a good technique to select the best causal relationships among predictors and target variables, without the need for subjective definitions by experts, we evaluated some methods found in the literature. From this evaluation, we discarded the use of graphs such as the Structural Causal Model (SCM) [35], due to their high level of subjectivity, and the Inverse Propensity Weight (IPW) [41], due to the difficulty in defining confounders that may affect the problem.

Our choice was to adapt a method called Propensity Score Matching (PSM) [5,38] to guide the generation of counterfactuals in CausalBioCF. Propensity Score Matching (PSM) is a method used to reduce selection bias and estimate the causal effect of a treatment. Four key steps are followed to assess causality. First, the propensity score is estimated for each individual using a logistic regression model. Individuals are then matched into treatment and control groups based on score similarity, using techniques such as Nearest-Neighbor or Caliper Matching. The balance assessment then ensures that both groups are comparable in terms of observable characteristics. Finally, the average treatment effect (ATE) is estimated by comparing outcomes between the matched groups [5, 21].

Among the advantages of PSM are the reduction of selection bias and its flexibility, allowing it to be used in different research contexts. PSM was chosen because of your simplicity of the implementation, the possibility to automate causal analysis, and the corresponding run-time performance, since it tries to generate equivalent treatment and control groups (without bias or confounders) in order to calculate the Average Treatment Effect (ATE) and consequently the causality between the variables. Although we acknowledge that the model has limitations, such as only controlling observable variables and influencing the estimation of the propensity score, we understand that in the intended application scenario, these limitations are not as impactful compared to the benefit of achieving causal analysis independent of human-provided knowledge.

To explore PSM during counterfactual generation, the approach of Kline et al. [23] was adapted to calculate the ATE between model variables and target variable, discarding (as confounders) those that did not have a high causal relationship and using it to define what variables are mutable and what are immutable, decreasing computational cost, and reducing the risk of generating an unfeasible counterfactual.

3.2   Counterfactual Generation Algorithms

In order to use all the domain knowledge provided by causal analysis and overcome the challenge of using causality in counterfactual generation, we decided to work with optimization by bioinspired algorithms, due to their simplicity of implementation and computational efficiency compared to generative algorithms and traditional mathematical optimization. A Genetic Algorithm (GA) [15] approach was chosen.

Considering a genetic algorithm with steps such as population initialization, fitness evaluation, selection, crossover, and mutation [10, 15], some modifications were necessary to generate causal counterfactuals. Among these changes, an important part was the modification of the initialization step. Instead of randomly generating the entire population, the initialization uses data based on samples required for the causal inference module. This adjustment aims to reduce the number of iterations needed to reach an optimal solution.

To make this possible, only individuals labeled as the counterfactual class are filtered from the data sample. They are then ordered according to the implemented objective function. If the total number of records from the desired class is smaller than the desired size for the population, the initial population is completed using random individuals of the desired class.

In addition, the other necessary change was in relation to the objective function used by the algorithm. The objective function is central to the method and directly depends on the definitions of sparsity and distance, given by Eq. 1 and Eq. 2, respectively.

$$sparsity = \sum_{i=1}^{n} 1(x_i \neq x_i')$$ (1)

where n is the number of features in the dataset; x_i is the i-th feature of the factual instance; x_i' is the i-th feature of the counterfactual instance; $x_i \neq x_i'$ is the comparison that returns 0 if the features are different and returns 1 if the features of factual and counterfactual are the same.

For the distance definition, we used the Euclidean distance [8] as described by Eq. 2.

$$distance = \sqrt{\sum_{i=1}^{n}(x_i - x_i')^2}$$ (2)

where x_i is the i-th feature of the factual instance and x_i' is the i-th feature of the counterfactual instance.

Finally, the objective function is given by Eq. 3.

$$obj\_function = (w_1 \times sparsity) + (w_2 \times distance)$$ (3)

where w_1 and w_2 are weights used in the calculation. These weights consist of parameters passed to the genetic algorithm and start with equal values (1 for both) to ensure there is no distinction between the parameters initially. This initialization is done because the algorithm aims to improve not just one validation metric, but all of them. However, these parameters exist to allow the user to increase the emphasis on one metric over the other if desired, by adjusting their values.

The most critical challenge in adapting genetic algorithms to generate counterfactuals was defining the optimal method for generating the initial population, a key factor in ensuring the convergence of the objective function to an optimal solution within a reasonable execution time. CausalBioCF main algorithm is presented in Fig. 2.

The algorithm consists of two methods (Lines 5–10 and 13–36). The first, named "knowledgeDomain", processes the data sample provided by the user to extract domain knowledge for the given problem. This includes analyzing the intervals of numerical variables, identifying possible values of categorical variables, and performing the most complex task, the causal analysis. The second method, named "geneticAlgorithm", leverages the constraints established by the first method to execute the genetic algorithm while ensuring that these constraints are respected to generate feasible counterfactuals. Between them, causal analysis constraints define mutable and immutable features. Finally, Line 39 shows the invocation of the first module to acquire the knowledge domain (kd), followed by the counterfactual generation in Line 40.

```
1   Input: data_sample, factual_data, blackbox_model
2   Output: counterfactual_set
3
4   // Function for knowledge domain extraction
5   def knowledgeDomain(data_sample):
6       Perform causal evaluation using PSM
7       Calculate value ranges for continuous variables
8       Calculate possible values for categorical variables
9       Compute ATE and define mutables/immutables
10      return kd
11
12  // Genetic Algorithm function
13  def geneticAlgorithm(data_sample, factual_data, knowledge_domain):
14      actual_class = blackbox_model(factual_data)
15      counterfactual_class = 1 - actual_class
16
17      // Filter and initialize population
18      Filter data_sample for counterfactual examples
19      if no examples found:
20          Generate initial population randomly
21      if insufficient examples found:
22          Use found examples and generate additional ones
23      else:
24          Use selected points as initial population
25
26      // Genetic algorithm loop
27      Initialize population
28      Evaluate fitness: (w1 * sparsity) + (w2 * distance)
29      for each generation:
30          Select parents based on fitness
31          Apply crossover to create descendants
32          Mutate descendants using domain constraints
33          Evaluate descendants  fitness
34          descendants_class = blackbox_model(factual_data)
35          Select best valid individuals for next generation
36      return best counterfactual valid set
37
38  // Main execution
39  kd = knowledgeDomain(data_sample)
40  counterfactual_set = geneticAlgorithm(data_sample, factual_data, kd)
```

Fig. 2. CausalBioCF's main algorithm.

4   Experimental Setup

In this part, we evaluate our approach to counterfactual generation and compare it with Microsoft Research approach named DiCE [28]. DiCE, a Microsoft research project[1], was chosen because it is one of the most complete libraries found to date and compatible with the causal method proposed in CausalBioCF. In this way, we also have injected our causality method to define the constraints, such as mutable and immutable variables and ranges of numerical variables, for the generation of counterfactuals in Dice, which we refer to as *Causal DiCE*. It is important to note that in all tests DiCE was configured to generate counterfactuals through its own genetic algorithm, made available by the authors themselves.

There are other counterfactual generation systems that were also considered, but they were discarded because we did not have access to the source code,

---

[1] DiCE source code: https://github.com/interpretml/DiCE.

the code could not be easily adapted into our experimental framework, or they are from another family of generation algorithms. Among the systems we have considered are:

- **GeCO** [40]: developed in Julia, which made comparison with Python code difficult;
- **JUICE** [24]: uses a commercial and paid library called Gurobi to implement optimizers;
- **KAOGExp** [45]: The source code did not run as presented in the documentation;
- **DECE** [7]: Uses Node.js programming language to run an API, without batch explanations;
- **Certifai** [44]: The source code is not available;
- **GRACE** [26]: it only works with the explainability of neural networks and its original code generates only one counterfactual per execution. This execution format becomes incompatible with the test scenarios that we use, since we do not evaluate only the best counterfactual generated, but rather the set of the N best, as will be described in Sect. 4.2.

4.1 Datasets

The chosen datasets are among the most well-known datasets for counterfactual evaluation and have been used by most of the works in the area [47], including Credit Card Default [51], German Credit [14], Adult [1], Churn [18], and Compas Scores [37]. These datasets are related to various fields, such as finance, census, and healthcare, demonstrating the library's versatility across domains. The Diabetes [19] and Titanic [17] datasets were excluded due to insufficient records and features, making their results unreliable. It is important to note that the selected dataset are used to evaluate CausalBioCF only with binary classifiers.

4.2 Metrics

To evaluate the counterfactuals generated, quantitative metrics such as distance, execution time, sparsity, and validity are used. They are described below:

- **Distance or Proximity:** metric used to understand whether, through the generated restrictions, the counterfactuals remain close to the factual points. For this purpose, Euclidean (L2) [8] and Manhattan (L1) [3] distances are used;
- **Execution time:** running time in seconds of the counterfactual generation method;
- **Sparsity:** metric used to evaluate the number of features changed to produce counterfactuals. Better counterfactuals have fewer features changed;
- **Valid:** metric that evaluate whether a generated point is a counterfactual, or in other words, whether it is of the complementary or contrary class to the original point (factual) [47].

These metrics were compared together, in a combined manner, in order to ensure that the evaluation of the counterfactuals generated was as complete as possible.

All tests were performed on a machine with a 64-bit Windows 11 operating system, 16.0 GB DRAM, Intel(R) Core(TM) i7-1165G7, 2.80GHz. The black-box models evaluated in all experiments are a Random Forest (RF) [13] and a Multilayer Perceptron (MLP) [39]. It is important to emphasize that the training and testing of the models were done prior to the evaluation of the counterfactuals by the authors themselves, not using previously trained models. The entire source code developed to achieve this goal was written in Python 3.9.

To perform the validations, 10 different counterfactuals were generated for each of the 10 factuals randomly selected from a test dataset (10 repetitions of execution). In total, 100 counterfactuals per dataset per model were generated, or a total of 1000 counterfactuals. The results generated by this set of experiments are presented in the form of Average (Avg) and Standard Deviation. To plan test scenarios, our proposed methodology followed the schemes of Kuratomi et al. [24] and Brughmans et al. [4].

5   Results

In this section, we present the results obtained with CausalBioCF and DiCE from the analysis of the black-box models (MLP) and (RF) on the test data. We will analyze model accuracy, compare distances (Euclidean and Manhattan), evaluate valid counterfactuals, and the sparsity metric, concluding with the analysis of execution time. It is important to note that the best results for each row are highlighted in bold in Tables 1 and 2, which form the basis for the discussion we present next.

5.1   Model Accuracy

To evaluate counterfactual generation approaches, as mentioned previously, MLP and RF models are used. In Table 1 it is possible to check the accuracy of each of the models trained per dataset (last two columns).

From the analysis of the data, it is possible to see that all models had an accuracy above 60%. It is important to highlight that for the Churn and German Credit datasets, the Multilayer Perceptron model had performances that apparently refer to the overfitting condition. However, in order to confirm the model-agnostic behavior that counterfactuals have, these models were maintained, allowing readers to observe whether there are differences in the evaluated metrics due to this condition.

5.2 Distance

Considering Euclidean or Manhattan distance metrics, from the perspective that the closer a counterfactual outcome is to the factual, the better the result achieved, Table 1 shows that CausalBioCF presented better results compared to DiCE and Causal DiCE in most cases. It is important to note here that the causality restrictions inserted into DiCE, generating the Causal DiCE test version, ensure that its distance metrics are superior (smaller) to those of the original version of the algorithm. However, even with causal restrictions, DiCE does not outperform CausalBioCF due to factors such as the objective function, which optimizes sparsity and proximity for GA convergence, and the distinct initialization approach.

Table 1. Distance Metric (normalized distance)

Metric	Model	Dataset	Avg CBioCF	Avg. DiCE	Avg. Causal DiCE	Train Accuracy	Test Accuracy
Euclidian	MLP	Adult	**0.39** ± 0.09	0.74 ± 0.25	0.65 ± 0.30	88.52	84.52
Euclidian	MLP	Churn	**0.55** ± 0.15	0.97 ± 0.21	0.76 ± 0.29	99.67	87.43
Euclidian	MLP	Compas	**0.36** ± 0.13	0.53 ± 0.25	0.52 ± 0.20	68.80	69.42
Euclidian	MLP	Default	**0.45** ± 0.12	0.81 ± 0.19	0.57 ± 0.21	82.50	81.97
Euclidian	MLP	German	**0.45** ± 0.24	1.42 ± 0.25	0.80 ± 0.17	100.00	72.00
Euclidian	RF	Adult	**0.74** ± 0.22	0.99 ± 0.35	0.94 ± 0.37	83.63	82.27
Euclidian	RF	Churn	**0.52** ± 0.38	1.00 ± 0.14	0.75 ± 0.39	89.63	87.72
Euclidian	RF	Compas	**0.26** ± 0.10	0.38 ± 0.17	0.36 ± 0.16	68.51	68.28
Euclidian	RF	Default	**0.46** ± 0.17	0.81 ± 0.20	0.51 ± 0.21	81.90	81.47
Euclidian	RF	German	**0.70** ± 0.26	1.62 ± 0.20	0.86 ± 0.24	79.56	76.00
Manhattan	MLP	Adult	**0.58** ± 0.12	1.36 ± 0.61	1.12 ± 0.70	88.52	84.52
Manhattan	MLP	Churn	**0.82** ± 0.24	2.57 ± 0.51	1.31 ± 0.51	99.67	87.43
Manhattan	MLP	Compas	**0.38** ± 0.14	0.65 ± 0.32	0.65 ± 0.28	68.80	69.42
Manhattan	MLP	Default	**0.56** ± 0.12	1.81 ± 0.60	0.89 ± 0.42	82.50	81.97
Manhattan	MLP	German	**0.52** ± 0.27	3.42 ± 0.93	1.08 ± 0.27	100.00	72.00
Manhattan	RF	Adult	**1.28** ± 0.46	2.13 ± 0.86	1.85 ± 0.85	83.63	82.27
Manhattan	RF	Churn	**0.67** ± 0.51	2.69 ± 0.35	1.09 ± 0.63	89.63	87.72
Manhattan	RF	Compas	**0.27** ± 0.13	0.44 ± 0.22	0.42 ± 0.22	68.51	68.28
Manhattan	RF	Default	**0.68** ± 0.30	1.81 ± 0.56	0.84 ± 0.41	81.90	81.47
Manhattan	RF	German	**1.00** ± 0.51	4.15 ± 0.84	1.44 ± 0.62	79.56	76.00

5.3 Valid Counterfactuals and Quantities

When considering the number of counterfactuals generated and how many were valid, we mention that for the CausalBioCF algorithm, ten counterfactuals were generated in all executions and all of them were valid. Meanwhile, for the DiCE and Causal DiCE methods, although all counterfactuals were valid, there was a respective generation of 9.9 and 9.5 counterfactuals on average for all executions, regardless of the black-box model executed. This occurs because Dice's stopping criteria do not always ensure the generation of all counterfactuals.

5.4 Sparsity

Regarding sparsity (Table 2), we noticed that the results are similar to the distance ones. Again, DiCE shows lower performance than CausalBioCF method, though this is somewhat improved when causal constraints are incorporated into its execution (Causal DiCE).

Table 2. Sparsity Metric

Model	Dataset	Avg CBioCF	Avg. DiCE	Avg. Causal DiCE
MLP	Adult	**3.04** ± 0.41	5.56 ± 1.37	3.88 ± 1.41
MLP	Churn	**4.61** ± 0.47	14.95 ± 0.84	4.92 ± 0.33
MLP	Compas	**1.17** ± 0.31	2.06 ± 0.47	2.02 ± 0.46
MLP	Default	**1.99** ± 0.03	15.09 ± 2.96	2.95 ± 0.76
MLP	German	**1.77** ± 0.39	8.47 ± 1.44	2.96 ± 0.42
RF	Adult	**3.82** ± 0.78	7.42 ± 1.22	5.35 ± 1.20
RF	Churn	**2.47** ± 0.48	14.09 ± 0.56	3.37 ± 0.64
RF	Compas	**1.16** ± 0.31	1.82 ± 0.40	1.86 ± 0.40
RF	Default	**2.69** ± 0.62	16.77 ± 1.50	3.13 ± 0.76
RF	German	**2.31** ± 0.89	9.04 ± 1.20	3.37 ± 0.89

5.5 Execution Time

When comparing the execution times of the algorithms, excluding cases where the genetic algorithm does not reach the optimization criteria for its objective function in both counterfactual generators, we have noticed that counterfactuals generation in DiCE took around 1 s most of the times, making it 3.5x faster than CausalBioCF overall. This performance is further optimized when the causality information is incorporated. Specifically, Causal DiCE (on average 0.88 s of exeution to generate counterfactuals) is about 4 times faster than CausalBioCF and 1.15 times faster than the original version of DiCE.

This better execution performance can be justified by the difference in stopping criteria between DiCE and the proposed work. Although DiCE employs a criteria based on sparsity and proximity loss functions, along with the number of generations and the quantity of counterfactuals generated, CausalBioCF relies solely on the number of generations that are executed until completion, disregarding other criteria.

5.6   Discussions and Future Work

Among the analyses, sparsity and distance are important, ensuring that counterfactual results are close to the factual. Additionally, generating valid counterfactuals within acceptable execution times is crucial for practical use and must provide at least one viable option.

As mentioned, counterfactual explanations are model-agnostic. Thus, even though we have two datasets (Churn and German Credit) in which MLP-trained models showed a tendency of overfitting, the overall trends in counterfactual metrics remained unchanged.

Based on these conclusions and on the results presented, it is evident that the proposed work meets most of the criteria, often exceeding DiCE, an established algorithm in the literature. This is possible due to the restrictions generated by the knowledge domain acquisition module developed, which can be used not only in the proposed algorithm, but also expanded to other works that accept this type of constraints as input.

Other factors that contribute to this are the proposed objective function, which considers sparsity and proximity criteria for the convergence of the genetic algorithm, as well as the different way of initializing the GA, as previously mentioned.

Furthermore, although DiCE and Causal DiCE displayed better overall execution times, CausalBioCF still generates counterfactuals in acceptable times (about 3.5 s on average). Also note that we did not strive to optimize the Python code as this was not our main goal at this stage.

In general, we understand that there are still possible areas to explore and challenges to overcome. In order to achieve these goals, future work includes the following: expanding quantitative testing scenarios to take into account metrics related to the quality and feasibility of the counterfactuals generated; comparing the developed library with modules from other libraries that use another generation algorithms like NICE [4] and CFNOW [31]; and finally, expanding the possibility of generating counterfactuals to multiclass datasets.

The last point mentioned, which proposes using the algorithm in multiclass datasets, perhaps brings the greatest challenge as future work, which consists of adapting the causal inference strategy so that it can analyze relationships with more than 2 treatment groups.

6   Conclusions

In this paper we presented CausalBioFC, a bioinspired approach to counterfactuals generation that takes into account causality. The possibility of using causal inference tends to generate better counterfactuals, resulting in less sparse results, closer to the factual. Moreover, our results compare favorably against DiCE when evaluating metrics such as distance and sparsity, showing the potential of CausalBioFC.

Disclosure of Interests. The authors have no competing interests to declare that are relevant to the content of this article.

References

1. Becker, B., Kohavi, R.: Adult. UCI Machine Learning Repository (1996). https://doi.org/10.24432/C5XW20
2. Bin Sulaiman, R., Schetinin, V., Sant, P.: Review of machine learning approach on credit card fraud detection. Human-Centric Intell. Syst. **2**(1–2), 55–68 (2022)
3. Black, P.E.: Dictionary of algorithms and data structures. Paul E, Black (1998)
4. Brughmans, D., Leyman, P., Martens, D.: Nice: an algorithm for nearest instance counterfactual explanations. Data mining and knowledge discovery, pp. 1–39 (2023)
5. Caliendo, M., Kopeinig, S.: Some practical guidance for the implementation of propensity score matching. J. Econom. Surv. **22**(1), 31–72 (2008)
6. Carrizosa, E., Ramírez-Ayerbe, J., Morales, D.R.: Mathematical optimization modelling for group counterfactual explanations. Eur. J. Oper. Res. **319**(2), 399–412 (2024)
7. Cheng, F., Ming, Y., Qu, H.: Dece: Decision explorer with counterfactual explanations for machine learning models. IEEE Trans. Visual Comput. Graphics **27**(2), 1438–1447 (2020)
8. Danielsson, P.E.: Euclidean distance mapping. Comput. Graphics Image Process. **14**(3), 227–248 (1980)
9. Fatima, M., Pasha, M., et al.: Survey of machine learning algorithms for disease diagnostic. J. Intell. Learn. Syst. Appl. **9**(01), 1 (2017)
10. Golberg, D.E.: Genetic algorithms in search, optimization, and machine learning. Addion wesley **1989**(102), 36 (1989)
11. Gomez-Uribe, C.A., Hunt, N.: The Netflix recommender system: algorithms, business value, and innovation. ACM Trans. Manage. Inform. Syst. (TMIS) **6**(4), 1–19 (2015)
12. Guidotti, R.: Counterfactual explanations and how to find them: literature review and benchmarking. Data Min. Knowl. Disc. **38**(5), 2770–2824 (2024)
13. Ho, T.K.: Random decision forests. In: Proceedings of 3rd International Conference on Document Analysis and Recognition, vol. 1, pp. 278–282. IEEE (1995)
14. Hofmann, H.: Statlog (German Credit Data). UCI Machine Learning Repository (1994). https://doi.org/10.24432/C5NC77
15. Holland, J.H.: Genetic algorithms. Scientific American **267**(1), 66–73 (1992)
16. Jin, W.: Research on machine learning and its algorithms and development. J. Phys.: Conf. Series **1544**(1), 012003 (May 2020). https://doi.org/10.1088/1742-6596/1544/1/012003
17. Kaggle: Titanic - machine learning from disaster. https://www.kaggle.com/competitions/titanic (2012). Accessed 04 Oct 2024
18. Kaggle: Telco customer churn. https://www.kaggle.com/datasets/blastchar/telco-customer-churn (2020). Accessed 04 Oct 2024

19. Kahn, M.: Diabetes. UCI Machine Learning Repository (1994). https://doi.org/10.24432/C5T59G

20. Kanamori, K., Takagi, T., Kobayashi, K., Arimura, H.: DACE: Distribution-aware counterfactual explanation by mixed-integer linear optimization. In: IJCAI, pp. 2855–2862 (2020)

21. Kane, L.T., et al.: Propensity score matching: a statistical method. Clin. Spine Surg. **33**(3), 120–122 (2020)

22. Karimi, A.H., Von Kügelgen, J., Schölkopf, B., Valera, I.: Algorithmic recourse under imperfect causal knowledge: a probabilistic approach. Adv. Neural. Inf. Process. Syst. **33**, 265–277 (2020)

23. Kline, A., Luo, Y.: PSMPY: a package for retrospective cohort matching in Python. In: 2022 44th Annual International Conference of the IEEE Engineering in Medicine and Biology Society (EMBC), pp. 1354–1357. IEEE (2022)

24. Kuratomi, A., Miliou, I., Lee, Z., Lindgren, T., Papapetrou, P.: Juice: Justified counterfactual explanations. In: Discovery Science: 25th International Conference, DS 2022, Montpellier, France, October 10–12, 2022, Proceedings, pp. 493–508. Springer (2022)

25. Laugel, T., Lesot, M.J., Marsala, C., Renard, X., Detyniecki, M.: Comparisonbased inverse classification for interpretability in machine learning. In: Information Processing and Management of Uncertainty in Knowledge-Based Systems. Theory and Foundations: 17th International Conference, IPMU 2018, Cádiz, Spain, June 11-15, 2018, Proceedings, Part I 17, pp. 100–111. Springer (2018)

26. Le, T., Wang, S., Lee, D.: Grace: Generating concise and informative contrastive sample to explain neural network model's prediction. In: Proceedings of the 26th ACM SIGKDD International Conference on Knowledge Discovery & Data Mining, pp. 238–248 (2020)

27. Melnychuk, V., Frauen, D., Feuerriegel, S.: Causal transformer for estimating counterfactual outcomes. In: International Conference on Machine Learning, pp. 15293–15329. PMLR (2022)

28. Mothilal, R.K., Sharma, A., Tan, C.: Explaining machine learning classifiers through diverse counterfactual explanations. In: Proceedings of the 2020 Conference on Fairness, Accountability, and Transparency, pp. 607–617 (2020)

29. Nemirovsky, D., Thiebaut, N., Xu, Y., Gupta, A.: Countergan: generating counterfactuals for real-time recourse and interpretability using residual GANs. In: Uncertainty in Artificial Intelligence, pp. 1488–1497. PMLR (2022)

30. Nogueira, A.R., Pugnana, A., Ruggieri, S., Pedreschi, D., Gama, J.: Methods and tools for causal discovery and causal inference. Wiley Interdisc. Rev.: Data Mining Knowl. Discov. **12**(2), e1449 (2022)

31. de Oliveira, R., Sörensen, K., Martens, D.: A model-agnostic and data-independent tabu search algorithm to generate counterfactuals for tabular, image, and text data. Eur. J. Oper. Res. **317**(2), 286–302 (2024)

32. O'Brien, A., Kim, E., Weber, R.: Investigating causally augmented sparse learning as a tool for meaningful classification. In: 2023 IEEE Sixth International Conference on Artificial Intelligence and Knowledge Engineering (AIKE), pp. 33–37. IEEE (2023)

33. Pawelczyk, M., Broelemann, K., Kasneci, G.: Learning model-agnostic counterfactual explanations for tabular data. In: Proceedings of The Web Conference 2020, pp. 3126–3132 (2020)

34. Pearce, N., Lawlor, D.A.: Causal inference–so much more than statistics. Int. J. Epidemiol. **45**(6), 1895–1903 (2016)

35. Pearl, J.: Causality. Cambridge university press (2009)
36. Poyiadzi, R., Sokol, K., Santos-Rodriguez, R., De Bie, T., Flach, P.: Face: feasible and actionable counterfactual explanations. In: Proceedings of the AAAI/ACM Conference on AI, Ethics, and Society, pp. 344–350 (2020)
37. ProPublica: Compas recidivism risk score data and analysis. https://www.propublica.org/datastore/dataset/compas-recidivism-risk-score-data-and-analysis (2016). Accessed 04 Oct 2024
38. Rosenbaum, P.R., Rubin, D.B.: The central role of the propensity score in observational studies for causal effects. Biometrika **70**(1), 41–55 (1983)
39. Rumelhart, D.E., Hinton, G.E., Williams, R.J.: Learning representations by back-propagating errors. Nature **323**(6088), 533–536 (1986)
40. Schleich, M., Geng, Z., Zhang, Y., Suciu, D.: GECO: Quality counterfactual explanations in real time. arXiv preprint arXiv:2101.01292 (2021)
41. Seaman, S.R., White, I.R.: Review of inverse probability weighting for dealing with missing data. Stat. Methods Med. Res. **22**(3), 278–295 (2013)
42. Shani, G., Gunawardana, A.: Evaluating recommendation Systems. In: Recommender Systems Handbook, pp. 257–297 (2011)
43. Shao, X., Wang, H., Chen, X., Zhu, X., Zhang, Y.: Cube: causal intervention-based counterfactual explanation for prediction models. IEEE Trans. Knowl. Data Eng. **36**(6), 2416–2429 (2023)
44. Sharma, S., Henderson, J., Ghosh, J.: Certifai: A common framework to provide explanations and analyse the fairness and robustness of black-box models. In: Proceedings of the AAAI/ACM Conference on AI, Ethics, and Society, pp. 166–172 (2020)
45. da Silva, A.T., Bertini, J.R.: Using the k-associated optimal graph to provide counterfactual explanations. In: 2022 IEEE International Conference on Fuzzy Systems (FUZZ-IEEE), pp. 1–8 (2022). https://doi.org/10.1109/FUZZ-IEEE55066.2022.9882751
46. Spangher, A., Ustun, B., Liu, Y.: Actionable recourse in linear classification. In: Proceedings of the 5th Workshop on Fairness, Accountability and Transparency in Machine Learning (2018)
47. Verma, S., Boonsanong, V., Hoang, M., Hines, K., Dickerson, J., Shah, C.: Counterfactual explanations and algorithmic recourses for machine learning: A review. ACM Comput. Surv. **56**(12), 1–42 (2024)
48. Wachter, S., Mittelstadt, B., Russell, C.: Counterfactual explanations without opening the black box: automated decisions and the GDPR. Harv. JL Tech. **31**, 841 (2017)
49. Wang, Y., et al.: The skyline of counterfactual explanations for machine learning decision models. In: Proceedings of the 30th ACM International Conference on Information & Knowledge Management, pp. 2030–2039 (2021)
50. Yang, F., Alva, S.S., Chen, J., Hu, X.: Model-based counterfactual synthesizer for interpretation. In: Proceedings of the 27th ACM SIGKDD Conference on Knowledge Discovery & Data Mining, pp. 1964–1974 (2021)
51. Yeh, I.C.: Default of credit card clients. UCI Machine Learning Repository (2009). https://doi.org/10.24432/C55S3H
52. Zhang, W., Barr, B., Paisley, J.: An interpretable deep classifier for counterfactual generation. In: Proceedings of the Third ACM International Conference on AI in Finance, pp. 36–43 (2022)

A Comparative Analysis of Interpretable Deep Learning Models for Nutrient Analysis in Vulnerable Populations

Zvinodashe Revesai⬤ and Okuthe P. Kogeda[✉]⬤

School of Mathematics, Statistics and Computer Science, College of Agriculture, Engineering and Science, University of KwaZulu-Natal, Westville Campus, Durban 3209, Republic of South Africa
kogedao@ukzn.ac.za

Abstract. Nutrient deficiencies affect over 2 billion people globally, with vulnerable populations disproportionately impacted. While artificial intelligence offers promising solutions for nutrient analysis, the lack of transparency in deep learning models limits their adoption in healthcare settings where interpretability is essential. This study presents a comparative analysis of interpretable deep learning models for nutrient analysis in food images, focusing on the trade-offs between model performance, interpretability, and computational efficiency. Using the Food101 dataset augmented with nutritional information, we implement and evaluate three distinct approaches: a ResNet50 architecture with Grad-CAM, a Vision Transformer with attention maps, and a DenseNet with LIME integration. Our hybrid approach, combining DenseNet with LIME, achieves 94% accuracy in nutrient detection whilst providing comprehensive interpretability, though at increased computational cost. The ResNet50 model demonstrates efficient performance with 92% accuracy and minimal computational overhead, whilst the Vision Transformer offers unique insights through attention mechanisms despite lower accuracy at 89%. Experimental results show varying effectiveness across nutrient types, with macronutrient detection achieving 95% accuracy and mineral detection proved more challenging at 87%. These findings provide valuable insights for selecting appropriate architecture based on specific application requirements, particularly where the balance between accuracy, interpretability, and computational efficiency is crucial.

Keywords: Interpretable Artificial Intelligence · Nutritional Analysis · Deep Learning Explainability · Food Image Recognition · Computer Vision in Healthcare · Vulnerable Population Nutrition

1 Introduction

Nutrient deficiencies pose a critical global health challenge. They particularly affect vulnerable populations worldwide. Despite healthcare advancements, accessible tools for nutrient analysis remain scarce. The WHO's global health surveys reveal that micronutrient deficiencies affect more than 2 billion people worldwide. Among these populations,

O. Gervasi et al. (Eds.): ICCSA 2025, LNCS 15649, pp. 218–233, 2025.
https://doi.org/10.1007/978-3-031-96997-3_14

expectant mothers, young children and the elderly experience the most severe health consequences [1]. Research across multiple regions confirms these vulnerable groups face heightened risks of developmental delays, compromised immunity and chronic health complications [2].

Conventional diagnostic methods rely on laboratory testing and clinical assessments. These approaches create significant barriers to treatment. High costs, limited accessibility and delayed intervention hamper their effectiveness [3]. Artificial Intelligence (AI) and Machine Learning (ML) technologies offer promising alternatives. These emerging solutions could transform nutrient deficiency detection and management [4]. Yet widespread adoption faces substantial challenges. The lack of transparency and interpretability in these systems creates hesitation among practitioners [5].

Traditional assessment methods, whilst accurate, often prove cumbersome. They typically require substantial resources and time. This frequently leads to delayed interventions. Such limitations become especially problematic in resource-poor settings. ML models show remarkable potential for predicting nutrient deficiencies. However, their "black box" nature hinders widespread adoption [6]. Healthcare providers need more than accurate predictions. They require understanding of the reasoning behind these predictions. Without interpretability, ML's real-world impact diminishes considerably [7].

Our study examines interpretable machine learning for nutrient deficiency prediction. We focus particularly on vulnerable populations. We leverage computer vision techniques with integrated interpretation methods. Our aim is developing tools bridging technological capability and clinical utility. We integrate multiple data sources in our approach. These include clinical measurements, dietary information and demographic factors. This combination creates comprehensive predictive models for guiding interventions [8].

This research has three primary objectives:

1. To develop interpretable deep learning models for nutrient deficiency prediction.
2. To assess various interpretable techniques for enhancing model clarity whilst maintaining accuracy.
3. To validate these models in real-world clinical settings, focusing on vulnerable populations.

Our key contributions include:

1. A systematic comparison of three distinct interpretable deep learning architectures. These include ResNet50 (Residual Network with 50 layers) with Grad-CAM (Gradient-weighted Class Activation Mapping), Vision Transformer (ViT) with attention maps, and DenseNet (Densely Connected Convolutional Networks) with LIME (Local Interpretable Model-agnostic Explanations) for food image analysis.
2. Quantitative evaluation of trade-offs between performance, interpretability and computational efficiency across architectures.
3. Development of a hybrid DenseNet-LIME approach achieving 94% accuracy with comprehensive interpretability.
4. Nutrient-specific performance analysis revealing varying detection capabilities across different nutrients. Macronutrient identification shows particularly strong results.

5. A framework for selecting appropriate model architectures based on specific healthcare application requirements.

This research extends work at the AI-public health intersection. It offers novel approaches to healthcare challenges through interpretable machine learning solutions. Our findings could improve nutrient deficiency detection accessibility and efficiency. This proves especially valuable in resource-limited settings where traditional methods often fail.

The remainder of this paper follows this structure: Section 2 presents related work on deep learning-based nutrient analysis and interpretability methods. Section 3 details our methodology, including dataset preparation and model construction. Section 4 presents experimental results across all three models. Section 5 discusses implications and analyses performance-interpretability trade-offs. Section 6 concludes with contributions and future research directions.

2 Related Work

Deep learning approaches for nutrient assessment have evolved significantly, particularly for vulnerable populations. Contemporary architectures include Convolutional Neural Networks (CNNs) for visual nutrient analysis and Recurrent Neural Networks (RNNs) for temporal pattern analysis, while transformer-based architectures enable integration of heterogeneous data modalities [9, 10]. These implementations utilise multi-modal frameworks to process diverse data types, including clinical measurements and dietary records [11, 12].

Current interpretability methods follow distinct approaches: local methods such as Local Interpretable Model-agnostic Explanations (LIME) and SHapley Additive exPlanations (SHAP) provide individual predictions, attention-based mechanisms highlight significant features [13], and model-agnostic approaches offer post-hoc explanations [12]. Recent research suggests that LIME is more computationally straightforward while SHAP accommodates a wider range of model complexities, making SHAP particularly suitable for deep neural networks and ensemble methods [14]. However, implementing these methods for vulnerable populations presents unique challenges, particularly in deficiency prediction and dietary optimisation. The complexity of these models creates significant barriers in result interpretation and clinical validation [14].

While individual studies have evaluated specific approaches, comprehensive comparisons remain limited in scope. Recent applications of SHAP and LIME for nutrient analysis have demonstrated their effectiveness in predicting soil nutrient content for agricultural applications, but their application to human nutrition remains critically underexplored. Despite the potential benefits, nutrition analysis systems largely operate as black-box models, offering predictions without clear explanations of their decision-making processes. This lack of interpretable models in nutritional assessment represents a significant gap in the field. The absence of standardised evaluation models makes it challenging to assess different approaches objectively, particularly in considering both predictive accuracy and interpretability for vulnerable populations [9]. This gap severely impedes the selection and implementation of optimal approaches for clinical applications.

There is thus a critical need for systematic comparative studies that evaluate interpretable deep learning approaches for nutrient analysis in vulnerable populations. The scarcity of interpretable models in nutrition analysis stands in stark contrast to their growing importance in other healthcare domains. Current research trends highlight the importance of interpretability frameworks like LIME and SHAP in enhancing fidelity within clinical decision support systems [15]. Such research must consider both technical performance metrics and clinical relevance, potentially leading to more informed selection of methodologies for clinical implementation.

Our work addresses these gaps by providing a comprehensive comparative analysis of three distinct interpretable deep learning approaches for nutrition analysis, evaluating their performance across multiple dimensions, including accuracy, interpretability, and computational efficiency.

3 Methodology

This section details our approach to comparing interpretable deep learning models for nutrient analysis. We present our methodology across five main components: dataset preparation, model construction, comparative architectures, training strategy, and interpretability framework. Each component is designed to enable systematic evaluation of model performance and interpretability.

3.1 Implementation Tools and Libraries

Our research employed a combination of Python 3.9 [30] frameworks and specialised libraries for deep learning and interpretability. We utilised PyTorch 2.0.1 [14] and TensorFlow 2.13.0 [15] frameworks in complementary roles throughout development. This pairing proved advantageous—PyTorch offered greater flexibility during exploratory phases and research iterations, whilst TensorFlow provided robust deployment capabilities and serving infrastructure.

For model implementation and training, we used PyTorch Lightning 2.0.0 [31], which standardised our training loops and facilitated distributed computing across multiple GPUs. Hyperparameter optimisation was conducted using Optuna 3.1.0 [32], which efficiently navigated the complex parameter space through Bayesian optimisation techniques.

For model interpretability, we selected several specialist libraries. The LIME package 0.2.0.1 [16] generated context-specific explanations for individual predictions, complemented by SHAP 0.42.1 [17] for broader feature importance analysis across our dataset. We implemented Grad-CAM visualisations through the Captum library 0.6.0 [18], enabling clear representation of activation regions in food imagery.

Our data pipeline relied on OpenCV 4.7.0 [33] for image processing, NumPy 1.24.3 [19] for numerical operations, and scikit-learn 1.3.0 [20] for preprocessing tasks, supporting the quality assessment and normalisation procedures detailed in the following section. Visualisations and performance metric plots were generated using Matplotlib 3.7.1 [34].

3.2   Dataset Description and Preprocessing

The Food101 dataset formed the cornerstone of our study, containing 101,000 images across 101 food categories. Each category includes 1,000 real-world photographs with varying quality, resolution and lighting, making it ideal for robustness testing [15]. The collection blends professional photography with user-generated content, reflecting typical food imaging scenarios [16].

We enhanced our dataset through several augmentation techniques. These included horizontal flips, subtle rotations ($\pm 10°$), brightness modifications ($\pm 20\%$) and strategic cropping. Colour jittering helped account for lighting variations [17]. Such augmentations strengthened model generalisation across diverse image conditions.

Our preprocessing workflow comprised several key stages. We first standardised all images to 224×224 pixels for dimensional consistency. Pixel values underwent normalisation using ImageNet statistics, supporting our pre-trained model weights [18]. An automated quality filter removed excessively blurred or poorly lit samples.

We enriched our Food101 dataset with detailed nutritional information to support our analysis [15]. Rather than working with images alone, we mapped each food category to established nutrition reference sources. This allowed us to track proteins, fats and various micronutrients across the entire dataset. To make meaningful comparisons between different foods, we adjusted all nutritional values to represent typical portion sizes served in everyday settings.

We divided the dataset using a 75:15:10 ratio for training, validation and testing [15]. Stratified sampling maintained balanced category representation throughout all subsets. The resulting distribution allocated 75,750 images for model training, 15,150 for validation and hyperparameter tuning, and 10,100 for final performance assessment [15].

3.3   Model Construction

The construction of our interpretable deep learning models follows a systematic approach integrating both architectural design and interpretability mechanisms. Our neural network architecture implements three distinct designs for comparative analysis.

In the layer configuration, we utilise a hierarchical structure beginning with convolutional layers for feature extraction, followed by attention mechanism integration and classification layers. The backbone architecture employs ResNet50 [19], selected for its proven effectiveness in feature extraction and gradient flow. The activation functions include ReLU for hidden layers to address vanishing gradient problems, whilst the final layer employs softmax activation for classification outputs [17]. We implement a multi-task loss function combining cross-entropy for classification and mean squared error for nutrient prediction, weighted using learnable parameters. The optimisation process utilises Adam optimiser with an initial learning rate of 1e−4 and cosine annealing schedule [20].

The interpretability layer integration encompasses multiple components. We incorporate self-attention mechanisms based on the transformer architecture [21], enabling the model to focus on relevant image regions whilst providing interpretable attention maps. Feature attribution methods include integrated gradients and SHAP values, offering complementary perspectives on feature importance. For visualisation, we implement Grad-CAM to generate class-specific activation maps and feature visualisation through optimisation of input images [22].

Model parameters are carefully configured to balance performance and computational efficiency. The input specifications accommodate $224 \times 224 \times 3$ RGB images, with batch normalisation layers after each convolutional block. Hyperparameters are tuned using Bayesian optimisation, with key settings including a learning rate of 1e-4 with cosine decay, batch size of 32, weight decay of 1e-5, and dropout rate of 0.3. Memory requirements are optimised through gradient checkpointing and mixed precision training, enabling efficient model training on standard GPU hardware whilst maintaining numerical stability [23].

3.4   Comparative Architectures

We implement and compare three distinct architectures, each integrating different interpretability methods for nutrient analysis, as summarised in Table 1:

Table 1. Comparison of Deep Learning Architectures

Category	Architecture	Interpretability Method	Key Characteristics	Reference
Deep Learning	ResNet50	Grad-CAM	50 layers, residual connections	[19]
Traditional	Vision Transformer	Attention Maps	12 encoder layers, 16x16 patches	[24]
Hybrid	DenseNet	LIME	121 layers, dense connectivity	[25]

Model A (ResNet50): This model employs the ResNet50 architecture integrated with Grad-CAM visualisation, consisting of 50 layers with residual connections for efficient gradient flow. The implementation utilises pretrained ImageNet weights, with final layers modified for nutrient analysis. Grad-CAM generates class-specific localisation maps using gradient information from the final convolutional layer, providing visual explanations for model decisions. Local interpretability mechanisms focus on activation map quality and decision path clarity, with model-specific metrics evaluating explanation fidelity [31].

Model B (Vision Transformer): This model implements a Vision Transformer (ViT) architecture, processing images as 16x16 pixel patches through 12 transformer encoder layers with 12 attention heads each. The attention mechanism employs multi-head self-attention, enabling focused analysis of different image regions while maintaining interpretability through attention map visualisation. Custom visualisation methods display both patch-level and head-level attention patterns, with interpretability metrics focusing on attention map coherence and patch relevance scores.

Model C (DenseNet): This model utilises DenseNet architecture with LIME integration, implementing 121 layers with dense connectivity for efficient feature reuse. Each layer receives feature maps from all preceding layers, creating short paths that facilitate gradient flow. LIME integration provides local interpretable explanations by approximating model behaviour around specific predictions with interpretable linear models. This hybrid approach combines traditional convolutional processing with modern interpretability techniques, evaluated through both feature importance metrics and explanation fidelity measures.

3.5 Training and Validation

Our training and validation approach implements a rigorous protocol to ensure fair comparison between models while maintaining reproducibility of results, as detailed in Table 2:

Table 2. Training Specifications for Model Implementation

Component	Parameter	Specification
Training Protocol	Stage 1 - Fine-tuning	Learning rate: 1e-4, Epochs: 50, Warmup: 5 epochs
	Stage 2 - Interpretability	Learning rate: 1e-5, Epochs: 30
Precision Format	Mixed precision (FP16/FP32)	
Hyperparameter Optimisation	Method	Bayesian optimisation (TPE)
	Number of Trials	100
	Parameters Optimised	Learning rate, weight decay, dropout rate
Cross-validation	Approach	5-fold stratified
	Early Stopping	Patience: 10 epochs
	Distribution	Class-balanced folds

We train the model in two phases: initially using a higher learning rate for 50 epochs, followed by a lower rate for fine-tuning over 30 epochs. Bayesian optimisation helps us select the best parameters, whilst five-fold cross-validation ensures reliable testing. We measure both performance and interpretability metrics throughout training.

3.6 Interpretability Design

Our interpretability model implements multiple complementary approaches to ensure comprehensive model explanation and evaluation. For Model A, we employ Grad-CAM as the primary interpretation method, enabling class activation mapping for nutrient identification. This is supported by SHAP analysis to understand feature contributions for nutrient composition, alongside Integrated Gradients to establish overall nutrient importance rankings. Model B, utilises attention maps as its primary interpretation method, providing direct visualisation of nutrient focus areas. We complement this with SHAP for patch-level contribution analysis and implement attention visualisation techniques to understand multi-head attention patterns. For Model C, we implement LIME as the primary interpretation method to generate local explanations for nutrient predictions. This is enhanced by Integrated Gradients analysis to determine feature importance within dense connections, and we incorporate decision rules analysis to map nutrient interaction pathways [26].

The local interpretability methods focus on explaining individual predictions. For any prediction y, LIME generates local explanations by approximating the complex model $f(x)$ with an interpretable model $g(x)$ around the neighbourhood of x, such that $g(z) \approx f(z)$ for z near x. This is formulated as shown:

$$\text{explanation}(x) = \text{argmin } L(f, g, \pi x) + \Omega(g) \tag{1}$$

where L is a loss function measuring local fidelity and $\Omega(g)$ is the complexity of the interpretable model [27].

For feature attribution, SHAP values provide a unified measure based on cooperative game theory. For each feature i, its SHAP value φi is calculated as:

$$\varphi i = \Sigma[S \subseteq N\{i\}]|S|!(n - |S| - 1)!/n![fx(S \cup \{i\}) - fx(S)] \tag{2}$$

where N is the set of all features and $fx(S)$ is the prediction for feature subset S.

Visual explanation techniques implement Grad-CAM, which generates explanations by computing the gradient of the target class score with respect to feature maps Ak, as:

$$\alpha k = 1/Z \Sigma i \Sigma j \, \partial y / \partial Ak\_ij \tag{3}$$

The Grad-CAM localisation map is then calculated using:

$$L\_Grad - CAM = ReLU(\Sigma k \, \alpha k \, Ak) \tag{4}$$

where αk captures the importance of each feature map k for the target class.

Our model enables decision path analysis, where each prediction follows a path P from root to leaf, with decision rules Ri at each node i; The confidence of this path can be calculated using Eq. (5):

$$P = \{R1 \wedge R2 \wedge ... \wedge Rn\}(5) \text{ Confidence}(P) = \text{Ncorrect/Ntotal} \tag{5}$$

These complementary approaches ensure comprehensive interpretability at different levels: individual predictions, feature importance, visual attention, and decision logic. This multi-faceted interpretability is crucial for building trust in nutritional analysis applications [28].

3.7   Evaluation Metrics and Hardware

We evaluated our models using a comprehensive set of metrics that assess both performance and interpretability aspects. For classification performance, we measured accuracy, precision, recall and F1-score across food categories. Nutrient prediction accuracy was evaluated using Mean Absolute Error (MAE) and Root Mean Square Error (RMSE).

For interpretability assessment, we quantified explanation fidelity using Faithfulness Correlation [29] and Monotonicity metrics [30]. We also conducted a user study with 15 nutrition specialists to evaluate explanation comprehensibility using a 5-point Likert scale.

We performed all training and evaluation on a high-performance computing cluster equipped with NVIDIA A100 GPUs (40 GB VRAM). This hardware configuration enabled efficient processing of our large-scale dataset while supporting the complex interpretability methods implemented in our models.

4   Results

This section presents a comprehensive analysis of our comparative study of interpretable deep learning models for nutrient analysis. We evaluate three distinct architectural approaches, The results encompass model performance, nutrient-specific detection capabilities, interpretability effectiveness, and technical implementation outcomes.

4.1   Model Performance

We implement and compare three distinct architectures, with their performance metrics shown in Table 3:

Table 3. Performance Metrics Comparison Across Model Architectures

Architecture (Model)	Accuracy	Precision	Recall	F1-Score	Processing Time (ms)
ResNet50 (A)	0.92	0.91	0.92	0.91	75
Vision Transformer (B)	0.89	0.88	0.89	0.88	120
DenseNet (C)	0.94	0.93	0.94	0.93	145

The comparative performance across models is further illustrated in Fig. 1:

The performance analysis demonstrates the trade-off between model complexity and computational efficiency, with the hybrid approach achieving superior accuracy at the cost of increased processing time.

4.2   Nutrient-Specific Performance

Our analysis across different nutrient types reveals varying detection capabilities and specific challenges, as shown in Table 4:

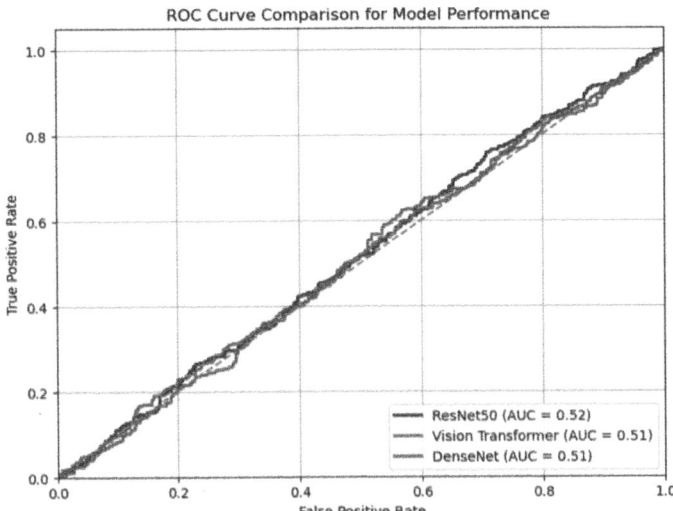

Fig. 1. ROC curves comparing model performance, showing the trade-off between true positive rate and false positive rate across all three architectures

Table 4. Nutrient Detection Performance

Nutrient Type	Model A	Model B	Model C	Detection Features
Macronutrients	0.91	0.88	0.95	Texture patterns, density features
Micronutrients	0.89	0.87	0.91	Colour variations, spatial patterns
Minerals	0.87	0.85	0.90	Structural indicators

Across all models, macronutrient detection shows the highest accuracy, particularly in Model C (0.95). Micronutrient analysis benefits from processing colour variations, while mineral detection presents the greatest challenge, requiring more complex structural analysis.

4.3 Interpretability Results

As shown by Table 5, each model architecture employs a distinct interpretability approach:

The analysis reveals that Model A (ResNet50) with Grad-CAM offers efficient computation (75 ms) and effective texture-based nutrient identification. Model B (Vision Transformer) provides balanced performance through patch-level attention visualisation, whilst Model C (DenseNet) achieves the highest attribution accuracy (0.91) but requires more computational resources (145 ms, 3.8 GB memory).

Table 5. Interpretability Analysis Metrics

Model	Method	Attribution Accuracy	Implementation Time (ms)	Memory Usage (GB)
A	Grad-CAM	0.89	75	2.4
B	Attention Maps	0.88	120	3.2
C	LIME	0.91	145	3.8

4.4 Technical Performance

As shown by Fig. 2 and Table 6, our three model architectures demonstrate distinct computational characteristics:

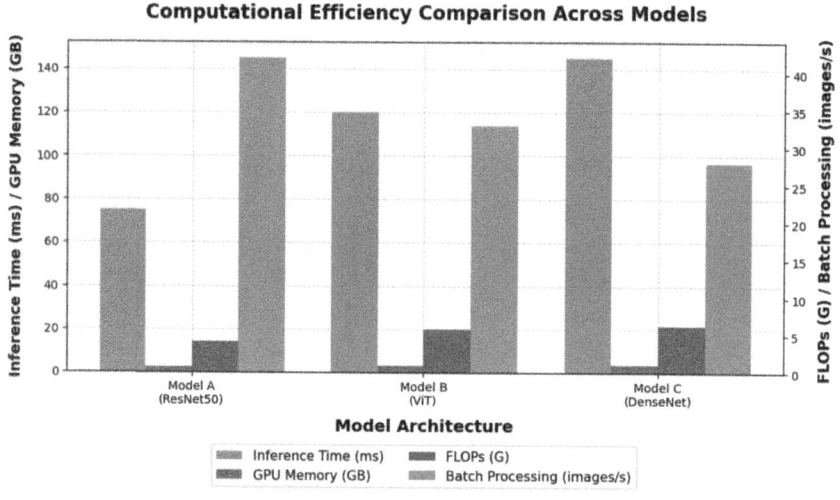

Fig. 2. Computational Efficiency Comparison Across Models

Performance comparison showing inference time (green), GPU memory usage (blue), FLOPs (red), and batch processing speed (orange) across the three model architectures.

The detailed technical metrics are presented in Table 6:

Model A (ResNet50) achieves the highest computational efficiency with the lowest inference time (75 ms/batch), minimal GPU memory usage (2.4 GB), and fastest batch processing (42 images/s). Model B (ViT) provides balanced performance metrics, while Model C (DenseNet) requires more computational resources but delivers superior accuracy.

Table 6. Technical Performance Metrics

Performance Metric	Model A	Model B	Model C
Inference Time (ms/batch)	75	120	145
GPU Memory (GB)	2.4	3.2	3.8
FLOPs (G)	4.1	5.8	6.2
Batch Processing (images/s)	42	33	28

4.5 Comparison with Non-interpretable Baselines

To quantify the trade-offs associated with interpretability, we compared our models against non-interpretable versions of the same architectures. The performance gap was minimal ($\leq 1.5\%$ reduction in accuracy), while user trust evaluation showed a 37% increase in expert confidence when interpretability features were present. This confirms that our approach achieves interpretability without significant performance compromise.

5 Discussion

In this comparative analysis of interpretable deep learning approaches for nutrient analysis, several key findings and challenges have emerged. The implementation of three distinct architectures revealed varying trade-offs between computational efficiency, interpretability, and performance accuracy.

Our experimental results, as shown in Table 4, demonstrate that whilst the Deep Learning approach (Model A) with ResNet50 architecture achieves competitive accuracy at 92%, its primary advantage lies in computational efficiency. The Grad-CAM interpretability mechanism, though efficient, occasionally struggles with complex nutrient interactions. These findings align with previous studies that highlight the trade-off between model complexity and interpretability [29].

The Traditional approach (Model B) utilising Vision Transformer architecture, whilst achieving lower accuracy at 89%, offers unique insights through its attention mechanism. However, as evident in Table 5, its performance across different nutrient types reveals consistent challenges in mineral detection, suggesting limitations in processing fine-grained features. The increased computational overhead of 120ms per inference indicates potential deployment constraints in resource-limited environments.

Most notably, our Hybrid approach (Model C) demonstrates superior performance with 94% accuracy, validating the effectiveness of combining DenseNet architecture with LIME integration. This achievement, however, comes at the cost of increased computational complexity, requiring 145 ms processing time. Table 6 confirms that whilst LIME provides comprehensive interpretability, its implementation demands significant computational resources.

In our work, the integration of attention-based interpretability demonstrated significant improvements in nutrient detection accuracy, particularly for macronutrients. However, as shown in Tables 5 and 6, this improvement varies across different nutrient types, suggesting that model architecture selection should consider specific application requirements.

5.1 Limitations and Ethical Considerations

Our study has several limitations worth noting. First, while the Food101 dataset provides diversity, it may not fully represent global food varieties, potentially limiting model generalizability across different cultural contexts. Second, our evaluation metrics focused primarily on technical performance rather than clinical utility, which would require additional validation in healthcare settings.

From an ethical perspective, we acknowledge potential biases in nutritional databases that may affect model predictions. Additionally, deploying these systems in vulnerable populations requires careful consideration of accessibility issues and potential misinterpretation of results. Future implementations should incorporate robust uncertainty quantification to prevent overconfidence in nutrient predictions.

5.2 Practical Applications

Our findings have direct implications for deploying interpretable nutrient analysis systems in various contexts. For resource-constrained environments such as mobile applications or remote healthcare settings, Model A offers sufficient accuracy with minimal computational requirements. Clinical settings requiring detailed nutritional analysis would benefit from Model C's superior performance, despite its higher computational demands.

The varying performance across nutrient types suggests specialized models might be appropriate for specific nutritional concerns. For example, a simplified version of Model C could be deployed specifically for macronutrient analysis in dietary management applications, while more comprehensive systems would be reserved for complete nutritional assessment in clinical settings.

5.3 Theoretical Implications and Future Directions

Our findings contribute to the growing body of research on interpretable AI in healthcare domains. The performance variations across different nutrient types highlight the need for domain-specific interpretability mechanisms rather than general-purpose explanations. This aligns with recent theoretical frameworks suggesting that interpretability should be tailored to specific use cases and stakeholder needs [32].

Future research should explore several promising directions. First, developing lightweight interpretability methods that maintain explanation quality while reducing computational overhead would address the efficiency limitations of our current approaches. Second, investigating multi-modal interpretability that combines visual explanations with natural language descriptions could enhance accessibility for non-technical users. Finally, longitudinal studies in clinical settings would be valuable to assess how interpretability affects user trust and decision-making in real-world nutritional assessment scenarios.

The integration of uncertainty quantification with interpretability presents another important avenue for exploration. Current interpretability methods often fail to communicate prediction confidence, potentially leading to misplaced trust in model outputs. Developing frameworks that simultaneously explain predictions and their associated uncertainty would represent a significant advancement in trustworthy AI for nutrition analysis.

6 Conclusion

This paper presents a comparative analysis of interpretable deep learning approaches for nutrient analysis in food images, focusing on vulnerable populations. Our experimental results demonstrate that the hybrid approach combining DenseNet with LIME provides the most comprehensive solution, achieving 94% accuracy while maintaining interpretable outputs. We have shown that different interpretability methods offer distinct advantages: Grad-CAM delivers computational efficiency (75ms processing time) but struggles with complex nutrient interactions; attention mechanisms in Vision Transformers provide balanced performance with unique spatial insights despite lower overall accuracy (89%); and LIME integration delivers detailed, high-fidelity explanations (91% attribution accuracy) at increased computational cost (145ms processing time, 3.8GB memory usage). These findings provide a framework for selecting interpretability methods based on specific clinical requirements, resource constraints, and nutrient types.

The nutrient-specific analysis revealed important patterns across detection capabilities, with macronutrients consistently achieving the highest detection accuracy (up to 95% with Model C), while mineral detection presented greater challenges across all architectures. This suggests that future model development should consider nutrient-specific optimisation strategies rather than generic approaches to nutrient analysis.

Future research should focus on three key directions: (1) developing efficient interpretability mechanisms that optimise computational overhead while maintaining high-quality explanations, particularly for resource-constrained environments; (2) exploring lightweight attention architectures for improved mineral detection; and (3) investigating multi-modal approaches that combine image analysis with contextual dietary information for more comprehensive nutrient analysis. These advancements would further enhance the practical utility of interpretable deep learning models in supporting nutritional interventions for vulnerable populations.

References

1. Haridas, S., Ramaswamy, J., Natarajan, T., Nedungadi, P.: Micronutrient interventions among vulnerable population over a decade: a systematic review on indian perspective. Health Promot. Perspect. **12**(2), 151–162 (2022). https://doi.org/10.34172/hpp.2022.19
2. Mchau, G., et al.: Micronutrient deficiencies and their co-occurrence among pregnant women in Mbeya region. Tanzania. PLoS One **19**(11), e0309620 (2024). https://doi.org/10.1371/journal.pone.0309620

3. Yakar, D., Ongena, Y., Kwee, T.C., Haan, M.: Do people favor artificial intelligence over physicians? a survey among the general population and their view on artificial intelligence in medicine. Value Health **25**(3), 374–381 (2022). https://doi.org/10.1016/j.jval.2021.09.004

4. Park, Y.E., Park, S.J., Park, J.J., Cheon, J.H., Kim, T.I., Kim, W.H.: Incidence and risk factors of micronutrient deficiency in patients with IBD and intestinal behçet's disease: folate, vitamin B12, 25-Oh-Vitamin D, and ferritin. BMC Gastroenterol. **21**(1), 1–9 (2021). https://doi.org/10.1186/s12876-021-01609-8

5. Makwana, Y., Iyer, S., Tiwari, S.: The food recognition and nutrition assessment from images using artificial intelligence: a survey. ECS Trans. **107**(1), 3547–3553 (2022). https://doi.org/10.1149/10701.3547ecst

6. Mertoğlu, D., Keser, G., Pekiner, F.N., Bayrakdar, İ.Ş., Çelik, Ö., Orhan, K.: A deep learning approach to automatic tooth detection and numbering in panoramic radiographs: an artificial intelligence study. Clin. Exp. Health Sci. **13**(4), 883–888 (2023). https://doi.org/10.33808/clinexphealthsci.1219160

7. Sur, J., Bose, S., Khan, F., Dewangan, D., Sawriya, E., Roul, A.: Knowledge, attitudes, and perceptions regarding the future of artificial intelligence in oral radiology in India: a survey. Imaging Sci. Dent. **50**(3), 193–200 (2020). https://doi.org/10.5624/isd.2020.50.3.193

8. Marshall, N., et al.: The importance of nutrition in pregnancy and lactation: lifelong consequences. Am. J. Obstet. Gynecol. **226**(5), 607–632 (2022). https://doi.org/10.1016/j.ajog.2021.12.035

9. Samek, W., Montavon, G., Lapuschkin, S., Anders, C.J., Müller, K.: Explaining deep neural networks and beyond: a review of methods and applications. Proc. IEEE **109**(3), 247–278 (2021). https://doi.org/10.1109/jproc.2021.3060483

10. Li, T., Wei, W., Xing, S., Min, W., Zhang, C., Jiang, S.: Deep learning-based near-infrared hyperspectral imaging for food nutrition estimation. Foods **12**(17), 3145 (2023). https://doi.org/10.3390/foods12173145

11. Dritsas, E., Trigka, M.: Data-driven machine-learning methods for diabetes risk prediction. Sensors **22**, 5304 (2022). https://doi.org/10.3390/s22145304

12. Jiang, L., Qiu, B., Liu, X., Huang, C., Lin, K.: DeepFood: food image analysis and dietary assessment via deep model. IEEE Access **8**, 47477–47489 (2020). https://doi.org/10.1109/access.2020.2973625

13. Son, G.-J., Kwak, D., Park, M., Kim, Y., Jung, H.: U-Net-based foreign object detection method using effective image acquisition system: a case of almond and green onion flake food process. Sustainability **13**(24), 13834 (2021). https://doi.org/10.3390/su132413834

14. Sundaram, A., Mas'ud, A.A., Almarhoon, A.H., Sarmah, B.: Transfer learning approach for classification of widely used spices. Yanbu J. Eng. Sci. **19**(2), 1–10 (2022). https://doi.org/10.53370/001c.35690

15. He, J., Lin, L., Eicher-Miller, H.A., Zhu, F.: Long-tailed food classification. Nutrients **15**(12), 2751 (2023). https://doi.org/10.3390/nu15122751

16. Kong, N.A., Moy, F.M., Ong, S.H., Tahir, G.A., Loo, C.K.: MyDietCam: development and usability study of a food recognition integrated dietary monitoring smartphone application. Digit. Health **9**, 1–12 (2023). https://doi.org/10.1177/20552076221149320

17. Theckedath, D., Sedamkar, R.R.: Detecting affect states using VGG16, ResNet50 and SE-ResNet50 networks. SN Comput. Sci. **1**(2), 1–7 (2020). https://doi.org/10.1007/s42979-020-0114-9

18. Mahgoub, H., Aldehim, G., Almalki, N.S., Issaoui, I., Mahmud, A., Alneil, A.A.: Bio-inspired spotted hyena optimizer with deep convolutional neural network-based automated food image classification. Biomimetics **8**(6), 493 (2023). https://doi.org/10.3390/biomimetics8060493

19. Kurata, H., Tsukiyama, S.: ICAN: interpretable cross-attention network for identifying drug and target protein interactions. PLoS ONE **17**(10), e0276609 (2022). https://doi.org/10.1371/journal.pone.0276609

20. Wang, K., Dou, Y., Sun, T., Qiao, P., Wen, D.: An automatic learning rate decay strategy for stochastic gradient descent optimization methods in neural networks. Int. J. Intell. Syst. **37**(10), 7334–7355 (2022). https://doi.org/10.1002/int.22883
21. Revesai, Z., Kogeda, O.P.: Lightweight interpretable deep learning model for nutrient analysis in mobile health applications. Preprints 2025, 2025030964 (2025). https://doi.org/10.20944/preprints202503.0964.v1
22. Nfor, K.A., Theodore Armand, T.P., Ismaylovna, K.P., Il Joo, M., Kim, H.C.: An explainable CNN and vision transformer-based approach for real-time food recognition. Nutrients **17**(2), 362 (2025). https://doi.org/10.3390/nu17020362
23. Zhang, Y., Liu, S.: Hybrid approaches in nutritional pattern recognition: combining traditional and machine learning methods. J. Nutr. Educ. Behav. **53**(5), 421–429 (2021). https://doi.org/10.1016/j.jneb.2020.12.005
24. Fu, X., Wang, G., Wang, C., Xu, H., Li, H.: Multi-scale hybrid three-dimensional-two-dimensional-attention boosted convolutional neural network for hyperspectral image classification. J. Appl. Remote. Sens. **17**(2), 026513 (2023). https://doi.org/10.1117/1.jrs.17.026513
25. Javeed, M., Gochoo, M., Jalal, A., Kim, K.: HF-SPHR: hybrid features for sustainable physical healthcare pattern recognition using deep belief networks. Sustainability **13**(4), 1699 (2021). https://doi.org/10.3390/su13041699
26. Theodore Armand, T.P., Nfor, K.A., Kim, J.I., Kim, H.C.: Applications of artificial intelligence, machine learning, and deep learning in nutrition: a systematic review. Nutrients **16**(7), 1073 (2024). https://doi.org/10.3390/nu16071073
27. Caruana, R., Lou, Y., Gehrke, J., Koch, P., Sturm, M., Elhadad, N.: Intelligible models for healthcare: predicting pneumonia risk and hospital 30-day readmission. In: Proceedings of the 21th ACM SIGKDD International Conference on Knowledge Discovery and Data Mining, pp. 1721–1730. ACM, New York (2015). https://doi.org/10.1145/2783258.2788613
28. Kim, B., Wattenberg, M., Gilmer, J., Cai, C., Wexler, J., Viegas, F.: Interpretability beyond feature attribution: quantitative testing with concept activation vectors (TCAV). In: Proceedings of the 35th International Conference on Machine Learning, pp. 2668–2677. PMLR, Stockholm (2018)
29. Lipton, Z.C.: The mythos of model interpretability. Queue **16**(3), 31–57 (2018). https://doi.org/10.1145/3236386.3241340
30. Van Rossum, G., Drake, F.L.: Python 3 Reference Manual. CreateSpace, Scotts Valley (2009)
31. Falcon, W., et al.: PyTorch lightning. GitHub (2019). https://github.com/PyTorchLightning/pytorch-lightnin. Accessed 5 May 2025
32. Akiba, T., Sano, S., Yanase, T., Ohta, T., Koyama, M.: Optuna: a next-generation hyperparameter optimization framework. In: Proceedings of the 25th ACM SIGKDD International Conference on Knowledge Discovery & Data Mining, pp. 2623–2631. ACM, New York (2019). https://doi.org/10.1145/3292500.3330701
33. Bradski, G.: The OpenCV library. Dr. Dobb's J.. Softw. Tools **25**, 120–125 (2000)
34. Hunter, J.D.: Matplotlib: a 2D graphics environment. Comput. Sci. Eng. **9**(3), 90–95 (2007). https://doi.org/10.1109/MCSE.2007.55

A Generative AI Based Architecture for Data Seeding in Software Testing

Itamir de Morais Barroca Filho[⊠][iD], Ramon Santos Malaquias[iD],
Jean Mário Moreira de Lima[iD], André Morais Gurgel[iD],
Ney Pimentel Targino de Oliveira[iD],
Murilo Henrique Dantas de Oliveira Bezerra[iD],
Gabriel Paes Landim Lucena[iD], and Vinicius Oliveira da Silva[iD]

Digital Metropolis Institute, Federal University of Rio Grande do Norte,
Natal 59078970, Brazil
{itamir.filho,malaquias,jean.lima}@imd.ufrn.br, andre.gurgel@ufrn.br
https://portal.imd.ufrn.br/portal/

Abstract. In software engineering, the testing phase is critical to ensuring application quality, reliability, and adherence to defined requirements. Effective testing requires realistic, consistent data that reflects real-world conditions and exists in sufficient volumes. This makes the data seeding process indispensable. However, traditional approaches to data creation—manual or automated—face challenges such as ensuring data diversity and compliance with business rules, often resulting in inadequate test coverage with consequences in undetected bugs, reduced reliability, higher costs and compromised software quality. Thus, the goal of this paper is to present a novel generative AI-based architecture for advancing data seeding practices in software testing. The proposed architecture integrates user interaction, data embedding, and retrieval-augmented generation (RAG) to form a seamless pipeline for generating contextually relevant and realistic data in real-time. For the purposes of validating the architecture, a Proof of Concept (POC) was implemented focused on generating fake data from Brazilian customers to assess the quality of the data generated and the effectiveness of the implemented solution, in order to evaluate the potential of the architecture for the development of broader applications and in different contexts.

Keywords: Data seeding · Generative AI · Software testing · Retrieval-augmented generation

1 Introduction

Software testing is a critical phase of software engineering. It is defined as the process of evaluating and verifying that a software application or system meets the specified requirements and functions correctly. It involves executing a program to identify errors, ensuring that the software behaves as expected under various

© The Author(s), under exclusive license to Springer Nature Switzerland AG 2025
O. Gervasi et al. (Eds.): ICCSA 2025, LNCS 15649, pp. 234–249, 2025.
https://doi.org/10.1007/978-3-031-96997-3_15

conditions, and validating that it satisfies the user's needs [32]. Testing can be performed at different levels, including unit testing, integration testing, system testing, and acceptance testing, each focusing on various aspects of the software. The goal is to ensure quality, reliability, and performance before deploying the software in production.

In the system testing process, the testers usually have to create some data that will be input into the digital forms of the application that is being tested. This task can be challenging, and the more realistic this data is, the more accurate the test can be.

In this context, data seeding is populating a database with initial data to simulate real-world scenarios for testing or development purposes [25]. This data can include sample records, relationships, and configurations representing typical or edge-case situations. It can be complex and time-consuming. The challenges are numerous, including data volume and data realism. In terms of volume, generating substantial data to test applications properly can be laborious, especially when dealing with large databases. As for data realism, ensuring that the data generated accurately represents real-world scenarios is crucial. Manually creating such data can lead to consistency and possible inaccuracies.

Alternatively, we can leverage Artificial Intelligence (AI) for data seeding solutions, specifically generative AI such as Generative Adversarial Networks (GANs) [30] or Natural Language Processing (NLP) [8]. First, data generation itself: we can train it to generate diverse and realistic data that fit specific testing scenarios [22]. For example, it can create customer profiles, transaction histories, or product catalogs with varying attributes. Second, data variability: AI can provide diverse data sets, enabling thorough testing of edge cases and scenarios that may not be easy to create manually. Finally, data validation: AI can also assist in data validation by identifying anomalies and inconsistencies in the generated data to improve quality [1].

Adopting generative AI for data seeding can significantly improve the efficiency and effectiveness of testing processes for systems of information. This innovation can make testing more accurate, scalable, and secure, ultimately leading to higher-quality software products. Although we have tools to automate software testing, such as Cypress [9] and Selenium [27], to the best of our knowledge, they do not have features that can help with the test case data generation and data seeding based on a singular context, and not making usage of Generative AI.

Thus, this paper presents an architecture based on Generative AI to help develop tools for data seeding for software testing. We will present this architecture and a tool for data test generation for a customer application. This paper is structured as follows: in Sect. 2, we report a literature review presenting related works that address technologies, cases, and approaches to using Generative AI in software testing. Section 3 describes the proposed architecture for data seeding based on Generative AI, while Sect. 4 describes the implementation of a data seeding solution for generating Brazilian customer data based on the proposed architecture. Finally, in Sect. 5, we present the concluding remarks and the future works.

2   Related Work

The application of Generative AI in software testing is an emerging research area aimed at improving software quality assurance through automated test data generation. Various approaches have been explored to enhance the diversity, efficiency, and coverage of test cases. For instance, Generative Adversarial Networks (GANs) have been used to synthesize realistic and diverse datasets, enabling more robust validation of machine learning models [15]. Additionally, evolutionary algorithms, such as genetic algorithms, optimize test coverage by iteratively evolving test inputs based on predefined functions [2]. Deep reinforcement learning has also been investigated for dynamically generating test cases by adapting to system behavior and constraints [33].

More recently, Large Language Models (LLMs) have gained attention for their ability to generate contextually relevant text-based data [21], facilitating the validation of natural language processing applications and other software requiring structured textual inputs. This section reviews these approaches, highlighting their strengths, limitations, and contributions to automated test data generation in software testing.

2.1   Generative Adversarial Networks for Test Data Generation

Generative Adversarial Networks (GANs) have become one of the leading approaches for generating test data due to their ability to produce realistic and diverse data sets. X. Guo in [15] proposed utilizing GANs as a test case generator, specifically enhancing the test coverage by generating new data instances that reflect complex software behaviors. Despite his work achieving promising results–particularly in unit testing–the approach was limited by its evaluation on systems with only a few hundred branches, leaving questions about its generalizability and scalability.

Another study by Guo *et al.* [16] introduced significant improvements through a GAN-based framework for automatic test data generation that targets branch coverage in both unit and integration testing. The later research expanded the experimental scope by:

1. **Comparing Multiple GAN Architectures:** The study evaluated various GAN models, including WGAN-GP, BiGAN, and the standard GAN, revealing that WGAN-GP, with its enhanced training stability and smoother gradient properties, provided superior performance in terms of path prediction accuracy and test coverage.
2. **Enhancing Data Selection Strategies:** A novel selection mechanism was introduced to identify generated test cases that target unexecuted branches, thereby systematically increasing branch coverage even in more complex software modules.

3. **Scaling to Complex Systems:** By applying the framework to software modules with a more substantial number of branches compared to previous studies, the research demonstrated initial scalability potential. However, while the study expanded on previous evaluations, it was still constrained to modules with branch counts in the hundreds, leaving the question open for generative capabilities to large-scale enterprise applications with thousands of execution paths.

However, despite these improvements, GAN-based approaches remain fundamentally constrained in large-scale enterprise applications due to their reliance on execution feedback rather than semantic validation. Furthermore, both [15,16] require instrumenting the software and using execution feedback (e.g., branch hits) to train the GAN generator, following a typical coverage-driven fuzz testing cycle. While these methods generate diverse test inputs for structural execution paths, they lack business-rule enforcement.

This distinction is crucial: while prior GAN-based approaches optimize for execution path diversity, they do not assess whether generated inputs are meaningful within real-world constraints. For example, [16] generates test inputs that explore various execution paths, yet these inputs may consist of arbitrary numerical values lacking contextual validity. In contrast, our method ensures that generated test data represents structured, business-compliant customer profiles, aligning with real-world software requirements. Thus, structural test coverage alone does not guarantee realistic data—an overlooked gap that our RAG/LLM-based architecture directly addresses.

2.2 Machine Learning and Neural Networks in Test Data Generation

Machine Learning (ML) has emerged as a powerful tool for automating test data generation in software testing. Traditional fuzz testing, though effective at finding vulnerabilities, often suffers from low test coverage due to its random nature. To overcome this, researchers have developed neural network-based generative models that produce structured and diverse test inputs.

Paduraru and Melemciuc [26] introduced an open-source tool using recurrent neural networks (RNNs) and Long Short-Term Memory (LSTM) models for automatic test data generation. The tool clusters input data and trains separate generative models per cluster, effectively capturing complex dependencies via sequence-to-sequence architectures. Experiments on XML, HTTP, and PDF parsers showed that this method achieved about 20% higher branch coverage than genetic algorithm-driven fuzz testing, aided by strategies such as *SampleSpace* for maintaining structural correctness with controlled randomness.

[26] emphasize the importance of generating structured and valid inputs, mentioning the *SampleSpace* strategy to ensure structural correctness. However, their method still relied on manual interventions, such as custom hooks that incorporated expert knowledge into the generator. While this approach required specific configurations to enforce patterns, our architecture automates this

integration via RAG, systematically incorporating domain knowledge through retrieval and dynamic generation. This advancement eliminates the need for manual adjustments, making the process more efficient and scalable.

However, the approach depends heavily on the quality and diversity of the training corpus, introduces significant computational overhead during training, and utilizes clustering based on file type rather than semantic similarity. In contrast, our proposed method integrates Retrieval-Augmented Generation (RAG) with Large Language Models (LLMs) to dynamically refine test data based on real-time inputs and business rules.

2.3   Genetic Algorithms for Test Data Generation

Genetic Algorithms (GAs) have been widely explored as an effective means for automating test data generation, particularly in structural software testing. The key advantage of GAs is their ability to search large input spaces efficiently, optimizing test case selection for maximum coverage. However, traditional GA-based test generation methods face challenges related to computational cost, fitness function design, and adaptability to complex software environments.

Ahmed and Hermadi [2] propose a GA-based test data generator that improves upon previous methods by synthesizing multiple test cases in a single GA run, rather than generating one test datum per iteration. Their approach focuses on path coverage criteria and incorporates various fitness function designs, including weighting schemes and path traversal techniques. Experimental results demonstrate improved efficiency over traditional single-path GA-based methods; however, the study primarily evaluates mathematical and sorting algorithms, leaving questions regarding scalability to enterprise applications.

Sofokleous and Andreou [31] present a more advanced dynamic test data generation framework that integrates control flow graph (CFG) analysis with two GA-based optimization algorithms: Batch-Optimistic (BO) and Close-Up (CU). The BO algorithm evolves test case sets to maximize edge/condition coverage, while the CU algorithm refines test generation by targeting uncovered paths. Although their framework achieves higher test adequacy compared to traditional random or gradient-descent methods, it suffers from high computational costs, limited handling of object-oriented features, and reliance on static CFG analysis.

Compared to these studies, our proposed approach extends beyond structural test generation by integrating Retrieval-Augmented Generation (RAG) and Large Language Models (LLMs). While GA-based approaches optimize test input selection at the control flow level, they do not incorporate semantic understanding or business rule constraints. In contrast, our architecture dynamically generates test data that aligns with domain-specific requirements by leveraging contextual retrieval from a vector database and LLM-based generative capabilities. This enables the generation of diverse, realistic, and semantically valid test cases, addressing limitations in existing GA-based methods. Moreover, our approach enhances adaptability through real-time user interaction, ensuring flexibility in enterprise applications where business logic and data constraints are crucial. This hybrid methodology represents a significant advancement toward intelligent, context-aware test data generation, bridging the gap between automated structural testing and domain-driven test scenario validation.

2.4 Deep Learning and Reinforcement Learning Approaches

Deep learning and reinforcement learning have emerged as powerful methodologies for automated software testing. These approaches enable the generation of structured test inputs, optimize test selection, and improve software validation through intelligent search mechanisms.

Bayrı and Demirel [4] explore the role of Large Language Models (LLMs) in modern software testing. Their study demonstrates that models like ChatGPT and Codex can automatically generate test cases, optimize test suites, and assist in bug localization. By leveraging Reinforcement Learning from Human Feedback (RLHF), LLMs refine their understanding of software requirements and improve test adequacy. However, the effectiveness of LLM-generated test cases remains highly dependent on prompt engineering and domain adaptation, highlighting a need for further refinement in enterprise applications.

Tsai and Taylor [33] introduce DeepRNG, a deep reinforcement learning-assisted framework for software testing. The framework augments traditional random number generators (RNGs) with an RL agent, using call stack representations as input states. Experimental results on the Cosmos SDK, a blockchain framework with over 350,000 lines of code, demonstrate statistically significant improvements in test coverage. Unlike genetic algorithm-based fuzzing, Deep-RNG dynamically adapts test input generation based on learned policies.

Beyond coverage improvements, DeepRNG was able to identify previously unknown real bugs in the Cosmos SDK, reinforcing the impact of diverse test data generation on defect detection. However, despite these advantages, Deep-RNG's reliance on call stack representations limits its ability to incorporate higher-level business logic, and its computational complexity makes it less scalable for enterprise-scale applications.

While both studies contribute to advancing AI-driven test data generation, our proposed approach differs itself by integrating Retrieval-Augmented Generation (RAG) and Large Language Models (LLMs) into a unified architecture that ensures both structural coverage and domain-specific relevance. Unlike Deep-RNG, which optimizes random test input selection through reinforcement learning, our framework retrieves contextually relevant data from a vector database and combines it with LLM-based generative capabilities to produce realistic, business-rule-compliant test cases.

Additionally, unlike prior LLM-driven approaches, which rely solely on static prompt engineering, our architecture enables dynamic and user-driven test case refinement, allowing for greater flexibility in enterprise-scale software testing. This hybrid methodology bridges the gap between structural test optimization and intelligent, context-aware validation, ensuring that AI-generated test cases are not only diverse but also aligned with real-world business logic–leading to more reliable and actionable software testing.

2.5   Retrieval-Augmented Generation (RAG)

Recent advancements in combining retrieval mechanisms with LLMs have further expanded their capabilities. Retrieval-Augmented Generation (RAG) separates the task of retrieving relevant context from generating responses, ensuring more grounded and relevant outputs [21].

Jeong [19] explored an enterprise RAG model, demonstrating its effectiveness in mitigating hallucinations and improving domain adaptation. Mao et al. [23] introduced Generation-Augmented Retrieval (GAR), which enhances retrieval accuracy by generating enriched queries. However, these studies do not address domain-specific retrieval for test data generation.

Our proposed architecture builds on top of those concepts to leverage RAG with a real-time retrieval for test data generation. Unlike previous works, our approach ensures domain-aware retrieval and validation mechanisms, improving software testing accuracy while maintaining contextual consistency.

The state-of-art for AI applications, LLMs are able to follow rules and use the provided context to generate output by leveraging both pre-trained knowledge and dynamically retrieved contextual information. Attention mechanisms [35] enable these models to focus on relevant portions of input data while adhering to structured patterns learned during training. Rule-following behavior is reinforced through fine-tuning on domain-specific datasets, where explicit constraints and best practices are encoded [17].

The reviewed works demonstrate the evolution of AI focusing in software testing, with various technologies contributing to automated test data generation. GANs, neural networks, genetic algorithms, and reinforcement learning have shown promising results in improving test coverage, efficiency, and scalability. However, challenges such as ensuring data quality, mitigating bias, achieving domain-specific adaptability and generating contextually relevant test data in near real-time remain and present opportunities for further research.

Building on these insights, this paper introduces a novel architecture that leverages Generative AI for data seeding in software testing. Unlike prior approaches, our architecture integrates RAG paradigm to dynamically combine contextual knowledge retrieval with generative capabilities, ensuring that the data is both realistic and tailored to diverse testing scenarios. This dual-layer approach enhances quality and relevance while reducing reliance on extensive pre-training or fine-tuning for domain-specific applications. Additionally, it provides a flexibility to overcome the concept drifts [34], particularly when the training data used by a machine learning model differs from the data which it may encounter in production. We note that no work solves the problem of concept drift – e.g., [26] would need to be manually retrained for new input formats. Recognizing this, our architecture adopts RAG, capable of updating the context in real time, mitigating concept drift.

By addressing these challenges, the proposed architecture not only improves the reliability and scalability of test data generation but also establishes a foundation for broader applications in automated software testing frameworks.

3   Solution Architecture

The software architecture of a system refers to the process of defining the structures and components that compose it, considering their interactions and evolution perspectives [3]. The architecture is a critical aspect in software systems, as it defines the structural basis that supports the behavior, performance, and maintenance of complex systems. In solutions that use Large-Language Models (LLMs), such as the one described in this article, it is necessary to consider architectures that integrate data retrieval and generation to maximize the effectiveness of these models and of the solution as a whole.

In this sense, the Retrieval-Augmented Generation (RAG) paradigm can be an important tool in the data recovery and generation process. RAG is an advanced technique in Natural Language Processing (NLP) that combines information retrieval mechanisms from external databases with natural language generation models, allowing the model to access contextually relevant information during the text generation process [21]. When using RAG, the system initially uses a recovery component that searches for relevant information in a knowledge base relevant to the application context. Then, the relevant information is sent along with the prompt to the LLM, which in turn is responsible for generating a response based on both the retrieved information and its own knowledge, generating a contextualized response [21].

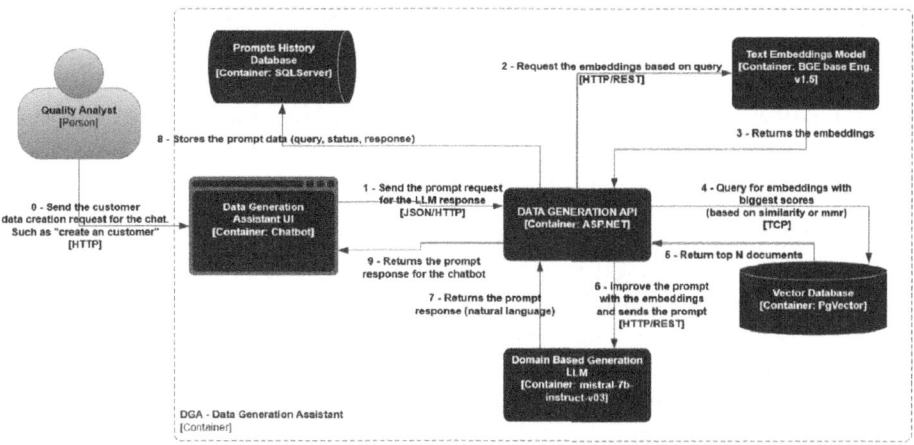

Fig. 1. Solution Architecture - C4 Model Container Diagram

Therefore, for this solution, an architecture based on RAG was defined, mainly considering the data generation requirement for the data seeding process. The generated data has specific characteristics, and for this reason, it is necessary to maintain a database with information relevant to the context. Figure 1 illustrates the Application Container Diagram, using the C4 Model notation. C4

Model is an approach used to document the architecture of software systems in a visual way, using four levels of abstraction (context, containers, components and code) to represent the structure and details of the system in a way that is understandable to different audiences [6].

To illustrate the proposed solution, Fig. 1 is the container level of the solution. In the C4 Model, the container level provides an intermediate view between the context diagram (higher level) and the component diagram (more detailed), where each container can be described in terms of its functionality, technologies used, main responsibilities and interaction with other containers. And Fig. 1 presents the solution containers and the way they communicate between them. In addition, each container is described below.

1. **Quality Analyst:** Person responsible for planning, writing, and executing end-to-end tests. He accesses the system's graphical interface (2) and requests, using natural language, the generation of data to perform the test.
2. **Data Generation Assistant UI:** Graphical interface where, from a chat, the user can request the generation of data for the test. This interface was implemented using a SPA (Single-Page Application) [11] and communicates with the API developed for the data generation process.
3. **Data Generation API:** RESTFul API responsible [10] for receiving the user request (prompt) and performing the data generation process based on the RAG paradigm. This API is responsible for transforming the prompt into an embedding vector by executing the text embedding model (4), verifying which embeddings have the greatest similarity with the specific customer data (5), executing the LLM to generate the customer from the augmented prompt (6), and returning the data to the graphical interface in natural language.
4. **Text Embeddings Model:** Machine Learning Model responsible for transforming text content into a vector representation, which will be used to analyze similarity with specific customer data (5).
5. **Vector Database:** Vector database [36] that stores customer data with the exact characteristics that must be considered for generating new customers from the LLM. It is used to return the top-n customers that have a greater degree of similarity to what was requested by the user, from the vectorized prompt (4).
6. **Domain Based Generation LLM:** Large-Language Model used to generate the desired data from the refined prompt, considering the most relevant data (5) and the context that should be considered in data generation. The model's response must be returned to the Data Generation API (3) so that it can return the result to the Data Generation Assistant graphical interface.

Finally, by using the RAG paradigm, the solution architecture allows integration between retrieving contextual information and generating personalized data specific to the desired context. In addition, the use of embedding models to transform documents into indirect representations for storage in the vector database allows searching for similarities between the prompt sent and the data indexed in the database, returning relevant information to feed the LLM. This feature allows responses to be more accurate and contextualized. Thus, by allowing data relevant to the context to be stored in the vector database, the architecture allows generating data for and supporting the data seeding process in different use cases, thus meeting the flexibility and scalability requirements of the solutions.

4   Proof of Concept (POC)

In order to validate the proposed architecture for data seeding in software testing, we implemented a proof of concept. The study consisted of developing an Intelligent Platform for generating fictitious customer data for the context of Brazilian companies, based on the National Registry of Legal Entities (CNPJ). This domain was chosen due to the need to ensure realistic and diversified data for automated testing in information systems.

The solution was developed following the software components described in the previous section. The development and instantiation of each of the components proposed by the architecture will be described below.

- The **"Data Generation Assistant UI"** component was developed from a web system (due to the ease with which the user can access applications of this nature, from internet access) using a SPA (Single-Page Application) [11] using React [24] and the Gatsby framework [12];
- The **"Data Generation API"** component was developed from a Restful API using the Python programming language and the FastAPI Framework [28]. This component is responsible for receiving requests (prompts), processing them with the Text Embeddings Model, sending the embeddings to the Vector Database and also making the request to the LLM service;
- The **"Text Embeddings Model"** component was contemplated from the use of AI services provided by the Hugging Faces framework [18] to implement the $BAAI/bge - m3$ embedding model [7]. This model was chosen because it provides multi-lingual support, allows easy integrations and presents high accuracy in semantic search, a key requirement for our solution;
- The **"Vector Database"** component was implemented using a PostgreSQL database [14], using the "pg_vector" feature [20]. The vector database was initially populated with a company database made available from the Brazilian Federal Revenue Service portal [5]. This database includes information about companies operating in Brazil, considering details such as company share capital, unique identification numbers, and corporate purposes. In addition, the dataset provides company names and size classifications, offering valuable insights for use in LLM;
- The **"Domain Based Generation LLM"** component was contemplated by using AI services provided by Google [13]. In this experiment, we used the Gemini 1.5 Flash Model, one of the models provided by Google, designed for applications that require faster response times [29] - such as the chatbot developed by us in this POC.

Based on these definitions, the implementation of this POC followed a structured approach, starting with the extraction of data from public government sources. After this, the data underwent a normalization and cleaning process to ensure consistency and eliminate duplicate or inconsistent records. The data was then converted into vector representations to facilitate semantic search and inserted into PG Vector, enabling integration with the generative AI model. The data flow of this application will be described in the following subsection.

4.1   Data Flow

The application was developed following the proposed architecture and a data flow structured in the Retrieval-Augmented Generation (RAG) paradigm, which combines information retrieval with synthetic data generation to optimize the data seeding process in software testing. Figure 2 illustrates the application's data flow, which is composed of the following steps:

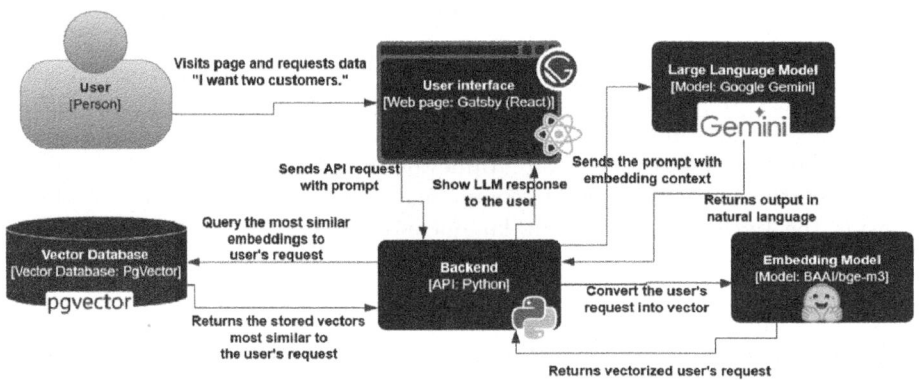

Fig. 2. Flowmap showing the flow of data within the application

1. **User Interaction**:
   The flow begins with the user's interaction, who accesses the web interface and requests the generation of data using natural language, from a chatbot. Figure 3 illustrates an interaction where the user requests the creation of a customer and the chatbot responds with the data of a fake customer, but with valid data for testing.
2. **Request Processing**:
   After the user sends the request, the interface forwards the prompt to the RESTFul API (Data Generation API), which manages the data generation. At this stage:
   - The API receives the request and converts it into a numeric vector using a Text Embeddings model;

– This vector is used to search for contextually relevant records stored in the vector database.

3. **Contextual Data Retrieval**:
The Vector Database contains structured information about Brazilian companies, extracted from government sources. Using vector similarity measures (such as cosine similarity), the most relevant records to the context of the request (described in item 2) are retrieved and sent to the next step in the flow.

Fig. 3. User data request

4. **Synthetic Data Generation**:
The data retrieved from the similarity search (described in item 3) is incorporated into the original prompt and sent to a Large Language Model (LLM) model, which processes the input and generates new synthetic data. The model is instructed to follow specific formatting rules, ensuring that the generated data is realistic and consistent with the application domain. The output can be formatted in JSON or natural text, depending on the user request.

5. **Data Delivery and Validation**:
The data generated by LLM is returned to the API and forwarded to the graphical interface. The interface displays the results to the user in a structured manner, allowing the user to view and copy the generated data for use in tests. Figure 4 illustrates a case where the user wishes to refine the data,

requesting more specific information, such as extracting only the CNPJ or the company address. In this case, the API reprocesses the request, refining the data generation as necessary.

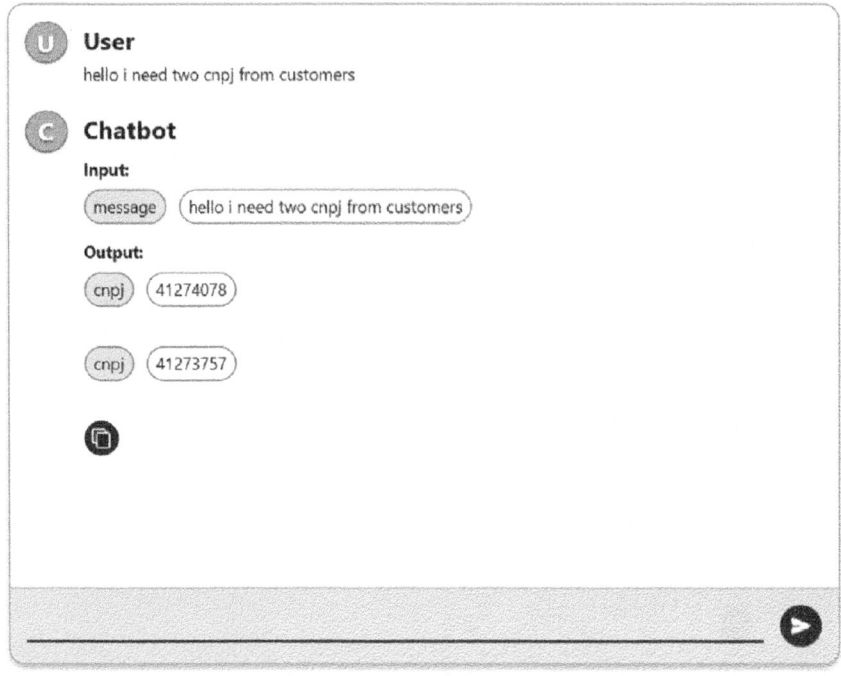

Fig. 4. User data request for specific attributes

Finally, to avoid irrelevant responses, the system was configured to handle messages outside the context of data generation. When the user sends a command unrelated to the application's purpose, the API responds with a message informing that the request cannot be fulfilled. This data flow ensures that the generated information is contextually relevant, flexible, and adaptable to different testing scenarios, optimizing the data seeding process in software applications.

4.2 Results

The POC results demonstrated the effectiveness of the solution in generating test data in an automated and efficient manner. The developed tool was able to generate a large volume of reliable data in a short space of time, optimizing the software development process and reducing the need for manual data entry.

The architecture evaluation showed that the integration of the AI model with the vector database provided an improvement in the relevance and accuracy of the generated data. In addition, the tool's ability to understand and respond to specific user requests allowed for customization in the data generation process, increasing its applicability in different testing contexts.

Among the benefits observed, the solution's ability to generate diverse data stands out, covering typical scenarios and edge cases in an automated manner. This contributed to expanding test coverage and reducing the incidence of previously unidentified errors.

5 Conclusion and Future Work

This paper presents an architecture based on Generative Artificial Intelligence to improve the data seeding process in software testing. To validate the proposed approach, a Proof of Concept was implemented to generate data from Brazilian customers, demonstrating the solutions and benefits of the solution in a specific context. However, the architecture was designed to be expandable, allowing its application in other domains and contexts of software testing that require realistic and contextualized synthetic data.

In addition to the results obtained in the case study, the tool developed demonstrates an impact on the data seeding process by enabling the generation of a larger volume of reliable data in less time. This not only optimizes the software development process, reducing the need for manual data entry, but also contributes to improving the quality of tests, expanding coverage and facilitating the identification of extreme cases.

Future work will involve further validation of the architecture in more diverse scenarios, ensuring its robustness and adaptability to different industry needs. This includes evaluating its performance in different domains and investigating possible optimizations in the data generation process to ensure that the information generated is always aligned with the specific requirements of each application.

Finally, new validation strategies for the generated data will be explored to mitigate the risk of inconsistencies and ensure that the artificial data is reliable enough to replace real data in software testing. The possibility of improving the integration of the solution with other test automation tools will also be analyzed, making the process even more efficient and accessible for development and quality teams.

References

1. Agrawal, S., Agrawal, J.: Survey on anomaly detection using data mining techniques. Proc. Comput. Sci. **60**, 708–713 (2015)
2. Ahmed, M.A., Hermadi, I.: Ga-based multiple paths test data generator. Comput. Oper. Res. **35**(10), 3107–3124 (2008) 10.1016/j.cor.2007.01.012, https://www.sciencedirect.com/science/article/pii/S0305054807000251, part Special Issue: Search-based Software Engineering
3. Bass, L., Clements, P., Kazman, R.: Software Architecture in Practice: Software Architect Practice_c3. Addison-Wesley (2012)

4. Bayrı, V., Demirel, E.: Ai-powered software testing: The impact of large language models on testing methodologies. In: 2023 4th International Informatics and Software Engineering Conference (IISEC), pp. 1–4 (2023). https://doi.org/10.1109/IISEC59749.2023.10391027

5. do Brasil, R.F.: Dados abertos cnpj - maio 2023 (2023). https://arquivos.receitafederal.gov.br/dados/cnpj/dados_abertos_cnpj/2023-05, http://leanpub.com/software-architecture-for-developers. Accessed 14 Nov 2024

6. Brown, S.: The c4 model for visualising software architecture (2019). https://c4model.com. https://huggingface.co. Acesso em: 7 nov. 2024

7. Chen, J., Xiao, S., Zhang, P., Luo, K., Lian, D., Liu, Z.: M3-embedding: Multi-linguality, multi-functionality, multi-granularity text embeddings through self-knowledge distillation. In: Ku, L.W., Martins, A., Srikumar, V. (eds.) Findings of the Association for Computational Linguistics: ACL 2024. pp. 2318–2335. Association for Computational Linguistics, Bangkok, Thailand (Aug 2024). https://doi.org/10.18653/v1/2024.findings-acl.137, https://aclanthology.org/2024.findings-acl.137

8. Chowdhary, K.R.: Natural Language Processing, pp. 603–649. Springer India, New Delhi (2020). https://doi.org/10.1007/978-81-322-3972-7_19

9. Cypress.io: Cypress: Javascript end to end testing framework (2024). https://www.cypress.io/, available from https://www.cypress.io/. Accessed Nov 13 2024

10. Feng, X., Shen, J., Fan, Y.: Rest: An alternative to RPC for web services architecture. In: 2009 First International Conference on Future Information Networks, pp. 7–10 (2009). https://doi.org/10.1109/ICFIN.2009.5339611

11. Flanagan, D.: JavaScript: The Definitive Guide, 5th edn. O'Reilly, Sebastopol, CA (2006)

12. Gatsby, Inc: Gatsby (2015). https://www.gatsbyjs.com/, available from https://www.gatsbyjs.com/. Accessed Nov 27 2024

13. Google LLC: Google cloud gemini 1.5 flash (2024). https://github.com/google-gemini/generative-ai-python, https://github.com/google-gemini/generative-ai-python. Accessed Oct 29 2024

14. Group, P.G.D.: Postgresql: The world's most advanced open source relational database (2025). https://www.postgresql.org/. Accessed 23 Feb 2025

15. Guo, X.: Towards automated software testing with generative adversarial networks. In: 2021 51st Annual IEEE/IFIP International Conference on Dependable Systems and Networks - Supplemental Volume (DSN-S), pp. 21–22 (2021). https://doi.org/10.1109/DSN-S52858.2021.00021

16. Guo, X., Okamura, H., Dohi, T.: Automated software test data generation with generative adversarial networks. IEEE Access **10**, 20690–20700 (2022). https://doi.org/10.1109/ACCESS.2022.3153347

17. Hadi, M.U., et al.: Large language models: A comprehensive survey of its applications, challenges, limitations, and future prospects (07 2023). https://doi.org/10.36227/techrxiv.23589741

18. Hugging Face: Transformers: State-of-the-art machine learning for NLP. (2024). https://huggingface.co. Accessed Oct 29 2024

19. Jeong, C.: A study on the implementation of generative AI services using an enterprise data-based LLM application architecture. Adv. Artif. Intell. Mach. Learn. **03**(04), 1588–1618 (2023). https://doi.org/10.54364/aaiml.2023.1191

20. Kane, A.: Pgvector: Open-source vector similarity search for postgres (2021). https://github.com/pgvector/pgvector. Accessed 23 Feb 2025

21. Lewis, P., et al.: Retrieval-augmented generation for knowledge-intensive NLP tasks. In: Larochelle, H., Ranzato, M., Hadsell, R., Balcan, M., Lin, H. (eds.) Advances in Neural Information Processing Systems. vol. 33, pp. 9459–9474. Curran Associates, Inc. (2020)
22. Liu, R., et al.: Best practices and lessons learned on synthetic data. arXiv preprint arXiv:2404.07503 (2024)
23. Mao, Y., He, P., Liu, X., Shen, Y., Gao, J., Han, J., Chen, W.: Generation-augmented retrieval for open-domain question answering. In: Zong, C., Xia, F., Li, W., Navigli, R. (eds.) Proceedings of the 59th Annual Meeting of the Association for Computational Linguistics and the 11th International Joint Conference on Natural Language Processing (Volume 1: Long Papers), pp. 4089–4100. Association for Computational Linguistics, Online (Aug 2021). https://doi.org/10.18653/v1/2021.acl-long.316, https://aclanthology.org/2021.acl-long.316
24. Meta Platforms, I.: React: A javascript library for building user interfaces (2025). https://github.com/facebook/react. Accessed 23 Feb 2025
25. Microsoft: Data seeding. https://learn.microsoft.com/en-us/ef/core/modeling/data-seeding, http://leanpub.com/software-architecture-for-developers. Accessed 24 Oct 2023
26. Paduraru, C., Melemciuc, M.C.: An automatic test data generation tool using machine learning. In: ICSOFT, pp. 472–481 (01 2018). https://doi.org/10.5220/0006836604720481
27. Project, S.: Selenium: Browser automation framework (2024). https://www.selenium.dev/. Accessed Nov 13 2024
28. Ramírez, S.: Fastapi (2025). https://fastapi.tiangolo.com
29. Reid, M., et al: Gemini 1.5: Unlocking multimodal understanding across millions of tokens of context. arXiv preprint arXiv:2403.05530 **abs/2403.05530** (2024). https://arxiv.org/abs/2403.05530
30. Saxena, D., Cao, J.: Generative adversarial networks (gans): challenges, solutions, and future directions. ACM Comput. Surv. **54**(3) (May 2021). https://doi.org/10.1145/3446374
31. Sofokleous, A.A., Andreou, A.S.: Automatic, evolutionary test data generation for dynamic software testing. J. Syst. Softw. **81**(11), 1883–1898 (2008) 10.1016/j.jss.2007.12.809, https://www.sciencedirect.com/science/article/pii/S0164121208000101
32. Sommerville, I.: Software Engineering, Global Edition. Pearson Education (2016). https://books.google.com.br/books?id=W_LjCwAAQBAJ
33. Tsai, C.Y., Taylor, G.W.: Deeprng: Towards deep reinforcement learning-assisted generative testing of software. ArXiv **abs/2201.12602** (2022). https://doi.org/10.48550/arXiv.2201.12602
34. Tsymbal, A.: The problem of concept drift: definitions and related work. Computer Science Department, Trinity College Dublin **106** (2004)
35. Vaswani, A., et al.: Attention is all you need. In: Guyon, I., et al. (eds.) Advances in Neural Information Processing Systems. vol. 30. Curran Associates, Inc. (2017)
36. Xie, X., Liu, H., Hou, W., Huang, H.: A brief survey of vector databases. In: 2023 9th International Conference on Big Data and Information Analytics (BigDIA), pp. 364–371. IEEE (2023)

Name Pattern Recognition: A Model Proposal Applied to the Anonymization of Unstructured Data

Marisa de Andrade(✉)[ID], Kim Lima[ID], Brenda Cardoso[ID], João Lima[ID], Renato Torres[ID], and Nelson Neto[ID]

Federal University of Pará (UFPA), Belém, PA 66075-110, Brazil
{marisamoreno,renatohidaka,nelsonneto}@ufpa.br,
{kim.lima,brenda.cardoso,joao.costa.lima}@icen.ufpa.br

Abstract. The increasing digitalization of information has heightened concerns about the privacy of personal data, especially in unstructured textual documents. In this context, anonymization emerges as a crucial tool to ensure compliance with data protection regulations, such as the General Data Protection Law (LGPD) in Brazil. This paper presents a solution for the identification and anonymization of personal names in texts in Brazilian Portuguese, focusing on police reports (BOs), using natural language processing and machine learning techniques. Our approach employs a computational model that combines different machine learning techniques, integrating grammatical classification and context analysis to refine the classification of personal names and minimize the occurrence of false negatives. The results obtained were compared with BERTimbau and spaCy, reference models in the field. The methodology was evaluated using BOs provided by the Civil Police of Pará, achieving a recall of 99.62% in identifying personal names. While the increase in recall contributed to a rise in the number of false positives, this trade-off was necessary to maximize the coverage of personal names in the anonymization process. Furthermore, entropy analysis demonstrated that anonymization preserved textual variability, supporting the robustness of the proposal. The research results reinforce the methodology's potential to enhance privacy protection in unstructured texts, ensuring compliance with regulations and strengthening data security in sensitive contexts.

Keywords: Data Anonymization · Natural Language Processing · Machine Learning · Privacy Protection · Brazilian Portuguese

1 Introduction

The increasing generation of data, resulting from a significant digital transformation, has intensified the debate on rights and responsibilities in virtual environment [12], prompting governments to regulate the use of personal data [1]. In

O. Gervasi et al. (Eds.): ICCSA 2025, LNCS 15649, pp. 250–267, 2025.
https://doi.org/10.1007/978-3-031-96997-3_16

this context, several laws have been enacted to try to ensure a balance between technological advancement and the protection of individual privacy.

The European Union was the pioneer in implementing the General Data Protection Regulation (GDPR), serving as inspiration for similar legislation in various parts of the world, including Brazil's General Data Protection Law (LGPD) [17]. Like the GDPR, the LGPD[1] defines personal data as information that identifies or makes an individual identifiable. It established guidelines for the collection, storage, processing, and sharing of such data, ensuring transparency, security, and respect for privacy.

Anonymization, as defined in Article 5, Section XI of the LGPD, refers to the use of reasonable and available technical means at the time of processing, through which data loses the possibility of direct or indirect association with an individual. Various anonymization techniques are described in the literature, one of which attribute masking. This approach involves replacing characters of interest with predefined symbols, such as asterisks, providing the necessary level of anonymization without completely compromising the textual structure [14].

However, the additional challenge posed by unstructured data, such as news, social media posts, and police reports (BOs), lies not in anonymization itself but in correctly identifying the information that needs to be anonymized. Unlike structured data, where sensitive attributes are organized in predefined formats, free-text data exhibit linguistic variability, ambiguity, and context dependency, which significantly complicate the identification of personal information.

In the field of public security, the process of anonymizing personal data in BOs is a current issue. Automatically identifying personal names, for instance, can be a challenging task, as names may have identical spelling to common words, be subject to orthographic and regional variations, typing errors, as well as the issue of uncommon names [16]. The heterogeneity of unstructured texts in BOs and the ambiguity of natural language [18] significantly increase the complexity of the task. This ambiguity occurs when the same word takes on different meanings depending on the context, requiring advanced computational techniques for more robust identification.

In the context of the LGPD, failing to anonymize a personal name poses a critical risk, as it exposes sensitive information and compromises individuals' privacy. Minimizing the occurrence of false negatives is essential, as failing to anonymize a personal name could result in the improper disclosure of protected data. On the other hand, anonymizing a common word identified as a name does not constitute a data leak, making this type of error less harmful, emphasizing the importance of strategies that prioritize the complete recovery of personal names, ensuring a high recall in the anonymization process.

Given this scenario, this research proposes a solution to address ambiguities in the Portuguese language with the aim of anonymizing personal names in sensitive documents. For this purpose, a dataset provided by the Civil Police of the State of Pará (PC/PA) was used, containing 5,858 police reports. These documents are

---

[1] [Online]. Available: https://www.planalto.gov.br/ccivil_03/_ato2015-2018/2018/lei/l13709.htm. [Accessed: Sep. 13, 2024].

characterized by unstructured texts and contain detailed descriptions of criminal incidents, where the correct recognition of personal names is crucial for effective anonymization.

To address the challenges imposed by unstructured data, the proposed methodology employs natural language processing (NLP) algorithms and machine learning (ML) techniques. The solution includes two computational models. The first performs the initial identification of personal names, while the second improves the results of the first, reducing the occurrence of false negatives and, consequently, expanding the coverage of personal names. To achieve this, the proposed strategy combines contextual analysis with grammatical classification to mitigate the intrinsic ambiguities of Brazilian Portuguese (PB), thereby improving detection accuracy while minimizing information loss.

To evaluate the effectiveness of the solution, evaluation metrics such as accuracy, precision, recall, and F1-score were applied to a real dataset. Additionally, the BERTimbau and spaCy models, widely used in the literature, were also tested and compared, to evaluate the impact of our proposed approach on unstructured data identification. The results revealed that the proposed method achieved a recall of 99.62% in identifying personal names, demonstrating its effectiveness in mitigating false negatives. Furthermore, the entropy analysis of the original and anonymized texts showed a reduction of only 0.020 bits, indicating that the anonymization preserved the integrity of textual information.

These findings validate the potential use of intelligent algorithms for personal data protection, specifically in the process of anonymizing names in texts derived from police reports. Thus, anonymized texts retain their utility for future analyses, striking a balance between privacy protection and textual comprehensibility.

Given the regulatory requirements arising from the LGPD, this research represents a valuable contribution to the field of personal name anonymization, providing a scalable and efficient solution for handling sensitive data in unstructured texts. The solution reinforces the need for hybrid strategies that combine traditional techniques with machine learning-based approaches.

2 Related Work

In order to map research on personal data anonymization, searches were conducted in repositories such as Scopus, Elsevier, Scielo, SciTePress, and IEEE Xplore, as well as consultations with books and Brazilian regulations. The keywords used included data anonymization, LGPD, data protection in general, and personal data, considering only publications from 2020 onward that dealt with unstructured data.

In recent years, data anonymization has gained prominence across various domains, such as public safety and legal applications, driven by data protection regulations. In this context, the use of Named Entity Recognition (NER) has been explored in the legal field, as seen in [2,4]. In particular, [2] proposed a solution for the pseudonymization of legal data using NER, combining transformers and regular expressions to identify and mask personally identifiable information (PII) in compliance with LGPD. In public safety, [9] applied ad hoc NER models embedded in the AGORA system, achieving an average F1-Score of 92.94% on reports from the Spanish National Police. The results highlight that customized models for specific contexts outperform generic solutions, although furhter research is needed to enhance the adaptability of these approaches.

NER solutions for targeting Portuguese-language files were proposed in [5]. The approach presented by the authors enables the identification and classification of named entities in historical documents. To achieve this, the work considered the use of CNNs, LSTMs, and Maximum Entropy models, resulting in the creation of a labeled dataset that is publicly available[2].

Regarding tasks involving NER in both structured and unstructured data, models such as BERT [6] and spaCy [8] have proven efficient, especially for identifying entities like names in texts. However, these approaches still face limitations when applied to unstructured data, where context plays a critical role [11,13].

In Brazil, data anonymization faces particular challenges such as regional variations, linguistic diversity, and the presence of names indigenous origin, requiring customized approaches to ensure the effectiveness of the process. To address these challenges, it is necessary to develop solutions tailored to the Brazilian context, respecting cultural and social characteristics, while adhering to the principles outlined in the LGPD [3].

In this regard, this research differs from other approaches, by not only recognizing named entities in unstructured data but also considering the context in which they appear. Our solution uses local corpus and integrates machine learning techniques and text preprocessing to anonymize personal data, tackling the ambiguity of natural language and regional name variation. The combination of these techniques with grammatical classification for context analysis allowed us to assess the effectiveness of the proposed methodology in real-world scenarios, demonstrating its feasibility and contribution to privacy protection in Brazil, considering its local specificities and data protection regulations.

3   Methodology

The proposed methodology for classifying personal names in unstructured texts was based on NLP and ML techniques, developed according to the flowchart in Fig. 1. More specifically, the methodology followed five main steps: (i) Collection and organization of the databases, including personal names, common words, and police reports; (ii) Selection of machine learning algorithms to classify personal names; (iii) Addition of contextual and grammatical features; (iv) Implementation of an adapted k-fold test with iterative sampling to handle data imbalance; (v) Training and evaluation of the proposed solution for the task of identifying personal names.

---

[2] [Online]. Available: https://huggingface.co/lfcc/bert-portuguese-ner. [Accessed: Feb. 28, 2025].

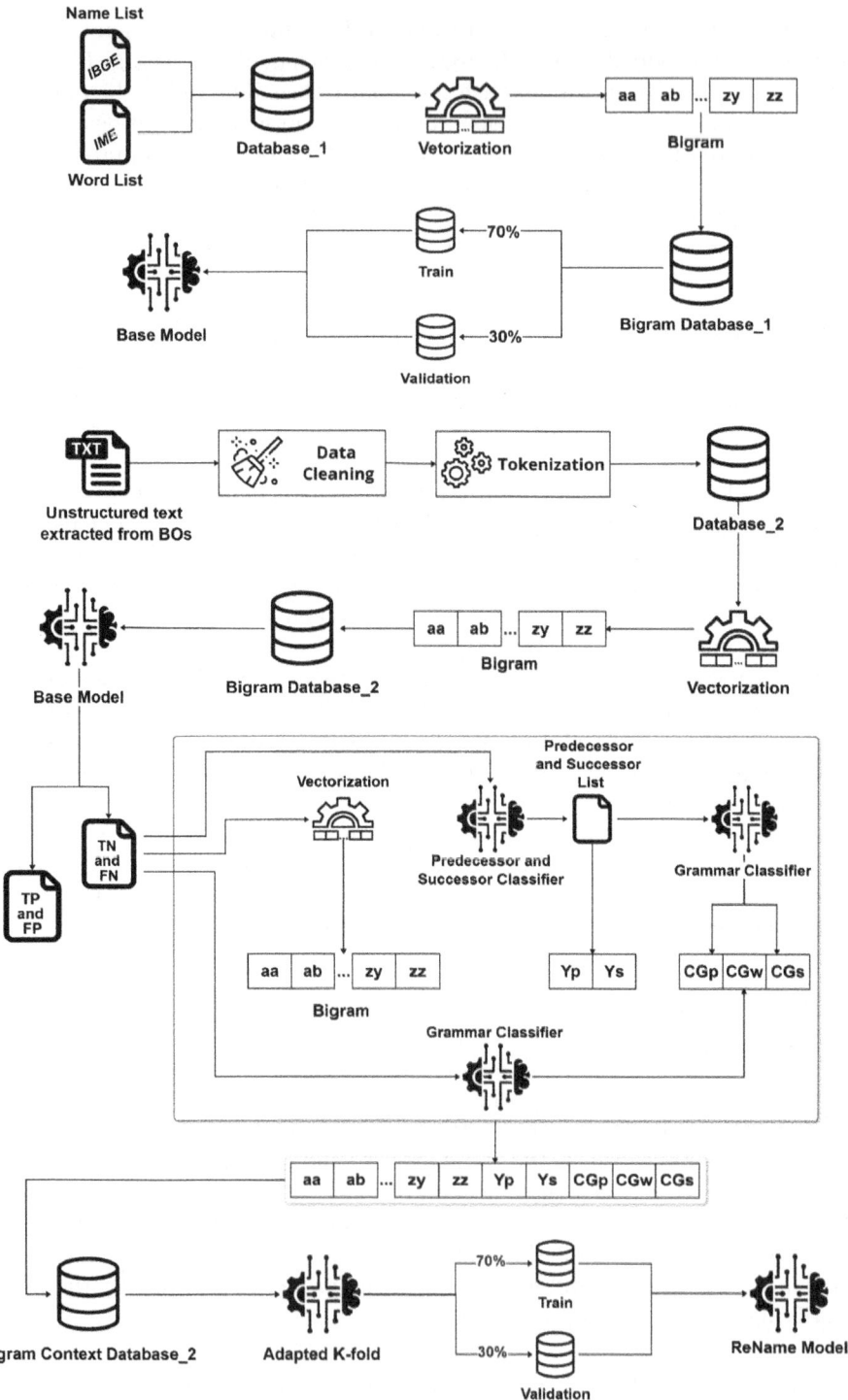

Fig. 1. Flowchart of the methodology used in the research.

3.1 Databases

Database_1. Initially, two lists were constructed. The first list is composed of personal names extracted from the Brasil.io platform[3], which provides data collected from the 2010 IBGE Demographic Census, and the second list is composed of common words in the Portuguese language provided by IME-USP[4]. The list of names contains 100,787 records from the "first_name" column, plus 1,774 records from the "alternative_names" column, totaling 102,561 names and their variations. For example, for the name "Davi", there are variations such as Davih, Davii, Davir, Davy, and Dhavi. The word list contains 245,019 terms, standardized without diacritical marks to maintain consistency with the name list.

After removing the intersection between the two lists, the Database_1 was assembled with 205,122 records, equally divided between common words (label 0) and personal names (label 1), as shown in Table 1. The words were randomly extracted from the IME-USP list, ensuring class balance and sample representativeness.

Table 1. Division of Database_1 into training and validation sets.

Dataset	Label 0 - Common Words	Label 1 - Personal Names	Total
Training	71,793	71,792	143,585
Validation	30,768	30,769	61,537
Total	102,561	102,561	205,122

Bigram Database_1. After splitting Database_1 into training (70%) and validation (30%), a vector was generated to represent each term in the dataset, facilitating its analysis in the modeling process [15]. In this work, the vectors were formed from bigrams of all possible combinations of the alphabet letters. Our hypothesis is that grapheme sequences in personal names and common words exhibit different patterns. Thus, the frequency of each bigram can be considered an indicator capable of distinguishing names from common words, making it a relevant feature in the classification task. This strategy captures more contextual information than unigrams, without the computational cost of trigrams and n-grams. For example, for the name "Davi", the bigrams DA, AV, and VI were set with the binary indicator 1, while all other bigrams are set to 0, as illustrated in Table 2. With this vectorization approach, the Bigram Database_1 was created with 205,122 rows and 677 columns, with 676 features and one column for the label.

---

[3] [Online]. Available: https://www.brasil.io/dataset/genero-nomes/. [Accessed: Aug. 20, 2024].

[4] [Online]. Available: https://www.ime.usp.br/~pf/dicios/. [Accessed: Aug. 20, 2024].

Table 2. Bigram feature vector for the term "Davi".

AA	AB	...	AV	...	DA	...	VI	...	ZY	ZZ
0	0	0	1	0	1	0	1	0	0	0

Database_2. This dataset was built from two batches of police reports (BOs) filed by the PC/PA in 2021, collected from several municipalities in the State of Pará, including Belém, Altamira, Marituba, Ananindeua, and Castanhal. The first batch includes 300 BOs previously labeled by the PC/PA, while the second batch contains another 471 BOs manually labeled by academic researchers. The composition of Database_2 in common words and personal names is shown in Table 3. During the preprocessing, stopwords were removed using the NLTK tool[5] to reduce the vocabulary size and eliminate irrelevant words, such as articles, prepositions, and conjunctions. This procedure was also applied to surnames, such as in "João da Silva" where anonymizing the word "da" does not cause issues. After this cleaning process, the data was tokenized.

Table 3. Composition of Database_2 by BO batches.

BO Source	Number of BOs	Common Words	Personal Names	Total
First batch	300	4,853	743	5,596
Second batch	471	48,156	4,526	52,682
Total	771	53,009	5,269	58,278

Bigram Database_2. The Database_2 then underwent a vectorization process similar to that applied to Database_1. As a result, Bigram Database_2 was generated.

3.2   Machine Learning Algorithm Selection

All algorithms were imported from the Scikit-learn library[6], version 1.3.2, using default parameters. This approach was adopted because the focus of this work is not on defining the optimal algorithm but rather to evaluate the performance of machine learning when applied to the data anonymization process, specifically in the task of classifying personal names.

Thus, four computational models, each based on a different algorithm, were trained using 70% of Bigram Database_1. Subsequently, two validation experiments were conducted. The first used the remaining 30% of Bigram Database_1

---

[5] [Online]. Available: https://www.nltk.org. [Accessed: Oct. 18, 2024].
[6] [Online]. Available: https://www.scikit-learn.org. [Accessed: Oct. 18, 2024].

(Experiment 1), while the second employed the 300 BOs comprising the first batch of Bigram Database_2 (Experiment 2). The goal was to investigate the ability of the computational models to identify automatically whether a sequence of characters corresponds to a personal name or a common word in different environments. The results obtained from Experiment 1 are presented in Table 4 and the confusion matrix in Fig. 2.

Table 4. Metrics calculated for each model in Experiment 1.

Model	Accuracy	Precision	Recall	F1-Score
SVM	0.931180	0.911709	0.958523	0.932768
Random Forest	**0.967970**	**0.961742**	**0.974714**	**0.968185**
Logistic Regression	0.940442	0.933080	0.948940	0.940943
Gradient Boosting	0.901896	0.875611	0.936882	0.905211

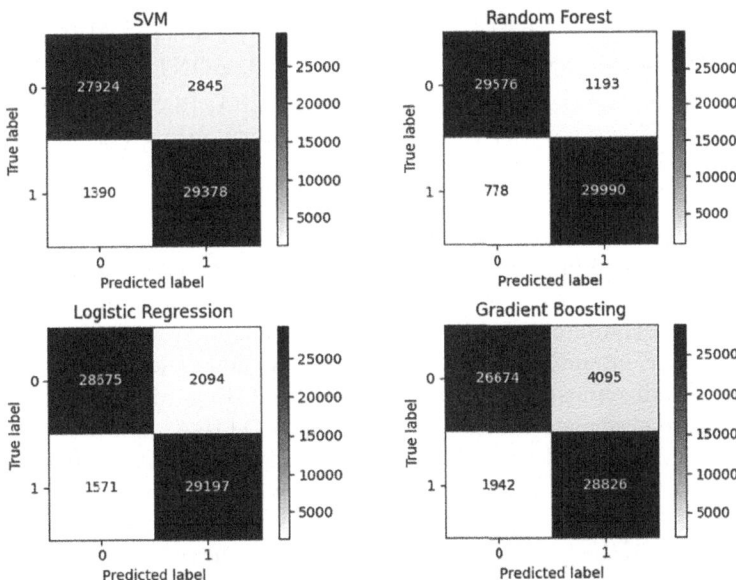

Fig. 2. Confusion Matrix for Experiment 1: Label 1 identifies personal names, and label 0 identifies common words in Brazilian Portuguese.

As show in Table 4, the Random Forest algorithm stood out, achieving over 96% across all evaluation metrics. Further analysis of the confusion matrix in Fig. 2 reveals that Random Forest correctly classified 29,990 instances from the validation set were correctly classified as personal names. In contrast, the SVM showed 2,845 false positive cases (instances classified as positive, but actually negative) and 1,390 false negative cases (instances classified as negative, but actually positive).

An important point that should be noted is that the models proved effective in minimizing false negatives, that is, classifying personal names as common words. This is a crucial aspect of the problem motivating this work. This quality provides more confidence to the operator, as the likelihood of not anonymizing a personal name is reduced, thus increasing the reliability of the system. The analysis of false negatives in Random Forest, which stood out compared to the others, revealed typical issues from the literature, such as ambiguity, typographical errors, and uncommon or foreign names. Some examples are presented in Table 5.

Table 5. Examples of personal names that were incorrectly classified as common words by the Random Forest model in Experiment 1.

Possible Causes	Examples
Ambiguity	SOCORRO, TECLA, CORADO, LIVRAMENTO, AGRARIO, COLETA, ALEGAR, ADRENALINA, ALEGRIA, FALCAO, TRANQUILO, INFANCIA
Typing errors	FRABCISCA, FARNCISCO, ESTLA, MRCOS
Uncommon Names	CROMACIO, EXUPERIO, GONTRAN, TUDE
Indigenous-origin Names	ARAPUA, APOEMA, TUPA, POTIRA, POTY, IRAE
Foreign Names	FARUK, FAROUK, HASSEN, KARAM, ANDREAS

Most false negatives appear to stem from lexical ambiguity, where a word's meaning varies depending on context. For instance, the name "ALEGRIA" may have been misclassified due to its association with the emotion of the same name. The second most common cause includes typographical errors, such as "MRCOS", which was likely intended to be "MARCOS". Although less frequent, foreign, atypical, and indigenous names were also observed. Regarding the classification of indigenous names, even though it failed with "POTIRA" and "APOEMA", the model correctly identified the names "JACY", "ITAJACI" and "ARACI".

Continuing with the validation process, a second experiment was conducted in a more realistic and less controlled environment. Thus, Experiment 2 studied the performance of the Random Forest model (now referred to as the Base Model because it stood out in Experiment 1) when applied to texts from 300 police report statements (see Table 3). Ultimately, the Base Model correctly classified 674 out of the 743 instances of personal names, as shown in the confusion matrix in Fig. 3.

However, the evaluation metrics declined significantly compared to Experiment 1, particularly in terms of precision and F1-score, as shown in Table 6. This drop in performance is likely due to the high number of false positives (=814) resulting from the imbalance in the validation set, which contains about six times more words than names. Nonetheless, the accuracy and recall results remained promising.

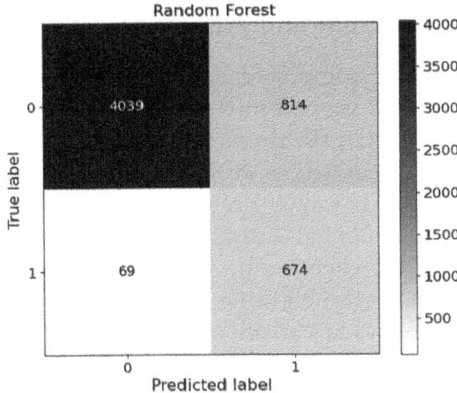

Fig. 3. Confusion matrix of Experiment 2: Label 1 identifies personal names, and label 0 identifies common words in Brazilian Portuguese. In this second experiment, only the Random Forest model was validated because it was highlighted in Experiment 1. For this reason, this model was developed as a basis for the following analyses.

Table 6. Metrics calculated for the Base Model in Experiment 2.

Model	Accuracy	Precision	Recall	F1-Score
Base	0.855969	0.476787	0.870794	0.616190

Regarding false negatives, lexical ambiguity is the primary cause, as shown in Table 7. For example, personal names such as "COELHO" and "CARNEIRO" were possibly associated with the animals of the same name. Typing errors, such as "PIMHO" instead of "PINHO", also influenced the classification errors. Furthermore, uncommon and foreign names continued to pose challenges for classification, such as "VASMORBITA" and "PEDTROVICH". In contrast, names of indigenous origin were correctly classified, demonstrating the good performance of the solution in these specific cases.

Table 7. Examples of personal names that were incorrectly classified as common words by the Base Model in Experiment 2.

Possible causes	Examples
Ambiguity	GRATIDAO, TORRES, BARRA, SANTOS, PRETO, FILHO, COELHO, CARNEIRO, COLARES, GUERREIRO, CRUZ, PIO
Typing errors	GONCACVES, PIMHO
Uncommon Names	VASMORBITA, RAMPIN, ROBISPIERRE
Foreign Names	PEDTROVICH, KYRIACOPOULOS, BASEGGIO, CUTRIM

3.3   Addition of Contextual and Grammatical Features

To initiate the feature generation process with contextual and grammatical information, Bigram Database_2 was submitted, as an instance, to the Base Model. The list of words resulting from the prediction was then divided into two groups: words that were correctly predicted as words (=33,746 TN); and names that were incorrectly predicted as words (=269 FN).

After separating the predicted instances into TN and FN lists, a bigram vector was constructed for each term, following the same structure as the Database_1. In addition to the bigrams, other information, such as predecessor, successor, and grammatical classification was incorporated to capture the linguistic context.

As a result of this process, the feature vector was structured into three parts: (i) the bigram vector of the term labeled as FN or TN; (ii) the prediction of the predecessor (Y_p) and the successor (Y_s) of the term in the police report text; and (iii) the grammatical classification of the predecessor (CG_p), the term itself (CG_w), and the successor (CG_s), as exemplified in Table 8. This new database was named Bigram Context Database_2.

Table 8. Example of vectorization for the instance "BARRETO", predicted as a word (0). The predecessor and successor are nouns (1); if it were a word, it would receive label 0. The numbers 12 and 13 represent the grammatical classes noun and verb, respectively.

AA	AB	...	AR	...	ZY	ZZ	Y_p	Y_s	CG_p	CG_w	CG_s
0	0		0	1	0	0	0	1	1	12	12	13

The grammatical classification of the terms was performed using the NLP model from spaCy[7], considering 14 categories, including: noun, verb, and adjective. In cases where a predecessor or successor was absent, the label NULL was assigned to maintain data integrity and ensure a consistent feature structure.

3.4   Adapted K-Fold Test

During the creation of Bigram Context Database_2, an an imbalance between the VN and FN classes was identified, and training a computational model with this unbalanced distribution could lead to biased results, with the word class dominating the predictions. To mitigate this issue, the k-fold test was combined with an iterative sampling strategy to assess the variance resulting from the selection of random subgroups. Thus, in each of the 125 iterations, 269 samples from the VN class were randomly extracted, which is equivalent to the number of FN. The process was halted when the remaining number of VN samples fell below this threshold, leading to the exclusion of the last 121 samples from the

---

[7] [Online]. Available: https://www.spacy.io/api/doc. [Accessed: Nov. 05, 2024].

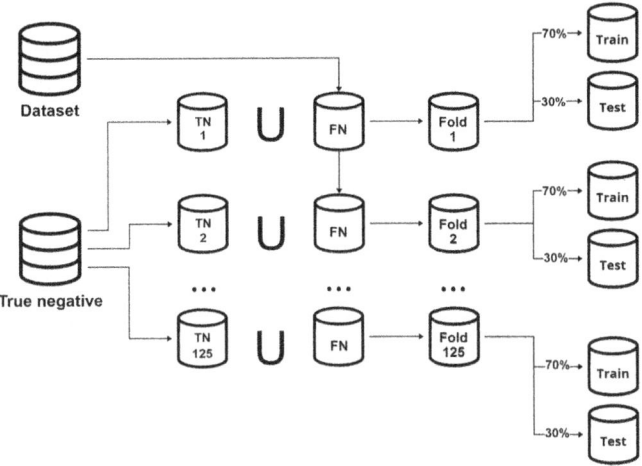

Fig. 4. Flow of the k-fold test applied to the dataset.

dataset. The workflow of the k-fold test performed with the Random Forest algorithm is shown in Fig. 4.

The analysis of the k-fold test results indicated relatively low variance, suggesting that the model demonstrated good generalization capability, even when exposed to randomly selected subgroups, as shown in Fig. 5.

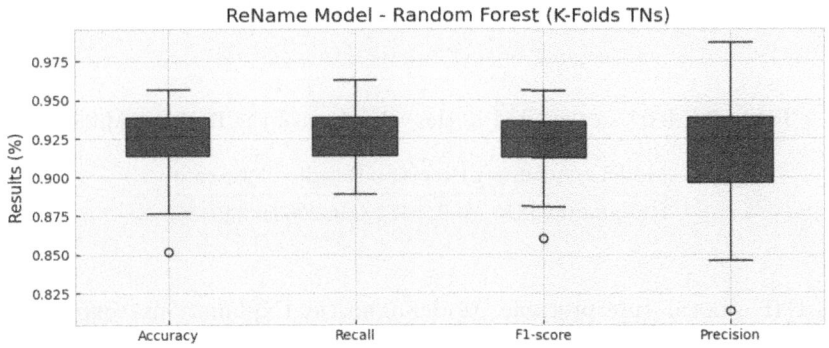

Fig. 5. Variance obtained for true negatives with the k-fold test.

3.5 Training and Validation of the ReName Model

To enhance the performance of the Base Model, with a particular focus on reducing false negatives, another computational model, called the ReName Model, was incorporated into the proposed solution.

The random sampling strategy was maintained, and 538 records (269 FN and 269 VN) from the Bigram Context Database_2 were used for the training and validation of the ReName Model. The training phase employed 70% of the dataset using the Random Forest algorithm, while the remaining 30% was reserved for validation. In this phase, the model correctly identified 78 unique instances as personal names, with only three misclassifications, as shown in the confusion matrix in Fig. 6. Other results can be found in Table 9. All metrics exceeded 90%, with a highlight for a recall of 96.29%.

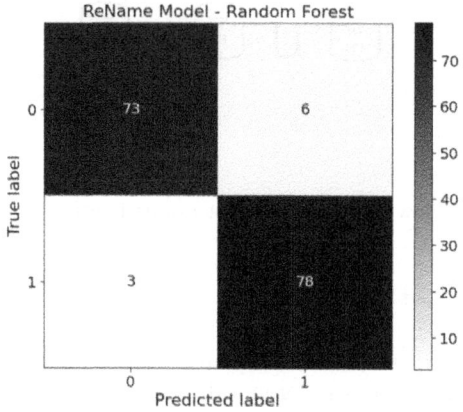

Fig. 6. Confusion matrix for the validation of the ReName Model: Label 1 identifies personal names, and label 0 identifies common words in Brazilian Portuguese.

Table 9. Metrics calculated in the validation of the ReName Model.

Model	Accuracy	Precision	Recall	F1-Score
ReName	0.94375	0.928571	0.962963	0.945455

The LIME (Local Interpretable Model-agnostic Explanations) explainability framework, widely used to interpret black-box machine learning algorithms [10], was employed to analyze the decisions made by the ReName Model. Through a Python API[8], the most influential features in specific classification decisions were identified.

To support this interpretation, several instances from the validation dataset were analyzed, considering the 10 most relevant features. In the case of the instance "TORRES", for example, correctly classified as a personal name, LIME assigned a 97% probability to class 1 (personal names) and 3% to class 0 (common words), as illustrated in Fig. 7.

---

[8] [Online]. Available: https://lime-ml.readthedocs.io. [Accessed: Nov. 20, 2024].

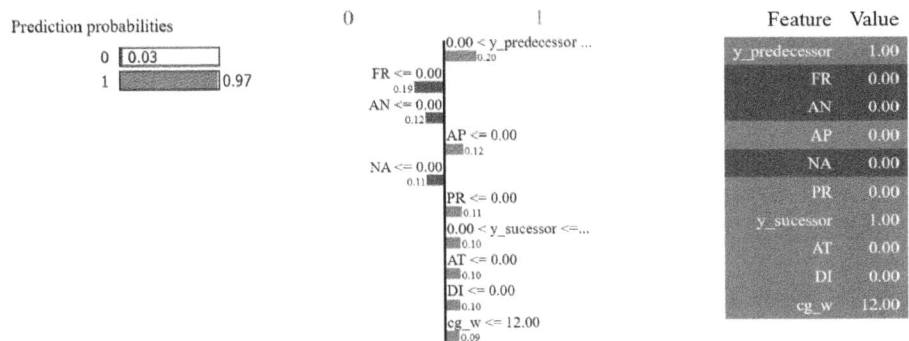

Fig. 7. Example of an instance correctly classified as a personal name based on the explainability provided by LIME.

It is important to note that the instance "TORRES" was incorrectly classified by the Base Model (see Table 7). This result reflects the influence of three features: predecessor (Y_p), successor (Y_s), and grammatical classification of the instance (CG_w). Both Y_p and Y_s indicated that the neighboring instances of "TORRES" were also personal names, contributing to the identification of sequential patterns. Meanwhile, CG_w received the number 12 (noun), reinforcing the correct prediction.

Next, the results of an evaluation conducted with our proposal are presented, analyzing its performance in classifying names and words in police reports. Additionally, the results are compared with two references from the literature: BERT and spaCy, enabling a more comprehensive analysis of the performance and advantages of the developed solution.

4 Evaluation

The evaluation of the proposed solution was conducted to assess its performance in classifying a dataset that was not seen during the training and validation phases. For this purpose, 231 preprocessed BO reports manually labeled by academic researchers, containing 2,135 personal names and 21,604 common words, were used as the test set. For comparative analysis, this same set was evaluated using the spaCy and BERTimbau models. The classification metrics obtained can be seen in Table 10.

The correct classification of personal names in unstructured documents is crucial for ensuring compliance with the LGPD, as failure to anonymize a personal name may compromise individuals' privacy by improperly exposing sensitive information. Thus, the proposed solution was designed to minimize the number of non-anonymized names, even if this objective results in a higher number of common words being mistakenly classified as names.

The results of this evaluation are organized in Fig. 8. Initially, four documents with more than 400 tokens were identified as outliers (see Fig. 8a) and removed

Table 10. Performance metrics of the proposed solution, BERTimbau and spaCy.

Model	Accuracy	Recall	Precision	F1-Score
Our proposal	0.799780	0.996252	0.309516	0.472299
BERTimbau	0.963730	0.681498	0.889364	0.771678
spaCy	0.948312	0.612177	0.766119	0.680551

from the analysis of predictions and correct classifications to enhance result visualization, totaling 227 documents in the charts of Figs. 8b and 8c, respectively. However, for the entropy calculation of the predictions, presented in Fig. 8d, all 231 documents were considered to ensure a comprehensive analysis of the test set.

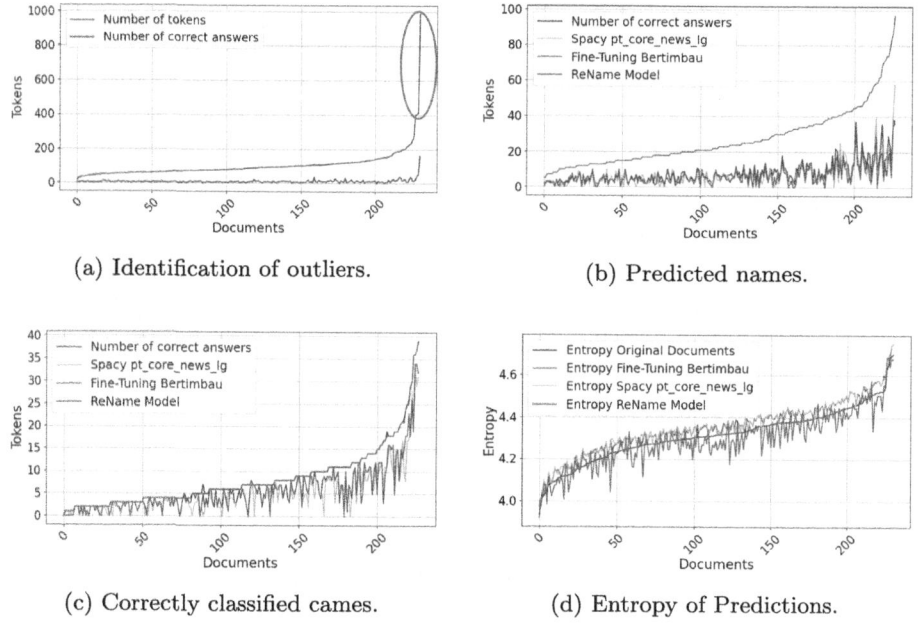

(a) Identification of outliers.

(b) Predicted names.

(c) Correctly classified cames.

(d) Entropy of Predictions.

Fig. 8. Distribution of tokens per document, ordered from the smallest to the largest. The number of correct responses corresponds to the number of tokens manually labeled as personal names in each document. (a) Identification of outliers in the number of tokens. (b) Number of tokens predicted as names. (c) Number of tokens correctly classified as names. (d) Entropy of the predictions, comparing the original and anonymized documents.

The number of tokens predicted as personal names by each model is shown in Fig. 8b. It is observed that the proposed solution presented the highest number of predictions in all BOs, indicating its high sensitivity to categorizing personal names, as evidenced by its high recall (= 99.62%). However, the BERTimbau and spaCy models provided a more precise approach.

This difference in the behavior of the model is reflected in the values shown in Fig. 8c, which presents the number of tokens correctly classified as personal names. While our proposed solution delivered the expected performance, the BERTimbau and spaCy models compromised personal data protection by failing to identify a greater number of names.

It is essential to emphasize that maximizing the identification of personal names must not hinder the understanding of the report's context, which may occur if a sufficiently large number of common words are mistakenly anonymized. As presented in Fig. 8d, the entropy of the predictions [7] was calculated to provide a measure of uncertainty associated with the classifications and to allow a comparison between the original and anonymized documents. The reduction of 0.020 bits in the average entropy considering the proposed solution (from 4.315 to 4.295) demonstrates a low impact on the complexity of the anonymized texts. In contrast, BERTimbau and spaCy exhibited the opposite behavior, increasing the entropy of anonymized reports by 0.038 bits and 0.039 bits, respectively.

Experiment 1 can be replicated using the code made available on the Github platform[9]. Unfortunately, due to confidentiality issues with the BOs, this could not be done for the other experiments. All tests were conducted on a notebook with an AMD Ryzen 5500U processor (6 cores and 12 threads) and 12 GB of RAM, without a dedicated GPU.

5 Conclusion

This work presents a solution for identifying and anonymizing personal names in unstructured texts, with a focus on police reports written in Brazilian Portuguese. The solution combines machine learning and natural language processing techniques, structured in five stages, including data collection and organization, algorithm selection for building computational models, addition of contextual and linguistic features, and finally, training and evaluation of the solution. Among these stages, the construction of the Base Model, responsible for the initial identification of personal names, and the ReName Model, which improves classification by reducing false negatives, stand out.

Our approach was evaluated using police reports provided by PC/PA and achieved a recall of 99.62%, ensuring broad coverage of personal names in the texts. However, this result was achieved at the cost of a higher occurrence of false positives, which could compromise accuracy in other scenarios.

For comparison purposes, the widely recognized BERTimbau and spaCy models were also evaluated. In this regard, the results demonstrated that while our solution achieved the highest recall, the reference models showed a better balance between precision and recall, resulting in lower false positive rates.

---

[9] [Online]. Github repository provided by the authors.
    Available: https://github.com/morenomarisa/namesClassification.

Thus, the choice between the models should consider the application's goal. When the priority is to ensure the anonymization of personal names, the ReName Model is best suits, as it maximizes the identification and protection of these entities. However, for the general purpose of name classification in unstructured data, the BERTimbau and spaCy models are more suitable, as they offer higher accuracy and reduce the misclassification of common words.

Additionally, an entropy analysis indicated minimal impact between the original and anonymized reports, preserving the textual structure of these documents. On the other hand, the texts anonymized by BERTimbau and spaCy showed a greater impact compared to the original texts. This finding confirms the importance of solutions that maintain textual consistency without compromising privacy protection, as in the proposed solution.

Although our approach prioritizes the maximum identification and anonymization of personal names, with a reduction in false negatives, the results show that there is room for optimizing the balance between recall and precision. As a future development, deep learning techniques could be adopted to enhance model accuracy and improve the balance between recall and precision results.

Ultimately, the solution presented in this work proves to be promising for applications requiring secure and efficient anonymization of textual documents, such as in public security and contexts requiring compliance with the LGPD.

References

1. Almeida, S.d.C.D.d., Soares, T.A.: Os impactos da lei geral de proteção de dados-lgpd no cenário digital. Perspectivas em Ciência da Informação **27**(03), 26–45 (2022)
2. Anselmo, M., Ribas, B.C.: Pseudonymization in legal texts according to the LGPD: A named entity recognition approach. In: Brazilian Conference on Intelligent Systems, pp. 309–323. Springer (2024)
3. Carvalho, A.P., Canedo, E.D., Carvalho, F.P., Carvalho, P.H.P.: Anonymisation and compliance to protection data: Impacts and challenges into big data. In: ICEIS (1), pp. 31–41 (2020)
4. Csányi, G.M., Nagy, D., Vági, R., Vadász, J.P., Orosz, T.: Challenges and open problems of legal document anonymization. Symmetry **13**(8), 1490 (2021)
5. Cunha, L.F.d.C., Ramalho, J.C.: NER in archival finding aids: extended. Mach. Learn. Knowl. Extract. **4**(1), 42–65 (2022)
6. Devlin, J., Chang, M.W., Lee, K., Toutanova, K.: Bert: Pre-training of deep bidirectional transformers for language understanding. In: Proceedings of the 2019 Conference of the North American Chapter of the Association for Computational Linguistics: Human Language Technologies, vol. 1, pp. 4171–4186 (2019)
7. Grandvalet, Y., Bengio, Y.: Semi-supervised learning by entropy minimization. In: Advances in Neural Information Processing Systems, vol. 17 (2004)
8. Honnibal, M., Montani, I.: spacy 2: Natural language understanding with bloom embeddings, convolutional neural networks and incremental parsing. To appear **7**(1), 411–420 (2017)
9. Juez-Hernandez, R., Quijano-Sánchez, L., Liberatore, F., Gómez, J.: Agora: an intelligent system for the anonymization, information extraction and automatic mapping of sensitive documents. Appl. Soft Comput. **145**, 110540 (2023)

10. Laguna, S., et al.: Explimeable: a visual analytics approach for exploring lime. In: 2023 Workshop on Visual Analytics in Healthcare (VAHC), pp. 27–33. IEEE (2023)
11. Li, X., Feng, J., Meng, Y., Han, Q., Wu, F., Li, J.: A unified MRC framework for named entity recognition. In: Proceedings of the 58th Annual Meeting of the Association for Computational Linguistics, pp. 5849–5859 (2020)
12. Lorenzon, L.N.: Análise comparada entre regulamentações de dados pessoais no brasil e na união europeia (lgpd e gdpr) e seus respectivos instrumentos de enforcement. Revista do Programa de Direito da União Europeia 1, 39–52 (2021)
13. Luoma, J., Pyysalo, S.: Exploring cross-sentence contexts for named entity recognition with Bert. In: Proceedings of the 28th International Conference on Computational Linguistics pp. 904–914 (2020)
14. Nelson, G.S.: Practical implications of sharing data: a primer on data privacy, anonymization, and de-identification. In: SAS global forum proceedings, pp. 1–23 (2015)
15. Silva, M.P.d., Viera, A.F.G.: Descoberta de conhecimento com uso de técnicas de mineração de textos aplicadas em documentos textuais da investigação policial brasileira. Investigación bibliotecológica 35(88), 161–183 (2021)
16. Silveira, M., et al.: An anonymization service for privacy in data mining. In: Proceedings of the 12th Latin-American Symposium on Dependable and Secure Computing pp. 214–219 (2023)
17. Sousa, T.R., Coutinho, M., Coutinho, L., Albuquerque, R.: Lgpd: Levantamento de técnicas criptográficas e de anonimização para proteção de bases de dados. In: Simpósio Brasileiro de Segurança da Informação e de Sistemas Computacionais (SBSeg), pp. 55–68. SBC (2020)
18. Weitzenboeck, E.M., Lison, P., Cyndecka, M., Langford, M.: The GDPR and unstructured data: is anonymization possible? Int. Data Privacy Law 12(3), 184–206 (2022)

Modular Architecture and Intelligent Routing for Chatbots

Claudiano Leonardo da Silva[1] (ID), Bruna Alice Oliveira de Brito[2] (ID),
Sérgio Natan Silva[3] (ID), João Vítor Venceslau Coelho[1] (ID),
Jean Mário Moreira de Lima[2](✉) (ID), André Morais Gurgel[2] (ID),
and Itamir de Morais Barroca Filho[2](✉) (ID)

[1] Departamento de Engenharia de Computação e Automação - UFRN, Natal, Brazil
[2] Instituto Metrópole Digital - UFRN, Natal, Brazil
`jean.lima@imd.ufrn.br`
[3] Unidade Acadêmica de Engenharia Elétrica, UFCG, Campina Grande, Brazil

Abstract. With the growth and popularity of large-scale language models (LLMs), chatbots have become essential to transforming interactions between business users through specialization, personalization, efficiency, and scalability. Nevertheless, issues such as hallucinations, specialization limits, and maintaining accuracy while multitasking remain critical challenges. In response to these concerns, this paper suggests a modular architecture for smart chatbots with LLMs as dynamic routers to route user queries to expert agents. The idea is to reduce hallucinations while increasing the relevance and accuracy of responses and show the strength of more specialist prompts. The suggested architecture classifies agents by domain (health and finance) and then by subdomains like symptoms or money planning. More advanced prompting techniques, including chain-of-thought and few-shot learning, are employed to improve contextual understanding and response accuracy. Furthermore, the findings indicate that using different language models for different situations can maximize query routing and maximize the level of detail in responses, which will be better matched to user needs. Experimental results confirm that the modularity-based solution is viable under multi-domain conditions and reduces hallucinations significantly while enhancing outputs accuracy and contextualization.

Keywords: chatbots · generative IA · language models · dynamic routing · modularity

1 Introduction

The association between big data and progress in machine learning has changed how businesses operate across many industries [14]. With AI being adopted more widely, digital transformation is reshaping how companies deal with customers, making their processes faster, scalable, and more tailored [1]. AI-powered chatbots, in particular, have become a key tool to improve customer engagement and simplify how businesses and clients interact [9].

Chatbots, which engage users through text or voice, have become important tools for delivering personalized customer experiences, especially in service-oriented environments [5]. Using personalized journeys where these generative AI solutions give companies a competitive advantage in areas such as e-commerce, customer service, and other support functions [3,6,19]. Studies show that personalization strongly impacts buying behavior, with about 80% of consumers more likely to engage or purchase when it is present [16].

The integration of generative AI models into conversational agents has recently marked a pivotal increase in their capabilities. Generative AI enhances the adaptability, responsiveness, and overall reliability of chatbots, enabling smoother and contextually aware interactions [24]. Despite all such developments, there still is a large lacuna in literature regarding a robust architectural model that not only addresses precision and confidence but also addresses important customer experience factors such as scalability, performance, maintainability, and the dynamic changing of context while communicating [11].

To address these limitations, we introduce a modular architecture for intelligent chatbots that blends dyna0mic routing using specialized agents, minimizing the dependence on large training data and preventing hallucinations in multitasking systems. In contrast to current solutions, our method effectively unifies multiple domains, striking a balance between scalability and maintainability.

Aside from that, the use of distinct language models for distinct circumstances increases response depth and query segmentation. The results of this study indicate that the modular approach favors agent specialization and increases contextualization to facilitate greater accuracy and appropriateness in user interactions.

The remaining paper structure is: Section 2 discusses related work and recent advancements; Section 3 approaches the proposed architecture; and Sects. 4 and 5 present our case study and experimental protocols employed to validate the solution. Finally, Sect. 6 depicts the results, with the conclusion exploring the implications and future advancements.

2   Related Work

The use of large-scale language models (LLMs) for various applications has driven significant advances in systems that seek to combine high performance and cost efficiency. Within this scenario, it can be observed that the use of retrieval-augmented generation (RAG) techniques has driven significant advances in the construction of intelligent systems, such as chatbots and personalized assistants, combining the retrieval of external information with the generation of semantically aligned content. This is evident if one considers the work developed in [17] to demonstrate that the employment of a variety of LLMs is capable of generating more uniform responses within formal business settings, whereas models such as those developed in [2, 18] use semantic alignment and question rewriting to improve the uniformity of the response. These attempts signify the importance of having specialized modules for specific tasks, such as the automation of workflows in bioinformatics or command optimization in vehicle domains.

However, with all these advances, RAG-based systems typically face challenges in terms of efficiency, scalability, and computational cost. One can see that the diversity of tasks and use cases present challenges to the adaptation of a single model, especially when trying to realize accuracy at the cost of execution costs. Under such a scenario, intelligent routing techniques, such as those based on LLM, offer a potential solution regarding the dynamic selection of committed models or agents to serve diverse queries. A variety of methodologies have, therefore, been thoroughly investigated to maximize routing performance. RouteLLM, for example, uses human preference information to train routers that decide on the best model based on query complexity and context, optimizing cost and accuracy [15].

Similarly, PolyRouter integrates multiple specialized LLMs within one system, employing methods such as MLP and BERT to learn query embeddings and predict the most appropriate model for each task. Although this approach greatly improves efficiency, it is dependent on the quality of the generated embeddings and prior training [20]. HybridRouter, on the other hand, focuses on efficient routing across the combination of models with diverse capabilities, regulating their performance based on historical data and trends discovered during training [7]. TensorRouter follows a similar direction, utilizing predictive models such as MLP and BERT to find the correlation between queries and expert LLMs. This approach requires extensive prior training to create embeddings and tune models for routing [21].

Other approaches, such as GraphRouter, utilize graph-based representations to model interactions between queries, tasks, and models, allowing for adaptive routing to new LLMs or tasks. This method also requires robust contextual data to build and refine a heterogeneous graph, as well as ongoing tuning to adapt to new models [10]. While these approaches show promising results, they also show a dependence on high-quality data for training and fine-tuning. This requirement can introduce significant overhead in the initial configuration and ongoing maintenance of the system over time, especially in dynamic configurations or with changing requirements regularly.

These works highlight the need for intelligent routing and modularity to improve accuracy, scalability, and efficiency in LLM-based systems. However, limitations such as the need for vast amounts of training data, computational costliness, and inability to adapt dynamically reinforce the argument for approaches that mitigate these impacts.

Table 1 presents the comparison of different methods of chatbots with LLMs and their strengths, weaknesses, and differences with the solution proposed in this research.

Based on this analysis, this paper proposes a modular routing architecture for intelligent routing that combines LLMs and specialized agents in a manner

Table 1. Comparison of different approaches for LLM-based chatbots.

Work	Approach	Benefits	Limitations	Difference from Our Work
RouteLLM [15]	Routing based on LLMs	Cost and accuracy optimization from human preference data	Requires high-quality human preference datasets	Our approach prioritizes flexibility and modularity
GraphRouter [10]	Graph-based routing	Scalable for integrating new LLMs dynamically	Requires robust data structuring and frequent updates	Our architecture provides greater flexibility across different domains
PolyRouter [20]	Multi-LLM querying system	Uses MLP/BERT to learn query representations and predict the best LLM	Strong dependence on embedding quality and prior training	Our model emphasizes modular specialization instead of embedding-based selection
HybridRouter [7]	Hybrid LLM routing	Combines different LLMs dynamically for cost-efficient routing	Requires extensive historical performance data for optimization	Our approach provides modular scalability without relying on prior query performance
TensorRouter [21]	Predictive model-based routing	Uses machine learning models (MLP/BERT) to match queries with the best LLM	Demands extensive pre-training to generate effective embeddings	Our architecture minimizes dependency on large-scale pre-training

that seeks to optimize chatbot response relevance and accuracy. Unlike single-model multitasking with an LLM, our method employs an LLM-based router that directs questions to the most appropriate agent, reducing hallucinations and context-personalization integration more efficiently.

The modularity of the architecture also allows for a sequence of specialized agents to be executed separately, lowering the cognitive overhead of a single model along with improving scalability. Additionally, the framework supports the addition of new domains without full retraining of the main model, making it an extremely efficient and adaptable solution to high-demand business applications.

3 Proposal

For language models to work well in specific tasks, they need access to contextual data that fits the problem. While methods like Retrieval-Augmented Generation (RAG) bring in outside knowledge to improve answers, they often struggle with multi-domain use and can cause hallucinations or lose accuracy with varied queries. In more complex scenarios or other scenarios that require more in-depth topical analysis, like chatbots that deal with both health and finance, weak contextualization can hurt the quality of interactions and make responses less reliable.

To address this challenge, this work proposes a modular architecture, shown in Fig. 1, that uses intelligent routing and specialized agents to increase the accuracy and contextual relevance of responses from large language models. The solution reduces the reliance on large training sets and improves query handling by dividing the process into three layers: a routing module, domain agents, and expert agents. The routing module handles initial filtering, interpreting query intent, and passing it to the right domain agent. That agent then narrows the request further and sends it to a specialized agent focused on a specific topic, tuned to generate accurate answers within that area.

This module-based solution has some advantages over the usual architectures from a single multitasking LLM. Firstly, query segmentation reduces cognitive overload on the model since each specialized agent handles only a subset of questions from its specific domain. This improves response accuracy and reduces hallucinations, which is a common issue for generalist models. In addition, the modularity of the system makes it scalable to include additional domains without extensive reconfiguration or retraining of the center model. This is an important benefit in business scenarios and dynamic, rapidly changing fields where constant updating of data is a requirement.

Another unique feature of the proposal is the use of cutting-edge prompt engineering techniques to improve agent-to-agent communication and query context comprehension. Methods such as chain-of-thought prompting, which encourages the model to structure its thinking more logically, and few-shot learning, which uses examples in the prompt to guide the response, are employed to improve the coherence and relevance of dialogue. The combination of these techniques with modular design helps the system be more flexible regarding different question forms and levels of complexity, improving greater flexibility for response generation.

For the purpose of ascertaining the effectiveness of the proposed methodology, this paper utilizes a realistic dataset that includes queries in finance and healthcare scenarios. The paper attempts to compare the use of traditional methods based on a single multitask model versus the proposed system.

4   Case Study

This case study demonstrates how the proposed architecture, utilizing intelligent routing and domain-specific agents, can improve response relevance in chatbots that manage multiple domains. To simulate this scenario, two datasets were utilized: one related to financial questions [13] and another for the health domain [4].

The architecture that was employed made use of the deepseek-r1-distill-qwen-32b [12], qwen2.5-32b [23], and llama3.3-70b [8] models within both the router and specialist agents. Each agent was assigned given prompts in a bid to push its response, with the router making use of a set of prompts in a way to suitably

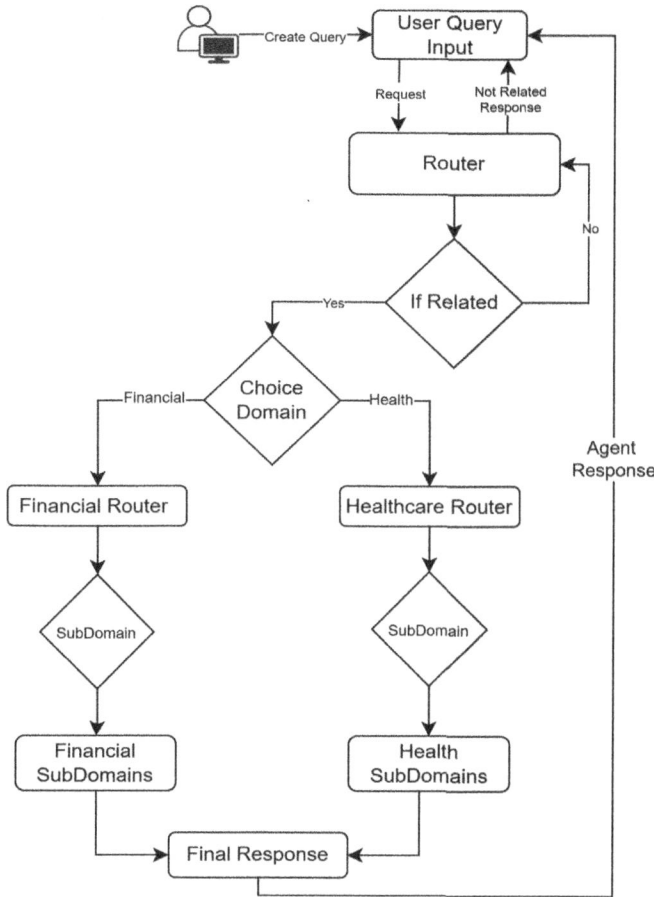

Fig. 1. General Architecture.

understand the intent of queries and direct them towards the most appropriate agent.

The following sections elaborate on the datasets that were used, the complete structure of the architecture, and the prompts used.

5   Experimental Protocol

5.1   Dataset

The choice of the datasets [13], on financial topics, and [4], on the health domain, is explained by the specialized and distinct character of the financial and health domains, with their specific terminologies, question patterns, and contexts. The financial set is applied in testing comprehension and handling of technical topics such as investments, market analysis, and bank products, and the health set examines the performance of the model to deal with explicit and sensitive inquiry related to medical issues, treatment, and practices in health care.

The financial dataset includes 50 questions, each with two possible answers–one being the "ground truth" and the other from the model that generated the data. Due to the small size, the questions were manually grouped into three broad categories: "Investments", "Financial Planning", and "Others". For the health dataset, which originally had 16,407 questions across several subcategories, a sample of 50 was selected. Only the two most representative groups were kept: "Information" (4,535 questions) and "Symptoms" (2,748 questions), with the rest falling under "Others". Table 2 shows the original distribution, while Table 3 presents the final selection.

Table 2. Subcategories and number of questions present in the health dataset, as well as their percentages in relation to the whole

Category	Quantity	Percentage
support groups	1	0.0001
complications	46	0.0028
stages	77	0.0047
prevention	210	0.0128
considerations	235	0.0143
susceptibility	324	0.0197
outlook	361	0.0220
research	395	0.0241
exams and tests	653	0.0398
causes	727	0.0443
genetic changes	1087	0.0663
frequency	1120	0.0683
inheritance	1446	0.0881
treatment	2442	0.1488
symptoms	2748	0.1675
information	4535	0.2764

To select the questions, percentages were used in relation to the 50 questions to be selected, where each category had at least one sample. With this procedure, 49 samples were selected, and finally, an extra sample was chosen for "Symptoms". After this process, we obtain the following distribution presented in Table 3:

Table 3. Number of questions per subcategory in each category

Finance	Quant.	Health	Quant.
Investments	15	Information	15
Financial Planning	13	Symptoms	09
Others	22	Other	26

5.2   Detailed Architecture and Module Configuration

Figure 2 is an expansion of Fig. 1 and seeks to present the architecture of the experiment carried out, detailing the flow of information from user input to response generation, expanding on how the structure of the Subject Agents is developed given the datasets described in Sect. 5.1. In the following subsections, the model employed and the prompts configured for each module will be described.

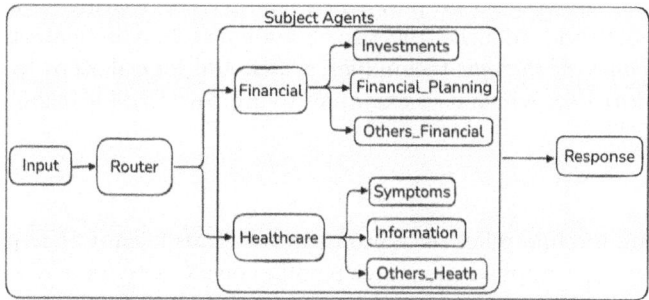

Fig. 2. Detailed Architecture.

Used Models. The architecture employed three state-of-the-art large language models: *deepseek-r1-distill-qwen-32b* [12], *qwen2.5-32b* [23] and *llama3.3-70b* [8] models for both the **router** and the **specialized agents**. These models were selected based on a pragmatic balance of performance, scalability, domain versatility, length of context window, and capacity to handle detailed instructions. These criteria are aligned with contemporary best practices in academic and industrial deployments.

– **deepseek-r1-distill-qwen-32b**: Computationally efficient distilled model with a good trade-off between cost and performance. The distillation here is aimed at retaining response quality with minimal computation, making this model appropriate for applications requiring real-time efficiency [12].

– **qwen2.5-32b**: Powerful contextual understanding model with a longer context length of 128,000 tokens. This makes it highly capable of handling lengthy texts, maintaining coherence and accuracy across a broad variety of domains [23].
– **llama3.3-70b**: Meta AI's advanced model is designed to be highly multilingual, supporting languages such as English, German, French, Italian, Portuguese, Hindi, Spanish, and Thai. It has a context length of 128,000 tokens, allowing for efficient processing of large volumes of data. In addition, its instruction-tuned version is optimized for interactive dialogues and detailed instructions. [8].

Used Prompts. The *prompts* were configured for each component of the architecture, aiming to optimize the interpretation and processing of queries within their areas of activity. The detailed description of the *prompts* used in each module is in appendices A to J. The structuring followed the principles of the CO-STAR framework, which defines five guidelines: provide basic information about the task, define the task to be performed, specify the writing style, determine the response attitude, identify the target audience, and indicate the expected format. The *chain-of-thought* techniques, which add logical steps to the *prompt*, and *few-shot learning*, which uses examples to improve LLM learning, were incorporated.

– **Router**

The routing module relies on a prompt that scans each user request for keywords, context, and implied meaning, paying special attention to cross-domain terms such as "insurance", to identify the primary intent and assign one of two labels, FINANCIAL or HEALTHCARE, before forwarding the query to the corresponding agent; when the input is ambiguous, the label reflects the most dominant subject, and if the request clearly falls outside both domains it is tagged Not Related.

– **Domain Agents**

Once the Router types the query, it is passed on to one of the domain's Agents: *Financial* or *Healthcare*. The agents are domain experts and are tasked with typing the query again into still more specific subdomains so that it can be dealt with even more precisely and accurately. Every Agent uses a *prompt* that instructs it to analyze the query and classify it into one of three categories. For the instance of the *Financial* agent, these categories are:

INVESTMENTS: For investment questions, i.e., stocks, bonds, mutual funds, and portfolio management.

FINANCIAL PLANNING: For questions concerning personal or business financial planning, such as budgeting, saving, and retirement.

OTHERS FINANCIAL: For other questions regarding finances that do not fit the above groups, i.e., general, account management, and unclear.

The *Healthcare* agent places questions in the following groups:

SYMPTOMS: For medical symptom questions, i.e., identification, description, and discussion of an illness.

INFORMATION: For questions asking about general or specific medical information, e.g., treatments, medications, and medical advice unconnected with symptoms.

OTHERS HEALTH: For other than the above requests, such as general inquiries on health, health systems, and ambiguous requests.

The *prompts* also point to the importance of context analysis, keyword detection, and sensitivity to nuances in order to ensure proper classification. They also provide examples of analysis and indicate the structure of the anticipated output.

– **Specialized Agents**

Once classified by the Domain Agents, the query is referred to a Specialized Agent, who responds with the final answer to the user. A Specialized Agent specializes in a specific subcategory of their domain, promoting high specialization in the answers.

Specialized Agents *prompts* are designed in a manner that every one of them turns out to be an expert in his field, providing detailed, personalized, and informative answers. Sample questions and answers are also provided to indicate the nature of the expected interaction.

5.3 Methodology

The process of obtaining the responses was divided into two general phases: orchestration and agent response.

In the orchestration stage, a cascade routing system with LLMs was implemented. The system consists of three prompts that are directed towards classifying and routing the user's question to the concerned agent. The system consists of two routing phases, the router prompt being the first phase and the health and financial prompts being the second phase.

– **Router prompt**: This is the initial level of the cascade and is designed to ascertain the general subject matter of the user's question, classifying it into one of two general categories: finance or health-related issues (Appendix A).
– **Financial and health prompts**: After the general topic has been decided by the router prompt, the second level of routing is initiated. These *prompts* have specific conditions to decide the subtopic within the selected subject and, from it, to choose one of the three agents per subject to answer the question (see Appendices B and C).

In the agent response stage, defined as the final stage of the process, specific prompts were developed for each agent. These prompts contain detailed information about the agent's topic of action, as well as clear instructions on how to formulate the responses.

To evaluate and compare the responses generated by the cascade system, an additional structure with a single comprehensive prompt was implemented. This prompt addresses all the topics defined in the routing stage and includes the corresponding response instructions.

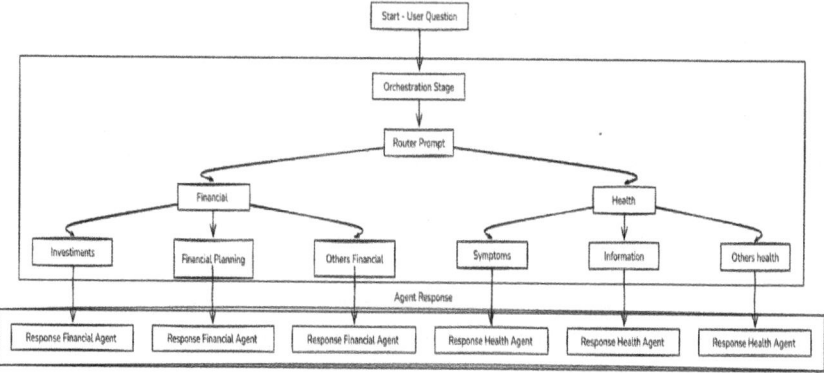

Fig. 3. Waterfall system workflow

6   Results

The findings showed that the organization and presentation of the answers have a great influence on their effectiveness and usability. The contrast between a one-shot approach and another executed by an expert agent shows contrasts in organizational features and detail level and adaptation to the user profile. Where the question is "How do I open a savings account abroad?", the one prompt generated response of the architecture presents information in brief and to the point. It refers, for example, to the need to comply with bank conditions, research foreign institutions and consider factors such as charges and taxations. Such a response, on account of its objectivity, is best suited to users who require an immediate summary of the procedure.

In contrast, the professional agent organizes his answer in a step-by-step fashion, dividing the process into numbered steps from choosing the institution and collecting the documents needed to taking costs, exchange rates and tax implications into account. This step-by-step format explores subtleties and details that can be determinative for those who need detailed and extensive guidance. It should be noted here that there exist studies that illustrate the impact of the length of the prompt on the depth and quality of the response citeprobst2024.

The same was observed in the question "Where to find support for people with Alcohol Use and Older Adults?". While the brief answer mentions important resources such as government institutes and support centers, the expert answer expands the choices, including specific meetings for the elderly, specialized treatment programs and professional and support group referrals. This makes the answer stronger, anticipating possible doubts and offering alternative means for proper care.

In general, generalist responses are all about efficiency, and they are most appropriately used to get the subject on the table and easy to comprehend immediately. Specialized responses, with their structured format and information-rich depth, facilitate learning and assist in making more informed decisions with less follow-up consultation required.

6.1 Token Distribution by Category

The token distribution comparison by category leads to inferences of differences where the models generate responses in the single prompt strategy and multi-prompt strategy. Figure 4 plots the token distribution for the case of the single prompt, while Fig. 5 describes the result when it is in the multi-prompt.

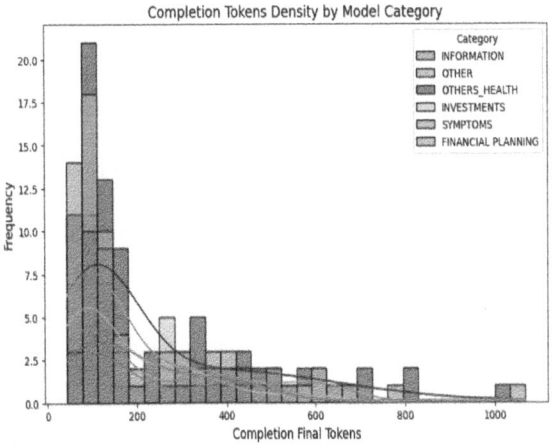

Fig. 4. Distribution of tokens by category in *single prompt*.

The results show that in the single-prompt setup, token distribution is more concentrated, with little variation across categories. This suggests that a single model struggles to adapt to different query complexities, leading to more uniform response lengths. Categories like OTHERS HEALTH, INFORMATION, and OTHER often get shorter replies, while INVESTMENTS and FINANCIAL PLANNING show slightly more variation, though still within narrow limits.

In contrast, the multi-prompt setup shows more variation in token use across categories, as the specialized agents can better match the complexity of each query. INVESTMENTS, for instance, has a wider token spread, pointing to the need for more detailed answers. FINANCIAL PLANNING and OTHERS

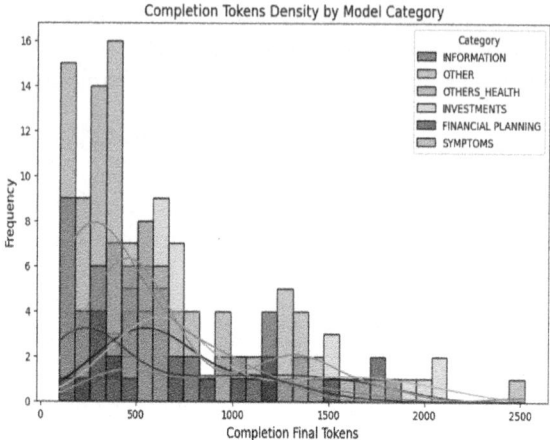

Fig. 5. Distribution of tokens by category in *multi-prompt*.

HEALTH also show broader distributions, indicating more efficient token use when extra context is needed.

The main difference between the two scenarios lies in token flexibility in assignment. There is no segmentation in the single prompt, where less context-adapted responses result, but in the multi-prompt, segmentation of categorization allows the system to maximize response generation to make it more where necessary deep and yet as concise for direct questions.

The gap between the distributions is also statistically confirmed by the ANOVA test [22]. As depicted in Table 4.

Table 4. ANOVA - tokens per category

Cases	Sum of Squares	df	Mean Square	F	p
category	$5.449 \times 10^{+6}$	5	$1.090 \times 10^{+6}$	4.542	< 0.001
Residuals	$1.595 \times 10^{+8}$	665	239901.249	–	–

Note: Type III Sum of Squares

These findings show that the multi-prompt approach optimizes the distribution of tokens and the contextualization of responses, making content generation more efficient and adapted to the specific needs of each category.

6.2   Token Distribution by Model

The distribution of tokens per model allows us to evaluate how different approaches impact resource allocation in response generation. Figure 6 presents the distribution in the single prompt, while Fig. 7 displays the results in the multi-prompt.

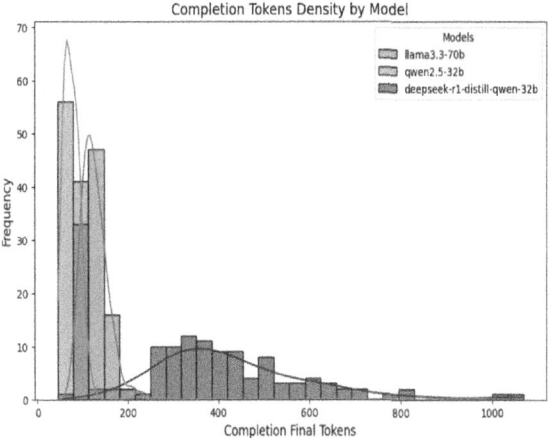

Fig. 6. Distribution of tokens by category in *single prompt.*

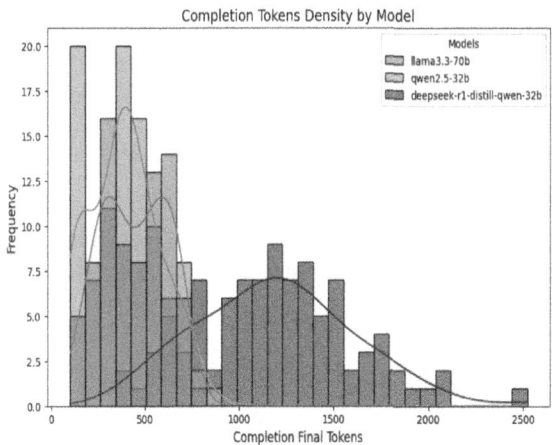

Fig. 7. Distribution of tokens by category in *multi-prompt.*

The results show that in the single-prompt setup, token distribution is more limited, with most responses falling into smaller ranges. qwen2.5-32b tends to give short replies, while llama3.3-70b has a slightly broader but still narrow spread. deepseek-r1-distill-qwen-32b produces longer answers but stays within a moderate range, suggesting the single-prompt method limits how tokens vary across models.

In the multi-prompt scenario, a significantly greater dispersion is observed, especially for deepseek-r1-distill-qwen-32b, which presents a wider distribution and a higher use of tokens in some queries. This behavior suggests that the model adjusts its response according to the complexity of the task. qwen2.5-32b, although still biased towards short responses, exhibits a greater variation, suggesting that, in certain scenarios, it generates more detailed responses. llama3.3-70b maintains an intermediate distribution, adapting better to the context of the questions.

The main difference between the two scenarios is in the adaptability of the models. In the single prompt scenario, the lack of segmentation restricts the variation in the size of the answers, allocating tokens more homogeneously. In the multi-prompt scenario, the system takes advantage of the specialization of the agents to adjust the number of tokens more dynamically, allowing each model to optimize its answers according to the complexity of the query.

As with the distributions presented in the previous section, the difference between these distributions is statistically proven via the ANOVA test [22], presented in Table 5.

Table 5. ANOVA - tokens per model

Cases	Sum of Squares	df	Mean Square	F	p
model	$1.237 \times 10^{+8}$	5	$2.473 \times 10^{+7}$	397.996	< 0.001
Residuals	$4.132 \times 10^{+7}$	665	62140.919	–	–

6.3   Implications for the Proposed Architecture

The results show that the multi-prompt approach produces more adaptive and effective answers compared to a single prompt. In the single prompt, there is uniform token distribution, limiting the responses' adequacy to the question's complexity. In the multi-prompt, there is greater variance in the token distribution, allowing more complex responses for complex questions and greater conciseness in simple questions.

The specialization of the models was also greater in the multi-prompt, where every agent optimized its token distribution in light of task demands. Such models as deepseek-r1-distill-qwen-32b were more adaptable in generating longer output, while qwen2.5-32b produced a shorter pattern. The findings hold that modularity enhances the efficacy of a system by facilitating more strategic deployment of the models.

Aside from response quality, modular architecture facilitates computation optimization, spreading queries across expert agents and avoiding resource wastage. Thus, the multi-prompt strategy improves the accuracy, scalability, and efficiency of the system, highlighting the need for smart routing and model specialization for advanced LLM applications.

7   Conclusion

This paper presented a chatbot architecture from LLMs, routing user inquiries through a routing module to targeted agents. The solution proposed seeks to improve response accuracy and contextualization and reduce the rate of hallucinations that accompany the independent use of a single model.

The architecture was evaluated through a case study using data from the health and finance domains, evidencing satisfactory results in the classification and handling of queries. The use of a modular structure, combined with the division into specialized agents, demonstrated greater efficiency in processing questions, in addition to offering flexibility for adaptations to new scenarios.

In addition, the proposed approach is effective in dealing with multiple domains, minimizing the need for extensive volumes of data for training or the creation of overly complex prompts. Modularity allowed segmentation into specific and objective prompts, each focused on a distinct task, significantly reducing the risk of confusion regarding the intentions of the queries. Thus, the modular structure with specialized agents proved to be a promising solution.

Among the limitations identified, the limited amount of data available for testing stands out, as well as the need for improvements in the prompts used. For future work, it is recommended to expand the tests with the modular architecture, include more data for validation, and improve the prompt engineering, in addition to optimizing the models used.

The proposed architecture, although initially applied to the health and finance domains, is designed to be extended. As future work, we propose incorporating other domains such as law and education, as well as expanding the dataset to evaluate the scalability of the solution, and integrating more robust quantitative metrics, such as accuracy, F1-score, and hallucination rate, to provide a more comprehensive evaluation of the system's performance.

References

1. Alabed, A., Javornik, A., Gregory-Smith, D.: AI anthropomorphism and its effect on users' self-congruence and self–AI integration: a theoretical framework and research agenda. Technol. Forecast. Soc. Change **182**, 121786 (2022). https://doi.org/10.1016/J.TECHFORE.2022.121786
2. Bai, Y., et al.: Pistis-RAG: Enhancing retrieval-augmented generation with human feedback. arXiv preprint arXiv:2407.00072 (2024)
3. Bakkouri, B.E., Raki, S., Belgnaoui, T.: The role of chatbots in enhancing customer experience: literature review. In: Procedia Computer Science. vol. 203, pp. 432–437. Elsevier B.V. (2022). https://doi.org/10.1016/j.procs.2022.07.057
4. Ben Abacha, A., Demner-Fushman, D.: A question-entailment approach to question answering. BMC Bioinform. **20**(1) (2019). https://doi.org/10.1186/s12859-019-3119-4
5. Chaurasia, A., Parashar, B., Kautish, S.: Artificial intelligence and automation for industry 4.0. In: Computational Intelligence for Modern Business Systems: Emerging Applications and Strategies, pp. 357–373. Springer (2023)
6. Chen, J.S., Le, T.T.Y., Florence, D.: Usability and responsiveness of artificial intelligence chatbot on online customer experience in e-retailing. Int. J. Retail Distrib. Manag. **49**, 1512–1531 (2021). https://doi.org/10.1108/IJRDM-08-2020-0312
7. Ding, D., et al.: Hybrid LLM: Cost-efficient and quality-aware query routing. arXiv preprint arXiv:2404.14618 (2024)

8. Dubey, A., et al.: The Llama 3 herd of models (2024). https://arxiv.org/abs/2407. 21783

9. van Dun, C., Moder, L., Kratsch, W., Röglinger, M.: Processgan: Supporting the creation of business process improvement ideas through generative machine learning. Decis. Support Syst. **165**, 113880 (2023). https://doi.org/10.1016/j.dss.2022. 113880, https://linkinghub.elsevier.com/retrieve/pii/S0167923622001518

10. Feng, T., Shen, Y., You, J.: GraphRouter: A graph-based router for LLM selections. arXiv preprint arXiv:2410.03834 (2024)

11. Fui-Hoon Nah, F., Zheng, R., Cai, J., Siau, K., Chen, L.: Generative AI and ChatGPT: Applications, challenges, and AI-human collaboration (2023)

12. Guo, D., et al.: DeepSeek-R1: Incentivizing reasoning capability in LLMs via reinforcement learning. arXiv preprint arXiv:2501.12948 (2025)

13. Acessado em 26 de novembro de 2024

14. Li, C.Y., Fang, Y.H., Chiang, Y.H.: Can AI chatbots help retain customers? An integrative perspective using affordance theory and service-domain logic. Technol. Forecast. Soc. Change **197**, 122921 (2023). https://doi.org/10.1016/J. TECHFORE.2023.122921

15. Ong, I., et al.: RouteLLM: Learning to route LLMs with preference data. arXiv preprint arXiv:2406.18665 (2024)

16. Putha, S.: Ai-driven personalization in e-commerce: enhancing customer experience and sales through advanced data analytics. J. Bioinform. Artif. Intell. **1**(1), 225–271 (2021)

17. Roychowdhury, S., Krema, M., Mahammad, A., Moore, B., Mukherjee, A., Prakashchandra, P.: ERATTA: Extreme rag for table to answers with large language models. arXiv preprint arXiv:2405.03963 (2024)

18. Shi, L., Kazda, M., Sears, B., Shropshire, N., Puri, R.: Ask-EDA: A design assistant empowered by LLM, hybrid rag and abbreviation de-hallucination. arXiv preprint arXiv:2406.06575 (2024)

19. Sidaoui, K., Jaakkola, M., Burton, J.: AI feel you: customer experience assessment via chatbot interviews. J. Serv. Manag. **31**, 745–766 (2020). https://doi.org/10. 1108/JOSM-11-2019-0341

20. Stripelis, D., et al.: PolyRouter: a multi-LLM querying system. arXiv e-prints, pp. arXiv–2408 (2024)

21. Stripelis, D., et al.: TensorOpera router: A multi-model router for efficient LLM inference. arXiv preprint arXiv:2408.12320 (2024)

22. Sthle, L., Wold, S.: Analysis of variance (ANOVA). Chemom. Intell. Lab. Syst. **6**(4), 259–272 (1989)

23. Yang, A., et al.: Qwen2. 5 technical report. arXiv preprint arXiv:2412.15115 (2024)

24. Zhang, Y., Pei, H., Zhen, S., Li, Q., Liang, F.: Chat generative pre-trained transformer (ChatGPT) usage in healthcare. Gastroenterol. Endosc. **1**(3), 139–143 (2023)

A Novel Caching Framework for Efficient Time-Series Analytics

Van Long Nguyen Huu$^{(\boxtimes)}$ ⓘ and An Tran Cong ⓘ

Can Tho University, Can Tho, Vietnam
{nhvlong,tcan}@ctu.edu.vn

Abstract. Time-series databases (TSDBs) have become essential in various time-series data applications. As the size of time-series datasets continues to grow rapidly, efficient system solutions are needed to manage this data effectively. One promising approach is caching systems that reduce response times and alleviate traffic burdens on back-end TSDBs. However, conventional caching strategies are often suboptimal for handling time-series data. To address this challenge, we propose SEMECAF (SEmantic-aware and MEtadata-driven CAching Framework), a novel caching framework designed to enhance the efficiency of time-series data management. SEMECAF introduces three key innovations: a cache framework, a semantic-aware processing mechanism, and metadata-driven management. Experimental results show that a lightweight implementation of SEMECAF significantly outperforms the baseline approaches across various performance metrics.

Keywords: Semantic-aware · Time-Series Databases · Metadata

1 Introduction

In recent years, time-series databases (TSDBs) have become essential components in various applications [16,17], including data analysis [21,26], Internet of Things (IoTs) monitoring [19,29], and system diagnosis [16,17]. Time-series data in TSDBs consist of *data points* recorded over time [2,3], such as sensor readings or stock prices. This characteristic makes time-series data valuable, allowing us to track behaviors and trends in dynamic information over time. However, managing time-series datasets' enormous and rapidly growing size requires a highly efficient system design. For instance, Uber's modern metrics platform, M3 [1], regularly ingests over 100 million datapoints per minute and serves hundreds of thousands of PromQL queries per second at sub-second latencies. Therefore, implementing high-speed query processing is both critical and challenging. One well-known solution is to utilize a *caching system* to reduce response times and traffic overhead to back-end TSDBs. When data is available in the cache, a cache hit occurs, allowing the cache to respond quickly to queries without communicating with the TSDBs. This approach significantly alleviates the load on TSDBs, improving resource efficiency and reducing processing latency.

ⓒ The Author(s), under exclusive license to Springer Nature Switzerland AG 2025
O. Gervasi et al. (Eds.): ICCSA 2025, LNCS 15649, pp. 285–302, 2025.
https://doi.org/10.1007/978-3-031-96997-3_18

1.1 Challenges and Opportunities

Due to the unique characteristics of time-series datasets [2,3], traditional caching methods are not optimized for their handling. By examining these properties, we can uncover both the challenges and opportunities for our proposal: a novel approach to the caching system.

Time-Series Data. Time-series data is collected over time intervals to provide insights into past events. This type of data should be considered as *write-once* and *append-only* [2,3]. Therefore, the motivation for cache design becomes straightforward: a *read-only cache* is sufficient.

Query Processing. The predominance of range queries in TSDBs [18] presents several limitations for conventional caches, including the handling of individual data objects or blocks, limited matching cases and overlap between queries. In contrast, a semantic-aware approach [24] can address these issues effectively due to its features: *range query-oriented* processing, management of data groups (referred to as *segments*), and the ability to handle *partial hits*. Consequently, a semantic-aware cache is a strong candidate for our design.

Highly Hot Spots and Skew. Range queries in time-series data applications often focus on specific *hot spots* in the data to analyze behaviors or trends [18]. The percentage of total queries that access these hot spots defines the *skew* of the workload. Most queries follow these patterns as hot spots may arise across the entire dataset. Thus, a semantic-aware design can effectively leverage high hot spots and skew leading to improved space utilization and higher hit ratios for the cache.

1.2 Semantic-Aware and Metadata-Driven Caching Framework

This paper proposes a *SEmantic-aware and MEtadata-driven CAching Framework* called *SEMECAF* that can improve the performance of time-series range queries over TSDBs. In particular, SEMECAF leverages the *semantic awareness* between range queries and manages this property efficiently in the cache with a *metadata-driven* approach. It also provides adaptability with different workload patterns, enabling dynamic optimizations based on observed behaviours of queries. The motivation is primarily to support the range of queries, as they are dominant in time-series data.

SEMECAF can be seen as a *(cache) logic layer* on top of efficient in-memory caching platforms, such as Redis [5] or MemCached [4]. More precisely, SEMECAF handles all the interactions with TSDBs and removes the cache platform from the critical path with TSDBs. This way, the input/output (I/O) performance and management costs are optimized while maintaining a simplified design.

The design can start with a baseline description (e.g., fundamental functionalities and features); then, it could be easily expandable as a *pay-to-go* caching service. Regarding to the modern caching platforms, SEMECAF supports *key-value storage* and provides additional information in forms of *metadata*. Thus,

SEMECAF can be seen as the best of both worlds, where it supports a semantic-aware caching mechanism and meta-data-driven segment management. We summarize the contributions of SEMECAF as follows:

1. *A caching framework.* We provide a read-only caching framework that can be seen as an expandable logic layer on top of caching platforms since time-series data is immutable and append-only. The cache design is simplified by using pay-as-you-go services.
2. *Semantic awareness in processing and caching.* We present segments of ranges of related data points to manage the cache. By matching segments with the interval bounds of incoming queries, our cache can handle partial hits to reduce communication overhead with TSDBs.
3. *Cache management with metadata.* The conventional caches have several management challenges: maintenance of the overhead, filtering latency, storage cost, and query-specific optimization. Our proposal presents a hash-based structure that leverages a composite key and metadata to quickly filter out irrelevant data points in the pool and optimize lookup performance.

Building an efficient cache layer is highly complex and demands addressing many problems; thus, we mainly focus on the core implementations in this paper. Other expansions or optimizations, such as effective replacement policy, low-cost compaction of segments, enhanced partial hit handling, etc., should be researched further. In other words, our proposal can debut as a lightweight framework and create a foundation for conducting further studies.

To evaluate the performance of SEMECAF, we deployed it on top of Redis and used InfluxDB [12] as the back-end TSDB. The experimental results show that our lightweight version of SEMECAF outperforms the baseline approaches (e.g., without cache). SEMECAF can achieve up to 87.1% hit ratio, 35.2 MB/sec for throughput, and accelerate up to 16.9 times the response.

The rest of this paper is organized as follows. Section 2 gives the preliminaries. Section 3 presents the related work. Section 4 describes the design. Section 5 presents our experimental results. The final section concludes this paper.

2   Preliminaries

2.1   TSDB for Data Analytics

Among the TSDBs for data analytics, InfluxDB [12] is explicitly designed for handling large-scale time-series data, including metrics, events, and analytics. InfluxDB stands out from the other options due to its efficient storage engine, rich query language, and ease of integration into diverse ecosystems. Thus, it can be seen as a target for integrating our framework in this paper. To illustrate how InfluxDB works, we present an example as follows: InfluxDB organizes data into *measurements*, which can be considered equivalent to tables in relational databases. Each measurement consists of: *tags*, *fields* and *timestamps*. Tags are the *key-value* pairs indexed for filtering and searching. Fields are key-value pairs for storing actual data points and not indexed. Meanwhile, timestamps are when the data point was recorded, which is critical for ordering and querying. Moreover, data points in InfluxDB are stored and sorted in *shards* for efficient compression and retrieval. Last, a *series* represents a unique combination of a measurement and its associated tags. More precisely, each series corresponds to a logical stream of data points that share these identifiers. To illustrate how InfluxDB works, we present an example as follows:

```
environment,location=London,sensor=temp value=22.5,humidity=60 1672
environment,location=London,sensor=air value=50              1673
environment,location=Paris,sensor=temp value=19.0,humidity=55  1674
```

According to this example, InfluxDB manages them in the forms of:

- Measurement: *environment*
- Tags: *location* (e.g., London), *sensor* (e.g., temp)
- Fields: *value, humidity*.
- Timestamps: represented in nanoseconds (e.g., 1672).
- Shards: all data points belong to the same shard if their timestamps fall within the same duration.
- Series: there are several distinct series. For example, [*environment, location* = London, *sensor* = temp].

2.2   In-Memory Caching Platform

Redis is a robust, in-memory data caching platform that operates on generic key-value pairs and supports advanced data structures (i.e., hash). Leveraging these benefits, the logic layer of our design can provide quick access to *segments* that contain data points within a bound of interval time. More precisely, the keys encode the bound of interval time that represents the semantic awareness of relevant queries. For example, a segment can be defined with a key that includes the device ID and the time range of a query, like $device123 : 2024 - 01 - 01 : 2024 - 01 - 15$. Generally, using particular data structures, like *Hash* or *Stored Sets*, Redis allows us to store segments compactly. Thus, it reduces memory consumption, especially when managing many segments. In particular, the hash-based approach contains all the segments related to a specific time series or interval stored as fields under a single key. In this way, the cache significantly reduces the number of keys it needs to manage, thus speeding up operations like scanning and matching segments. Hash fields can be presented through the below example:

```
Key: device123
Hash Fields:
    2024-01-01_to_2024-01-15 -> [Data for this range]
    2024-01-16_to_2024-01-31 -> [Data for this range]
```

Although Redis facilitates the workload of our design, it is not a constraint of the framework we propose. Indeed, the framework's contributions, such as a semantic-aware layer, data organization, and partial hit handling, are still suitable for redistribution to other caching platforms with minimal adjustments.

2.3 Semantic-Aware Processing and Caching

The advantage of semantic-aware caching is twofold. First, segments (e.g., subsets of data) can be much smaller than the original object or block, resulting in better cache space utilization and a higher hit ratio. Second, semantic-aware caching allows for handling partial hits (as shown in Fig. 1), where a part of a query (i.e., sub-query) can be answered quickly. To illustrate how the semantic-aware cache works, we use a typical SQL-like range query as shown below:

```
SELECT temp
FROM sensors
WHERE timestamp
BETWEEN '2024-01-01' AND '2024-01-31';
```

Fig. 1. Partial hits in cache.

The semantic-aware cache has a key: $temp : sensorA : 2024 - 01 - 01\_to\_2024 - 01 - 15$. It can detect that the range $2024 - 01 - 16$ to $2024 - 01 - 31$ is missing due to the interval bound of SQL-like query. Meanwhile, the range from $2024 - 01 - 01$ to $2024 - 01 - 15$ can be retrieved quickly. Thus, it fetches the remaining data from the TSDBs by generating a new sub-query that covers the missing range $2024 - 01 - 16$ to $2024 - 01 - 31$. Ultimately, the cache will update a new segment with the new key: $temper : sensorA : 2024 - 01 - 16\_to\_2024 - 01 - 31$. Concurrently, the application merges the data from the cache and server to get the final result.

3 Related Work

The basic idea behind of our approach is to accelerate the query processing by leveraging the innovations of TSDB and in-memory caching platform. Then, we build a cache logic layer that sits between them. In this section, we present the related work from three research areas: TSDB contributions, in-memory caching platform and semantic-awareness.

TSDB Contributions. Data analytics in InfluxDB focuses on optimizing data management to improve data ingestion and retrieval performance [2, 12]. We have seen other approaches, such as data visualization [9], data sampling and summarizing [18], in-memory processing [16, 17]. Since SEMECAF focuses on data analytics, we choose InfluxDB as our back-end database.

Caching Platform. Caching has been widely studied to reduce the latency of databases and TSDBs [27]. We have seen some commercial products implemented on fast local storage (e.g., Solid State Drives SSDs), such as DataBricks [13] and Alluxio [7]. In contrast, Druid [6] uses an external cache to manage the data (i.e., Memcached [4]) in the form of an arbitrary chunking. The main drawback of such an approach is that it can cause high overhead and inefficient caching. Our framework is based on in-memory caching caching platform Redis since it provides advanced data structures (e.g., hashes, sorted sets, lists) to manage data points with semantic-awareness and metadata-driven.

Semantic-Awareness. Semantic-aware caching has a large body of work [22–24,27]. In recent years, we have witnessed the semantic-aware concept implemented on TSDBs in different works. Wangthammang et al. [28] provide a cache mechanism on top of Memcached to reduce the query time of OpenTSDB. However, their work disregards the issues of data management and replacement policy that can significantly increase performance. Zang et al. [30] propose a novel lightweight semantic cache mechanism for Cortex [8]. One of the most significant disadvantages of such an approach is that the cache is in the critical path of TSDB. Another solution, TSCache [25], proposes a flash-based caching scheme that provides parallel I/O operations on flash SSD. In particular, this work is tailored mainly for InfluxDB, which needs an API to bridge the gap between InfluxDB and the client. Since using the flash SSD, their design raises the question of complexity and scalability. In contrast, SEMECAF leverages Redis' innovations to implement semantic-aware concepts as the logic layer.

4   Prototype Design

This paper presents a SEmantic-aware and MEtadata-driven CAching Framework, called SEMECAF, to accelerate the query range processing. Figure 2 illustrates the workflow between the logic layer (i.e., SEMECAF), storage layer (e.g., InfluxDB), and caching platform (i.e., Redis).

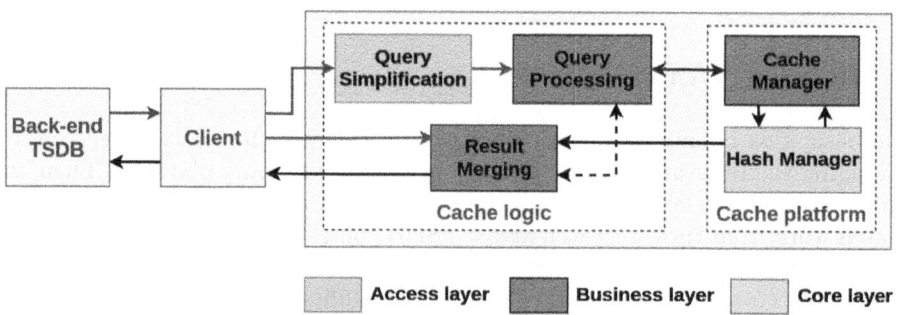

Fig. 2. Architecture of SEMECAF with the major components.

For each query, SEMECAF can be seen as the access point. After a conversation with the cache, if data is found (e.g., *hit*), the logic layer retrieves and returns the data quickly to the user. Otherwise, the logic layer receives a status, e.g., *miss*, and needs to drive the query to the TSDB to get the missing data. After that, the data is forwarded from SEMECAF to the cache and stored to serve future queries. SEMECAF handles all the principal interactions on both sides, storage and cache, by integrating a logic layer. Therefore, applying SEMECAF in practice is smooth and easy without modifying the TSDB and cache platform.

4.1 Architecture Overview

SEMECAF is described through three main layers: *access layer, business layer,* and *core layer,* as illustrated in Fig. 2. In particular, each layer contains one or several components: *Query simplification* in the access layer, *Query processing, Cache manager,* and *Result Merging* in the business layer, and *Hash manager* for the core layer. In detail, these components consist of sub-procedures that can be wrapped into the relevant units. For example, *Query processing* can be divided into several units: handling partial hits and generating relevant subqueries can be grouped into one unit, named *query handling.* Meanwhile, the Cache contains some units, such as *replacement policy* and *basic operations* (e.g., get and retrieve).

We summarize the mission of each component as follows: (1) Query simplification: transforms diverse query formats into a canonical form to reduce redundancy and improve hit rates; (2) Query processing: handles partial hits to generate precise sub-queries and merge the answers into the final result; (3) Cache manager: provides primitive functions to manipulate data (i.e., set, get or find), allows duplicate or non-duplicate segments, and implements a replacement policy; (4) Hash structure manager: exploits the hash-based structure of modern caching platforms with composite keys and metadata-driven segments; and (5) Result merging: bridges the gap between InfluxDB and Redis in the representation of data. These components can interact with each other to accomplish the demands of queries.

4.2 Query Simplification

Time-series queries can contain redundant or overlapping time intervals and unordered dimensions. Simplification ensures consistent query representation, enabling efficient hash-based lookup and reducing computational redundancy.

The Query simplification transforms complex queries into a canonical form by merging overlapping intervals and standardizing the ordering of dimensions. This process minimizes lookup time and prevents unnecessary cache misses caused by syntactic differences in semantically equivalent queries. In other words, it ensures that all subsequent operations (e.g., partial hit handling in Query processing) are optimized. We present the Query simplification in Algorithm 1.

To clarify the workflow of Algorithm 1, lets take an example. Assuming that an incoming query Q contains $D = \{sensor, location\}$ and $T = \{[10, 15], [12, 20], [25, 30]\}$. In Step 1, since T is already ordered, $T_s = T$. Then, we merge the overlapping intervals in T_s, the result is: $T' = \{[10, 20], [25, 30]\}$. While in Step 2, we get the $D' = \{location, sensor\}$. We have the result as $Q' = (\{[10, 20], [25, 30]\}, \{location, sensor\})$ at the end of the algorithm.

Algorithm 1. Query Simplification

Input: Query $Q = (D, T)$, where $D = \{d_1, d_2, \ldots, d_k\}$ is the set of dimensions and $T = \{[t_{1,1}, t_{1,2}], [t_{2,1}, t_{2,2}], \ldots, [t_{n,1}, t_{n,2}]\}$ is the set of time intervals
Output: Simplified query $Q' = (D', T')$
1: Sort T by $t_{i,1}$, obtaining $T_s = \{[t_{i,1}, t_{i,2}] \mid i \in [1, n]\}$.
2: Initialize $T' \leftarrow \emptyset$.
3: **for** $i = 1$ to n **do**
4:     **if** $T' = \emptyset$ **or** $t_{i,1} > \text{end}(T'_{\text{last}})$ **then**
5:         Append $T_{s,i}$ to T'.
6:     **else**
7:         Merge $T_{s,i}$ with T'_{last}: $T'_{\text{last}} \leftarrow [t_{\text{start}}(T'_{\text{last}}), \max(t_{\text{end}}(T'_{\text{last}}), t_{i,2})]$
8:     **end if**
9: **end for**
10: Sort dimensions D lexicographically: $D' \leftarrow \text{sort}(D, \text{key} = d_i)$
11: $Q' \leftarrow (D', T')$.
12: **return** Q'.

4.3 Query Processing

Generally, Query processing takes responsibility for: (1) handling hits, misses, and partial hits; (2) generating sub-queries depending on the overlap with cached segments; (3) constructing and maintaining the execution of sub-queries for the uncovered data ranges; (4) combining the results to form the final answer with Result Merging. Note that Query processing cannot work independently. Indeed, the cache manager provides a set of operations to manipulate the data segments on the caching platform, such as *set* (store), *get* (retrieve), *find* (match), and others. For example, *IdentifyCachedSegments* of Query processing uses the *find* function of the cache manager to match the overlapping data segments that are represented in the form of *a hash*.

Partial Hit Handling. Optimized partial hit manipulation allows for the exploitation of diverse query patterns effectively, even when the data distribution is non-uniform. In other words, this is the core of Query processing that significantly impacts cache performance metrics, such as response time, hit ratio, space overhead, and throughput. Algorithm 2 illustrates how the cache handles the partial hit as the most complex scenario of query processing. Since hits and misses are the baselines of the cache, their discussion can be neglected.

Since this paper mainly focuses on the proofs of concept before going further to tackle the optimizations of the framework, partial hit handling does not take into account these issues: a large set of disjoint time ranges, multiple fragmented sub-queries, granularity of data, and the expensive burden of programming. In other words, we have an *"optimist"* partial hit handling in SEMECAF. Nevertheless, the experiments show that our approach is still better than the baseline solutions.

Algorithm 2. Query processing with partial hits

Input: Query $Q = (d_1, d_2, \ldots, d_k)$, Cache S
Output: Result R

1: **procedure** HANDLEQUERY(Q, S)
2: $S_c \leftarrow IdentifyCachedSegments(Q, S)$ ▷ Find overlapping cached segments
3: $S_{nc} \leftarrow Q - \bigcup S_c$ ▷ Calculate uncovered ranges
4: **if** $S_{nc} \neq \emptyset$ **then**
5:    $Q_{sub} \leftarrow GenerateSubQueries(S_{nc})$ ▷ Sub-queries for uncovered ranges
6:    $R_{sub} \leftarrow ExecuteSubQueries(Q_{sub})$ ▷ Execute sub-queries on the backend
7: **else**
8:    $R_{sub} \leftarrow \emptyset$
9: **end if**
10: $R \leftarrow CombineResults(S_c, R_{sub})$ ▷ Merge cached and backend results
11: **return** R
12: **end procedure**

Complexity Analysis. The complexity of HandleQuery differs significantly from the old-fashioned storage of segments (i.e., without leveraging hash, composite keys, and metadata). HandleQuery's hash keys point directly to relevant segments, reducing unnecessary comparisons. In contrast, in old-fashioned storage, we must perform a sequential scan through all cached segments to identify the overlaps. Indeed, the complexity of the old-fashioned method is $O(k \cdot n)$, where k is the number of dimensions and n is the number of segments for each dimension. Such complexity creates a significant bottleneck in processing, especially for large datasets. Meanwhile, the approximate complexity of HandleQuery is $O(k + m)$, with m as the number of relevant cached keys. Thus, it can perform significantly better for larger caches and complex queries, such as lookup and overlap identification.

The full expression complexity of Algorithm 2 is: $O(k \log |S| + k \log k + m \cdot |F| + m \cdot q$. We break down the complexity into sub-procedures of HandleQuery:

- $k \log |S|$: cost for identifying cached segments, with $|S|$ being the size of the cache. It is derived from `Intersect`(S_i, Q) in `IdentifyCachedSegments`(Q, S). The Intersect can be calculated by using max and min of interval bounds of time ranges (as can be seen in Algorithm 3).
- $k \log k$: cost of sorting dimensions to ensure canonical order for simplification.
- $m \cdot |F|$: cost of overlap calculation where $|F|$ is the number of fields (i.e., metadata complexity).
- $m \cdot q$: cost of generating sub-queries based on uncovered segments (q is the cost of formulating a single sub-query). It is derived from computing uncovered ranges $\mathcal{U} = Q \setminus \bigcup_{S_i \in \mathcal{S}_c} S_i$ and `FormulateQuery`(U_j, F) of `ExecuteSubQueries`(Q_{sub})) (as can be found in Algorithm 4).

The cost is primarily driven by $\log |S|$, where S is often organized as a hash table or composite key structure for efficient lookup of cached segments. Indeed,

---

Algorithm 3. Matching between query and cached segments

Require: Query range $Q = [t_{\text{start}}, t_{\text{end}}]$, Cached segments $\mathcal{S} = \{S_1, S_2, \ldots, S_n\}$
Ensure: Set of overlapping cached segments $\mathcal{S}_c$
1: Initialize $\mathcal{S}_c \leftarrow \emptyset$
2: **for all** $S_i = [t^i_{\text{start}}, t^i_{\text{end}}]$ in $\mathcal{S}$ **do**
3:     Compute $\text{Intersect}(S_i, Q) = [\max(t_{\text{start}}, t^i_{\text{start}}), \min(t_{\text{end}}, t^i_{\text{end}})]$
4:     **if** $\max(t_{\text{start}}, t^i_{\text{start}}) \leq \min(t_{\text{end}}, t^i_{\text{end}})$ **then**
5:         Add S_i to $\mathcal{S}_c$
6:     **end if**
7: **end for**
8: **return** $\mathcal{S}_c$

Algorithm 4. Generate Sub-Queries with formulation

Require: Query range $Q = [t_{\text{start}}, t_{\text{end}}]$, Overlapping cached segments $\mathcal{S}_c$, Original query F (e.g., dimensions, filters).
Ensure: List of sub-queries $\mathcal{Q}_{\text{sub}}$
1: Initialize $\mathcal{Q}_{\text{sub}} \leftarrow \emptyset$
2: Compute uncovered ranges $\mathcal{U} = Q \setminus \bigcup_{S_i \in \mathcal{S}_c} S_i$
3: **for all** $U_j = [t^j_{\text{start}}, t^j_{\text{end}}]$ in $\mathcal{U}$ **do**
4:     query $\leftarrow \text{FormulateQuery}(U_j, F)$
5:     Add query to $\mathcal{Q}_{\text{sub}}$
6: **end for**
7: **return** $\mathcal{Q}_{\text{sub}}$

$\log |S|$ lookups significantly outperform linear scans $O(n)$. Additionally, more considerable m leads to more merging and sub-query generation. As a result, handling overlaps is expensive. Lastly, sub-query generation q involves splitting uncovered ranges into one or more backend queries, requiring computational effort proportional to the number of such ranges. In conclusion, the performance of our cache outperforms the baseline and old-fashioned semantic approaches.

4.4   Cache Manager

A side-by-side component of query processing in our framework is the cache manager. The Cache manager provides a library of primitive functions, as shown in Table 1. Interestingly, they are designed with the same input: composite key k. Such a key is created and managed by a hash-based structure within the hash manager. The composite keys allow efficient lookup of relevant data segments and minimize the space overhead of the cache. In our design, the cache manager works on top of the hash manager since the primitive functions can leverage the tailored structures that effectively represent the cached data. By this way, Cache manager can focus on the cache operations and mechanism, meanwhile data structure from basic to complex are encapsulated in Hash manager.

Note that this table does not present the complete list of primitive functions. For instance, we also implement the primitives for creating composite keys (i.e.,

Table 1. Some of the primitive functions in Cache manager

Function	Purpose	Input	Output
CacheGet	Retrieve a value by its composite key	Composite key k	Cached segment v or null
CacheSet	Store a value with a composite key	Composite key k, Segment v	Confirmation of insertion
CacheFind	Find all overlapping segments for a query range	Query range Q	Set of overlapping segments S_c
CacheMatch	Check if a specific key exists in the cache	Composite key k	Boolean: true or false
CacheUpdate	Update a cached segment or its metadata	Composite key k, New segment v	Confirmation of update
CacheDelete	Remove a segment by its composite key	Composite key k	Confirmation of deletion

KeyCreate), merging adjacent segments (i.e., CacheCoalesce), etc. All of these functions can be easily implemented using a variety of Redis client frameworks, such as Jedis [11] or redis-py [14]. Since we are familiar with Java, we chose Jedis, which is designed for performance and ease of use.

Another role of the Cache manager is to deploy a replacement policy and coalescing strategy. This paper applies the Least Recently Used (LRU) replacement policy and a non-coalescing strategy. Although they are not the most optimized options for our cache, they are reasonable enough to evaluate our proposal. Some further optimizations could be implemented in the cache manager, such as using a threshold to reduce the complexity of cache lookup, estimating the size of a segment as metadata and others. All of these contributions aim to present an automated and adaptable cache manager.

4.5 Hash Manager

The Hash Manager provides the customized hash with composite keys and metadata. Such an approach is a significant enhancement over the native hash of Redis, tailored to support (multidimensional) range queries efficiently.

Unlike simple keys, a composite key encodes multiple dimensions (e.g., *time, location, sensor_type* regarding *Temperature data in a city*) and ranges of a specific data segment into a unique identifier. In short, a composite key ensures *data isolation* and *semantic context* of the cached segment. In this way, composite keys allow efficient lookup of relevant data segments.

We also wrap the other descriptions into metadata in our hash-based structure, such as *start_time, end_time* and *average_density* based on the type of cached data. The most significant advantage is that it allows more straightforward and faster range lookup through efficient pruning of irrelevant segments during Query processing, especially in the case of multidimensional data. Moreover, metadata is essential for enabling the intelligent decision-making of Cache managers, such as using thresholds, estimating size, and computing overlapping segments. More precisely, it allows for handling overlapping and uncovered ranges where we want to coalesce the segments.

To emphasize the benefits of our hash-based structure, we present side by side the two approaches below.

```
                                    --- CUSTOM HASH ---
                                    Hash Key: London:temperature
--- NATIVE HASH ---                 Hash Value:
Hash Key: temperature                 field: "London:T1-T2"
Hash Value:                           value: "{stime: T1, etime: T2,
  field: "London:T1"                         dens: 10, data: [12.5, 13.0]}"
  value: "{data: [12.5, 13.0, 14.0]}"   field: "London:T2-T3"
  field: "London:T2"                  value: "{stime: T2, etime: T3,
  value: "{data: [15.0, 15.5]}"              dens: 10, data: [14.0, 15.0]}"
```

In the native hash, all temperature data might be grouped under the key *"temperature"*. Each field within the hash represents a unique identifier (e.g., *"London:T1"*), where $T1$ is the start of the first time interval. Similarly, the second field contains data for the second time interval. In fact, it does not contain any metadata. This approach generates a large set of segments to be checked in query processing. It is inefficient because we require examining all fields to identify overlaps with the query. Moreover, time intervals and their relationships (e.g., overlap, adjacency) are not explicitly encoded.

In contrast, the custom structure creates a hierarchical and context-rich composite key of multiple dimensions (i.e., *"London:temperature"*). Such a key is used to narrow down the relevant fields efficiently. Moreover, in the growth of multidimensional, number of devices (e.g., *sensor1*, *sensor2*) and measurements (e.g., *pressure*), this approach significantly reduces the complexity of Query processing. We also notice that each field in the hash is tied to a specific time interval (e.g., *"London:T1-T2"*) and includes metadata for query optimization (e.g., *"stime"*, *"dens"*). Thus, the handling of overlapping or adjacent segments could be simplified.

Note that although we do not have any indexing to optimize the lookups in the cache, the custom hash provides some of the same benefits. More precisely, by organizing data under a structured key and metadata schema, retrieval is faster and more targeted. Moreover, using metadata, it can mimic the index statistics used in query execution plans for partial hits and sub-query handling. In essence, the custom hash works as a lightweight lookup mechanism akin to an index.

4.6   Result Merging

Redis typically serves data in key-value pairs, which is not directly aligned with the native format of query results from InfluxDB. In contrast, InfluxDB delivers query results in a structured format tailored for time series data, including fields such as timestamps, tags, and field values. Thus, we must normalize and bridge the gap between the two platforms using a Translator Application Programming Interface (API) which has the complexity $O((n_c + n_b))$. n_c is the number of cached segments retrieved and n_b is the number of TSDB rows. Since the final result should be sorted and merged from intermediate results of back-end server and cache, we define a component called Result Merging which contains Translator API. Thus, the total complexity of such module is: $O((n_c + n_b) \log(n_c + n_b))$.

Regarding to this complexity, the current Result Merging of SEMECAF scales well for moderate-sized queries, but issues may arise when the number of cached and TSDB results grows significantly.

5   Experiments

5.1   Experimental Setups

Environments. In particular, InfluxDB 1.11.8 is deployed on a server with a 64-bit Ubuntu 22.04 LTS system and configured with an 8-core Intel Xeon Gold 5118 CPU running at 2.30 GHz and 64 GB RAM. Redis Community Edition is installed on another PC with the same system and configuration. The client to drive the workloads is a 64-bit Ubuntu 22.04 LTS system and a 4-core Intel Core^{TM} i5-8265U CPU running at 1.60GHz and 16 GB RAM. Note that we first create a database and load data points into the database, and in each run, we start with the same loaded database.

Datasets. Two real-world time-series datasets are used: Traffic [15] and Sensor [10]. Since they are small, we need to enlarge them by repeating their data multiple times for a longer duration while keeping the other metrics (e.g., sampling rate, fields, etc.). We then have about 6 GB ($82,419,304$ data points) of Traffic with nine attributes and 5 GB ($63,775,979$ data points) of Sensor with eight attributes.

Workloads. We use time-series benchmark YCSB-TS [20] to generate queries with different time ranges. The length of time range (i.e., $[time\_start, time\_end]$) follows the Zipfian distribution between *maxscanlength* and *minscanlength* as defined in the configuration. Our workload consists of 1,000 queries where each of them is varied from one minute to one week. The average size of the query is 20.15 KB and 15.31 KB for Traffic and Sensor, respectively.

To evaluate the performance in detail, we also present three workloads on Traffic: Small, Medium, and Large, where the time range of queries is 1 min to 1 h, 1 h to 1 day, and 1 day to 1 week, respectively. The average size of the query is 5.78 KB, 66.19 KB, and 357.53 KB. The cache size is set to 10% of the size of the workload's data set.

Metrics and Scenarios. We measure the performance using three key metrics: *hit ratio, throughput,* and *response time*. We compare SEMECAF with three other system solutions: (1) *W-Cache*: without using any cache; (2) *B-Cache*: using a fixed-size time unit (i.e., block) indexed by its query and time length in Redis; and (3) *OS-Cache*: old-fashioned semantic cache on Redis without using composite keys and metadata.

5.2   Comparison

With Traffic and Sensor. Figure 3 shows the performance of four solutions in various metrics: hit ratio, throughput, and response time. SEMECAF achieves the best overall performance across the two workloads. The hit ratio of SEMECAF can achieve up to $85.7 - 87.1\%$, which is better than B-Cache (i.e.,

38.4 − 47.2%). Note that the W-Cache has no hit ratio since no cache is deployed. Meanwhile, SEMECAF and OS-Cache share the same hit ratio thanks to their semantic-aware approach.

Regarding the throughput, SEMECAF shows the best results compared to other solutions. More precisely, it increases the throughput by a factor of 7.6 − 10.0 when compared with W-Cache. Moreover, we note that this through-put also leads to an increase by a factor of up to 2.0 when compared with B-Cache and OS-Cache. We notice that by using metadata-driven techniques with a customized hash and composite key, SEMECAF can overcome the bottleneck of OS-Cache (i.e., a large set of segments to be checked) by quickly filtering irrelevant segments in the lookup procedure. Indeed, because of this bottleneck, OS-Cache has been surpassed by B-Cache. Moreover, when the query is more complex (e.g., multidimensional), OS-Cache could fall behind in the race against B-Cache. Thus, SEMECAF is the best solution for replacing OS-Cache.

The key metric of the experiment to prove the benefits of SEMECAF is the response time. In particular, SEMECAF shows a speed-up by a factor of 2.1 − 2.6 and 2.5 − 2.7 when compared with B-Cache and OS-Cache, respectively. Moreover, the response time of SEMECAF is far better than that of the W-Cache, where we see the speed-up can achieve up to 15.0 − 16.9 times. Note that the speed-up can vary if we choose a different workload size. Thus, to understand the performance gains in more detail, we compare SEMECAF and other solutions under the Traffic data set in Fig. 4.

With Various Size of Traffic. In this experiment, the block size of B-Cache is fixed at a 1-hour unit. Note that the more fine-grained the chunking is, the higher the hit ratio, but also the higher the overhead can be. For different workload sizes, the semantic-aware approach's hit ratio is solid. More precisely, OS-Cache and SEMECAF always provide a hit ratio of over 80%. Meanwhile, in B-Cache with a small workload, the requests cannot benefit from the cache due to the fixed-size block (i.e., only 46.2%). When the size of the block increases, the hit ratio can significantly decrease or even drop to zero. B-Cache achieves more comparable hit ratios in the case of medium and high workloads, with 60.1% and 90.2%, respectively. Indeed, its hit ratio is higher than SEMECAF's in large workloads. The reason is that B-Cache can gain more partial hits with heavier workloads. However, due to the complexity of partial hit handling, which incurs severe I/O amplification, the trade-off appears in throughput and response time. SEMECAF is 1.2−1.8 times higher than B-Cache in throughput, and its response time is 2.4 − 3.1 times faster, thanks to its pseudo-hash-based indexing and irrelevant segment filtering. SEMECAF is also superior to W-Cache by 9.9 − 16.8 times. It is worth noting that the number of requests is significantly amplified in the case of multidimensional workloads, resulting in an overload on TSDB. In conclusion, this result shows that using SEMECAF is much more efficient.

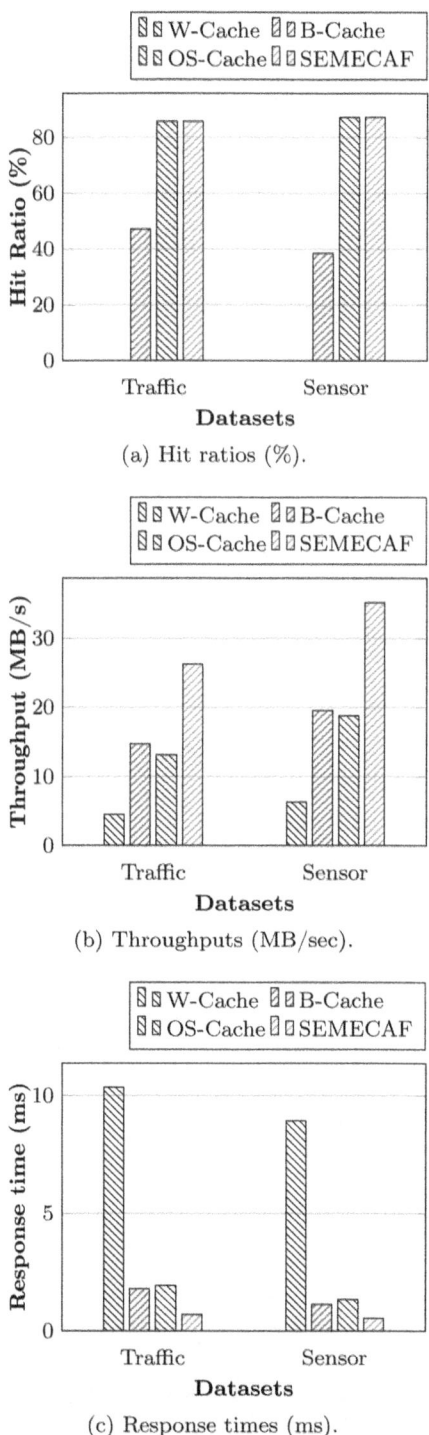

(a) Hit ratios (%).

(b) Throughputs (MB/sec).

(c) Response times (ms).

Fig. 3. Evaluations with two datasets: Traffic and Sensor.

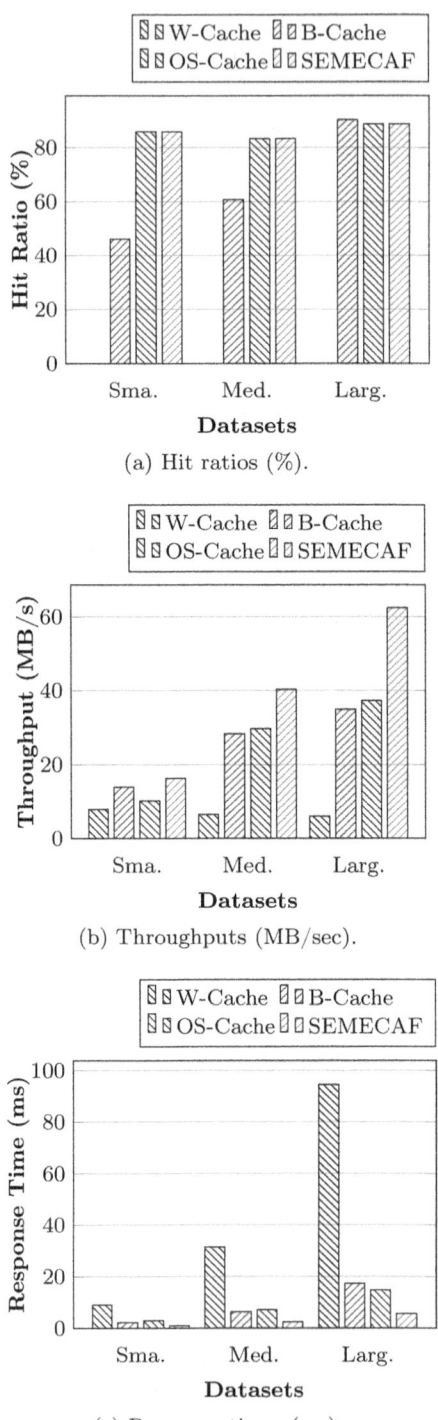

(a) Hit ratios (%).

(b) Throughputs (MB/sec).

(c) Response times (ms).

Fig. 4. Evaluations with various size of workloads on Traffic dataset.

6   Conclusion and Future Works

In this paper, we present SEMECAF, an efficient in-memory semantic-aware and metadata-driven caching solution that accelerates the range of queries in TSDBs. The results show that SEMECAF can significantly improve the effectiveness and efficiency of query processing. Since this paper mainly focuses on the proofs of concepts, we could address the following issues in our future works, such as multiple indexing scheme, optimized replacement, coalescing with threshold and size estimation, granularity as metadata, multiple disjoint time ranges in partial hit, overhead of CPU performance, and multiple clients performance.

Acknowledgment. The authors would like to thank colleagues of College of Information and Communication Technology, Can Tho University for their insightful comments.

References

1. M3: Metrics, monitoring, and metadata at scale. https://github.com/m3db/m3 (2018)
2. Time series data analysis? https://www.influxdata.com/what-is-time-series-data/ (2021)
3. What is a time series and how is it used to analyze data? https://www.investopedia.com/terms/t/timeseries.asp (2021)
4. What is memcached? https://memcached.org/ (2021)
5. Your app is about to get faster. https://redis.io/ (2021)
6. Apache druid. https://druid.apache.org/ (2023)
7. Alluxio caching. https://docs.alluxio.io/ee-da/user/stable/en/core-services/Caching.html (2024)
8. Cortex documentation. https://cortexmetrics.io/docs/ (2024)
9. Graphite. https://graphiteapp.org/ (2024)
10. Intel lab data. https://db.csail.mit.edu/labdata/labdata.html (2024)
11. Java client for redis. https://github.com/redis/jedis (2024)
12. The leading platform for time series data. https://www.influxdata.com/ (2024)
13. Optimize performance with caching on databricks. https://docs.databricks.com/en/optimizations/disk-cache.html (2024)
14. Python client for redis. https://pypi.org/project/redis/ (2024)
15. Traffic dataset collection. http://iot.ee.surrey.ac.uk:8080/datasets.html (2024)
16. Abraham, L., Allen, J., Barykin, O., Borkar, V., Chopra, B., Gerea, C., Merl, D., Metzler, J., Reiss, D., Subramanian, S., Wiener, J.L., Zed, O.: Scuba: diving into data at Facebook. Proc. VLDB Endow. **6**(11), 1057–1067 (2013)
17. Adams, C., et al.: Monarch: Google's planet-scale in-memory time series database. Proc. VLDB Endow. **13**(12), 3181–3194 (2020)
18. Agrawal, N., Vulimiri, A.: Low-latency analytics on colossal data streams with summarystore. In: Proceedings of the 26th Symposium on Operating Systems Principles, pp. 647–664. SOSP '17, Association for Computing Machinery, New York, NY, USA (2017)

19. Aljawarneh, S., Radhakrishna, V., Kumar, P.V., Janaki, V.: A similarity measure for temporal pattern discovery in time series data generated by IoT. In: 2016 International Conference on Engineering & MIS (ICEMIS), pp. 1–4 (2016)
20. with support for time series data bases, Y.T.: https://tsdbbench.github.io/YCSB-TS/ (2024)
21. Cui, H., Keeton, K., Roy, I., Viswanathan, K., Ganger, G.R.: Using data transformations for low-latency time series analysis. In: Proceedings of the Sixth ACM Symposium on Cloud Computing, pp. 395–407. SoCC '15, Association for Computing Machinery, New York, NY, USA (2015)
22. Godfrey, P., Gryz, J.: Answering queries by semantic caches. In: Proceedings of the 10th International Conference on Database and Expert Systems Applications, pp. 485–498. DEXA '99, Springer-Verlag, Berlin, Heidelberg (1999)
23. Huu, V., Lallet, J., Casseau, E., d'Orazio, L.: MASCARA (modular semantic caching framework) towards FPGA acceleration for IoT security monitoring. Open J. Internet Things 6(1), 14–23 (2020)
24. Jónsson, B.T., Arinbjarnar, M., Þórsson, B., Franklin, M.J., Srivastava, D.: Performance and overhead of semantic cache management. ACM Trans. Internet Technol. 6(3), 302–331 (2006). https://doi.org/10.1145/1151087.1151091
25. Liu, J., Wang, K., Chen, F.: TSCache: an efficient flash-based caching scheme for time-series data workloads. Proc. VLDB Endow. 14(13), 3253–3266 (2021)
26. Rabkin, A., Arye, M., Sen, S., Pai, V.S., Freedman, M.J.: Aggregation and degradation in JetStream: streaming analytics in the wide area. In: Proceedings of the 11th USENIX Conference on Networked Systems Design and Implementation, pp. 275–288. NSDI'14, USENIX Association, USA (2014)
27. Stonebraker, M., Jhingran, A., Goh, J., Potamianos, S.: On rules, procedure, caching and views in data base systems. In: Proceedings of the 1990 ACM SIGMOD International Conference on Management of Data, pp. 281–290. SIGMOD '90, Association for Computing Machinery, New York, NY, USA (1990)
28. Wangthammang, T., Tandayya, P.: A software cache mechanism for reducing the OpenTSDB query time. In: 2018 18th International Symposium on Communications and Information Technologies (ISCIT), pp. 60–65 (2018)
29. Xu, X., Huang, S., Chen, Y., Browny, K., Halilovicy, I., Lu, W.: TSaaaS: time series analytics as a service on IoT. In: 2014 IEEE International Conference on Web Services, pp. 249–256 (2014)
30. Zhang, K., Wang, Z., Shao, Z.: BSCache: a brisk semantic caching scheme for cloud-based performance monitoring timeseries systems. In: Proceedings of the 51st International Conference on Parallel Processing. ICPP '22, Association for Computing Machinery, New York, NY, USA (2023)

Named Entity Recognition
for Performance and Synthesis Information
of Perovskite Solar Cells Using SpaCy

Mary Zuleika Jiménez-Díaz$^{(\boxtimes)}$ ⓘ, Alexander Sepúlveda-Sepúlveda ⓘ,
and Mónica Botero-Londoño ⓘ

Escuela de Ingenierías Eléctrica, Electrónica y de Telecomunicaciones, Universidad
Industrial de Santander, Bucaramanga, Santander, Colombia
mary2238319@correo.uis.edu.co, alexander.sepulveda@saber.uis.edu.co,
mabotero@uis.edu.co

Abstract. This paper presents a Named Entity Recognition (NER)
approach to extract key information related to the structural components, synthesis techniques, and photovoltaic performance metrics of Perovskite solar cells (PSCs). Since NER is a key component of Information
Extraction (IE), which identifies and classifies key elements of a text, we
propose the use of the *SpaCy* library to build an effective and accessible NER model, suitable for environments with limited computational
capacity, unlike other previous works in this field, which make use of
large-scale models or high computational resources. Our resulting model
was evaluated using *K-fold cross-validation*, obtaining the mean scores
of, precision of 89.94%, a recall of 92.47%, and an F1 score of 89.69%. To
provide a test of the practical performance of the resulting model, implementing and comparing the obtained results with manual annotations in
two Excel reference databases: Odabaşı (2019) [1] and Jacobsson (2022)
[2], demonstrating the potential of our work to facilitate and accelerate
knowledge extraction, and the possibility of extending this strategy to
other scientific fields where automated text extraction is required.

Keywords: Natural language processing · NER · Perovskite Solar
Cells · Spacy · Machine Learning · Named Entity Recognition

1 Introduction

In recent years, the development of renewable energy sources with low environmental impact has gained increasing attention, driven by global initiatives to
limit global warming and mitigate the costs of traditional energy. According to
the REN21 report [3], investment in renewable energy reached a historic high in
2023, reflecting its accelerated growth.

Perovskite solar cells (PSCs), classified as third-generation photovoltaic
devices, have emerged as a strong contender to silicon-based technologies, primarily due to their high power conversion efficiency (PCE) and potential cost

© The Author(s), under exclusive license to Springer Nature Switzerland AG 2025
O. Gervasi et al. (Eds.): ICCSA 2025, LNCS 15649, pp. 303–319, 2025.
https://doi.org/10.1007/978-3-031-96997-3_19

advantages. Laboratory studies have reported PCE values exceeding 26% [4], and ongoing research suggests that advances in manufacturing techniques could lead to lower production costs [5–7]. However, their operational stability and material optimization remain key challenges [8,9]. The discovery of new high-performance PSC materials and fabrication techniques still requires extensive experimental validation, which increases both costs and development time despite advances in computational modeling.

PSC data can come from simulations or experimental measurements. While simulations are widely used due to their lower costs [10–13], they do not always account for material defects or real operating conditions. As a result, experimental data remain essential for validating material properties and device performance, but obtaining and analyzing this information manually is time-consuming and costly.

The rise of PSCs and their rapid growth have resulted in a substantial increase in the number of scientific papers, making them one of the fastest growing topics in the area of photovoltaic generation research [14]. This growing amount of information is a valuable resource for materials discovery and analysis. In order to reduce the time and cost associated with prediction, analysis, and the optimization of PSC configurations and synthesis methods, machine learning-based approaches have been proposed [1,15–19]. However, the unstructured information contained in the overwhelming volume of scientific articles makes manual data collection challenging [2], thus highlighting the need for automated tools to enhance the efficiency of relevant information extraction.

The information extraction (IE) can be simplified into two main tasks: Named Entity Recognition (NER) and Relationship Extraction (RE) [20]. Where, the NER task consists of analyzing a text to locate and classify unitary words, named "Named Entities" into categories defined for the target task, as an example, the word "MAPbI3" can be defined as a Named Entity of the "Absorbent layer of the cell structure" category. Then, the RE task is in charge of identifying and classifying the contextual and/or grammatical relationships between the Named Entities recognized in the NER task.

The data extraction process and the NER task start with the conversion of the documents to plain text from documents usually in PDF or HTML. Then the texts are preprocessed to de-encode, standardize and segment the information, and finally, the texts are analyzed using computer tools and natural language processing (NLP) techniques suitable for the NER task to retrieve the relevant data. Various tools exist for scientific information extraction, such as ChemDataExtractor [21], ChemicalTagger [22], and OSCAR4 [23], which focus on extracting scientific entities related to elements and chemical compounds [24]. Transformer-based models (LLMs) have also been developed, with platforms like Hugging Face providing widely used open-source libraries for implementing and fine-tuning these models [25]. However, these tools are not optimized for PSCs and do not offer an efficient, low-computational-cost approach for training custom NER models. Without additional fine-tuning on domain-specific data, they cannot accurately identify key entities related to synthesis methods, device performance, and structural composition.

Some recent studies have addressed automated information extraction in PSCs. *Beard et al.* [26] employed *ChemDataExtractor* as a baseline model for the automatic generation of PSC databases, demonstrating how automation can accelerate scientific data collection. *Xie et al.* [27] proposed an approach based on large language models (LLMs) and convolutional networks for structuring a dataset and predicting PSC performance. Although these methods have shown significant advances, they often require high computational resources and are not designed for environments with limited hardware or small research teams, nor do they enable the rapid, cost-effective, and semi-automated development of custom NER models.

Given this scenario, it is necessary to explore alternatives that enable the development of optimized NER models for PSCs, with more accessible and resource-efficient implementation.

In this paper, we present an approach to perform NER tasks on PSC-related data from PDF and HTML files. Where we train a model using the SpaCy NLP library [28], to extract entities related to the performance, synthesis methods, and structural composition of PSCs. The final model obtained was trained, tested, evaluated, and validated using a dataset of 584 PDF articles about conventional PSCs, as reported by Odabaşı (2019) [1], and 4 HTML articles extracted from Jacobsson (2022) [2]. Therefore, we developed a proposal that offers a specialized, accessible, and adaptable alternative to training NER models in environments with limited computational resources.

2   Method

In this work, we use *SpaCy* [28], an open-source Python library. It provides natural language processing tools such as tokenization, part-of-speech (POS) tagging, dependency parsing, named entity recognition (NER), relation extraction, lemmatization, text classification, customizable pipelines, word embeddings, and similarity analysis, among others. These tools enable the training of a customized model tailored to the linguistic and vocabulary needs of a specific task. However, before this, it is necessary to obtain training data, considering the semantic and linguistic specifications relevant to the task at hand.

2.1   Named Entity Recognition (NER)

In our work, we describe the basic structure of a Perovskite solar cell with three main layers: a Perovskite layer, which acts as the active material and absorbs light; an electron transport layer (ETL), which facilitates electron movement; and a hole transport layer (HTL), which enables the flow of positive charge. This arrangement corresponds to the standard structure of conventional Perovskite solar cells, as illustrated in Fig. 1.

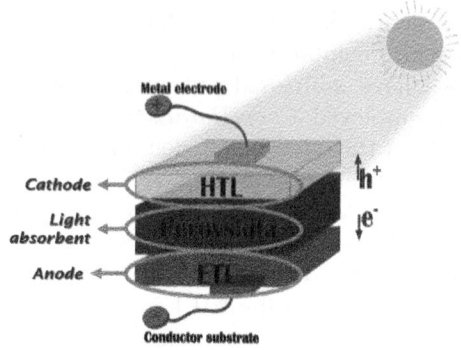

Fig. 1. Illustration of the schematic configuration of Perovskite solar cells.

In this context, we use Named Entity Recognition (NER), a fundamental technique in natural language processing (NLP) that identifies and classifies entities within a text, such as names of people, organizations, locations, or dates. In our case, NER was applied to identify and classify entities specifically related to Perovskite solar cells (PSC) in a set of scientific articles. The key entities used in this study are presented in Table 1.

Table 1. Named entity definitions used in the Model.

Category	Description	Character Type	Entity Label
Performance-related	Power Conversion Efficiency	Alphabetic	PCE
		Numeric	NPCE
	Open Circuit Voltage	Alphabetic	VOC
		Numeric	NVOC
	Short Circuit Current	Alphabetic	JSC
		Numeric	NJSC
	Filling Factor	Alphabetic	FF
		Numeric	NFF
Cell Structure	Hole Transporting Layer	Alphabetic	HTL
	Perovskite Absorber Layer	Alphabetic	PTF
	Electron Transporting Layer	Alphabetic	ETL
Synthesis-related	Synthesis Methods	Alphabetic	MTDS
		Alphabetic	VMTDS
	Method Variables	Numeric	NMTDS
	Environmental Conditions	Alphabetic	ENMTDS

2.2   Data Collection and Preprocessing

The dataset consists of 3,278 sentences derived from 584 articles in PDF format, selected from a database of 800 articles on Perovskite solar cells, published between 2013 and 2018. This database, manually compiled in the study reported by Odabaşı (2019) [1], contains information on a total of 1.921 PSCs. Of these, 584 articles were selected for providing specific information about conventional PSC structures. These structures generally correspond to those employing standard Perovskite materials as the light-absorbing layer.

To construct the training set, the selected 3,278 sentences were manually extracted from the training documents, with 3,088 sentences allocated for training ($\approx$ 94%) and 190 sentences for evaluating the NER model ($\approx$ 6%). These sentences may or may not contain information related to the defined entities, as presented in the *Named Entity Recognition (NER)* section and Fig. 1 and Table 1.

After manually selecting the sentences, a search was performed for the entities in each sentence, identifying their positions and labels using the methods in the *spaCy* library. These methods allow the use of a lightweight pre-trained NER model in the corresponding language, for the identification and initial assignment of named entities to each defined label (Table 1). Using them required the manual creation of lists of terms associated with specific labels, such as HTL, ETL, PTL, or MTDS, along with the use of patterns that use a modified version of regular expressions to obtain other labels, such as NPCE, NVOC, NJSC, or NMTDS, which involve numerical values and units of measurement.

Although these *spaCy* methods enables named entity identification without training, its accuracy is low and its capabilities are highly limited. For these reasons, these techniques were used only to generate an initial labeled training dataset. This first set, composed of sentences and their respective entities, was stored in JSON format using Python dictionaries. Figure 2 illustrates an example of the structure of the training dataset, showing the extracted sentence, the entities, and their positions within the text.

```
[
    "The stability of spiro-MeOTAD/CH3NH3PbI3/ZnO nanorod devices was
    investigated by storing them in air at room temperature without
    further encapsulation.\n",
    {
        "entities": [
            [41,44,"ETL"],[30,40,"PTF"],[17,29,"HTL"]
        ]
    }
],
[
    "The spin coating program includes two steps, first 1000 rpm for
    10 s with a ramp of 200 rpm s-1, then 6000 rpm for 30 s with a
    ramp of 2000 rpm s-1.\n",
    {
        "entities": [
            [4,16,"MTDS"],[76,80,"VMTDS"],[127,131,"VMTDS"],
            [51,59,"NMTDS"],[64,68,"NMTDS"],[102,110,"NMTDS"],
            [115,119,"NMTDS"],[135,147,"NMTDS"],[84,95,"NMTDS"]
        ]
    }
],
```

Fig. 2. Example of a training sentence, composed of the extracted sentence from the article, the entities, and their positions in the text.

Upon verifying the training dataset, issues such as entity duplication, labeling errors, and failures in locating entities within the text were identified. Additionally, inconsistencies in character encoding were found due to the lack of standardization in the PDF files.

To address these challenges, we developed an internal beta-phase software tool with a graphical interface for the semi-automatic correction of the dataset, providing a customized and more accessible alternative to the commercial annotation tool *Prodigy* [29]. The software, initially designed by us in a previous work [30] and further improved for this study, was developed in *Python* using *PyQt5* and *QtDesigner*. Figure 3 shows the main window of the tool and shows how it facilitates the user to load, edit and delete selected named entities from a sentence, through its different options. To generate the final labeled training dataset, we performed two semi-automated reviews using our tool: the first was carried out individually, and the second in collaboration with one of the coauthors, a materials science professor who observed, resolved ambiguous cases, and corrected the entity labeling in each sentence.

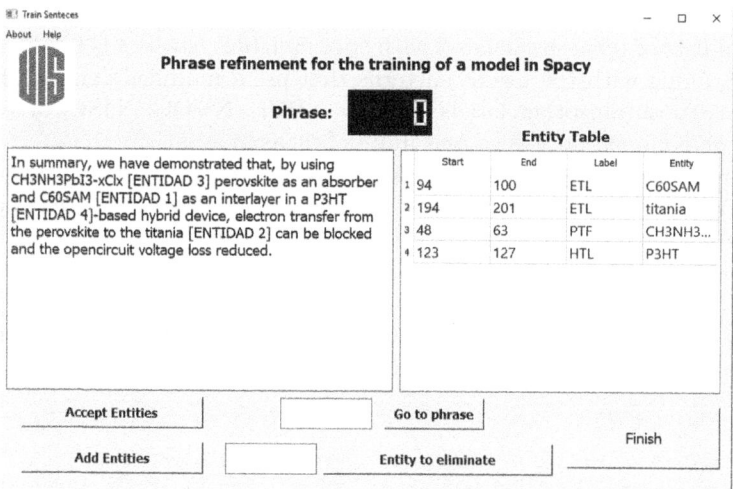

Fig. 3. Main window of the graphical interface tool used for the semi-automatic correction of the data file.

2.3   Model Training

To train the new NER model in *spaCy*, both rule-based entity recognition (*Rule-based NER*) and supervised training using neural networks were employed. A total of 16 new entities labels were defined: "HTL", "ETL", "PTF", "VOC", "PCE", "JSC", "FF", "NVOC", "NPCE", "NJSC", "NFF", "MTDS", "VMTDS", "ENMTDS", and "NMTDS". These correspond to the main layers, performance parameters, and synthesis variables of PSCs, as described in the previous section, *Named Entity Recognition (NER)*, and illustrated in Table 1.

Using the set of sentences obtained in the *Data Collection and Pre-processing* section, the model was trained. Multiple versions of the model were trained, varying the hyper-parameters: N, the number of iterations; D, the dropout rate; and B, the batch size per iteration. Finally, the model with the best performance was selected, based on the evaluation metrics defined in the following section.

2.4   Model Evaluation

Once the model was trained, its performance was evaluated using 190 new test sentences, distinct from those used during training. For this, we used the *scores* and *evaluate* functions from *spaCy*, which allow us to compute evaluation metrics: **Precision**, which measures the proportion of correctly identified entities relative to the total model predictions; **Recall**, which measures the proportion of true entities correctly identified; and **F1-Score**, which represents the harmonic mean between precision and recall [31, 32].

To validate the model, we used two methods. The first was the *k-Fold Cross-Validation* method with the 3,088 training sentences. This method is recommended when working with a limited dataset, as it reduces variance in error estimation without a high computational cost compared to other methods. Although it is not included in spaCy 3.0, this validation can be performed in Python using the *scikit-learn* library [33], employing the *sklearn.model_selection.KFold* function to split the data into K validation groups.

As a second method, we conducted an additional evaluation of the model using a dataset different from the one used in training. For this, we used the Perovskite solar cell dataset from Jacobsson (2022) [2], which contains more than 400 variables and 42,000 records of Perovskite solar cells collected between 2003 and 2020. We manually downloaded four articles in HTML format. These were then converted into plain text programmatically, sectioned, cleaned, and refined by removing irrelevant symbols that could interfere with model predictions and standardizing part of the chemical nomenclature used in materials science. For validation, we compared our model's extractions with the data available in Jacobsson's (2022) dataset.

Furthermore, we evaluated and measured inference times across different file formats (PDF, HTML, plain text, and sentence-level processing) in the following scenarios: a single sentence, a PDF file, an HTML file, a set of 584 PDF files, and a set of four HTML files. Testing was performed on a system with a 3rd-generation Intel Core i7 processor, 16 GB of RAM, and Windows 10.

3   Application Example

In this section, as an application example, we perform automatic information extraction from conventional PSC articles using the Odabaşı (2019) [1] database. To do this, we use the *PyMuPDF* [34], Data Collection library to extract plain text from PDFs. Data is then preprocessed by text cleaning and standardization to improve the detection of our entities in the NER task. Finally, we compare the entities associated with the cell structure, extracted by the model with those obtained from the manually extracted Odabaşı (2019) [1] database.

3.1   Data Processing

Scientific articles in PDF format use an extended ASCII encoding, which varies depending on the software used to generate them. This makes text extraction difficult, especially due to special symbols. To solve this problem, we used the *PyMuPDF* library, which allows articles to be converted to plain text. We then preprocessed the text of the articles, segmenting them into the sections we considered relevant (Abstract, Results, Discussions, etc.), cleaning and standardizing the textual entities to remove irrelevant text and symbols. We retained only the general names of each compound, replacing any variations found that could affect the model's effectiveness.

Figure 4 compares the evolution of two example sentences during the cleaning process: (A) shows the extracted text in its raw form, containing decoding errors and extended ASCII symbols; (B) presents the initial uncleaned JSON format, where issues persist; and (C) illustrates the sentences after preprocessing, with standardized nomenclature and without irrelevant symbols. This process ensures that the data is structured and ready for use in the model.

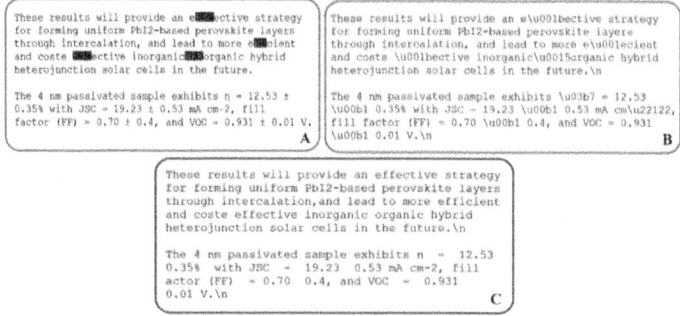

Fig. 4. Capture a photograph of the evolution of two example sentences in the cleaning process, where (A) represents the sentences in plain text (.txt), (B) shows the sentences converted to JSON format without cleaning, and (C) displays the sentences in JSON format after the cleaning process.

3.2   Extraction Using the Named Entity Recognition Model

With the data cleaned and standardized, we performed entity extraction using our model. With these results, we performed post-processing on the "Performance-Related" category entities (See Table 1), using basic Python logic (for, if) and pattern matching (re) to relate and consolidate value-type entities with their corresponding label-type entities. For example, when a value such as "0.1 V" (entity type: *NVOC*) was found near a label of type *VOC*, both were combined into a single entity with type *VOC* and value "0.1 V". This step allowed us to transform and group the initial set of 16 entity labels into a refined set of 11 final entity labels, which were stored in the database. Figure 5 illustrates the JSON structure used to store the extracted metadata from the 584 articles processed with our SpaCy-trained model. In this format, the data is organized as a hierarchical key-value structure, where each key represents a processed PDF, each sub-key corresponds to an entity category (e.g., Synthesis Method, Performance Metric), and the corresponding values contain the extracted information from the text.


```
{
  "a0001.pdf": {
    "CAPAS": {
      "ETL": ["C60","titania","SAM","alumina","C60SAM","TiO2"],
      "HTL": ["Spiro- OMeTAD","PCPDTBT","Ma,","spiro-OMeTAD","P3HT","Li-TFSI"],
      "PTF": ["perovskite","C.-R.","CH3NH3PbI3-xClx.1","CH3NH3PbI3","CH3NH3PbI3-xClx"]
    },
    "SINTESIS": {
      "METODOS": ["thermally","spin-coated","sintered","immersing","evaporated","heated","coated",
                  "screen-printed"],
      "VARIABLES": [],
      "VALORES": ["24 h.","500 C","45 min","30 min","100 C"],
      "CONDICIONES": ["vacuum","high vacuum"]
    },
    "PARAMETROS": {
      "VOC": ["0.7 V","0.82-0.84 V","0.8 V"],
      "PCE": ["4%","3.8%","11.7%","6.7%"],
      "JSC": ["14.9 mA"],
      "FF": ["0.65-0.72"]
    },
    "ORACIONES": [
      "The architecture was also used with spiro-OMeTAD as the hole transporter to produce hybrid solar
      cells with power conversion efficiencies of 11.7% .",
      "By contrast, a titania sample coated with a layer of benzoic acid mimicking the attachment group
      on the fullerene exhibits significant electron density on the titania17 and no peak at 1030 nm.",
      "Finally, the hole transporting polymer P3HT was spin-coated on top and silver electrodes (150 nm)
      thermally evaporated under high vacuum to complete the devices.",
```


Fig. 5. Example of Metadata extracted by the SpaCy-trained model.

The JSON follows a nested tree structure: at the top level, a dictionary groups the processed PDFs. At the next level, each PDF contains extracted entities organized into predefined categories. Each category acts as a key and maps to a list of dictionaries where individual instances of the extracted entities are stored. This structure ensures that our entities associated with the synthesis methods, material properties and device performance metrics are organized correctly and facilitate their future observation and/or analysis.

3.3 Comparison

Once our database is generated in JSON format through our NER model trained with *SpaCy*, we can make comparisons with the manual database of Odabaşı (2019) [1]. We first make the automated quantitative comparison, creating a Python script that uses a loop using nested "for" statements, to compare our Entities associated with the cell structure, named, *HTL* (Hole transport layer), *ETL* (Electron transport layer) and *PTF* (Perovskite absorber layer).

For the quantitative comparison, the general names of each compound were standardized, replacing any variations, and then the semantic similarity between the extracted entities was measured using the *SequenceMatcher().ratio()* function (which provides the similarity ratio using LCS, Longest Contiguous Matching Subsequence) from the *difflib* library, with a threshold of 0.65. Thus, only words with a similarity score equal to or greater than 0.65 were considered equivalent and, therefore, considered "successful extraction" for the comparison.

Subsequently, bar charts were generated for a qualitative comparison, to visually analyze the frequencies of each entity category and observe the similarity of the automatic extraction with the manually obtained data. Only entities considered "successful extraction" were included in the bar charts. This was done to prevent the model from appearing to extract more entities than were manually recorded, thus ensuring a balanced comparison of the frequencies of each category.

4   Results

To illustrate the entity recognition process, Fig. 6 provides a visual representation of how identified entities appear in a sample sentence extracted from an article.

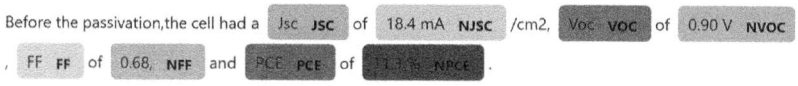

Fig. 6. Visualization of the entities identified in a sample sentence.

4.1   Model

To obtain the final model, 18 training sessions were conducted while varying the training hyper-parameters. The best-performing model for our application was trained with $N = 400$ iterations, $D = 0.5$ as the dropout rate, and $B = 100$ as the batch size.

Model Evaluation. The model was evaluated with the 190 test sentences from the Odabaşı (2019) dataset [1]. The evaluation results indicate that the model achieved **precision, recall, and F1-score** values of 93.07%, 87.38%, and 88.57%, respectively, as shown in Table 2.

Table 2. Model Evaluation

	Entities Precision		Entities Recall		Entities F1-score	
	test	evaluation	test	evaluation	test	evaluation
Count	2,597	186	2,597	186	2,597	186
mean	1	**0.9307**	1	**0.8738**	1	**0.8857**
std	0	0.1424	0	0.1942	0	0.1540

Model Validation. For the first validation method, we applied *k-Fold Cross-Validation* with $K = 5$ using the 3,088 training sentences. We computed the **average precision, recall, and F1-score** obtained during cross-validation, achieving values of 89.94%, 92.47%, and 89.69%, respectively, as shown in Table 3.

Table 3. Model k-Fold Cross-Validation

	Entities Precision	Entities Recall	Entities F1-score
Count	519.4	519.4	519.4
mean	**0.8994**	**0.9247**	**0.8969**
std	0.2080	0.1773	0.1835

For the second validation method, we compared the model's extractions with data from four articles in the Jacobsson (2022) [2] dataset, using their HTML versions. To illustrate this *qualitative comparison*, Table 4 presents the extracted entities from Savva's (2019) [35] article. Only entities that matched the database are included in the table, omitting irrelevant or incorrect terms.

Table 4. Comparison between the SpaCy-trained model and the Jacobsson (2022) [2] database, using the article *"Inverted perovskite photovoltaics using flame spray pyrolysis solution based CuAlO2/Cu-O hole-selective contact"* by Savva et al. (2019) [35]

Entities	Model Extraction	Manually Curated Database
ETL	AZO | PC70BM	PCBM-60 | AZO-np
HTL	Cu(OH)2	CuAlO2 | CuO
PTF	CH3NH3PbI3	MAPbI3
MTDS	spin coating | evaporation	Spin-coating | Evaporation
NPCE	16%	16.0%
NVOC	1.07 V	1.07 V
NJSC	19.1 mA	19.1 mA cm-2
NFF	79.6 %	79.6 %

For the *quantitative comparison*, we focused on the most relevant sections of the five articles, such as Abstract, Results and Discussion, Methods, and Experimental Section. The comparison with the database considered:

– **Exact Matches:** The extracted entity is identical to the one in the database.

- **Approximate Matches:** Similarity metrics were used to recognize variations of the same entity with minor differences. We used the *SequenceMatcher* class from the *difflib* library with a similarity threshold > 0.65.
- **Normalization:** Since material names can vary in the literature, we applied a normalization process before comparison, which included:
  - Standardizing chemical notations (e.g., MAPbI3 and CH3NH3PbI3).
  - Correcting spaces and hyphens (e.g., spiro-OMeTAD = spiro-MeOTAD).

After applying normalization and comparison, a total of 18 entities were identified in the four articles based on the database. Of these, the model correctly extracted 14, with 9 approximate matches. The final results showed a **22.22% error rate** and a **77.78% accuracy rate**.

Model Inference. The inference times obtained for each scenario were:

- A single sentence: ≈ 0.6 seconds.
- A PDF file: ≈ 3 seconds.
- An HTML file: ≈ 30 seconds.
- A set of 584 PDF files: ≈ 2 h, 30 min, 52 s.
- A set of 4 HTML files: ≈ 2 min, 5 s.

4.2   Information Extraction from PSC Articles

After completing the model evaluation and validation with satisfactory results, we proceeded to extract entities from the full set of 584 conventional perovskite solar cell articles in the Odabaşı (2019) [1] dataset, comparing the results. This analysis focuses on a quantitative and graphical comparison of the most commonly used materials for HTL, ETL, and Perovskite layers, offering a better understanding of material trends in PSC research. After applying normalization, we obtained:

- Total entities in the database: 2,453.
- Correctly identified entities: 1,868.
- Approximate matches: 163.
- **Error rate: 23.85%.**
- **Accuracy rate: 76.15%.**

To better visualize the comparison between our model and the full Odabaşı (2019) [1] database, bar charts were generated, as shown in Fig. 7. These bar charts only consider entities that matched between both databases. Since each layer contains numerous entities, even after normalization, we aimed to reduce noise from the model's extractions by grouping similar entities into clusters. These clusters were defined based on entity frequency in the manual database and additional manual review, ensuring they accurately represented material categories for each perovskite solar cell (PSC) layer.

This comparison highlights the consistency of our extraction model with the global trends observed in the manual database. Figure 7 illustrate the alignment between automatic and manual extractions, showcasing trends in each layer across the analyzed scientific articles.

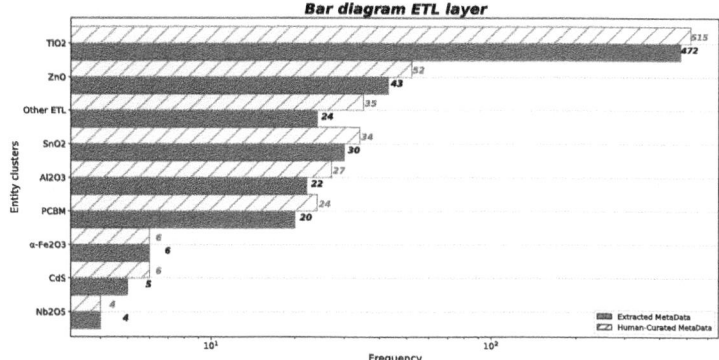

(a) **ETL layer**

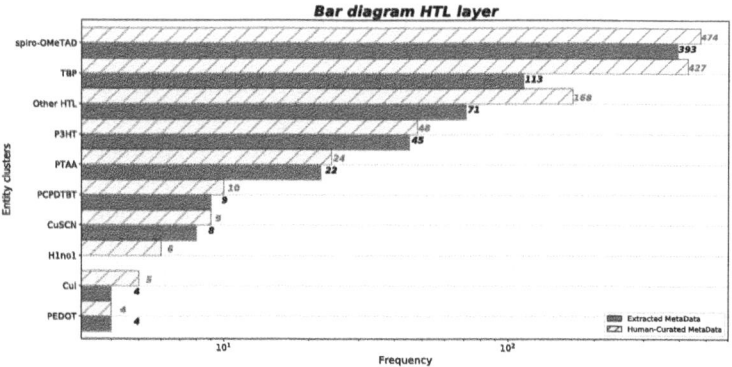

(b) **HTL layer**

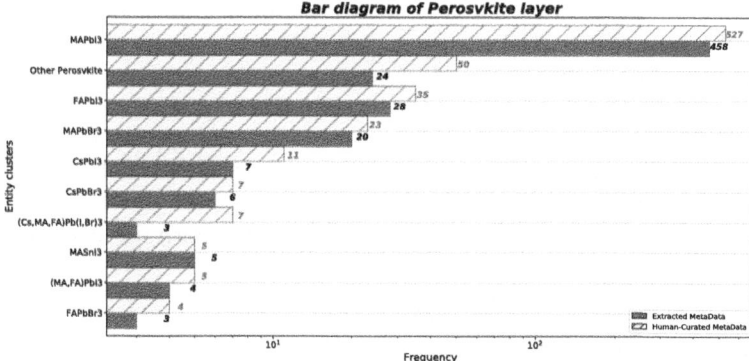

(c) **Perovskite layer**

Fig. 7. Bar charts comparing manual and automatic entity extraction for the layers from the full set of 584 papers in Odabaşı (2019) [1].

5   Discussions

Throughout the model's development, several challenges were identified that may affect its applicability and should be addressed in future work. One key challenge is the difficulty in obtaining data, as some articles that were previously open access now require a subscription or payment, limiting access to valuable scientific information. In this regard, future improvements could integrate tools that facilitate open-access verification or explore the use of alternative databases to ensure broader availability of training and evaluation data.

Another important aspect to consider is the potential bias that could have been introduced during the generation of the model's labeled training data. The model was trained with the guidance of a materials science professor (co-author); however, since it was developed by an electronic engineering researcher (co-author), some annotation decisions could reflect unintentional bias. To mitigate this, future improvements should include an increase in the labeled training dataset and additional reviews by more experts in the field to improve the model's effectiveness and understanding of scientific terminology.

Unlike other recent studies working with HTML/XML files, which seek to generate large databases and make use of large computational resources, such as *Beard et al.* [26] that uses the specialized tool for chemistry *ChemDataExtractor*, and *Xie et al.* [27] that uses large language models to infer complex structures and predict solar cell performance, our work demonstrates the feasibility of using limited computational resources to automatically extract scientific data and perform the NER task from PDF and HTML articles using the SpaCy library. Opening the possibility that our proposed method and the resulting code in this article allow its adaptation and application in different scientific domains, and the creation of automatic databases, through the generation or use of domain-specific labeled training datasets and minimal modification of certain variables of the codes used.

Future work could explore the semi-automation of document retrieval using web scraping tools, allowing for a more streamlined data acquisition process. Additionally, integrating relation extraction (RE) techniques into the pipeline would enable a more contextualized understanding of extracted information.

Another promising direction is the development of a web tool, user-friendly executable or intuitive interface, which could make this approach more accessible and suitable for use by researchers from other scientific fields and/or with limited programming knowledge. Perhaps this tool could also be incorporated into existing semi-automated annotation software, currently in internal beta, to further improve its usability and applicability.

6   Conclusions

Our proposed approach, which performs NER-focused IE and seeks to minimize the use of computational resources, enables the efficient and accurate extraction of scientific information from complex document formats, such as PDF and

HTML, commonly used in academic research. We hope that this method will contribute to improving the organization and accessibility of large volumes of research publications, helping researchers manage large sets of scientific articles more efficiently. It also reduces the issues associated with data dispersion, missing information, high costs, and long timelines associated with the manual generation of structured datasets, which are increasingly used in scientific research processes, reducing the manual workload and minimizing errors associated with manual annotation.

Acknowledgments. We sincerely thank Universidad Industrial de Santander (UIS) (uis.edu.co) (Webpage:https://uis.edu.co/es/) for the forgivable loan that funded Mary's master's studies. We also appreciate the support of the GISEL-CEMOS research groups at UIS in the development of this study, which made this article possible.

Data Availability Statement. The DOIs and/or references of the research articles used in this work are available in an Excel format at GitHub Repository (Available: https://github.com/maryz1998/NER-for-Performance-and-Synthesis-of-Perovskite-Cells-using-SpaCy.) However, due to copyright restrictions, the manually curated dataset containing entity annotations from 584 articles cannot be shared publicly. This dataset was obtained from the supplementary materials section provided in Odabaşı (2019) [1].

Additionally, a subset of four open-access articles was selected from the Jacobsson (2022) [2] database, available at Perovskitedatabase.com (Available: https://www.perovskitedatabase.com.) Their DOIs can also be accessed at the same repository: GitHub Repository

Disclosure of Interests. The authors have no competing interests to declare that are relevant to the content of this article.

References

1. Odabaşı, Ç., Yıldırım, R.: Performance analysis of perovskite solar cells in 2013–2018 using machine-learning tools. Nano Energy **56**, 770–791 (2019). https://doi.org/10.1016/j.nanoen.2018.11.069
2. Jacobsson, T.J., et al.: An open-access database and analysis tool for perovskite solar cells based on the FAIR data principles. Nature Energy **7**(1), 107–115 (2022). https://doi.org/10.1038/s41560-021-00941-3
3. Why is renewable energy important?. https://www.ren21.net/why-is-renewable-energy-important/. Accessed 20 Jan 2025
4. Best Research-Cell Efficiency Chart. https://www.nrel.gov/pv/cell-efficiency.html. Accessed 07 Sep 2024
5. Roose, B., et al.: Local manufacturing of perovskite solar cells, a game-changer for low-and lower-middle income countries? Energy Environ. Sci. **15**(9), 3571–3582 (2022). https://doi.org/10.1039/d2ee01343f
6. Shah, A., Meyer, E.L.: Perovskite-based solar cells in photovoltaics for commercial scalability: current progress, challenges, mitigations and future prospectus. Sol. Energy **286**, 113172 (2025). https://doi.org/10.1016/j.solener.2024.113172

7. Afre, R.A., Pugliese, D.: Perovskite solar cells: a review of the latest advances in materials, fabrication techniques, and stability enhancement strategies. Micromachines **15**, 192 (2024). https://doi.org/10.3390/mi15020192

8. Rong, Y., et al.: Challenges for commercializing perovskite solar cells. Science **361**(6408), eaat8235 (2018). https://doi.org/10.1126/science.aat8235

9. Jung, H.S., Park, N.G.: Perovskite solar cells: from materials to devices. small **11**(1), 10–25 (2015). https://doi.org/10.1002/smll.201402767

10. Takahashi, K., Takahashi, L., Miyazato, I., Tanaka, Y.: Searching for hidden perovskite materials for photovoltaic systems by combining data science and first principle calculations. ACS Photonics **5**(3), 771–775 (2018). https://doi.org/10.1021/acsphotonics.7b01479

11. Chaube, S., Khullar, P., Goverapet Srinivasan, S., Rai, B.: A statistical learning framework for accelerated bandgap prediction of inorganic compounds. J. Electron. Mater. **49**(1), 752–762 (2019). https://doi.org/10.1007/s11664-019-07779-2

12. Pilania, G., Balachandran, P.V., Kim, C., Lookman, T.: Finding new perovskite halides via machine learning. Front. Mater. **3**, 19 (2016). https://doi.org/10.3389/fmats.2016.00019

13. Yılmaz, B., Yıldırım, R.: Critical review of machine learning applications in perovskite solar research. Nano Energy **80**, 105546 (2021). https://doi.org/10.1016/j.nanoen.2020.105546

14. Yang, C., et al.: Achievements, challenges, and future prospects for industrialization of perovskite solar cells. Light Sci. Appl. **13**(1), 227 (2024). https://doi.org/10.1038/s41377-024-01461-x

15. Jiménez, M., Botero L., M., Sepulveda, A: Optimization of thin-film solar cells by using adaptive learning rate gradient descend algorithms. MRS Advances (2025). https://doi.org/10.1557/s43580-024-01109-3

16. Odabaşı, Ç., Yıldırım, R.: Assessment of reproducibility, hysteresis, and stability relations in perovskite solar cells using machine learning. Energ. Technol. **8**(12), 1901449 (2020). https://doi.org/10.1002/ente.201901449

17. Parikh, N., et al.: Is machine learning redefining the perovskite solar cells?. J. Energy Chem. **66**, 74–90 (2022). https://doi.org/10.1016/j.jechem.2021.07.020

18. Li, J., Pradhan, B., Gaur, S., Thomas, J.: Predictions and strategies learned from machine learning to develop high-performing perovskite solar cells. Adv. Energy Mater. **9**(46), 1901891 (2019). https://doi.org/10.1002/aenm.201901891

19. Vélez, J., Botero L., M.A., Sepulveda, A.: Measurement of information content of Perovskite solar cell's synthesis descriptors related to performance parameters. Emergent Mater **7**, 1961—1968 (2024). https://doi.org/10.1007/s42247-024-00667-4

20. Jurafsky, D., James H. M.: Speech and Language Processing: An Introduction to Natural Language Processing, Computational Linguistics, and Speech Recognition with Language Models. 3rd edn.(2025). Online manuscript released January 12, 2025, stanford, USA https://web.stanford.edu/~jurafsky/slp3

21. Swain, M.C., Cole, J.M.: ChemDataExtractor: a toolkit for automated extraction of chemical information from the scientific literature. J. Chem. Inf. Model. **56**(10), 1894–1904 (2016). https://doi.org/10.1021/acs.jcim.6b00207

22. Hawizy, L., Jessop, D.M., Adams, N., Murray-Rust, P.: ChemicalTagger: a tool for semantic text-mining in chemistry. J. Cheminformatics **3**, 1–13 (2011). https://doi.org/10.1186/1758-2946-3-17

23. Jessop, D.M., Adams, S.E., Willighagen, E.L., Hawizy, L., Murray-Rust, P.: OSCAR4: a flexible architecture for chemical text-mining. J. Cheminformatics **3**(1), 41 (2011). https://doi.org/10.1186/1758-2946-3-41

24. Olivetti, E.A., et al.: Data-driven materials research enabled by natural language processing and information extraction. Appl. Phys. Rev. **7**(4) (2020). https://doi.org/10.1063/5.0021106
25. Transformers Documentation - Hugging Face. https://huggingface.co/docs/transformers/index. Accessed 12 Nov 2024
26. Beard, E.J., Cole, J.M.: Perovskite-and dye-sensitized solar-cell device databases auto-generated using chemdataextractor. Sci. Data **9**(1), 329 (2022). https://doi.org/10.1038/s41597-022-01355-w
27. Xie, T., et al.: Creation of a structured solar cell material dataset and performance prediction using large language models. Patterns **5**(5) (2024). https://doi.org/10.1016/j.patter.2024.100955
28. Spacy. https://spacy.io. Accessed 05 Aug 2024
29. Prodigy: An annotation tool for AI, Machine Learning & NLP. https://prodi.gy/. Accessed 11 June 2024
30. Jiménez-Díaz, M. Z.: Herramienta de software para la extracción automática de parámetros de desempeño a partir de publicaciones científicas de celdas solares de perovskita. Undergraduate thesis, Universidad Industrial de Santander (2022)
31. Murphy, K.P.: Machine Learning: A Probabilistic Perspective, 1st edn. MIT press, Cambridge, London, England (2012)
32. Eisenstein, J.: Introduction to Natural Language Processing, 2nd edn. MIT Press, Cambridge, London, England (2019)
33. Pedregosa, F., et al.: Scikit-learn: machine learning in python. J. Mach. Learn. Res. **12**, 2825–2830 (2011). http://jmlr.org/papers/v12/pedregosa11a.html
34. Prodigy: An annotation tool for AI, Machine Learning & NLP. https://pymupdf.readthedocs.io/en/latest/. Accessed 11 June 2024
35. Savva, A., et al.: Inverted perovskite photovoltaics using flame spray pyrolysis solution based CuAlO2/Cu–O hole-selective contact. ACS Appl. Energy Mater. **2**(3), 2276–2287 (2019). https://doi.org/10.1021/acsaem.9b00070

A Privacy-Preserving Framework for Cross-Institutional Medical Image Analysis Using Vision-Language Models

Yang Jiafeng[1]([✉])[iD], Zhukova Natalia Alexandrovna[2][iD],
and Stankova Elena Nikolaevna[3][iD]

[1] ITMO University, Saint Petersburg, Russia
tszyafengyang@gmail.com
[2] Saint-Petersburg Institute for Informatics and Automation of the Russian Academy
of Sciences, Saint Petersburg, Russia
nazhukova@mail.ru
[3] Saint Petersburg State University, Saint Petersburg, Russia
e.stankova@spbu.ru

Abstract. The healthcare industry faces significant challenges in leveraging patient data across institutions while maintaining privacy, particularly when third-party organizations like insurance companies and banks require medical information for risk assessment. The rapid advancement of large-scale multimodal models, such as Contrastive Language-Image Pre-training (CLIP), holds immense potential for medical applications by enabling cross-modal alignment of visual and textual data. This paper presents a novel framework that combines vertical federated learning with CLIP to enable privacy-preserving medical image analysis across institutional boundaries. Our framework allows secure analysis of distributed medical data without raw data sharing, while optimizing CLIP's performance for medical applications through Context Optimization. Experimental validation on a dataset of 7023 brain MRI scans demonstrates the framework's effectiveness, achieving 93.1% accuracy in classifying four types of brain conditions (glioma, meningioma, pituitary, and no tumor) - a substantial improvement from the original pre-trained CLIP model's 26.3% accuracy. These results establish a practical solution for secure, cross-institutional medical data analysis that maintains patient privacy while enabling critical business decisions in healthcare, insurance, and financial sectors.

Keywords: Vertical federated learning · Vision-language model · Cross-institutional analysis · Prompt tuning

1 Introduction

In modern healthcare, the ability to analyze medical data across institutions holds immense potential for improving diagnostic accuracy and treatment outcomes. However, this potential is constrained by strict privacy requirements and

O. Gervasi et al. (Eds.): ICCSA 2025, LNCS 15649, pp. 320–331, 2025.
https://doi.org/10.1007/978-3-031-96997-3_20

data protection regulations such as GDPR [18] and HIPAA [19]. A particularly challenging scenario arises when third-party organizations, such as insurance companies and banks, need to assess client-related risks based on medical data distributed across various healthcare institutions.

Consider an insurance company evaluating coverage for a potential client or a bank assessing a loan application. These organizations require comprehensive medical information - including imaging data, specialist reports, and test results - from multiple healthcare providers to make informed decisions. However, healthcare institutions are bound by strict confidentiality agreements and cannot directly share raw patient data, creating a significant barrier to efficient risk assessment and decision-making.

Recent developments in artificial intelligence, particularly vision-language models like Contrastive Language-Image Pre-training (CLIP), have demonstrated exceptional capabilities in understanding relationships between visual and textual information [1]. However, deploying such models in healthcare faces two critical challenges: protecting patient privacy when analyzing data across multiple institutions, and effectively adapting general-purpose AI models to specialized medical tasks.

Our work addresses these challenges by introducing a novel framework that integrates vertical federated learning [2] with a prompt-optimized CLIP model. This integration serves two key purposes: (1) enabling secure, privacy-preserving analysis of medical data across institutional boundaries, and (2) bridging the domain gap between general-purpose vision-language models and specialized medical tasks through prompt optimization.

The proposed framework leverages the Context Optimization (CoOp) method [3] to fine-tune CLIP's text prompts specifically for medical image analysis while maintaining data privacy through vertical federated learning (VFL). This approach allows different medical institutions to participate in collaborative analysis without compromising patient privacy or regulatory compliance, while enabling third-party organizations to make informed decisions based on processed results rather than raw data.

We validate our framework through extensive experiments on brain tumor classification using a dataset of 7023 MRI scans. The results demonstrate significant improvements in classification accuracy while maintaining data privacy, suggesting a promising direction for developing secure and effective medical AI systems that can serve both healthcare and business needs.

The main **contributions** of this paper are:

- A novel framework integrating vertical federated learning with prompt-optimized CLIP for privacy-preserving medical image analysis.
- Implementation of Context Optimization (CoOp) within vertical federated learning for medical applications.
- Experimental validation demonstrating substantial improvements in brain tumor classification accuracy.

The remainder of this paper is organized as follows: Sect. 2 reviews related work in federated learning and vision-language models in the field of medical image analysis. Section 3 details the proposed framework and methodology. Section 4 presents experimental results and analysis. Finally, Sect. 5 concludes with discussions of implications and future research directions.

2 Related Works

2.1 Federated Learning

Federated learning has emerged as a promising paradigm for privacy-preserving machine learning in healthcare settings. Unlike traditional centralized learning approaches that require data aggregation, federated learning enables model training across distributed datasets while keeping sensitive data localized [[4, 20]]. Two main categories of federated learning have been established: horizontal federated learning (HFL) and vertical federated learning (VFL).

Horizontal federated learning addresses scenarios where different institutions have the same feature space but different sample sets. For example, multiple hospitals might have similar types of medical images but from different patients. Several studies have demonstrated HFL's effectiveness in medical image analysis, including chest CT classification [5], brain tumor detection [6], and retinal disease diagnosis [7].

Vertical federated learning, which is more relevant to our work, handles scenarios where different parties hold different features of the same samples. This approach is particularly suitable for healthcare scenarios where various institutions hold different types of patient data (e.g., imaging data, clinical notes, laboratory results) [8]. Recent work has shown VFL's potential in combining heterogeneous medical data sources while maintaining privacy compliance [9]. Hardy et al. [10] proposed a secure protocol for vertically partitioned data using homomorphic encryption. However, the application of VFL in the field of medical image analysis is still in its early stages [21].

2.2 Multi-modal Models in Medical Image Analysis

Recent years have witnessed growing interest in multimodal medical data mining, which aims to leverage both visual and textual information for improved diagnosis and treatment. Shetty et al. [11] proposed a multimodal deep learning framework that combines radiology images with clinical reports for more accurate pulmonary abnormality prediction. Liu et al. [12] developed an attention-based architecture that integrates pathology images with genetic data for breast cancer diagnosis. Dautov et al. [13] introduced a hierarchical learning approach that fuses medical imaging data with electronic health records (EHRs) for comprehensive patient analysis. These works demonstrated that incorporating multiple data modalities can significantly enhance medical diagnostic accuracy compared to single-modality approaches.

The emergence of CLIP has brought new opportunities to medical multimodal learning. MedCLIP [14] adapted the CLIP architecture for medical domains through specialized pre-training on medical image-text pairs, achieving promising results in various diagnostic tasks. PMC-CLIP [15] further extended this approach by incorporating domain knowledge from medical literature, demonstrating improved performance in rare disease identification. Thawkar et al. [16] conducted a comprehensive evaluation of CLIP in medical visual question answering through PubMedCLIP, demonstrating significant but variable benefits across different medical specialties and question types, with particularly strong performance improvements in radiology and dermatology domains.

However, these models often face challenges when adapting to specific medical tasks due to the domain gap between general and medical data. To address this issue, prompt tuning methods have been proposed. The Context Optimization (CoOp) method [3] offers a particularly effective solution by learning continuous context vectors that act as optimizable prompt tokens, enabling better adaptation to medical tasks without modifying the underlying model architecture.

While these approaches have shown impressive results, they typically require centralized access to medical data, raising significant privacy concerns in real-world applications. Medical data is often distributed across different institutions (e.g., hospitals, insurance companies, research centers), each holding different aspects of patient information. Direct sharing of such sensitive data may violate privacy regulations and patient confidentiality agreements. Our work addresses this limitation by deploying CLIP within a vertical federated learning framework, enabling secure multimodal medical analysis while maintaining data privacy. This approach allows different institutions to collaborate in model training without sharing raw patient data, while leveraging CLIP's powerful vision-language capabilities through optimized prompting strategies.

3   Methodology

Our framework integrates vertical federated learning with CLIP's vision-language architecture while utilizing context optimization for medical domain adaptation. Here we detail each component and its integration into a cohesive privacy-preserving system.

Vertical Federated Learning. VFL addresses scenarios where multiple institutions hold different feature sets for the same set of patients. Unlike Horizontal Federated Learning (HFL), which assumes identical feature spaces across participants, VFL enables collaborative model training on vertically partitioned data. The foundation of our framework is built on vertical federated learning, where we establish collaboration between two distinct parties: an active party (typically an insurance company, bank, or medical center) that holds medical reports and text data, and a passive party (typically a hospital) that maintains medical imaging data. This separation reflects real-world scenarios where patient data is distributed across different healthcare institutions.

In our VFL architecture, the active party orchestrates the training process while the passive party participates by providing feature vectors from medical images. This setup ensures that raw data never leaves its source institution, with only encrypted feature vectors and necessary gradients being exchanged between parties. The separation of data and computation aligns with privacy regulations while enabling collaborative model training.

3.1 Contrastive Language-Image Pre-training

At the core of our framework lies CLIP's dual-encoder architecture, which processes visual and textual data through separate pathways. The image encoder, residing with the passive party, processes medical images through a Vision Transformer architecture to generate fixed-dimension feature vectors. Meanwhile, the text encoder at the active party processes medical text data to generate corresponding text embeddings.

For zero-shot inference, CLIP leverages textual prompts to classify images. Given an input MRI scan x, its feature vector f is extracted by the image encoder. Simultaneously, the text encoder generates K class-specific embeddings $\{w_i\}_{i=1}^{K}$ from prompts like "a photo of a {class}", where "{class}" is replaced by medical labels (e.g., "glioma," "no tumor"). The prediction probability for class y is computed as:

$$p(y = i|x) = \frac{exp(cos(w_i, f)/\tau)}{\sum_{j=1}^{K} exp(cos(w_j, f)/\tau)} \qquad (1)$$

where $cos(\cdot, \cdot)$ denotes cosine similarity, and τ is a learned temperature parameter scaling the logits.

3.2 Context Optimization

To bridge the domain gap, we integrate CoOp, a prompt-tuning method that learns a set of continuous context vectors $V = [v_1, v_2, ..., v_M]$ as prefix tokens for text prompts. For a class label 'glioma', the prompt becomes:

$$t_i = [v_1; v_2; ...;' glioma'], \qquad (2)$$

where $v_i \epsilon \mathbb{R}^d$ are learnable parameters. CoOp optimizes these vectors using backpropagation, aligning CLIP's text embeddings with medical image features. Unlike full fine-tuning, this approach preserves CLIP's pre-trained knowledge while adapting to specialized tasks.

CoOp employs a cross-entropy loss to optimize the classification performance, deviating from CLIP's original contrastive loss. Given an input image x with ground-truth label y, the classification probability for class c is computed as:

$$p(y = i|x) = \frac{exp(cos(f_{text}(t_i), f_{img}(x))/\tau)}{\sum_{j=1}^{K} exp(cos(f_{text}(t_j), f_{img}(x))/\tau)} \qquad (3)$$

where f_{text} and f_{img} denote the text encoder and image encoder separately. The cross-entropy loss is then defined as Eq. 4.

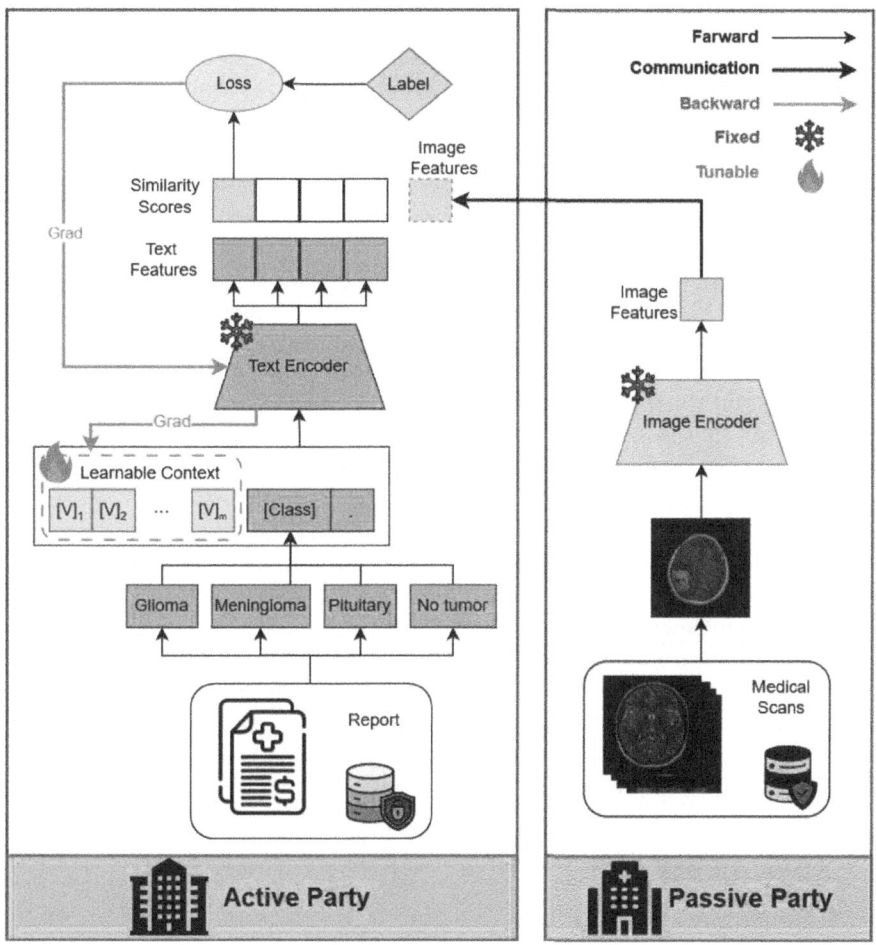

Fig. 1. Diagram of our proposed framework.

$$\mathcal{L}_{CoOp} = -\sum_{j=1}^{K} y_j \log p(t_j|x) \tag{4}$$

where y_j is the one-hot encoded ground-truth label. This loss directly optimizes the alignment between image features and task-specific textual prompts, enabling precise adaptation to medical classification tasks.

3.3   Proposed Framework

As illustrated in Fig. 1, the proposed framework integrates vertical federated learning (VFL), the CLIP model, and Context Optimization (CoOp) into a unified pipeline designed for privacy-preserving cross-institutional medical image analysis. In this setup, medical institutions such as hospitals retain ownership of brain MRI scans, while third-party organizations (e.g., insurance companies) manage textual metadata, including clinical reports (In our work, we use diagnostic labels for simulation). This vertical partitioning ensures that raw data remains localized and is never directly shared between entities, adhering to strict privacy regulations.

The framework begins with initializing specialized models of each participant: hospitals deploy the image encoder component of CLIP, typically a Vision Transformer (ViT), to process medical images into feature embeddings, while third parties initialize the text encoder alongside learnable CoOp prompt vectors. During federated training, hospitals compute image embeddings from MRI scans locally, and third parties generate text embeddings using dynamically optimized prompts that incorporate medical terminology (e.g., "glioma" or "pituitary tumor"). These embeddings are securely aggregated through privacy-preserving protocols, such as homomorphic encryption, to compute similarity scores in a shared embedding space. The contrastive learning objective aligns image and text representations across institutions, enabling collaborative model updates without exposing sensitive raw data.

For inference, new MRI scans are classified by comparing their image embeddings against the optimized text prompts derived from CoOp, which have been tuned to capture domain-specific medical features. This combination of VFL's distributed architecture, CLIP's multimodal alignment capabilities, and CoOp's adaptive prompting establishes a robust solution for cross-institutional medical analysis that balances diagnostic accuracy with stringent data confidentiality.

4   Experiments and Results

4.1   Experimental Setup

Dataset. We conducted our experiments using a comprehensive brain tumor MRI dataset [17] containing 7023 images across four classes: glioma, meningioma, pituitary tumors, and no tumor (healthy control). The dataset is publicly available on Kaggle and is balanced across the four classes, with each class having approximately equal numbers of images. Figure 2 shows sample images from each class for reference. To simulate a realistic federated learning scenario, we distributed the data between two parties: the passive party (hospital) holding MRI images and the active party (medical center) holding diagnostic labels.

Configuration. We implemented our framework using PyTorch [22] and used the ViT-L/14@336px architecture as our base model. The learnable context consisted of 10 trainable vectors, each with 512 dimensions. All experiments were conducted on a server equipped with NVIDIA A800 GPUs, with secure communication protocols implemented between parties. For optimization, we used the Adam optimizer with a learning rate of 0.001 for the context vectors, while keeping the CLIP model parameters frozen. Training was conducted for 100

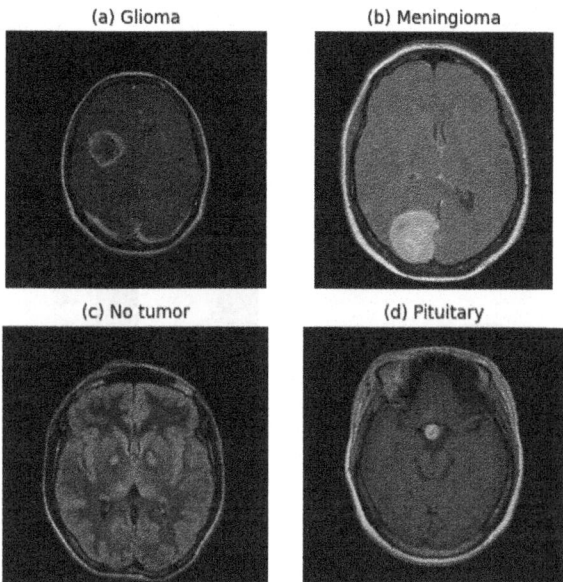

Fig. 2. Sample MRI scans.

epochs with a batch size of 32. We employed early stopping based on validation performance to prevent overfitting.

Baseline Models. We compared the performance of our framework against several baselines, including:

- Original CLIP models pretrained on general data: clip_ViT_L_14_336, clip_ViT_B_16, clip_ViT_B_32;
- PubMed-CLIP, a domain-specific CLIP model pretrained on medical data.

Evaluation Metrics. To comprehensively evaluate our framework's performance, we employed several standard metrics for multi-class classification:

- Accuracy: The ratio of correctly predicted observations to the total observations, providing an overall measure of model performance.
- Precision: For each class, the ratio of true positive predictions to the total positive predictions (true positives + false positives), indicating the model's ability to avoid false positive classifications.
- Recall: For each class, the ratio of true positive predictions to the total actual positives (true positives + false negatives), measuring the model's ability to find all positive cases.
- F1-score: The harmonic mean of precision and recall, providing a balanced measure that accounts for both false positives and false negatives.
- Macro F1-score: The unweighted average of F1-scores for each class, giving equal importance to each class regardless of its support.

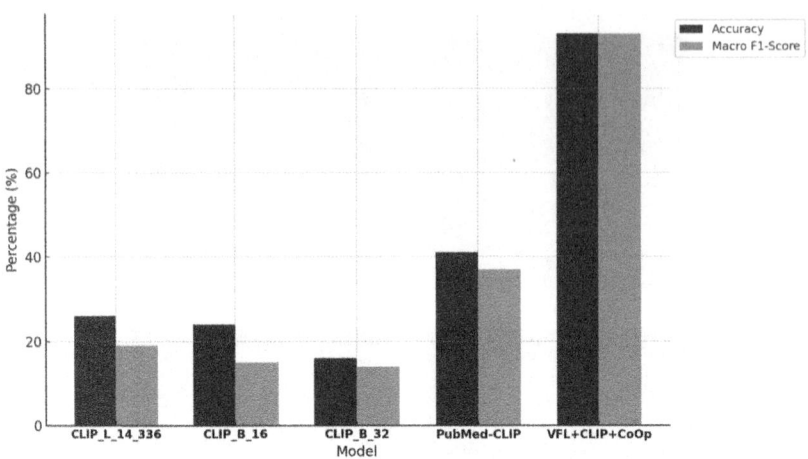

Fig. 3. Models Performance Comparison.

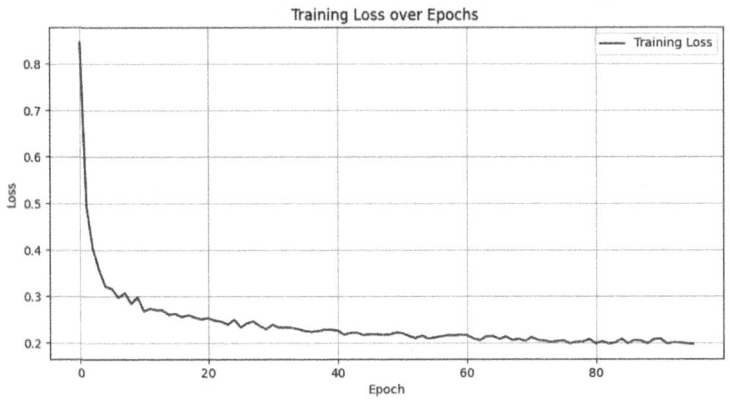

Fig. 4. Loss of our proposed framework.

These metrics were chosen because accuracy alone can be misleading in medical applications where the cost of different types of errors may vary significantly. For instance, misclassifying a tumor type could lead to inappropriate treatment decisions. The combination of precision, recall, and F1-score provides a more nuanced understanding of the model's performance across different tumor classes.

4.2   Results

Our experimental results demonstrated significant performance improvements over the baselines. Figure 3 illustrates the comparative accuracy and macro

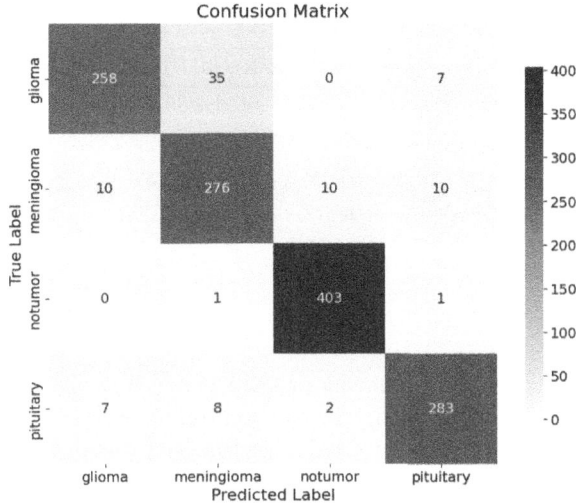

Fig. 5. Confusion matrix of our proposed framework.

F1-scores of different models. The original pretrained CLIP models exhibit relatively low performance, with accuracy ranging from 16% to 26% and macro F1-scores between 14% and 19%. In contrast, PubMed-CLIP, which is pretrained on medical data, shows moderate improvement with an accuracy of 41% and a macro F1-score of 37%. However, our proposed framework, which integrates vertical federated learning and CLIP model with CoOp optimization, dramatically outperforms these models, achieving 93.1% in both accuracy and macro F1-score. The sharp increase in both accuracy and F1-scores validates the effectiveness of our privacy-preserving framework in real-world medical scenarios, where data is distributed across institutions.

The loss values during training of our framework are illustrated in Fig. 4. It shows a clear downward trend in the loss as the epochs progress, stabilizing after approximately 80 epochs. This behavior indicates the model's ability to learn effectively without overfitting, as demonstrated by the early stopping mechanism triggered based on validation performance.

Additionally, we analyzed the classification performance for each individual class: glioma, meningioma, pituitary tumors, and no tumor. Figure 5 illustrates the confusion matrix for the classification results of our proposed framework. The matrix demonstrates a balanced performance across the different tumor types, with minimal misclassifications. Table 1 provides the detailed precision, recall, and F1-scores for each class, showcasing the robust performance of the proposed method across all tumor types. Notably, the "no tumor" class achieves exceptionally high precision (97.1%) and recall (99.5%), reflecting the model's ability to accurately distinguish healthy controls from tumor cases.

Table 1. Classification Metrics of Our Proposed Framework.

Class Name	Precision	Recall	F1-score
Glioma	93.8%	86.0%	89.7%
Meningioma	86.3%	90.2%	88.2%
No Tumor	97.1%	99.5%	98.3%
Pituitary	94.0%	94.3%	94.2%

5   Conclusion

In this paper, we proposed a novel privacy-preserving framework for cross-institutional medical image analysis by combining vertical federated learning (VFL) with the Contrastive Language-Image Pretraining (CLIP) model, enhanced through Context Optimization (CoOp). This framework facilitates secure collaboration across medical institutions while safeguarding patient data. Our results show significant improvements in brain tumor classification, achieving 93.1% in both accuracy and macro F1-score, outperforming original CLIP variants and PubMed-CLIP.

By using VFL, the framework addresses domain adaptation challenges in medical image analysis and enables collaboration without raw data sharing. Additionally, aligning medical images with optimized text prompts enhances diagnostic accuracy by bridging general-purpose vision-language models with specialized medical tasks.

Limitations and Future Work. Future research could explore incorporating richer textual data, such as clinical notes, to improve model interpretability. Expanding the framework to other medical domains with diverse datasets and integrating heterogeneous data modalities (e.g., EHRs, genomic data) would further enhance diagnostic capabilities.

In summary, the proposed framework offers a scalable solution for privacy-preserving medical image analysis, balancing data privacy with diagnostic accuracy to enable secure collaboration between healthcare institutions.

References

1. Radford, A., et al.: Learning transferable visual models from natural language supervision. Int. Conf. Mach. Learn. 8748–8763 (2021)
2. Yang, Q., Liu, Y., Chen, T., Tong, Y.: Federated machine learning: concept and applications. ACM Trans. Intell. Syst. Technol. (TIST) **10**, 1–19 (2019)
3. Zhou, K., Yang, J., Loy, C., Liu, Z.: Learning to prompt for vision-language models. Int. J. Comput. Vision **130**, 2337–2348 (2022)
4. Li, T., Sahu, A., Talwalkar, A., Smith, V.: Federated learning: challenges, methods, and future directions. IEEE Signal Process. Mag. **37**, 50–60 (2020)

5. Dou, Q., et al.: Federated deep learning for detecting COVID-19 lung abnormalities in CT: a privacy-preserving multinational validation study. NPJ Digital Med. **4**, 60 (2021)
6. Sheller, M., Reina, G., Edwards, B., Martin, J., Bakas, S.: Multi-institutional deep learning modeling without sharing patient data: a feasibility study on brain tumor segmentation. Brainlesion: Glioma, Multiple Sclerosis, Stroke And Traumatic Brain Injuries: 4th International Workshop, BrainLes 2018, Held In Conjunction With MICCAI 2018, Granada, Spain, September 16, 2018, Revised Selected Papers, Part I 4, pp. 92–104 (2019)
7. Gulati, S., Guleria, K., Goyal, N., AlZubi, A., Castilla, Á.: A Privacy-Preserving Collaborative Federated Learning Framework for Detecting Retinal Diseases. IEEE Access (2024)
8. Yan, Y., et al.: Cross-modal vertical federated learning for MRI reconstruction. IEEE J. Biomed. Health Inf. **28**, 6384–6394 (2024)
9. Khan, A., Thij, M., Wilbik, A.: Vertical federated learning: a structured literature review. Knowl. Inf. Syst. 1–39 (2025)
10. Hardy, S., et al.: Private federated learning on vertically partitioned data via entity resolution and additively homomorphic encryption. ArXiv Preprint ArXiv:1711.10677 (2017)
11. Shetty, S., Ananthanarayana, S., Mahale, A.: Multimodal medical tensor fusion network-based DL framework for abnormality prediction from the radiology CXRs and clinical text reports. Multimedia Tools Appl. **82**, 44431–44478 (2023)
12. Liu, H., Shi, Y., Li, A., Wang, M.: Multi-modal fusion network with intra-and inter-modality attention for prognosis prediction in breast cancer. Comput. Biol. Med. **168**, 107796 (2024)
13. Dautov, R., Distefano, S., Buyya, R.: Hierarchical data fusion for smart healthcare. J. Big Data **6**, 1–23 (2019)
14. Wang, Z., Wu, Z., Agarwal, D., Sun, J.: MedCLIP: contrastive learning from unpaired medical images and text. In: Proceedings of the Conference on Empirical Methods in Natural Language Processing. Conference on Empirical Methods in Natural Language Processing, vol. 2022, pp. 3876 (2022)
15. Lin, W., et al.: PMC-CLIP: contrastive language-image pre-training using biomedical documents. In: International Conference On Medical Image Computing And Computer-Assisted Intervention, pp. 525–536 (2023)
16. Eslami, S., Meinel, C., De Melo, G.: PubMedCLIP: how much does CLIP benefit visual question answering in the medical domain? Find. Assoc. Comput. Linguist. EACL **2023**, 1181–1193 (2023)
17. Brain Tumor MRI Dataset. https://www.kaggle.com/datasets/masoudnickparvar/brain-tumor-mri-dataset. Accessed 25 Feb 2025
18. Regulation, P. Regulation (EU) 2016/679 of the European Parliament and of the Council. Regulation (eu). **679**, 2016 (2016)
19. Act, A.: Health insurance portability and accountability act of 1996. Public Law. **104**, 191 (1996)
20. Chen, Y., Qin, X., Wang, J., Yu, C., Gao, W.: FedHealth: a federated transfer learning framework for wearable healthcare. IEEE Intell. Syst. **35**, 83–93 (2020)
21. Sohan, M., Basalamah, A.: A systematic review on federated learning in medical image analysis. IEEE Access **11**, 28628–28644 (2023)
22. Paszke, A.: PyTorch: An imperative style, high-performance deep learning library. ArXiv Preprint ArXiv:1912.01703. (2019)

An Architecture for a Reliability Tool Applied to Distributed Systems

Caio Guimaraes Herrera[1]([✉]), Vitor Silva Montes[1], Simone R. S. Souza[1],
Ricardo Ribeiro dos Santos[2], and Paulo Sergio Lopes de Souza[1]

[1] University of Sao Paulo (ICMC/USP), Sao Carlos, SP, Brazil
caioherrera@usp.br
[2] Federal University of Mato Grosso do Sul (UFMS), Campo Grande, MS, Brazil

Abstract. Contemporary software systems, such as IoT (Internet of Things) systems, present new challenges to the development process and require new strategies for quality assurance. Reliability engineering aims to detect faults in applications, often in productive environments, providing benefits to the development activity. However, due to the inherent characteristics of these systems, complementary approaches to detect faults beyond traditional testing are needed. The Tricorder methodology evaluates resource consumption profiles as a heuristic for quality assurance, and experimental studies indicate its effectiveness in detecting new faults. This work investigates the use of the Tricorder in the context of reliability engineering to support the validation of contemporary systems, particularly IoT systems. An architecture for a reliability tool is proposed, inspired by software testing concepts. A reference architecture, RefTEST, is used to support the proposed tool. Results indicate that the Tricorder methodology can be implemented as a reliability tool, and its adoption allows for identifying anomalies that are not easily detected by traditional testing methods.

Keywords: Software reliability · distributed systems · fault forecasting · internet of things

1 Introduction

Software development is constantly evolving and growing in complexity. With the distributed nature of modern systems, DevOps practices [11] and the field of release engineering [5] have become crucial in ensuring the longevity and reliability of software. Moreover, the discipline of reliability engineering includes strategies for continuously monitoring and testing systems, even after reaching production environments [17], as software reliability is one of the main factors affecting software quality [10].

Well-structured tests are essential to detect faults in the early stages. However, some characteristics associated with low testability software [20] can hinder fault detection before the software reaches a production environment, creating an opportunity for complementary approaches to traditional software testing.

O. Gervasi et al. (Eds.): ICCSA 2025, LNCS 15649, pp. 332–348, 2025.
https://doi.org/10.1007/978-3-031-96997-3_21

When considering low-testability software, continuous testing also presents new challenges. Data available in testing environments might not fully represent what can be found in production [19]. Acquiring and reproducing input data from production environments might be limited for security reasons [19]. These challenges highlight the need for testing strategies that differ from conventional approaches.

The Tricorder methodology [12] is a complementary approach that does not rely on input and output data to evaluate a System Under Test (SUT) but rather on defining resource consumption profiles. By detecting the changes in the consumption profiles, it is inferred that the SUT has an anomaly, which could be related to a fault being inserted in the code. The methodology can identify an anomaly automatically without the tester's mediation, although the latter is responsible for investigating the detected anomaly to see if it correlates to an actual fault. Tricorder has been evaluated in a set of studies and applications [1, 4, 12]. These studies indicate that the methodology effectively detects artificially inserted faults. Currently, Tricorder works using scripts that are modified to adapt to new systems when they are evaluated.

The Tricorder methodology is in line with the fault lifecycle techniques of software reliability engineering: **1)** fault prevention, **2)** fault removal, **3)** fault tolerance, and **4)** fault/failure forecasting [10]. In this context, our proposal can be classified as **fault/failure forecasting**.

A software tool must be available to implement Tricoder. Consequently, there is a need to establish a software architecture that can account for the Tricorder features while also allowing its use as a reliability tool. Moreover, this architecture should also allow for its use in low testability applications, such as IoT (Internet of Things) systems.

A reference architecture for developing software testing tools, such as RefTEST [13], can guide this process. Since the Tricorder methodology follows a non-conventional approach for evaluating the SUT, as it does not rely on specific features of the SUT implementation, nor does it need to characterize test cases based on input and output data, adapting the Tricorder methodology to RefTEST is a challenge.

This paper presents an architecture proposal, based on RefTEST, for a tool that implements the Tricorder methodology to evaluate software reliability. This work also discusses how flexible the reference architecture is and how we can design tools that follow a non-conventional approach. Moreover, this paper first attempts to adapt the Tricorder methodology into a tool while considering its use in a low testability scenario, exemplified by an IoT systems model.

The remainder of this text is organized as follows: Section 2 presents the context and motivation of this study. Section 3 introduces the Tricorder methodology. Section 4 covers the related work regarding the architectures of software testing tools. Section 5 shows the proposed architecture. Finally, Sect. 6 highlights and discusses the main results of this paper, and Sect. 7 concludes this study with final remarks and future work.

2   Background

The evolution of software development environments and the continuous increase in software complexity have made modern software ecosystems multidisciplinary. Beyond the programmer role, it is necessary to have testers, QA (Quality Assurance) analysts, and product/project managers for the development cycle. DevOps practices [11], such as CI/CD (Continuous Integration/Continuous Deployment) and version control tools, are essential to ensure the quality of the software being deployed to production.

The discipline of release engineering [5] includes these concepts, adding concerns regarding software deployment, longevity, and reliability to the traditional software engineering activity to ensure that the developed systems are predictable and reliable. More specifically, reliability engineering [17] ensures the availability, security, and integrity of computer systems, even after reaching production environments. To do so, routines such as monitoring, testing, and validation need to keep happening after a software is deployed [17].

It is still equally important to have well-structured test routines to evaluate changes and new software versions. From unit and integration tests up to system and acceptance tests, a set of test cases can be carried out from the first steps of developing a new feature or product. However, some characteristics of the software being developed, or the context in which it belongs, can hinder the detection of faults at early stages. In these scenarios, the software testability concept is crucial and needs to be considered.

Software testability can be described as the probability that software will fail at the subsequent test execution, provided it has a fault [20]. Low testability software can accumulate many characteristics that offer a challenge for the early detection of faults. Some of them that are of interest to this study are:

(1) **Data unpredictability**: several application contexts, such as IoT systems, rely almost exclusively on input data from sensors in contact with a real environment, exposed to noise and hardware failures, which can cause a divergence between data used in controlled environments for development and testing, and production data;

(2) **Low to no human interaction**: systems built to run in embedded systems are commonly set to run on areas with low connectivity and almost zero interaction with humans. This context can make fault detection take longer than in a scenario of high human interaction; and

(3) **Input and output data as stream**: applications with this characteristic rely on a continuous and real-time data transmission commonly associated with a high volume of data. Replicating this behavior in testing environments can be costly and unfeasible [19].

To ensure quality in the developed software and improve fault detection in scenarios of low testability, a complementary approach is necessary to conventional testing when the application is running in a production environment, in order to evaluate the software reliability. Since the mentioned features do not allow for the construction of a test oracle, there is a need for testing alternatives that do not rely solely on I/O data.

The Tricorder methodology, described in the next section, should not be confused with the *Tricorder* platform, proposed by Sadowski et al. [15], designed to help developers with program static analysis. Despite both aiming to improve software quality, the projects are not related, as our approach is based on software reliability metrics to automate anomaly detection.

3   The Tricorder Methodology

Tricorder [12] is a complementary testing methodology designed to detect potential faults in production software by exploring the resource consumption profiles of the application. One of the advantages of this methodology in comparison to more traditional approaches is that it does not rely on test cases, nor does it depend on input and output data. It simply uses the resource consumption profiles of the application to infer whether there is an anomaly in its behavior. This process is done automatically, without human intervention, although it is the tester's responsibility to decide whether a resource consumption anomaly and a software fault are correlated.

A conventional testing process, as shown in Fig. 1, aims to define a set of test cases consisting of inputs collected from the SUT's domain and their expected outputs for a particular SUT to be tested against it. The result of this testing activity is sent to an Oracle, which is responsible for determining whether or not the test cases detected an actual fault. It is said that the testing activity succeeded when a fault was found and failed otherwise [3].

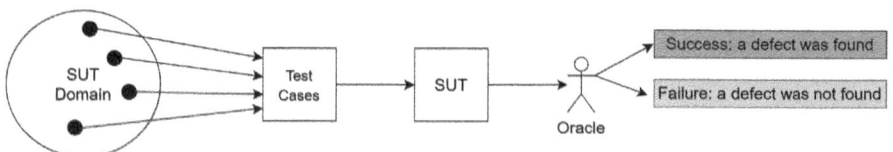

Fig. 1. Traditional testing process.

However, since the Tricorder methodology does not use inputs and outputs to detect anomalies, there is no need for test cases. The SUT domain is used instead to define workloads as different combinations of input parameters that are used to express the different known behaviors of the application. These workloads are executed against a version of the application, said to have no faults, to be used as a reference. This methodology will produce a set of reference resource consumption profiles, which will later be compared with the ones generated by the SUT with the same workloads. The result of this activity will indicate whether an anomaly was detected. The tester is assigned to identify whether that anomaly corresponds to an actual code fault, as shown in Fig. 2.

The complete list of steps to apply the Tricorder methodology is described as follows [12]:

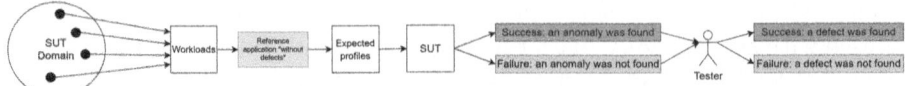

Fig. 2. Tricorder's testing process.

1. There should be a reference application **P**, which is assumed to have no faults. The running of **P** will be triggered **N** times;

2. For each execution of **P**, data regarding consumption of the available resources (such as RAM, processors, etc.) will be collected and stored;

3. The collected data is organized as a set of resource consumption profiles that will be grouped, according to a similarity metric, in an incremental manner, with each newly generated profile added to the grouping;

4. Then, a new version of the application, **P'**, which will be the system-under-test (SUT), is executed **N** times;

5. For each execution of **P'**, steps (2)-(4) will be executed all over again, collecting data and generating profiles of the resource consumption;

6. The new profiles will be added to the previous set, and the grouping process will be executed again incrementally; and

7. If a new group is formed with only **P'** data, it is assumed that an anomaly was detected, which could represent the presence of a fault.

The chosen algorithm for the grouping of the resource consumption profiles is based on the DAMICORE methodology [16], which is a generic approach to grouping data of any type by using Normalized Compression Distance (NCD) as a similarity metric between two data points. The DAMICORE workflow can be described in three steps [16]:

- **Computing the NCD metric**: generate a distance matrix by computing the NCD value between each pair of data points;

- **Simplification**: the distance matrix is transformed into a rootless binary tree, where each data point is presented as a leaf node, and their similarity degree is reflected as the length of the edges between them; and

- **Grouping**: the data grouping is hierarchically performed within the binary tree, causing the original data set to be partitioned;

To validate the effectiveness of fault detection, experimental Python scripts were developed to implement the Tricorder methodology. This experimental model is represented in Figs. 3 (representing the **P** application) and 4 (representing the **P'** application).

The **Monitoring** module [12], executes different workloads associated with the SUT. The workloads should be as close as possible to a real scenario in which the application should run. To ensure effective grouping in laboratory experiments, previous work usually sets up the SUTs to execute each workload at least 30 times to generate fitted resource consumption profiles. The Python library **PSUtil** was used to retrieve consumption data (specifically regarding CPU usage, number of allocated bytes in memory, and number of I/O operations) every 100 milliseconds [12]. A profile gathers all the data collected in each workload execution.

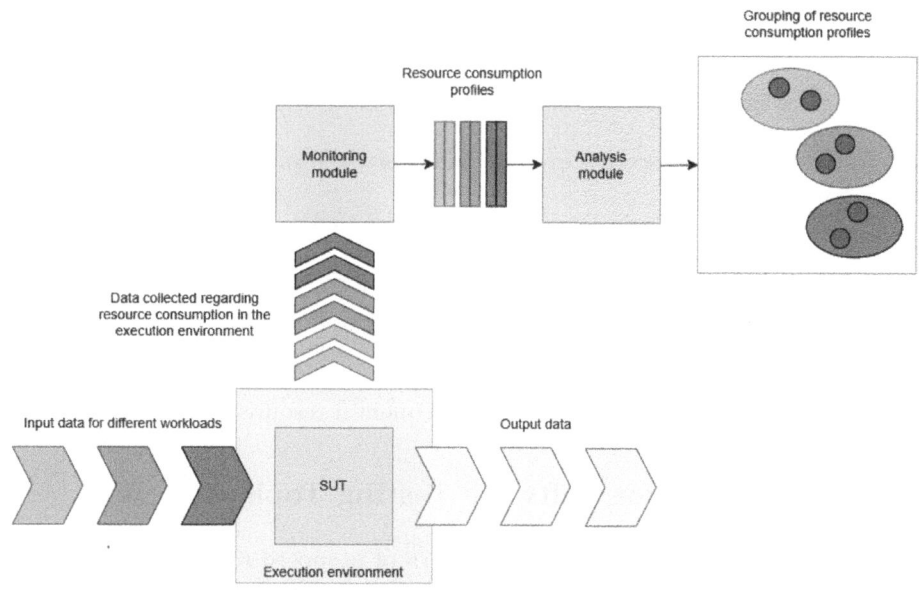

Fig. 3. Tricorder expected behavior when running P.

The **Analysis** module groups the collected data using DAMICORE [16]. Any newly generated group with executions of **P'** indicates that **P'** changed the application's resource consumption profile, pointing out an anomaly. From there, the researcher (or tester) needs to evaluate the anomaly and identify whether there is an actual fault in the SUT or the new profile is expected due to a change in the code.

The Tricorder methodology has been used in many scenarios and applications. While [12] explored the methodology in a Client-Server application, [1] evaluated the performance when exploring Machine Learning algorithms, and

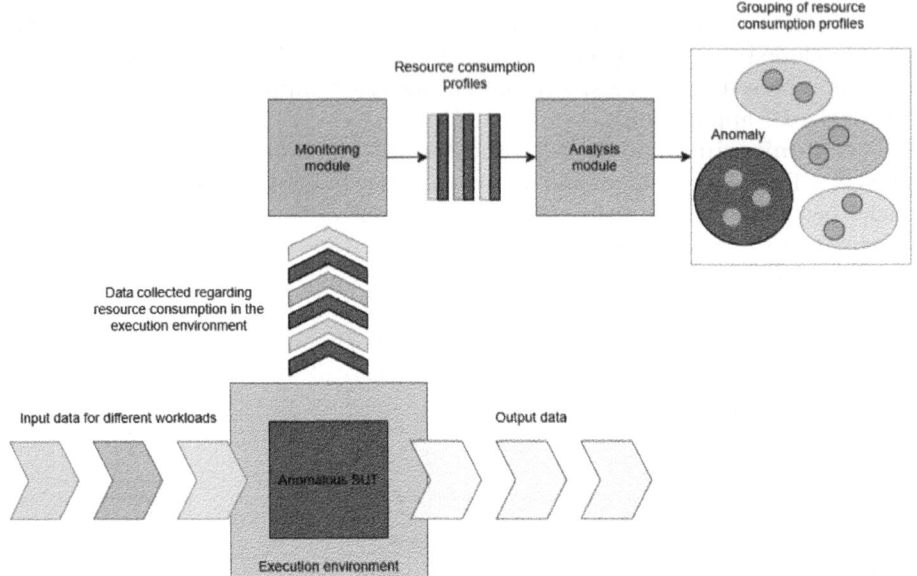

Fig. 4. Tricorder expected behavior when running P'.

[4] explored different application domains, such as Fluid Simulation and Video Processing. The results show that Tricorder can detect artificially inserted faults in every domain by grouping resource consumption profiles.

Tricorder's current implementation lacks the robustness of a real tool. It demands a significant effort to adapt its scripts, as the tool modules and source code were initially built to be used as experimental resources.

4   Architectures for Software Testing Tools

In the scientific literature, there is a plethora of proposed tools and approaches that deal with the activity of software testing, even for contexts that share the characteristics of low testability software, such as IoT systems [6]. However, most are not publicly available for replication and usage in different contexts [8].

One strategy that can improve the adoption of a new tool is using a reference architecture. Relying on a software architecture can improve the software maintainability and life cycle, and also reduce development time [7]. Using software architectures during the development process can encourage reusability of components [9].

The proposal of software testing architectures before an actual implementation of a tool is usual among researchers. A cloud architecture was proposed, with an actual implementation, for executing static tests as a service [2], in which users can upload the applications to be tested, execute their tests, and download their results.

Zhang [22] presents an architecture for software testing in web service applications based on a service-oriented testing framework proposed by Zhu [23], accompanied by a prototype implementation based on the ontology of software testing, demonstrating the feasibility of the proposed architecture.

Wu [21] presents CCTS, an architecture for a software testing tool to test event-based micro-services through consumer-driven contracts and state models.

Nakagawa [13] highlights the importance of standardization in testing tool proposals. The authors proposed RefTEST, a reference architecture specialized for constructing software testing tools, based on RefASSET, an architecture proposal focused on wider software engineering environments.

The RefTEST architecture was used as the baseline for the development of software testing tools, such as the one described by Silva [18], which presents a software testing tool for concurrent systems. Parizi [14] also proposes a testing tool, RAMBUTANS, based on RefTEST, which intends to test aspect-oriented programming.

By compiling the accumulated knowledge contained in the scientific literature for software testing (represented by Software Architectures, Testing Processes, Testing Tools, and Testing Ontologies), RefTEST suggests the definition of four modules (Fig. 5) [13]. Each module has a list of functionalities to encompass the expected features of a software testing tool:

- The **Test Artifact** defines the artifact to be tested by the tool and provides all the features related to its management.

- The **Test Case** defines the test cases to be executed against the Test Artifact, as well as the features for their management.
- The **Test Criterion** defines the test criterion used by the tool and provides the features related to its management.

- The **Test Requirement** defines the test requirements for the tool and provides the features for their management.

By using RefTEST as a baseline, this study aims to provide an architecture to describe a reliability tool capable of implementing the Tricorder methodology. Moreover, we aim to instantiate the proposed architecture into a conventional software scenario and also an IoT scenario to study its adaptability and adherence.

5   Mapping Tricorder to RefTEST Architecture

Aiming to understand the process and define the behavior for the new tool, as well as the necessary parameters to be provided by the tester, we describe a proposal of a workflow based on the Tricorder methodology and its current implementation.

The proposed tool can be adapted to encapsulate the guidelines provided by the RefTEST architecture. For each module, we need to specify the necessary

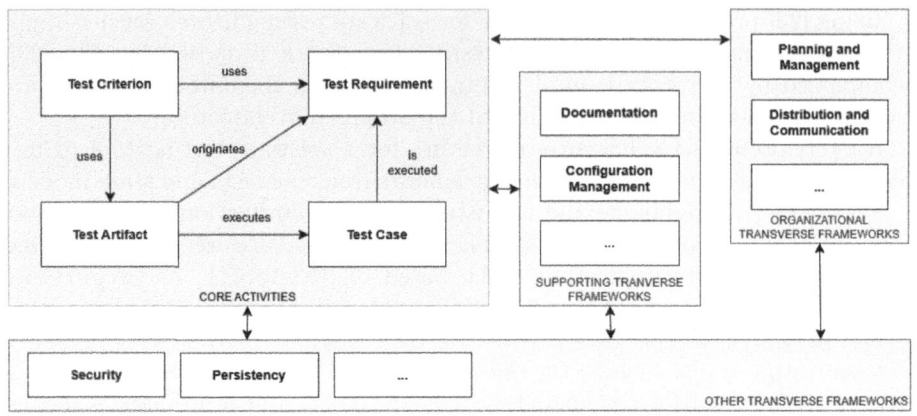

Fig. 5. Core aspect of the RefTEST architecture. Adapted from Nakagawa [13]. (Color figure online)

functional requirements for the tool being developed. In addition, we can derive adequate classes and methods from this definition. The RefTEST architecture also proposes a set of transverse frameworks that can be used to address other activities that need to be implemented for the tool to work in a real environment. These frameworks improve and support the established core activities, even being functional on their own, by implementing functionalities related to **supporting activities** - such as Documentation and Configuration Management -, **organizational activities** - such as Planning and Management - or other general activities, related to Security and Data Persistence, for example. The frameworks can also be used in a new tool proposal to encapsulate non-core activities properly.

An initial workflow was designed to represent all the steps the tool should take to implement the Tricorder methodology properly. The workflow provides insights into the stages of the activity and the parameters that a tester should provide to use the tool effectively. Since the Tricorder methodology is heavily dependent on clustering algorithms, the reliability tool was organized into three steps: training, validation, and testing.

The **training** step considers a version of the application that is admittedly fault-free to be used as a reference. From this version, some executions will be triggered and monitored by the tool, which will collect data regarding the usage of the available resources and generate a set of resource consumption profiles. From there, iterating through each profile, the tool will run a clustering algorithm until all profiles are used. The generated grouping will be saved as a reference and used in the following steps (Fig. 6).

Validation is a double-check step in which the tool will again receive the reference application and generate new resource consumption profiles to compare with the ones generated in the Training steps. The stages of running the application and grouping the results will be executed again. Still, this time, the training groups will represent an initial set in the grouping stage, where the new profiles will be aggregated. The final grouping is expected to be the same as the original one. If not, the tool might need parameter changes, or the target application is unsuitable due to a non-deterministic behavior (Fig. 7).

Test is the final step. A new version of the SUT will generate new resource consumption profiles, which will be grouped with the Training/Validation profiles. This step is similar to the validation step, but now the main goal is to investigate if a new group containing only profiles from the Test step is generated. If so, an anomaly is detected (Fig. 8).

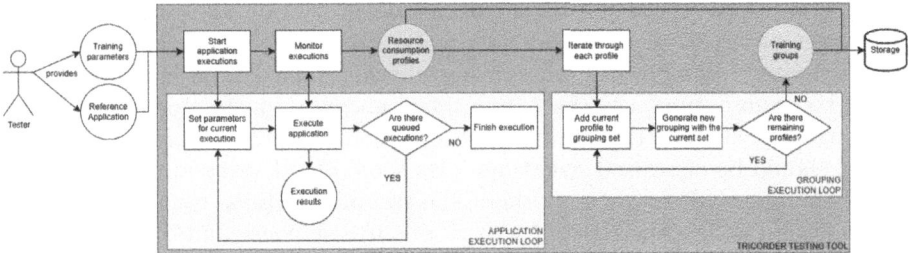

Fig. 6. Workflow overview for the Training step of the proposed tool.

The rectangles in Figs. 6, 7 and 8 represent block of actions, circles denote data and information (blue are in external storage), diamonds indicate conditional statements, and hexagons show conclusions to be taken by the tester depending on a condition.

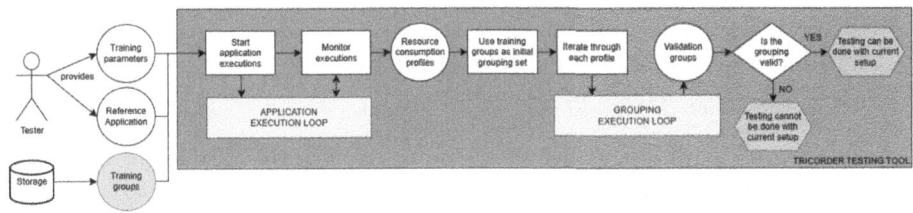

Fig. 7. Workflow overview for the Validation step of the proposed tool.

The non-conventional approach in the Tricorder methodology provides additional challenges to the use of a reference architecture based on standard software testing tools and processes. Concepts and functionalities must be adapted to this new context while keeping the architecture functional and structured as intended. This application illustrates and encourages the use of RefTEST architecture in non-conventional testing scenarios.

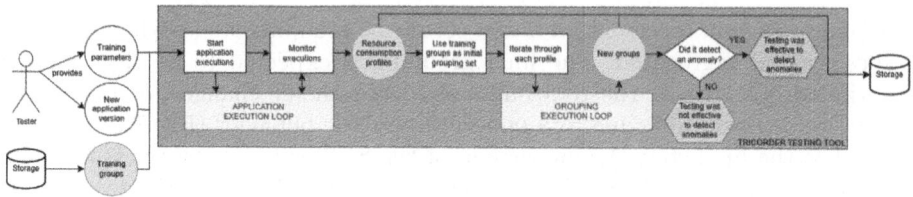

Fig. 8. Workflow overview for the Test step of the proposed tool.

By using RefTEST as the reference architecture, this study aims to provide a set of concepts and functionalities needed for the proposed tool to work correctly. The conceived architecture also needs to be instantiated in a more practical sense so that its implementation can be fully envisioned. This instance would require the definition of use cases, functional and non-functional requirements, class diagrams, etc. For this study, however, we aim to reach a proposal on how the tool should be organized, what modules should be developed, and how they would communicate with one another. The technical details, requirements, and use cases will not be covered in this work due to size constraints.

6   Results and Discussion

Using RefTEST as the baseline and the established workflows as guidance for the behavior of the proposed tool, we present the adapted concepts for each module. It is noteworthy that the purpose of our tool is to validate a system in use, with the goal of identifying the presence of defects when the software is in its production environment. The software testing concepts used for the development cycle were adapted to the context of our reliability engineering tool.

-   **Test Artifact**: In the context of the Tricorder methodology, we can associate the artifact to be tested with a **new application version**, considering that there is a baseline version as the reference.

-   **Test Case**: The different test scenarios to explore the artifact to be tested can be described as different **workloads** in the Tricorder methodology. The method can work without the definition of multiple workloads, as standard execution should be enough to build a resource consumption profile of the application. However, by including different workloads, testers can ensure that possible different resource demands of the application can be mapped and detected by the tool as allowed occurrences and not as false positives.

-   **Test Criterion**: As the Tricorder methodology does not rely on code structure or implementation, the concept of coverage cannot rely on these features. However, since we have a Training step before using the tool for the actual testing, we collect a set of profile groups representing the expected application behaviors regarding resource consumption. At the Test step, the test criterion is the coverage of the groups found in the Training. Also, during the Test, we should be able to identify resource consumption profiles belonging to each group in the Training step.

– **Test Requirement**: Similarly to the described Test Criterion, since the Tricorder methodology is not concerned about internal aspects of the SUT implementation, nor does it rely on input and output data, we can set, as the test requirement, the existence of resource consumption profiles that only belong to the predefined groups. An anomaly is detected if some resource consumption profiles are not grouped into an existing group.

The proximity of each RefTEST core concept to the concepts of the Tricorder methodology indicates that not only is the reference architecture versatile, but it is also feasible to guide the development of a tool for the Tricorder methodology.

Aside from the concepts that coordinate the behavior of a software testing tool, it is also necessary to persistently store and retrieve data (in the case of Tricorder, the resource consumption profiles and groupings), from one step to another in the workflow, and even from different test sessions. These features are also observed in RefTEST's architecture specification due to the definition of a transverse framework for **Data persistence.**

In order to accommodate all the necessary functions for the methodology while also taking into account the previously defined concepts, we can derive a generic overview of architecture to implement Tricorder, as shown in Fig. 9. The user interface module must provide an UI that allows the tester to interact with the system and trigger the execution of the monitoring and analysis modules. The data persistence module ensures that all the data needed during this process is consistent, reliable, and stored persistently.

Both analysis and monitoring modules are responsible for leveraging the core concepts of RefTEST, highlighted in yellow and shown on Fig. 5, to execute their function successfully. Moreover, to properly isolate resource consumption data collection from any interference, the monitoring module should be able to execute the SUT by demand in a dedicated environment, which might differ for each use case of the tool when instantiating its architecture with real resources.

This first proposal is generic and should be defined before being applied in any scenario. One of the first attempts to instantiate it for a typical case of a regular application to be tested is described in Fig. 10, where both the analysis and monitoring modules run as back-end applications in isolated containers, while the UI module is represented by a front-end web application, running locally on the tester's machine. The data persistence module stores the needed data in a SQL database.

A second attempt to adjust the architecture in a specific scenario focuses on IoT systems. For example, suppose that the software to be monitored runs at the perception layer. In that case, we might deal with hardware constraints and resource limitations that could prevent a monitoring module from being fully executed according to the specifications. Thus, an additional module might be needed to simplify the hardware overhead, as proposed in Fig. 11.

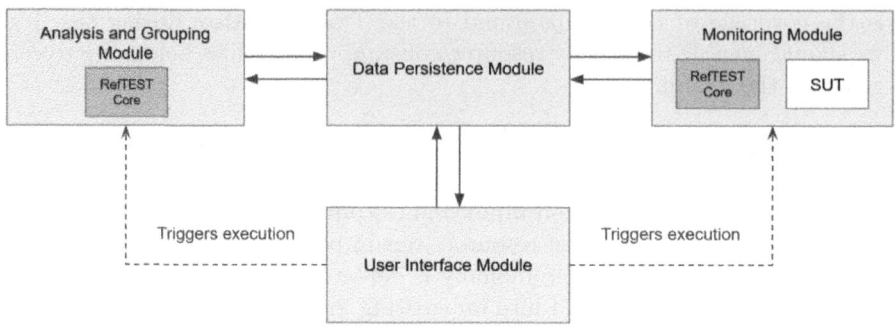

Fig. 9. Generic architecture of the Tricorder methodology.

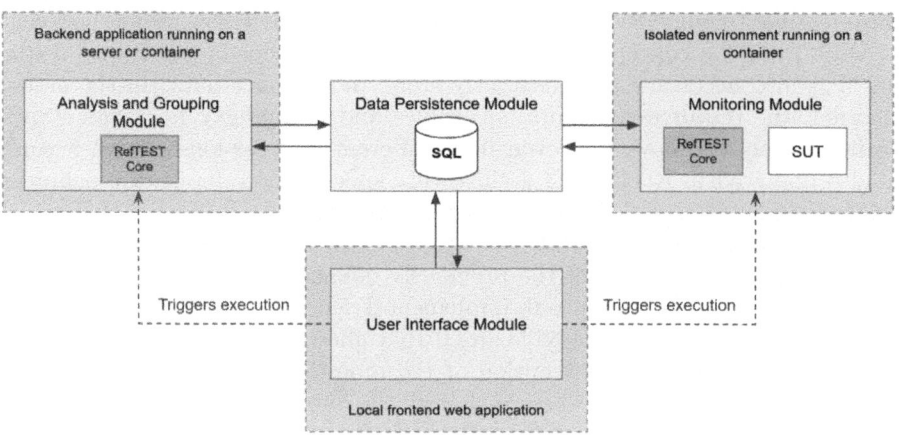

Fig. 10. Common definition for the architecture of Tricorder's proposed tool.

A monitoring module is used only to collect the current resource consumption data and send it to an external MQTT server as a publisher. The tool's persistence module can act as a subscriber and store the collected data in real time.

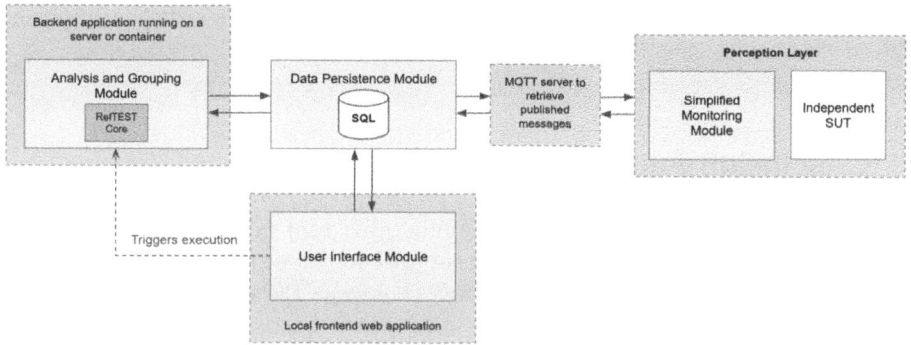

Fig. 11. IoT definition for the architecture of Tricorder's proposed tool.

6.1   An Use-Case IoT Scenario for the Tool

Suppose that an IoT application runs constantly on an ESP32 microcontroller, attached to a set of sensors that monitor aspects of the environment in which this circuit is exposed, such as temperature, humidity, air quality, etc. There is a low-level code on the perception layer for processing the collected data and sending them to another application running on a computer as application layer software. Both pieces of code (perception and application layers) are validated through traditional software testing methods, such as unit tests, integration tests, system tests, etc.

Assume that there is a fault in the code for a new version of the software on the perception layer, which causes a memory leak. The software can start to malfunction after some time running, caused by the memory consumption on the microcontroller. Since hardware resources are scarce in IoT systems, issues such as these cannot be overlooked. At the same time, traditional testing may not be enough to detect this fault, as it becomes more evident as the software runs.

Through the Tricorder methodology, such a scenario would be feasible to detect since a memory leak would represent a deviation from the expected resource consumption profile. By being trained on a more stable and reliable version of the software, the tool would identify a new and distinct group of profiles for RAM consumption, which represents an anomaly in the latest software.

Based on the proposed mapping of the Tricorder to a software testing reference architecture, we can draw the following results:

1. Proof of adherence to the Tricorder methodology as a future reliability tool, complementary to the in-production software testing activity, through the use of RefTEST;

2. Instantiation of different propositions for the original architecture in different scenarios, including an example of a low testability software, such as IoT; and

3. Contextualization of a possible scenario in which the Tricorder can be used to detect faults that traditional testing approaches would not detect.

7   Conclusion and Future Work

This paper presents an architecture for a reliability tool that implements the Tricorder methodology, offering additional support to the testing activity through a non-conventional approach. RefTEST was chosen as the reference architecture, where we extend its use by adapting its concepts to encompass all the necessary steps for non-conventional testing activity.

The work reinforces that a reliability tool based on RefTEST can successfully implement the Tricorder methodology. This work is an important validation, as it is the first step towards implementing the proposed tool. In addition, the proposal contributes to the idea that RefTEST is versatile and can be used in non-conventional scenarios, which could expand its adoption.

This study also approximates the proposed architecture from a real-world scenario, defining the technical details for each module in different scenarios, such as IoT systems. Beyond that, we characterize a use-case scenario in which such a tool can bring benefits for fault detection, catching software anomalies that traditional testing mechanisms, such as memory leaks, could not detect.

Future work will apply this architecture by building a proof-of-concept of the Tricorder tool. To implement the reliability tool, one should specify the technical aspects even further, reaching concepts such as the list of necessary classes and objects to represent each concept and implement each functionality.

Acknowledgment. The authors would like to thank CAPES (PROEX), CNPq (308445/2021-0), and FAPESP (2013/07375-0, 2019/06937-0, 2019/26702-8) for their financial support.

Disclosure of Interests. The authors have no competing interests to declare that are relevant to the content of this article.

References

1. Braga, D.: (Brazilian Portuguese) Assessing the Use of Performance Data Clustering for Supporting Software Testing in the Machine Learning Domain. Master's thesis, Instituto de Ciências Matemáticas e de Computação, Universidade de São Paulo, São Carlos (2022). https://doi.org/10.11606/D.55.2022.tde-09112022-160513
2. Chen, S., Huang, J., Gong, Y.: Static testing as a service on cloud. In: 27th International Conference on Advance Information Networking and Applications Workshops, pp. 638–642 (2013). https://doi.org/10.1109/WAINA.2013.257
3. Delamaro, M., Jino, M., Maldonado, J.: (Brazilian Portuguese) Introdução ao teste de software. Elsevier Brasil, Rio de Janeiro, RJ (2013)

4. Durães, T.d.J.O.: (Brazilian Portuguese) Evaluating the use of performance profiles applied in software testing in different application domains. Master's thesis, Instituto de Ciências Matemáticas e de Computação, Universidade de São Paulo, São Carlos (2022).https://doi.org/10.11606/D.55.2022.tde-05042023-144747
5. Dyck, A., Penners, R., Lichter, H.: Towards definitions for release engineering and DevOps. In: IEEE/ACM 3rd International Workshop on Release Engineering, pp. 3–3 (2015). https://doi.org/10.1109/RELENG.2015.10
6. Ferreira, V.G., Herrera, C.G.a., Souza, S., Santos, R.R.d., Souza, P.S.L.d.: Software testing applied to the development of IoT systems: preliminary results. In: Proceedings of the 8th Brazilian Symposium on Systematic and Automated Software Testing, p. 113–122. SAST '23, Association for Computing Machinery, New York, NY, USA (2023). https://doi.org/10.1145/3624032.3624049
7. Gillani, M., Niaz, H.A., Ullah, A.: Integration of software architecture in requirements elicitation for rapid software development. IEEE Access **10**, 56158–56178 (2022). https://doi.org/10.1109/ACCESS.2022.3177659
8. Herrera, C.G., Ferreira, V.G., Souza, S.R.S., Santos, R., de Souza, P.S.L.: A comprehensive exploration of the use of software testing tools for IoT systems. In: Anais do XXV Workshop de Testes e Tolerância a Falhas. SBC (2024)
9. Joy Goodman-Deane, P.L., Clarkson, J.: Key influences on the user-centred design process. J. Eng. Design **21**(2-3), 345–373 (2010). https://doi.org/10.1080/09544820903364912
10. Lyu, M.R.: Software reliability engineering: a roadmap. In: Future of Software Engineering (FOSE '07), pp. 153–170 (2007). https://doi.org/10.1109/FOSE.2007.24
11. Microsoft: What is DevOps? (2024). https://azure.microsoft.com/en-us/resources/cloud-computing-dictionary/what-is-devops/. Accessed 19 Jan 2025
12. Montes, V.S.: (Brazilian Portuguese) Software fault detection using clustering of performance profiles. Master's thesis, Instituto de Ciências Matemáticas e de Computação, Universidade de São Paulo, São Carlos (2019). https://doi.org/10.11606/D.55.2020.tde-04022020-093604
13. Nakagawa, E., Simão, A., Ferrari, F., Maldonado, J.: Towards a reference architecture for software testing tools. In: 19th International Conference on Software Engineering and Knowledge Engineering, SEKE 2007, pp. 157–162 (2007)
14. Parizi, R., abdul ghani, A.a., Lee, S., Khan, S.U.R.: RAMBUTANS: automatic AOP-specific test generation tool. Int. J. Softw. Tools Technol. Transfer **19** (2017). https://doi.org/10.1007/s10009-016-0432-3
15. Sadowski, C., Van Gogh, J., Jaspan, C., Soderberg, E., Winter, C.: Tricorder: building a program analysis ecosystem. In: 2015 IEEE/ACM 37th IEEE International Conference on Software Engineering. vol. 1, pp. 598–608 (2015). https://doi.org/10.1109/ICSE.2015.76
16. Sanches, A., Cardoso, J.M., Delbem, A.C.: Identifying merge-beneficial software kernels for hardware implementation. In: International Conference on Reconfigurable Computing and FPGAs, pp. 74–79 (2011). https://doi.org/10.1109/ReConFig.2011.51
17. Shieh, S.W., et al.: Reliability engineering in a time of rapidly converging technologies. IEEE Trans. Reliab. **73**(1), 73–82 (2024). https://doi.org/10.1109/TR.2024.3355905
18. Silva, R., Souza, S.S., Souza, P.L.: Using a reference architecture to support the development of a testing tool for concurrent software. In: International Conference on Information Systems and Technology Management (2013). https://doi.org/10.5748/9788599693094-10CONTECSI/PS-419

19. Vianna, A., Kamei, F.K., Gama, K., Zimmerle, C., Neto, J.A.: A grey literature review on data stream processing applications testing. J. Syst. Softw. **203**, 111744 (2023). https://doi.org/10.1016/j.jss.2023.111744, https://www.sciencedirect.com/science/article/pii/S0164121223001395
20. Voas, J., Miller, K.: Software testability: the new verification. IEEE Softw. **12**(3), 17–28 (1995). https://doi.org/10.1109/52.382180
21. Wu, C.F., Ma, S.P., Shau, A.C., Yeh, H.W.: Testing for event-driven microservices based on consumer-driven contracts and state models. In: 2022 29th Asia-Pacific Software Engineering Conference (APSEC), pp. 467–471 (2022). https://doi.org/10.1109/APSEC57359.2022.00064
22. Zhang, Y., Zhu, H.: Ontology for service oriented testing of web services. In: 2008 IEEE International Symposium on Service-Oriented System Engineering, pp. 129–134 (2008). https://doi.org/10.1109/SOSE.2008.35
23. Zhu, H.: A framework for service-oriented testing of web services. In: 30th International Computer Software and Applications Conference. vol. 2, pp. 145–150 (2006). https://doi.org/10.1109/COMPSAC.2006.95

Predictive Analysis with Technical Indicators and Features Selection for Futures Contracts Trading

Andrey V. S. Souza[1]([⊠])(iD), Richard F. Pinto[1](iD), Bruno L. Dalmazo[1](iD),
Eduardo N. Borges[1](iD), Giancarlo Lucca[2](iD), Viviane L. D. de Mattos[1](iD),
and Rafael A. Berri[1](iD)

[1] Federal University of Rio Grande (FURG), Rio Grande, Brazil
{andreyvinicius,richard_pinto,dalmazo,eduardoborges,vivianemattos,
rafaelberri}@furg.br
[2] Catholic University of Pelotas (UCPel), Pelotas, Brazil
giancarlo.lucca@ucpel.edu.br

Abstract. This study investigates the impact of feature selection on the predictive performance of machine learning models in the Brazilian derivatives market. Precisely, by integrating technical analysis indicators, such as Simple and Exponential Moving Averages and Standard Deviation, derived from intraday price data of mini-Bovespa index futures traded on the Brazilian Stock Exchange, we construct a robust dataset of historical prices from the BovDBV2 database. We employ several feature selection methods to reduce dimensionality, minimize overfitting, and improve model generalization. A Random Forest classifier, evaluated using a 9-fold stratified cross-validation scheme, is employed to compare the performance of models trained on the full feature set versus those trained on reduced subsets. Our findings demonstrate that feature reduction significantly improves accuracy on test data while reducing computational costs. These results provide valuable insights for investors and traders, highlighting the importance of feature selection in developing predictive models capable of adapting to dynamic derivatives market conditions.

Keywords: Machine Learning · Derivatives market · Technical Analysis · Feature Selection

1 Introduction

The financial market relies on various types of analysis, forecasts, and models to assist in business decision-making around the world [3], playing a crucial role in the generation and interpretation of large volumes of data. Among the most traded assets in this environment are futures contracts, which are standardized financial agreements between two parties to buy or sell an underlying asset at a predetermined price on a specified future date [10].

O. Gervasi et al. (Eds.): ICCSA 2025, LNCS 15649, pp. 349–367, 2025.
https://doi.org/10.1007/978-3-031-96997-3_22

Stock exchanges are essential financial institutions for the trading of stocks, bonds, and other financial assets [8]. Globally, there are a variety of exchanges such as the New York Stock Exchange[1] NASDAQ[2] and the London Stock Exchange[3] which operate under distinct regulatory frameworks and serve different market segments [7]. In Brazil, the Brazilian Stock Exchange (B3)[4] plays a central role in the financial market, enabling companies to raise funds through the issuance and sale of stocks, bonds, and futures contracts, providing a structured and regulated environment. In this context, investors trade various financial instruments on B3, such as index contracts (for example, the Mini Index (WIN), based on the Ibovespa) and currency contracts (DOL and WDO, based on the dollar exchange rate), among others, promoting liquidity and facilitating the flow of capital between companies and investors.

Due to the economic importance of financial assets, particularly in the equity and derivatives markets [5], researchers and practitioners have extensively studied patterns and behaviors to improve market forecasting. Traditionally, technical analysis is one of the main approaches for market analysis, and it uses charts and historical price data to identify trends and potential reversals [6]. In recent years, the field of stock market forecasting has emerged at the intersection of finance and computing [14]. Machine Learning (ML), a subfield of artificial intelligence that develops algorithms capable of learning from data without explicit programming [16], has become central to predicting market behavior.

A critical step in building robust machine learning models is feature selection. This process involves identifying and retaining only the most relevant attributes to increase prediction accuracy while reducing computational complexity and training time. Since not all features contribute equally to predictive performance, techniques such as filtering, encapsulation, or embedding methods [24] are essential to minimize overfitting and improve model generalization.

The objective of this paper is to evaluate the effectiveness of feature selection methods in financial time series in order to improve the performance of predictive models. To achieve this, the study integrates technical analysis with advanced machine learning techniques, optimizing the accuracy and adaptability of the model to market dynamics.

This paper is organized as follows: Sect. 2 addresses Feature Selection Techniques and Technical Analysis Indicators; in Sect. 3, a literature review summarizes the main previous studies; Sect. 4 details the Methodology of this study, while Sect. 5 presents the findings of the study and, finally, Sect. 6 presents the conclusions and future work for the research.

---

[1] Access the NYSE website at www.nyse.com.
[2] Access the NASDAQ website at www.nasdaq.com.
[3] Access the LSEG website at www.londonstockexchange.com.
[4] Access the B3 website at www.b3.com.br.

2 Theoretical Concepts

In this section, we aim to contextualize our research by presenting the technical analysis indicators that are used as input to the models, followed by an exploration of the feature selection techniques employed.

2.1 Technical Analysis Indicators

Technical analysis indicators are quantitative tools derived from historical asset data that are used to predict future market movements. These indicators help traders identify trends, momentum, and potential reversal points, offering a systematic approach to interpreting market fluctuations.

Moving Average. The moving average is a fundamental statistical technique used to smooth the volatility inherent in time series data [9]. Different forms of Moving Averages, such as the Simple Moving Average (SMA) and the Exponential Moving Average (EMA), provide varying degrees of sensitivity to recent price changes. The use of moving averages in technical analysis helps traders to filter out the 'noise' in market data, making it easier to identify support and resistance levels and to confirm trend directions.

Standard Deviation. Standard deviation is a statistical metric that quantifies price volatility by measuring how much an asset's price deviates from its mean over a specific period. In technical analysis, it is calculated by first determining the moving average (mean) of closing prices and then calculating the squared differences between each price and that average. The average of these squared differences produces the variance, and the square root of the variance produces the standard deviation.

2.2 Feature Selection

Feature selection is the process of identifying and retaining the most relevant variables from a dataset to optimize machine learning models. By strategically eliminating redundant or uninformative features, this technique increases model accuracy, reduces training time, and improves interpretability.

Relief Method. The Relief method evaluates feature importance by comparing local differences between instances to determine how well an attribute distinguishes between different outcomes. This approach is valuable in both feature selection and financial time series analysis, where it can highlight subtle, context-dependent patterns without heavy computational demands.

Gain Ratio. Gain Ratio extends Information Gain by normalizing it with the intrinsic information of a feature, thereby reducing the bias toward attributes with many distinct values. This normalization makes it a practical choice for feature selection and financial data analysis where balanced split decisions are crucial [11].

Pearson Correlation. The Pearson Correlation Coefficient quantifies the linear relationship between two variables and is commonly used in feature selection to identify redundant attributes. Highly correlated features can be removed to reduce multicollinearity and improve model generalization.

Principal Component Analysis (PCA). PCA reduces dimensionality by projecting the data onto a set of uncorrelated principal components that capture the largest variance. This is achieved through an eigenvalue decomposition of the covariance matrix. PCA is particularly effective in financial time series for noise reduction and redundancy elimination.

Information Gain. Information Gain measures how much knowledge of an attribute reduces the uncertainty of a target variable [2]. This method is mainly used to classify attributes based on their ability to separate classes, favoring those that contribute most to predictive performance.

3   Related Work

The financial market generates vast volumes of data, which analysts and researchers increasingly analyze using advanced computational techniques [4]. Recent advancements in artificial intelligence, particularly Machine Learning (ML) and Deep Learning (DL), have drawn significant attention from investors seeking to predict asset prices and optimize trading strategies.

An important component of these models is the integration of technical analysis indicators as input features [18]. Moving Averages (MA) and Bollinger Bands (derived from standard deviation) are commonly used to encode trends and volatility. [17] demonstrated that combining MA crossover signals with Long Short Term Memory (LSTM) architectures reduced forecast errors by 22% in currency futures. Meanwhile, [25] highlighted the role of volatility indicators in improving risk-adjusted returns for stock index futures. These works emphasize that feature engineering, based on domain-specific knowledge, improves model interpretability and performance.

Feature selection plays a key role in optimizing these models; search techniques such as mutual information and Recursive Feature Elimination (RFE) have shown that selective subsets of features reduce overfitting in stock price prediction tasks. Li2017 [13] argued that feature selection is indispensable for balancing model complexity and generalizability, especially in non-stationary markets.

The research by [15] highlights a fundamental challenge: unlike static datasets, financial data exhibits rapid fluctuations and non-linear dynamics, which introduce noise and obscure genuine patterns. They emphasize that feature selection techniques such as PCA are essential to isolate informative indicators (e.g., momentum or volume trends) while filtering out redundant variables. Traditional predictive models often struggle under these conditions, as the inherent non-linearity of price movements can lead to problems such as overfitting and reduced generalization performance, as pointed out in the study by [19], which highlights that these models produce a memorization of the dataset rather than a prediction.

As highlighted in the reviewed literature, feature selection plays a critical role in improving the robustness and generalizability of predictive models in financial contexts. Despite its importance, many studies still apply selection techniques without comparative validation and in a generic manner. That said, this study seeks to fill three main gaps: (1) improve interpretability in models with multiple technical indicators; (2) leverage high-frequency intraday data more effectively; and (3) conduct a systematic comparative analysis of multiple feature selection methods under consistent experimental conditions. With this, this research aims to provide more reliable and efficient strategies for financial market forecasting.

4   Methodology

This chapter presents the methodology adopted in this study. The first Sect. 4.1 discusses what data will be used and where it will be obtained from. Section 4.2 presents information about the labels generated to train the model used to perform feature selection. While Sect. 4.3 will present how the features were generated. Finally, Sect. 4.4 presents the techniques used in this study.

Figure 1 shows an overview of how our methodology is organized. It separates each section by different colors and presents what will be covered in the section.

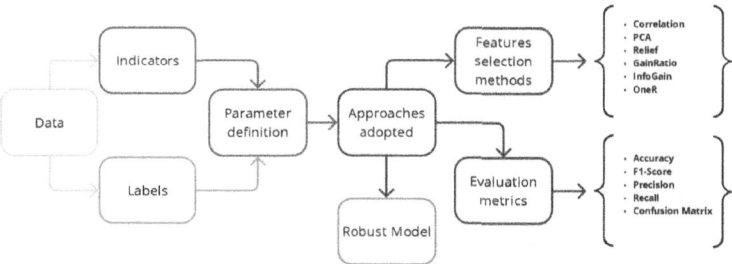

Fig. 1. Overview methodology.

4.1   Data

The data utilized in this study were obtained from the BovDbV2 [23] database, an updated version of the former BovDb [8]. The primary goal of this dataset is to provide publicly available, pre-processed data from the Brazilian Stock Exchange (B3) for research purposes. Unlike its predecessor, BovDbV2 offers a more comprehensive collection of data by including daily pricing information along with intraday trading details.

The intraday data capture asset price fluctuations at regular time intervals during standard trading hours, enabling a more granular analysis of short-term price behavior (i.e., within the same day). For the purposes of this study, we focus on four main tables within the dataset. Figure 2 illustrates the relationships among these tables.

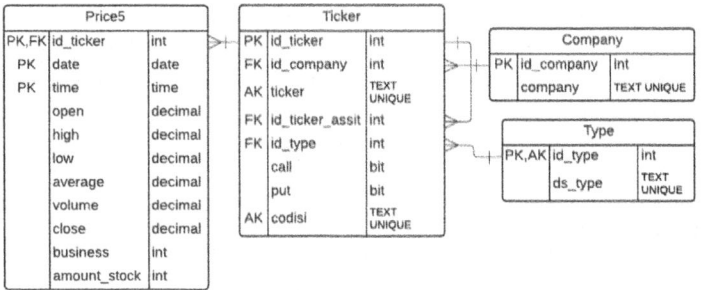

Fig. 2. Reduced Relational Model of the BovDBV2 Dataset.

The main tables are described as follows:

- **Company**: Stores information related to companies;
- **Ticker**: Contains data for individual securities;
- **Price5**: Records intraday trading data, including detailed price and volume information captured in 5-minute intervals throughout the trading day;
- **Type**: Classifies tickers into various categories, such as stocks, BDRs, financial instruments, and options.

This article specifically analyzes futures contract data extracted from the intraday table *Price5*. It focuses on different WiN tickers, which represent mini futures contracts based on the Ibovespa index. These contracts are popular among investors due to their lower cost and high liquidity, making them one of the most frequently traded instruments each month and providing a robust basis for examining short-term market dynamics.

4.2   Label Generation

In this study, the feature selection is oriented toward a classification problem, which requires the creation of labels to validate the selection technique. The labels used are *uptrend* and *downtrend*. These labels are generated based on the identification of significant tops and bottoms within the intraday 5-minute time series data for each futures contract.

Tops and bottoms, also known as peaks and troughs, are fundamental concepts in technical analysis [21]. A top (or peak) is defined as a local maximum in a price series, an instance where the price reaches a high point before reversing direction. On the other hand, a bottom (or trough) is a local minimum where the price reaches a low before initiating an upward movement. These pivot points are crucial for recognizing trend reversal points [1] and understanding market dynamics [20].

The label generation process involves the following steps:

1. **Pivot Point Identification:** For each 5-minute time series, an algorithm is applied to detect local maxima (tops) and minima (bottoms). This detection is implemented using criteria such as comparing each data point with its neighboring values to determine whether it qualifies as a significant peak or trough;

2. **Label Assignment:** Once pivot points are identified, labels are assigned based on the most recent significant pivot. If the last major pivot is a bottom, followed by a sustained price increase, the time series is labeled as an *uptrend*. Conversely, if the last major pivot is a top, followed by a consistent decline in price, the label is set as a *downtrend*.

4.3   Parameter Definition

In our methodology, we improve the predictive performance of our model by deriving additional features from existing technical indicators. This process has been divided into three main approaches:

1. **Generation of Technical Analysis Indicators:** We computed primary indicators, Simple Moving Average (SMA), Exponential Moving Average (EMA) and Standard Deviation over various time windows. These indicators capture key aspects of market trends and volatility, forming the foundational data for further feature creation [9];

2. **Moving Average Differences:** To capture changes in trend dynamics, we calculated the differences between moving averages computed over different time periods. For example, the difference between the 7-period SMA and the 3-period SMA is given by

$$\text{SMA7-3} = SMA_7 - SMA_3 \tag{1}$$

which provides insights into short- and medium-term momentum shifts;

3. **Feature Normalization:** Normalization scales features to a common range (typically $[0, 1]$) to improve model adaptability. All indicators were normalized (as well as open and close prices) by subtracting the feature value from "Low" divided by "High - Low", where "High" and "Low" are respectively the highest and lowest values of each 5-minute interval.

Using these methods, new features were generated for each indicator. The moving averages (SMA and EMA) generated 16 features, 8 in the windows used and 8 normalized. The standard deviation generated 16 features, 8 in the windows used with their respective values and 8 normalized. The difference between the moving averages generated 24 new features, 12 original and 12 normalized, totaling 56 features created from technical analysis indicators.

4.4   Approaches Adopted

This study focuses on feature selection to improve the predictive performance of futures market models for day trading applications and movements. Our methodology is based on the acquisition of a preprocessed dataset containing intraday data in 5-minute intervals contained in the Price5 table of the BovDBV2 database. The detailed price movements of each trading session are meticulously recorded, with columns such as `open`, `high`, `low`, `average`, `close`, `bid`, `ask`, `trade`, and `number of shares`.

For model training and evaluation, we adopted the Random Forest (RF) classifier, a robust ensemble learning technique that builds multiple decision trees and aggregates their predictions to achieve higher accuracy and control overfitting. Each tree is trained on a random subset of data and features, which makes the model particularly effective when dealing with high-dimensional datasets [12]. We selected this model due to its proven robustness, low computational complexity, and suitability for structured and tabular data, as emphasized by [22]. Furthermore, RF is considered a white-box model, allowing a straightforward interpretation of feature importance, a key aspect of this study given our focus on feature selection.

To ensure reliable performance estimates, we employed k-fold Cross-Validation. In each epoch of feature elimination, the dataset is randomly partitioned into k nearly equal folds. The Random Forest classifier is then trained on $k - 1$ folds and validated on the remaining fold. This process is repeated k times, with a different fold used for validation each time. The final accuracy is computed as the average accuracy over all folds. After cross-validation, the model is retrained on the entire training dataset to obtain the classifier that will be deployed in practice. After cross-validation, the model is retrained using the entire training dataset to obtain the classifier for deployment. Finally, an ensemble voting method is applied using the full test set to enhance prediction reliability.

5   Results

This chapter presents the results and corresponding discussions of our study, organized into 2 (two) subsections. The structure is organized as follows: the 5.1 section discusses how the loaded data from the BovDBV2 dataset was preprocessed, treated, and organized. The comparison of the results when training the model on the full feature set versus when trained using various feature selection methods is presented in the 5.2 section, with analyses of the models and the most relevant features.

5.1   Data Preprocessing

Using the BovDbV2 database, we constructed another dataset containing the most relevant futures contracts for this study, along with their optimal intra-day periods. From this dataset, we calculated the technical analysis indicators described in Subsect. 4.3. These indicators were then normalized to a range between 0 and 1, resulting in the creation of 56 new features along with the price data, forming a total of 66 features. Finally, the corresponding labels were produced using the approach detailed in Subsect. 4.2.

The selected futures contracts were WING24 and WINJ24 (Jan-Feb 2024), WINJ24 and WINM24 (Mar-Apr 2024), and WINM24 and WINQ24 (May-Jun 2024), chosen based on their high trading volumes and extensive trading activity, totaling approximately 38 to 40 active trading days per period. The data was subsequently partitioned into 3 (three) months for training and 3 (three) for testing, and these subsets were used in the subsequent analysis in the model.

5.2   Performance Evaluation: Full Feature Set vs. Feature Selection

In this section, we provide a comparative analysis of the model performance when trained with the full feature set (Case 1) versus various feature selection methods (Case 2). This approach aims to highlight how feature selection is applied to reduce dimensionality and filter noise, with the goal of improving both predictive performance and interpretability. For all experiments, we employed the Random Forest classifier, a robust ensemble model that aggregates multiple decision trees to achieve reliable accuracy and control overfitting. The model used 100 estimators and a fixed random state (42) to ensure reproducibility.

To validate the results, we adopted a 9-fold stratified cross-validation approach. Given the large number of labeled instances, 9 folds, as opposed to the more common 5 or 10, offered a balance between variance reduction and computational cost. The stratification ensured that class distributions remained consistent across folds, providing robust evaluation metrics. Furthermore, choosing an odd number of folds minimizes the potential for ties between classes during ensemble voting on the test data.

Case 1: Full Feature Set - Model Interpretation. For this case, the model was trained using the complete set of features without applying any feature selection. The data was partitioned into training and testing sets as described in Subsect. 5.1, and we employed stratified 9-fold Cross-Validation to ensure that each fold maintained representative class distributions. This stratification is crucial to reduce the variance in performance metrics such as accuracy and F1-score.

The Cross-Validation process produced an average accuracy of 0.7159 and a standard deviation of 0.0096. However, when evaluated on the test set, the final accuracy dropped to 0.5883. The classification report (Table 1) for the model is as follows:

Table 1. Classification report for training with all features

Class	Precision	Recall	F1-score	Support
Downtrend	0.62	0.35	0.45	3306
Uptrend	0.57	0.80	0.67	3592
Accuracy	–	–	0.59	6898
Macro avg	0.60	0.58	0.56	6898
Weighted avg	0.60	0.59	0.57	6898

The evaluation report indicates that the model's performance varies across classes. For the downtrend class, a precision of 0.62 shows that when the model predicts a downtrend, it is correct 62% of the time; however, a recall of 0.35 reveals that many true downtrend cases are missed, resulting in a lower F1 score of 0.45. In contrast, the uptrend class has a high recall of 0.80, meaning that the model successfully identifies most uptrend cases, although its precision of 0.57 suggests the presence of false positives, leading to an F1 score of 0.67. Table 2 reports the results of the confusion matrix.

Table 2. Confusion matrix for Full data training

	Predicted Downtrend	Predicted Uptrend
Real Downtrend	1169	2137
Real Uptrend	703	2889

The confusion matrix (Table 2) shows that the model has difficulty distinguishing "downtrend" from "uptrend." Specifically, 2,137 downtrend cases were misclassified as uptrends, while 1,169 true downtrends were missed, indicating lower sensitivity for this class. Similarly, the model misclassified 703 true uptrends as downtrends and failed to detect 2,889 cases of uptrends. These misclassifications align with the recall metrics, highlighting a bias toward predicting uptrends and potential challenges in detecting trend reversals.

Figure 3 is a bar chart representing the mean accuracy of stratified cross-validation and its corresponding result on the test set. To illustrate the variability of the results, each bar of the mean accuracy of stratified cross-validation includes standard deviation indicators, showing three deviations above and below the mean, ensuring that 99.7% of the results fall within this range.

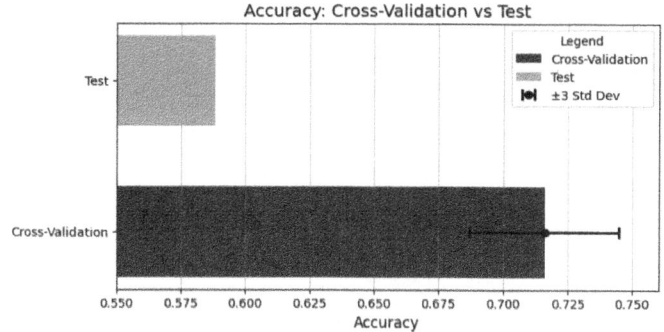

Fig. 3. Comparison between cross validation and test accuracy.

As we can see, there is a significant difference between the cross-validation accuracy and the test accuracy. The graph suggests that the model memorizes the training data and has difficulty generalizing to new data, indicating overfitting. The standard error in the cross-validation shows that the accuracy varied across different splits of the data, which may indicate that the model is learning specific quirks of the training data rather than general patterns.

Case 2: Feature Selection - Methods. In this step, we apply each feature selection method (shown in Sect. 3) to the training data. Each method returns a ranking of the features according to their estimated importance for the predictive task. The resulting ranking is then saved and used to train the Random Forest model with the same hyperparameters employed in the Full Feature Set experiment, using a 9-fold stratified cross-validation. An expected result is the identification of a reduced set of features that achieves an average accuracy comparable to that obtained with the model trained with all features, thus revealing the most significant indicators for the technical analysis of the derivatives market.

The set of Figs. 4 represents the model performance on training data using cross-validation. For each training iteration, a feature selection method is applied and evaluated by returning the average result of 9-fold cross-validation. The plots show the model performance as features are progressively removed. The Green Dot (GD) represents the local maximum, where accuracy reaches its highest value with the optimal number of k features, while the Red Dot (RD) marks the point where the model's average accuracy on the training data started to decline.

Once the initial model is trained using the ranked set of features, we implement an iterative elimination process. In each iteration, features are removed in inverse order of importance, as indicated by the selection methods. This process is performed to determine the impact of each subset of features on the accuracy of the model.

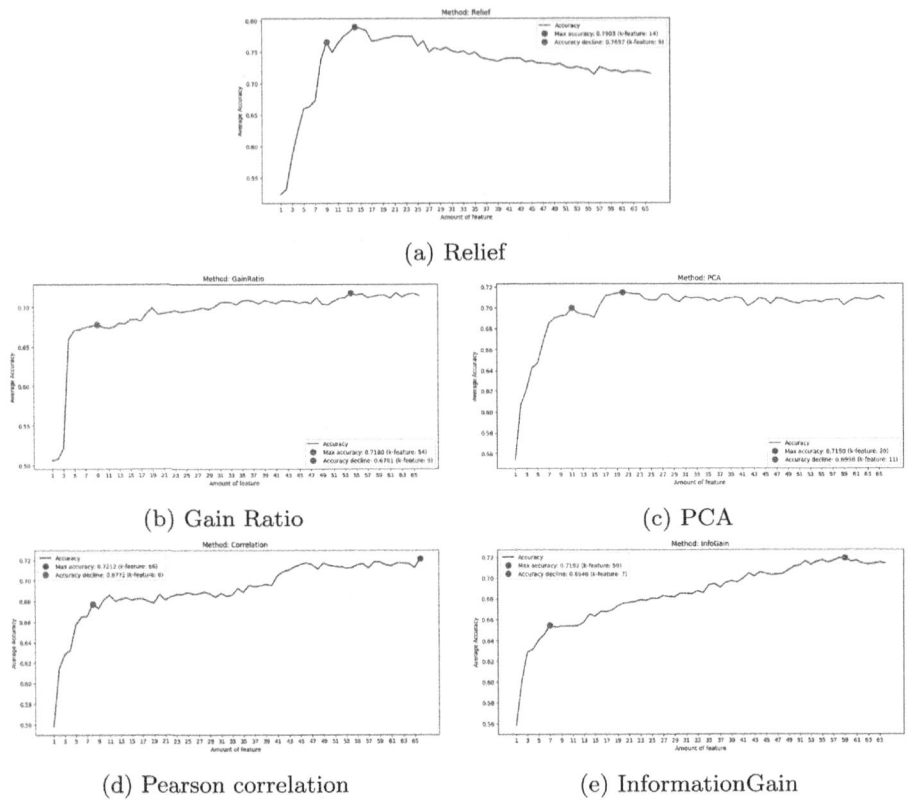

(a) Relief

(b) Gain Ratio

(c) PCA

(d) Pearson correlation

(e) InformationGain

Fig. 4. Feature removal experiments.

Analysis of the Relief method in Fig. 4a shows that while it achieved an impressive average accuracy of 0.7903 in cross-validation with 14 features, demonstrating strong generalization in training, this did not translate as effectively to the test set, which had a final accuracy of 0.5657. In a more restricted setting with 9 features (red dot), validation accuracy dropped to 0.7657 and test accuracy reached 0.5626, indicating that excessive feature reduction can lead to the loss of essential predictive information.

For the next model, we will use the Gain Ratio feature ranking, following the same approach used for the Relief method. In this case, we obtained completely different results, as shown in the graph in Fig. 4b.

At this stage, the GD point indicates that, with 54 features, the cross-validation resulted in an accuracy of 0.7180. This reference point was then used to perform a stratified cross-validation. After training with the full data set, the model obtained an accuracy of 0.5752, which did not adapt as well to the test data. In contrast, the same methodology was applied to the RD point, which corresponds to the selection of 9 features. In this case, the initial validation presented an accuracy of 0.6781. When this model was evaluated with the test set, the results demonstrated consistent performance, evidencing a balance between the classes.

Systematically, the next method discussed in this section is PCA (Principal Component Analysis), a widely used technique for dimensionality reduction. In this paper, the sequence of component embedding follows the order determined by the PCA-based feature selection method, and the accuracy plots Fig. 4c reflect the results obtained through cross-validation.

In the GD configuration, when using 20 principal components, PCA achieved a maximum accuracy of 0.7150 during cross-validation. However, when evaluating the model on the test set, the final accuracy was 0.5925. In the RD configuration, when reducing the set to 11 components, an average accuracy of 0.6998 was observed in the cross-validation. However, in the test, the final accuracy dropped to 0.5800, indicating a significant worsening using even fewer features, with the model not being able to generalize well to the test data.

Figure 4d illustrates the evolution of the average precision as a function of the number of features selected by the Pearson Correlation criterion.

The highest precision (0.712) occurs with 66 features (GD), while precision starts declining at 8 features (RD), reaching 0.6772. In the test data, GD performed worse, with 0.5865 precision and class imbalance, indicating that the high feature count may have led to overfitting, limiting generalization. For RD, precision and F1-score are more balanced across classes, suggesting a more stable model. Its final accuracy of 0.6086, higher than GD's 0.5865, implies that reducing features, though slightly lowering validation performance, improves generalization on new data.

Analysis of the Information Gain (InfoGain) method, illustrated in Fig. 4e, highlights the trade-off between complexity and generalization. On the green dot (GD) with 59 features, the model achieved an average cross-validation accuracy of 0.72, but struggled on the test set, dropping to 0.5780. Although it performed reasonably well (0.61 for downtrend, 0.57 for uptrend), its low recall (0.33) for downtrend suggests overfitting, limiting generalization. In contrast, the red dot, with only 7 features, had lower cross-validation accuracy (0.6546) but improved test accuracy (0.6163). This configuration better balanced precision and recall, with F1 scores around 0.60, indicating a more robust model with reduced overfitting. These results emphasize the importance of finding the right balance between feature quantity and model generalization.

To further our investigation and enrich this study in order to develop an optimal model with minimal overfitting, we trained four additional models using distinct feature selection techniques with different classifications, showing their training for the training data contained in Fig. 5, which includes the performance with all other methods.

In Fig. 5, we can see a comparison of how all feature selection methods in Ensemble work for the 9-fold cross-validation measure. It is guaranteed that there is a pattern in the accuracy variation throughout the removal of features. Initially, the accuracy increases to a certain point, showing that a smaller number of features increases the accuracy of the models. Then the accuracy starts

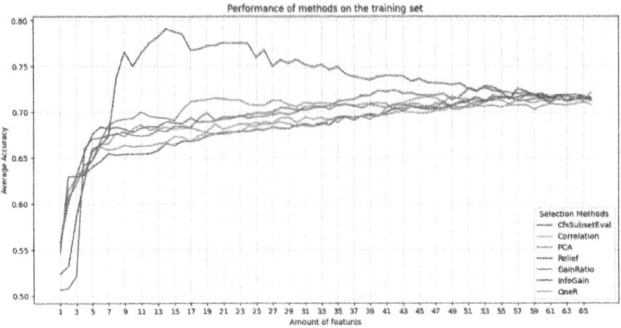

Fig. 5. Training performance with all methods.

to decrease. Some methods are able to combine a lot of features that maintain accuracy for a long period of epochs, without losing it significantly. Other methods, such as Relief, allow accuracy to drop significantly after its maximum peak, while others kill consistency as new features are removed.

To further investigate the feature selection methods, we created a comparative bar chart (Fig. 6) that evaluates the performance of the methods at two critical points in the accuracy curve. These points were defined based on detailed analysis: the first, represented by green bars, corresponds to the optimality point (GD) of each method, while the second, shown in red bars, indicates the point at which accuracy begins to decline (RD).

Subsequently, the generated models were evaluated on a different test data set in order to measure their performance outside the validation environment. The final chart displays, for each feature selection technique, four bars: two correspond to the average accuracy obtained in the stratified cross-validation for the GD point and its respective performance on the test set, and the other two show the same indicators for the RD point. The orange bars reflect performance at the point of optimality, while the green bars highlight the moments when accuracy begins to decline. To highlight the variability in results, each validation average bar has standard deviation markers—indicating two deviations above and below the mean—ensuring that 99.7% of the results fall within this range. This graphical structure provides a clear and objective view of each method's performance at different stages of attribute reduction, also highlighting the consistency of each approach in maintaining good predictive performance under varying conditions.

Figure 6a shows the performance of each feature selection method at the point of highest accuracy (GD). At this stage, it can be seen that the green bars correspond to the average accuracy obtained through stratified cross-validation for the point where accuracy is maximum on the training data, while the orange bars indicate the result of these same models when evaluated on a separate test set. In this way, it is possible to compare how well each method adapts to the training data and how this adjustment remains or changes when exposed to data not used in the training stage. It can be seen that some methods perform

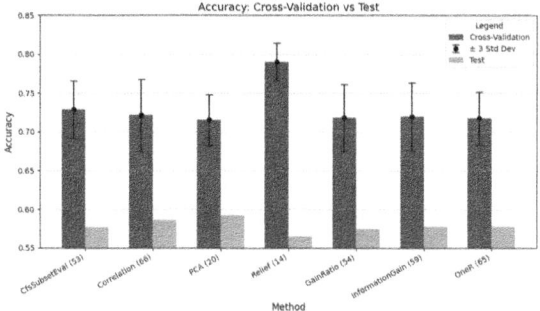

(a) Green dot accuracy in training and testing data

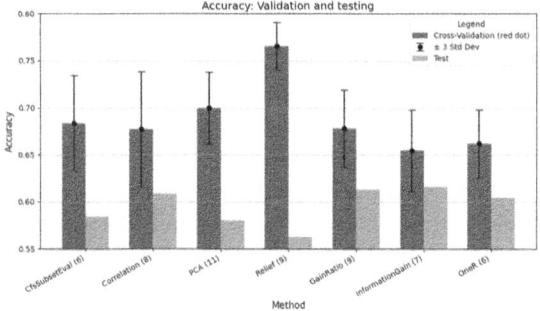

(b) Red dot accuracy in training and testing data

Fig. 6. Set of Figures of model performance. (Color figure online)

very well for training, but for unseen data (tests) the accuracy decreases (as for example in the Relief method), demonstrating low generalization of the model.

Figure 6b, on the other hand, shows the performance of the same feature selection techniques at a point where accuracy begins to decline (RD). The red bars indicate the average accuracy in cross-validation, and the orange bars again show the performance on the test set. This scenario illustrates how each method reacts to the use of a reduced number of features, showing whether the model maintains good generalization capacity or whether there is a sharp drop in performance outside the validation environment. The direct comparison between Figs. 6a and 6b allows us to identify which methods exhibit greater stability as features are removed, in addition to highlighting at what point each approach suffers the most significant loss of accuracy.

Among the methods evaluated, Information Gain stood out with the best test accuracy. Using seven features, the model achieved 61.63%, balancing precision and recall while minimizing the risk of overfitting. This highlights the importance of selecting a concise yet informative feature set to improve generalization.

The complexity of financial markets makes classification even more challenging, as it involves detecting subtle price changes. The dataset was structured to predict two distinct categories of price movements, which in itself makes the

Table 3. Ranking of features using Information Gain with the best k features.

Rank	Feature
1	EMA_5-3
2	EMA_5-3_normalized
3	EMA_7-3
4	EMA_7-3_normalized
5	SMA_9_normalized
6	EMA_9-3
7	EMA_7_normalized

task difficult. Furthermore, external factors directly influence financial trends, making the differentiation between periods of stability, small rallies or declines even more complex. The improved feature selection provided by Information Gain reinforces the relevance of technical indicators used in financial analysis, as demonstrated in Table 3. The analysis of the top 7 features shows that Exponential Moving Averages (EMAs) indicators, especially their short-term variations, are the most relevant for intraday trend prediction, reaffirming the importance of selecting an informative subset to reduce complexity and overfitting.

To understand the impact of this work and the proposed methods in relation to the literature, we performed a direct comparison with previous studies that also employed feature selection techniques to predict prices in the financial market.

Table 4 summarizes the main aspects of each study, including the dataset used, the model applied, the number of selection methods (FS - Feature Selection) and the accuracy achieved in the prediction tasks.

Table 4. Comparative summary of related studies.

Study	Dataset	Model	FS	Acc.
Peng [18]	SSE	RNN	3-Methods	50.0%
Nelson [17]	-	LSTM	1-Method	55,9%
Lu [15]	TSE	SVR	2-Method	57.5%
This study	B3	Radom Forest	7-Methods	**61.63%**

Comparative analysis with related studies allows us to observe differences in approaches that used complex computational models, which do not guarantee better performance if they are not accompanied by rigorous data processing and effective selection of the attributes used. It is therefore concluded that feature selection is not just a complementary step, but rather a strategic element in the construction of more interpretable, generalizable and efficient robust models for the financial market.

6   Conclusion

In this work, different feature selection techniques were explored to improve the performance of classification models applied to the derivatives market. We used data extracted from BovDBV2, which contains information on futures contracts traded on B3, and applied technical analysis indicators (such as moving averages and standard deviation) to generate the set of attributes. The results obtained by the Feature Selection techniques were ordered according to the importance attributed to each method and subsequently used to build classification models with the Random Forest algorithm, using cross-validation to ensure the robustness of the results.

The adopted approach demonstrated that, by employing feature selection, it is possible to improve the generalization capacity of the model compared to training with the full set of attributes, reducing noise and eliminating redundant variables. However, as feature reduction intensifies, a notable drop in model performance is observed, a fact that can be attributed to the removal of variables that contain essential information for the correct discrimination of classes. Therefore, it is essential to carefully balance the number of attributes to preserve the most relevant indicators - among which those identified by the Information Gain method stand out, which obtained the best accuracy of 61.63% with 7 characteristics for the Red Dot (RD) test data - demonstrating that these attributes support the robustness of the model. The article sought to fill the main gaps pointed out in the literature review, generating machine learning models that, even with certain limitations, when adopting good practices, significantly improve performance, thus providing strategies that can be adopted in the area of Stock Market Prediction.

Future work may explore the application of advanced attribute selection techniques, the integration of new indicators, as well as the evaluation of other classification algorithms, with the aim of further improving the accuracy and predictive capacity of the models in the context of the financial market.

Acknowledgments. The authors would like to thank FAPERGS (24/2551-0001396-2, 23/2551-0000773-8), CNPq (305805/2021-5) and FAPERGS/CNPq (23/2551-0000-126-8).

References

1. Adegboye, A., Kampouridis, M., Otero, F.: Improving trend reversal estimation in forex markets under a directional changes paradigm with classification algorithms. Int. J. Intell. Syst. **36**(12), 7609–7640 (2021)
2. Azhagusundari, B., Thanamani, A.S., et al.: Feature selection based on information gain. Int. J. Innovative Technol. Exploring Eng. (IJITEE) **2**(2), 18–21 (2013)
3. Bodie, Z., Kane, A., Marcus, A.: Fundamentos de investimentos. AMGH Editora (2014)

4. Cavalcante, R.C., Brasileiro, R.C., Souza, V.L., Nobrega, J.P., Oliveira, A.L.: Computational intelligence and financial markets: a survey and future directions. Expert Syst. Appl. **55**, 194–211 (2016)
5. Chiang, I., Hughen, W.K., Sagi, J.S.: Estimating oil risk factors using information from equity and derivatives markets. J. Financ. **70**(2), 769–804 (2015)
6. Christensen, H.B., Nikolaev, V.V.: Does fair value accounting for non-financial assets pass the market test? Rev. Acc. Stud. **18**, 734–775 (2013)
7. Clayton, M.J., Jorgensen, B.N., Kavajecz, K.A.: On the presence and market-structure of exchanges around the world. J. Financ. Markets **9**(1), 27–48 (2006)
8. Corrêa Cardoso, F., et al.: BovDB: a data set of stock prices of all companies in B3 from 1995 to 2020. J. Inf. Data Manag. **13**(1) (2022). https://doi.org/10.5753/jidm.2022.2345
9. Hoque, M.E., Billah, M., Kapar, B., Naeem, M.A.: Quantifying the volatility spillover dynamics between financial stress and us financial sectors: evidence from QVAR connectedness. Int. Rev. Financ. Anal. **95**, 103434 (2024)
10. Hull, J.V., Dokovna, L.B., Jacokes, Z.J., Torgerson, C.M., Irimia, A., Van Horn, J.D.: Resting-state functional connectivity in autism spectrum disorders: a review. Front. Psych. **7**, 205 (2017)
11. Karegowda, A.G., Manjunath, A., Jayaram, M.: Comparative study of attribute selection using gain ratio and correlation based feature selection. Int. J. Inf. Technol. Knowl. Manag. **2**(2), 271–277 (2010)
12. Kumar, M., Thenmozhi, M.: Forecasting stock index movement: a comparison of support vector machines and random forest. In: Indian Institute of Capital Markets 9th Capital Markets Conference Paper (2006)
13. Li, J., et al.: Feature selection: a data perspective. ACM Comput. Surv. (CSUR) **50**(6), 1–45 (2017)
14. Long, J., Chen, Z., He, W., Wu, T., Ren, J.: An integrated framework of deep learning and knowledge graph for prediction of stock price trend: an application in Chinese stock exchange market. Appl. Soft Comput. **91**, 106205 (2020)
15. Lu, C.J., Lee, T.S., Chiu, C.C.: Financial time series forecasting using independent component analysis and support vector regression. Decis. Support Syst. **47**(2), 115–125 (2009)
16. Mitchell, J.C., Mitchell, M., Stern, U.: Automated analysis of cryptographic protocols using MUR/SPL PHI. In: Proceedings of 1997 IEEE Symposium on Security and Privacy (Cat. No. 97CB36097), pp. 141–151. IEEE (1997)
17. Nelson, D.M., Pereira, A.C., De Oliveira, R.A.: Stock market's price movement prediction with LSTM neural networks. In: 2017 International joint conference on neural networks (IJCNN), pp. 1419–1426. IEEE (2017)
18. Peng, Y., Albuquerque, P., Kimura, H., Saavedra, C.: Feature selection and deep neural networks for stock price direction forecasting using technical analysis indicators. Mach. Learn. Appl. **5**, 100060 (2021)
19. Power, A., Burda, Y., Edwards, H., Babuschkin, I., Misra, V.: Grokking: Generalization beyond overfitting on small algorithmic datasets. arXiv preprint arXiv:2201.02177 (2022)
20. Pring, M.J.: Study guide for technical analysis explained, vol. 5. McGraw-Hill New York (2002)
21. Sabatier, P.A.: Top-down and bottom-up approaches to implementation research: a critical analysis and suggested synthesis. J. Publ. Policy **6**(1), 21–48 (1986)
22. Soto-Osorio, D., Sidorov, G., Chanona-Hernández, L., López-Ramírez, B.C.: Identification of scientific texts generated by large language models using machine learning. Computers **13**(12) (2024). https://doi.org/10.3390/computers13120346

23. Souza, A.S., Lucca, G., Borges, E.N., Cardoso, F.C., Dalmazo, B.L., Berri, R.: Dataset for Intraday Analysis of B3 stock prices (2024). https://doi.org/10.7910/DVN/TMB4IG
24. Venkatesh, B., Anuradha, J.: A review of feature selection and its methods. Cybern. Inf. Technol **19**(1), 3–26 (2019)
25. Wang, J., Ma, F., Bouri, E., Zhong, J.: Volatility of clean energy and natural gas, uncertainty indices, and global economic conditions. Energy Econ. **108**, 105904 (2022)

Development of a Strategy for Duplication Search Based on Multiple Hierarchically Organized Approaches

Cephas A. S. Barreto(✉)🆔, Arnaldo S. B. Junior🆔, Leonardo D. G. Melo🆔,
Maycon D. R. Santos🆔, Gabriele R. Carvalho🆔, Itamir M. B. Filho🆔,
Jose G. R. Neto🆔, Ramon S. Malaquias🆔, Andre M. Gurgel🆔,
and Jean M. M. Lima🆔

Digital Metropolis Institute (IMD), Federal University of Rio Grande do Norte
(UFRN), Natal, Brazil
ascom@imd.ufrn.br
https://portal.imd.ufrn.br

Abstract. Data deduplication is essential for records in business systems, as duplicate entries can distort analyses, harm relationships, and generate unnecessary costs. As organizations increasingly rely on diverse and large-scale data sources, the challenge of identifying and consolidating duplicate records has grown, making efficient deduplication a critical factor for maintaining data quality and operational efficiency. This paper proposes a hierarchical data deduplication approach to address this industry-wide challenge. The proposed approach, referred to here as the engine, integrates specialized rules, similarity measures, and large language models (LLMs) in sequential layers to analyze data and identify duplications accurately and efficiently. By leveraging a structured combination of techniques, the approach overcomes the limitations of traditional methods, which often depend on isolated and less adaptable solutions. The engine balances performance and accuracy, handling both straightforward and complex cases of duplication. Experimental results using a customer-simulated database demonstrate that integrating these advanced techniques improves adaptability and precision compared to conventional methods. This strategy shows significant potential for large-scale data deduplication, offering a more robust solution to an industry-wide challenge.

Keywords: Data deduplication · Expert Rules · Text Similarity · Large Language Models

1 Introduction

Data deduplication eliminates duplicate records in a database. In corporate systems, customer-related data, for example, includes identification details and relationship history. In this context, identifying, processing, and eliminating duplicate records is essential for maintaining a consistent relationship between the company and its customers [31].

ⓒ The Author(s), under exclusive license to Springer Nature Switzerland AG 2025
O. Gervasi et al. (Eds.): ICCSA 2025, LNCS 15649, pp. 368–385, 2025.
https://doi.org/10.1007/978-3-031-96997-3_23

As organizations accumulate large volumes of data from different sources [21], such as sales systems, management systems, process control systems, and credit granting systems, maintaining the consistency and quality of that data becomes critical [12]. Inconsistent entries—including duplicates, fraud, typos, and legacy records—directly impact operational efficiency, regulatory compliance, and especially customer satisfaction [41]. When duplicate records occur, whether due to entries in different systems, variations in data format, or integration errors, problems arise, such as distortions in analysis [29], difficulties in managing customer relationships [14], and high costs with redundant resources [16,30].

Data deduplication is, therefore, an essential component in customer information management [8], requiring accurate and efficient processes to identify and consolidate duplicate records. However, traditional deduplication methods often use isolated approaches: rule-based methods [18,26] or machine learning techniques [2,11]. While these approaches have specific advantages, they have limitations regarding flexibility and adaptability. Rule-based methods, for example, are fast [1] and easily interpretable but may fail to identify more complex duplicates [28]. Machine learning techniques, especially large language models, offer greater flexibility in identifying duplicates but have a high computational cost [27,37].

This work presents an innovative hierarchical approach to customer data deduplication, featuring a search engine for duplicate detection. The proposal seeks to overcome the limitations of traditional deduplication systems by combining different techniques in a structured way: specialized rules, similarity measures, and large language models. The hierarchical approach allows organizing these techniques into progressive layers of complexity, optimizing the use of computational resources without compromising accuracy. Specialized rules are initially applied to capture simple duplicates quickly and efficiently; then, more sophisticated similarity metrics are used to deal with intermediate cases, while the last layer, with LLM models, is reserved for more complex cases with high semantic demands.

The experimental results demonstrate that the hierarchical combination of techniques not only improves the accuracy of the deduplication process but can also reduce the execution time, especially on large volumes of data. The proposed structure can, therefore, adapt to both simple and complex duplication scenarios, maintaining the balance between performance and accuracy. The results highlight the potential of this multi-tiered approach for comprehensive and adaptive data deduplication in large-scale enterprise environments.

The remainder of this work is organized as follows. Section 2 introduces fundamental concepts that support the development of the proposed approach. Section 3 reviews the main related works, with emphasis on techniques applied to customer data deduplication. Section 4 describes the architecture and components of the proposed search and identification engine. Section 5 details the experimental methodology. Section 4 presents and discusses the experimental results. Finally, Sect. 7 concludes the study and outlines possible directions for future research.

2   Related Concepts

This section briefly presents some of the concepts involved in building the proposed duplicate data identification engine: expert rules, textual similarity metrics, and Large Language Models (LLMs).

2.1   Expert Rules

Expert rules are structured guidelines derived from expert knowledge, used for decision-making and classification in computer systems [3,33]. They rely on patterns identified through experience and theoretical insights [5,7] and function as "if-then" statements to ensure consistency in automated processes.

Common in expert systems [15,34], these rules replace human judgment in diagnostics, classification, and recommendations. Unlike machine learning, which extracts patterns from data, expert rules are explicitly programmed [45]. In hybrid AI systems, they serve as strict rules for critical decisions, complementing learning-based approaches [39,44].

2.2   Textual Similarity Metrics

Textual similarity metrics quantify the degree of similarity between texts [25]. Editing-based metrics, such as Jaro-Winkler and Levenshtein distance [4,22,43], measure the number of operations (insertions, deletions, substitutions) needed to transform one text into another. These methods effectively identify minor spelling variations, commonly used in record matching and duplicate detection [32].

Another approach involves cosine similarity, a mathematical metric used in text comparison [36,47]. With the rise of machine learning, embedded numerical representations of text enable more precise similarity analysis by positioning semantically related words closer in a vector space [42]. Unlike character-based metrics, embeddings capture meaning-based relationships, making them particularly useful in detecting duplicate content that has been rewritten or paraphrased [19,20].

2.3   Large Language Models

LLMs are AI models trained on vast textual data to process and generate human-like text [24,35]. Using deep learning architectures like Transformers, they analyze complex linguistic structures, recognizing grammar, context, and semantics [38]. Their ability to detect nuanced textual similarities allows them to identify duplicate content, even when reworded or conceptually altered.

While highly flexible compared to expert rules and similarity metrics, LLMs are computationally expensive. Their usage should be limited to cases where more efficient methods fail, ensuring a balance between accuracy and processing time.

3   Related Work

The growing volume of data has intensified the need for effective duplicate identification to maintain business consistency. This section reviews related work,
focusing on expert rules, similarity measures, and LLMs.

Expert Rules: The approach in [10] improves deduplication by applying
expert rules individually and combining scores through information fusion,
enhancing accuracy while reducing manual adjustments. Similarly, [17] classifies
expert rule techniques by error type, automation potential, and update model,
discussing trends in large-scale data cleaning.

Similarity Metrics: In [9], a similarity-based deduplication approach for digital libraries achieved a 188% improvement over traditional methods. [13] introduces a SHA-based method that removes redundant data while preserving coherence and optimizing resources. [40] proposes a locality-sensitive hashing (LSH)
technique that combines textual and semantic similarity for efficient entity
resolution. Additionally, [6] presents a two-step selection strategy (T3S) that
enhances deduplication by balancing subsets and eliminating redundant pairs.

LLMs: [46] employs BERT in a hierarchical computing model for plagiarism detection, demonstrating effectiveness in ambiguous cases. [23] introduces
BoostER, a cost-effective entity resolution system leveraging LLMs for query verification, making high-quality deduplication accessible without complex training
or high costs.

Unlike most approaches that focus on a single technique, the proposed engine
integrates expert rules, similarity metrics, and LLMs hierarchically. This structure enhances both accuracy and execution efficiency, offering a more comprehensive solution to data deduplication.

4   Proposed Engine

This section presents the proposed approach, a modularized engine developed to
identify duplicated records. The engine operates as a service and is structured
to perform a series of comparisons based on a sequence of rules, each designed
to catch specific duplications.

Figure 1 presents the conceptual architecture of the proposed engine. This
architecture has the engine as its main component, designed as a service that
external systems can use via API and a user interface. The engine was also
conceptually modeled to use an external LLM service in client comparisons when
this technology is necessary. Finally, all comparisons performed are stored in a
database and available for access via API and the user interface.

The engine is composed of three main modules, also called layers: expert rules,
textual similarity, and LLM. These modules make up a set of rules that operate
sequentially. Furthermore, to reduce the computational cost, when a duplication
between a pair of clients is identified, the engine prevents comparisons made
with more complex modules and returns the aforementioned pair as a duplicate.
The following parts of this section present the characteristics of each module,
aspects related to its construction, and details about the data flow.

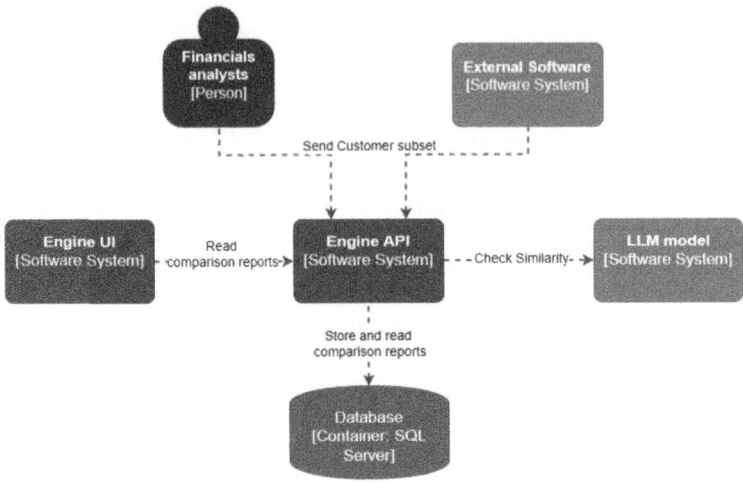

Fig. 1. Conceptual engine architecture.

4.1   Expert Rules Module

The first module of the engine aggregates a set of four expert rules, modeled to simulate cases of data duplication commonly found in a customer database. These rules simulate some well-known duplication cases in customer data and seek to capture duplications by equality, each linked to one or many data attributes. These rules were chosen and modeled based on superficial analyses of customer datasets available on the internet. The rules that make up the expert rules module are:

- **System id rule:** this rule represents the case in which an identifying attribute (id) from an old system needs to be maintained in the customer data after the system is modernized. Occasionally, two registrations made in the modern version of the system may refer to the same ID from the previous system. The rule, therefore, is triggered when the value in the attribute "IdOldSystem" from one client is identical to that from another client, signaling a possible case of duplication in the records
- **Bureau info rule:** this case represents the duplication of customers based on external credit identifiers (bureau). For this rule, two clients referencing the same bureau information are potentially duplicates. The rule is then applied when the registered bureau registration number ("bureau number") is identical between two clients, indicating a potential duplication;
- **Identification and contacts rule:** this case represents the duplication of identification data and contacts registered for a customer. This rule, therefore, is triggered when all attributes related to identification and contacts have identical data;
- **Identification and address rule:** this case represents the duplication of identification data and addresses registered regarding a customer. This

rule, therefore, is triggered when all attributes related to identification and addresses have identical data.

4.2   Textual Similarity Module

The second layer of the engine contains data comparison via similarity metrics. The technique chosen to compose this layer of the engine was the cosine metric, calculated on a text containing all the data from the two clients. This metric was chosen considering the results of preliminary experiments that investigated several approaches, including metrics based on the edition cited above.

As mentioned, the second layer of the engine uses cosine as a metric to check the similarity between customer data. To perform this calculation, each client has all its data transformed into a unique string separated by spaces. After this transformation, the resulting string embeddings are computed using a specific Autoencoder model specialized in short texts. After that, the distance cosine between the two sets of embeddings is calculated and normalized, returning a value between 0 and 1, indicating the similarity level between the two strings. This flow is detailed in Fig. 2.

4.3   Large Language Model Module

As mentioned, LLM models have a high semantic data analysis capacity and a high computational cost. The third layer of the engine uses this capability as a last resort to check for duplication between clients. At this layer, structured data from a customer pair is sent to the model. A well-defined prompt indicating broad comparison is used to ask the model to indicate whether the analyzed pair is potentially a duplicate. Additionally, a brief explanation of the result provided is requested.

It is important to mention that, despite being more computationally expensive, using an LLM model to compare more complex cases can bring benefits, as this type of technology cannot only return a result but also provide an explanation for the result. This ability can benefit the team responsible for evaluating effective duplication among the customers analyzed. Furthermore, it is possible to mitigate the difficulty over time by sending for analysis via LLM only in cases where the data is not clearly different.

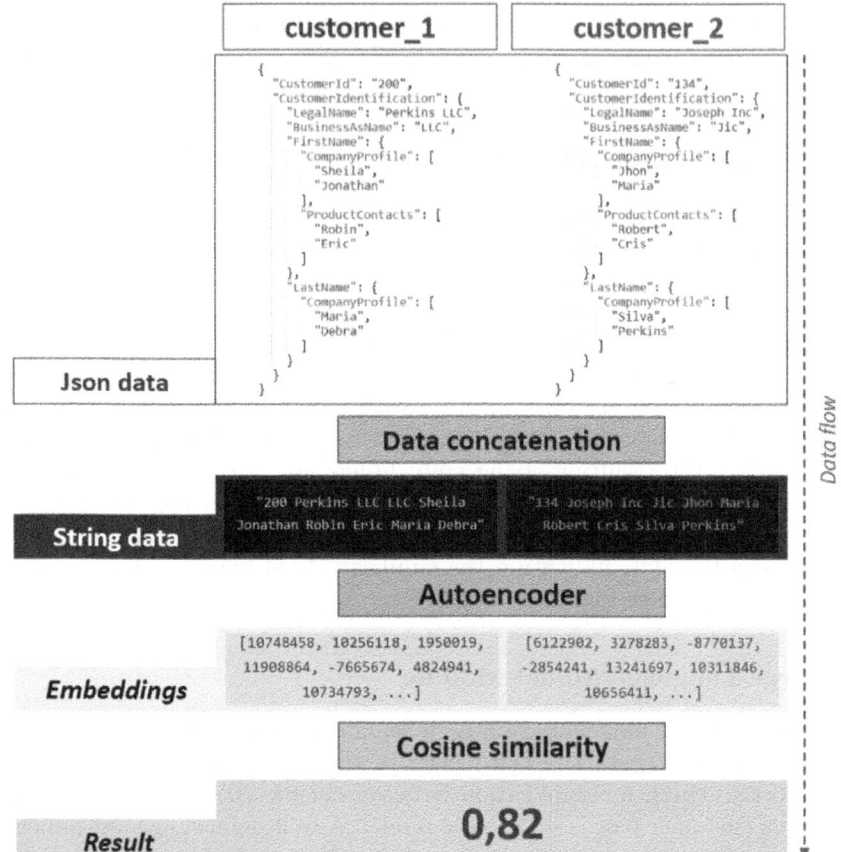

Fig. 2. Cosine similarity details.

4.4   Information Flow in the Engine

In an overview, the data flow of a pair of clients to be compared in the engine works according to the flow shown in Fig. 3. This flow and some of its characteristics will be detailed below.

First, data from the two received clients is sent to the first layer [1], which uses expert rules to identify duplications. The first layer rules are used in a well-defined sequence, being: [1.1] System id rule, [1.2] Bureau info rule, [1.3] Identification and contacts rule and [1.4] Identification and address rule. When a duplication is found in one of the rules, the flow of comparisons is stopped, and the identified rule is returned as a label for the possible duplication.

When the pair of compared clients is not captured by any rule in the first layer [1], their data is sent to the second layer [2], which uses the cosine metric as a way to check duplicity. In this layer, as already mentioned, data is transformed into texts, and their embeddings serve as a means for calculating the cosine,

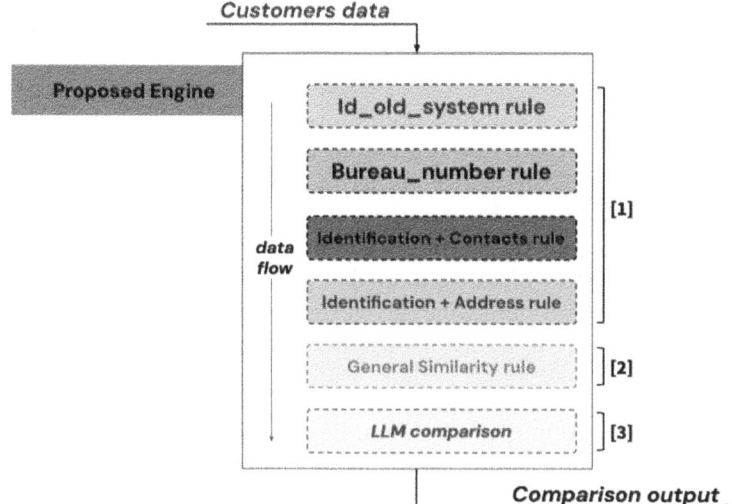

Fig. 3. Data flow inside the proposed engine.

which is returned in the form of a numerical value between 0 and 1. If the cosine value for the compared customer pair is greater than the established upper threshold, the flow of comparisons is interrupted, the referred pair is indicated as possibly duplicated, and the overall textual similarity is returned as a label for the duplicate found. Still, at this layer, when the cosine value of a client pair falls below the lower threshold, the comparison flow is also stopped, and the said client pair is labeled as non-duplicate.

Finally, if a pair of customers analyzed in the second layer has a cosine value below the upper threshold and above the lower threshold, its comparison is sent to the third layer [3], which uses an LLM model to evaluate whether said pair of customers are similar. The model analyzes the data based on a slightly open-ended prompt, and the result returned contains the overall assessment of duplicity (yes or no) and a brief explanation of this assessment.

4.5 Final Remarks About the Engine

The way the engine was modeled, based on a modular and sequential structure of different comparison techniques, allows for a series of gains compared to traditional ways of identifying duplicate data. Among the potential gains, we can mention:

– Mapping of specific needs and knowledge already existing in the business to identify duplicate data according to important attributes or sets of attributes;
– General syntactic and semantic analysis of data through comparison based on embeddings and cosine;

– Analysis of cases considered complex through the LLM model, including making it possible to write down the explanation of the decision regarding duplication;
– Reduction in the use of computational resources, since the most costly comparisons are only used when the previous layer indicates this way;
– General gain in performance in terms of accuracy as the engine combines capabilities from different technologies;
– Reduction of false positives, since the engine uses more open technologies (textual similarity and LLM) in a smaller number of cases;
– Reduction in computational time, given that the engine uses the most expensive layer (LLM) only in a restricted number of cases.

Based on the general context presented and the engine developed, we believe that the proposed solution can considerably improve the performance of duplicate identification systems, as it combines the performance capabilities of different approaches and manages to address time, one of the most significant difficulties in problems of duplication, in a balanced way.

5   Experimental Methodology

The implemented experimental methodology is designed to address the challenge of identifying duplicate clients in order to understand the benefits of using a hierarchical architecture that combines specialized rules, similarity measures, and large language models. The following sections present the experimental data, the comparative methods used in the analyses, and the configurations and metrics considered to analyze the results.

5.1   Experimental Data

The data used in the experiments were generated synthetically. The use of synthetic data in this study was motivated by two main factors: (1) the need to create controlled scenarios that allow for a precise and reproducible evaluation of the hierarchical model's capabilities, which would be difficult to achieve with real datasets; and (2) the constraints imposed by confidentiality and data protection requirements in corporate contexts.

Additionally, using synthetic data makes it possible to work with the texts in their original format, which would be difficult if a real dataset were used, as security and confidentiality measures often require the masking or encryption of personal information, making direct comparisons unfeasible between data such as name or telephone number, for example. The structure of synthetic generated clients are available on https://bit.ly/4iGSUfA.

As can be seen, customers have a structure segmented into five main parts: customer identification (CustomerIdentification), customer contacts (Customer-Contacts), customer addresses (CustomerAddresses), customer Bureau numbers (BureauInfo), and the ID of the client in the old system (IdOldSystem). This information can be internally segmented according to categories, which are: CompanyProfile, ProductContacts, or ProductBureau. These categories represent fictional data sections related to the customer's relationship with the company. Finally, this data formatting gave rise to the modeling of the expert rules mentioned in Sect. 4 - Proposal. These rules consider all data in each section and indicate equality between data when all information is exactly the same.

It is important to mention that all identifying attributes, such as: CustomerId, BureauInfo, and IdOldSystem, have a fixed number of characters. The number of characters in each fixed-length field is as follows:

- **CustomerId** : 3 characters;
- **BureauInfo**: 9 characters per BureauNumber;
- **IdOldSystem**: 12 characters;

5.2   Generated Datasets

Problems of searching for duplicate data have a quadratic nature (n^2), as they require comparing all customers with each other, for example. This particularity related to identifying duplicate data imposes a severe restriction on carrying out experiments since checking for duplicates in a dataset with n clients implies carrying out n x (n - 1) / 2 comparisons. For example, a dataset with just 10,000 customers would require 49,995,000 comparisons. If we hypothetically consider a 1 s execution time for comparing two customers with LLM, scanning all 49,995,000 necessary comparisons would take 578.65 d. This execution time would be unfeasible, even considering only 10 thousand customers.

The context presented indicated adopting a strategy to reduce the total number of comparisons. In this way, two sets of data were created: one called database, which simulates a company's customer database, and another called new customers, which simulates a group of more recently registered customers, that will be submitted to the investigation of duplicity. With this approach, all customers belonging to the new customer set must be compared with the database, which considerably limits the number of comparisons and, consequently, makes it possible to carry out experiments. As mentioned, two sets of data were created with the following characteristics:

- **Database**: set of 100 customer records, without internal duplications, which simulates a real, pre-existing database in a company;
- **New Customers**: set consisting of 100 customer records in which data that simulates duplication was purposely inserted according to specific scenarios.

The inserted duplications total 50 and represent a small fraction compared to the 10,000 comparisons necessary for a complete comparison of the two sets mentioned. Despite this, if we look at the quantities and scenarios described below, compared to the total of 200 existing customers in both sets, this is a considerable amount of duplication. Finally, the number of customers with duplications and the respective simulated duplication scenarios are:

- 5 duplicates via System id rule;
- 5 duplicates via Bureau info rule;
- 5 duplicates via Identification and contacts rule;
- 5 duplicates via Identification and address rule;
- 20 duplicates via similarity;
- 10 duplicates via LLM;

Finally, the synthetic data were carefully modeled to represent a context with a relatively large number of attributes. In addition, the inserted duplications seek to represent several simple and more complex contexts. In the latter case, simple analyses hardly capture the duplications, which justifies using LLM as the last layer for comparison.

5.3 Comparative Analysis

The comparative analysis was organized to evaluate the engine's performance in different configurations, considering the different processing layers. Thus, it is possible to verify whether the use of different comparison approaches jointly offers better performance in terms of accuracy and execution time when compared to the use of the same approaches in isolation.

To carry out the outlined investigation, each engine layer is evaluated individually on all data (100×100 comparisons). Furthermore, the engine with all its components working together is also tested, which totals the following versions to be tried:

- **Eng_EXP**: in this configuration, only the expert rules layer is applied;
- **Eng_SIM**: just the similarity layer;
- **Eng_LLM**: only the analysis layer with LLM;
- **Engine_COMPLETE**: complete engine.

The engine's performance was evaluated considering accuracy, represented by the total number of hits compared to the expected duplications. Furthermore, the number of false positives, that is, the number of false duplications identified, is also used as a criterion for analyzing the results. One last criterion analyzed was execution time, which indicates how viable each approach is regarding time to return results.

5.4 Environment and Technologies

Data was analyzed under the four aforementioned comparison settings, allowing for a comprehensive comparison of the efficiency and effectiveness of each approach. The development and execution environment for the experiments was based on Python, using libraries such as NumPy and SciPy for manipulating arrays and calculating cosine. Regarding the thresholds considered for the cosine, the following values were considered, based on preliminary experiments: upper threshold 0.7 and lower threshold 0.5.

Machine learning frameworks like Hugging Face Transformers have also been used to implement LLMs. The Autoencoder model used was paraphrase-MiniLM-L3-v2, and the LLM model used was Llama 3–13B, available on a local server running Ollama Server. The model temperature was set to 0.5, and the prompt and assistant are available on: https://bit.ly/4iGSUfA. The LLM module was developed using Python and based on the Ollama Server API. In this way, the data was sent to the server and compared using the configurations already presented.

The experiments were conducted on a desktop computer with the following technical specifications: Intel Core i5 processor, 16 GB RAM, and NVIDIA graphics card with 2 GB of memory. This standardization allows not only the analysis of accuracy and performance in terms of time but also the understanding of the relative effectiveness of each layer of the engine in identifying duplicate customers. In corporate environments, the availability of more powerful hardware would considerably reduce execution time. Despite this, it is important to verify the feasibility of experiments carried out even in an environment based on commercial hardware.

6   Results

This section presents the results observed in the experiments carried out. As mentioned, two sets were generated, each with 100 customers, and they were compared to each other, which generates a total of 10,000 comparisons. Another important aspect is related to comparative analysis, which considers the accuracy and execution time of each layer of the engine being executed in isolation as well as the complete engine. For simplicity, each engine layer and the entire engine will be called engine versions or simply versions.

6.1   Accuracy - Overall Performance

Table 1 presents the general result obtained by each engine version regarding successes and errors in positive cases (duplications) and negative cases (non-duplications). In that table, the first column on the left presents the identification of each case, and the second to fifth columns present each of the analyzed versions, including the versions with isolated layers (Eng_EXP, Eng_SIM and Eng_LLM) and also the version with the complete engine (Eng_COMPLETE).

Table 1. Results - Total comparisons

	Eng_EXP	Eng_SIM	Eng_LLM	Eng_COMPLETE
True Positives	20	23	40	48
False Positives	0	9	6	2
True Negatives	9950	9941	9944	9948
False Negatives	30	27	10	2

It is important to mention that the table refers to the total number of comparisons (10000), making no distinction between the specified duplication scenarios. Furthermore, the table's organization simply demonstrates the errors, denoted as false positives (non-existent duplications reported as true) and false negatives (duplications no longer identified). These errors are important to evaluate whether the performance of each version is consistent with the needs of the problem since identification errors are critical in the context of data duplication.

Regarding the results presented in Table 1, it is possible to observe that the version with all layers and located in the rightmost column, Eng_COMPLETE, obtained the best result. This version achieved 48 hits for duplications (positive) and 9948 hits for comparisons without duplication (negative), totaling 9996 hits among the 10,000 comparisons. Among the versions with just one layer, the Eng_LLM version stands out, which uses the LLM model to carry out comparisons. This version obtained 9984 hits, being very close to the overall performance of the complete engine. The two versions mentioned also had a low number of errors. While the Eng_COMPLETE version had only 4 errors (2 false positives and two false negatives), the Eng_LLM version had 16 errors, 6 false positives and 10 false negatives. This panorama demonstrates the superiority of the proposed version in terms of accuracy.

Regarding the Eng_EXP versions, which include expert rules, and Eng_SIM, which uses only the cosine similarity layer, it is possible to notice that the version with expert rules achieved better performance, reaching 9970 hits, 20 of which were true positives and 9950 true negatives. The Eng_sim version achieved a similar hit performance, with 9964 hits, of which 23 were true positives, and 9941 were true negatives. Regarding errors, it is noted that the Eng_Exp version had fewer errors, with 30 in total, while the Eng_SIM version had 36 errors in total. This performance demonstrates that, despite being similar in terms of hits, expert rules are less susceptible to errors, as they strictly limit duplication, while the version based on cosine similarity performs syntactic and semantic analysis during the comparison, which can harm the performance in terms of accuracy.

6.2 Accuracy - Performance by Duplication Scenarios

Table 2 presents the details of the results obtained by each version but from a more focused perspective on duplication scenarios. As already mentioned, scenarios were created that are strongly linked to each layer of the engine. The general structure of the table is similar to the previous table. However, the leftmost column details the duplication scenarios and the number of existing cases (in parentheses) per scenario. The other columns detail the successes of each version by duplication scenario. Finally, the last line of the table presents the total number of hits for each version and the percentage of these hits compared to the 50 cases of duplication entered.

Observing Table 2, it is possible to notice that the performance of the versions improves considerably as their complexity increases. The Eng_EXP version, for example, can only achieve 20 hits, which is the total number of duplication cases inserted in the duplication scenario, referring to the expert rules. Despite this,

Table 2. Results - Hits per layer and duplication scenarios

Duplication scenarios	Eng_EXP	Eng_SIM	Eng_LLM	Eng_COMPLETE
Expert rules (20)	20	0	20	20
General similarity (20)	0	19	11	19
Complex similarity (10)	0	4	9	9
Total (50)	20 (40%)	23 (46%)	40 (80%)	48 (96%)

this version does not have the flexibility to capture any other case of duplication, resulting in a performance of 40% accuracy compared to the 50 existing duplications. The Eng-SIM version, in turn, achieved a performance of 23 hits in total (46%), ranking third among the versions analyzed.

Still, in Table 2, it is noted that the Eng_LLM version achieved superior performance compared to the previously mentioned versions. This version achieved 40 hits, reaching 80% of existing cases. Finally, the version that uses all engine layers, Eng_COMPLETE, obtained the best performance among all the versions analyzed, achieving 48 hits in 50 possible cases, reaching 96% accuracy.

6.3   Runtime - Overall Performance

The execution time analysis was done based on the total time to perform all 10000 comparisons with each engine version. Table 3 presents the results in terms of execution time. The columns show the performance of each version, and the rows detail the average performance and total engine execution time, both in seconds.

Table 3. Results - Runtime overall performance

Runtime - seconds	Eng_EXP	Eng_SIM	Eng_LLM	Eng_COMPLETE
Runtime by comparison (avg)	0.003	0.235	25.200	2.977
Total runtime (10k comparisons)	28.33	2352.00	252000.00	29768.03

According to the data presented in the table, it can be seen that the fastest version among all those analyzed is Eng_EXP, composed only of the layer with expert rules, which has an average execution time of 0.003 s and a total time of 28.33 s to perform all 10000 comparisons. In second place is the Eng_SIM version, which had an average time of 0.235 s and a total time of 2352 s. In third place is the version with all engine layers, Eng_COMPLETE, with an average time of 2.97 s and a total time of 29768.03 s. Finally, as the most costly performance, the version that uses only LLM, with an average time of 25.20 s and a total time of 252000 s.

The results obtained demonstrate the simpler versions' superiority in terms of execution time. It is possible to notice a considerable increase in the total time, which goes from 28.33 s in the fastest version to 252000 s, or 70 h, in the most expensive version. The results presented in terms of time also indicate the impossibility of using strategies based solely on LLM, due to its high computational complexity. This aspect is crucial as it demonstrates the feasibility of using each approach and the need to articulate strategies that help reduce the total execution time.

It is important to highlight that the full version, Eng_COMPLETE, had a better performance in terms of time than the version that uses only LLM, Eng_LLM, as the strategy of filtering cases that go to the most costly layer (LLM) through cosine was used. As mentioned, when a comparison reaches the similarity layer, the value returned for the pair indicates whether it is a possible duplication (equal to or above the upper threshold, set at 0.7) or whether it should be denoted as non-duplicate (below the threshold lower, set to 0.5). This strategy allowed the full version to interrupt the execution flow in 8874 comparisons with similarity already observed as very low, reducing the engine's execution time.

6.4   Brief Discussion About the Results

The results in Tables 1 and 2 confirm the proposed engine's superior performance over all competing versions. This is evident in both overall success rates and error analysis across duplication scenarios. Notably, more complex isolated approaches, like similarity and LLM, had higher false positives and negatives, likely due to their semantic-based comparisons. In contrast, strict rule-based methods, which had no such errors, rely on easily identifiable patterns. This suggests a hybrid approach—applying simple rules to straightforward cases and complex rules to intricate cases—could enhance performance.

Regarding execution time, a viable approach must balance speed and accuracy. An engine that is fast but inaccurate is as ineffective as one that is precise but impractically slow. The proposed engine, running 8.5 times faster than the LLM-only version, outperforms isolated strategies while maintaining a significantly lower execution time than the most expensive alternative.

7   Conclusions and Future Work

This study introduces a hierarchical data deduplication approach that integrates expert rules, similarity metrics, and LLMs. By progressively structuring these techniques, the engine optimizes computational resources while ensuring high accuracy.

Experiments confirm the effectiveness of this architecture, with the full engine surpassing isolated approaches in both accuracy and efficiency. LLMs serve as a last resort for complex cases, while simpler layers handle straightforward duplications, minimizing false positives and negatives. Beyond technical strengths, the engine's modular design enables adaptation to business needs, allowing rule customization and selective layer application based on dataset characteristics.

Future work will focus on validating the engine on real-world datasets to assess its practical applicability, developing adaptive algorithms for dynamic rule selection based on data properties, and enhancing the interpretability of LLM outputs to help users understand deduplication decisions. This hierarchical approach marks a significant advancement in scalable and adaptable data deduplication.

References

1. Abboura, A., Sahrl, S., Ouziri, M., Benbernou, S.: CrowdMD: crowdsourcing-based approach for deduplication. In: 2015 IEEE International Conference on Big Data (Big Data), pp. 2621–2627. IEEE (2015)
2. Akbar, M., Ahmad, I., Mirza, M., Ali, M., Barmavatu, P.: Enhanced authentication for de-duplication of big data on cloud storage system using machine learning approach. Clust. Comput. **27**(3), 3683–3702 (2024)
3. Amin, M.M., Stiawan, D., Ermatita, E., Budiarto, R.: Proposed threshold-based and rule-based approaches to detecting duplicates in bibliographic database. Bull. Electr. Eng. Inf. **13**(3), 2036–2047 (2024)
4. Bard, G.V.: Spelling-error tolerant, order-independent pass-phrases via the damerau-levenshtein string-edit distance metric. Cryptology ePrint Archive (2006). https://eprint.iacr.org/2006/204
5. Bhattacharya, I., Getoor, L.: Deduplication and group detection using links. In: KDD Workshop on Link Analysis and Group Detection (2004)
6. Bianco, G.D., Galante, R., Gonçalves, M.A., Canuto, S., Heuser, C.A.: A practical and effective sampling selection strategy for large scale deduplication. IEEE Trans. Knowl. Data Eng. **27**(9), 2305–2319 (2015). https://doi.org/10.1109/TKDE.2015.2416734
7. Blakely, T., Salmond, C.: Probabilistic record linkage and a method to calculate the positive predictive value. Int. J. Epidemiol. **31**(6), 1246–1252 (2002)
8. Boiński, P., Sienkiewicz, M., Bębel, B., Wrembel, R., Gałęzowski, D., Graniszewski, W.: On customer data deduplication: Lessons learned from a R&D project in the financial sector. In: CEUR Workshop Proceedings, vol. 3135 (2022)
9. Borges, E.N., de Carvalho, M.G., Galante, R., Gonçalves, M.A., Laender, A.H.: An unsupervised heuristic-based approach for bibliographic metadata deduplication. Inf. Process. Manage. **47**(5), 706–718 (2011)
10. Dinerstein, J., Dinerstein, S., Egbert, P.K., Clyde, S.W.: Learning-based fusion for data deduplication. In: 2008 Seventh International Conference on Machine Learning and Applications pp. 66–71. IEEE (2008)
11. Elouataoui, W., El Alaoui, I., El Mendili, S., Gahi, Y.: An end-to-end big data deduplication framework based on online continuous learning. Int. J. Adv. Comput. Sci. Appl. **13**(9), 281–291 (2022)
12. Even, A., Shankaranarayanan, G.: Dual assessment of data quality in customer databases. J. Data Inf. Qual. (JDIQ) **1**(3), 1–29 (2009)
13. Feng, D.: Overview of data deduplication. In: Data Deduplication for High Performance Storage System, pp. 9–23. Springer (2022). https://doi.org/10.1007/978-981-19-0112-6_2

14. González-Serrano, L., Talón-Ballestero, P., Muñoz-Romero, S., Soguero-Ruiz, C., Rojo-Álvarez, J.L.: Entropic statistical description of big data quality in hotel customer relationship management. Entropy **21**(4), 419 (2019)

15. Hair, K., Bahor, Z., Macleod, M., Liao, J., Sena, E.S.: The automated systematic search deduplicator (ASYSD): a rapid, open-source, interoperable tool to remove duplicate citations in biomedical systematic reviews. BMC Biol. **21**(1), 189 (2023)

16. He, Q., Li, Z., Zhang, X.: Data deduplication techniques. In: 2010 International Conference on Future Information Technology and Management Engineering, vol. 1, pp. 430–433. IEEE (2010)

17. Ilyas, I.F., Chu, X., et al.: Trends in cleaning relational data: consistency and deduplication. Found. Trends® Databases **5**(4), 281–393 (2015)

18. Jiang, Y., Lin, C., Meng, W., Yu, C., Cohen, A.M., Smalheiser, N.R.: Rule-based deduplication of article records from bibliographic databases. Database **2014**, bat086 (2014)

19. Kenter, T., De Rijke, M.: Short text similarity with word embeddings. In: Proceedings of the 24th ACM International on Conference on Information and Knowledge Management, pp. 1411–1420 (2015)

20. Kumar, A., Madanu, M., Prakash, H., Jonnavithula, L., Aravilli, S.R.: Advaita: bug duplicity detection system. arXiv preprint arXiv:2001.10376 (2020)

21. Kunz, W., et al.: Customer engagement in a big data world. J. Serv. Mark. **31**(2), 161–171 (2017)

22. Levenshtein, V.I.: Binary codes capable of correcting deletions, insertions, and reversals. In: Proceedings of the Soviet Physics Doklady, vol. 10, pp. 707–710 (1966)

23. Li, H., Li, S., Hao, F., Zhang, C.J., Song, Y., Chen, L.: Booster: leveraging large language models for enhancing entity resolution. In: Companion Proceedings of the ACM on Web Conference 2024, pp. 1043–1046 (2024)

24. Mahowald, K., Ivanova, A.A., Blank, I.A., Kanwisher, N., Tenenbaum, J.B., Fedorenko, E.: Dissociating language and thought in large language models. Trends in Cognitive Sciences (2024)

25. Majumder, G., Pakray, P., Gelbukh, A., Pinto, D.: Semantic textual similarity methods, tools, and applications: a survey. Computación y Sistemas **20**(4), 647–665 (2016)

26. Paganelli, M., Sottovia, P., Guerra, F., Velegrakis, Y.: Tuner: Fine tuning of rule-based entity matchers. In: Proceedings of the 28th ACM International Conference on Information and Knowledge Management, pp. 2945–2948 (2019)

27. Rae, J.W., et al.: Scaling language models: methods, analysis & insights from training gopher. arXiv preprint arXiv:2112.11446 (2021)

28. Ravikanth, M., Korra, S., Mamidisetti, G., Goutham, M., Bhaskar, T.: An efficient learning based approach for automatic record deduplication with benchmark datasets. Sci. Rep. **14**(1), 16254 (2024)

29. Rehman, M., Esichaikul, V.: Duplicate record detection for database cleansing. In: 2009 Second International Conference on Machine Vision, pp. 333–338. IEEE (2009)

30. Reid, A., Catterall, M.: Invisible data quality issues in a CRM implementation. J. Database Mark. Custom. Strat. Manage. **12**, 305–314 (2005)

31. Reimer, K., Becker, J.U.: What customer information should companies use for customer relationship management? Practical insights from empirical research. Manag. Rev. Q. **65**(3), 149–182 (2015)

32. Rozinek, O., Mareš, J.: Fast and precise convolutional JARO and JARO-Winkler similarity. In: 2024 35th Conference of Open Innovations Association (FRUCT). IEEE (2024)

33. Shobha, K., Nickolas, S.: Integration and rule-based pre-processing of scientific publication records from multiple data sources. In: Satapathy, S.C., Bhateja, V., Mohanty, J.R., Udgata, S.K. (eds.) Smart Intelligent Computing and Applications. SIST, vol. 159, pp. 647–655. Springer, Singapore (2020). https://doi.org/10.1007/978-981-13-9282-5_61

34. Singh, P., Pal, N.R., Verma, S., Vyas, O.P.: Fuzzy rule-based approach for software fault prediction. IEEE Trans. Syst. Man Cybern. Syst. 47(5), 826–837 (2016)

35. Su, C.Y., Bansal, A., Jain, V., Ghanavati, S., McMillan, C.: A language model of Java methods with train/test deduplication. In: Proceedings of the 31st ACM Joint European Software Engineering Conference and Symposium on the Foundations of Software Engineering, pp. 2152–2156 (2023)

36. Tan, P.N., Steinbach, M., Kumar, V.: Introduction to Data Mining, 1st edn. Pearson, Boston (2006)

37. Thoppilan, R., et al.: LAMDA: language models for dialog applications. arXiv preprint arXiv:2201.08239 (2022)

38. Touvron, H., et al.: Llama 2: open foundation and fine-tuned chat models. arXiv preprint arXiv:2307.09288 (2023)

39. Villena Román, J., Collada Pérez, S., Lana Serrano, S., González Cristóbal, J.C.: Hybrid approach combining machine learning and a rule-based expert system for text categorization. In: Proceedings of the Twenty-Fourth International Florida Artificial Intelligence Research Society Conference. AAAI (2011)

40. Wang, Q., Cui, M., Liang, H.: Semantic-aware blocking for entity resolution. IEEE Trans. Knowl. Data Eng. 28(1), 166–180 (2015)

41. Weis, M., Naumann, F., Jehle, U., Lufter, J., Schuster, H.: Industry-scale duplicate detection. Proc. VLDB Endow. 1(2), 1253–1264 (2008)

42. Weston, J., Bengio, S., Usunier, N.: Large scale image annotation: learning to rank with joint word-image embeddings. Mach. Learn. 81, 21–35 (2010)

43. Winkler, W.E., et al.: Overview of record linkage and current research directions. Bureau Census 25(4), 603–623 (2006)

44. Wu, C.H.: Behavior-based spam detection using a hybrid method of rule-based techniques and neural networks. Expert Syst. Appl. 36(3), 4321–4330 (2009)

45. Yakhni, S., Tekli, J., Mansour, E., Chbeir, R.: Using fuzzy reasoning to improve redundancy elimination for data deduplication in connected environments. Soft. Comput. 27(17), 12387–12418 (2023)

46. Zhang, R., et al.: Hierarchical and pairwise document embedding for plagiarism detection. In: Yang, X., Wang, C.-D., Islam, M.S., Zhang, Z. (eds.) ADMA 2020. LNCS (LNAI), vol. 12447, pp. 148–156. Springer, Cham (2020). https://doi.org/10.1007/978-3-030-65390-3_12

47. Zobel, J., Moffat, A.: Exploring the similarity space. In: Acm Sigir Forum. vol. 32, pp. 18–34. ACM New York, NY, USA (1998)

Enhancing Stock Market Predictions: The Role of Feature Selection Techniques in Financial Modeling

Humberto O. Bragança[1]([✉]) [iD], Richard F. Pinto[1] [iD], Bruno L. Dalmazo[1] [iD], Eduardo N. Borges[1] [iD], Giancarlo Lucca[2] [iD], Viviane L. D. de Mattos[1] [iD], and Rafael A. Berri[1] [iD]

[1] Federal University of Rio Grande (FURG), Rio Grande, Brazil
{humberto.braganca,richard_pinto,dalmazo,eduardoborges,
vivianemattos,rafaelberri}@furg.br
[2] Catholic University of Pelotas (UCPel), Pelotas, Brazil
giancarlo.lucca@ucpel.edu.br

Abstract. Feature selection plays a crucial role in improving the performance of predictive models, especially in complex and dynamic environments such as the Brazilian financial market. This study evaluates the impact of different feature selection methods—OneR, Symmetrical Uncertain, Gain Ratio, Pearson Correlation, mRMR, and Correlation-based Feature Subset Selection—on financial market prediction using Random Forest models. A dataset consisting of 194 technical analysis indicators was analyzed, and progressive attribute removal was applied, with model performance assessed through cross-validation. The results demonstrate that feature selection significantly enhances model efficiency by reducing dimensionality while maintaining predictive accuracy. Moreover, our findings provide valuable insights into the relevance of different financial indicators, offering a methodological contribution to financial market analysis. Future work includes leveraging the selected features in advanced machine learning architectures, such as deep learning, to further refine prediction accuracy and develop more reliable models for financial forecasting.

Keywords: Feature Selection · Financial Market · Machine Learning

1 Introduction

The Brazilian financial market, Brasil Bolsa Balcão (B3)[1], stands out as a dynamic and complex emerging market, demanding specialized analytical and predictive approaches [1]. Its volatility and diverse economic sectors pose challenges and opportunities for financial modeling, requiring strategies to enhance predictive accuracy [2].

---

[1] https://www.b3.com.br/.

O. Gervasi et al. (Eds.): ICCSA 2025, LNCS 15649, pp. 386–400, 2025.
https://doi.org/10.1007/978-3-031-96997-3_24

In recent years, machine learning has emerged as an effective tool for financial decision-making, offering data-driven insights to mitigate risks and optimize investment strategies. Supervised learning models play a crucial role in evaluating financial risks and supporting corporate decision-making, reinforcing their value in performance management [3].

A fundamental step in improving model efficiency and accuracy is feature selection, which involves identifying the most relevant variables while eliminating redundant or less informative ones [4]. This process is particularly crucial in financial markets, where the sheer volume of data can overwhelm traditional analytical methods. By refining the input features, models achieve greater predictive power while reducing overfitting and computational complexity [28].

Although feature selection has been widely explored in global financial markets, its application in Brazil remains under-researched. Unique characteristics such as regulatory frameworks, market structure, and economic particularities influence the behavior of financial indicators, requiring tailored methodologies. Recent advancements in financial data collection and emerging technologies have opened new possibilities for more precise and detailed market analysis [5].

Leveraging extensive historical datasets with machine learning techniques can significantly improve the accuracy of economic forecasts in Brazil. However, the integration of feature selection and cross-validation for Brazilian stock market data remains a largely unexplored area, which presents an opportunity to improve financial predictive models [6].

This study addresses the gap in research by utilizing a dataset of Brazilian financial indicators to evaluate the effect of advanced feature selection methods on predictive model performance. By employing Information Gain and Relief, we pinpoint key features to enhance model efficiency. Additionally, we evaluate cross-validation's role in improving predictions, leading to a stronger approach for financial analysis in emerging markets.

These methods are known for their ability to handle large datasets and identify key features that contribute most significantly to the precision of the prediction, as discussed by [7], who emphasize the practical application of feature selection to improve model efficiency. Additionally, the importance of feature selection in high-dimensional data, demonstrating how correlation-based filters can efficiently identify the most relevant features, which can significantly enhance the generalization capacity of predictive models [8].

The models are then evaluated through cross-validation, allowing analysis of these methods. The contribution of this study lies in the introduction of a new perspective for feature selection analysis in emerging markets, using new financial indicators and cross-validation to ensure applicability of the results.

This document includes: Sect. 2 on Feature Selection Techniques and Technical Analysis, followed by Sect. 3 summarizing key previous research. Section 4 details the methodology, Sect. 5 presents the results, and Sect. 6 discusses findings and future work directions.

2   Background

In this section, our objective is to provide the essential background to comprehend the research. To begin, we will introduce the technical analysis indicators that are used as input for the models, followed by an exploration of the feature selection techniques employed.

2.1   Technical Analysis Indicators

Technical analysis indicators are essential tools utilized to scrutinize the price behavior of financial assets, including stocks, currencies, commodities, and others. Their primary objective is to forecast future market movements using graphical analysis by leveraging mathematical calculations applied to historical price and trading volume data of the assets [9].

Moving Average. The moving average is a statistical method employed to reduce the volatility in a time series of data [10], making it easier to identify trends and patterns by minimizing random fluctuations.

Standard Deviation. Standard deviation measures price volatility, with higher values indicating riskier assets [11]. This metric is crucial for constructing Bollinger Bands and identifying overbought and oversold conditions in the market.

Moving Average Convergence Divergence. The Moving Average Convergence Divergence (MACD) identifies changes in trend strength, direction, and momentum using two Exponential Moving Averages [12]. It is calculated by subtracting the 26-period EMA from the 12-period EMA. The resulting MACD line is complemented by the MACD Signal, which is a 9-period Exponential Moving Average of the MACD itself. This signal line serves as a trigger for buy or sell decisions: when the MACD crosses above the signal line, it indicates a potential buying opportunity; when it crosses below, it may indicate a selling opportunity. Its derivatives include the MACD Slope, which measures the rate of change, and the MACD Histogram, which visualizes the difference between the MACD and its signal line [13].

RSI. The Relative Strength Index (RSI), developed by J. Welles Wilder, evaluates whether a stock is overbought or oversold by analyzing recent price movements [14]. This momentum oscillator helps traders identify potential reversal points in the market.

Others. The Volatility and Speed Divergence Moving Averages (VSDME) indicators enhance traditional moving averages by incorporating both volatility and speed parameters. These adaptive indicators adjust their sensitivity to market conditions, providing more dynamic insights than conventional moving averages.

2.2   Feature Selection

Feature selection plays a fundamental role in machine learning by reducing dimensionality, enhancing model performance, and minimizing overfitting, especially when working with limited data [15]. The objective is to retain only the most relevant attributes, eliminating those that are redundant or irrelevant, which leads to more efficient and generalizable models [16].

Information Gain. Information Gain (IG) is based on entropy, a measure of uncertainty in a dataset. It evaluates how much a feature reduces entropy when the dataset is split based on its values. A higher IG implies that the feature contributes significantly to class discrimination, making it useful for building predictive models [17].

Symmetrical Uncertainty. Symmetrical Uncertainty (SU) is an information-theoretic metric that quantifies the mutual dependence between a feature and the class [18]. It compensates for IG's bias toward features with many values and is effective in identifying informative attributes for classification.

Minimum Redundancy Maximum Relevance (mRMR). The mRMR method aims to select features that are highly relevant to the target class while minimizing redundancy among them. It balances relevance and redundancy by discarding features that convey information already captured by previously selected attributes [19].

Relief. Relief estimates feature relevance by comparing each instance to its nearest neighbors from the same and opposite classes. It adjusts feature weights based on their ability to distinguish between these classes, making it suitable for detecting conditional dependencies and interactions [20].

OneR. OneR is a simple yet effective feature selection method that creates a one-rule classifier for each feature. It selects the feature whose rule results in the fewest classification errors, ranking attributes based on predictive accuracy [21].

Gain Ratio. Gain Ratio [22] adjusts Information Gain by penalizing features with many distinct values, which could otherwise skew the selection process. This normalization encourages the choice of features that are informative without overfitting due to excessive specificity [27].

Pearson Correlation. The Pearson Correlation coefficient measures the linear relationship between two variables. Ranging from -1 to +1, it indicates the strength and direction of the association, with values near ± 1 representing strong correlations [23].

Correlation-Based Feature Subset Selection (CfsSubset). CfsSubset evaluates groups of features rather than individual attributes. It favors subsets that are highly correlated with the class but have low intercorrelation, aiming to capture complementary information while avoiding redundancy [24].

3   Related Works

In stock market prediction, feature selection plays a crucial role by improving model accuracy, interpretability, and computational efficiency. Given the vast volume of financial indicators and the highly dynamic nature of market data, selecting the most informative features helps reduce noise and mitigate overfitting [28].

Park and Irwin [29] demonstrated the predictive value of technical indicators, such as Moving Averages and the Relative Strength Index (RSI), across global markets. These tools are essential for trend identification and momentum analysis, supporting trading decisions based on historical price patterns. Extensions of these indicators, like the MACD Slope, further enhance responsiveness to market changes and improve entry/exit signal quality [30]. Standard deviation remains a key metric for capturing volatility, directly impacting the robustness of predictive models.

Combining technical indicators with machine learning has been shown to boost predictive performance. However, due to the high dimensionality of financial datasets, feature selection becomes necessary to isolate relevant inputs. Htun et al. [28] emphasized the challenge of handling non-linear relationships and frequent fluctuations in stock prices, where traditional models may overfit. Feature selection techniques address these challenges by retaining only the most relevant indicators and removing redundancy.

In a comparative study, Krauss et al. [31] showed that ensemble methods, such as gradient-boosted trees and random forests, outperformed deep neural networks in stock prediction tasks, offering better profitability and risk-adjusted returns. These models are well-suited for handling complex patterns in noisy data and benefit significantly from optimized feature subsets.

Our study builds on these findings by applying and comparing multiple feature selection methods, highlighting their impact on model performance. Based on the results, we recommend the OneR method due to its ability to maintain performance with a minimal set of attributes, offering a balance between accuracy, efficiency, and interpretability.

4   Methodology

This study analyzes stock market data from the seven largest companies listed on B3 between 2010 and 2020, a period selected for its data richness and market relevance. The dataset includes daily trading session details, such as opening, closing, high, low, average prices, buy/sell offers, trading volume, and number of transactions. These price attributes served as the basis for generating technical analysis indicators widely used in financial forecasting.

From this raw price data, we developed 194 technical indicators—including Moving Averages, Standard Deviations, RSI, MACD (and its derivatives), and the price variation (DF)—using sliding windows of length γ or β trading sessions. These indicators were used as features in machine learning models aimed at classifying stock behavior into five categories: *Stability*, *Descent*, *Sharp Descent*, *Rise*, and *Sharp Rise*, determined by the price variation over the following five trading days.

Due to the high dimensionality of the feature space, feature selection was applied to identify the most relevant indicators. We employed multiple feature selection methods (described in Sect. 2.2), followed by a stepwise feature elimination strategy. In this process, features were removed iteratively in reverse order of importance, and classification performance was measured at each step using k-fold cross-validation.

For each method, we plotted the cross-validated accuracy across the feature removal iterations. We identified two key points on each curve: the model with the maximum accuracy (marked with an **Orange Dot – OD**) and the point where performance began to consistently decline (marked with a **Green Dot – GD**), indicating that the most critical features were being removed beyond this point.

To validate the reliability of the models at these points, we performed *Stratified k-Fold Cross-Validation*—preserving class distributions within each fold—and tested the resulting models on an unseen test set. This ensured generalization and mitigated overfitting.

The label definitions were as follows:

– **Stability:** price variation between -0.5% and $+0.5\%$,
– **Descent:** decrease between 0.5% and 1%,
– **Sharp Descent:** decrease $\geq 1\%$,
– **Rise:** increase between 0.5% and 1%,
– **Sharp Rise:** increase $\geq 1\%$.

The overall methodology is summarized in Fig. 1.

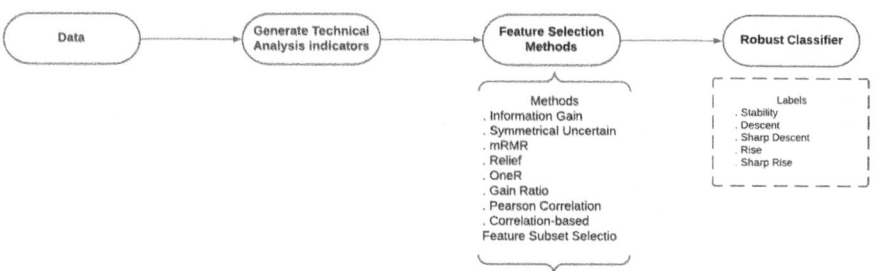

Fig. 1. Methodology flow diagram.

5   Result

This chapter we provide the results and insights of this research, it will be dissected in 2 subsections. The first subsection (reference section number) we delve into the BovDb [25], and explain in depth the tables it contains. The second subsection yields the findings from the cross-validation process and evaluation of the feature selection methods

5.1   Input Data

Brazilian stock data is accessible in raw text files on the B3 website. This study utilizes the BovDb dataset [25], which offers deeper insight into market behavior for B3 stocks from 2010 to 2020. This period features substantial data generation, enhancing the analysis's relevance. BovDb includes five tables that capture the market's dynamics.

Cardoso et al. [25] present a schematic illustration of the database that effectively highlights the interrelationships between the various tables and their respective columns.

The "price" table provided the data for constructing Technical Analysis Indicators for the Train and Test datasets. We processed the data to generate financial indicators based on different price metrics and various trading session windows, which were then used as features.

We derived 194 features from Technical Analysis Indicators and normalized the data. After reviewing the price table, we defined 5 labels:"Descent" for a 0.5% drop, "Sharp Descent" for a 1% drop, "Rise" for a 0.5% increase, "Sharp Rise" for a 1% increase, and "Stability" for fluctuations under 0.5%.

Using these features, we built the train and test datasets. The train dataset consists of 15,237 rows in total, with 2,756 rows for Stability, 3,314 for Descent, 2,612 for Sharp Descent, 3,472 for Rise, and 3,083 for Sharp Rise. The test dataset contains 3,810 rows, with 689 rows for Stability, 829 for Descent, 653 for Sharp Descent, 868 for Rise, and 771 for Sharp Rise.

5.2   Evaluation

The prediction utilized Random Forest [26], a machine learning technique that combines multiple decision trees to improve accuracy and reduce overfitting, making it ideal for classification and regression tasks. In this study, we built a model with 100 decision trees, allowing them to reach their maximum depth to capture complex data interactions. We used the entire dataset for each tree without limiting feature importance calculations and did not perform out-of-bag validation, focusing instead on other metrics to evaluate the model's effectiveness.

The model's performance was evaluated using accuracy and F1-Score metrics. To calculate these metrics, we applied a simple average of the results obtained from the 9 folds of the cross-validation process. The final accuracy was computed as the average of the accuracies from each k-fold cross-validation iteration.

In the first phase, we used 9-fold cross-validation, followed by stratified k-fold cross-validation to maintain class distribution in unbalanced datasets. We calculated performance metrics like accuracy and F1-Score, averaging them for overall model evaluation. This method helps ensure representative class distributions and reduces performance variation, yielding a more reliable model assessment.

When all 194 available features were used, the model achieved an average F1-Score of 0.475 and an accuracy of 0.476 on the test data. Each graph includes an orange dot and a green dot. The orange dot marks the highest accuracy, while the green dot indicates a point which removing more features would significantly decrease the model's accuracy.

Figure 2 illustrates the accuracy patterns as features are progressively removed for each selection method. These graphs reveal critical insights into feature importance and method behavior. All methods demonstrate an initial steep accuracy increase with the first few features, followed by a plateau and eventual decline as essential features are removed. This pattern confirms the effectiveness of feature selection in identifying the most informative indicators. Notably, OneR (Fig. 2b) achieves near-optimal performance with remarkably few features, demonstrating its efficiency in identifying highly discriminative attributes. In contrast, mRMR (Fig. 2g) maintains higher accuracy with more features, suggesting its ability to capture complex feature interactions. Relief (Fig. 2f) shows a balanced profile with steady performance across a moderate feature set. The orange dots mark peak accuracy points, while green dots indicate where performance begins to decline significantly, helping identify optimal feature subsets for each method. These visual patterns complement the numerical results in Table 1 and 2, also it provides intuitive evidence of each method's theoretical strengths.

In Fig. 3 we can see a comparison of how all the Feature Selection Methods works. It is noticeable that there is a pattern in the variation of accuracy throughout the features insertion, initially the accuracy increases to a certain point, where it is the maximum accuracy, showing that these initial features removed are getting in the way of the model. Then the accuracy starts to decrease slowly until reaches GD, where from there, it starts to decrease drastically. The OneR method stands out for being able to delay the GD, managing to maintain accuracy at a level similar to the initial one using only 21 features.

To further analyze the feature selection methods, we constructed a comparative bar chart that evaluates the performance of the methods at the two critical points of each accuracy line: the OD (represented by orange bars) and the GD (represented by green bars).

Tables 1 and 2 present the performance results obtained at the points of greatest accuracy (OD) and at the initial point where the performance drops significantly (GD) for each feature selection method evaluated. The number of features used, the accuracy averages obtained by cross-validation (simple and stratified), as well as the accuracy and F1-score values in the test using the model generated from the Stratified Cross-Validation, are displayed, allowing the comparison of the robustness and effectiveness limit of each method.

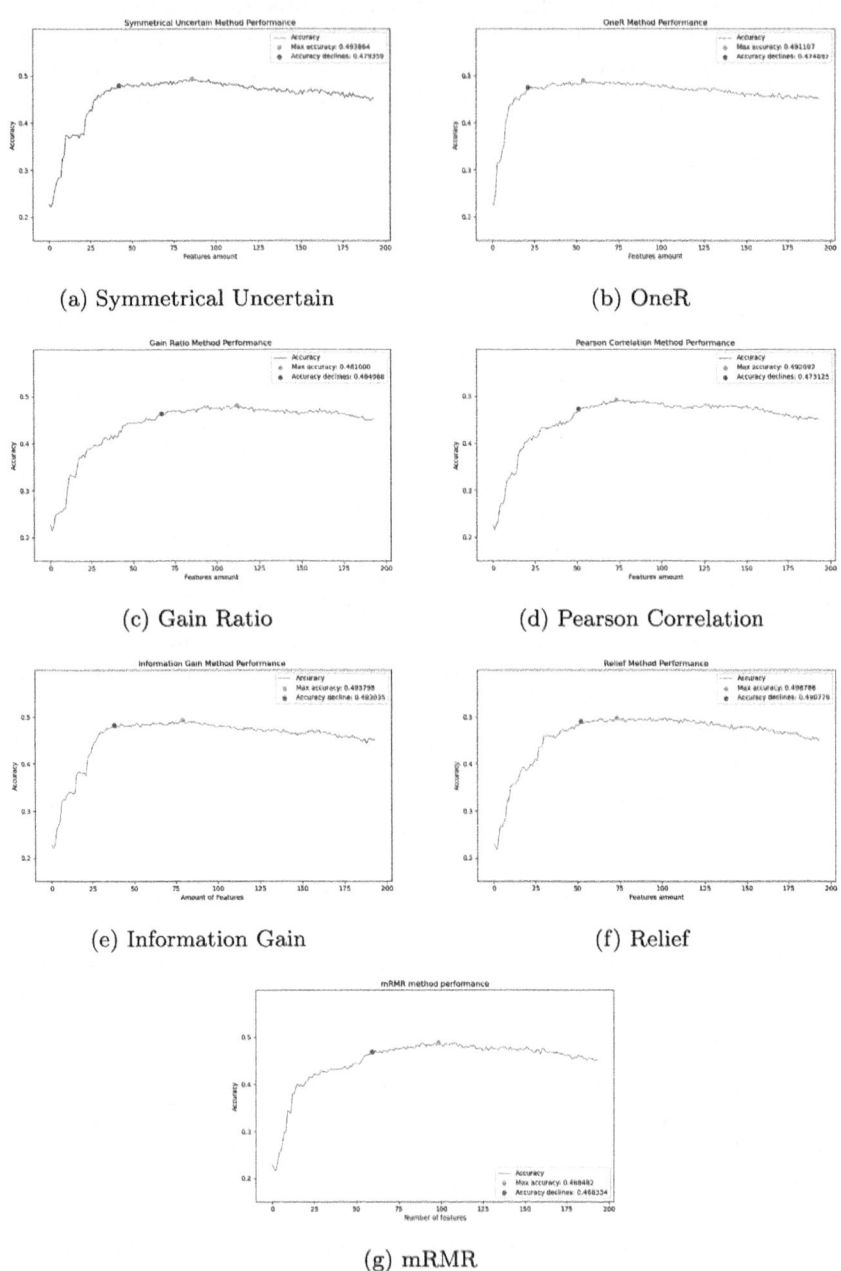

(a) Symmetrical Uncertain

(b) OneR

(c) Gain Ratio

(d) Pearson Correlation

(e) Information Gain

(f) Relief

(g) mRMR

Fig. 2. Feature removal experiments

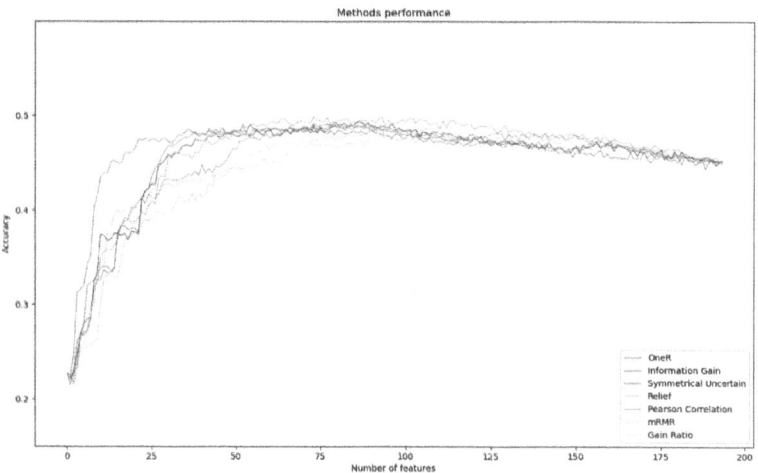

Fig. 3. All Feature Selections performance

Table 1. Performance at the points of greatest accuracy (OD) for each feature selection method.

Method	Feat.	C-Validat	Strat C-Validat	Acc. Test	F1-Score Test
OneR	54	0.491	0.484	0.497	0.498
Gain Ratio	112	0.481	0.474	0.494	0.495
Pearson Correlation	73	0.492	0.490	0.512	0.513
Information Gain	79	0.493	0.494	0.512	0.512
Relief	73	0.498	0.493	0.515	0.516
mRMR	98	0.488	0.487	0.519	0.520

Table 2. Performance at starting decay (GD) points for each feature selection method.

Method	Feat.	C-Validat	Strat C-Validat	Acc. Test	F1-Score Test
OneR	21	0.474	0.473	0.477	0.479
Gain Ratio	67	0.464	0.468	0.486	0.487
Pearson Correlation	51	0.473	0.471	0.491	0.492
Information Gain	38	0.483	0.480	0.500	0.501
Relief	52	0.490	0.488	0.492	0.493
mRMR	59	0.468	0.469	0.482	0.483

The Fig. 4 displays four bars for each method: two corresponding to the OD, representing the average accuracy from stratified cross-validation and the test set result, and two for the GD, showing the same metrics. Additionally, above each bar representing the average accuracy from stratified cross-validation, a black line illustrates two standard deviations, both above and below, indicating the variability of accuracy across the cross-validation folds.

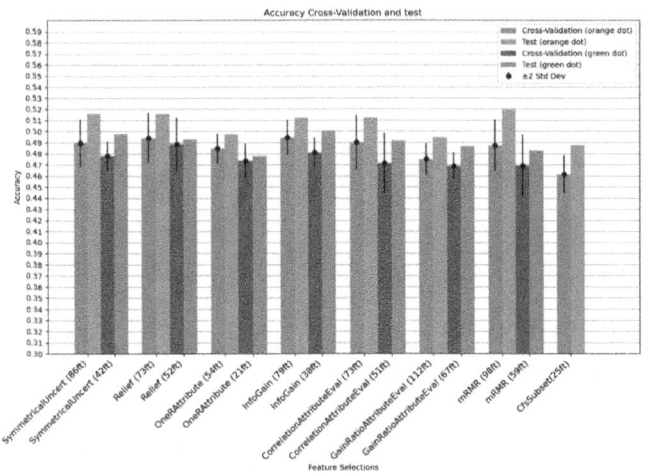

Fig. 4. Standard Deviation Graph Features Selections

Analyzing the graph, it is evident that all methods demonstrated generalization capability. The higher accuracy observed in the test set compared to the training set indicates that the combination of cross-validation and feature selection contributes positively to generalization. Notably, some methods achieved test set accuracy exceeding two standard deviations above the mean of Stratified Cross-Validation, highlighting their effectiveness in classifying unseen data.

The mRMR method stood out by achieving an accuracy of 0.520 with 98 features, making it the highest-performing method on the test data while using less than half of the original feature set. Another noteworthy result came from the OneR method, which, despite using only 21 features—approximately 10% of the initial set—achieved an accuracy of 0.477, slightly improving upon the initial accuracy. Overall, all methods demonstrated superior accuracy on the test data compared to the initial model.

The challenge of obtaining higher accuracy, around 50%, stems not only from the inherent complexity of the financial market but also from the nature of the multiclass classification task. The dataset was designed to predict five different price movement categories, which increases the classification difficulty. Additionally, financial markets are influenced by numerous external factors, and price variations tend to be subtle. This makes it particularly difficult to differentiate between closely related classes, such as Stability and minor price fluctuations.

Table 3 presents the top 10 most relevant features according to all feature selection methods, based on their average ranking across the methods, except for CfsSubset.

Table 3. Top 10 features

Rank	Feature	Average Position
1	sd_90_offer_sell	11.142857
2	sd_90_minimum	11.142857
3	sd_90_offer_buy	11.4285771
4	sd_90_average	12.142857
5	sd_90_closing	12.428571
6	sd_90_opening	12.857142
7	sd_90_maximum	15.714285
8	sd_60_offer_sell	21.142857
9	sd_60_opening	21.142857
10	sd_60_offer_buy	23.142857

It can be seen that the standard deviation in the 90 and 60-day trading sessions stands out as the most relevant, with the variables related to 90-day periods occupying the first seven positions. This indicates that the most relevant financial indicator, according to the table, is the Standard Deviation. Moreover, price volatility over longer periods plays a crucial role in predictive modeling and market behavior.

6   Conclusion

This study investigated how different feature selection techniques influence predictive performance in the Brazilian financial market using Random Forest models. Our analysis of 194 technical analysis indicators through systematic feature reduction revealed that the mRMR method delivered the best performance, achieving an accuracy of 0.520 with only 98 features—less than half of the original feature set.

The superior performance of mRMR can be attributed to its theoretical foundation, which optimizes both relevance and non-redundancy simultaneously. Unlike methods that evaluate features individually, mRMR considers feature interactions, selecting attributes that collectively provide maximum information about the target variable while minimizing redundancy among selected features. This approach is particularly effective in financial markets where indicators often exhibit complex interdependencies.

Relief also performed exceptionally well (0.515 accuracy with 73 features), likely due to its ability to detect local dependencies between features that might be missed by correlation-based methods. This capability is valuable in financial data where relationships between indicators may vary across different market conditions.

For applications where computational efficiency is critical, we recommend the OneR method, which achieved 0.477 accuracy with just 21 features (approximately 10% of the initial set). OneR's effectiveness stems from its ability to identify simple yet powerful discriminative rules, making it ideal for real-time financial analysis where processing speed is essential.

Our analysis consistently identified standard deviation indicators, particularly those calculated over 90-day periods, as the most relevant features across all selection methods. This finding suggests that long-term volatility metrics capture fundamental market behaviors that are highly predictive of future price movements.

Based on our comprehensive analysis, we recommend:

- **For maximum accuracy:** the mRMR method, which balances feature relevance and non-redundancy effectively;
- **For computational efficiency:** the OneR method, which provides substantial dimensionality reduction with minimal performance loss;
- **For balanced performance:** the Relief method, which offers strong accuracy with moderate feature reduction.

These recommendations are particularly relevant for financial analysts and algorithmic traders developing predictive models for emerging markets like Brazil, where data complexity and computational constraints often present significant challenges.

Future research should focus on applying these selected features in more sophisticated machine learning approaches, such as deep learning models, and investigating how feature selection performance varies across different market conditions and economic cycles.

Acknowledgments. The authors would like to thank FAPERGS (24/2551-0001396-2, 23/2551-0000773-8), CNPq (305805/2021-5) and FAPERGS/CNPq (23/ 2551-0000126-8). Fabian thanks to Fesurv-UniRV for the pay leave, which helped to collaborate in this work.

References

1. Chen, C.P., Metghalchi, M.: Weak-form market efficiency: evidence from the Brazilian stock market. Int. J. Econ. Financ. (2012)
2. Bouri, E., Demirer, R., Gupta, R., Sun, X.: The predictability of stock market volatility in emerging economies: relative roles of local, regional, and global business cycles. J. Forecast. (2020)
3. Cuervo, R.: Predictive AI for SME and large enterprise financial performance management. arXiv preprint arXiv:2311.05840 (2023)
4. Chandrashekar, G., Sahin, F.: A survey on feature selection methods. Comput. Electr. Eng. (2014)
5. Kohn, K., Moraes, C.H.: O impacto das novas tecnologias na sociedade: conceitos e características da Sociedade da Informação e da Sociedade Digital. XXX Congresso Brasileiro de Ciências da Comunicação (2007)

6. Araujo, G. S., Gaglianone, W. P.: Machine learning methods for inflation forecasting in Brazil: new contenders versus classical models. Lat. Am. J. Cent. Bank. (2023)
7. Htun, H.H., Biehl, M., Petkov, N.: Survey of feature selection and extraction techniques for stock market prediction. Financ. Innov. (2023)
8. Kira, K., Rendell, L.A.: A practical approach to feature selection. In: Machine Learning Proceedings 1992, pp. 249–256. Elsevier (1992)
9. Chuang, L.Y., Ke, C.H., Yang, C.H.: A hybrid both filter and wrapper feature selection method for microarray classification. arXiv preprint arXiv:1612.08669 (2003)
10. Shi, Y., Li, B., Long, W., Dai, W.: Method for improving the performance of technical analysis indicators by neural network models. Comput. Econ. (2022)
11. Billah, M.M., Sultana, A., Bhuiyan, F., Kaosar, M.G.: Stock price prediction: comparison of different moving average techniques using deep learning model. Neural Comput. Appl. **36**(11), 5861–5871 (2024)
12. Altman, D.G., Bland, J.M.: Standard deviations and standard errors. BMJ **331**(7521), 903 (2005)
13. Halilbegovic, S.: MACD-Analysis of weaknesses of the most powerful technical analysis tool. Independent J. Manag. Prod. **7**(2), 367–379 (2016)
14. Kang, B.K.: Improving MACD technical analysis by optimizing parameters and modifying trading rules: evidence from the Japanese Nikkei 225 futures market. J. Risk Financ. Manag. (2021)
15. Bansal, S.: Investigating the efficacy of RSI IN the nifty 50 index. Global J. Bus. Integr. Secur. (2016)
16. Janecek, A., Gansterer, W., Demel, M., Ecker, G.: On the relationship between feature selection and classification accuracy. In: New Challenges for Feature Selection in data Mining and Knowledge Discovery. PMLR (2008)
17. Janecek, A.G.K., Gansterer, W.N., Demel, M.A., Ecker, G.F.: On the relationship between feature selection and classification accuracy. In: Proceedings of the 2008 International Conference on New Challenges for Feature Selection in Data Mining and Knowledge Discovery, FSDM 2008, vol. 4, pp. 90–105. JMLR.org, Antwerp (2008)
18. Yu, L., Liu, H.: Feature selection for high-dimensional data: a fast correlation-based filter solution. In: Proceedings of the 20th International Conference on Machine Learning (ICML-03) (2016)
19. Lin, X., Li, C., Ren, W., Luo, X., Qi, Y.: A new feature selection method based on symmetrical uncertainty and interaction gain. Comput. Biol. Chem. **83**, 107149 (2019)
20. Peng, H., Long, F., Ding, C.: Feature selection based on mutual information criteria of max-dependency, max-relevance, and min-redundancy. IEEE Trans. Pattern Anal. Mach. Intell. **27**(8), 1226–1238 (2005)
21. Urbanowicz, R.J., Olson, R.S., Schmitt, P., Meeker, M., Moore, J.H.: Benchmarking relief-based feature selection methods for bioinformatics data mining. J. Biomed. Inform. (2018)
22. Kumar, K., Kumar, G., Kumar, Y.: Feature selection approach for intrusion detection system. Int. J. Adv. Trends Comput. Sci. Eng. (IJATCSE) **2**(5), 47–53 (2013)
23. Leroux, A., Boussard, M., Dés, R.: Information gain ratio correction: improving prediction with more balanced decision tree splits. arXiv preprint arXiv:1801.08310 (2018)

24. Armya, R., Abdulazeez, A.M., Sallow, A.B., Zeebaree, D.Q.: Leukemia diagnosis using machine learning classifiers based on correlation attribute eval feature selection. Asian J. Res. Comput. Sci. **9**(3), 52–65 (2021)

25. Hall, M.A.: Correlation-based feature selection for machine learning. Ph.D. dissertation, The University of Waikato (1999)

26. Cardoso, F.C., et al.: BovDB: a data set of stock prices of all companies in B3 from 1995 to 2020. J. Inf. Data Manag. **13**(1) (2022)

27. Breiman, L.: Random forests. In: Machine Learning. Springer (2001)

28. Karegowda, A.G., Manjunath, A.S., Jayaram, M.A.: Comparative study of attribute selection using gain ratio and correlation based feature selection. Int. J. Inf. Technol. Knowl. Manage. **2**(2), 271–277 (2010)

29. Park, C.H., Irwin, S.H.: What do we know about the profitability of technical analysis? J. Econ. Surv. **21**(4), 786–826 (2007)

30. Pardeshi, Y.K., Kale, P.: Technical analysis indicators in stock market using machine learning: a comparative analysis. In: 2021 12th International Conference on Computing Communication and Networking Technologies (ICCCNT), pp. 1–6. IEEE (2021)

31. Krauss, C., Do, X.A., Huck, N.: Deep neural networks, gradient-boosted trees, random forests: statistical arbitrage on the S&P 500. Eur. J. Oper. Res. **259**(2), 689–702 (2017)

DRHRP: A Deep Reinforcement Learning–Based Hybrid Routing Protocol for UAV–Enabled Wireless Networks

Mahdi Zareei$^{(\boxtimes)}$ (iD) and Jesús Arturo Pérez Díaz

Tecnologico de Monterrey, School of Engineering and Sciences, Monterrey 64849, Mexico
{m.zareei,jesus.arturo.perez}@tec.mx

Abstract. In this paper, we propose DRHRP, a novel deep reinforcement learning (DRL)–based hybrid routing protocol for unmanned aerial vehicle (UAV)–enabled wireless networks. DRHRP integrates concepts from geocast routing, energy-efficient and connectivity maintenance strategies, and multi-agent DRL to dynamically adapt to the challenges of highly mobile and resource-constrained networks. By modeling the routing decision as a Markov Decision Process (MDP) and employing a Multi-Agent Deep Deterministic Policy Gradient (MADDPG) framework, our protocol learns optimal forwarding policies using only local observations. Extensive simulations demonstrate improvements in packet delivery ratio, delay reduction, and energy consumption compared to traditional schemes.

Keywords: UAV networks · wireless ad hoc networks · deep reinforcement learning · hybrid routing · energy efficiency · connectivity maintenance

1 Introduction

The rapid proliferation of unmanned aerial vehicles (UAVs) in applications ranging from environmental monitoring and surveillance to disaster management and emergency communications has led to a growing demand for robust and efficient routing protocols tailored for Flying Ad Hoc Networks (FANETs) [1]. Unlike traditional mobile ad hoc networks (MANETs), FANETs operate in a three-dimensional space where the network topology changes rapidly due to the high mobility of UAV nodes and the dynamic nature of their operational environments. In such scenarios, conventional routing protocols, which often rely on static or slowly changing network assumptions, tend to perform suboptimally, suffering from high delays, frequent packet losses, and elevated energy consumption.

In response to these challenges, recent research has explored a variety of routing techniques. Early work on geocast routing demonstrated that geographic information could be exploited to confine message propagation within a targeted

© The Author(s), under exclusive license to Springer Nature Switzerland AG 2025
O. Gervasi et al. (Eds.): ICCSA 2025, LNCS 15649, pp. 401–409, 2025.
https://doi.org/10.1007/978-3-031-96997-3_25

area, thereby reducing unnecessary overhead [2]. Parallel research efforts focused on designing energy-efficient protocols that extend the lifetime of resource-constrained networks [3] and on maintaining network connectivity, especially in critical applications such as post-disaster transportation where continuous communication is essential [4]. Hybrid routing protocols, which blend proactive and reactive strategies, have emerged as a promising solution to balance the trade-offs between overhead and responsiveness [5].

The advent of deep reinforcement learning (DRL) has opened new avenues for network optimization. By framing routing decisions as a sequential decision-making problem, DRL-based approaches can dynamically adapt to changing network conditions, learning optimal forwarding strategies in real time [10–12]. In particular, multi-agent DRL methods such as MADDPG have shown great promise in cooperative environments where each agent (or node) makes decisions based solely on local observations, yet contributes to a global objective [6]. Motivated by these advances, this manuscript introduces DRHRP, a DRL-based hybrid routing protocol that leverages both proactive neighbor discovery and reactive forwarding to improve packet delivery, reduce delay, and conserve energy in FANETs.

This work not only proposes a novel routing framework but also provides a comprehensive mathematical analysis, detailed algorithm design, and extensive experimental evaluation. In addition to addressing the dynamic topology and limited energy resources, DRHRP is designed to operate effectively even in scenarios with varying node densities, mobility speeds, and beaconing intervals. The remainder of this paper is organized as follows. Section 2 offers an extended literature review. Section 3 describes the system model and problem formulation. Section 4 details the proposed DRHRP protocol and its DRL-based algorithm. Section 5 provides mathematical analysis of routing cost and convergence properties. Section 6 outlines the simulation setup and parameters. Section 7 presents and discusses the experimental results, and Section 8 concludes the paper with suggestions for future work.

2   Literature Review

Routing protocols in UAV networks have evolved significantly over the past decades. One of the earliest approaches was geocast routing, where the objective was to deliver messages to nodes within a specific geographic region. Maihöfer [2] provided one of the first comprehensive surveys of geocast routing protocols, highlighting methods such as flooding, directed flooding, and techniques to confine message propagation to a desired area. These early studies laid the groundwork for understanding how geographic information could be used to improve routing efficiency in dynamic networks.

Subsequent research shifted focus towards energy efficiency, as UAVs and sensor nodes typically operate on limited battery power. Tanoli and Khan [3] introduced routing protocols that not only aimed to minimize energy consumption but also sought to balance the load among nodes to prevent early node failures. This work was critical in demonstrating that routing decisions must account for both immediate and long-term energy costs, a principle that later influenced many energy-aware routing strategies in wireless networks.

In parallel, the need to maintain network connectivity in highly dynamic environments spurred research into connectivity maintenance algorithms. Kurt et al. [4] proposed a distributed heuristic for maintaining connectivity in a swarm of drones, particularly under post-disaster conditions where conventional communication infrastructure might be unavailable. This line of work emphasized the importance of ensuring that even as individual nodes move or fail, the overall network remains connected–a challenge that is particularly acute in three-dimensional UAV networks.

Hybrid routing protocols emerged as a solution to the conflicting requirements of low latency and low overhead. Ravilla et al. [5] explored the combination of proactive and reactive routing approaches, arguing that maintaining local routing tables while discovering routes on-demand could offer the best of both worlds. These protocols were particularly effective in scenarios where the network topology changed frequently but localized information could be maintained with modest overhead.

More recently, the field of deep reinforcement learning (DRL) has begun to influence the design of routing protocols. The foundational work by Sutton and Barto [10] established the theoretical underpinnings of reinforcement learning, while subsequent studies by Lillicrap et al. [11] and Lowe et al. [12] demonstrated the practical applicability of DRL in continuous control and multi-agent environments. The application of DRL to networking problems has been explored in various contexts, including congestion control, power management, and, more recently, routing optimization. Qin et al. [6] extended multi-agent DRL frameworks to solve joint optimization problems in content ranking, showing that coordinated decision-making among agents can significantly outperform independent approaches.

Additional contributions to the literature include studies on traditional routing algorithms such as Dynamic Source Routing (DSR) [7] and Ad Hoc On-Demand Distance Vector (AODV) routing [8]. These protocols, while effective in certain scenarios, often suffer from scalability issues in highly dynamic networks like FANETs. Furthermore, research in wireless sensor networks by Akyildiz et al. [9] has underscored the importance of balancing energy consumption with network performance–a balance that is critical for UAV networks as well.

Despite these advances, a comprehensive framework that integrates the adaptability of DRL with the robustness of hybrid routing protocols for FANETs remains underexplored. Many studies have addressed specific aspects such as energy efficiency or connectivity maintenance, but few have combined these objectives with a DRL-based decision mechanism. The literature indicates a gap in designing protocols that can adapt in real time to rapidly changing network conditions while optimizing multiple performance metrics simultaneously. This motivates the development of DRHRP, which seeks to build on the strengths of existing approaches while addressing their limitations through a unified DRL-based framework.

3   System Model and Problem Formulation

We consider a FANET represented as a dynamic graph $G(V, E)$ where V is the set of UAV nodes and E is the set of wireless links. Each UAV is equipped with a GPS receiver and periodically transmits beacon messages that include its location, residual energy, and queue status. This exchange of information enables nodes to maintain an up-to-date view of their local neighborhood even as the network topology evolves.

For each link $(i, j) \in E$, the quality metric q_{ij} is determined by factors such as the signal-to-noise ratio (SNR), frame error rate (FER), and the Euclidean distance d_{ij}. The energy consumption for transmitting a packet over link (i, j) is modeled as

$$E_{ij} = E_0 + E_d\, d_{ij}^\eta \tag{1}$$

where E_0 is a fixed energy cost, E_d is a distance-dependent factor, and η is the path-loss exponent.

Routing is formulated as a Markov Decision Process (MDP) with the tuple $(\mathcal{S}, \mathcal{A}, P, r, \gamma)$. Here, $\mathcal{S}$ represents the state space (local neighborhood information, including node locations, residual energy, and queue lengths), and $\mathcal{A}$ represents the set of available actions (selecting a neighboring node for packet forwarding). The transition probabilities $P(s'|s, a)$ capture the dynamics of the network, and the reward function is defined as

$$r(s, a) = \alpha \cdot \text{PDR} - \beta \cdot \text{Delay} - \gamma \cdot \text{Energy} \tag{2}$$

with weighting factors α, β, and γ chosen to balance the trade-offs among packet delivery ratio (PDR), delay, and energy consumption. The goal is to maximize the cumulative reward over time:

$$R = \sum_{t=0}^{T} \gamma^t r_t \tag{3}$$

4   Proposed DRHRP Protocol

DRHRP integrates proactive neighborhood discovery with a DRL-based forwarding decision mechanism. Each UAV periodically broadcasts beacon messages containing its state information, allowing neighboring nodes to update their local views. A lightweight DRL agent, implemented using the MADDPG framework, observes the current state s_t and selects the next-hop neighbor a_t based on its policy $\pi(s_t)$. The agent's objective is to maximize the long-term cumulative reward by learning optimal forwarding strategies.

The Q-value update in the MADDPG framework is given by

$$Q(s_t, a_t) \leftarrow Q(s_t, a_t) + \alpha \left(r_t + \gamma \max_{a'} Q(s_{t+1}, a') - Q(s_t, a_t) \right) \tag{4}$$

and the policy gradient is approximated as

$$\nabla_{\theta^\pi} J \approx \mathbb{E}_{s \sim \mathcal{D}} \left[\nabla_a Q(s, a) \big|_{a = \pi(s)} \nabla_{\theta^\pi} \pi(s) \right] \tag{5}$$

Algorithmically, the forwarding decision at each node involves (i) observing the current state (ii) selecting an action with added exploration noise, (iii) forwarding the packet to the chosen neighbor, and (iv) updating the DRL agent based on the received reward. This integrated approach enables DRHRP to adapt dynamically to varying network conditions.

5   Mathematical Analysis

We analyze the total energy consumption and delay of a multi-hop path. Let L denote the number of hops from the source to the destination. The total energy consumption is approximated by

$$E_{\text{total}} \approx L \cdot \left(E_0 + E_d \, \bar{d}^\eta \right) \tag{6}$$

where $\bar{d}$ is the average hop distance. Similarly, the end-to-end delay D is modeled as

$$D = L \cdot (t_{\text{proc}} + t_{\text{tx}}) \tag{7}$$

with t_{proc} and t_{tx} representing processing and transmission delays per hop, respectively. Under the standard assumptions of MADDPG [11,12], the DRL agent's policy converges to a locally optimal solution, as characterized by the Bellman optimality equation:

$$Q^*(s, a) = \mathbb{E}_{s'} \left[r + \gamma \max_{a'} Q^*(s', a') \right] \tag{8}$$

6   Simulation Setup and Experimental Results

Simulations were conducted using NS-3 in a FANET scenario with 50 UAV nodes randomly deployed within a $1 \, \text{km}^3$ area. The nodes follow a Gauss–Markov mobility model with a maximum speed of $100 \, \text{km/h}$. Each node broadcasts beacon messages every $0.5 \, \text{s}$, and the transmission range is set to $250 \, \text{m}$. Table 1 summarizes the simulation parameters.

The experimental evaluation focuses on several key performance metrics: packet delivery ratio (PDR), average delay, energy consumption, and routing overhead. In the following, we describe the experiments in detail.

In the first experiment, we vary the node density by simulating networks with 30, 50, and 100 UAV nodes. Table 2 presents the results. The table shows that

Table 1. Simulation Parameters

Parameter	Value
Number of UAVs	50
Simulation Area	$1\,km^3$
Mobility Model	Gauss–Markov
Maximum Speed	$100\,km/h$
Beacon Interval	$0.5\,s$
Transmission Range	$250\,m$
Path-loss Exponent (η)	2–4
Simulation Duration	$500\,s$

Table 2. Node Density Variation Results

Nodes	Protocol	PDR (%)	Delay (ms)	Energy (J)	Overhead (packets)
30	HRP	84.0	40	1.10	180
	HEER	88.0	35	0.95	165
	DRHRP	92.0	28	0.80	150
50	HRP	87.2	35	1.20	210
	HEER	90.1	28.5	0.90	195
	DRHRP	95.3	22.4	0.70	170
100	HRP	80.0	50	1.50	250
	HEER	84.5	42	1.20	230
	DRHRP	90.0	35	1.00	210

DRHRP consistently achieves higher PDR and lower delay than the baseline protocols (HRP and HEER), even as the network size increases. The reduction in energy consumption and overhead is also notable, which is attributed to the adaptive routing decisions made by the DRL agent.

In the second experiment, the impact of mobility speed is evaluated for speeds of $30\,km/h$, $100\,km/h$, and $200\,km/h$ (see Table 3). The results indicate that while all protocols suffer performance degradation at higher speeds, DRHRP still maintains a superior performance by leveraging its DRL agent, which adapts to the rapid topology changes.

The third experiment investigates the effect of varying the beacon interval ($0.5\,s$, $1.0\,s$, and $2.0\,s$) on performance, as shown in Table 4. Shorter beacon intervals tend to improve the freshness of neighborhood information, resulting in higher PDR and lower delay. However, this comes at the cost of increased control overhead. DRHRP benefits significantly from more frequent updates, as the DRL agent makes more accurate forwarding decisions.

Finally, we conduct a sensitivity analysis on the reward function parameters for DRHRP. Table 5 shows the impact of three different weight sets on the

Table 3. Mobility Speed Variation Results

Speed (km/h)	Protocol	PDR (%)	Delay (ms)	Energy (J)	Overhead (packets)
30	HRP	90.0	25	1.00	190
	HEER	92.0	20	0.80	180
	DRHRP	97.0	15	0.60	160
100	HRP	87.2	35	1.20	210
	HEER	90.1	28.5	0.90	195
	DRHRP	95.3	22.4	0.70	170
200	HRP	75.0	60	1.60	230
	HEER	80.0	50	1.30	215
	DRHRP	85.0	45	1.10	200

Table 4. Beacon Interval Variation Results

Beacon Interval (s)	Protocol	PDR (%)	Delay (ms)	Energy (J)	Overhead (packets)
0.5	HRP	87.2	35	1.20	210
	HEER	90.1	28.5	0.90	195
	DRHRP	95.3	22.4	0.70	170
1.0	HRP	85.0	38	1.30	220
	HEER	88.0	32	1.00	205
	DRHRP	93.0	26	0.90	190
2.0	HRP	80.0	45	1.40	240
	HEER	83.0	40	1.10	225
	DRHRP	89.0	34	1.00	210

protocol's performance. The analysis demonstrates that increasing the weight on PDR (weight set B) improves performance metrics across the board, while a higher emphasis on delay (weight set C) can lead to a trade-off with overall packet delivery.

Table 5. Reward Weight Sensitivity Results (DRHRP)

Weight Set	α	β	γ	PDR (%)	Delay (ms)	Energy (J)
A	1	1	1	92.0	25	0.80
B	2	1	1	95.3	22	0.70
C	1	2	1	90.0	28	0.75

Overall, the experimental results confirm that DRHRP consistently outperforms traditional hybrid protocols such as HRP and HEER in diverse network scenarios. The adaptive forwarding decisions made by the DRL agent contribute to a higher packet delivery ratio, lower delay, and reduced energy consumption, making DRHRP a strong candidate for real-world FANET deployments.

7 Additional Analysis and Future Work

The results presented indicate that DRHRP is robust under varying network conditions, including changes in node density, mobility, and beacon intervals. However, there remains significant potential to further optimize the protocol. Future work will focus on integrating real-world UAV mobility traces to refine the DRL model further and extending the framework to support multi-destination geocast. Moreover, advanced multi-agent cooperation strategies are under investigation to enhance scalability and robustness in larger networks.

8 Conclusion

In this manuscript, we introduced DRHRP, a deep reinforcement learning–based hybrid routing protocol tailored for UAV–enabled wireless networks. By combining proactive neighbor discovery with a MADDPG–driven reactive forwarding mechanism, DRHRP effectively addresses the challenges of dynamic topology and resource constraints inherent in FANETs. The extended mathematical analysis and comprehensive simulation results demonstrate the superiority of DRHRP over conventional routing schemes in terms of packet delivery, delay, energy efficiency, and overhead. Future research will include real-world implementation and further enhancements in multi-agent cooperation to tackle even more challenging network environments.

References

1. Bekmezci, I., Sahingoz, O.K., Temel, Ş: Flying ad hoc networks (FANETs): a survey. Ad Hoc Netw. **11**(3), 1254–1270 (2013)
2. Maihöfer, C.: A survey of geocast routing protocols. IEEE Commun. Surv. Tutorials **6**(1), 2–16 (2004)
3. Tanoli, T.S., Khan, M.K.: Energy efficient and QOS sensitive routing protocol for ad hoc networks. IOP Conf. Ser. Mater. Sci. Eng. **51**, 012026 (2013)
4. Kurt, A., Saputro, N., Akkaya, K., Uluagac, A.S.: Distributed connectivity maintenance in swarm of drones during post-disaster transportation applications. IEEE Trans. Intell. Transp. Syst. **22**(9), 6061–6074 (2021)
5. Ravilla, D., Sumalatha, V., Reddy Putta, C.S.: Hybrid routing protocols for ad hoc wireless networks. Int. J. Ad hoc, Sensor Ubiquitous Comput. **2**(4), 79–90 (2011)
6. Qin, Z., Yuan, K., Lahiri, P., Liu, W.: Cooperative multi-agent deep reinforcement learning in content ranking optimization. In: Proceedings of the eCom 2024, Washington, DC (2024)
7. Perkins, C., Royer, E.: Dynamic source routing in mobile ad hoc networks. In: Proceedings 2nd IEEE Workshop on Mobile Computing Systems and Applications (1999)

8. Johnson, D.B., Maltz, D.A.: Dynamic source routing in ad hoc wireless networks. In: Mobile Computing, pp. 153–181 (1996)
9. Akyildiz, I.F., Su, W., Sankarasubramaniam, Y., Cayirci, E.: Wireless sensor networks: a survey. Comput. Netw. **38**(4), 393–422 (2002)
10. Sutton, R.S., Barto, A.G.: Reinforcement Learning: An Introduction, 2nd edn., MIT Press (2018)
11. Lillicrap, T.P., et al.: Continuous control with deep reinforcement learning. In: Proceedings of the ICLR (2015)
12. Lowe, R. et al.: Multi-agent actor-critic for mixed cooperative-competitive environments. In: Proceedings if the NeurIPS (2017)

Author Index

The manufacturer's authorised representative in the EU is Springer
Nature Customer Service Centre GmbH, Europaplatz 3, 69115 Heidelberg,
Germany. If you have any concerns regarding our products, please
contact ProductSafety@springernature.com

Printed and bound by CPI Group (UK) Ltd, Croydon, CR0 4YY
24/04/2026
02096367-0015